U.S. SUBMARINES THROUGH 1945

U.S. SUBMARINES THROUGH 1945

AN ILLUSTRATED DESIGN HISTORY

By Norman Friedman

Ship Plans by Jim Christley and Norman Friedman

Naval Institute Press
Annapolis, Maryland

© 1995
by the U.S. Naval Institute
Annapolis, Maryland

All photographs are official U.S. Navy

ISBN-13: 978-1-55750-263-6

Library of Congress Cataloging in Publication Data

Friedman, Norman, 1946–
    U.S. submarines through 1945 : an illustrated design history /
Norman Friedman.
        p.   cm.
    Includes bibliographical references and index.
    ISBN 1-55750-263-3 (alk. paper)
    1. Submarine boats—United States—History—20th century.
2. United States.   Navy—Submarine forces—History—20th century.
I. Title.   II. Title: U.S. submarines through 1945.
V858.F75   1995   94-29958
623.8′257′0973—dc20

Printed in the United States of America on acid-free paper ⊗

10 09 08 07   9 8 7 6 5

CONTENTS

List of Tables   vii

Preface   ix

List of Abbreviations   xi

1   Introduction   1

2   Beginnings: The Age of Manpower   11

3   Holland and His Rivals   19

4   Harbor Defense   33

5   The General Board's Coastal Defense
Submarines   75

6   Fleet Submarines   99

7   The S-Boats   117

8   World War I   149

9   Submarines for a Pacific War   163

10   Submarines for Mobilization   195

11   Detour: The Return to Limited
Dimensions   221

12   World War II   233

Appendices

A   Submarine Propulsion   255

B   Periscopes   267

C   U.S. Submarines Through 1945   285

D   Submarine Data   305

Notes   313

Index   367

TABLES

6–1   Steam Submarine Studies, May 1920   113

8–1   General Board Submarine Program, 20 April 1918   157

9–1   Cruiser Submarine Proposals, February 1920   168

9–2   C&R Sketch Designs for Long-Radius Submarine, 1919   170

9–3   Cruiser Submarine Proposals, June 1920   171

9–4   C&R Cruiser Submarines, 1920   171

9–5   C&R Cruiser Submarines, 1922   173

9–6   C&R Schemes for V-7, 8 May 1928   186

9–7   V-7 Design Alternatives, June and August 1929   187

9–8   Number of Submarines on Station, 1930   191

9–9   The 1930 Submarine Designs (V-8 and V-9)   192

11–1   Small Submarines for Admiral Hart, 12 October 1937   222

11–2   Electric Boat Designs for Small Submarines, 1934 and 1938   223

11–3   Small Submarine Designs, 1939   227

11–4   Portsmouth's Proposed Redesign of *Marlin*, 1941   227

11–5   SubLant's Comparison of *Mackerel* and *Marlin* Designs, 1942   229

12–1   Torpedo Firing Doctrine: Hits Required   234

12–2   Average Detection Ranges for Submarine Sensors, 1945 (kyd, 50 percent detections)   241

12–3   Submarine Characteristics, May 1945   250

A–1   Early U.S. Navy Diesels   257

A–2   Comparison of BuEng and German MAN Engines, 1928   259

A–3   Lightweight Diesels   261

B–1   Some Typical U.S. Periscopes, Pre-1919   270

B–2   Foreign Periscopes Bought by C&R Through 1927   271

B–3   Standard Periscopes, Post-1919   278

PREFACE

Propulsion is treated in Appendix A. Readers should keep in mind the distinction between an air-breathing *engine* (diesel, gasoline, steam) and an electric *motor*. Periscopes are described in Appendix B.

Fiscal year (FY) refers to the year ending on 30 June. For example, FY 14 began on 1 July 1913 and ended on 30 June 1914; "Submarine 1914" was the submarine built under the FY 14 program.

The main documentary sources consulted for this work are the correspondence of Secretary of the Navy/Chief of Naval Operations (RG 80) in the U.S. National Archives (NARS), the correspondence of the Bureau of Construction and Repair (RG 19 in NARS), the papers of the General Board (now in NARS), the papers of the Board on Construction (NARS, RG 80), and the papers of the Underwater Warfare Division of the Office of the Chief of Naval Operations (Operational Archives, U.S. Naval Historical Center). I also greatly benefited from a microfilm series of miscellaneous plans of the Bureau of Construction and Repair that are filmed in numerical order (the originals of the rolls are now held by the Portsmouth Naval Shipyard). They include some summaries of bids for early U.S. submarines. Other sources, such as the papers of the Naval War College, are cited specifically in the text.

A printed source that deserves special mention is John D. Alden, *The Fleet Submarine in the U.S. Navy* (Annapolis, Md.: U.S. Naval Institute, 1979).

I am very grateful to Jim Christley (who illustrated this book) and to John Alden, both of whom kindly read and criticized a draft of the book; Mr. Christley also greatly assisted my research. Commander Alden very kindly allowed me access to his correspondence with Admirals Andrew McKee and Armand F. Morgan, written in connection with his fleet submarine book. Nicholas Lambert assisted me with, among other things, access to the draft of his new book, tentatively titled *The Influence of the Submarine upon Naval Strategy 1898–1914* (an expanded version of his Oxford University D.Phil. thesis), to be published in 1995. He, too, read and criticized a draft of this book. I benefited from their comments, but I am responsible for whatever errors remain. As always, I want to thank the staff of the Naval Historical Center, particularly of its Operational Archives and of the Navy Department Library, and the staff of the military records division of the U.S. National Archives, particularly Dr. Richard von Doenhoff. Thanks also go to A. D. Baker, III, Ned Beach, Mary Cherpak of the Naval War College Archives, Steve Finnegan of the Submarine Force Museum (*Nautilus* memorial), Chuck Haberlein, Mark Henry, Paul Lepinski of Kollmorgen Corp., Terry Lindell, Dr. E. R. Lewis, Michael Pokalyko, James Patton, and C. C. Wright.

This book could not have been written without the loving support and encouragement of my wife, Rhea. Her equanimity and her excellent sense of humor sustained me through a difficult, complex, and lengthy project, much of it conducted during a year which was difficult for both of us. She particularly encouraged me to follow up the many and often labyrinthine issues my research raised, and she served as a very friendly, yet perceptive, critic of my draftsmanship.

ABBREVIATIONS

AC	alternating current		dB	decibel
Adm.	Admiral		DC	direct current
ADP	automatic data processing		DCDI	depth charge direction indicator
amp	ampere		DCNO	Deputy Chief of Naval Operations
amp-hr	ampere-hour		DCRE	depth charge range estimator
A/S	anti-submarine		DD	direct drive
ASNE	American Society of Naval Engineers		DRT	dead-reckoning tracer
ASWORG	Anti-Submarine Warfare Operations Research Group		ED	electric drive
ASW	anti-submarine warfare		EDO	engineering duty officer
			EHP	effective horsepower
B&L	Bausch & Lomb		ELINT	electronic intelligence
BDI	bearing deviation indication		EXPO	expanded Posiedon
BHP	brake horsepower			
BOT	battle order telephone		FCS	fire-control system
BT	bathythermograph		FIAT	Fabrica Italiano Automobile Torino (Turin Italian Automobile Factory)
BuEng	Bureau of Engineering		FM	frequency modulated; Fairbanks-Morse
BuOrd	Bureau of Ordnance		FoV	field of view
BuNav	Bureau of Navigation		ft	foot/feet
BuShips	Bureau of Ships		FY	fiscal year
BWL	beam on waterline		FTC	false target can
			FTS	false target shell
Capt.	Captain			
CIC	combat information center		gal	gallon(s)
CinC	Commander in Chief		GE	General Electric
CinCLant	Commander in Chief, Atlantic		GM	General Motors; metacentric weight
CinCPac	Commander in Chief, Pacific		GRT	gross tons
CinCUS	Commander in Chief, U.S. Fleet			
CIP	class improvement plan		HF	high frequency
cm	centimeter		HP	horsepower
CNO	Chief of Naval Operations		hr	hour(s)
CO	commanding officer		HTS	high-tensile steel
CO₂	carbon dioxide		Hz	Hertz (one cycle per second)
Comdr.	Commander			
Cominch	Commander-in-Chief, U.S. Fleet (also Office of)		IFF	identification friend or foe
			IHP	indicated horsepower
ComSubPac	Commander, Submarines, Pacific (World War II)		in	inch(es)
			INSURV	Board of Inspection and Survey
C&R	Bureau of Construction and Repair			
CRT	cathode-ray tube		JANAC	Joint Army-Navy Assessment Committee
CT	conning tower			
cu ft	cubic foot/feet			

Note: CO₂ = CO_2

K&E	Keuffel & Esser
kHz	kiloHertz (one thousand cycles per second)
kt	knot(s)
kw	kilowatt(s)
kwh	kilowatt-hour(s)
kyd	kiloyard(s) (one thousand yards)
lb	pound(s)
LBP	length between perpendiculars
LOA	length overall
LP	low pressure
Lt.	Lieutenant
Lt. Comdr.	Lieutenant Commander
LWL	length on waterline
m	meter(s)
MAD	magnetic anomaly detection
MAN	Maschinenfabrik Augsburg Nürnburg
MATD	mine and torpedo detection
MBT	main ballast tank
MHz	megaHertz
mi	mile(s)
min	minute(s)
MIT	Massachusetts Institute of Technology
Mk	mark (number—ordnance designation)
mm	millimeter(s)
mo	month(s)
mph	miles per hour
MS	mild steel
msec	millisecond
MTB	maintenance of true bearing
NARS	National Archives and Records Service
NAVSEA	Naval Sea Systems Command
NDRC	National Defense Research Committee
NELSECO	New London Ship and Engine Company
NLM	noise level monitor
nm	nautical mile(s) (2 kiloyards equal about 1 nautical mile)
NRL	Naval Research Laboratory
OL	object locator
ONI	Office of Naval Intelligence
ONR	Office of Naval Research
OOD	officer of the deck
OpNav	Office of the Chief of Naval Operations
Op-O2	Deputy Chief of Naval Operations
PPI	plan-position indicator

psi	pounds per square inch
PUFFS	passive underwater fire control feasibility
Q	quickdive (tank)
R&D	research and development
RLI	right-left indicator
rpg	rounds per gun
SE	Steam Engineering (Bureau of)
sec	second(s)
SecNav	Secretary of the Navy
SF	submarine, fleet (designator briefly used)
SHP	shaft horsepower
SNAME	Society of Naval Architects and Marine Engineers
SOD	small object detector
SORG	Submarine Operational Research Group
sq ft	square foot/feet
SS	submarine
STS	special treatment steel
SubDiv	Submarine Division
SubLant	Submarine Commander Atlantic
SubPAC	Submarine Commander Pacific
Subron	Submarine Squadron
TBT	target bearing transmitter
TDC	torpedo data computer
TDM	torpedo detection modification
TFCS	torpedo fire control system
TLR	triangulation listening ranging
TVG	temperature, voltage, gassing
UCDWR	University of California Division of War Research
V	speed (used in tables)
VCNO	Vice Chief of Naval Operations
WAA	wide aperture array
WCC	weapon control console
wk	week(s)
WW I	World War I
WW II	World War II
XO	executive officer
yd	yard(s)
yr	year(s)

U.S. SUBMARINES THROUGH 1945

1

Introduction

THE TYPE OF submarine described in this book no longer exists. Essentially a surface ship that could submerge to hide, it had limited underwater performance and endurance. Underwater power, once exhausted, had to be renewed by an air-breathing (usual diesel) surface plant. Only on the surface could the submarines make much distance. They kept to the surface whenever that was safe: at night in enemy waters and in daylight away from enemy eyes. Radar allowed U.S. World War II submarines to surface in daylight, even in waters nominally controlled by the enemy, by warning them in time to dive as aircraft approached. After the submarines' enemies received their own radars, the surface was no longer safe, day or night. The Germans and Japanese encountered this situation during World War II. At the end of the war, the U.S. Navy assumed that its own submarines would face the same sort of opposition, and it developed a different kind of submarine (often converted from the earlier types). The new submarines are the subject of a companion volume, *U.S. Submarines since 1945: An Illustrated Design History*.

Who designed U.S. submarines? Responsibility was split among three independent bureaus, each responsible only to the secretary of the navy: (1) Construction and Repair (C&R) for hulls and overall configuration; (2) Steam Enginering (SE, later Engineering; both are denoted by BuEng in this book) for propelling machinery; and (3) Ordnance (BuOrd) for weaponry.[1] In theory, the Bureau of Navigation (BuNav), the operations and personnel branch, represented fleet views.[2] C&R and BuEng merged in 1940 to become the Bureau of Ships (BuShips). Although

BuOrd had lost control over the design of torpedo craft in 1894, its Naval Torpedo Station at Newport, Rhode Island, was the main experimental base. As long as submarines were considered experimental craft (i.e., to about 1904), they were assigned to BuOrd on completion.

Any warship is a compromise among the ship qualities that the materiel bureaus represented, so the bureaus' independence and equal status caused problems. In 1889, the secretary sought to coordinate the bureaus by forming the Board on Construction, an advisory board consisting of the bureau chiefs (including the senior line officer, the chief of BuNav).

The U.S. Navy found itself in this position because Congress abhorred the idea of any permanent military staff. It sought to ensure civilian control by concentrating authority in the hands of the civilian secretary. The system's inability to develop and implement consistent naval policy had little noticeable impact on U.S. surface ship designs of the late 19th and early 20th centuries. Technology was evolutionary, and the implications of particular decisions were well understood. However, this "nonsystem" was ill suited to the development of entirely new types of warships, such as submarines.

The Spanish-American War shook the 19th-century naval administration just as the U.S. Navy bought its first usable submarine. Clearly, the secretary could not be his own operational commander. Because Congress rejected a naval general staff, Secretary of the Navy Herbert Long formed an advisory war planning organization, the General Board. War planning was the first sustained conscious

The submarines described in this book were submersible surface warships, diving mainly to conceal themselves in the face of the enemy. Much of the World War II submarine development in the United States was intended to improve their surface performance, including their ability to detect enemies in time to dive. USS *Mingo* (SS 261) is shown at Mare Island, 17 July 1945, with changes circled. On deck, forward of her bridge fairwater, she has a twin 20-mm mount (with guns removed); firing over it is a single manually operated 40 mm gun. Aft on deck, a single 5 in/25 wet mount has been installed. The short whips circled atop her periscope shears are SPR-1s intended to detect enemy radars. Her own SJ and SV radars, circled, were expected to detect enemy aircraft and to make possible night surface attacks. The circled object atop the bridge is a target-bearing transmitter (TBT) used to designate targets in night surface attacks.

analysis of U.S. naval policy. Plans naturally carried implications for the overall shape of the nascent U.S. fleet. From October 1900 on (for the fiscal year ending 30 June 1902), the General Board prepared an annual building program. In 1903, it added comments on the appropriate characteristics of the ships. The Board on Construction commented on these proposals, and a conference committee had to be called to reconcile the differences between the two boards. From then until 1909, the Board on Construction prepared its own annual recommended building programs.

The General Board gained enormous prestige from its first chief, Adm. George Dewy (Admiral of the Navy, and thus the most senior naval officer). Members included the chief of BuNav and the chief intelligence officer and his principal assistant (after 1901, this seat was filled by the president of the Naval War College). In theory (as expressed in 1901 by Admiral Dewey), the combination of the General Board, the Naval War College, and the Office of Naval Intelligence corresponded to a German-style Great General Staff—naval intelligence collected information, the General Board made plans on the basis of that information, and the War College evaluated the plans and also trained the staff officers who would execute the war plans. Before 1914, the General Board met each summer at the Naval War College. Its Newport location placed it close to the fleet's exercise grounds, as well as the Naval Torpedo Station. Students at the War College would have come into close contact with the pre-1914 submarines, based at Newport, that exercised in Narragansett Bay.

As the navy's "think tank," the Naval War College used its students to test both war plans and many proposed warship types on its gaming floor. For example, it was partly responsible for early U.S. interest in fleet submarines. War College gaming was also responsible for some important post–World War I submarine tactics that helped to shape submarine design.

Some younger naval officers, including Comdr. William S. Sims, the future admiral who would command U.S. naval forces in Europe during World War I (WW I), saw the General Board as the means by which the fleet's views could prevail over the technological conservatism of the bureaus. The advent of all-big-gun battleships was their opportunity. The bureaus opposed this innovation.[3] The reformers charged that even when the bureaus did design modern battleships, the ships were terribly flawed. In 1908, the General Board was made responsible for the formal characteristics to which U.S. warships would be designed. To many, the innate conservatism of the bureaus (or their unwillingness to admit technical error) was most strikingly illustrated by BuOrd's World War II refusal to admit that the MK 10 magnetic exploder of its Mark 14 submarine torpedo was dangerously flawed. The General Board did not, and could not, altogether solve the problem.

Consequently, from 1909 on, U.S. warship designs were tied to U.S. war plans. Between the two world wars,

for example, ships were designed specifically to fight the most likely enemy, Orange (Japan). Typically, a specialist on the General Board developed tentative "single sheet characteristics" for a projected class. C&R preliminary designers developed alternative sketch designs in the spring ("spring styles," after women's fashions, because data were needed for appropriations bills that had to pass before the beginning of the fiscal year on 1 July). Representatives of the materiel bureaus and the fleet testified at General Board hearings held to draft characteristics for submission to the secretary of the navy. The characteristics generally reflected a chosen sketch design. The level of design detail involved in a spring style varied considerably. By the end of WW I, the secretary's approved characteristics generally reflected a fairly elaborate preliminary design. Once the characteristics had been set, this was developed into a contract design on the basis of which shipyards could bid. The lead shipyard for a class developed detailed plans (working drawings) from the contract design. BuEng practice was quite different: contract drawings generally left a blank space for machinery, and a contactor developed preliminary and detailed machinery arrangements.

C&R had no experience designing submarines. The navy therefore bought complete designs, just as it bought airplanes. Most importantly, C&R could not offer the navy any independent judgment of the trade-offs inherent in submarine design. Consequently, to a great extent, the navy had to accept the design policy chosen by the inventor-producer.[4] Enjoying a near-monopoly, Electric Boat Company largely shaped early U.S. submarine evolution. In 1909, for example, the General Board turned to Lawrence Y. Spear, the company's designer, rather than to a U.S. Navy constructor, to be educated about trade-offs in submarine design. There were other influences; the growing corps of U.S. submariners had definite ideas, but Electric Boat remained dominant prior to 1914. Submariners sometimes alleged that the company retarded progress by always incorporating its patented devices in its submarines.[5]

Electric Boat angered some naval officers by what they saw as undue use of political influence. In its early years, the company considered it necessary to use Congress to overcome a conservative naval establishment. The Board on Construction was particularly skeptical of Electric Boat's claims because USS *Plunger*, designed by John P. Holland (who originated Electric Boat's submarines), had been such an abject failure.[6]

The navy needed its own submarine designers and builders. It designated Portsmouth Navy Yard its specialist builder and, in June 1914, ordered a Lake boat (L-8). In 1916, Electric Boat's design O-1 was ordered from the same yard. Emory S. Land, a naval constructor, had been assigned to submarine duty with the C&R preliminary design office in 1915. To gain practical knowledge, he went to sea on board as many Atlantic Fleet submarines as he could. His experiences convinced him that the submari-

NIXON'S JAN. 18 TH. 1901, 7 E.

On the stocks at the Lewis Nixon yard on 18 January 1901, A-1 illustrates typical single-hull construction. The pressure hull is wrapped around the frames, and any tankage is inside. Bulkheads for some tanks have already been installed. Framing for another boat is visible through the frames. (*Submarine Force Museum and Library*)

ners were right in opposing the small coastal submarines espoused by Electric Boat and the General Board. He championed the 800-tonner they wanted and prepared its preliminary design (for the Navy version of the S-class submarine, alongside competitive designs by Lake and Electric Boat). Now that C&R had adequate expertise, it claimed responsibility for all future submarine preliminary (outline) designs. Portsmouth prepared working plans of Land's submarine and built several to its design.

Electric Boat nearly went bankrupt when new submarine construction essentially ceased after WW I.[7] It was saved largely because its subsidiaries made diesel engines, electric motors and associated equipment, and motor yachts. U.S. submarine construction was kept alive by

the Portsmouth Navy Yard, which did not need a steady stream of contracts to justify maintaining its skilled design and construction staffs. With one exception, after Electric Boat reentered the program in the 1930s, it never again designed a submarine all the way from initial concept to final drawings. Like Portsmouth, it functioned as design agent that developed contract as well as working plans. Postwar, Electric Boat developed both preliminary and detailed designs for many nuclear submarine power plants but not preliminary designs for complete submarines. (It did develop many contract designs.)

The General Board's supremacy could not last; it was not designed to run an operational navy. The Office of Operations (OpNav), headed by the chief of naval operations (CNO), was formed in 1915. The CNO was senior

Launched incomplete on 20 September 1946, *Walrus* illustrates a typical U.S. submarine hull form: double hull amidships and single hull at the ends. The free-flooding superstructure was not fitted. The structure visible amidships was a trunk leading up to the conning tower (which was not fitted). *Walrus* was never completed. (*Electric Boat*)

Under construction at Mare Island on 2 January 1941, the submarine *Silversides* illustrates double-hull construction. The inner circular section is the pressure hull; the framing, which surrounds it, supports a thin streamlined outer hull. Such a configuration leaves the interior of the pressure hull unencumbered by framing and allows for a streamlined outer hull whose shape is not determined by the need to resist water pressure.

naval officer but he had no direct authority over operating forces or over the independent bureaus. OpNav responsibilities grew enormously once war broke out in 1917. Op-Nav also gained precedence over the bureaus, though they revived their independence after the war. In 1917, OpNav established a London Planning Section to support Admiral Sims, commander of U.S. naval forces in Euopean waters. After the war, this section was folded into OpNav. It naturally became concerned with both characteristics and the overall shape of the building program, and for a time in 1920 it was not clear whether the General Board would retain its responsibility for characteristics. The board's primacy was reaffirmed, although the CNO was its presiding officer until 1931. OpNav took over the primary war planning and training roles. The boundary between its responsibilities and those of the General Board began to blur; OpNav's offices included more submarine expertise than the General Board could muster. Too, the CNO served as acting secretary of the navy when the latter was absent or incapacitated, a particularly important consideration during the administration of Franklin D. Roosevelt.

Submarine development was retarded (compared with that in Europe) partly because, before 1915, the submarine service was quite decentralized and lacked a school to develop unified doctrine and to propose new materiel. In June 1907, in connection with a query about developing submarine tactics, the General Board suggested that an officer of command rank be appointed to the Bureau of Navigation (i.e., to the closest approximation of a naval staff) and, to ensure continuity, be in charge of developing the torpedo flotilla, which then included submarines. Although he never had a title, Comdr. (later Capt.) Charles C. Marsh became the BuNav submarine specialist who evaluated various proposals submitted by the submariners.[8] Between 1909 and 1911, Lt. Comdr. Ridley McLean served as the General Board's submarine specialist.[9] On leaving, he proposed that a chief submarine officer be appointed to the staff of the new aide for operations (a forerunner of the CNO) to oversee both characteristics and operations. These ideas bore fruit during WW I. A postwar proposal to form a separate submarine bureau (analogous to the Bureau of Aeronautics) failed, but an OpNav undersea warfare division eventually grew into Op-02, Deputy Chief of Naval Operations for Undersea Warfare (now N87).

In June 1915, all submarines other than two small divisions in the Philippines were grouped under Adm. A. W. Grant, who flew his flag in the old cruiser *Chicago*.[10] He started the submarine school at New London. It became a center for submarine thinking and for the evaluation of new materiel. Grant was relieved by Adm. S. S. Robinson after Grant opposed sending U.S. submarines to Europe in 1917, on the justifiable (but unacceptable) ground that they were unprepared for European conditions. The Navy Department selected Capt. Thomas C. Hart, who had made a name as commander of the submarine division in Hawaii, as Robinson's chief of staff. Robinson naturally wanted to appoint his own man, so he offered Hart the submarine school. Hart demurred, and he was appointed instead to command submarines assigned to European waters.

In July 1918, Hart was brought home as OpNav director of submarines. Admiral Robinson was still in New London and far from the center of policy making in Washington. Hart became, in effect, the senior U.S. submariner. He approved the Q-boat operations (see chapter 6). Admiral Robinson's centralized submarine command was broken up, partly (according to Hart) because his flagship was badly wanted for escort duty. By October 1918, Hart was, for all practical purposes, commander of the U.S. submarine force. About the time of the Armistice, he began to hold Submarine Officers Conferences in Washington; these conferences were responsible for postwar cruiser submarine concepts. Hart left office in June 1920, and his submarine desk was eliminated in June 1922, but he continued his close involvement with submarines. Serving on the General Board in 1936–1939, he was responsible for the decision to build two smaller submarines of the *Marlin* type.

When the fleet moved to the Pacific in 1919, the direct tie between the naval establishment in Washington and the operational submarine fleet lapsed. Hart's successful solution was to reestablish a regular Submarine Officers Conference consisting of submariners assigned to Washington duty. It first met in October 1926. The conference seems to have been most important very early in its career when U.S. submarine design was changing most radically.

OpNav would not become preeminent again until WW II. In December 1941, Adm. Ernest J. King would become commander in chief of operational U.S. naval forces and in March 1942, also CNO. Through his vice chief of naval operations (VCNO), he would control naval materiel, including submarine production and outfitting.

The central problem of submarine design is underwater control. A submarine could easily take on enough water to make her submerge. Unfortunately, water generally has the same density throughout its depth. Once beneath the surface, a submarine heavier than water just keeps sinking. The hull contracts under water pressure, so as the submarine goes deeper, she becomes more dense and loses more buoyancy. Similarly, if enough water is pumped out to make her lighter than water, she rises until she surfaces. Yet, to be useful, a submarine has to be controllable below the surface and able to rise and dive at will.

Robert Fulton seems to have been the first to try a dynamic solution: water flowing over a hydroplane (a horizontal rudder), in effect, a wing in the water, could generate sufficient force to keep a slightly buoyant submarine below water (the hull itelf also generates some dynamic force). As long as the submarine kept moving through the water, she could stay down. Slight buoyancy made for safety because the submarine would pop to the surface as soon as she lost way. Dynamic forces can also keep a slightly heavy submarine from sinking deeper. Such a submarine is an underwater airplane.[11]

Holland realized that Fulton had also solved another problem. Many 19-century submarines were inherently very unstable underwater because they were designed to dive with partly filled ballast tanks (e.g., to compensate for local variations in water density, to maintain exactly neutral buoyancy underwater, and thus not to sink uncontrollably). If the submarine trimmed slightly fore or aft, water rushed to one end of the tank; this free-surface effect increases the up or down angle. Inventors tried to compensate by pumping water fore or aft or by moving weights, but such methods were never effective. The underwater airplane did not have to be neutrally buoyant. She could dive with full ballast tanks, whose contents could not slosh back and forth. Small tanks near her center of gravity, where free surfaces had little effect, could be used for fine adjustments.

Submarines varied in the arrangement of their hulls and ballast tanks. *Single-hull* submarines, such as Holland's, had ballast tanks inside their pressure hulls. *Double-hull* submarines had thin outer hulls wrapped

Launched on 22 November 1942, *Puffer* illustrates the typical combination of hull and superstructure. The streamlined double hull (with single-hull ends) is surmounted by a free-flooding superstructure ("casing," in British parlance). The limber holes along its side forward of the bridge allow air inside to escape quickly as the submarine dives. The holes farther forward are to flood the bow buoyancy space (vents on top trap air in it). Earlier double-hull submarines had no separate superstructure, only a ship-shaped outer hull.

partly or completely around their pressure hulls, with tankage in between. Often, the outer hull was ship-shaped for better surface running (the pressure hull has to be more or less cylindrical, for strength underwater). Submarines were generally double-hulled over only part of their length. A double-hull submarine could have her framing between the hulls, thus increasing useful space inside the pressure hull but making access to the ballast tanks more complicated. There was also an intermediate type, the *saddle-tank* submarine, in which the ballast was carried in bulges alongside the pressure hull. All three types also had

free-flooding superstructures (casings, in British parlance) above their pressure hulls and tanks. The superstructure provided freeboard for surface running, and sometimes it was partly watertight to provide extra buoyancy to ride over waves.

Simon Lake's submarines were unusual in having partly watertight (controlled-flooding) superstructures above what amounted to single hulls with internal ballast tanks. In Lake's gasoline-powered boats, the superstructure generally contained the fuel tanks. Lake's submarines were described as double-hulled but were quite different

A hull section at the World War II Manitowoc Shipyard illustrates typical U.S. double-hull construction, with tankage wrapped completely around the circular-section pressure hull. The ends of such a "fleet boat" were single hull because it was difficult to get into very narrow tanks to maintain them and the pressure hull inside.

from conventional double-hull submarines, in which the outer hull was wrapped more or less completely around the inner hull.

Some other points of hull nomenclature are important. A submarine's *conning tower* is a pressure hull structure attached to the main pressure hull. This structure is not generally streamlined, so it is surrounded by a nonwatertight *fairing,* or *fairwater* or *fairwater/bridge* (the entire structure above the submarine's deck is often erroneously called a conning tower). Often, the fairwater is surmounted by *shears* that support the retractable periscopes and masts.

U.S. submarine designers were much influenced by German U-boat practice, largely as revealed by U-boats like this one, taken briefly after World War I. *U-111* is shown in American service.

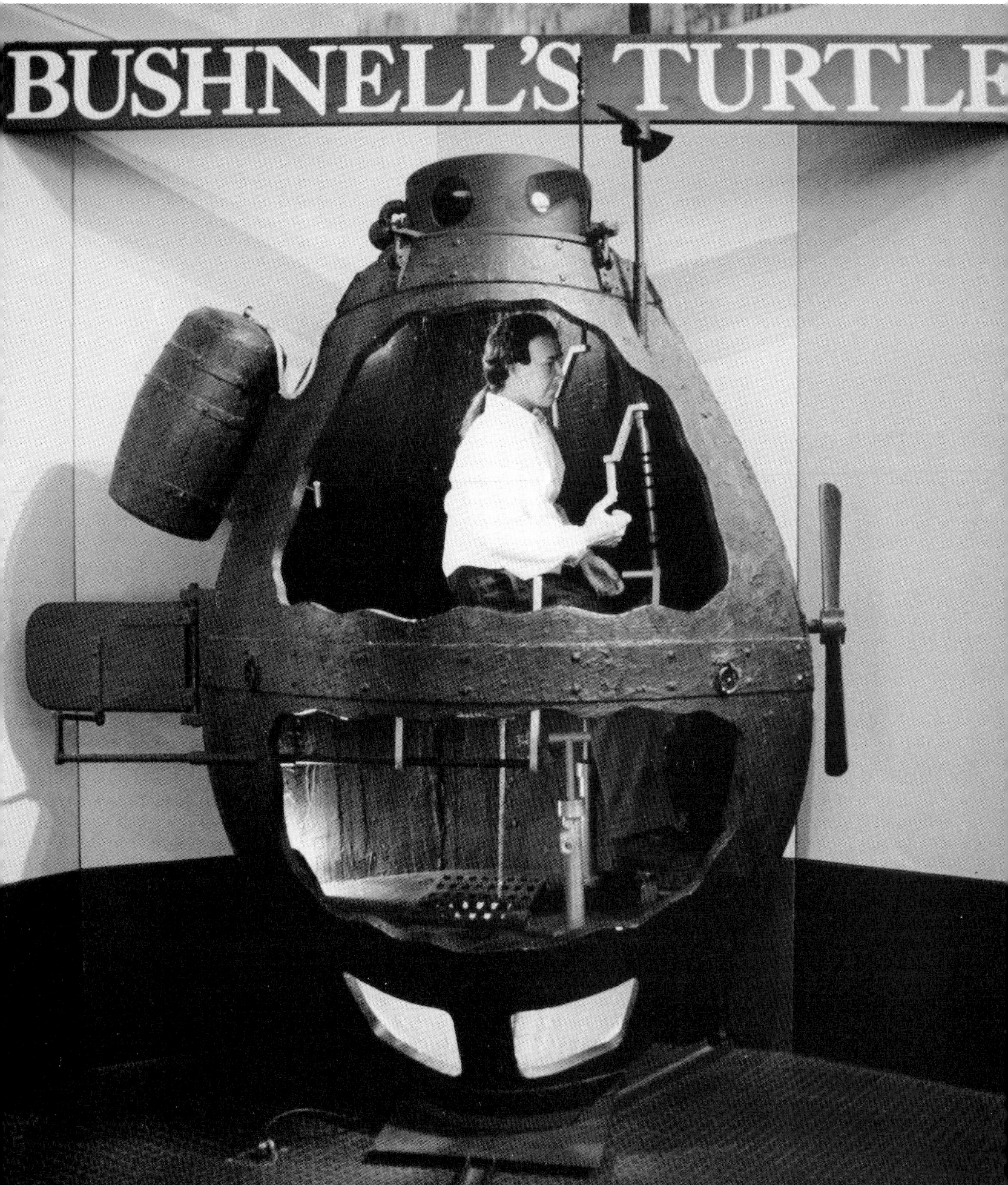
BUSHNELL'S TURTLE

2

Beginnings: The Age of Manpower

A LINE CAN be drawn from the first American submarine inventor, David Bushnell, to the precursor of all modern U.S. submarine designers, John P. Holland. Bushnell seems to have inspired Robert Fulton. Fulton's successful experiments probably inspired craft used by both sides during the Civil War. Their successes led to the foundation of the Naval Torpedo Station at Newport in 1869. *Torpedo* then meant a moored mine or a charge on a spar projected ahead of a submarine or small boat (self-propelled "automobile" torpedoes were in their infancy). The officers at Newport studied not only the weapons but also their carriers, which were sometimes difficult to distinguish from the weapons. The station naturally became a focus for those trying to sell submarines to the navy, and the officers gained insight into the problems of submarine design. One of them, W. W. Kimball, recognized in Holland's work the first workable solution he had seen. His encouragement (described in chapter 3) was one key to Holland's acceptance and success.

In 1775, Bushnell designed and built the submersible *Turtle* for the specific purpose of breaking the British blockade of New York harbor. He seems to have worked on underwater warfare, initially on the problem of building a successful mine, while attending Yale College (1771–75).[1] Bushnell substituted propellers for the oars of previous inventors. *Turtle* had slight positive buoyancy and normally floated with 6–7 in of conning tower above the surface. To submerge, the operator used a foot pedal to flood the bilges. He could eject water by means of a pump.

Once the boat was at near-neutral buoyancy, depth could be adjusted by turning a vertical (haul-down) screw, apparently the first to be designed for a submarine. She was propelled by a second screw, mounted in her bow and operated by a hand or by foot pedal. For safety, she could jettison her 200-lb lead keel (there were also 700 lb of fixed lead ballast). Alternatively, her operator could surface completely by pumping out the bilges. When near the surface, the operator could breathe through a tube, which closed automatically when *Turtle* submerged.[2] As a measure of how little changed during most of the 19th century, this design still seemed quite sophisticated when *Turtle* was included among newer submarines in an 1875 lecture at the Newport Naval Torpedo Station. Real change awaited the appearance of a practical underwater power plant.

Completed at Saybrook, Connecticut, in October or November 1775, *Turtle* had been financed largely by Bushnell but with some money from the state of Connecticut. Word almost immediately leaked to the British. Aware of the submarine's threat, they presumably kept a more alert lookout and posted picketboats whose crews might have been able to sink the small *Turtle* as she porpoised during her approach to the target. Bushnell canceled his orignal plan to attack in Boston Harbor when British forces evacuated that city in March 1776. Bushnell then turned to New York Harbor. When his chosen operator, his brother Ezra, fell ill, Bushnell requested Gen. George Washington ask for volunteers. Sgt. Ezra Lee was chosen. He set out on the night of 6 September 1776. After having been towed

Bushnell's *Turtle* was the first American submarine. This cutaway model is in the submarine museum at Groton, Connecticut. The cask on the back of the submarine is its weapon, containing 150 lbs of black powder with a clockwork time fuse, for a delay of up to 12 hours. Abaft the vertical propeller atop the hull is the screw by which means the bomb (which was roped to it) would have been attached to the hull of a target. Once the screw was firmly attached, the boat was expected to submerge to release it and the bomb. The operator's hands hold cranks for both propellers; there were also foot pedals.

Visible in the lower part of the boat are the forcing pump for water ballast and the rudder control rod (the control bar would be depressed for port and raised for starboard). The operator sat on a transverse beam not visible here (it was inside the reinforcing band). Visible atop the hull is the hatch with its deadlights and, on the left, a ventilation pipe with a valve that would seal underwater. Not visible are 200 lbs of lead ballast that could be released on a 50-ft line, to be recovered if possible. (*Submarine Force Museum and Library*)

as far as possible, Lee submerged to attack HMS *Eagle*, the British flagship. He later reported that he had been unable to fasten his limpet mine to the ship's hull. As he withdrew in failure, the British spotted his craft and a boat pursued him. When Lee cut the mine loose, it drifted toward the British anchorage, where it exploded spectacularly and apparently caused the British to move their ships downstream. Bushnell tried twice more, from Fort Lee, New Jersey, later in September. On 6 October, the British sank the sloop carrying *Turtle*. The submarine was salvaged but seems to have seen no further action.

In 1797, Robert Fulton, probably inspired by Bushnell, offered a submarine to France.[3] The following year the minister of marine rejected the favorable report of a commission convened by the Directory (the governing body). Then Napoleon came to power; the new minister of marine, P. A. L. Forfait, had been a member of the 1798 commission. On 13 July 1800, Fulton first tested his submarine *Nautilus* on the Seine.

Fulton used diving planes instead of Bushnell's haul-down screw. His cigar-shaped (elongated) hull accommodated a multi-man crew, driving his screw by hand cranks rather than by Bushnell's foot pedals. Fulton was the first to provide a submarine with a separate cruising power plant for surface mobility, in this case sails. She was soon provided with a flat deck, 20 ft × 6 ft, for use on the surface. Jars of oxygen supplemented the air in the boat.[4]

On her first trial, *Nautilus* carried a three-man crew underwater for 45 min. (Fulton later estimated that the air in his boat would last a four-man crew 3 hr.) Forfait then recommended another test further downstream at Rouen, where the river was deeper. After diving twice in 25 ft, *Nautilus* moved to the sea at Le Havre. Fulton once stayed at sea for 3 days in September 1800. A gale once forced him down for 6 hr; he breathed through a metal tube. Two British brigs weighed anchor before he could attack them.[5]

Fulton was given 10,000 francs in March 1801 for more tests at Brest. He installed a large deadlight to supplement the candle he usually burned. He also developed a towed "submarine bomb," to swing into a target. During the summer of 1801, Fulton cruised off Brest and looked for targets, but the British were aware of him and took appropriate precautions. Disappointed, he broke the boat up that fall. He later wrote that he had lost interest in the submarine because it was difficult to manage underwater; he was more interested in mine warfare. Forfait was interested mainly in the submarine. In October 1801, he was replaced by a more traditional officer, Adm. Denis Decres, who abandoned the Fulton project altogether.[6]

Fulton left for England in 1804. There he designed a much improved double-hull submarine, with the boat-shaped outer hull measuring 35 ft × 10 ft × 8 ft (depth) and the cylindrical inner (pressure) hull, 24 ft × 6 ft.[7] As in later double-hull submarines, the space between was for ballast. The inner hull would accommodate six people and sufficient provisions for 20 days at sea. As in the

earlier boat, Fulton estimated that the air inside would suffice for 3 hr. Like the French boat, the new submarine would have two breathing tubes, one for discharge and one for intake. She would carry 30 bombs, each containing 100 lb of powder. Unlike *Nautilus*, this boat would have a haul-down screw at the bow but no diving planes. Apparently, Fulton planned to lie submerged in ambush (either at anchor or using the haul-down screw) until after dark, then surface to attack. The submarine, Fulton wrote, "must be considered as a masked battery which can lie secure in the neighborhood of an Enemy, watch for an opportunity to deposit her cargo of Bombs, and retire unperceived." The Admiralty was far more interested in Fulton's drifting mines, which it tried unsuccessfully in combat.

At least one later potential sponsor, President Thomas Jefferson, was far more interested in Fulton's submarines than in his mines. Fulton published an account of his ideas on mining (including primitive surface torpedo boats), *Torpedo War and Submarine Explosions*, in 1810. He conducted some U.S. tests but never got the backing he sought.

Presumably inspired by Fulton's experiments, Congress passed the Torpedo Act of 3 March 1813: anyone who destroyed a British ship would be paid half her value.[8] At least three "torpedo boats" operated unsuccessfully against the British fleet off the U.S. coast that year. One might have been a Bushnell-type true submarine built at Norwich, Connecticut. She dived "like a porpoise" after attacking HMS *Ramilles* in August 1813.[9] Silas Halsey reportedly operated another submarine in New London harbor in 1814.[10]

Fulton's book was reprinted at least once in the United States (in 1834), and it was translated into French. Although interest tended to be concentrated in mines, they were often related to submarines. For example, Germany's Wilhelm Bauer, one of the more successful submarine inventors during the mid–19th century, designed a submarine for the purpose of attaching a 500-lb mine to an enemy ship.[11] It is not clear to what extent Bauer was inspired by Fulton's success, but by his time Fulton's ideas and, more important, the knowledge that *Nautilus* had been a technical success, were certainly widely circulated.

Like the American Revolution and the War of 1812, the Civil War excited many would-be submariners. When the Confederates seemed to have the upper hand in the form of their ironclad *Merrimack* (CSS *Virginia*), the U.S. government badly wanted a submarine capable of dealing with her. Once *Monitor* won her battle, the Confederates were clearly at a gross disadvantage and became much interested in submarines.

A Frenchman, Brutus de Villeroi, designed the first submarine commissioned into the U.S. Navy: *Alligator*, built by Neafie & Levy of Philadelphia, Pennsylvania, under government contract.[12] She was 46 ft × 4½ ft × 6 ft (depth), powered by folding oars, with a crew of 16 plus her commander. She had a pair of air purifiers (one chemi-

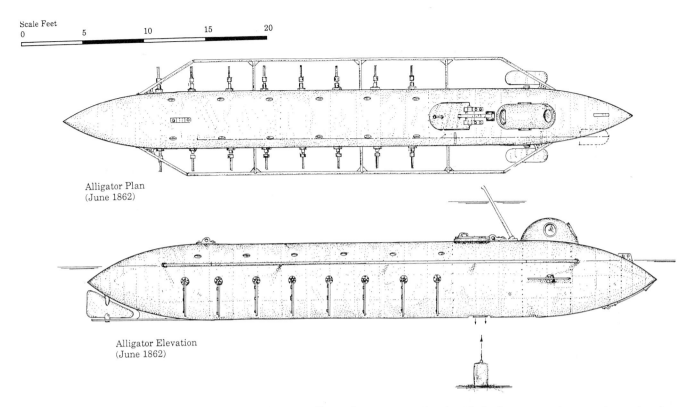

Scale Feet
0   5   10   15   20

Alligator Plan
(June 1862)

Alligator Elevation
(June 1862)

Alligator was the first submarine bought by the U.S. Navy. She is shown as completed, with feathering oars for propulsion (they were later replaced by a conventional propeller). The object below the boat in the elevation drawing is its explosive charge. Waterlines are shown for both the awash and fully submerged conditions; note the air pipe for use when fully submerged (at shallow depth). (Jim Christley)

cal to make oxygen, one a bellows to force air through lime) and was armed with two explosive charges. *Alligator* was launched 30 April 1862 and officially taken over by the U.S. Navy in June 1862. She arrived under tow at Hampton Roads on 23 June after a trip through the Chesapeake and Delaware Canal. A proposed attack on an important railroad bridge at Petersburg, Virginia, on the Appomattox River, was abandoned because the river was too shallow there and flowed too fast. *Alligator* was towed to the Washington Navy Yard for trials and then for refit (installation of a 3-ft screw propeller in place of the earlier oars); she returned to Hampton Roads on 24 March 1863.[13] By this time, de Villeroi was gone, taking with him the secret of his air purifier. *Alligator* departed in tow of *Sumpter* for Port Royal on 1 April 1863 but ran into a storm and foundered the next day. She had no successors in the Union navy.

The Confederates did not always distinguish between true submarines and semisubmersibles intended to attack awash, with the idea that their low silhouettes would not be seen until it was too late. Many of the latter were called "Davids" (as in David versus Goliath). The first Confederate submarine might have been built in 1861 by the Tredegar Iron Works of Richmond, Virginia, for operation on the James River. Most records of Confederate special attack craft were deliberately destroyed be-

fore the end of the war, so no details of this craft have survived.[14]

The first Confederate privateer submarine was the three-man *Pioneer*, built in New Orleans, Louisiana, in 1861–62 by John K. Scott, Robert F. Barrow, Baxter Watson, and James R. McClintock. They were granted a letter of marque on 31 March 1862 but had to scuttle their boat to avoid capture when New Orleans fell. Like Fulton's *Nautilus*, she was cigar-shaped but not cylindrical. She had diving planes at her fore end and rudders at both ends (connected, for control by one man) and an air pipe. Two men drove the crankshaft of the propeller. The commander, well forward, controlled the rudders, diving lever, and air cock; he had a compass and a depth gauge. The weapon was probably a towed charge, with the submarine diving under her target.[15]

The sureties for the bond (for the letter of marque) were H. L. Hunley (Barrow's brother-in-law) and H. J. Leovy. After the fall of New Orleans, Hunley joined McClintock and Watson to build a somewhat larger submarine at Park and Lyons, Mobile, Alabama. The boat reportedly foundered in bad weather in Mobile Bay en route to picking up her first crew. Like *Pioneer*, she was not cylindrical (she was later described as of oblong section). She was better streamlined fore and aft and, unlike *Pioneer*, had only a single, conventional rudder aft.[16]

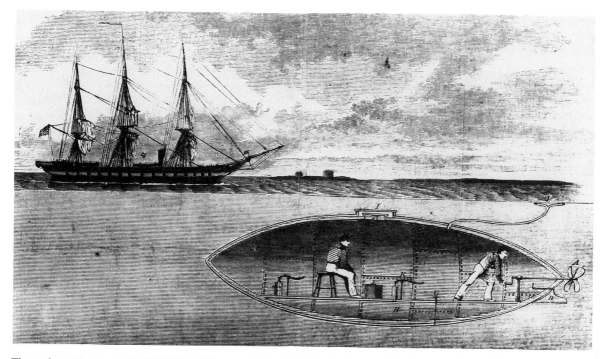

Throughout the Civil War the Confederacy sought to deny the Union the advantages of its larger fleet. This sketch, which appeared in *Harper's Weekly* (2 November 1861), was probably the first to show a Confederate submarine. The boat was purportedly intended to operate on the James River, specifically to destroy the Union squadron—headed by USS Minnesota—there. The following year the Confederate ironclad *Virginia* (ex-*Merrimack*) almost achieved this end, though *Minnesota* survived.

The Confederate submarine *Pioneer* is shown at the Spanish Fort on Lake Ponchartrain, northeast of New Orleans, about 1880. Her propeller hub (without blades) is on the stern at the left; the rudder and diving planes are in the bow, at right.

A contemporary sketch shows the Confederate submarine *H. L. Hunley*, which made the first recorded successful underwater attack. The spar torpedo projects to the left.

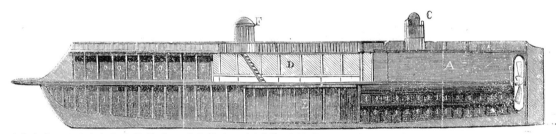

A. Engine-Room.—C. Smoke-Stack.—D. Munition-Room.—E. Coal-Bunkers.—F. Look-Out.—1, 1, 1. Compartments for Air or Water.—0, 0, 0. Compartments for Compressed Air

LONGITUDINAL SECTION OF SUBMARINE BATTERY.

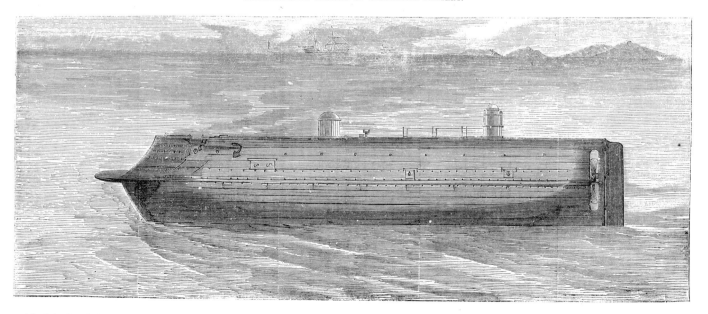

Alstilt's Confederate submarine, as shown in *Harper's Illustrated Weekly*, 10 June 1864. It is by no means clear that this boat was actually built, but a similar drawing appeared in Lt. Barber's 1875 lecture on submarines, which John P. Holland read. This seems to have been the first proposal for a dual power plant boat, with steam for surface running and batteries for use submerged.

Hunley then built another submarine at Park and Lyons, the famous *H. L. Hunley*. She was basically a lengthened version of the earlier boat (for greater propulsive power, eight rather than four men, for a speed of about 4 kt).[17] She was elliptical, rather than boatlike, in section, about 35 ft × 5½ ft.[18] Like *Pioneer*, she had diving planes forward and ballast tanks in the tapered sections at her ends. She also had a sectional drop keel. As did her predecessor, *Hunley* had a breathing tube, in this case two 4-ft lengths of 1.5-in pipe with elbows. Also, like *Pioneer*, she was originally designed to pass under her target as she towed a 90-lb charge on a 200-ft line. She could stay submerged for ½ hr without using the air tubes; her crew relied on a burning candle to indicate oxygen consumption on board. *Hunley* spent most of her time awash, sometimes with the two hatches open for ventilation.[19]

Privateering was soon abandoned, and *Hunley* was offered to Confederate Gen. P. G. T. Beauregard. With little chance of action at Mobile, Beauregard ordered *Hunley* shipped overland to Charleston, where she arrived on 15 August 1863; her intended target (which she was unable to attack) was the big, ironclad *New Ironsides*. Two weeks later, the swell of a passing steamer swamped her at the dock. Only her commander, Lt. J. A. Payne, who was in the open hatchway, escaped. While lying near Fort Sumter, she capsized and again sank (Payne and two crewmen survived). During a submerged run on 15 October 1863, she became unmanageable and sank, killing all on board, including Hunley.[20] Like many other submarines of her time, *Hunley* found it difficult to level off, and thus tended to dive into the bottom. Beauregard refused to let her dive again; she would attack only awash.

Armed with a 90-lb charge on a spar, she went out on 17 February 1864 under command of Lt. George E. Dixon of Mobile, one of her two builders. Attacking the Union corvette *Housatonic*, she was sunk, probably swamped by the explosion of her spar torpedo. This time she was not recovered. *Housatonic* was the first operational warship sunk by a submarine.

Late in 1863, a Confederate by the name of Alstilt reportedly built a much more sophisticated submarine, *American Ram*, out of sheet iron. She was about 65 ft long, with an internal deck running her length. The machinery, compressed air, and gear for operating the two rudders (horizontal and vertical) were above the deck; below were compartments for water, coal, and other supplies. Alstilt's boat was driven by steam on the surface and by two electric motors when submerged. Alstilt dived by flooding ballast tanks fore and aft and expected to cruise 3 ft below the surface, where there was still enough light by which to steer. He seems to have been the first to use a dual power plant of more or less a modern type. (Although storage batteries had been recently invented, it is unlikely that Alstilt used them, so his steam engine would not have charged the batteries in modern fashion.) Presumably, Alstilt's boat was scuttled before Mobile surrendered, but she was included in a lecture by Lt. F. M. Barber (BuOrd), "Submarine Boats and Their Application to Torpedo Operations," at the Naval Torpedo Station, Newport, in 1875 (Holland probably obtained a copy).[21]

The Union navy was well aware of the Confederate submarines but developed none of its own; there was no massive Confederate fleet to counter. Small boats were armed with spar torpedoes to destroy the few Confederate ironclads blocking major rivers; one of them blew up *Albemarle* in a celebrated 1864 action.

The other important U.S. submarine of this period was the "Intelligent Whale," a private venture presumably inspired by the naval events of the Civil War and by reports of the French submarine *Le Plongeur*. Designed by Scovel S. Meriam, she was begun in Newark, New Jersey, in 1863 by Augustus Price and Cornelius S. Bushnell.[22] They provided the capital for what became the American Submarine Co. A government loan also might have been involved, and ownership was litigated for some years. The *Whale* was completed in 1866, by which time the boat (along with, theoretically, the secrets of her construction) was controlled by O. S. Halstead of Newark. Halstead apparently decided to sell her to the government, until then not an interested party. The report of an Army Corps of Engineers test was signed by Gen. T. W. Sweeney (who apparently ordered the test), Col. John Michal, Col. T. R. Tresilian, and Maj. R. C. Bocking. The *Whale* dove successfully with her full crew of 13 in the Passaic River. After submerging to 16 ft, General Sweeney emerged from the air lock in a diving suit to attach a 25-lb mine to a scow. Reports of this test almost certainly inspired John Holland, who later made his own experiments on the Passaic River.[23]

The boat-shaped *Whale* had dimensions of 26 ft 8 in × 7 ft × 9 ft (depth) and a crew of 6 to 13 (4 men were needed to drive the single four-bladed screw at 4 kt). She had vertical and horizontal (diving plane) rudders aft and two main ballast tanks that could be blown by medium-pressure air or emptied by pump. She could anchor submerged to let her diver out. Reportedly, she could be effectively controlled while submerged.

After Sweeney's successful test, the Navy Department appointed a committee to consider the whale: Commodore C. M. Smith, Commodore Augustus L. Chace (chief of BuOrd), and Edward O. Mathews (chief of the Torpedo Board) recommended that she be bought for $50,000. Ownership was still being litigated. When title was finally established, she was sold (by sheriff's sale) to the Navy Department on 29 October 1869; most of the price was to be paid after a successful trial. Another condition was that Halstead furnish full details of the boat, including those of his air purifier. The government took over the *Whale* on 27 May 1870 and made a first payment of $12,050 against a total of $25,000. The first navy trial in September 1872 was a complete failure, and the secretary of the navy stopped payment. Halstead died (apparently murdered, presumably by other creditors), and the project was abandoned.

The *Whale* sat in the Brooklyn Navy Yard for many years; she is currently at the Washington Navy Yard.[24]

Other inventors, inspired by the Civil War experience (and probably also aware that BuOrd was quite interested in submarines), submitted their designs to Newport. None had much impact. In Europe, meanwhile, Robert Whitehead built his first self-propelled torpedo in 1866. It was a truly successful (if unmanned) submarine. Holland would later make much of the analogy between his diving submarine and the diving Whitehead torpedo.

The "Intelligent Whale" was a man-powered submarine bought by the U.S. Navy after the end of the Civil War but never placed in service. Her success on trial apparently inspired John Holland's far more successful work. The "Whale," shown on display at the old Brooklyn Navy Yard, is now at the Washington Navy Yard.

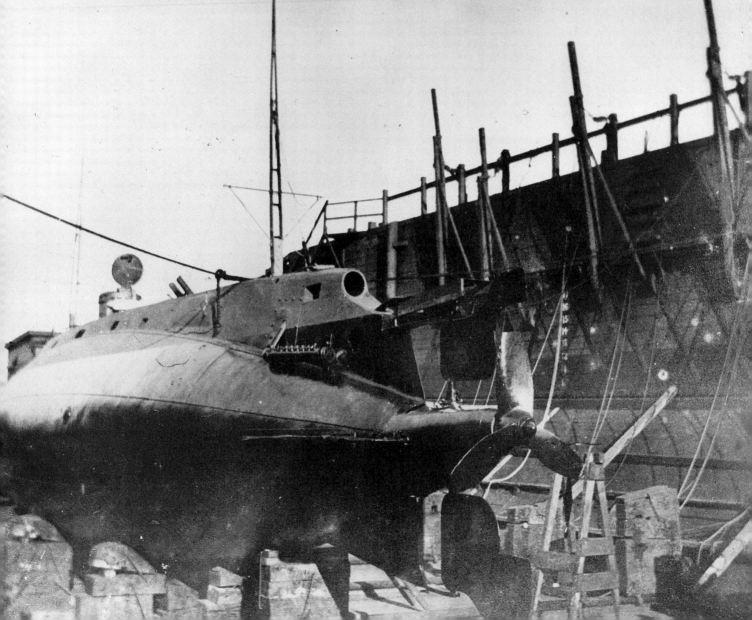

3

Holland and His Rivals

THE INTERNAL COMBUSTION engine, lead-acid storage battery, and self-propelled torpedo, the three technological developments that made modern submarines practical, all reached maturity at about the same time that the U.S. Navy began to revive during the 1880s. The American designer John Holland combined them into a successful prototype for submarines adopted by the U.S. Navy and several foreign navies, including the British Royal Navy. At about the same time, the French Navy was developing its own submarines quite independently. Holland designed a single-hull submarine emphasizing underwater performance, whereas Maxime Laubeuf, a French designer, developed double-hull craft, which he conceived as surface torpedo boats capable of submerging to hide. He inspired submarine designers in Germany and Italy.[1]

Most late 19th-century submarine inventors used vertical propellers (haul-down screws) to pull down their boats on an even keel. Holland, preferring to dive at an angle, used water flowing over planes (diving rudders) to generate the necessary forces. In effect, he offered an underwater "airplane"; his rivals designed underwater "helicopters." Freed from the problems of synchronizing two or more separate haul-down engines or motors, Holland could concentrate on underwater control. Because the planes continuously applied strong forces, they could hold down Holland's boat (or keep her up), even if she was not neutrally buoyant. She could avoid free-surface problems by diving with full tanks. Rival boats had to come far closer to neutral buoyancy; they generally dived with tanks only partly full. Water was generally pumped in or out to change depth. That could not be satisfactory: once water was pumped in to make a boat go deeper, she would keep sinking until enough was pumped out to make her light (and so to reverse the process). Then she would rise until enough water was added to make her heavy enough to begin sinking again. This sort of instability was bad enough, but fore-and-aft instability was far worse. Water in a partly filled tank sloshes forward when the tank tilts forward (as it does in a submarine trimmed by the bow). Similarly, it runs aft when the submarine tilts aft. In each case, the added weight forward or aft increases the boat's trim, usually suddenly and disastrously. Designers were aware of the problem, but their remedies were grossly insufficient. They could not pump water fore or aft quickly enough to balance off free-surface motion, nor were weights moved fore and aft nearly sufficient. Holland avoided these problems. Because his main ballast tanks were always full, a small trim did not quickly grow into an uncontrollably large one. Trim was a static, not dynamic, problem, correctable by pumping small amounts of water into or out of tanks small enough that their free surfaces had little effect. As for Holland's rivals, many boats advertised as level divers were anything but that type. For example, on her 1886 official trial, Thorsten Nordenfeldt's Turkish steam submarine plunged by the stern upon firing a torpedo submerged (i.e., upon suddenly lightening herself by the bow).

Detractors argued that a Holland boat might well go straight to the bottom if she failed to pull out of her initial dive. Holland's answer was that because she was held down only by hydrodynamic forces, she would bob to the surface if her motor stopped. Holland's very responsive boat could easily porpoise, coming up briefly to give her operator a good view through the conning tower deadlights and then diving. Holland sometimes argued that a porpoising submarine needed no periscope.

Holland claimed that he first thought about the submarine problem in 1863, while he was still living in Ireland.[2]

Holland's *Fenian Ram* (top) incorporated most of the features of his successful *Holland VI* (bottom), except for an inadequate power plant. The *Ram*, now in the Paterson, New Jersey, city museum, is shown on the grounds of the New York State Marine School, Clason Point, where she was displayed between 1916 and 1927. *Holland VI* is shown in her original configuration, with rudders forward of the propeller and the muzzle of the after pneumatic gun, at the Erie Basin Dry Dock in Brooklyn, New York, between 26 May and 1 June 1898. (*Submarine Force Museum and Library*)

His interest in flight probably led to his concept of the submarine as an underwater airplane.[3] Holland apparently felt that only a submarine could get close enough to have much chance of hitting a target with the slow torpedoes then in existence. About 1870, he conceived a two- or three-man, torpedo-armed harbor defense submarine. To compensate for the large weights of the torpedoes as they fired, Holland planned to admit water automatically to the spaces they had occupied. Any postfiring dive would be stopped by compressed air blowing water from the ballast tanks.[4]

Holland emigrated to the United States in 1872. He was offered financial backing if he could interest the government in his submarine. He contacted Secretary of the Navy George M. Robeson, who passed him to Capt. (later Rear Adm.) Edward Simpson of the Naval Torpedo Station. Simpson rejected Holland's sketch design for a treadle-powered, 15.5-ft one-man submarine; without any means of vision while the boat was submerged, her operator, Simpson claimed, could not navigate. He also disliked the design for its lack of motive power. That led Holland to

adopt Brayton's newly patented oil (petroleum) internal combustion engine.[5] Holland argued that a compass would suffice. F. M. Barber included the design in his 1875 submarine lecture at Newport (see chapter 2). Holland built a 30-in clockwork model of this design and tested it successfully at Coney Island, New York, in 1875.

In 1876, Holland was introduced to the Fenians, a group of Irish exiles who saw his submarine as a counter to British seapower. They financed his *No. 1*, built at the Albany Iron Works in New York City. Like the 1875 sketch, this 2.25-ton boat (14 ft 6 in × 3 ft; 2 ft 6 in high, excluding the conning tower) was man-powered. Like Holland's later boats, she maintained stability, both longitudinal and transverse, by keeping her center of gravity always fixed. Her diving planes were at the center of buoyancy, just forward of the conning tower (turret), where they added considerable underwater resistance. Holland learned that he could reduce their resistance by moving them aft. *No. 1* was launched on 22 May 1878. Later that year, she was moved to J. C. Todd & Co. in Paterson, New Jersey, partly for installation of a Brayton engine. To keep her details

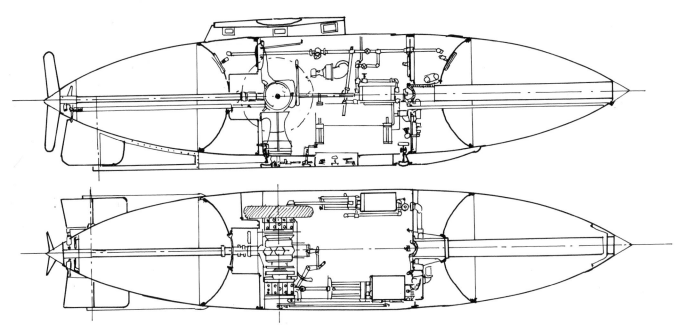

The *Fenian Ram*, John P. Holland's first full-size submarine (31 ft × 6 ft, 19 tons), embodied many of the features of the *Holland* that he would build nearly two decades later. In this drawing, the plan view is at the bottom. The operator sat above the crankshaft of the Brayton engine, whose two cylinders lay horizontally, roughly on the boat's axis (the flywheel, shown as a dashed line in the side view, is shaded in the plan view). Through a crank, the flywheel drove an air compressor mounted forward, above a high-pressure air tank (a second compressor was mounted to starboard). The engine exhausted overboard through a check valve and took its intake air from the central compartment. Control was exerted through the lever shown (there were two: the left for the rudder, the right for the diving planes). Holland continued to use levers in his successful *Holland* of 1897–98. The crew comprised an engineer and a gunner. The domed tanks at the ends were air spaces to provide positive buoyancy. Inboard of each was a water ballast tank; Holland hoped that, by placing water ballast closer to amidships, he could avoid the longitudinal instability that plagued other submarine inventors. He kept the after tank full and the forward tank nearly full (allowing some air to compensate for changing weights, such as oil consumption and projectiles fired; later Holland boats would have separate compensating tanks). Kingstons for flooding the tanks are visible in the boat's keel. Both tanks were connected to the Kingstons by a duct keel, a feature of later Holland and Electric Boat designs. The duct keel made it possible for centrally located Kingstons to control the flooding of the tanks and thus greatly simplified the boat's arrangement. The tube forward was a 9-in pneumatic ("dynamite") gun, credited with a range of 50–60 yd underwater, that fired a 100-lb projectile 6 ft long. Presumably, the boat could be trimmed so that the gun could be fired through the air, to a range Holland estimated as 300 yd. (In the later "Zalinski Boat" and *Holland*, the dynamite gun was canted up at an angle; Holland abandoned underwater fire.)

secret, Holland scuttled the boat in the Passaic River after completing his experiments. It was later raised and placed in the Paterson Museum, where it remains.[6]

Encouraged by Holland's experiments, the Fenians bought a second boat, built by the Delameter Iron Works in New York City (which built USS *Monitor*), with their skirmishing fund.[7] The 19-ton *Fenian Ram*, with dimensions of 31 ft × 6 ft × 7 ft 4 in (depth), was launched about 1 May 1881.[8] Built of $\frac{11}{16}$-in charcoal flange iron, she had both a ram and a 9-in pneumatic gun firing through a bow cap.[9] The commander, sitting in a bucket seat under the turret deadlights, controlled both rudder and diving planes (diving rudders) with levers. The boat also carried an engineer and a gunner. Holland placed ballast tanks fore and aft, with two tanks nearer amidships to adjust the longitudinal center of gravity (the after tank was always full, but some free surface was left in the forward tank).

Ram's improved two-cylinder double-acting Brayton engine was rated at 15–17 HP. Holland hoped to run her submerged on air stored in tanks but then decided to use the air in the boat (he thought it would suffice for crew and engine). Holland also thought that the engine could exhaust overboard against back pressure at depths as great as 40 ft. His wildly optimistic estimate that he could remain submerged for 3 days with the engine running was never tested. Holland claimed that *Ram* made 9 mph on the surface (and a similar speed underwater, though that was not measured).[10] While testing *Ram*, he had a scale model submarine (16 ft long, 1 ton) built at Gannon & Cooper in Jersey City, New Jersey, to test planned improvements.

Many Fenians felt that the submarines had crowded out more direct anti-British action. For awhile, it appeared that the boats might be legally attached. Fenians stole the *Ram* and the scale model from their pier in late November 1883. The model sank in tow, and the *Ram* was laid up at New Haven, Connecticut. It is now in the Paterson Museum.[11]

By this time, Holland had met Lt. William W. Kimball, USN, at the Naval Artillery Station at the New York Navy Yard. Kimball was impressed by Holland's ideas, as illustrated in the 1875 Newport lecture notes. His attempt to have BuOrd hire Holland was frustrated because Congress was out of session (hiring even one draftsman required congressional action). Kimball introduced Holland to Lt. Edmund L. Zalinski, U.S. Army Artillery, who was stationed at Fort Hamilton in Brooklyn. Zalinski owned the Pneumatic Gun Company (which eventually armed the "dynamite cruiser" *Vesuvius*). He considered Holland's porpoising submarine particularly well adapted to his dynamite gun. Using a periscope, the helmsman could spot the target while running submerged, bring the bow to the surface at an appropriate angle, fire, then dive.

Zalinski hired Holland; together they formed the Nautilus Submarine Boat Company. He ordered a 50-ft × 8-ft demonstration boat built of wood on iron frames by Cyrus Plant of Brooklyn. The boat was large enough to provide the operator with a platform from which he could reach all of the controls. Like her predecessors, the boat had a

Brayton engine. An automatic steering vane (tested on the 16-ft model) was mounted above the rudder, and there were eight tubular air tanks (4-in diameter, each about 20 ft long). Holland complained that the periscope (camera lucida) was useless. Zalinski was unlucky; his great opportunity for a sale, the Sino-French War (in the course of which France seized Indochina), ended before the boat was complete. She was damaged on launch (4 September 1885). Raised and repaired, she ran some trials during the summer of 1886, but the company went bankrupt and the boat was soon broken up.

By now, Holland had real rivals, both foreign and domestic. The French were beginning a series of electrically powered short-range submarines. Their *Gymnote* (1888) was the first submarine ever accepted by a major naval power.[12] Nordenfeldt, a major Swedish arms manufacturer, managed to convince many of his contemporaries that his steam-powered boats were successful, and he sold them to Greece and Turkey.[13] They became the standard against which the U.S. government, among others, judged new submarine proposals.[14]

Nordenfeldt used three engines: one for forward propulsion and two to drive air blowers when awash and to run two haul-down propellers. For power submerged, Nordenfeldt stored steam generated on the surface at 150 psi in hot-water tanks, but their free surface caused great problems. Steam built slowly; it took 12 hr to generate enough steam to manage much underwater endurance. Diving was also slow, taking 20–30 min. Horizontal bow planes, connected to weighted pendulums hanging in a tank of oil and water, were intended to maintain trim. An internal counterweight was intended to keep her down angle within limits when she dived. Neither helped much; the Nordenfeldt had far too much free water surface to be stable. Seagoing versions were credited with 15 kt surfaced and 5 kt submerged, with a surface endurance of 450 nm (10 nm submerged).

In the United States, Professor Josiah H. L. Tuck completed his first boat (30 ft × 7 $\frac{1}{2}$ ft × 6 ft) about 1883 at the Delameter Iron Works. She was all-electric and had vertical and horizontal propellers clutched to the same shaft, with a 20-ft breathing pipe and an air lock for a diver.[15] Tuck's larger *Peacemaker* (1885) used a fireless (caustic soda) patent boiler to power a 14-HP Westinghouse steam engine. She made several short trips in New York Harbor. Her planned weapon was a limpet mine.

About a decade later, George C. Baker of Chicago, Illinois (who was already offering a design) built a 40-ft × 14-ft, 75-ton submarine at the Detroit Dry Dock Co. on the Detroit River and tested it at Chicago. The axes of the propellers on either beam could be rotated to drive the craft up, down, ahead, or abaft, much as in contemporary French/Russian Goubet/Drzwiecki submarines (whose single screws, however, were at the after end and could not have their axes turned through 90 degrees). As in later submarines, her air-breathing surface plant (steam in this case) could be clutched to charge the battery. Her 4 tons of reserve buoyancy left about 2 ft of hull, with a small conning tower, above the water when surfaced. The 6-in wooden hull was designed to resist water pressure at 75 psi.[16]

Reports from France and Nordenfeldt's self-promotion convinced many that practical submarines were at hand. BuOrd had long been waiting for just this moment. By the fall of 1886, three or four tentative submarine designs were on offer. Kimball was at BuOrd in Washington. Secretary of the Navy William C. Whitney strongly supported competitive bidding for all naval contracts. Kimball suggested asking for bids for a submarine. No specifications existed. By writing them (subject to BuOrd approval), Kimball could largely control the outcome of the contest.[17] He was not altogether successful. For example, the bureau chief, Capt. (later Commodore) Montgomery Sicard, demanded that the submarine be able to hover, which Kimball realized required haul-down screws. Kimball argued unsuccessfully that a dynamically controlled boat, such as Holland's, could maintain depth near any desired place simply by circling. On other points, however, Kimball headed Nordenfeldt off by emphasizing qualities only Holland could match.

The Circular of Requirements, issued 26 November 1887, distinguished among surfaced, covered (submerged to a shallow depth, with water over the highest point of the shell, but not necessarily cut off from connection with the atmosphere and with a view of the target), and fully submerged conditions. It was almost certainly based on Nordenfeldt's contemporary claims, demanding 15 kt surfaced, 12 kt covered, and 8 kt submerged (endurance 30 hr covered, 2 hr submerged at 8 kt, with provisions for 90 hr). The boat had to dive to 150 ft and quickly change direction by 10 degrees in the vertical, which greatly favored Holland. She had to maintain positive buoyancy except when sinking to pass under an obstacle. Air capacity, with purification, had to suffice for 12 hr submerged. Tactical diameter in any condition could not exceed four lengths. The boat could displace 40–200 tons, probably would be powered by 1,000-HP engines, and would be armed with torpedoes. The winner could expect a $2 million appropriation.[18]

William Cramp & Sons of Philadelphia, the largest U.S. shipyard, offered both Holland's and Nordenfeldt's designs. Tuck and Baker also competed. All the bids were thrown out because they lacked performance guarantees. Holland won a reopened competition in 1889 with a single-screw, steam-powered design.[19] Then the first Cleveland administration ended; new Secretary of the Navy Benjamin Tracy spent the money to complete surface ships.

By the time that Cleveland was reelected in 1892, Nordenfeldt's star clearly had fallen. Whatever his merits, Holland had no boat to show. Baker completed a steam/electric boat in 1892 and was ready to demonstrate it on Lake Michigan. He thought he could win easily, and he had the political influence to restart the competition. Holland hoped to repeat his 1888 success. There was also a new entrant, Simon Lake, who would become Holland's most bitter American rival.[20] Congress appropriated $200,000 on 3 March 1893; designs were due on 1 April 1893.[21]

Holland had already formed a new Holland Torpedo Boat Co. on 5 February 1891. His plans won again. Baker tried to block the contract, but it was let on 3 March 1895 and signed on 26 March after Holland had made several approaches to foreign navies. Congress took responsibility for the Holland boat despite the opposition of the Board on Construction. Secretary of the Navy H. A. Herbert dithered but, as he said later, ultimately decided to go ahead because he had the authority and "if we don't make experiments we are not apt to keep abreast of the world." In October 1900, Chief Constructor Philip Hichborn recalled that "when Mr. Herbert became in a mood to accept the contract for the *Plunger*," he asked whether it would succeed; Hichborn recalled saying that "she would be in advance of anything that had ever been completed up to that time," although surely she would later be superseded. Chief Engineer George W. Melville, however, recalled saying at a public meeting in the secretary's office that "he did not believe the *Plunger* would amount to a row of pins."

Holland later blamed the navy for demanding haul-down screws (two in sleeves, fore and aft). Twin screws were replacing single screws in surface craft. BuEng advised Holland to use twin screws, whatever else he did. Because he wanted a screw on the axis of his spindle hull (to push it up and down), Holland adopted triple screws, which he did not want. Kimball recalled that since Capt. "Condor" (Sir Charles) Beresford in England had set the fashion of twin torpedo tubes, BuOrd demanded twin bow tubes. Holland feared they would ruin his hull lines.[22]

The net result was disastrous: five screws and three steam engiens, far from the simplicity to be expected in an experimental craft. Three triple-expansion steam engines (one 300 indicated horsepower [IHP] and two 600 IHP), driving triple screws for a speed of 15 kt awash, filled the middle of the hull and divided it almost completely. The big Mosher boiler directly beneath the conning tower created intolerable heat. There was also a small compound engine to charge storage batteries. The 70-HP electric motor was expected to drive *Plunger* at 8 kt submerged. Substantially larger than earlier Holland boats (85 ft × 11 ft 6 in, 154 tons light and 168 tons submerged), she was built at the Columbian Iron Works and Dry Dock Co., Locust Point, Baltimore, Maryland, and armed with two torpedo tubes (five torpedoes).

Plunger was never completed. Launched on 7 August 1897, she failed dock trials. She became far too hot when her steam engine ran and was also inherently unstable. Later, about 1899, Holland offered to replace the steam

---

The U.S. Navy's first *Plunger* (*facing page*), as designed (top) and as completed (bottom), shows Holland's trademark centerline propeller on the hull axis, to drive the submarine along the line of the hull (which would be angled up or down by the stern planes). A pair of more conventionally located propellers and a pair of vertical thrusters (bow and stern) were added. The camera lucida was an abortive periscope. (Jim Christley)

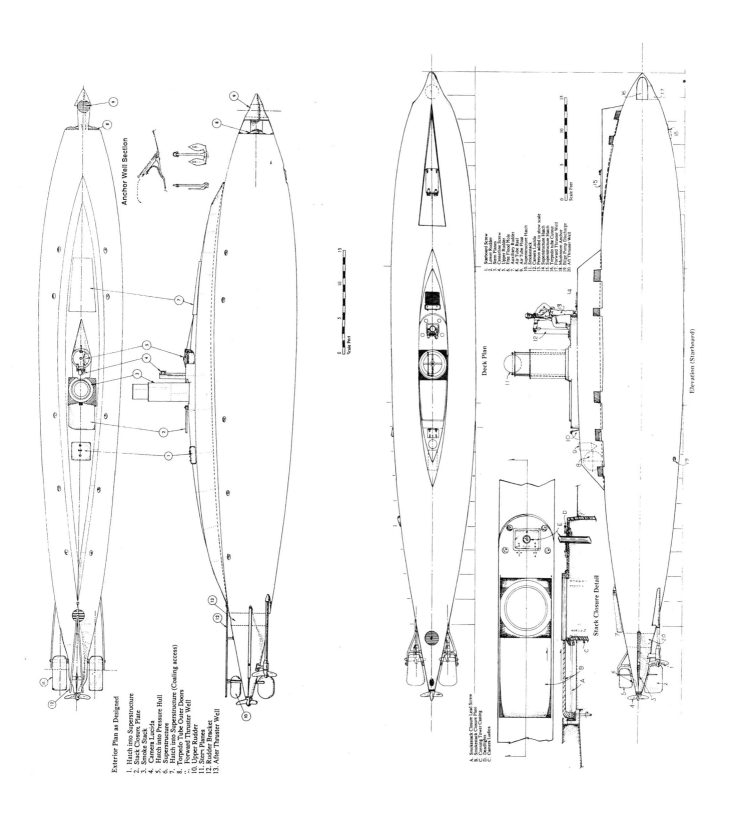

Anchor Well Section

Exterior Plan as Designed

1. Hatch into Superstructure
2. Stack Closure Plate
3. Smoke Stack
4. Camera Lucida
5. Hatch into Pressure Hull
6. Superstructure
7. Hatch into Superstructure (Coaling access)
8. Torpedo Tube Outer Doors
9. Forward Thruster Well
10. Upper Rudder
11. Stern Planes
12. Rudder Bracket
13. After Thruster Well

Scale Feet

Deck Plan

1. Starboard Screw
2. Lower Rudder
3. Stern Planes
4. Centerline Screw
5. Upper Rudder
6. Free Flood Hole
7. Auxiliary Rudder
8. Air Tube Float
9. Air Tube Float
10. Superstructure Hatch
11. Smokestack
12. Camera Lucida
13. Pivots added to show scale
14. Superstructure Hatch
15. Superstructure Hatch
16. Torpedo Tube Cutout
17. Forward Thruster Well
18. Mushroom Anchor
19. Bilge Pump Discharge
20. Aft Thruster Well

A. Smokestack Closure Lead Screw
B. Smokestack Closure Plate
C. Conning Tower Casting
D. Deadlight
E. Camera Lucida

Stack Closure Detail

Elevation (Starboard)

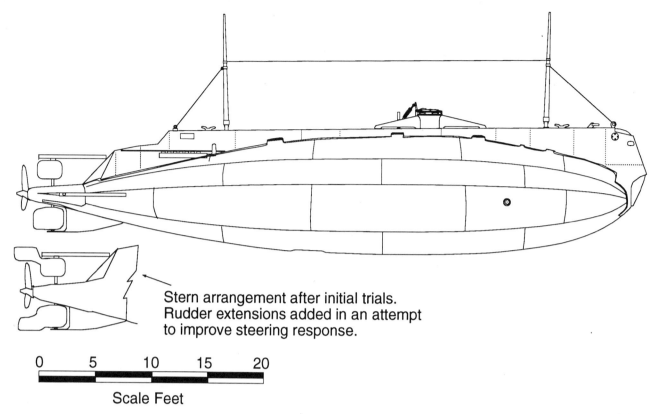

Stern arrangement after initial trials.
Rudder extensions added in an attempt
to improve steering response.

```
0      5      10     15     20
```
Scale Feet

Holland's successful boat, Design No. 6, is depicted as launched on 17 May 1897 with planes and rudders forward of the propeller and with a second dynamite gun to be fired aft out of the superstructure. (Jim Christley)

engine with an internal combustion engine, but the idea was abandoned as too expensive. When Holland and his new partner, railroad financier Isaac Rice, realized that *Plunger* never could be made satisfactory within any price range even close to the appropriation, they tried to convince the navy to take back most or all of the progress payments and to buy an "improved Holland" as a replacement (see below).[23] The hulk of *Plunger* was later brought to New Suffolk on Long Island, New York, and used to train navy divers at New London, Connecticut, during WW I. Holland's failure to deliver *Plunger* blocked his attempts to sell the navy what he considered a much more satisfactory submarine. A Congressional act of 10 June 1896 had authorized two more such submarines, each of which was to cost $175,000, but they were to be built only if *Plunger* proved successful.

Holland later claimed that he was always unhappy with the compromises reflected in *Plunger's* design. He convinced his backers to finance another boat, *Holland VI*, reflecting his own ideas. They were encouraged by the exaggerated claims made by Holland's navy supporters before the House and Senate naval affairs committees that had led to the June 1896 Act.[24]

Holland used an internal combustion engine this time. He chose a 50-HP Otto (gasoline) engine used to light a private house at an exhibition of electrical equipment in Madison Square Garden. Substantially smaller than *Plunger* (53 ft × 10 ft 3 in, 63/74 tons), the new boat had a circular-section pressure hull surmounted by a flat superstructure with a small midships conning tower (18 in high,

about 2 ft in diameter). There was no periscope; the operator had to porpoise. Surface speed was 6–7 kt (1,500-nm endurance) and submerged speed, 5 kt (40-nm endurance: 8 hr). Armament was a single bow torpedo tube (three torpedoes) and pneumatic ("dynamite") guns fore and aft (six projectiles).

Three Kingston valves closed the ballast tanks from below.[25] As in a torpedo, depth was maintained by diaphragms (sensing water pressure), with balancing springs controlling the diving rudder (stern plane). A pendulum amidships (as on a torpedo) kept the boat from taking too sharp a down angle. Depth was measured by a sounding machine (a weight on a wire passing out of the boat). The boat was steered by a compressed air engine.

This prototype of all modern U.S. submarines was built in 1896–97 at the Crescent Shipyard, Elizabethport, New Jersey. Accidentally flooded on the night of 13–14 October 1897, she was salvaged to begin trials on 25 February 1898. She first dived on 11 March.

The Spanish-American War had just begun. On 10 April, Assistant Secretary of the Navy Theodore Roosevelt suggested buying the new boat.[26] Kimball, now commanding the torpedo boat flotilla, wanted to use her at Havana, but the Navy Department refused. A board of inspection was formed to observe a diving trial: Capt. C. S. Sperry (an expert on surface torpedo craft), Comdr. William Swift, and Assistant Naval Constructor G. H. Rock (later chief constructor, but then responsible for *Plunger*). Washington moved very slowly. Secretary of the Navy Herbert Long did not arrange a full official trial until 12 November; the

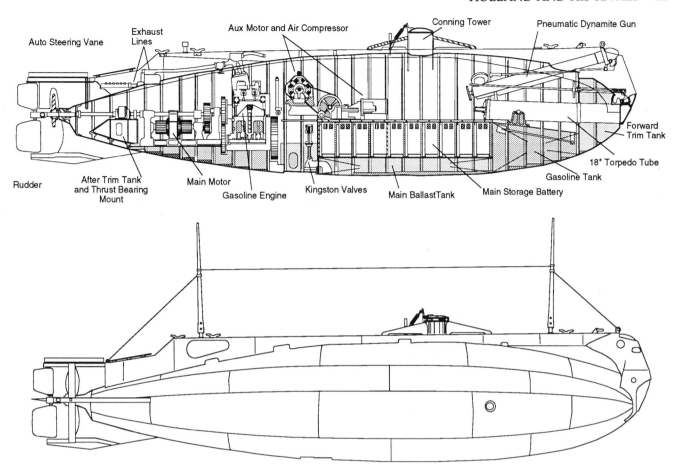

Holland's boat was modified for U.S. naval service in 1900, with planes and rudders moved abaft the propeller and the after pneumatic dynamite gun removed. This boat was never fitted with a periscope. Note that the engine, whose shaft was low in the hull, had to be geared to the propeller shaft so that the latter could run along the axis of the hull. The main ballast tank was brought up the boat's sides outboard of the battery; its top was U-shaped. Holland patented this configuration, which he (and then Electric Boat) used in later designs. It made for relatively easy flooding and formed a bilge down the boat's centerline. The U shape contributed structural strength. Largely because the U-shaped tank had been patented, Simon Lake had to use flat-topped tanks, which caused him serious problems. In this boat, the air compressor was driven by an auxiliary motor; in later Holland and Electric Boat designs, auxiliaries were geared to the propeller shaft or shafts. (Jim Christley)

war was over. The boat fired a torpedo, made 6 kt on the surface, and dived 19 times. Unfortunately, the inexperienced crew took too long to ballast for diving.

She steered erratically, yawing underwater and on the surface. The trial board thought that might be due to her captain's inexperience. However, Holland's test captain, Frank T. Cable, described steering as "the most unsatisfactory task I have ever undertaken" and suggested moving the rudders and planes aft of the propeller, where they might bite more firmly. Holland disagreed but was finally convinced. There was also a more basic problem. In Holland's earlier boats, a single operator was responsible for both planes and rudder; he could not steer and dive simultaneously. To simplify operation, he typically put the planes hard down until the boat bottomed. For safety in deeper water, Cable wanted separate operators for planes and rudder. The boat lacked either a good depth gauge (she used a modified steam pressure gauge) or a clinometer (one was patented in 1900). The operator had to rely on "feel."

First trials encouraged Holland's congressional backers

to pass a new act (3 March 1899) amending the 1896 act to make the new boats similar to *Holland VI*. Holland could look forward to two repeat orders if he could only survive a navy trials board.

The boat was rebuilt during the winter of 1898–99 at the Gas Engine and Power Company, Morris Heights, New York, on the Harlem River. The after dynamite gun was removed to provide space for an improved gasoline engine exhaust. Two new after trim tanks were fitted on either side of the propeller shaft, and small compensating tanks were added. Holland felt that a series of small tanks did not present the free surface danger of a single large, partially filled tank.[27] The hull was shortened aft and a skeg added to support the diving planes and rudders. Relaunched 24 March 1899, *Holland VI* made her first dive on 13 May 1899. She made a successful naval trial run at New Suffolk, Long Island, on 6 November 1899, despite trouble with sections of her armature motors damaged in the 1897 sinking. The new trials board, however, was still influenced by *Plunger's* failure; only Chief Constructor Hichborn supported Holland.

Modified to her final form, *Holland VI* (*above and facing*) is shown at Greenpoint, Long Island, in 1899. Rudders have been moved abaft the propeller. The box above is probably Holland's auto-steering device. The after pneumatic gun has been removed. Forward, the bow cap has been raised (hauled up) to reveal the blanked-off muzzle of the single torpedo tube. The two masts folded down when the boat submerged.

Holland was broke because he had not yet delivered *Plunger*. His major asset was his new submarine, which clearly had considerable sales potential. She had attracted Rice, who, on 7 February 1899, formed a new holding company, Electric Boat Company, with the Holland Torpedo Boat Co. as its major subsidiary. Rice's Electric Storage Battery Co. controlled the key 1888 patent on the storage batteries (chloride "accumulators") that powered the submarine underwater. He was already president of Elco (Electric Launch Co.), which had been formed to supply electric launches to the Chicago World's Fair of 1893.

Holland became Rice's employee.[28] He wanted to continue developing his submarine, but Rice had a different priority: selling submarines. This shift in control, from inventor to investor/salesman, is probably inevitable for any inventor of a successful product. Holland became embittered, particularly at the way in which he was maneuvered out of control of the company he had created (he would leave Electric Boat in 1904).

By late 1899, Rice and Holland were fairly desperate, yet hopeful that the amended 1896 act would provide them with new orders. Although *Holland VI* had cost $236,615 to build, she was offered to the navy on 23 November 1899 for $165,000 ($170,000 if modified).[29] Holland also offered

an improved version with more power (180 BHP surfaced, 70 rather than 50 HP submerged) and an improved dynamite gun that he had patented. Without the gun, the boat could accommodate five, rather than three, torpedoes.

Rice and Holland asked that *Plunger* be returned to them for completion under the 1895 contract. The Board on Construction argued that the 1896 act could not apply until *Plunger* was completed and accepted by the government. There was some question as to whether her successful completion was still a legal precondition for buying any further Holland boats.

To apply pressure, Rice and Holland demonstrated *Holland VI* in Washington, D.C.; she arrived at the Washington Navy Yard in December 1899. On 14 March 1900, *Holland VI* ran an official trial before Adm. George Dewey (now head of the new General Board), the bureau chiefs, the new assistant secretary of the navy (Charles H. Allen), and a variety of senators and representatives.[30] She submerged in 12 sec, steered a straight course underwater at 6 kt for 10 min (maintaining depth within 6 in), surfaced, fired a torpedo, dived, turned while submerged, ran 5 min submerged to show her ability to escape after attacking, then surfaced again.

Dewey was most impressed. Two years before, at Manila Bay, he had been badly worried by reports of Spanish

mine fields. A single submarine might have deterred him altogether. Now that the United States had the Philippines, it would probably have to defend them against Japan without being able to concentrate its own fleet in the Far East. Submarines seemed to answer the problem. Also among the observers was a Lieutenant Ide of the Japanese Navy, who was later in charge of building Holland boats for Japan.

On 11 April 1900, the U.S. Navy bought Holland's boat, which became USS *Holland,* for $150,000 (the original contract price of the abortive *Plunger*) under the amended 1896 act.[31] A contract for six more submarines, described as an "improved Holland type," was drawn 25 August 1900. Each was to cost no more than $170,000. The first was bought under the 1896 act; five more were bought under a further act of 7 June 1900. In October 1900, the Holland Torpedo Boat Co. (by then, a subsidiary of Electric Boat) offered to refund the $93,000 already paid for *Plunger* and to sell the navy a seventh new submarine. The seven "improved Hollands" were the *Adder* class (later redesignated the A class). Electric Boat designated the new design EB 7 (*Holland,* John Holland's sixth submarine, was considered the EB 6 design). In line with its practice through WW I, Electric Boat did not actually build these submarines; instead it subcontracted to two yards (Lewis Nixon's Crescent Shipyard of Elizabethport, New Jersey, which had

built *Holland,* and Union Iron Works of San Francisco, the main West Coast shipyard), for completion in 1901–02.[32] Electric Boat considered the *Adder*s so great an advance over the original *Holland* that it ordered a prototype, *Fulton,* to full naval specifications, from the same Crescent shipyard that built *Holland* and the East Coast *Adder*s.

Fulton was launched on 12 June 1901 and left for Electric Boat's trials base at New Suffolk, Long Island, early that July. During construction, it was discovered that weights and volumes had not been calculated precisely enough. Only three of the planned five long (Whitehead Mk II) torpedoes could be carried (the *Adder*s were armed instead with short tubes: they carried five short 18-in weapons).[33] Nearly half of the air flasks had to be omitted and part of the main ballast tanks blanked off. A planned large auxiliary pump, driven by a 10-HP motor, would have taken up half the space in a boat and so was never installed. Air-driven engines for the rudders and planes, which had not been useful in the original *Holland,* were discarded (they were never installed in the *Adder*s).[34] Speed trials also vindicated Electric Boat's decision to build a private prototype: *Fulton* did not reach 6 kt until her propeller was changed.

In November, *Fulton* successfully spent 15 hr on the floor of Peconic Bay, Long Island, New York, much beyond the endurance of any earlier submarine. She acciden-

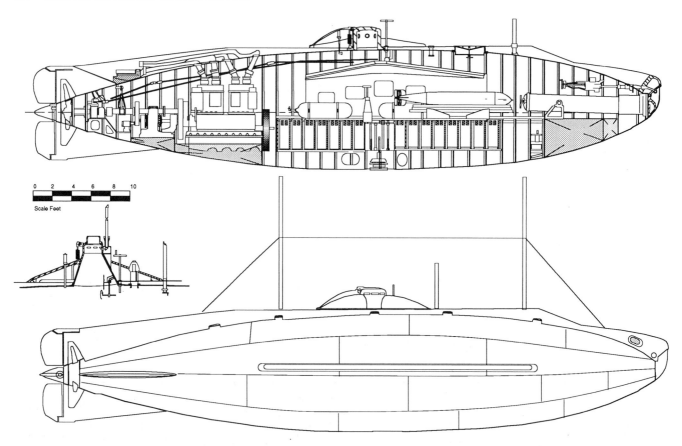

The A (*Adder*) class was, in effect, an enlarged production version of *Holland* with a much more powerful gasoline engine. With the dynamite guns omitted, the decking at the ends was no longer necessary and the superstructure was drastically reduced. The hull was enlarged so that men could move about erect on its internal deck, with plenty of headroom. In 1900, when advocating this design, Electric Boat argued that she would be handier and livelier than *Holland*, despite her greater size, because weights would be concentrated better near her center of gravity. For example, whereas *Holland*'s ballast tanks were spread along her length, in this design the main ballast tank was no longer than the storage battery. It was designed to avoid the air pockets (with their free-surface effect) that could form in the earlier boat's ballast tanks. The air compressor had much increased capacity. The company argued that the most important single improvement was provision of a compensating tank that made it easy to operate in fresh or salt water (*Holland* had failed a 20 April 1898 trial because she was trimmed wrong for New York harbor, with its mixture of fresh and salt water). The scrap drawing shows the periscope and conning tower modification applied to *Plunger*. In the inboard profile, note the rods high in the hull that connect the steering gear to the control surfaces aft. (Jim Christley)

tally sank at her dock in December 1901. After being raised, she made the long run from New Suffolk to the Delaware Breakwater in April 1902; she made slightly more than 8 kt on the first leg through Long Island Sound to New York. This run ended with a battery gas explosion, blamed on saltwater damage sustained by the battery in the 1901 sinking. By this time, *Fulton* had validated the *Adder* design; she was laid up while Electric Boat concentrated on completing the *Adder*s and thus earning contract payments.

None of the *Adder*s was even close to being on time, possibly, in part, because construction had to await the *Fulton* trials. *Adder*, the first, did not begin trials until November 1902; she was commissioned on 12 January 1903. Three boats were each about 2 years late. These delays had serious consequences for Rice and Holland. Because no submarines had been completed, Congress appropriated no money for new ones in 1901 (for FY 02) or in 1902 (for FY 03). By 1902, Electric Boat badly needed cash.

Ominously, its product was unpopular with senior naval officers. Rear Adm. Charles O'Neil of BuOrd grumbled

that, for all the praise, *Holland* had made only slow surface runs and short submerged runs, always in carefully selected places and under the most favorable conditions. Chief Engineer Melville thought Congress liked submarines only because they seemed to justify cuts in the naval budget: when the *Adder*s were added to the FY 01 budget (over the opposition of the Board on Construction), all funds for battleships and cruisers were deleted. The board also considered Electric Boat's prices extortionately high; Melville estimated that fully $100,000 of the $170,000 per boat was profit. Ton for ton, a submarine was far more expensive than a surface ship. Part of that cost could be traced to its complex design, but some of it was also Holland's profit for his long years of largely unpaid research. There was also a strong feeling, which persisted through WW I, that Electric Boat exploited its patents against the U.S. Navy.[35] The Board on Construction did not include submarines in its annual budget proposals.

Less senior officers were more impressed. In a fall 1900 war game at Newport, just before *Holland* was formally

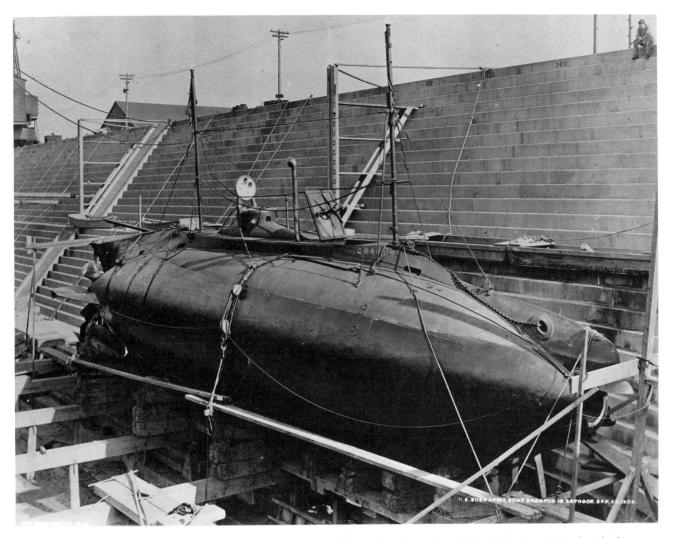

In dry dock, probably at Mare Island, *Grampus* (A-3) illustrates the initial configuration of the *Adder* class. Note that the bow cap swings up rather than lifts up. Unlike Holland, this design shows a deck only amidships. The short stub immediately abaft the ventilator is for the surface steering wheel.

commissioned, she sortied at sundown, trimmed awash (6 in of freeboard), and "sank" the flagship *Kearsage*. Her new naval commanding officer (CO), Lt. Harry H. Caldwell, concluded that she "could in all probability have torpedoed three blockading vessels without being discovered." Electric Boat knew, however, that the navy could not really explore the potential of submarines until more were in commission.

The construction of the *Adder*s had another important consequence for Electric Boat. In 1899, Rice had guaranteed Holland, who was then his only submarine designer, 5 years of employment in exchange for his patents. Holland designed the *Adder*s. As was its standard practice, the navy appointed a trained naval constructor, Lawrence Y. Spear, to supervise the *Adder*s' construction. In 1902, Rice hired Spear as vice president and naval architect. Spear was particularly important to Rice because he understood the navy's unexpressed needs. Rice was well aware that Congress, not the naval establishment, had bought the *Adder*s. He knew that active naval support was needed to maintain any continuing submarine program.

Spear moved Electric Boat away from Holland's nearly pure submarine and toward the seagoing type the navy would need but did not yet envisage. He was probably the reason why Holland bitterly complained that naval officers were subverting his concept of a pure submarine, optimized for underwater performance, in favor of a boat with a substantial superstructure that could cruise extensively on the surface. Holland and Spear collaborated on the *Viper* (B) class, which was a major step in that direction. At the same time, Holland developed a new design to achieve higher underwater speed. He was disappointed when, despite encouraging model basin results, the U.S. Navy did not buy it.[36] With Spear on board, Rice was free to abandon Holland, who left Electric Boat in March 1904. Spear designed the next, *Octopus* (C), class. For many years, he was a major force in U.S. submarine development.

The *Adder*s were essentially enlarged *Holland*s with much more powerful engines. A single 4-cylinder, 160-BHP Otto engine drew its air through the conning tower hatch and also through a 10-in ventilator near the fore end.[37] Holland insisted that, to avoid producing any up or down force of its own, the propeller had to thrust directly along the axis of the hull. Because the engine was one of the heaviest weights in the boat, however, it had to be as low as possible. Both in *Holland* and in the A-boats, Holland's solution was to gear the engine (which drove the generator/motor directly) to the propeller shaft, to the high pressure air compressor, and to the main bilge pump. Gearing was extremely noisy, a defect that became particularly serious when A-boats in the Philippines were fitted with submarine bells (for acoustic signaling). Experience with *Fulton* convinced Electric Boat to replace standard marine cast iron gearing with steel. Similarly, the cast iron Kingstons were replaced with steel Kingstons.[38] Like *Holland*, *Fulton* was not internally subdivided. It was argued that bulkheads would block the commander's view of the engines and motors. It soon became clear that gasoline fumes could circulate far too easily in an unsubdivided boat.

Because her engine was so much more powerful than *Holland*'s, Fulton could run at 6 kt while charging batteries. Maximum surface speed was 8.5 kt. Radius was 400 nm at maximum speed and 560 nm at 8 kt. Semiawash, *Fulton* could make 7 kt (range 340 nm). A 70-BHP motor fed by 60 storage cells (total 1,900 amp-hr at 4-hr rate) drove her submerged at 7 kt (range 21 nm; 35 nm at 5.25 kt).[39] Ready to dive, with only the conning tower showing, she could make 3 kt (range 100 nm). During November 1902 trials in sheltered waters (Peconic Bay), *Adder* and her sister *Moccasin* exceeded their contract speeds; *Adder* made 8.86 kt in light condition, 8.12 kt awash, and 7.08 kt submerged. *Moccasin* was somewhat slower surfaced but slightly faster submerged.[40]

The process of submerging was lengthy. Three ventilator pipes and their cowls had to be removed and stowed and several valves closed (e.g., those of the exhaust ventilator and muffler). The boat was generally trimmed down to dive while these preparations were being made. Main ballast tanks flooded via two 7-in Kingstons, enclosed in a special tank that could be closed off if the valves failed (the tank was generally not used).[41] Designed test depth was 100 ft; however, *Porpoise* (A-6) survived after bottoming in 144 ft, 19 August 1904.[42]

The conning tower, somewhat larger than that of *Holland* (21-in diameter, about 2 ft high), was protected with 4-in armor. There was no bridge as such. A man in the conning tower could steer the boat on the surface by using a horizontal wheel forward of the conning tower, offset to port. The two levers controlling *Holland*'s steering engine were replaced by a conventional vertical wheel accessible to a man standing up in the conning tower and looking through its deadlights. The navy considered the levers unacceptable because they provided no steering at all if the steering engine (which needed a great deal of compressed air) lost power. The steering shaft was carried to the port side of the conning tower; it was connected by bevel gear to the main wheel inside the conning tower and to a shaft for a horizontal wheel to be used on deck when the boat was surfaced. Later, a second internal wheel was added, and all three wheels were clutched so that the boat could be steered from any one of them. The boat reportedly steered poorly underwater because of her great beam, compared with length.[43] There was no periscope; like *Holland*, this boat was intended to porpoise, with her commander looking out periodically through the conning tower deadlights. The hull also had deadlights for illumination at or near the surface.

The planes were controlled by a second horizontal diving wheel near the conning tower. Each horizontal wheel controlled a pair of steering surfaces through push rods passing through the upper part of the hull. The planesman's wheel was to port, immediately adjacent to the conning tower, so that he could work closely with the helmsman. Opposite it were a large depth gauge and a very sensitive clinometer. Below the gauge was a (diving) rudder (i.e., plane) angle indicator geared directly to the diving shaft. Manually controlled planes were balanced so that they could be turned with minimum effort (to a 12-degree dive angle or an 18-degree rise angle). Successful control required the planesman (diver) to anticipate the boat's motions. For example, while diving, he had to begin putting on rise to check a dive before the boat showed she was completely obeying the initial down angle on the planes. That would require great expertise: *Adder*'s trials board concluded that boats had to be kept continuously in commission to train divers adequately. Members of the board noted that the trim angle changed very gradually when the boat was submerged. The average angle was 6–7 degrees (maximum during trials was 11 degrees). For example, at 7 kt, with the planes set for 6–7 degrees of dive, the actual down angle was 3–4 degrees. The *Adder* trials board considered that the boat's success was due largely to "absolute freedom from automatic devices of any character in connection with her diving mechanism, and convenient grouping of her various fittings used in directing change in depth."[44]

The *Adder* trials board noted several design defects. Access to some of the tanks would require removal of much of the superstructure. The ventilator over the gasoline engine was inadequate.[45] The switchboard, abreast and near the working side of the gasoline engine, could arc and thus cause a gasoline explosion. The 30-ft depth gauge was inadequate in a boat designed to dive to 100 ft. The single torpedo tube at the bow was closed by a cap raised by a bell-crank. The tube had to be flooded (by opening the cap) before the torpedo could be fired. If the submarine had to run submerged for any great distance with the cap open, water flowing around the torpedo sometimes turned the small arming propeller in its nose sufficiently to arm the weapon.[46]

Electric Boat sold near-duplicates of the *Adder*s to several foreign navies (see chapter 4). Externally, *Fulton* and the *Adder*s could be distinguished from the foreign boats because their floodable superstructures (casings) did not extend all the way to the bow. They were cut away to leave a rounded bow topped by a narrow fairing (for a hawse-pipe and the bell-crank that raised the bow cap over the torpedo tube); in profile, their decks appeared to be broken forward. *Plunger* was unique in having her fairing extended straight forward from the deck to the bow.[47] At least the Royal Navy carried long Whitehead Mk II torpedoes in its *Adder*s.[48]

Holland's only competitor, Simon Lake, had a different outlook of marine salvager and explorer. Lake initially had little interest in the very difficult problem of depth control. He was content to run his boat along the bottom on wheels. His first demonstrator, *Argonaut Junior* (1894), was wheeled along the bottom by two men. The full-scale *Argonaut* (36 ft × 9 ft, 1897) was driven by a 30-HP gasoline engine. Like Holland's boats, the hull was spindleform; however, she had two driving wheels forward and

a third, connected to the rudder, aft. When running on the bottom, her engine drew air through a flexible rubber tube extending to a surface buoy; later, she used a 50-ft pipe. Gasoline vapor leaked into the boat and threatened to explode; Lake moved the fuel tanks outside the pressure hull. When the engine backfired, carbon monoxide escaped into the hull. Lake installed an induction tank between the engine and its air intake. A backfire closed the check valve that normally let in oxygen; the carbon monoxide was caught in the tank and sucked into the engine again on the next stroke. A lack of reserve buoyancy made a run on the surface somewhat difficult. In 1899–1900, Lake rebuilt *Argonaut* with a shiplike superstructure that increased reserve buoyancy to 40 percent. The superstructure emptied when the boat was on the surface and filled when she submerged.

This 1912 photograph shows the breech of A-4's single torpedo tube plus two reloads on wooden skids. It appears that, like the loading trays of modern nuclear submarines, the skids slid across for loading. (U.S. Navy photograph courtesy of Phillip H. Wilson)

4

Harbor Defense

SUBMARINES IN THIS and later chapters are designated by the letters and numbers applied to them after fish names were abolished on 17 November 1911. *Adder*s became the A class; *Viper*s, B class; *Octopus*es, C class, and *Narwhal*s, D class. Lake's *Seal* became G-1, part of a later group. Names were revived in 1931, but only for post–WW I submarines.

Holland evidently imagined his submarines operating in sheltered waters and defending harbors. He concentrated on underwater performance. Naval officers were more interested in greater range, for true coastal defense, in choppy waters. The *Adder* trials board complained that boats should be tested, not in sheltered waters, but in the open sea, for example on the 50-nm run between Electric Boat's New Suffolk base and Great Salt Point on Block Island, Rhode Island, running at least 10 of those miles submerged at 7 kt.

Adder ran her 3-hr endurance trial with an 8-ft nonrotating periscope (installed in November 1902) rigged through her port forward ventilator. Like the periscopes of contemporary Holland-designed British submarines, it had a fixed upper window (with a 30-degree arc of vision).[1] A similar periscope was installed on board *Moccasin* about mid-1903. The trials board was impressed: the boat was able to remain submerged for over 2 hr without having to surface to navigate. It considered the periscope almost as important when the submarine ran awash; in that case, the conning tower ports were so close to the surface that little could be seen through them. The board wanted a trainable periscope offering a wider arc of vision. A reference line on the periscope would permit an observer to measure a target's bearing against an attached arc. The board wanted a relatively short periscope, on the theory that a submarine could easily place it above the surface by porpoising. A longer instrument always projecting above water, however, might allow a helmsman to observe continuously.

In October 1903, the trials board's Naval Constructor J. W. Woodward proposed that each boat be fitted with two steering stations, each with a compass, and one with a hand-turned 20-ft or 21-ft periscope. Electric Boat argued that anything over 15 ft would vibrate, but that the periscope had to allow the boat to cruise with at least 10 ft of water over her deck to avoid broaching or creating a visible disturbance and also to avoid ramming by shallow-draft craft, such as destroyers.

In October 1903, Lt. Arthur McArthur, CO of the two West Coast boats *Pike* and *Grampus*, urged that they be fitted with periscopes; he wanted to operate them submerged, never porpoising to find targets. The first three (fixed) periscopes had proved unsatisfactory, so C&R decided to test rotating units. Electric Boat developed a fixed-eyepiece type, which it installed on board *Plunger*. Revolving periscopes were also installed for tests on board *Shark* and *Porpoise*.[2] For details of these and later periscopes, see Appendix B. Woodward also proposed other improvements.

In close touch with the first generation of submarine officers, Electric Boat was well aware that the *Adder*s were inadequate. It was also aware of the conclusions reached by the trials boards of the first *Adder*s. By early 1903, Electric Boat planned to rebuild *Fulton* to compete against Lake's *Protector* for expected FY 04 orders. The planned modifications matched most of those proposed for the *Adder*s by the trial board and later ordered by the navy. The first new material was ordered in June 1903. As of July 1903, the following major improvements were planned:

- A higher and larger conning tower to provide the commander (standing in the hull) a better view on the surface, especially in bad weather. The space below the conning tower was enlarged, giving the commander a better view of the submarine's interior. A

The coastal defense submarines grew very rapidly. In dry dock at San Diego, *Grampus* shows her rudimentary superstructure and a single tall periscope abaft her enlarged conning tower. *Cuttlefish*, launched somewhat earlier, shows a much more extensive superstructure (but as yet no portable bridge platform). (*R. C. Richards*)

new midships quick dive (Q) tank roughly matched the displacement of the conning tower when the submarine was in diving trim. Blowing it popped the conning tower out of the water; flooding it put the submarine quickly under water (in 2 sec). The Q tank became a standard submarine feature.[3]

- Eight new tanks at the center of buoyancy, each with a capacity of about 75 lb of water, to compensate for small added or deleted weights. Existing boats could not add or subtract small fixed weights because there was no way of precisely measuring flow into or out of the big main ballast tanks. These auxiliary tanks (albeit fewer in number) also became standard features.

- Improved torpedo compensating and loading gear to permit the tubes to be loaded without any change in trim (underwater reloading was difficult in the *Adders*).

- Each row of battery cells sealed with marine glue to reduce the danger of a short circuit caused by acid slopping out of the jars.

- The exhaust and air valve cams of the Otto engine to be rearranged so that all could be closed when the engine was shut down (i.e., when there was no exhaust pressure to keep water out). In the *Adders*, water leaking into an exhaust pipe could enter the engine via an open valve to short out the spark plugs. The gasoline pump was redesigned to work when the engine was stopped, so that the engine did not have to be jacked over to start. A special thermometer on

the middle bearing allowed the engine operator to check its temperature.

Woodward's list largely matched the improvements planned for *Fulton*. Woodward also wanted periscopes and two sea-keeping improvements. Unlike Electric Boat, he wanted a watertight false bow (with flooding valves) to provide buoyancy for better surface sea-keeping: the bow wave was too high. Trials outside Newport in the fall of 1903 showed that boats often could not run their engines on the surface because in rough water hatches had to be kept closed for fear of flooding. No A-boat had the false bow, but it was incorporated into the B class that followed.[4] A boat in the Pacific had recently shorted out her battery while rolling heavily on the surface. Woodward wanted a heavy framework to carry the weights of the battery plates, with the heavy rubber jars merely carrying the weight of the contained liquid.

Electric Boat estimated that the modification package would cost about $9,700; it included several minor improvements to prevent leakage of gas fumes, to reduce the time needed to trim and ballast for diving, and to better regulate buoyancy. The Board on Construction approved these changes on 18 December 1903. *Plunger*, the last East Coast A-boat to be completed, was chosen in March 1904 as the prototype and modernized by Electric Boat at her builder, Crescent Shipyard, between March and November.[5] She emerged with a power periscope, whose eyepiece was let into one of the conning tower deadlights, so that it was usable from the enlarged conning tower (upper steering station).[6] The CO could use either dead-

Plunger (A-1) was the prototype modified *Adder*. This 1907 photograph clearly shows her enlarged conning tower and her single tall periscope, at its fore end. Note also that her bow casing differed from those of her near sisters. The original photograph was signed by her 1907–1909 commanding officers—Lt. C.P. Nelson, Lt. P. P. Bassett, and Lt. C. W. Nimitz—whose submarines would contribute so much to winning the Pacific war more than three decades later. (*Fleet Admiral Nimitz via the Naval Historical Center*)

In the *Dewey* floating dry dock at Olongapo in the Philippines, three A-boats show standard features: a single tall periscope abaft the conning tower; a conning tower fairing; and a bridge structure atop the conning tower, with the surface wheel atop it. This photograph was taken sometime between 1910 and 1912, before boats had been fitted with forward periscopes. (*Phillip H. Wilson Collection via the Naval Historical Center*)

lights or periscope to conn the boat. A separate steering station (without a periscope) was set up in the body of the boat just forward of the conning tower. Tanking and piping were revised, and separate blowing and flooding arrangements were provided for the gasoline tank so that gas could not be introduced into the main pipelines.[7]

By April 1904 the boats at Newport had shown sufficient promise for the Board of Inspection and Survey to recommend that they be formed into an operational flotilla to work with the coast defense monitors, under the command of an officer on board a mother ship. Their commander at Newport, Lt. Charles P. Nelson, argued that they needed modifications, particularly installation of usable periscopes, before that could be done.[8]

Alterations to *Porpoise* and *Shark* were approved in January 1905.[9] They had tall periscopes abaft their enlarged conning towers and secondary steering stations (with conventional vertical wheels) beneath them in the hull. Binnacles and surface steering stations were placed abaft the conning tower. Periscopes and enlarged conning towers were proposed for the other four *Adders* in February 1906; in October, the Board on Construction recommended that similar changes be made in *Holland* and the remaining four *Adders* (only *Holland* was never modernized).[10]

There were several further improvements, the most significant probably being a temporary "flying" bridge for better surface seakeeping, which became a prominent

feature of pre-1917 U.S. submarines.[11] All of the *Adders* were eventually fitted with second periscopes.[12]

With no new submarines authorized, Electric Boat had offered *Fulton* to the Navy in July 1903 for $170,000. The company proposed a new boat of the same size to attain 1.5 kt more on the surface and nearly 1 kt more submerged. It hoped to develop a larger 100- to 110-footer, "which type meets with the approval of some of your experts, and which is the type of boat now being built by the British Admiralty." These proposals led to the B and C classes.[13]

At that time, Electric Boat was staying alive by selling licenses to its designs and patents. Under a 35-year license, Vickers had entered the submarine field by building *Adders* for the Royal Navy (*Holland No. 1* through *Holland No. 5*).[14] Laid down in February 1901, the first boat had been launched that October and had run sea trials in February and April 1902, well before USS *Adder*.[15] Vickers then began to design its own submarines, based loosely on the Holland design. The British considered the single-hull Hollands poor seaboats that were dangerously unstable longitudinally when surfaced. Given other demands on space, internal ballast tanks could take up no more than about 10 percent of the submarine's hull (i.e., reserve buoyancy, their volume, was limited to about that). In its 1905 D class, Vickers solved the surface sea-keeping problem by moving main ballast into saddle tanks outside the pressure hull, where they could be much larger. In

Off New York Navy Yard, *Porpoise* (A-4) displays her enlarged conning tower and tall periscope (its lens points dead ahead). The other two pipes are a ventilator and the engine induction. Note how the deck has been extended outboard around the enlarged conning tower. The purpose of the object on the bow is unknown.

1906, the design was modified to be powered by diesel engines; Electric Boat later adopted Vickers' diesels for the U.S. E-boats and F-boats.

In 1902, when Electric Boat's U.S. orders dried up, Vickers's cash kept it alive. By 1903, Rice and Vickers held the major share of Electric Boat stock (Vickers had at least 30 percent by 1904). Vickers also held much of Electric Boat's debt, particularly after the panic of 1907. The U.S. Navy was probably unaware of this connection. It demanded that Electric Boat keep all navy designs to itself and was shocked when the British magazine *Engineering* published a detailed account of Electric Boat submarines in November 1911. Only in 1914 did Vickers have to sell its holdings in Electric Boat. The close connections of Electric Boat, Vickers, and British-oriented Bethlehem Steel probably explains Electric Boat's enthusiasm for the secret project to build H-class submarines for Britain in 1914.

Fulton was demonstrated to foreign representatives, including Admiral Tadema, chief of the Dutch Naval Staff, and Comdr. Beklemisheff of the Russian Navy.[16] In 1904, as war broke out between them, Japan and Russia both eagerly sought U.S.-built submarines. Japan ordered five *Adder*s (Nos. 1 through 5, EB 7P design) that year. Prefabricated by Fore River, they arrived at Yokosuka on 12 December 1904. Assembly was relatively slow, and they were not launched until May 1905, too late for the war. They differed from the *Adder*s in having a broad reinforcing strip of bronze plating around their hulls. Test depth increased to 125 ft. These boats were completed with conning tower periscopes.

The Russians ordered six *Adder*s (EB 7P) from Electric Boat's licensee, Nevskiy-Works in Petersburg, under their 1904 emergency program. A month later, they bought *Fulton* (EB 7A) as a pattern boat for the series. Only *Fulton* (renamed *Som*) and *Shchuka* arrived in Vladivostok before the end of the war; they became operational in April and November, respectively, 1905.[17]

K. M. "de Schelde" in Flushing, Netherlands, built an EB 7P on its own account as *Luctor et Emergo* (laid down June 1904, completed July 1906). On 20 December 1906, she became the first Dutch Navy submarine, *0.1* (*Onderzeeboot I*). This brought the total of *Adder*s to 25. Brazil reportedly had planned to buy five Hollands (presumably *Adder*s) but instead bought three Italian boats. Portugal also reportedly considered buying *Adder*s but eventually bought Italian boats. Sweden had sent naval engineer Carl Richson to the United States to learn about submarines. His *Hajen* (lauched in 1902) resembled the *Adder*s but was

In the Philippines about 1915, A-2 (ex-*Adder*) shows her false bow and two periscopes protruding from her enlarged conning tower fairing. The object abaft the second periscope is an underwater bell for signaling; the noisy geared drives in these boats often rendered such devices useless. (*Phillip H. Wilson Collection via the Naval Historical Center*)

a pirated derivative, rather than a licensed copy. Three improved *Hajen*s were launched in 1909 (*Undervattensbaten No. 2* class), followed by more Richson designs, *Delfinen*, 2 *Laxen* (improved *U.2*) and 2 *Abborren* (improved *Laxen*).

After he resigned from Electric Boat in March 1904, Holland tried to go into competition with his former employer. During the Russo-Japanese war, he sold Japan two boats of a new type, which he claimed could operate well out to sea, perhaps by virtue of their greater surface power (300 BHP).[18] Holland incorporated a new Submarine Boat Co. in May 1905, but he could not long remain in business. He had already assigned exclusive rights to his key patents to Electric Boat, which understandably refused to allow him to use those patents to compete with it.

The flying bridge was proposed by Lt. Guy W. S. Castle, who commanded the First Submarine Flotilla (the Atlantic A-boats), on 19 January 1908; this is a redrawn version of his sketch.

Electric Boat's further export submarines are described later in this chapter. While the company struggled to survive on export orders, its rival, Simon Lake, perfected his own very different submarine.

Back in January 1901, after having found insufficient interest in his salvage submarines, Lake had decided to compete for U.S. Navy contracts. That June, he had asked the Board on Construction to review his designs for a one-man boat (31 ft 6 in, to be carried on board a larger ship), a 65-ft boat for coast defense, and a 125-footer for extended cruising. He hoped that unofficial endorsement of the 65-footer (which he planned to build himself) would lead the navy to buy the boat if Congress provided money in 1902. Chronically underfunded, Lake was probably trying to encourage potential backers. The board respected him. Its members resented Electric Boat's political machinations and feared an Electric Boat monopoly. It reported that Lake's design would be worth considering *if* Congress wanted more boats.

Lake had expected his *Protector* to be ready by March 1902, but she was not launched until 1 November. At Lake's invitation, Chief Constructor Francis T. Bowles sent David W. Taylor (later a chief constructor) to inspect her. On 15 December, Lake asked that an official trials board test *Protector*. A board was appointed on 19 Janauary 1903 and reported early in Febraury that *Protector* was incom-plete and unable to submerge or even to run awash. The board could not rely on the mere "expectations and hopes of her builders."[19] Lake's latest complete submarine, the bottom-running *Argonaut*, could not maintain depth and maneuver underwater. Lake failed to have his new submarine included in the 1903 summer maneuvers off Newport.

Unlike Holland's, Lake's boat was designed to dive on an even keel using amidships planes, which exert no turning force.[20] Lake considered even-keel diving an important safety feature. Partly to ensure longitudinal stiffness, he raised the submerged center of buoyancy by providing a large separate conning tower (accommodating up to five men). He lowered the center of gravity by providing a 5-ton drop keel. Because he did not intend to porpoise, Lake provided a periscope (omniscope).

Like *Argonaut*, *Protector* had an outer free-flooding hull for sea-keeping. Lake's submarine was far larger, hence far roomier than Holland's: submerged, *Protector* displaced 174 tons, compared with *Adder*'s 122 tons.[21] Diving was slower, however—20 min against 3.5 min for *Adder*.[22] Lake's was not a double-hull submarine in the later sense because it did not use the space between superstructure and pressure hull for ballast tanks. This difference (in addition to much of the historical record) calls into question Lake's later claims to have inspired such European submarine builders as Krupp.[23]

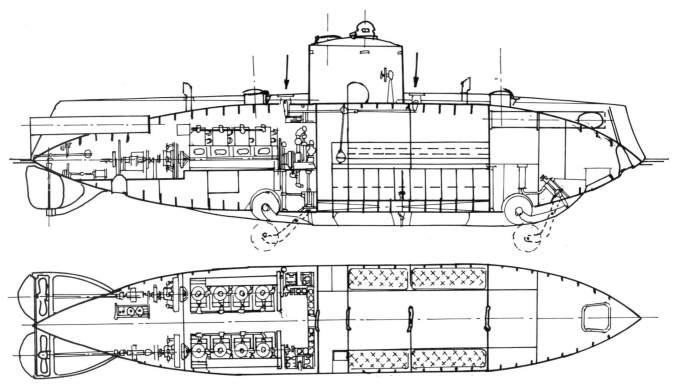

Protector was Simon Lake's first naval submarine. These sketches are adapted from drawings in *Sudostroyenie*, a Russian magazine. They do not show Lake's characteristic midships planes (but the plane axes are indicated here by arrows; note that the two planes are linked to work together). Note also the couches for the crew, indicated by x's in the plan (they were buttoned leather). Also not shown here is the engine exhaust that extended well above the deck and allowed the engine to operate while the submarine was awash.

Lake's *Protector* was his rival to Electric Boat's *Fulton*. She was clearly designed as a submersible surface ship, with high freeboard, a wide flat deck, and a large conning tower. The pipe aft is the engine exhaust. Lake sold this type of submarine to Russia.

Because his submarine submerged on an even keel, Lake was not much concerned with the up or down force the propeller might exert when the boat was trimmed to dive or surface. Therefore, Lake did not have to place the screw on his boat's axis. He used twin screws, each with its own power train (gasoline engine, generator, and motor). As in later twin-screw submarines, one gasoline engine could charge the battery while the other drove the submarine. For a quick dash, the electric motors could be driven by battery to supplement the gasoline engines.[24] Because the engines drew their air through the tall conning tower, Lake expected to run them even when the boat was nearly submerged and thus nearly invisible to a target. She could approach on gasoline power and save the battery for a submerged escape.[25] The engine induction valve was designed to close automatically when a wave passed over it. This idea, which the U.S. Navy adopted in pre–WW I submarines, led directly to at least one 1915 snorkel proposal.

Lake initially used adjustable-pitch propellers but later switched to fixed-pitch. He promised 10 kt surfaced (radius 350 nm) and 7 kt submerged (radius 21 nm). On the Newport measured mile, *Protector* made only 7.5 kt surfaced (on both gasoline engines, total output 240 BHP) and only 4.6 kt submerged (75-BHP electric motors, at the 3-hr rating). Lake blamed poor propeller design and promised to do better before delivery.

Twin engines and motors left enough space aft for a stern 18-in torpedo tube, in addition to two bow tubes. There were no reloads, although there was sufficient internal space; torpedoes were typically loaded through the tube muzzles.[26]

Protector retained Lake's trademark sea-bottom wheels and diver's air lock. Hung by pivoted steel jaws, the unpowered wheels were housed in pockets in the submarine's bottom. They were intended to cushion the submarine when she ran along the bottom. Another unusual feature was a pair of half-ton anchoring weights, with which the boat could anchor while submerged. Lake argued that divers might be as important as torpedoes because they could cut communication cables, control mines, and connect a bottomed or anchored boat with the shore via bottom cables. As yet, there was no efficient means of communicating with a submerged or awash submarine offshore.

Despite intense lobbying by both Electric Boat and Lake, Congress had appropriated no money for submarines in 1902.[27] Chief Constructor Bowles told the House Naval Affairs Committee that further submarine construction should await the trials of the *Adders*. Given the number of new submarine proposals, however, he suggested that $500,000 be appropriated for two experimental boats, chosen on the basis of competitive tests, to be ordered during FY 04. Congress passed an act to this effect in March 1903.[28]

Ready for launch at Bridgeport, Lake's *Protector* shows his characteristic twin-screw stern and a single after torpedo tube. The two port-side hydroplanes are visible at the deck edge near the conning tower; the pipe farther aft is the engine exhaust. This photograph was taken no more than a month before the submarine was launched on 1 November 1902. (*Submarine Force Museum and Library*)

On 1 June, Lake formally requested a test in the hope of competing against a standard *Adder*. In July, however, Electric Boat persuaded the secretary of the navy to approve its modified *Fulton*, instead, for October trials on Narragensett Bay off Newport. Materiel, particularly the new conning tower, was arriving late; in September, the Board of Inspection and Survey agreed to postpone trials to 16 November. Convinced that the improvements to *Fulton* were crucial, Electric Boat specifically rejected the government's offer to lend it an *Adder*. Lake became impatient; his financing clearly depended on the outcome. He therefore persuaded the board to test only a single competitor, if necessary, and not wait for the other submarine. This would prove to be a fatal miscalculation.

Protector arrived at Newport on 17 November. Drydocked to repair her damaged starboard propeller-reversing mechanism, she was reported ready for trials on 2 Janaury 1904. By then, Narragansett Bay was badly iced; trials were postponed until spring.

Lake asked the trial board to take into account the better efficiency he expected of his new propeller design. Like Holland, he could always devise improvements; unlike Holland, he had no Rice to force him to freeze a design to sell it. The secretary of the navy asked that he certify his boat to be complete and that he would accept the tests as final. The outcome had to be based on the condition of the boat as tested, not as promised. Lake seemed too insistent that, no matter how the trials came out, he wanted to make further improvements before delivery to the navy.[29]

Meanwhile, Lake offered his boat to the army, which was responsible for fixed U.S. coastal defenses, including controlled mine fields. After a successful Janaury 1904 test, the School of Submarine Defense at Fort Totten, New

York, recommended using it as a bottom workboat, for example, to repair mine field junction boxes. Five boats were needed: one for experiments and one each for Long Island Sound's eastern entrance, the Chesapeake Bay entrance, San Francisco, and Puget Sound. A torpedo-carrying submarine would be a natural extension of the fixed shore torpedo tubes then under discussion. Despite Senate approval, the army submarine died. The navy, claiming responsibility for all mobile elements of coastal defense, gained jurisdiction over all submarines. The competitive test became absolutely crucial for Lake.

No test had been conducted during 1903. New legislation of 27 April 1904 increased the total appropriation to $850,000 for up to five submarines. On 19 April, an acci-

dent had disabled one of *Fulton*'s engine cylinders. Electric Boat reported that *Fulton* finally would be ready on 30 May 1904 and certified that it would accept the trial as final. Badly undercapitalized, Lake refused to sell out, as Holland had done (in this case, to Percy Maxim). He jumped at a Russian offer to sell his *Protector* (as *Osetr*).[30] With *Protector* out of the way in Russia, only *Fulton* was available for trials and, therefore, the only submarine in position to win the big U.S. Navy competition. Lake's insistence that the navy accept trials even if only one boat was available killed his chance of getting any U.S. FY 05 orders.

The *Fulton* trials began on 1 June 1904. Using a new periscope and running submerged, Fulton launched a tor-

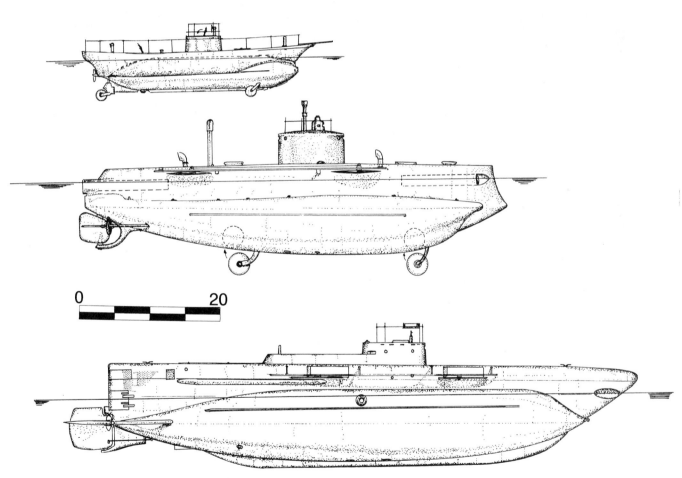

Depicted are three of Simon Lake's designs that were in competition with Electric Boat's submarines. *Argonaut*, as shown in 1903 (top) was lengthened (from 36 ft to 56 ft) and fitted with a boatlike hull and smaller wheels. Her reserve buoyancy increased from 12 percent to more than 40 percent. The bowsprit was a hydraulic device to cushion against underwater collision when the boat was running along the bottom; the stay under it would raise the bow over an obstruction. This was the first time that Lake used a watertight superstructure as a ballast tank (*Argonaut* initially had a single hull, like a Holland boat). In 1903, *Protector* was fitted experimentally with a trestle to protect her superstructure when she dove beneath ice. The next year, she would be sold to Russia. As *Lake XV*, *Defender* (1906) (bottom) was defeated by Electric Boat's *Octopus* in 1907. Midships planes (fore and aft of the conning tower) are visible in both *Protector* and *Defender*. (Jim Christley)

The three B-boats (*Cuttlefish, Tarantula, Viper*) share a snowy dry dock at the New York Navy Yard, probably in 1907. Note that each one still has a single tall fixed periscope, with a flagstaff above it. Boats running submerged flew flags on these staffs to warn surface ships against running them down. Note, too, the running lights affixed to boards on the foremasts. (*Collection of Rear Adm. Henry Williams*)

pedo attack against a target 10 mi away. She was rated on how often the periscope was exposed. Her compass was inaccurate, and a considerable sea made it impossible to find the target after a 5-nm run and again after a 3-nm run. First sighting the target after another mile, she found herself about 25 degrees off course. She did not actually fire because the sea was so heavy that there was a real possibility of losing a torpedo. In a second trial, *Fulton* porpoised, with her commander relying on the conning tower deadlights as though the periscope had been shot away. She was exposed only twice, for only a few seconds each time. Finally, she stayed down successfully for 12 hr.

The trial board recommended buying two versions of an improved *Fulton*, as prototypes of future submarines: three boats about 75 ft long (150 tons) and one enlarged boat about 100 ft long (250 tons). The board wanted to reserve another $30,000 for an open competition for a small submarine about 45 ft long. The submariners had been discussing the two enlarged sizes for some time. Electric Boat offered a 76-footer for $200,000 and a 100-footer for $250,000. Having accomplished her most important mission, *Fulton* was hoisted aboard a steamer en route to Russia on the evening of 28 June 1904 (she arrived early in July).

The trials board report was leaked to the press, and Lake vigorously pretested what he called a biased report. Secretary of the Navy William H. Moody, who was planning to leave at the end of June, deferred any decision to his successor. Lake used Russian payments for five new *Protector*s to finance a new *Lake X*.[31] He could therefore look forward to a new round of comparative trials. On 1 July 1904, he gave ''reasonable notice,'' as required by the April 1904 act, to request a test on the third Tuesday in November 1904.

Again, as in 1902, Lake's work was delayed. In September, Newport News could promise only that the submarine would be ready by 22 December (*Lake X* was launched on 27 October 1904). Now it was Electric Boat's turn to protest further delays. Bowles testified in September that the 1904 act had never intended a delay in contract award merely to hold further trials and that the money had to be spent during FY 05 (i.e., by 30 June 1905). This question had been explicitly asked and answered on the floor of the House of Representatives during debate on the bill.

In New York harbor for the 1909 naval review, *Viper* (B-1) shows both her periscopes and a substantial false bow (superstructure) above her pressure hull. There were few limber holes because these boats were not expected to dive quickly. Note the temporary bridge for surface navigation.

Moored alongside one another in the Philippines about 1919, B-1 (left) and A-7 (right) both show the submarine bells used for underwater communication (B-1's is on her foredeck, A-7's abaft her conning tower). Note how rudimentary their bridges were. (*Mr. Arthur B. Furnas via the Naval Historical Center*)

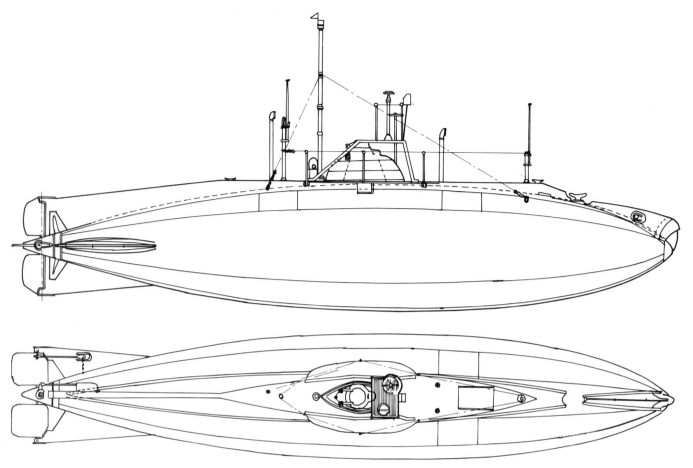

These drawings represent the two Pacific Coast A-boats *Grampus* (A-3) and *Pike* (A-5), modernized, but before installation of the second periscope. Taken from a November 1911 C&R sketch of an improved hoisting arrangement, it shows the arrangement of the *Porpoise* as modernized (from which the Pacific modernizations were copied). The big rectangle forward of the bridge is the torpedo hatch. The circular object on the bridge is a pelorus, for taking bearings. A portable compass was mounted alongside the wheel. By January 1912 *Grampus* had been fitted with a submarine bell abaft her periscope, nearly at the break of the deck aft. Abaft the tall periscope is a binnacle, which holds a magnetic compass clear of the magnetic mass of the hull.

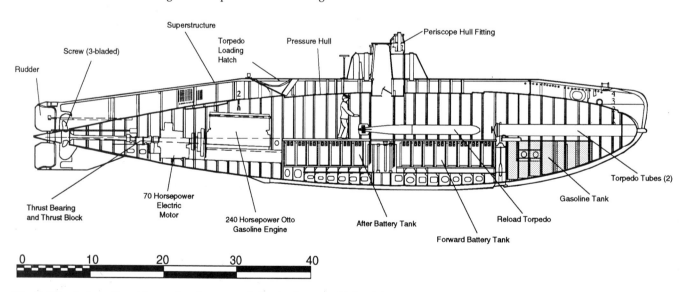

The B (*Viper*) class, the ultimate development of the single-screw *Holland* design, introduced a much more extensive superstructure for sea-keeping. As designed, *Viper* had only the single periscope shown; as in *Plunger,* it was let into the conning tower. A second (hull) periscope was later added. Engine gearing had been abandoned; the propeller shaft no longer coincided precisely with the axis of the hull. Air compressors and main bilge pumps were driven from the main shaft via clutches and gears; they could be operated by either the motor or the engine. Note that, in a boat this small, a reload torpedo occupied much of the hull. An Electric Boat 75-ft × 7-ft design, dated 23 February 1905, was apparently an alternative to the *Viper* design. Unlike *Viper,* the 75-footer would have had one tube above the other, with a common bow cap swinging up. This arrangement made for a much slimmer hull than the side-by-side tubes of the *Viper* class. Electric Boat later adopted it for several small submarines for Russia (EB 27B) and Norway. (Jim Christley)

The secretary of the navy refused to grant Lake a trial unless he certified that his boat was finally complete. Lake refused; he could always envisage improvements. In January 1905, he asked the Navy to return his plans and complained that some of their features had been used without his consent.

The new Electric Boat submarines were EB 16 (81-ft B class [*Viper*]) and EB 17 (105-ft C class [*Octopus*]). The four boats were built at Fore River, which became Electric Boat's sole East Coast subcontractor.[32] Electric Boat submitted specifications on 22 December 1904. These designs incorporated Woodward's floodable superstructures extending all the way to the bow, and the boats would have substantial conning towers surrounded by streamlined fairwaters. Each was completed with a single motorized periscope looking into conning tower deadlights, as in *Plunger*, but reinforced by streamlined shears. The boats were designed

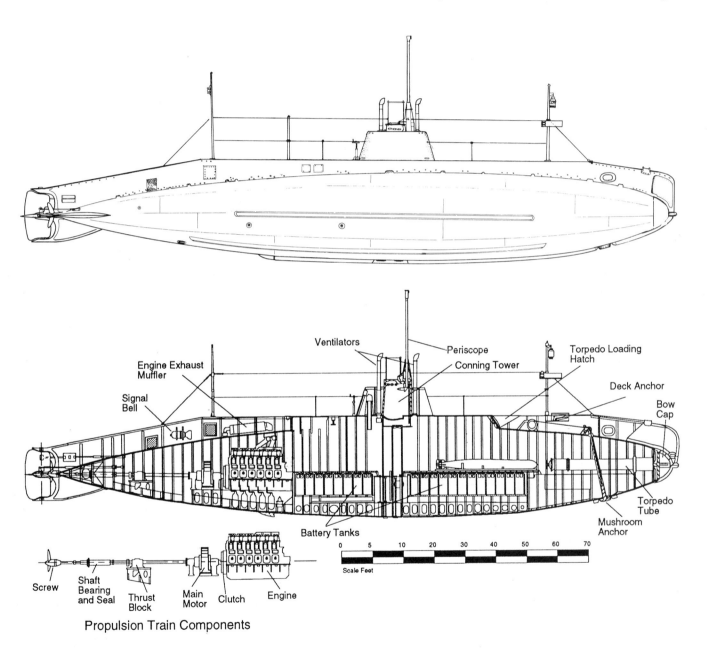

The C (*Octopus*) class was the first designed entirely by L. Y. Spear (Holland had left Electric Boat). As in the *Viper* design, the periscope was a fixed-eyepiece type let into the conning tower. Note the scoop directly under the engine to collect cooling water; until the 1930s, U.S. submarine engines used seawater as a coolant. The high-speed diesels introduced at that time used closed-circuit cooling, in which fresh water circulated around the cylinders and surrendered its heat to a heat exchanger (radiator) in contact with the sea. This design introduced Electric Boat's characteristic stern, with two propeller shafts nearly parallel to the axis of the hull, rudders and stern planes arranged symmetrically around that axis, and heavy skegs protecting and supporting planes and rudders. This was also the first class of U.S. submarines completed with a bell for underwater signaling (it was later fitted to earlier boats). Air-operated signal bells were superseded in later designs by electrically operated Fessenden oscillators, which could put out stronger signals. (Jim Christley)

Octopus (C-1) illustrates Electric Boat's rotating bow cap, which has exposed the muzzle of her port torpedo tube. (*Submarine Force Museum and Library*)

with the awkward horizontal diving and steering wheels of the *Adder* class, but much more convenient vertical wheels (driving horizontal control shafts through belts) were substituted. Vertical wheels (along the side of the boat for diving planes, the helm athwartship) were standard in all later classes.

The *Viper*s, the last U.S. harbor defense submarines, were closer to the *Adder*s than to anything that came afterward. They enjoyed twice the range of the earlier boats, however, and were designed to dive twice as deep. The main innovation in the *Viper* class was a second torpedo tube. Both tubes were closed by a single rotating cap pivoted on the centerline. To fire, both tubes were flooded and the cap unseated and rotated. Therefore, it was impossible to fire only a single torpedo and leave the other one dry for later use. Each boat carried four short (18-in) torpedoes. The *Viper*s were also equipped with submarine bells, an early form of underwater communication (though not with receivers).[33] Unlike the A-class boats, their engines (and those of later U.S. submarines up to the 1930s) drove the motor and propeller shaft directly, via clutches between engine and motor and between motor and shaft. The motor drove the two main auxiliaries, the air compressor, and the bilge pump. Propeller pitch could be changed when the boat stopped. For example, during *Viper*'s trials, her propeller pitch was decreased to a minimum when her batteries were connected in parallel, for minimum speed and maximum endurance.

Octopus, Spear's first design, was the first U.S. submarine that could be described as seagoing. Electric Boat hoped that her performance would be so impressive as to inspire more navy contracts. More than twice as large as *Adder* (273 tons), she was also the first U.S. Navy twin-screw submarine. (Holland was no longer present to demand that any screw be on the boat's axis.) In addition, she had twice as many battery cells (120, in two banks of batteries) as her predecessors.

As in the *Viper*s, each motor drove a set of auxiliaries, mainly a bilge pump and an air compressor, whether or not the engine on that side was running. The friction clutch connecting engine and motor could accidentally engage, turning over an engine down for repair and crushing those working on it. Boats were so cramped that such an overhaul on one side generally interfered with machinery on the other; any attempted major overhaul at sea would shut down the entire boat. These problems persisted until the L class.

Like the *Viper*s, *Octopus* had two bow torpedo tubes, with a total of four torpedoes.[34] *Octopus* was the first U.S. submarine to have both a submarine bell and a receiver.[35] She was tested with a primitive radio antenna, although it was not permanently installed. Consisting of 30-ft masts and 50 ft of wire, the antenna could be used when the submarine ran surfaced or awash. Range was about 40 nm.

Octopus and later Electric Boat single-hull submarines

were largely optimized for underwater performance. The concessions to surface sea-keeping were the superstructure and the bridge. The pressure hull was a body-of-revolution similar in form to that of a modern nuclear submarine. Because its axis was well below the waterline, the submarine's conical stern was submerged. Twin screws were carried to port and starboard parallel to the axis of the pressure hull, with the stern planes immediately abaft them, in their wash. The balanced rudder was symmetrical above and below that axis. The reserve buoyancy of Electric Boat's single-hull submarines was limited (typically to about 12 percent) because only so much ballast tankage could be accommodated inside the pressure hull. The axis-of-revolution hull naturally had most of its buoyancy amidships, where the hull was widest. Without much buoyancy in the bow, it tended to root under waves in-

stead of riding over them. Aft, propellers and diving planes lacked any buoyant structure above them to help reduce pitching. In rough weather, they could come out of the water and pound down into it; stern planes sometimes pounded so hard that they were broken off. At times, seas carried away the after part of the superstructure. Eventually, the skegs of the diving planes had to be stiffened and welded (rather than riveted) to hulls, and the after part of the superstructure discarded altogether. These problems persisted through the S-boats of WW I.[36] They explain the later U.S. shift to double hulls after WW I.

On trial, *Octopus* achieved 11.57 kt (average 11.02 kt) surfaced and 10.03 kt submerged (at periscope depth), well beyond the navy's expectations. She dived extremely fast. The gasoline engine could be disconnected in 5 sec

Lake's *Defender* was modified from his *Lake XV,* which competed unsuccessfully with Electric Boat's *Octopus* in the 1907 official U.S. Navy trials. Built by Newport News, she was launched on 27 February 1906. At that time she had a short ram bow—similar to that of Lake's earlier boats—and triple amidships planes in a protective frame. She was later rebuilt with the sharply raked bow seen here, and her topsides were changed (the triple planes and their single frame were replaced by the twin planes shown). As rebuilt, *Defender* is shown ready for launch at Lake's Bridgeport base. Above her twin propellers is the shutter of a stern torpedo tube. Lake's characteristic pair of amidships planes have been folded up (they are forward and abaft the big conning tower).

After the sinkings of the S-4 and S-51, Lake and his submarine commander, Capt. Sloan Danenhower, refitted *Defender* for submarine salvage trials, which were to have begun in January 1929. Lake and Danenhower argued that salvage work conducted from a submerged submarine would not be affected by rough surface weather. In April, however, the boat was offered to Sir Hubert Wilkins for Arctic exploration (the larger O-12 was rebuilt in her place).

Plans for the salvage trials were revived, and on 26 June 1929 *Defender* made a successful test dive to 156 ft off Block Island. The submarine dropped her mushroom anchor and then followed it down. A diver from the submarine successfully attached air hoses to a pontoon simulating a sunken submarine. The tests ended in a dispute with the navy; in December 1929 Rear Adm. J. D. Beuret, the chief constructor, reported that Lake's test, conducted in smooth water, proved little, and work was abandoned.

Reportedly *Defender* was to have participated in Lake's June 1930 search for gold aboard the sunken British frigate *Hussar,* but instead she remained moored at New London. In February 1932 she developed a leak and nearly sank, but she was saved, only to sink several times at the dock. In December 1937 it was announced that she would be scrapped. Instead, she was beached on a mud flat at Old Saybrook, Long Island, then scuttled in 1946 by the U.S. Army Corps of Engineers. (*Submarine Force Museum and Library*)

and the electric motor turned on in 7 sec; at an 8-degree angle, the boat reached 26 ft in 40 sec. At maximum underwater speed, she could maintain depth within less than 12 in.[37] She remained underwater for 24 hr (albeit not under way), twice what *Fulton* had managed 3 years earlier. Trials included a 4-hr motor endurance run, with the submarine's bow up against the dock. *Octopus* was much stronger than her predecessors and could better withstand accidental deep dives. For the first time, the navy specified a test depth, in this case 200 ft, to be sustained for 15 min. *Octopus* was suspended at this depth from a floating derrick, 6 mi east of Boston Light.

On 29 June 1906, Congress authorized $1 million to be spent on submarines following tests to occur within nine months (i.e., by 29 March 1907). The bill was later amended (2 March 1907) to extend the test period to 29 May 1907 and to increase the pot to $3 million.[38] Although *Octopus* was not commissioned until 30 June 1908, she was ready for trials during the crucial spring of 1907. Newport News launched a new *Lake XV* (*Defender*, 85 ft × 11 ft 3 in) on 27 February 1906, with delivery on 25 June.[39] Electric Boat and Lake both offered enlarged versions of their boats for future construction.

Electric Boat won the trials.[40] Lake's midships diving planes failed to submerge *Lake XV* on an even keel; she broached 18 times. The trials board also considered *Defender* far more difficult to control than *Octopus* because her captain had to handle helm, planes, and ballast. In *Octopus*, these tasks were split among the CO, planes operator, and ballast operator. A scale model of a third competitor, a semisubmersible boat, did well, but she was not a true prototype and could not compete with a true submarine.

The trials board wanted a faster, enlarged *Octopus* with independently fired torpedo tubes. On 22 June 1907, the Board on Construction recommended another compromise: four *Octopus*es and four larger (340-ton, 133-ft) submarines. It also wanted the guaranteed underwater speed of the repeat *Octopus* class raised from 8 kt to 9 kt (to match demonstrated *Octopus* performance), and it wanted

Electric Boat to guarantee 9.5 kt, rather than 8 kt, for its enlarged design. The repeat *Octopus* group (EB 17C) had 250-BHP gasoline engines, rather than the 150-BHP units in *Octopus* and the *Viper*s.

Based on experience with earlier classes, Electric Boat included a second periscope, a radio, and underwater signaling bells in its FY 08 bids.[41] The Board on Construction found the bids ($313,000 for a 105-footer, $380,000 for a 133-footer) far too high; it decided that the company should provide only a single periscope and no radio or underwater signal outfit. That cut the C-boat down to $285,000; the board accepted $360,000 for the larger boat on the ground that the new type was riskier. Even so, the order for 133-footers had to be cut to three.

Electric Boat's proposals were based partly on improvements proposed in August 1907 by the *Octopus* trials board for future submarines. Chief among the board's suggestions were a second periscope equipped with torpedo firing gear, a second pair of torpedo tubes, a quick-acting torpedo tube cap (preferably with independent caps for each tube), subdivision of the boat, independent air supply for automatic tank blowing, lowering of the adjusting tank into the auxiliary tank, reduction of engine noise, and making the engines reversible.[42]

Although the Board on Construction rejected Electric Boat's offer of a second periscope in the C and D classes, early experience with *Octopus* and the *Viper* class revived interest in such an instrument.[43] When it was fitted to the *Viper*s (B class), their surface (external) steering wheels had to be moved from forward to abaft the conning tower fairwater, which also carried a pair of ventilators fore and aft. The contract for the repeat C class (FY 08) was changed to provide second periscopes. Installation proved straightforward.

The larger Electric Boat design (EB 18) became the *Narwhal* (D) class. As the *Octopus* board wanted, two more torpedo tubes were added; all four torpedoes were stowed in the tubes. The conning tower was shaved to a narrow cylinder, without a steering wheel. The external steering wheel was eliminated, leaving a wheel only in the body

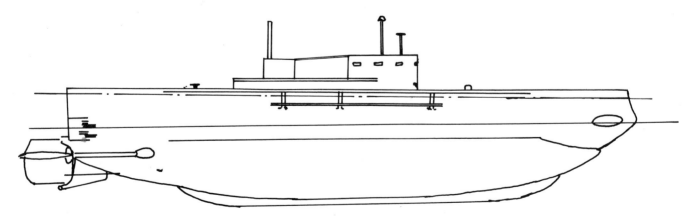

Lake XV was Simon Lake's unsuccessful competitor against Electric Boat's *Octopus*. This approximate sketch is based on contemporary launch and running photographs. The solid waterline is for the light condition; the dot-and-dash line well above it is for the awash condition. The vertical lines along the hull amidships are supports that could swing out to connect with a hydroplane guard when the planes were folded out for use. *Lake XV* was later rebuilt as *Defender*, with a narrower superstructure (above the spindle pressure hull) and a raked bow.

D-3 (*Salmon*) is shown at the October 1912 naval review in New York harbor. This was the last Electric Boat class of gasoline- powered submarine.

of the boat, with the diving station forward of it. For the first time, the boat was internally subdivided: bulkheads now cut off the commander's view of part of the boat. The bulkheads were both insurance against collision damage and a way of making the hull more rigid (presumably without adopting deeper frames, which would consume more internal space). In this design they were placed fore and aft of the controls amidships; other bulkheads separated the torpedo room forward from the officers' quarters abaft it, and the crew's quarters abaft the control space from the engine/motor room abaft it. Because the commander could no longer see or speak into the torpedo room, the new bulkheaded design suggested a need for some form of torpedo-firing gear (initially a buzzer at the commander's periscope, later a torpedo director) in the control room.[44] Electric Boat's proposed deadlights in the bulkheads did not solve the problem of oversight for the rest of the boat; they offered views only into the two adjacent spaces, used for quarters.

There were still considerable habitability problems.[45]

The new submarine was designed to survive flooding (by collision) of any one compartment; this limited compartment size. The control room had to be quite short (this compartment included the conning tower above, as there was no watertight hatch between hull and conning tower). A mock-up demonstrated that the control room could accommodate not only the men usually there but also the commander, who would move down from the conning tower to use the new second periscope. To keep the control room short, Electric Boat wanted to let the second (forward) periscope into the hull forward of the control room bulkhead, with the fixed eyepiece projecting through it.

When the navy revived the second periscope, Electric Boat offered its original fixed-eyepiece design. Much of the pressure for a second periscope was directed, however,

toward providing the commander with a walk-around instrument.[46] Electric Boat protested that any changes, if practicable, would be expensive. The first two boats were completed to much the original design, with fixed-eyepiece periscopes at the fore ends of their control rooms. About 1911 these instruments were replaced by German-made Goerz fixed-eyepiece instruments, in which images remained erect as the tubes turned. By mid-1908 Electric Boat had developed a modified EB 18A design, which it would offer the navy for FY 09; the three EB 18s of FY 08 were modified to match.[47]

It proved possible to modify *Salmon*, the third boat, because her completion was delayed by late engine delivery. In some FY 09 proposals Electric Boat provided only two bulkheads, one at the forward end of the engine room and one at the after end of the torpedo room. *Salmon* was completed with this arrangement, which left sufficient space free for the CO's walk-around periscope with a torpedo director. The necessary contract change was formally approved in March 1910. In September 1909 Electric Boat proposed installing new 130 HP interpole motors on board *Salmon*. Although they were the same size and weight of the original motors, they were designed to take a 100 percent overload for 1 hour so that they could discharge the boat's battery in one hour (rather than in the 3 hr for which it was normally rated). Spear promised a gain of 1 to 1.5 kt. The new motors were also approved in March 1910. Before *Salmon* was handed over to the navy, she was experimentally fitted with special higher-capacity rheostats, to make 12.4 kt underwater (her normal maximum rating was 11.35 kt).[48]

During WW I, re-engining with modern diesels was proposed. Initially rejected, it was carried out because usable submarines were needed so badly: D-1 received her new engines at Philadelphia in October 1918, D-2 and

D-3 in February 1919. A similar planned re-engining of the C-boats was stopped in 1919, with C-1 and C-4 stripped for work to begin and the engines already delivered to the boats' base at Coco Solo, Panama.

There were now four bow torpedo tubes (with six torpedoes), but they could not fire independently; as in the B and C classes, they shared a single bow cap. It had two openings and had to be rotated to allow the other pair of tubes to fire. The nest could not be reloaded until all four had fired and the cap had been reseated. From this class on, U.S. submarines were required to be able to fire two tubes simultaneously. In 1910, *Salmon*, the last of the D-boats, showed that she could fire all four of her torpedoes within 1 min. Tubes proved defective and were only slowly fixed. (Problems with the B class, revealed in 1907 trials, were not cured until the fall of 1909.) Because submarines fired dummy, rather than real, torpedoes on trials, it was not always clear where the responsibility for tube performance lay. Given the poor records of some

types of torpedoes, a contractor might be forgiven for refusing to run firing trials (i.e., to risk rejection as a result of torpedo, rather than submarine, defects).

A-class through D-class submarines originally fired short, 45-cm (18-in) Whitehead Mk III torpedoes (3.55 m long) from 5-m tubes. About 1912, the short tubes of the C and D classes were replaced by long ones that could fire any U.S. 5.2-m × 45-cm torpedo.[49] C-boats and D-boats had Bliss-Leavitt Mk IV and IV-1 (1,452 lb, 139.5-lb charge, 2,000 yd at 30 kt). E through H classes all had Bliss-Leavitt Mk VI (1,500 lb, 200-lb charge, speed 35 kt). K-boats introduced Bliss-Leavitt Mk VII (1,628 lb, 326-lb warhead, 6,000 yd at 35 kt). It was the last U.S. 18-in torpedo; Mk X armed the R-boats and S-boats of WW I. The gyros of Bliss-Leavitt torpedoes could be angled, but submarine torpedo tubes at that time apparently lacked facilities to set gyro angles. Four-tube submarines typically had two set to run straight and two set to run 5 degrees each way.

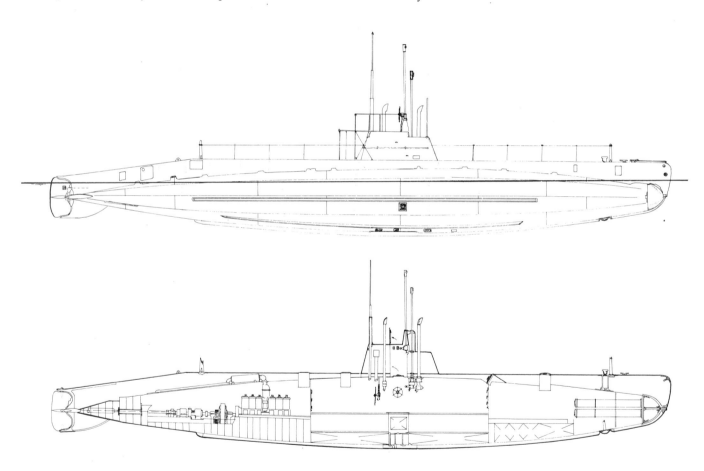

D-3, the last of her class, introduced some features planned for the following E and F classes. Unlike the first two D-boats, she had only two bulkheads, one at the after end of the torpedo room and one at the fore end of the engine room. Pushing out the bulkheads left much more space in the control room (and thus simplified periscope arrangement), but it also made the compartments so large that the boat was unlikely to survive if any one of them flooded. This decision, to arrange bulkheads for more efficient operation, might explain why several U.S. submarines were lost to collision during the 1920s. Quite aside from simplifying internal arrangement, placing the two periscopes very close to each other made it possible to brace both against vibration, a very serious problem in the *Octopus* class. The telescoping radio mast is visible at the after end of the conning tower fairwater. As in earlier Electric Boat designs, control rods for the planes and rudders were carried overhead, along the inside of the pressure hull. That is why the ship's wheel had to be suspended from the overhead, as is clear here, so that it could connect to the appropriate rod. (Jim Christley)

Lake attributed his many defeats to politics. On 29 June 1907, soon after the Board on Construction had decided in favor of Electric Boat's *Octopus,* Lake's attorney, former Sen. John Mellen Thurston, argued that the law required the Navy Department to purchase any boat proven superior to any U.S. submarine either on hand or on order as of 2 March 1907. The department had erred in deciding to buy the type demonstrated superior in the trials. On 30 July, the attorney general certified Thruston's interpretation. Lake publicly charged that Electric Boat had gained its effective monopoly on U.S. submarine construction through corruption.[50]

Secretary of the Navy Victor H. Metcalf saw a simple way out. He offered Lake a contract: the resulting submarine would not be accepted until it had proved itself equal or superior to any boat either in service or on order as of 2 March 1907 (i.e., *Octopus*). No progress payments would be made, so Lake had to raise all his building capital. He had made his point and had to be taken into account in all future submarine programs. A contract for a 500-ton submarine, to be delivered in 27 mo at a cost of $450,000, was signed on 3 February 1908. Lake promised that she would be faster than any submarine in service: 14.5 kt surfaced (for 4 hr, with sufficient fuel for 70 hr, compared with 13 kt for Electric Boat) and 9.5 kt submerged (as in the Electric Boat craft). Underwater endurance speed (for 3 hr) would be 8 kt. Batteries could be recharged on the surface with the submarine running at 6 kt. Minimum acceptable speeds were 12.5 kt surfaced (60-hr endurance, compared with 12.5 kt and 50-hr endurance for Electric Boat) and 9 kt submerged (as in Electric Boat's craft). In 1908 congressional testimony, Secretary of the Navy Metcalf pointed out that Electric Boat had generally exceeded its guaranteed performance; Lake had no comparable record because he had not previously built any submarines for the U.S. Navy.[51]

By this time, Lake had designed and built two further generations of submarines, for Austria-Hungary and then for Russia (see below). The Russian *Kaiman* class introduced trainable deck torpedo tubes and a patented form of pressure hull. Instead of being symmetrical around a straight axis, the hull curved up at the ends. Lake claimed

that this form made for easier diving and surfacing. Underwater, it raised the center of buoyancy and improved rolling stability. Lake apparently delayed laying down his *Seal* (G-1) until he had a design ready, late in 1908, for the FY 09 competition.[52] He ordered it and the FY 09 boat (G-2) from Newport News. G-1 retained Lake's trademark features: his bottom wheels (two single wheels in tandem this time), his diving compartment (usable at 35–75 ft), and floodable tankage in the watertight superstructure above the pressure hull.[53] Critics argued that the superstructure flooded relatively slowly: G-1 took 5 min to submerged from "light" condition, and 4 min from "awash" condition, compared with 3 and 2 min, respectively, for an E-boat or F-boat.[54] Compared with a single-hull Electric Boat submarine, G-1 had a more satisfactory (more buoyant) stern, albeit with lightly built diving planes, but she had insufficient reserve buoyancy and hence was not seaworthy. Her most unusual feature, inherited from the *Kaiman*s, was a pair of twin deck tubes that could be trained while the boat was stopped underwater or at speed on the surface.[55] She also had two bow tubes, with the first independent shutters in U.S. service.

The G-1 trials board disliked Lake's superstructure tankage. It feared that, as the boat worked at sea, gasoline lines would not remain pressure-tight. The tanks were inaccessible for repairs, and, because Lake had provided no gauges, it was impossible to tell how much gasoline remained in any of them (superstructure plating had to be removed to sound the tanks). On trial, G-1 demonstrated an endurance of 66.73 hr (versus 70 hr guaranteed) and an average submerged speed of 10.109 kt (1-hr battery rate). It took 5 min 25 sec to go from full ahead surfaced (14.10 kt) to 8.91 kt submerged (3-hr battery rate). G-1 also demonstrated her inventor's claim that she could hover underwater.

G-1 differed from other U.S. submarines in having four (rather than two) gasoline engines, two in tandem on each shaft with a clutch between. This arrangement was unsuccessful; the two forward engines were removed in 1916. The engine foundations proved far too light. Crankshafts often broke, putting G-1 out of service. Through mid-1916, her longest trips were from New York to

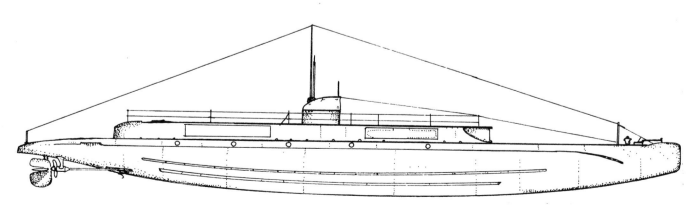

G-1 (*Seal*), as built (1912), shows the deck torpedo tube positions fore and aft of the bridge. (Jim Christley)

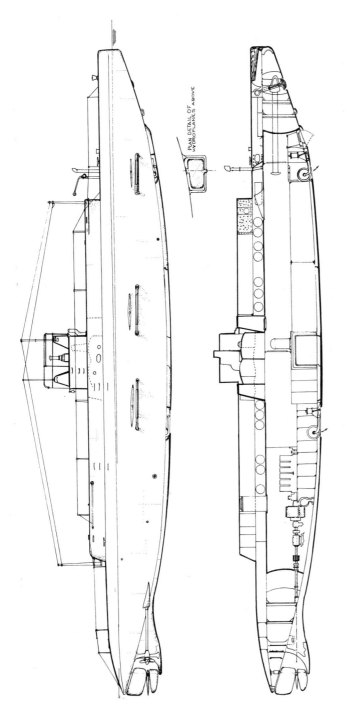

PLAN DETAIL OF
HYDROPLANES ABOVE

G-1 (ex-*Seal*) is depicted in December 1916 after a refit at the New York Navy Yard. Note Lake's trademark wheels and the trap door from the diver's compartment. G-1's forward pair of engines had been removed, which halved her surface power to 600 BHP. Her deck torpedo tubes had been removed, leaving only the two bow tubes in the main hull. Unlike Electric Boat, Lake was happy to blister his tubes out from the main hull. Moving them well apart left space for the diver's compartment between them. G-1 retained Lake's wheels. Although this boat was generally described as double-hulled, she had a conventional circular-section (spindle) pressure hull with a partly watertight superstructure; as in Electric Boat submarines, ballast tanks were inside the pressure hull (mainly under the machinery and at the ends). Gasoline was stowed at the ends, outboard of ballast tanks that presumably protected the interior of the submarine from possible explosions. The bridge fairwater shows Lake's practice of separating the navigating turret (forward) from the captain's turret (aft), with a separate conning tower protruding from the superstructure between them. Forward of both is a separate hatch trunk into the pressure hull, and the captain's turret has its own hatch trunk at its after side. Abaft the engine room hatch is a well for a marker buoy. The battery is concentrated forward of the immersion tank (presumably equivalent to a Q-tank) below the conning tower; above that tank is an equilibrium control tank, and abaft it is a final adjusting tank. Lake argued that his type of battery housing was far superior to Electric Boat's battery tanks, but there was some question as to how much more space it required. (Jim Christley)

Lake's *Kaiman*s, built for Russia, incorporated many of the features of the later *Seal*, but they were extensively modified before they were accepted. *Alligator* is shown here. The trainable torpedo tubes originally mounted forward of the bridge were replaced by the dropping frames visible here, and the superstructure extended toward bow and stern. As first completed, these ships closely resembled *Seal*. (*A Private Collection*)

Simon Lake's first U.S. Navy submarine was *Seal* (G-1). The raised superstructure covers trainable torpedo tubes fore and aft. Unlike contemporary Electric Boat submarines, she had housing periscopes. (*Newport News Shipbuilding and Drydock Co.*)

In dry dock at Philadelphia, *Seal* clearly shows her after torpedo tubes and her stern configuration, quite unlike that of contemporary Electric Boat craft for the *Seal's* propellers are well below the axis of the hull.

Charleston, South Carolina, during the June 1916 war game. She was credited with excellent submerged handling qualities, although she suffered from some problems in submerged control. G-1 and the later Lake boats were all fitted with radios. G-1's greatest claim to fame was a record 256-ft dive in 1914. Because Lake was chronically undercapitalized, his submarines took far too long to build: G-1 was delivered 2 yr, 5 mo, and 15 days late. By 1918, G-1 was condemned as a slow diver, her engines worn out. On the other hand, her last Board of Inspection

Lake's G-1 (*Seal*) shows her trainable torpedo tubes fore and aft of her conning tower fairwater. Note the horizontal surface steering wheel atop the fairwater, at its fore end. (*Submarine Force Museum and Library*)

and Survey (INSURV) report describes her as uneconomical but fairly reliable.

While these boats were being built, ideas on their use crystallized. In 1905, the fleet was concentrated in the Atlantic, with only limited forces on the West Coast. Japan's victory in the Russo-Japanese War had released the main restraint on its seapower, and tensions were rising between the United States and Japan. A hostile Japan would certainly threaten the Philippines, and people in many communities on the West Coast feared Japanese naval attack. Yet, the main U.S. industrial infrastructure required for sustained fleet support was in the East, and U.S. strategists considered the potential European threat very important. Anything short of full concentration of the entire fleet would leave weak forces that could be picked off in detail. As the Spanish-American War had demonstrated, however, concentration of the fleet left civilians in the major coastal cities feeling quite vulnerable. They demanded close-in naval protection. To avoid splitting up the battle fleet, the navy had to maintain a force of torpedo boats and monitors to supplement the army's forts. The Spanish-American War had even inspired construction of new monitors, clearly at the expense of battleships. To continue building and maintaining such craft would detract from the vital concentrated battle fleet.

In 1904, the Taft Board began the first formal review of U.S. coastal defenses (particularly the division of effort between army and navy) since the Endicott Commission of 1886.[56] Initially, the General Board argued for a larger army role. Given improvements in naval gunnery and warship performance, however, the Taft Board concluded that fixed defenses offered relatively little protection; the United States would have to rely mainly on mobile warships (submarines and destroyers) and mine fields.

The board seems to have been heavily influenced by a 1905 report on developments in the two most advanced submarine powers, Britain and France. Reportedly, the British had decided to transfer much of the responsibility for coastal defense from the army's controlled mine fields to the navy's submarines and small surface torpedo craft.[57] The U.S. Navy cited this British experience in its disputes with the army over jurisdiction for coastal defense, as in the 1904 army attempt to buy Lake's *Protector*. The U. S. attaché in London reported that the 1904 British maneuvers (the results of which were not made public) had demonstrated that submarines could keep blockading destroyers and torpedo boats at least 10 nm offshore. French experience had shown that submarines could operate effectively well out to sea: in 1901, *Gustave Zede* was towed about 150 nm from Toulon to attack a squadron at Ajaccio and then returned under her own power at 8 kt; in July 1902, four boats from Cherbourg successfully penetrated and returned from the Brest roadstead, 200 nm away.

Initially, the General Board had argued that submarines were not yet reliable enough for coastal defense. By 1906, however, its position had changed. Submarines were far

preferable to revival of coastal monitors. They could back up the concentrated battle fleet and compensate for any error that might allow an enemy's fleet to slip past it. Should the United States fight Japan, submarines were the only way to defend the West Coast until the battle fleet could arrive from the East Coast. Moreover, submarines were the obvious solution to the serious problem of defending the vulnerable Philippines and the vital U.S. naval base at Subic Bay until the fleet could cross the Pacific. In June 1904, the General Board had endorsed a request forwarded by Rear Adm. W. Fogler, commander in the Philippines, for two submarines, but the Navy Department had rejected it.[58]

Once the fleet moved to the Pacific, submarines on the East Coast would be needed to deter any possible European involvement. The pre-1914 U.S. Navy also had to defend the Western Hemisphere against a possible European (most likely German) attempt to establish a new colony in defiance of the Monroe Doctrine. In this case, the U.S. fleet might have to develop an advanced base in the Caribbean; submarines cruising out with the fleet would help to defend it. An important caveat, however, applied to each possible scenario: submarines were attractive only so long as their cost did not rise to the point of threatening the battle fleet itself, which was always seen as the decisive naval arm. For the next decade, submariners and the General Board fought over the unit size, and thus the unit cost, of submarines.

By this time, European navies were building submarines for offensive operations in enemy waters. The crucial difference between their submarines and the defensive U.S. craft was geography. European nations were close together; little was required to transform a submarine capable merely of going beyond the horizon into an offensive weapon that could reach into enemy harbors. The only foreign waters in which short-range U.S. submarines could expect to operate would be around French or British bases in the Western Hemisphere. The ideal—transoceanic performance for offensives into enemy home waters—was not yet attainable. U.S. submarines intended for coastal defense, however, had to go well out into the Atlantic and Pacific oceans. By European standards, they were oceangoing boats.

In April 1907 the General Board study of submarine deployment turned out to govern FY 09 building policy. Until that time, all but two A-boats had been built on the East Coast. Only the A- and B-boats were small enough to go abroad (to the Philippines) as deck cargo on colliers. Nothing larger could possibly make it across the Pacific. Nor could any boat built on the East Coast steam around Cape Horn to the Pacific. U.S. boats were never designed for transcontinental transportation in knocked-down form. In order of importance for submarine protection, vital strategic points were Narragansett Bay, Hampton Roads, Puget Sound, San Francisco, Olongapo in the Philippines, Guantánamo, and Honolulu. Although important, Key West was not listed as a potential submarine base. So that they could be concentrated as needed, groups of about 4 coastal submarines would be based on mobile tenders. The board's distribution, therefore, implied that 12 submarines would be based on each coast, with another 4 in the Philippines.

In September 1907, Admiral Dewey formally requested four or more submarines to defend Subic. At about the same time, the board proposed that, of the FY 08 C-boats and D-boats, two of each class be delivered on the Atlantic Coast, then 2 D-boats on the West Coast and 2 C-boats in the Philippines (manufactured in the United States but assembled at Cavite or Olongapo in the Philippines). The Board on Construction decided that any such arrangement should be the subject of a separate contract. Money was tight; the boats were all built and delivered on the East Coast. Two *Adders*, however, were ordered to the Philippines in January 1908; in September, the General Board asked that the remaining East Coast *Adders* go to the Philippines (two of the three went in 1909). The only West Coast submarines, the two A-boats built there, had to remain there until 1915, when they could be replaced by new larger boats. Two B-boats went to the Philippines in 1913, to be joined in 1915 by B-1.

For FY 09, the secretary of the navy asked for four submarines. Congress bought eight (act of 13 May 1908). The original intention apparently was to buy only somewhat improved versions of the most recent Electric Boat design, but Lake had made that impossible. Too, the navy badly wanted to find alternatives to the effective Electric Boat monopoly, at least to enforce naval desires and requirements on Electric Boat. Therefore, in October 1908, it welcomed another potential contractor, the American Laurenti Co., which offered submarines designed by Cesare Laurenti of Italy.

By September 1908, the General Board considered it so urgent to build modern submarines on the West Coast that it wanted six of the eight FY 09 boats built there (BuNav had proposed five). Because of its connection with Union Iron Works, only Electric Boat could build on the West Coast. Lake offered to build a boat at Bath Iron Works or at an unspecified West Coast yard (he soon opened his own Lake Torpedo Boat Co. yard at Bridgeport). Because he had not yet begun work on his first U.S. submarine, he could not be awarded more.

Laurenti had arranged for Cramp, a major East Coast yard, to build any boats for which it received contracts. Although Laurenti would use a proven Italian design, the Board on Construction deemed it imprudent to award the new company more than one boat. Rather than award the other six to Electric Boat, the board proposed that the navy build two West Coast boats at Mare Island Navy Yard. Electric Boat could build two at Union Iron Works and offered to build two more at an unspecified West Coast yard. (It eventually chose Moran in Seattle, which had not previously built submarines.)

BuEng wanted to use a new and unproven double-acting gasoline engine, probably offered by the Standard Motor Construction Co. of Jersey City. Electric Boat offered its version of the Vickers diesel. The Board on Con-

struction appreciated the potential of the diesel; initially, it wanted Electric Boat to build two diesel and two gasoline boats (Mare Island would build repeat D-boats).

Electric Boat clearly feared competition from a navy yard. It refused to provide the navy with working drawings of boats (D-class) still under construction, with the argument that it could not guarantee their accuracy. (Its highly trained shipyard workmen could work around errors, but an inexperienced Mare Island work force might not, to the company's cost.) Electric Boat offered working plans of its earlier C class (this experience probably explains why the first navy yard–built submarine was a Lake design). The board retreated and abandoned Mare Island on the ground that the yard would be fully occupied with building its assigned FY 08 collier. That left a navy yard on the East Coast. By late January 1909, the board knew that there was insufficient money: Electric Boat would build the two East Coast boats.

Electric Boat also vigorously protested building any more gasoline boats. The major foreign submarine navies (England, France, Germany, Russia, and Japan) had abandoned gasoline. Surely, the U.S. Navy should not be left behind. Lake offered to install a foreign diesel engine, but Electric Boat had already tested its own engine. The board liked diesels but observed that, in service, they were not yet as satisfactory as gasoline engines; it would be best to limit diesels to two boats. Electric Boat retorted that the particular gasoline engine in question was a risky proposition—untested and sharply criticized by many engineers. The company claimed that its diesel was superior to those causing problems abroad.

Electric Boat offered three basic designs: the 340–375 ton EB 18 and EB 19 and the 400–435 ton EB 20.[59] EB 18A was essentially a D-boat lengthened by 1 ft 6 in and provided with a second periscope (its eyepiece in the control room), a torpedo firing control, a hatch at the base of the conning tower, a portable extension bridge (with hatch trunk), and submarine signal apparatus. She fell a knot short of the required 14 kt. EB 19, very nearly a dieselized D-boat, was rejected for the same reason. EB 20A and EB 20D were diesel- and gasoline-powered 14-kt submarines; the diesel-powered EB 20B was unacceptable because it was too slow (13.5 kt).

The board chose two EB 20As and two EB 20Ds for the West Coast. Money was tight, so it favored the least expensive alternative, two EB 18Cs boosted to 14 kt, for the East Coast. Electric Boat objected to both choices. EB 20D lacked the endurance to go from the West Coast to Hawaii. Late in 1908, the company offered to increase EB 20B's speed by modifying the engine. As modified, EB 20B was faster underwater than EB 20A and had a much better radius of action than EB 20D (though still slightly shorter than EB 20As). Four EB 20Bs became the U.S. Navy's F class.

In EB 18C, the requisite extra $\frac{1}{2}$ kt could be gained only by cutting tonnage (batteries and motors) at a cost in endurance (70 hr versus 85 hr at full power), underwater speed (10.25 kt versus 11.25 kt), and even stability. EB 19

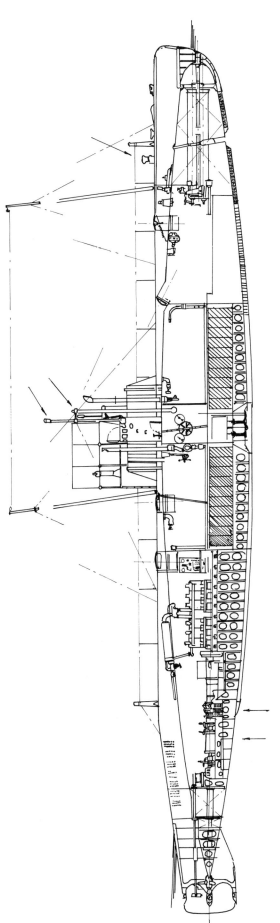

(A)

These drawings show how the standard Electric Boat design evolved. In each drawing, batteries have been shaded in for clarity.

(A) D-1, shown in March 1918, was the first such boat to be subdivided for survivability. The compartments defined by the bulkheads had to be small (i.e., bulkheads had to be close together) so that the submarine (surfaced) would survive flooding any one of them. They greatly complicated internal access, and bulkheading was drastically reduced in the last boat of the class, *Salmon* (D-3). Changes made late in construction included a second periscope, entering the hull just abaft the bulkhead at the fore end of the control room, and an air-operated signaling bell, indicated on deck. This drawing clearly shows Electric Boat's duct keel, draining the ballast tanks fore and aft, controlled centrally by Kingstons operated directly from the control room. Aft, the watertight duct ran up into the bilge pump, which was driven by the propeller shaft. This was a very neat arrangement: the single pump aft could easily pump out all the main ballast tanks fore and aft, by putting suction on the duct. Without a single watertight drain running fore and aft, Lake had to provide each tank with its own connection to pump suction. It was therefore natural for him to locate pumps amidships, under the control room. There they could not be driven directly by the main motors or engines; they required their own motors. Electric Boat's duct keel made for a neat internal arrangement but also for relatively slow flooding. In the company's production S-boats (S-18 and above), the forward ballast tanks had their own remotely-controlled Kingstons, and the watertight duct keel ended just forward of amidships. These tanks, which would bring the boat's head down for diving, could therefore flood particularly quickly. Post-World War I U.S. submarines eliminated the duct keel altogether in favor of individual Kingstons in each tank, with remotely-controlled vents (driven by British-style hydraulic telemotors). Riding the vents (i.e., with Kingstons open), a submarine could dive quickly merely by opening the vents and letting out the air that kept the tanks empty. The S-boats and their predecessors, however, generally could not ride the vents because their ballast tanks were too leaky. They had to rely on their Kingstons to the end of their service lives.

Electric Boat also considered the duct keel and the ballast tanks safety features, protecting a boat if she grounded; the company argued that the tanks, which were built to withstand full sea pressure (since they would be flooded when the boat dove), formed, in effect, an inner bottom over the forward part of the hull.

Just below the control room was the adjusting tank, with its own side-by-side Kingstons (also operated directly from the control room). Using this tank, the boat could be trimmed from the control room, using Electric Boat's patented trim line. This type of direct control was extremely important in an era predating the reliable remote control of individual valves.

This drawing also shows Electric Boat's characteristic power train, with auxiliaries driven by the propeller shaft: the bilge pump, with an air compressor abaft it, and the thrust block (note arrows). The temporary bridge, with its portable canopy frame, and the external ladder, which could be protected by a portable trunk, can also be seen. Note also that the bulkheads fore and aft of the control room each covered part of the deck above the battery. The forward bulkhead could not be pushed much farther forward—to clear a walk-around periscope—because it would then block access to the battery. Electric Boat also argued that the head (at the fore end of the battery space) could not be enclosed because any enclosure would block access on deck forward and the two periscopes. (The object forward of the first periscope is a ventilator; note how the eyepiece of the forward periscope is just inside the forward bulkhead of the control room.)

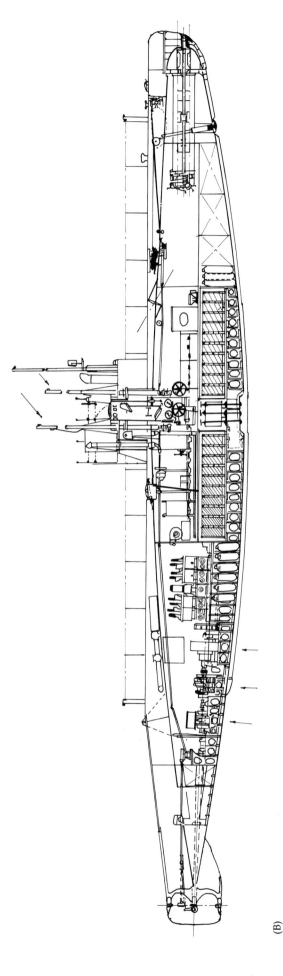

(B)

(B) E-2 was, in effect, a diesel-powered D-boat incorporating the changes ordered in 1908. The signaling bell was included late in the design process, so it is still on deck (forward) unusable when the submarine is surfaced. The after part of the bridge structure shows a ventilator leading into the control room and providing intake air for the engine. Access to the bridge was only via the conning tower hatch and the external hatch abaft the conning tower fairwater. A temporary trunk that led from the hatch in the deck up to the bridge could be fitted, but it was much disliked. The space abaft the control wheels contains the switchboard and the rheostats (under the ventilating fan shown).

In this design both periscopes pass into the control room, with a narrow conning tower between them. Forward of the forward periscope is a big ventilator; the telescoping radio mast lies forward of it. Note that the only ship's wheels are on the bridge and in the control room. When submitting this design (and the companion F-class design), Electric Boat argued that the volume of the conning tower should be minimized to give the maximum elevation at minimum reserve buoyancy when the submarine ran awash, ready to dive. It should be limited, therefore, to a surface conning station. For submerged work, the company argued that the commanding officer should not only be near the quartermaster's station (the helm) but also near the diving gear, depth gauges, air manifolds, and the valves controlling the main ballast tanks—i.e., in the control room. He needed a periscope with torpedo controls; the second periscope was for the lookout.

Furthermore, the company reasoned, in the event of a collision with a surface ship, the conning tower was the most likely watertight part of the submarine to be hit. Consequently, it was designed to yield without opening up the hull. The surface bridge was in two parts. A small platform atop the conning tower was expected to suffice for good weather or for short runs in bad weather. Although it could be disassembled, it was small enough not to add much underwater drag. For long runs a portable section could be added, together with a trunk leading up from the hatch abaft the conning tower, to provide access without interfering with the conning tower itself.

The trunk proved to be quite unpopular. E- and F-boats were powered by non-reversing diesels. Friction clutches connected the main engines to the motors. As a result, the engines could be disconnected while running and the propellers could be reversed by the motors for maneuvering on the surface. It later turned out that friction clutches were unreliable; positive-engagement (claw) clutches were used in later submarines. Arrows indicate the two periscopes and, aft, the motor, bilge pump, and air compressor.

(C)

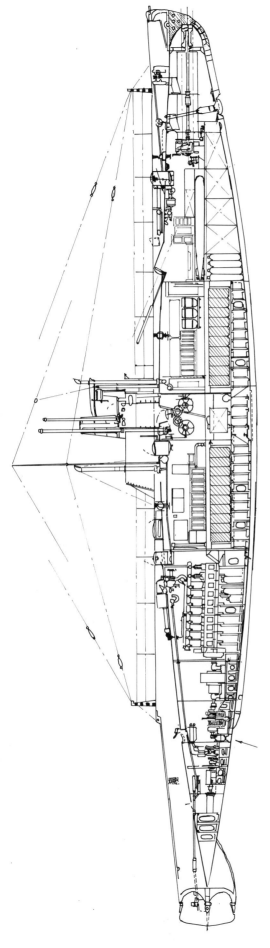

(C) H-2, shown as in 1918, displays the standard World War I "chariot" bridge but not standard wartime listening equipment. In this design the conning tower was greatly enlarged (in response to submariners' complaints) and a periscope restored to it, with sufficient space to make it a walk-around unit. The conning tower fairwater enclosed the external hatch just abaft the conning tower, so there was foul-weather access to the bridge (outside the conning tower) without using a temporary trunk or external ladder. The ventilator abaft the conning tower—the telescoping radio mast is just forward of it—fed the main induction (engine room air intake), with a valve leading into the main diving gear station abaft the control room.

Another ventilator, at the fore end of the bridge, fed forward spaces and ventilated the battery. The tube just abaft it (the rattail) carried radio lines down into the radio room just forward of the control room. Note the streamlined shears carrying the two periscopes and reinforcing them against vibration. In the control room the two wheels controlling the forward and after planes are shown with the ship's wheel. (There is a second ship's wheel on the open bridge.) At its after end, the space abaft the control room contained the battery-charging and motor-control panel and the rheostats used to control the motors. The prominent horizontal shaft running between the torpedo tubes forward turned the bow cap, which uncovered the tube muzzles.

A temporary torpedo loading tray is shown on deck above the torpedo hatch forward. The three cone-shaped objects in the quarters just abaft the torpedo room, pointing down, are stowed torpedo warheads. Abaft the motor are the main auxiliaries driven by the propeller shaft: the main bilge pump and air compressor, then the thrust block (the signal bell, arrowed, is between the bilge pump and the air compressor). By the time this design was begun, signal bells were a standard requirement, so Electric Boat placed one on the keel aft, where it could be used even when the boat was surfaced. This location was standard in later Electric Boat designs.

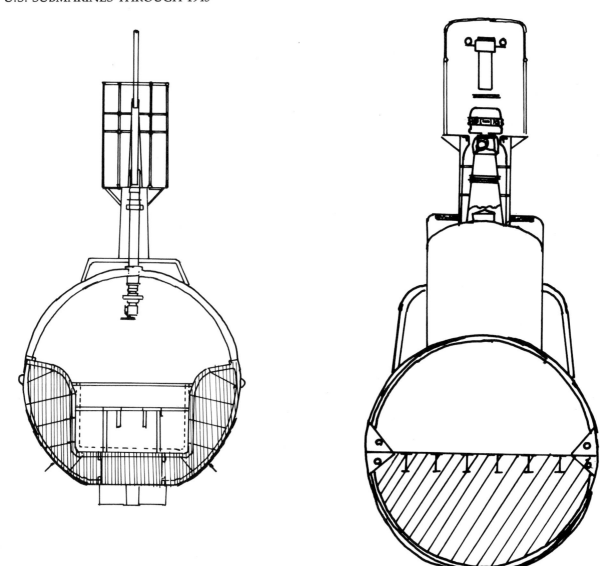

A midships cross section of E-2 (left) illustrates Holland's patented U-shaped tank, in this case surrounding the boat's safety (adjusting) tank. A similar cross section of Lake's G-1 is shown at right. Because Holland had patented the U-shaped ballast tank, Simon Lake had to use inefficient flat-topped tanks. For example, he had to place his batteries on top of the tanks (limiting overhead space), where Holland could surround batteries with tankage. In both drawings, shading indicates ballast water. Note that E-2's hull is not perfectly circular; it has a flat bottom where the pressure hull joins the duct keel.

could be easily boosted $\frac{1}{2}$ kt without any cost in battery or motor, partly because its hull form was easier to drive. Engine power would be increased by enlarging the cylinders (for 12 in × 12 in to 12$\frac{3}{4}$ in × 13 in). Full-power endurance would fall from 125 hr to a still very impressive 115 hr. Endurance at 11 kt was 2,475 nm (3,465 nm with fuel in ballast tanks), compared with a maximum of 1,380 nm at 10.5 kt for EB 18C. Electric Boat offered the modified EB 19A for the same price as EB 18C; she became the E class.

A skeptical Board on Construction was mollified by a contract guarantee that if the new engine did not prove as satisfactory as the earlier gasoline type during the first 6 mo, Electric Boat would have to replace it with a specified type at no cost. Although in theory diesels were a great advance, in practice they were quite unreliable: typically,

they had to be rebuilt after 500 mi. Theoretical cruising radius, based on fuel efficiency rather than reliability, was 2,400 nm. Both E and F classes had to have their engines replaced. The F-boats also suffered from weak battery enclosures that allowed acid to leak into their bottoms and thus to destroy their hulls (F-4 foundered for this reason).

Almost certainly in the interest of streamlining, Electric Boat had already drastically reduced the size of the conning tower to near-uselessness in the D class. It took the next step, moving the conning tower periscope down into the body of the boat, in the E and F classes.[60] The other (now longer) periscope was mounted abaft the conning tower, nearer the steering station. Although the conning tower was little more than a trunk, it retained its deadlights (presumably for surface navigation in severe weather). Surface operation in rough weather demanded a real

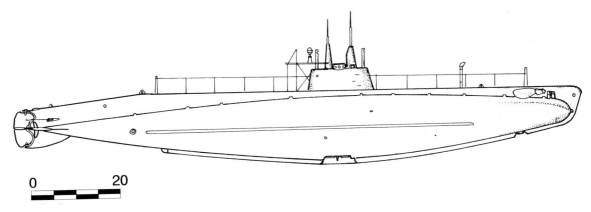

0   20

USS *Skipjack* (E-1). (Jim Christley)

bridge, and the external steering wheel was restored in the form of a conventional steering stand at the fore end of the conning tower (whose hatch was hinged aft to give access). A binnacle was mounted on the bridge platform, which extended aft from the conning tower roof. Unfortunately, moving the CO down into the operating compartment resulted in great congestion.[61]

These classes introduced bow diving planes to Electric Boat practice. The effect of adding bow planes was to separate dynamic control of angle on the boat from control over the angle of dive or rise in the water. Bow planes were used for precise depth control and to keep a boat from broaching after firing a torpedo.[62] Stern planes in the propeller slipstream were typically used to control the angle on the boat. As Electric Boat craft grew, they no longer dived at steep angles. By 1911, a typical diving angle was 2.5 degrees (4–5 degrees when diving rapidly); boats could also dive at 1 degree, but that took longer. It was no longer possible (or, for that matter, desirable) to porpoise.[63] These classes introduced electric power for

their stern planes. Like the D-boats, E-boats and F-boats carried six torpedoes.[64] They were the first U.S. submarines with permanent radios on board.

For FY 09 Lake offered both a 135-footer and a 161-footer similar to G-1.[65] He seems to have assumed that the obvious superiority of the latter would cause its selection and was shocked when the Board on Construction selected the less expensive 135-footer. He seems to have ordered G-1 to the larger design in expectation of the repeat order. Presumably he expected to economize by using the same hull drawings (lofting) for both boats. Progress payments on G-2 would pay for this work. He therefore offered the navy an austere version of the 161-ft boat for the same price as the 135-footer. The Board on Construction was happy to accept.[66]

Thus, Lake's FY 09 boat, *Tuna*, repeated the G-1 hull but lacked deck tubes; instead she had three bow tubes and one stern tube (the first internal stern tube in a U.S. submarine). Her flat upper deck ran virtually her whole length; G-1's raised superstructure ran only far enough

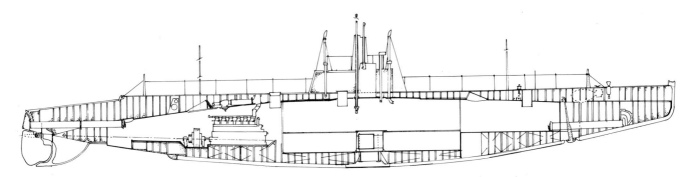

Electric Boat designed EB-19B for Chile (as *Antofagasta*), but the deal fell through; just before the outbreak of World War I, the premier of British Columbia bought her for Canada. When the central Canadian government approved the purchase, she became CC 2 (because of her resemblance to the British C class). Ordered to Europe, the two CC-boats were the first submarines to transit the Panama Canal. Upon arrival at Halifax, however, they were judged unfit to cross the Atlantic. They were discarded in 1920. CC 2 was an E-class submarine redesigned with two fewer tubes forward and with a single tube on the centerline aft, as shown here. Reloads were carried for each of the bow tubes (note that they have individual shutters, not the contemporary U.S. rotating bow cap). There is no separate after torpedo room. The boat's stern form resembles that of the larger double-hull Russian cruiser (EB 31) and of M-1. This design inspired U.S. Navy demands for one or two stern torpedo tubes in what became the K class. Note that, unlike the E class, this boat had a conning tower periscope, as well as one let into the central compartment. CC 1 (ex-*Iquique*) was the somewhat shorter EB-19E (144 ft 3.5 in × 14 ft × 11 ft 6 in, compared with 157 ft 6½ in × 14 ft 11½ in × 11 ft; displacements were 313/373 tons and 310/373 tons, respectively), which had four bow tubes. Both were rated at 13 kt surfaced (600 BHP) and 10 kt (260 HP) submerged. (Jim Christley)

The closely related E- and F-boats were the first U.S. submarines with diesel engines and the first Electric Boat submarines with bow planes. F-2 (*Barracuda*) is shown ready for launch, March 1912, at Union Iron Works in San Francisco. She was virtually complete then, since she was commissioned (after preliminary trials) only three months later.

to cover the two trainable torpedo tubes. One forward and the one after tube were mounted inside this extended casing. Unlike G-1 and the later G-3, G-2 lacked Lake's diving chamber. G-2 was the last submarine Lake built at Newport News. She was almost complete (2 yr, 2 mo, and 16 days late) when Lake declared bankruptcy on

6 November 1913. *Tuna* was placed in service but did not begin preliminary trials until 30 November 1915. She was then turned over to Lake's reorganized company for further trials and completion. by this time, her design was quite dated.[67]

Lake received another submarine contract in FY 10,

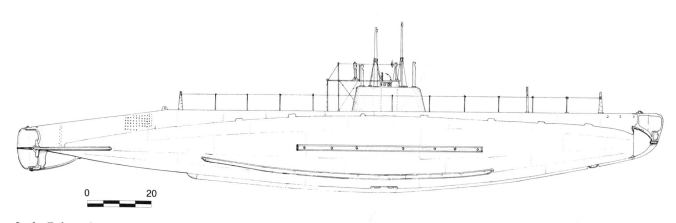

In the F class, the conning tower is shown in dashed vertical lines between the two periscopes. This class and the E class introduced bow planes into Electric Boat practice. (Jim Christley)

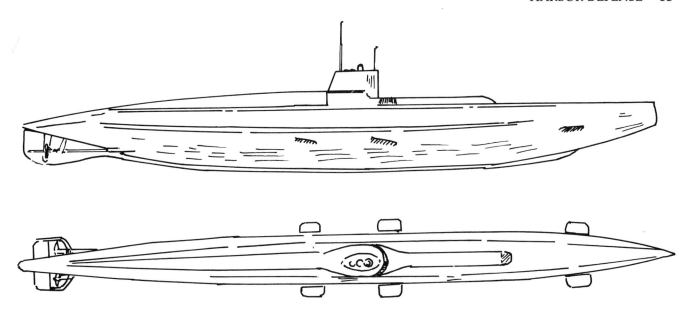

In 1908, Simon Lake bid on the U.S. FY 09 submarine contract. He offered both a 135-footer and a 161-footer, the latter clearly related to G-1 (*Seal*). Obviously, he hoped to sell the larger design; he seems to have believed that by going beyond the navy's stated requirements to produce the best possible ship, he could overturn Electric Boat's effective monopoly. To prove that his claims were realistic, he had a towing-tank model of his 161-footer built and towed in the navy's experimental tank at the Washington Navy Yard. He also had Bath Iron Works make a dummy hull section, which he tested to prove it could withstand pressure at the standard 200-ft test depth. These drawings are adapted from Lake's photographs of the towing-tank model, which presumably represents his proposed 161-footer. This boat would have displaced about 400 tons surfaced and 518–535 tons submerged, including 68 tons of water in the watertight superstructure. Armament would have been two bow and four superstructure (twin-mounted, trainable) torpedo tubes, the latter (like those in G-1) firing over a 120-degree arc on either broadside. The surface power plant would have been four 6-cylinder, 300-BHP White & Middleton gasoline engines, two clutched in tandem on each shaft, with 10,700 gal of gasoline. Each of two motors would have generated 300 HP (375 HP for 2-hr overload, 450 HP for 3 min) served by a 120-cell battery (3,840 amp-hr at the 3-hr rate). Lake claimed a design diving depth of 300 ft. He expected the boat to dive in 6 min (in 15 sec from wartime cruising condition). To Lake's disappointment, C&R and BuEng suggested that the navy buy the less expensive 135-footer. After the contract had been signed, Lake offered to build an austere version of the 161-footer at the same price, and the navy agreed. The two technical bureaus were happy to forgo such features as wheels and the diver's chamber, on the ground that they had never really been wanted in the first place. This boat was G-2 (*Tuna*).

Although conceived as a duplicate *Seal*, *Tuna* (G-2) dispensed with trainable tubes in favor of fixed tubes at her ends. The shutters of her paired stern tubes are visible in this pre-launch photograph. (*Newport News Shipbuilding and Drydock Co.*)

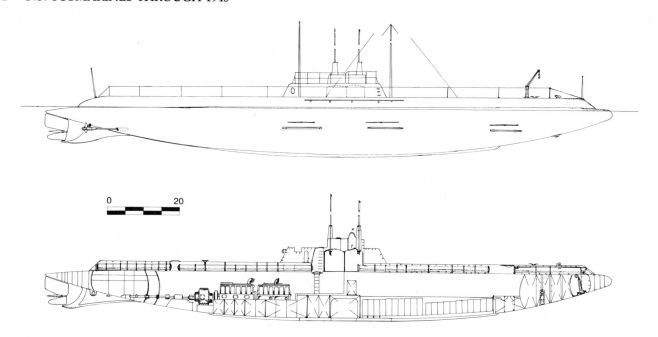

Tuna (G-2) was Lake's second submarine for the U.S. Navy. Note Lake's trademark features: his midships and bow diving planes (each with its guard below it), his ship-shaped stern (unlike Electric Boat's), and his paired conning towers, one for the commanding officer and a separate one for the navigator. Lake's watertight superstructure accommodated both torpedo tubes and torpedo stowage fore and aft. Another pair of bow tubes (not visible in the inboard profile) were blistered out from the pressure hull. Note also the tandem gasoline engines. (Jim Christley)

for G-3 (*Turbot*). Laid down at a new yard he opened at Bridgeport, she was similar to G-2 but had diesel engines and twin, rather than single, tubes at each end of the raised superstructure, for totals of four bow and two stern tubes and 10 instead of 8 torpedoes. After Lake went bankrupt, G3 was delivered to New York Navy Yard for completion on 31 December 1913 and was ready for tuning-up trials in April 1915. It then turned out that she lacked reserve buoyancy and stability; the reorganized Lake Co. had to install blisters (sponsons). She was not ready for preliminary trials until 1916. Lake's G-boats were never fully operational, perhaps partly because their nonstandard design would have complicated logistics.[68]

The Laurenti submarine was G-4. Laurenti, a former Italian naval constructor, was already a well-known submarine designer.[69] In the 1906 Italian maneuvers, two of his boats ran 600 mi from Taranto to Venice under their own power and twice attacked the Italian fleet in the Mar Grande—once in daylight, once at night. In the 1907 maneuvers, they ran 1,300 nm from Venice to La Spezia. G-4 was the last U.S. gasoline-powered submarine. As with Lake's boats, she was very late (by 2 yr, 10 mo, and 28 days). By then, she was quite obsolete. Her machinery proved too light, she rolled excessively (a stabilizer had to be fitted), she needed more rudder area, and her planes had to be modified. In 1916, however, the Submarine Flotilla liked her despite her problems.

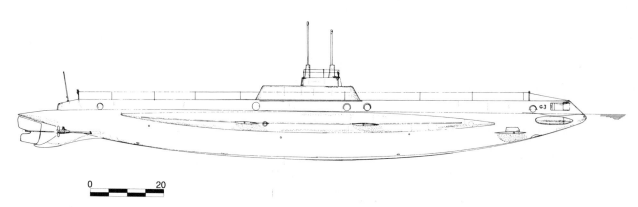

Lake's G-3 had to be blistered, as shown, before she was accepted. Note her two amidships planes, in addition to conventional fore and aft planes. The big openings in the sides of the hull are flooding ports. (Jim Christley)

Hauled up on the marine railway at Lake's yard in Bridgeport, Connecticut, G-3 shows the blisters added to provide adequate stability. Note also the separate shutters of her hull and superstructure bow torpedo tubes and the torpedo crane on deck. This photograph was taken on 9 December 1915. (*Submarine Force Museum and Library*)

Submarines grew quickly before World World I. Lake's big G-3 is shown alongside Electric Boat's much smaller D-1 at New London, 4 May 1920. Both show the standard wartime modification, a permanent metal ("chariot") bridge. G-3 also shows a radio mast aft, a torpedo loading crane forward, and the shutter of one of her above-water bow tubes (the other tube on this side was below the surface). (*Adm. John S. McCain, Jr., via the Naval Historical Center*)

Laurenti's G-4 (*Thrasher*) was a typical early double-hull design in which the ship-shaped outer hull formed the entire outside of the submarine; there was no floodable ("self-baling," in contemporary parlance) superstructure.

Like Laubeuf, Laurenti emphasized surface performance: he thought of a submarine as a surface torpedo boat that could submerge at will. He used a boat-shaped, rather than circular-section, pressure hull to increase usable internal volume. For example, a man could stand upright in any part of the machinery space. When the boat was submerged, her commander could work from within the spacious control room rather than from an external conning tower; Laurenti claimed that this central position made for better control and greatly reduced the chance of an accident. The structure between the two hulls supported both of them (an elliptical hull is inherently far weaker than a more conventional circular-section hull).

Like Lake, Laurenti sought increased power by placing two engines on each propeller shaft. Unlike Lake, he pro-

vided no clutch between the fore and aft engines, so (unlike G-1) G-4 could not have her forward engines removed; she retained all of her engines to the end. They were never considered reliable (possibly, in part, because it was difficult to obtain spares during WW I), and the boat could exceed 10.5 kt for only a few hours at a time. Laurenti also paired electric motors in tandem on each shaft.[70]

Unlike most of his contemporaries, Laurenti used watertight bulkheads. These saved a boat from flooding when an engine cooling jacket burst during the 1906 Italian maneuvers. Bulkheading also made diving quicker; because the engine room could be sealed off, the engine did not have to be cooled first. This practice proved unfortunate. After they had been shut down, the engines had to be ventilated for several minutes before a dive. When G-4

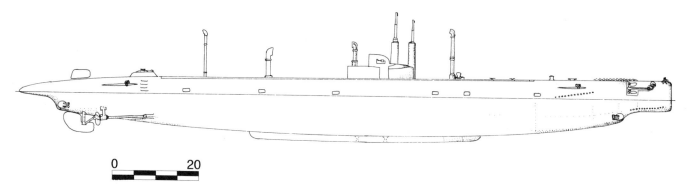

0   20

Cramp's Laurenti-designed *Thrasher* (G-4), unlike contemporary Electric Boat craft, had her ventilators on deck, where access (to prepare for diving) was likely to be difficult in rough weather. Note the droppable safety keel. (Jim Christley)

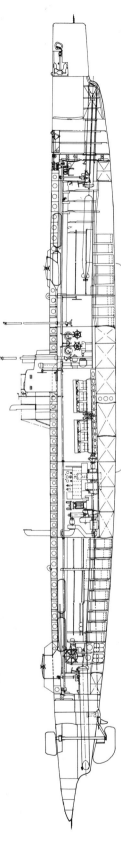

G-4 was essentially a submersible surface torpedo boat. For example, her conning tower resembled that of contemporary small steam torpedo boats. The flasks shown above each pair of torpedo tubes (fore and aft) contain firing impulse air. The rods connecting the plane control wheels to the planes are shown, as is the safety keel. Note the paired gasoline engines *and* electric motors on each shaft. This arrangement convinced U.S. submariners that power could be easily increased to achieve greater speed. The device abaft the two motors (abeam the electrical switchboard) is the air compressor, with the main ballast pump abaft it. Crew accommodation is shown forward of the control room and abaft the after vent fan (under the after ventilator). Batteries are fore and aft of the main ballast tanks.

tried to crash dive, several crewmen were overcome by fumes.

Even with freeing-ports open, Laurenti's superstructure was substantially watertight, as in a Lake submarine. During diving, water was let into the large ballast tanks below the waterline, below the center of gravity, before the superstructure was filled. Lake tended to fill his superstructure first, so that he risked losing stability at a critical moment (his solution was to provide a heavy lead keel).

Unlike Electric Boat, Laurenti used linked fore and aft diving planes, which were supposed to provide firmer depth control. The Laurenti boat also differed from its contemporaries in having a topside rudder in addition to the usual one. The design included a pair of haul-down screws, but they were not installed.

Laurenti claimed a surface speed of 14 kt and a submerged speed of 9.5 kt; endurance was 980 nm at 14 kt or 2,200 nm at 8 kt surfaced (submerged, 3 hr at 8 kt, the standard rate, or 45 nm [7.5 hr] at 6 kt). Diving time from full speed on the surface to 8 kt submerged was given as 6 min. Armament was four torpedo tubes, paired fore and aft, with four reloads.

European builders showed little interest in licensing their designs to U.S. builders. They might have feared that Electric Boat and Lake would sue them for patent infringement. Frustrated in their attempts to secure access to foreign ideas, C&R and BuEng suggested jointly in March 1913 that an FY 14 boat be ordered abroad. That

June, Secretary of the Navy Josephus Daniels formally approved the project, provided that the submarine was at least equal to U.S. types (L and M classes) but materially cheaper (attachés were told that about $600,000 would be available). As might have been expected, Electric Boat complained bitterly that foreign purchases would kill off the U.S. naval shipbuilding industry. The program died, however, only because WW I intervened. Its failure made the navy's own program to develop a design and production capacity more urgent.

It took some years for these boats to achieve their theoretical performance. By November 1910, the D-boats were considered good for continuous 50-hr engine runs, and their effective range was 500 nm. By early 1911, exercises showed that the C-boats could remain at sea for about 4 days and the D-boats somewhat longer.[71] It was considered a major achievement when four C-boats and three D-boats ran from Newport to Gloucester, Massachusetts, in mid-1911, most of the 190 nm submerged; the run was made in segments, the boats anchoring in harbor overnight.[72] Gasoline fumes caused some problems; some in the submarine flotilla wanted a bulkhead to isolate the engine and its fumes from the forward part of the boat. There was some fear that gasoline engines would not run properly after long submerged runs.

Changes to propellers and engines during 1912 were expected to make the C-boats and D-boats practically self-sustaining for up to 10 days (i.e., within a surface radius

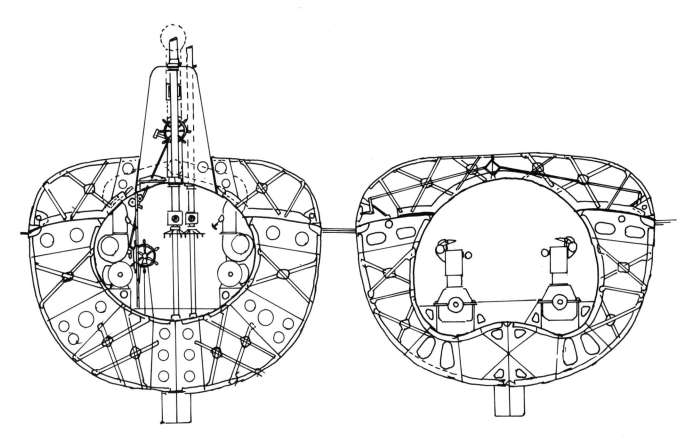

Cross sections of Laurenti's G-4 (*Thrasher*) at the control room (left) and at the engine room (right) show this boat's characteristic elliptically shaped pressure hull, heavily braced against her outer hull.

of 1,000 nm). They were credited with a submerged radius of 35 nm at about 8 kt, or 75 nm at about 5 kt. In 1912, these boats cruised without escorts as far north as Gloucester and as far south as Norfolk, Virginia. In February 1913, the C-boats, accompanied by the monitor *Ozark*, completed the longest cruise to that date by U.S. submarines, 700 nm from Guantánamo Bay, Cuba, to Cristóbal, Panama, without serious engineering problems.[73] The word *seagoing*, however, could be exaggerated. During FY 15, average mileage for the two classes considered by BuEng to have proved their mechanical reliability was 927 nm for the C class and 1,163 nm for the D class. In 1916, the Atlantic Submarine Flotilla asked that the gasoline engines of both classes be replaced with diesels. Initially vetoed, this was later approved and completed in the D class but never carried out in the C-boats.[74]

A big week-long May 1915 exercise provided a more realistic test of these submarines. D-1's CO thought the exercise demonstrated that she could remain 7 days away from a base and that she could have remained away another 2 days. She was reliable, but the CO considered her unsuited to long-range coastal work because of fumes, dampness, and constipation of her crew.[75] D-2 did worse. On 21 May, she had to be towed for a time when the port crankshaft broke while the starboard engine was out of commission. Both engines were inoperable for 30 hr.

E-1 spent only 2 days at sea. Both of her engines broke down on 22 May and had not yet been repaired when the exercise ended on 27 May. Her radio did not work at all. Nor could she always dive: her CO thought all her Kingstons were stuck by bitumastic paint in the ballast tanks (but "afterwards found not to be so" was written in pencil). E-2 had one engine out of commission for 2 days. Her CO considered her engines fair, "better than can be relied upon for future performance." Even so, he considered her good for the 7 days of the exercise, and capable of staying out another 2 days. The crew's health was "fair, probably due to good weather," but the CO complained of "insufficient berthing space, sleeping on deck, noise, vibration, engine fumes, dampness, constipation." Nor was her radio effective: she could receive only at 3 nm.

Although she had not yet run official trials, G-2 participated in the maneuver. Her CO considered her too small for the work demanded of her. Her effective full speed was 12.5 kt, but her best reliable patrol speed was about 9.5 kt. She remained 7 days away from base and could have remained efficient for 3 more days. Health was good, except for effects of gasoline fumes on the engineer's force and poor ventilation of the living compartment. The CO did not consider G-2 seaworthy in a rough sea; ventilation of the living compartment was very poor at all times. She was able to receive radio messeges at 25 nm (at 75 nm from high-powered stations), using 6-ft masts fore and aft and aerials rigged to a yard on the forward periscope. She was not always ready to dive because of inexperienced personnel and leaky outboard exhaust valves; the CO had not previously submerged.

Her CO considered G-4 too small for the required work, but he also thought that she had demonstrated greater endurance (10 days) than any of the other boats (7 days each), and that she could have remained out for another 2 days. Engines were "excellent," but one was out of commission for 5 hr (it was repaired). The CO kept his batteries two-thirds charged at all times.

Both Electric Boat and Lake tried hard to sell their submarine designs abroad. Many Electric Boat export designs were probably versions of U.S. Navy types, their origins concealed (to avoid legal action) by coding their design designations. The two digits of the EB design number were reversed and separated by a zero, so that the export version of EB 26 (the H-boat) was EB 602. These designations were used even when the U.S. Navy did not buy the design.

During 1905, the two companies competed directly in Austria-Hungary. Having failed to obtain a satisfactory home-designed submarine, that navy ordered competitive prototypes from Electric Boat, Germania (Krupp), and Lake, each about 100 ft long. Electric Boat's licensee was Whitehead (in Fiume). It assembled two boats (U 5 and 6, EB 17B design derived from USS *Octopus*, EB 17A), largely prefabricated in the United States and launched in February and June 1909. Poorly installed gasoline engines nearly suffocated their crews. Whitehead built a modified third unit on speculation (EB 17E design, launched in March 1911). The Austrian Navy did not buy it because the competitive trials had not yet been completed, and the company offered it to Brazil, Bulgaria, the Netherlands, Peru, and Portugal. The Austrian Navy took it over as U 12 at the outbreak of WW I.[76]

Marley F. Hay, who was probably trained by Electric Boat, became submarine designer for Whitehead and for Denny, an associated British builder (his boats were called either Hay-Whiteheads or Denny-Hays). About 1910, the Royal Netherlands Navy began buying his submarines: four *O-2* class (design A-3) and one *K-1* class (design K-1). Electric Boat considered them licensed versions of its designs.[77] Whitehead and Copenhagen Navy Yard built six somewhat larger single-screw diesel submarines (*Havmanden* class, design T-3, launched in 1911–14). Austria-Hungary ordered four boats of this Hay-Whitehead design, U 20–23, on 27 March 1915.[78] Electric Boat sometimes cited the success of Hay designs in Danish competition as proof of the superiority of its single-hull type, but it is not clear to what extent they were Electric Boat designs. Newport News offered a Denny-Hay design in the U.S. FY 16 competition.

The Austrians considered Lake's U 1 and U 2, built at Pola Navy Yard, superior for diving and steering, although their gasoline engines were unsatisfactory (they could not reach contract power). The Austrian Navy leased the engine until they could be replaced by Austrian-made diesels. There were no reorders. Although it had an Electric Boat license, Krupp built French-derived double-hull submarines. In the Austrian trials, its U 3 and U 4 had the worst diving qualities and smoked badly but were considered the most reliable and most habitable.

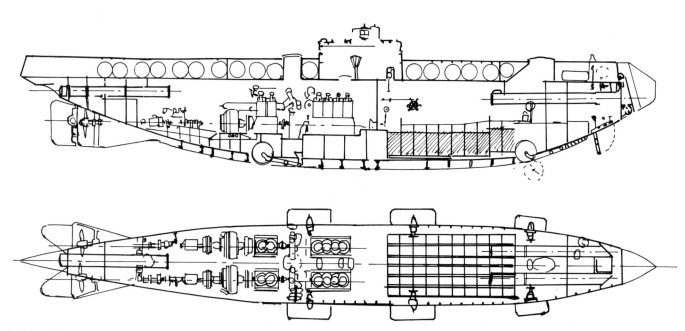

Lake sold Austria a pair of 100-ft submarines, essentially enlarged *Protectors,* designated U 1 and U 2. Dimensions were 26.55 m between perpendiculars (30.48 m overall) × 3.6 m (equivalent to 87.1/100 ft × 11.8 ft); displacement was 230/270 tons (metric). The surface power plant was a pair of engine sets, each consisting of a two-cylinder cruising engine (120 BHP) and a four-cylinder boost engine (240 BHP) clutched together. Each electric motor developed 100 HP. Maximum speed was 10.3 kt surfaced, 6 kt submerged; endurance was 950 nm at 6 kt surfaced, 15 nm at 5 kt submerged, or 40 nm at 2 kt submerged. Armament was two bow and one stern 45-cm (18-in) torpedo tubes (the boats carried no reloads) and one machine gun. The single periscope (not shown here) was supplied by Goerz. The contract was signed on 24 November 1906; construction began at Pola on 2 July and 18 July 1907. Unfortunately, construction was slow because of Lake's delay in supplying detailed plans (presumably so that he could add improvements). Like other Lake boats, these had wheels and a diving compartment (the trap door, under the bow, is shown opened). The circles in the boat's superstructure (visible in the side view) are gasoline tanks; Lake claimed that such external stowage was far safer than the internal tankage of an Electric Boat submarine. On trials, the boats behaved well under water; the diving planes could be left unattended for half an hour, with the boat maintaining depth. Even Lake pronounced himself impressed by this behavior. The gasoline engines were considered unsuccessful, however; in 1915, they were replaced by diesels.

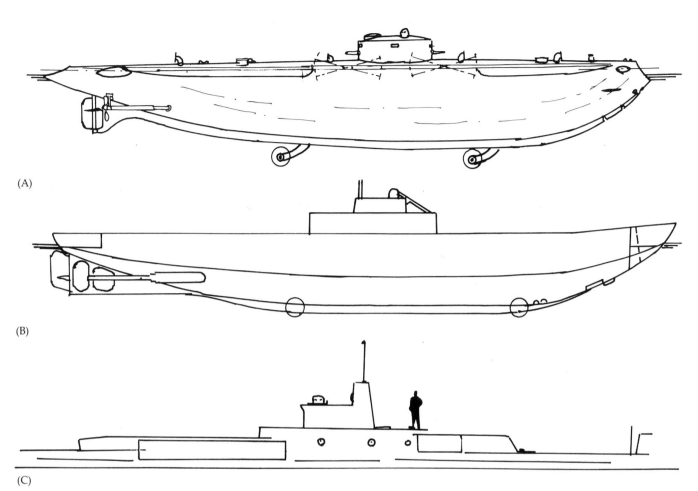

(A)

(B)

(C)

Lake designed the 125-ft cruiser (A) in parallel to his 65-ft *Protector;* he offered her to the Board on Construction in 1901. The two hydroplanes (diving planes) are indicated amidships. Lake called another pair of planes, in the bow and just abaft the propellers, ''level vanes.'' As in later Lake submarines, water ballast was carried both in internal hard tanks (below the level of the internal deck) and in the watertight superstructure above the hull. This design was Lake's first to incorporate a pressure hull with the axis curving up at the ends. He claimed that this patented feature overcame the tendency of more conventional cigar-shaped hulls to dive by the head and increased both surface speed and surface stability (metacentric height). In 1906, Lake sold this design to the Russians, who badly wanted long-range submarines. The Russian boats, the *Kaiman* class, were completed to a very different design: Lake liked to tinker with his designs after boats had been laid down. The middle drawing (B) shows the boat, as redesigned in 1907, with a modern raked bow. The bottom drawing (C) shows *Kaiman* completed for trials in 1908. The large rectangle forward is the downward-opening cover for a pair of trainable torpedo tubes, a feature Lake apparently added quite late in construction. He called this his 1905 design and offered a 135-foot version to the U.S. Navy in November 1908 (for the FY 09 program). Dimensions would have been 135 ft × 12 ft 6 in (300/410–415 tons). As offered at that time, the boat would have been armed with two bow and two trainable torpedo tubes (like *Kaiman*) and powered by a pair of 300-BHP White & Middleton gasoline engines (8,350 gal of gasoline). Submerged power would have been provided by a pair of 200-HP motors (capable of 250 HP for 2 hr, or 300 HP for 3 min of overload) drawing on a 120-cell battery (3,000 amp-hr). The Russians demanded considerable changes (including elimination of the trainable tubes) to *Kaiman* before she could be accepted, so the boat never entered service as Lake had intended.

Lake was luckier with the Russians. In 1906, he sold them the design for a modified version of the 125-ft cruiser he had first sketched in 1901. The submarines were launched in 1907–08. Lake later described the four *Kaiman*s as the largest in the world at the time, with a displacement of nearly 500 tons submerged. Unfortunately, they were rejected upon completion in December 1910 because of numerous problems, including about 12 tons of overweight. To prevent the builder, Crichton of St. Petersburg, from selling them abroad, the Russian Naval Ministry took them over without making the final payments. This money was spent instead on modifications, including replacement of a 3-cylinder section of each gasoline engine by a new ballast pump, to reduce diving time from 10 min to 3 min.[79] These boats had twin trainable torpedo tubes forward, apparently the first of their kind in the world. The Russians soon replaced them with drop-collars for two more torpedoes.

Trainable tubes obviously impressed the Russians; they were included in Electric Boat's big EB 31 design (*Narval* class), three of which they bought in 1911.[80] When the large EB 31A was described in a November 1911 article in *Engineering*, it inspired U.S. interest in a fleet submarine (which also had twin trainable tubes). EB 31A was strikingly unlike contemporary Electric Boat submarines for the U.S. Navy; she carried her propellers well below the axis of the hull. Much the same hull form was repeated in the company's T-class fleet boats for the U.S. Navy. At the other end of the scale, Russia bought the smallest of all Electric Boat submarines, three EB 27B midgets (33 tons) for use in coastal defense by the Russian army in the Black Sea.

Chile ordered two modified E-boats built in Seattle (designs EB 19B and 19E); they were taken over by Canada as CC 1 and CC 2 at the outbreak of war in 1914. Each had a stern torpedo tube, which the U.S. E class lacked. One boat had two bow tubes, and the other had four.

Electric Boat benefited from the outbreak of WW I, which cut navies off from their European suppliers. In 1914, K. M. "de Schelde," the company's licensee, laid down a 190-ton coastal submarine (O 6) to the EB 803G (EB 38G) design for the Royal Netherlands Navy at the same time that Fijenoord built a Hay-Denny boat. "de Schelde" then built five longer-range (K, Kolonien) double-hull boats for service in the East Indies: two 105Bs (EB 51B: *K III* class) and three 105Gs (EB 51G: *K VIII* class). Each class had two bow and two stern tubes; EB 105B also had two deck torpedo tubes, an unusual feature for the time. EB 105B and EB 105G were almost certainly variations on Electric Boat's M-1 (EB 39) for the U.S. Navy. This type was also built for Spain.

Norway shifted to Electric Boat after buying five Krupp (Germaniawerft) submarines (the A class), the last of which the German Navy took over at the outbreak of war in 1914. Six B-class submarines (EB 406B; i.e., 64B) were ordered in 1915. Presumably, the company's great advantage was the neutrality of the United States at that time,

so it could still sell submarines abroad (the Norwegians also considered firms in England, Germany, and Italy). These 415-ton (four-tube) boats were broadly similar to the U.S. H class then being built for England, Italy, and Russia. In July 1916, Norway ordered two smaller (220-ton, two-tube) submarines, the C class (EB 407A; i.e., EB 74A). The supply of materiel from the United States was stopped by the war. Electric Boat tried to sell Norway six H-boats that could not be delivered to Russia because of the revolution; they were taken over by the U.S. Navy instead. Although laid down in 1915, the B-class submarines were completed postwar (1923–30). The C-boats were canceled. In 1931, the Norwegian navy asked for replacement designs. One of eight competitors, Electric Boat was soon rejected. (After a very lengthy selection process, a German design related to the Type VII U-boat of WW II was adopted; two were on order when Norway fell in 1940.)[81] .

Spain bought its first modern submarines under a 1913 Navy Law (program), which included 3 of them. A law of 17 February 1915 authorized 10 more. The first 3 (A class) were Laurentis. Then Spain turned to Electric Boat for a prototype, *Isaac Peral* (EB 903L; i.e., EB 39L design) very similar to the double-hull U.S. M-1. She was followed by 6 improved versions (B class: EB 105F; i.e., EB 51F, with four bow tubes). In 1919, Spain was credited with 12 Electric Boat submarines under construction, including 6 B-boats that entered service in 1926–27. The remaining 5 submarines did not materialize (3 remained to be built under the 1915 law).

Electric Boat's great WW I success, the H-class program for Britain, Italy, and Russia, is described in chapter 5.

The company's export fortunes collapsed after the war. Navies that bought wartime H-boats were unlikely to import submarines postwar. Of the other three wartime export customers, Norway was no longer in the market; postwar Dutch submarines were apparently of domestic design. Spain bought six C-boats (EB 309; i.e., EB 93), somewhat larger than U.S. S-boats, with two stern tubes, which the Electric Boat version of that class lacked (they were sometimes described as enlarged B-boats).[82] For the successor D class (three boats), Electric Boat lost out to its former licensee, Vickers, which built the boats at Cartagena.

Electric Boat competed for several contracts, but its only new postwar foreign customer was Peru, which bought six submarines (EB 707D, essentially a modernized R-boat [EB 77a]) in the 1920s; these were the first submarines to be built in Groton, Connecticut. They had the same lines as an R-boat but were redesigned internally; the company claimed the boat achieved much the same performance as an S-boat on an R-boat's tonnage. Peru bought six replacements (based on the *Mackerel*) after WW II.[83]

One other major theme of U.S. submarine development deserves comment here: the continuing effort to ensure against loss. In 1907, *Plunger* tested a marker (reel) buoy, which a submarine on the bottom could release to indicate its position. Then, in 1909-10, a pair of foreign losses seem to have made a considerable impression. The British C-11 was rammed and sunk by the steamer *Eddystone* on 14 July 1909. The Japanese *No. 6* was lost on 15 April 1910 when the chain drive to her main induction valve broke and the valve jammed open. Probably as a consequence,

U.S. submariners showed intense interest in submarine escape and salvage. Several men successfully escaped from torpedo tubes and from conning towers rigged as air locks. In addition, money was spent to develop a standard messenger buoy carrying a telephone.[84]

Perhaps the most important harbors submarines had to defend were those in the Philippines, which had to be held until the fleet could steam across the Pacific. Early U.S. submarines could not transit all the way there, so they were transported aboard colliers. Here *Adder* (A-2) is unloaded from the collier *Caesar* in 1908.

5

The General Board's Coastal Defense Submarines

FOR THE PRE-1914 U.S. Navy, coast defense meant attacking battleships.[1] Submarines had four bow tubes because it was assumed that four hits would disable or sink any capital ship. U.S. coastal waters would not be infested with enemy nets and mines (as in foreign waters in Europe), so there was no need for periscopes to house (retract into the hull), as in other navies. A fixed periscope presented no hazard to the submarine, and Holland-type submarines could easily porpoise to raise their hulls (and their periscopes), albeit risking broaching (exposing the hull itself). Nor were U.S. submarines expected to operate in water so shallow that they could not dive deep enough to cover their periscopes.

According to tactics first formalized in 1908, a U.S. submarine would approach a target on the surface and dive only to avoid detection. Tests in Buzzard's Bay showed that a submarine could spot a large surface ship about 1½ mi away before beign spotted. Later tests showed that if she had to approach submerged, with 4 ft of periscope out of the water, she could generally spot a large ship at 7–8 nm (C-5 easily saw the masts and smoke of USS *Dixie* at 9 nm). After taking the target's bearing and estimating her course and speed, she ran in submerged, using her periscope sparingly, never showing more than a foot, and never for more than 4 sec. A periscope feather could sometimes be seen at 7,000 yd. The closing submarine tried to remain undetected mainly to avoid giving the prospective target sufficient time to evade her. When close enough that the target could not evade (within torpedo range), the submarine, no longer having to hide, kept her periscope on the target for effective fire control. There was apparently no fear that, having spotted the periscope, the target or a consort would ram the approaching submarine; presumably, it was supposed that she could always dive to protect herself. Similar ideas applied to offshore group tactics: submarines would try to approach unseen to within maximum torpedo range; in 1912, this was about 2,000 yd. The new feature was that the boats, typically five to a group, had to submerge ½ mi apart to avoid

underwater collision. Seeking a position on the target's bow, they were expected to fire at 500–1,000 yd.[2]

To deal with fast warships, the U.S. Navy emphasized relatively high underwater speed (albeit far inferior to surface ship speed) at the expense of surface sea-keeping. Even then, many prewar U.S. submariners wondered whether their boats could run fast enough or long enough underwater. Submarines often failed to catch their targets in maneuvers, even when they knew target courses and speeds in advance. Batteries might be exhausted during the approach, and the submarine might be unable to escape on the surface to recharge them. The solution would be to run air-breathing engines underwater, as the submarine closed in on her target. In May 1909, the Navy Department approved what later would be called a simple proposed snorkel: the existing ventilator (engine air intake pipe) would be extended to within about a foot of the top of the fixed periscope. A snorkeling submarine would shut down her engine and dive deep before her periscope and snorkel could be spotted.[3]

Apparently untested at the time, this idea was revived in June 1914 by Lt. (jg) R. S. Edwards. He proposed to mount a periscope-like ventilator, along with the periscopes, that would discharge air directly into the bilges to feed the diesels when the submarine was submerged to a shallow depth. The engine would use its existing exhaust and work against back pressure when submerged. BuEng estimated that a C-boat would need a 12-in air pipe; it would use about a quarter of its engine power to suck in air.[4] Submariners planning to try running engines awash during winter exercises in 1914–15 asked what would happen if the engine continued to run after waves closed the snorkel. In heavy weather off Cape Hatteras, North Carolina, during the winter of 1909, C-1 had run her engines with the ventilators sealed but the conning tower hatch (analogous to the snorkel) open. When waves began to come over the conning tower, the officer and men, who were lashed to its top, stepped on the hatch to seal the boat. The engines accelerated briefly, then grad-

The O-boats were the oldest U.S. submarines to survive to serve in World War II. O-3 (SS 64) is shown in much her original form with a 3 in/23 disappearing mount forward of her bridge fairwater and her two periscopes in faired shears. O-7 (SS 68) is shown on October 1944 in the Atlantic, south of Fishers Island.

ually slowed. Two inches of pressure were lost as the engines sucked air out of the boat. The partial vacuum made it very difficult to reopen the hatch, but clearly the boat could have handled a somewhat smaller pressure drop. The experiments were aborted in 1915 because the U.S. submarine force was so badly stretched and the international situation so threatening that no operational submarine could be spared. Edwards's idea did not reemerge for another three decades.[5]

The other U.S. attempt to maintain high underwater speed, the Cage (later Neff) system, was a 1912 private proposal. Cage planned to run diesels underwater on air stowed under pressure.[6] A. R. Neff bought Cage's Los Angeles Submarine Boat Co. in 1915 and continued to promote his system after WW I. The navy objected that the exhaust would surely leave a visible wake and that it was impractical to compress the exhaust to store it on board. Neff eventually proposed to use the diesels only for high speed; at lower speeds, the boat would run on compressed air. High-speed underwater endurance would far exceed that offered by conventional batteries because the fuel contributed so much energy. Compressed air could not store as much energy as chemicals in a battery, however, at 5 kt, Neff managed only half the endurance of an S-boat. In tests using N-2, BuEng found that diesels running underwater were quite noisy. Rejecting Neff in 1922, the General Board argued that batteries and motors had so much scope for development that they might well exceed anything he could achieve with internal combusion engines.

For efficient mobile coastal defense, submarines loitering offshore had to be cued by surface scouts farther out to sea. By about 1912, submarines could receive radio messages, though initially not at very long range. The first units built with radios, E-1 and E-2, received at 90 nm and sent at 50 nm; they used an aerial strung between two folding masts. Unfortuanetly, a boat could not dive with her antenna rigged.

Submarines could also communicate by an underwater bell or, later, a Fessenden oscillator. With machinery stopped, two submarines could hear each other at 8 nm under ideal conditions (boats on opposite courses could hear each other at only $\frac{1}{2}$ mi apart). Oscillators were widely used during WW I, often to exchange recognition signals. Because virtually all navies used them, however, they could be expected to alert a prospective target. In 1912, Lt. (later Admiral) Chester Nimitz described a typical use. He imagined a group of harbor defense submarines attacking, with each boat running at maximum speed to get within torpedo range of a target assigned while they lay at anchor in port: "They must . . . take the risk of collision. On this final charge, the submarine bells may be rung continuously to assist the submarines to stay clear of each other."[7] As in other aspects of U.S. pre–WW I submarine tactics, there seems to have been little fear of detection and counterattack by the target or by screening destroyers.

The General Board first set characteristics in 1909 for the FY 10 program. That March, the Naval War College proposed that the submarine force consist of 6-boat flotillas; two long-range flotillas for each coast (at Narragansett Bay, Hampton Roads, Puget Sound, and San Francisco), plus single flotillas for Hawaii, the Philippines, the West Indies, and Panama, and a half flotilla for Guam, for a total of 51 submarines. The sheer size of the Philippine archipelago required long-range submarines. Short-range units could defend localized points (Guantánamo, Guam, Tutuila, and Pearl Harbor). A 25 percent reserve of 13 boats would maintain strength despite the frequent repairs these delicate craft required (2 mo for repair, plus 12 days' travel time). This considerably increased the requirement for Pacific boats. Unfortuanetly, as of 30 November 1908, the U.S. Navy had only 12 boats on hand (8 of them restricted to harbor defense), 7 boats on order, and 8 more authorized (the Royal Navy had 60 built or in process). To be sufficiently mobile under the War College proposal, each submarine flotilla would require at least one tender. Because of the submarines' limited endurance, each tender had to be able to tow five at a time and fuel each boat at least once under way. Through WW I, Congress was far more willing to supply submarines than the tenders to make them effective.

The General Board's early view of submarine design was much shaped by L. Y. Spear's careful April 1909 presentation on design trade-offs. He saw little point in much growth (up to 650 tons submerged in some European craft) because size did not buy invisibility, handiness, or any proportionate growth in firepower. This argument would be revived by opponents of large submarines during the interwar period. Spear did not point out that size might give submarines sufficient speed and cruising radius to accompany the battle fleet. The General Board would not seriously consider this role for another two years.

Spear pointed out that strategic mobility (the long-range surface mobility that got the submarine to the point of action) was always traded off against tactical mobility within a given hull. Surface speed also had a tactical role; after sighting her target, the submarine approached to within a few miles before diving. Surface speed (engine size and appetite for fuel) was traded against radius of action (fuel capacity). Spear argued that future submarines should be able to cruise with the fleet (whose economical speed was 11 kt) and to reach outlying U.S. posessions under its own power (radius at least 3500 nm): from the East Coast to the Caribbean or Panama and the West Coast, and from the West Coast to Hawaii and the Philippines. Spear did not envisage the submarines operating with the fleet in battle. Like his contemporaries, he imagined the U.S. fleet convoying its train to a distant area and setting up an advanced base. Submarines would help to protect the base from enemy counterattack. Endurance could be best increased not by enlarging submarines but by adopting more efficient engines and denser fuel with greater heat content.[8] Underwater, motor weight (power:

maximum speed) was traded against low-speed endurance (battery weight, therefore capacity). Spear assumed that low speed would be used mainly to retire after attacking. He arbitrarily made motor power sufficient to exhaust the battery in 1 hr.[9] Using a simple (but arbitrary) mathematical model of the standard attack, Spear justified the 14-kt surface speed and 11.25 kt submerged speed of the then current F class.

Spear sought the smallest submarine (about 340 tons) that would provide the largest possible torpedo salvo, four tubes (as in the D class and later boats).[10] He considered that a sufficiently seaworthy submarine with these characteristics could be built on 350–450 tons, with a surface speed of 13.5–14.5 kt. The navy had already fixed hull strength by requiring a safe depth (test depth) of 200 ft. Significantly for later developments, Spear did not associate net submarine size, hence sea-keeping and habitability, with strategic mobility. Later, U.S. submariners would bitterly criticize the General Board for its failure to realize that small submarines were not really seaworthy. They blamed Electric Boat's commercial interest in multiplying the number of submarines, given a fixed overall congressional appropriation. On the other hand, contemporary discussions of warship design show little explicit attention to either sea-keeping or habitability.

Some submariners suggested that Spear's single-minded pursuit of the coastal defense role against battleships might be far too limited. In November 1909, one suggested a special fast, long-range submarine (albeit with low submerged speed) to attack an enemy's dockyards or "lay in wait in enemy's channels in beginning of a war." The necessary technology did not yet exist. Another submariner suggested that the new European practice of mounting guns on board might be intended to allow submarines to fight enemy submarines on the surface.

Submarine officers equated endurance with engine reliability (which meant space for maintenance), storeroom space, and even space in which to overhaul torpedoes, none of which figured explicitly in Spear's calculations. Fearing that the theoretical approach, so appealing to the General Board, would outweigh their operational experience, they periodically appealed to the board.

For FY 10, the secretary of the navy requested, and Congress provided (act of 3 March 1909), four submarines. The General Board wanted them all built on the Pacific Coast, but one contract (for G-3) went to Lake. Electric Boat built the others on the West Coast (EB 26: H-1 through H-3), two at Union Iron Works and one at Moran. Unit cost rose slightly; $3.5 million had bought eight FY 09 boats, but $2 million bought four in FY 10.

The General Board only slightly modified the F-class circular of requirements for the new H class. The main change, ordered in January 1910, was that engines had to be reversible. The alternative of shutting down diesels and switching to motors for maneuvering seemed unacceptable. The board ordered this change on the unanimous recommendation of four submarine COs. Electric Boat had to switch from 4-cycle Vickers diesels to 2-cycle MAN diesels, which caused enormous problems in the H, K, L, and M classes. The board also required one reload per torpedo tube (total of eight torpedoes).

By this time, the submariners wanted separate conning towers equipped with periscopes.[11] The H-class conning tower was modified to permit installation of a walk-around periscope. The operating compartment instrument was in

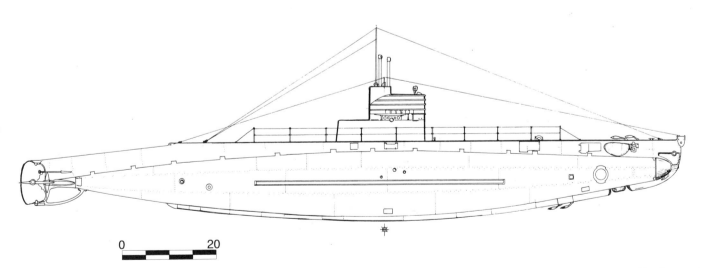

0   20

Electric Boat's H-1 is shown as modified during World War I, with a permanent (chariot) bridge and Y-tube sound gear (visible above and below her hull, forward). U.S. sound gear was installed on H-boats completed for Britain after the United States entered World War I. For example, early in 1918 H-11 had a C-tube installed on her upper deck but not on her keel. Her British CO liked this position for its easier access. He also argued, incorrectly, that a keel location was noisier, because even when the propellers were stopped, their shafts conducted hull noise into the water. Although few such boats were built for the U.S. Navy, Electric Boat built many during World War I for Britain, Italy, and Russia; some were transferred to Chile in payment for ships taken over by Britain. (Jim Christley)

the same position as the after periscope of an E-boat or F-boat, with its eyepiece near the steering station. Each periscope had torpedo-firing gear.

The circular called for a sustained surface speed of 12.5 kt (20-hr trial in the open sea), with a maximum surface speed (4-hr trial) of at least 14 kt, and full-power endurance of at least 80 hr. Submerged speed was to be at least 9.5 kt at the 1-hr rate and 8.5 kt at the 3-hr rate. The boat had to submerge, from full-ahead on the surface to 8 kt underwater (at periscope depth), in not more than 10 min. The prewar U.S. Navy did not imagine that submarines would have to crash-dive. Apparently for the first time, the submarine had to be able to fire all her torpedoes while surfaced in light trim.

The H-boats were the last built under contracts that allowed plans to be offered directly to foreign governments. Although Electric Boat apparently sold slightly modified plans of later U.S. submarines (see chapter 4), the company would have found it far more embarrassing if it had actually built or prefabricated them in the United States, where it might have been subject to U.S. naval inspection. When Britain secretly negotiated to buy Electric Boat submarines in 1914, the company therefore offered H-boats, rather than more modern K-boats or L-boats.[12] Britain ordered 20 boats: 10 to be assembled by Vickers in Montreal (to avoid U.S. neutrality laws) and the other 10 to be delivered "after the war" from the United States (in fact, by Fore River). The first 10 boats, completed in May–June 1915, crossed the Atlantic under their own power. The others were held in the United States until this country entered the war in April 1917, but their engines, motors, and other fittings were sent to Vickers for incorporation into Vickers-built H-boats (H 21 class). Of the interned series, 6 were transferred to Chile to compensate for ships taken over by the Royal Navy. Canadian Vickers assembled another 8 boats for Italy. Russia ordered 18 boats (as the AG class) under its 1915 emergency program. They were delivered in knocked-down form for assembly at Petrograd and Nikolaev. Delivery of the last 6 (AG 17–20, 27, 28) was canceled because of the Russian revolution; the U.S. Navy took them over as H-4–H-9.[13]

The General Board (and therefore the secretary of the navy) asked for no submarines for FY 11.[14] If Congress bought any, the board wanted them built or delivered on the West Coast.[15] Congress authorized four (act of 24 June 1910), but these Electric Boat submarines (EB 30B: K-1 through K-4) were split between the two coasts.[16] The board was more concerned with the lack of submarine tenders. Submarine flotillas could not be mobile without them. At least six were needed: three for each ocean. Two would replace the obsolescent Mohican and Severn. The ex-gunboat Castine would do only for a flotilla of older boats. A new tender had to be able to tow up to five boats (flotilla strength was variously given as five and six), refueling each at least once and charging their batteries under way. She would carry distilled water and electrolyte for their batteries. The board wanted her to have a cable

ship–type bow to lift a damaged submarine out of the water and a boom aft to lift the tail of a submarine so that her propellers could be changed. Congress preferred to buy combatant ships.

The General Board submitted characteristics on 13 October 1910. Because money was limited, the board cut submerged speed (to 10.5 kt) and maneuverability (tactical diameter eight lengths). The new Salmon (D-3) had just made 11.1 kt on trial, and her tactical diameter was slightly over six lengths. Sustained (3-hr) underwater speed was cut to 8.5 kt (D-3 made almost 9 kt on her 3-hr trial). The board asked for 14.5 kt on the surface, with an endurance of 80 hr at maximum speed (960 nm), 2,300 nm cruising at 11 kt (4,000 at 11 kt with maximum oil fuel load).[17] Speed and endurance were comparable to those demanded of contemporary units of the fleet train that steamed with the fleet to its advanced base (auxiliaries were required to have a maximum speed of 14 kt, and the fleet had to stop about every 3,300 nm for coal). U.S. submarine endurance figures were unrealistic; they took into account neither lubricating oil nor battery water, and neither was carried in amounts proportional to fuel oil capacity.[18]

The board allowed either diesel or steam power. The French were still using steam in their Laubeuf submarines, and this clause may have been intended to allow for U.S. purchase of a Laubeuf-type boat. Diesels, in fact, were used. The 200-ft test depth was retained. Armament was the usual quartet of 18-in tubes (5.2 m long), with one reload per tube carried nearby, but the Board also wanted a new feature, one or two tubes firing astern. Both C&R and the submariners much disliked them. The EB 30B design selected had two stern tubes (plus its four bow tubes), but it was soon reordered to match the next year's EB 32, which was similar but lacked stern tubes.[19]

K-2, K-5, and K-6 participated in the week-long May 1915 strategic exercise. K-2's CO considered her large enough for coastal operation but not for independent work. Her best reliable speed of 9 kt was insufficient for patrol. The CO encountered trouble with both his motors (commutators) and batteries (rapidly deteriorating). Crew health was poor from lack of exercise and improperly cooked food. Radio messages were received at 20 nm. K-5's CO thought her endurance had been limited to 10 days only by lack of fresh water; otherwise, she could have remained out for another 2 days. At the end of the exercise, he was beginning to suffer commutator trouble in his motors and his batteries were deteriorating. Unlike K-2's crew, his did not suffer from poor health, though he did complain of engine gases and rolling. He could not dive at all times because of crew inexperience (10 of 26 unqualified) and only half motor power available on the starboard side; however, "in actual war could and would have submerged, but could not have handled vessel in most efficient manner." K-6's CO also complained of insufficient fresh water; his batteries were usable but "deteriorating very rapidly." Later K-boats were the first U.S. submarines sent to Europe in WW I.

The submariners, represented initially by the com-

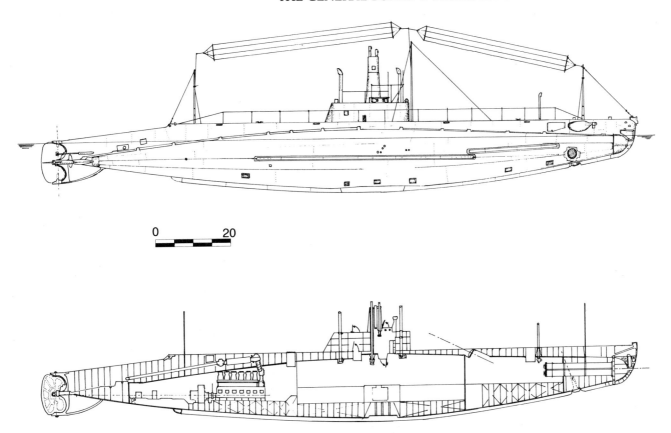

Electric Boat's K-5 is shown as built, with faired periscope shears. The shaded circle under her fore planes is a Fessenden oscillator, the replacement for the earlier signal bell. (Jim Christley)

mander of the Altantic Torpedo Flotilla, considered the General Board far too conservative. In August 1910, they asked for much higher speed (18 kt surfaced, 15 kt cruising, 14 kt submerged). A larger submarine could be compartmented, hence protected against damage caused by grounding or collision. The noisy engine room could be shut off from the operating compartment. All major valves could come under central supervision in the control room. Size would also buy the stores (as much as 50 percent over the usual surface ship allowance) the submarine needed to loiter in her patrol area. It was at this time that the submariners asked for the conning tower with a periscope, which the General Board retroactively included in the H-boat requirement; the K-boats had an enlarged conning tower.

The bureaus asked the three contractors for their views on the submariners' big "sea-keeping" boat. Electric Boat protested that its own experience in designing a 17/11-kt submarine for Russia proved that high surface speed would require not only more power but also a ship-shaped hull with increased underwater resistance and thus slower underwater. A really fast submarine would have to be about twice as large (hence twice as expensive) as an H-boat. Laurenti initially demurred; it could provide 18 kt surfaced, but 14 kt submerged would be a very different proposition. Lake refused to comment.

Laurenti soon offered a new Italian design for a 20-kt (10-kt submerged) submarine (214 ft 1 in × 20 ft × 14

ft, 750/900 metric tons), which it claimed could replace existing torpedo craft. Characteristics aproached those that the General Board later wanted in a fleet submarine: radius of action, 2,000 nm at 20 kt or 6,000 nm at 10 kt; submerged endurance, 24 nm (3 hr) at 8 kt or 95 nm (21¼ hr) at 4 kt. She would have four diesels paired on two shafts (total 4,000 BHP). Laurenti argued that no more than 10 kt submerged was worthwhile; above that, a submarine could not use her periscope.[20] Chief Constructor Richard M. Watt rejected this $1 million design on the ground that Congress had appropriated $2 million for four FY 11 submarines.

The General Board's mobile defense still needed submarine tenders. By September 1910, there was only the inadequate *Castine*. The board recommended against buying any more submarines until new tenders could be built. In November, however, instead of asking for three tenders, the secretary of the navy asked for two submarines and one tender for FY 12. About this time, obsolete (and apparently unmodified) monitors were pressed into service as interim submarine tenders. Congress bought four submarines and the tender *Fulton* (act of 4 March 1911). This time, Lake's bid was rejected.[21] All four submarines were built by Electric Boat (EB 32: K-5 through K-8). The General Board chose to repeat the FY 11 design with minor changes.

Commenting on the K-boat characteristics in April 1911, the Submarine Detachment of the Atlantic Torpedo Fleet

Dry docked in Honolulu about 1916, K-8 displays the typical Electric Boat bow cap, which rotated to expose the torpedo tube muzzles (the holes in the cap were on the centerline, at top and bottom, when the cap was closed). Her periscopes were fixed, with large heads. The temporary bridge structure has been removed, leaving only a streamlined fairwater.

argued that submarines could not realistically expect to porpoise to hide their periscopes during the approach to a target. They might well have to fire as soon as the feather of the periscope was spotted, (i.e., at greater range). The submariners wanted the new 21-in torpedo that was then superseding the 18-in on board U.S. destroyers. They also wanted an independent cap for each tube, so that all four could be fired (and reloaded) in quick sequence. The General Board feared that any such changes would greatly enlarge the submarine; the 10,000 yd promised for the new version of the 18-in torpedo was surely enough.[22] The board did accept a suggestion that a loitering submarine needed 50 percent greater stores endurance than a surface ship. The board also adopted some other changes. The FY 12 submarines would be protected against grounding and damage as a result of going alongside. Main ballast tanks had to be fillable in 1 min (as suggested by the Atlantic Torpedo Fleet). Final characteristics issued in the summer of 1911 showed slightly greater required cruising radius (3,000 nm at 11 kt, 5,000 nm with maximum oil fuel, and capable of making a 3,000-nm passage in any weather). Required surface speed was reduced to 14 kt,

and the characteristics included both maximum (10.5-kt) and 3-hr rate (8.5-kt) underwater speeds.

In January 1912, the secretary of the navy reacted to submariners' criticism by forming a board of submarine officers to review design and construction policy. The submariners' proposal for a fleet submarine led to the T and V classes, described in chapter 6. They argued that a double hull was needed to protect against collision and grounding. The officers clearly disliked the small conning towers of the H-boats and K-boats. They wanted a large oval structure (8 ft × 4 ft) fitted as an escape chamber with its hatch hinged on the fore side, so that no one at the steering station could accidentally slip back into it). It would carry a 2-in breathing pipe to refresh the air in the boat (as yet, there was no way to remove carbon dioxide) and a fixed-eyepiece periscope. A walk-around periscope would be let into the body of the boat. Both were to house flush with the tops of the periscope shears.

The officers rejected a proposed innovation, a vertical-base range finder, on the ground that it introduced excessive complication and was as yet untested. The engine room, motor room, galley, and radio room were to be

On the Mississippi near St. Louis in 1919, K-5 displays some standard World War I modifications: passive sound gear forward (the three "rats" of a Y tube forward of the forward planes and an SC tube forward of the forward hatch); a permanent chariot bridge; and housing periscopes.

enclosed; they wanted an air regenerator (which they would not get until WW I). The main bilge pumps would be in separate compartments, one in the engine room and one in the motor room, and an emergency high-pressure bilge pump would be outside the engine room. The cry for 21-in torpedoes was revived. Finally, the officers wanted a reliable radio. In a 1911 night attack on battleships off Block Island, Rhode Island, only three of seven boats managed to attack because the others had never been alerted.

In May, C&R agreed readily enough that some advance in submarine characteristics was needed, but the submariners wanted too mcuh on too few tons. More tonnage should be used to provide a double hull; watertight subdivision (bulkheads with the same test depth as the submarine herself), including enclosed engine and motor rooms; and higher submerged speed (11 kt for 1 hr). Growth to 800 tons submerged (compared with 550 tons of the K class) would buy about 2 more kt on the surface (16 kt), a surface radius at full speed of at least 2,000 nm (vice 1,680 nm now guaranteed), and a cruising radius of 5,500 nm (as in the K class). An 800-ton (submerged) boat would accommodate 21-in torpedoes, with one reload per tube. She might mount a small gun; the submariners had *not* suggested this, but it was beginning to appear abroad. Unit cost probably would be $750,000–$800,000. Alternatively, some of the board's detail ideas could be incorporated in a repeat K-boat.

C&R included provision for the small gun in the L-class bidders' package, with the proviso that the gun could be included or deleted later on (approved by the General Board in January 1913). The board considered a gun useful to a U.S. submarine forced to surface in the face of enemy submarines and light picket vessels. The 3-in gun was streamlined by being placed in a disappearing mount forward of the bridge; only the barrel was visible when it was housed. Even so, it cost about $\frac{1}{2}$ kt in speed at a time when submerged speed seemed all important.[23]

In May 1911, the General Board proposed five submarines and two submarine tenders for FY 13 (FY 12's appropriation did not suffice for the one authorized tender). In December 1911, the secretary of the navy asked for no submarines, but Congress bought eight plus a second tender, *Bushnell* (act of 22 August 1912). The General Board decided that all eight submarines would be repeat K-boats. Largely as a result of the submariners' demands, they were modified to become the L class, split between Electric Boat and Lake. They had provision for 3-in guns, though the first batch of Electric Boat units was completed without them. The submariners' preferred large conning tower was abandoned; this class reverted to a pair of hull periscopes. The tower might have been cut to a trunk to compensate for the added drag of the 3-in guns. The L class introduced the strong internal bulkheads sought by the submariners since 1910. Electric Boat units finally had their

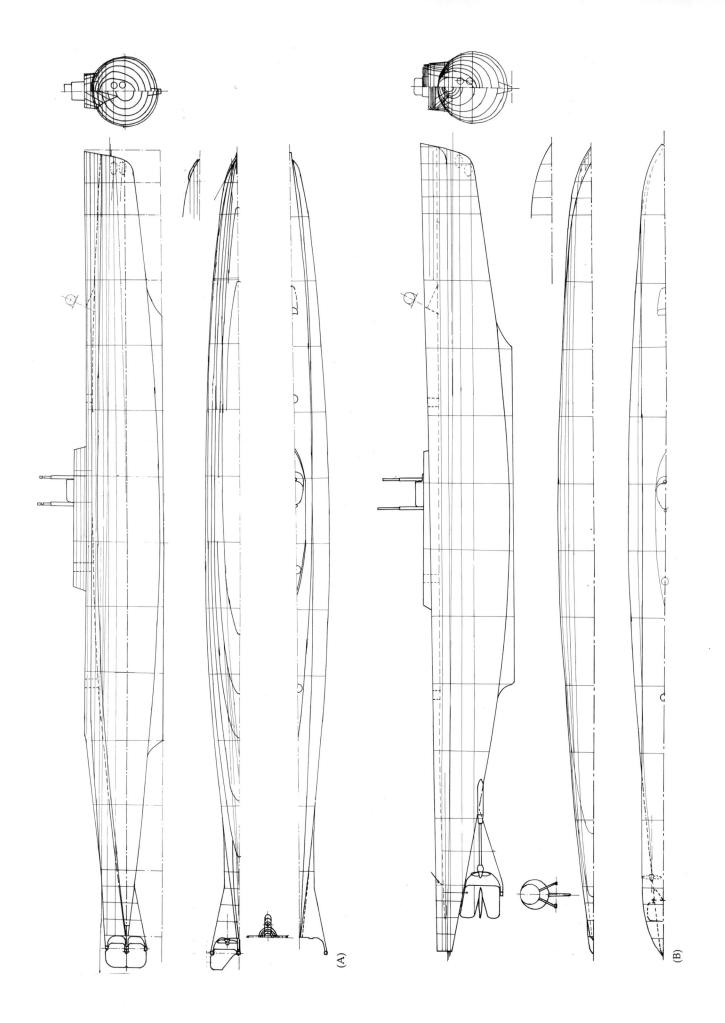

(A)

(B)

L-10 was a typical Electric Boat L-boat, shown here running trials off Provincetown, 25 May 1916. Note her temporary canvas bridge screen and fixed (non-housing) periscopes. The object forward of her bridge fairwater is a disappearing 3 in/23 gun.

main auxiliaries removed from the main motor shafts and driven by separate electric motors (mounted forward of the main engines). Independent bow caps were finally provided for torpedo tubes. Virtually nothing was done on the three Lake boats before Lake was declared bankrupt in November 1913. They were reordered (to improved designs) from the reorganized Lake Co. Presumably, the navy was loath to eliminate Electric Boat's only important American competitor. OpNav found Lake's L-boats inferior to the Electric Boat L-boats, although their Busch-Sulzer engines might be considered superior.

In September 1912, the General Board expected to buy eight more K-boats during FY 14. Chief Constructor Watt protested that no advances could be made unless at least a few of them were larger and more offensively oriented. Although hardly a fleet boat, the double-hull boat proposed by C&R that May would be a distinct step forward. C&R and BuEng much preferred step-by-step evolution to anything riskier. The General Board feared that anything short of a spectacular improvement would cause Congress to cut the number in the FY 14 budget. Therefore, it suggested that the FY 14 program include one advanced fast submarine, its displacement not to exceed 750 tons submerged. On 22 October 1912, the General Board asked C&R to prepare sketch plans for submarines larger than the K-boats.[24] Within a few weeks, the bureau was able to estimate appropriate dimensions and characteristics: double-hull, 190 ft × 15 ft (450/600 tons), 16 kt surfaced, and 11 kt submerged.

In December, the General Board convinced the secretary of the navy to use some of the FY 14 money to replace one of the FY 13 submarines with C&R's double-hull type (M-1). The other seven were split between Electric Boat (EB 37G: L-1–L-4) and Lake (L-5–L-7).[24] For FY 14, it asked for six coastal boats plus a submarine tender and a special submarine testing/salvage pontoon dock. Congress bought four repeat L-boats (act of 4 March 1913): the Lake-type L-8 built at Portsmouth (the first navy-built submarine) and Electric Boat's EB 37H: L-9–L-11.

The experimental M-1 (EB 39E) was slower than Watt had hoped. With a double hull and the military characteristics of an L-boat, she was about 20 percent larger than a Lake L-boat and had far more reserve buoyancy (27 percent, compared with 15.5 percent for an Electric Boat L-boat or 11 percent for a Lake L-boat). She was far more seaworthy but too small to take full advantage of her configuration. Probably to save weight in the pressure hull, her test depth was reduced to 150 ft. She was much more cramped internally and in the tanks between her hulls than the single-hull boats. Because of poor ballast tank arrangement, she became unstable when surfacing or diving and sometimes listed heavily. M-1 was considered unsuccessful, but her design was repeated in slightly modified form by several foreign Electric Boat customers (see chapter 4).

Bids for the six FY 14 boats were opened on 2 December 1913. Electric Boat offered seven designs: EB 32E, 37H, 38H, double-hull EB 39J and 39K, and two fleet submarines, EB 42C and 49B. EB 32E would have been a modified repeat K-boat; EB 37H was the L-boat chosen. The company was clearly aware of interest in larger submarines; to buy them, the navy would have to drastically cut the

---

These C&R submarine sketches (*facing page*) reflecting requirements stated by the Submarine Flotilla board in January 1912 might have been the first submarines designed by U.S. Navy constructors. Although undated, the drawings probably were executed in mid-1912, and they reflect the two configurations Electric Boat had developed. Scheme A (top three drawings) is a conventional Electric Boat body-of-revolution (i.e., single-hull) design (204 ft 6 in overall × 17 ft 6 in, 604/755 tons). Scheme B (bottom three drawings) shows the sort of vertical-chisel stern Electric Boat introduced in its big Russian cruiser (EB 31A) and an elliptical-section hull form, presumably housing an inner pressure hull. Dimensions were 197 ft 6 in × 17 ft 6 in (604/780 tons). Each version shows four torpedo tubes with the independent shutters favored by the flotilla. The corresponding inboard profiles seem not to have survived.

L-9 (AL-9) shows typical war modifications: a chariot bridge and retractable (housing) periscopes. U.S. L-boats serving in British waters were given AL-designations to distinguish them from the unrelated British L-boats.

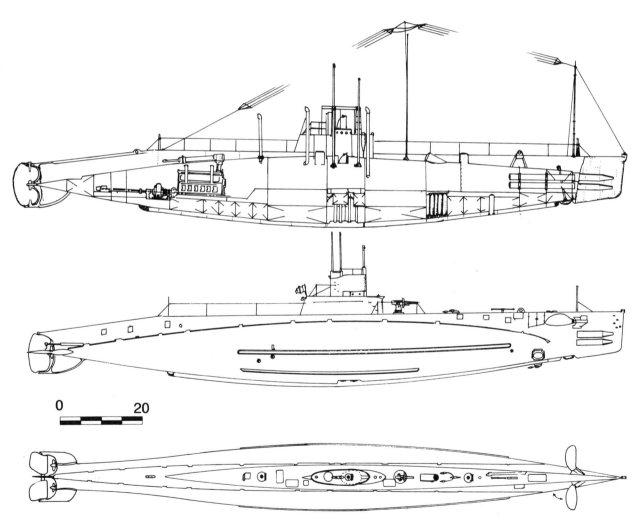

0   20

Electric Boat's L-1 is shown as designed (inboard, top) and during World War I (outboard and plan views, middle and bottom), when she served in British waters as AL-1. Wartime modifications included installation of a disappearing mount for the 3-in/23 gun and sound gear (Y-tubes on deck and on the keel and a T-shaped SC-tube on deck forward of the deck Y-tube), as well as a permanent sheltered bridge. The disappearing gun mount was inspired by a German 3.5-in (88-mm) gun seen on board prewar U-boats. This was Electric Boat's first class to use independent torpedo tube shutters, rather than a single rotating bow cap. (Jim Christley)

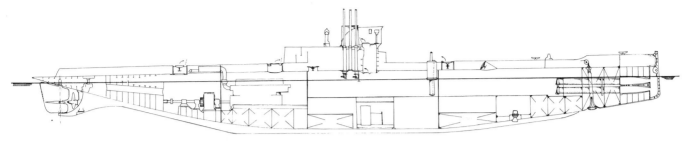

Simon Lake's L-8 (built by Portsmouth) shows his characteristic ship-type stern, with its horizontal chisel shape, which C&R preferred to Electric Boat's much less buoyant one. The cylinder forward of the bridge houses a 3-in Mk IX gun. The bankruptcy of Lake's original company delayed construction of these boats; when completed, they embodied such war modifications as chariot bridges and retracting (housing) periscopes. Note the signal bell set into the keel forward. During World War I, such bells were superseded by Fessenden oscillators, which used plates set into flooded tanks. The battery tanks were set above the two main ballast tanks, one below the torpedo room forward and one below the control room amidships. Note that Lake subdivided his boats more completely than did Electric Boat, with separate engine and motor rooms aft, and with a separate tiller flat abaft the after trim tank (which was abaft the motor room, connected to it by an access trunk). He concentrated pumps and other auxiliaries in the large space beneath the control room, rather than (as in Electric Boat designs) along the propeller shafts abaft the motors. The two periscopes flank the retractable antenna mast. This class incorporated Lake's patented air lock abaft the conning tower. (Jim Christley)

size and cost of any other boats it bought at the same time. It therefore offered a tiny EB 38H: 116 ft × 12 ft 9½ in, 185.5/228.6 tons, driven by a single 300-BHP 6-cylinder diesel, armed with only two bow tubes (four torpedoes). Test depth was reduced to 150 ft. This design foreshadowed the N class.[25] The fleet submarine designs are described in chapter 6.

FY 15 characteristics for a repeat K-boat, with a 3-in gun and bulkheading sufficient to survive flooding of one compartment at 50 ft, had been approved on 15 July 1913. The new features were made retroactive to FY 13 and FY 14 submarines, which became the separate L class. In order to buy a single fleet submarine, however, Congress

(apparently *not* the navy), by act of 30 June 1914, cut the available money per coastal submarine to $440,000 (an L-boat cost about $530,000). By this time, work on characteristics for FY 16 was already under way. C&R and the General Board assumed that Congress would impose the same cost limit. The Navy Department used the 1916 characteristics (see below) for the FY 15 submarines to produce the N class, but it proved far too small to be useful. As in FY 13, the class was divided between Electric Boat (EB 61B: N-1–N-3) and Lake (N-4–N-7). Lake's N-boats were considered inferior to Electric Boat's because of poor detail design, complicated machinery, and relatively poor habitability.

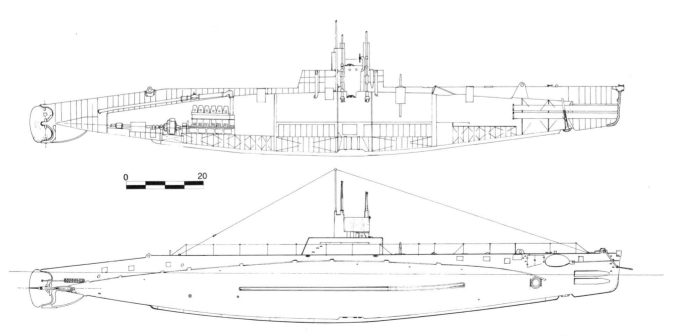

0   20

Electric Boat's L-11 was a unit of the repeat L class. The circular plate on the hull forward covers a Fessenden oscillator for underwater signaling. The 3-in/23 gun forward of the bridge is shown in stowed position. (Jim Christley)

Portsmouth's L-8 displays Lake's trademark bulky watertight superstructure, with limber holes to allow the bow portion to flood quickly for a fast dive.

Work on 1916 characteristics apparently began in May 1914; the General Board formalized them in June. The new submarines were described as harbor, rather than coastal, defense boats, with a maximum submerged displacement of 400 tons (compared with 550 tons for an L-boat). They would operate largely in the presence of enemy forces, hence mainly submerged. The General Board wanted both higher burst speed (11.5 kt rather than 10.5 kt; given a limited appropriation per boat, C&R could offer only 11 kt) and longer endurance (5 hr at medium speed after 1 hr at 11 kt, compared with 2 hr at 5 kt after 3 hr at 8.5 kt in the abortive FY 15 submarine). Because the boat had to attack battleships, she still needed four bow tubes (one reload each); surfaced in light condition, however, she could fire only the lower two. To have immersed the other two would have cost too much tonnage. No gun would be needed near a U.S. harbor. The main concession was 1 kt less on the surface (13 kt). Surfaced endurance would be cut to 2,500 nm at 11 kt. Supplies were cut from 30 days to 12. The board rejected a C&R proposal to cut test depth to 150 ft.

C&R suggested other details to achieve savings. Auxiliaries once again could be run from the main shafting. Diesels could be nonreversing, with the boat maneuvering on her motors; Electric Boat could revert to 4-cycle designs, which proved far more reliable and would soon replace the 2-cycle units of the H-boats and K-boats. Permanent torpedo warhead stowage could be omitted because all of the boats would operate from bases.

These characteristics (which were actually used for the FY 15 submarines) were approved (for FY 16) on 29 October 1914. By that time, the German U-boats were beginning to demonstrate their potential. In December 1915, the secretary of the navy asked for eight FY 16 submarines, including a second fleet boat. Bids were requested for SS 62–67 (i.e., for only six boats); C&R was expected to design the fleet submarine. Electric Boat offered a modified L-boat (EB 37L and 37M) or M-boat (EB 39M) or a new design (EB 68A, the one bought). All had 4-cycle engines (6-cylinder, except 8-cylinder for EB 39M) in place of the 2-cycle type used in the H through M classes, which was performing very poorly. Union Iron Works independently offered EB designs.[26] Lake offered a variety of designs. Lake's new West Coast affiliate, California Shipbuilding Corp. (CALSHIP), built three of the six boats he was awarded.[27] There were also some new bidders.[28]

The General Board wanted 3 more fleet submarines (to make up a division of 4) and 16 coastal submarines. Congress bought 16 coastal boats (O class, act of 3 March 1916) at a fixed cost of $550,000, about that of an L-boat; it also bought 2, rather than 3, fleet submarines. The General Board withdrew its harbor defense characteristics. The FY

Lake boats show their distinctive sterns at Philadelphia Navy Yard in 1919: O-boats, plus Lake's prototype G-1 (the small submarine third from left). After World War I the U.S. Navy standardized on Lake's flat stern, whose buoyancy kept the propellers and diving planes down in the water.

14 (L-boat) characteristics were revived, except for one surviving feature of the original FY 15/16 characteristics—a higher underwater speed of 11 kt. The 14-kt surface speed was restored, and surface radius was 3,150 nm at 11 kt (maximum 5,500 nm, using ballast tanks for fuel oil). Again, contracts were divided between Electric Boat (EB 68A: O-1–O-10) and Lake (O-11–O-16). Two Electric Boat units (O-1 and O-2) were built in navy yards (Portsmouth and Puget Sound, respectively). The Electric Boat units survived to WW II.

These were the first U.S. submarines with really satisfactory diesels. In April 1918, Emory S. Land, C&R's submarine expert, was particularly impressed by the Electric Boat O class because "two boats [actually] completed trials in accordance with the contract requirements. That is really remarkable for our service. . . . These boats are reasonably satisfactory. They not only made the contract speed but they beat it."[29] The O-boats also had major improvements in habitability. For the first time, every man in the normal complement had his own berth (albeit narrower than on surface ships) and locker. This class also introduced evaporators, which were heated by the battery and thus wasted power, but they were rarely used.

With the post-1919 shift to Pacific priorities, the coastal defense submarines were inevitably relegated to training and the defense of particular points, such as important bases and the Panama Canal. The C-boats were stricken in 1920. On 25 July 1921, the General Board recommended that surviving units of the A, B, and C classes (of which only 1 B-boat and 3 D-boats still existed) be scrapped immediately; Secretary of the Navy Edwin Denby agreed on 30 July. The board considered the H class obsolete because of its poor habitability and short radius of action. The larger K-boats retained some value for coastal defense.[30]

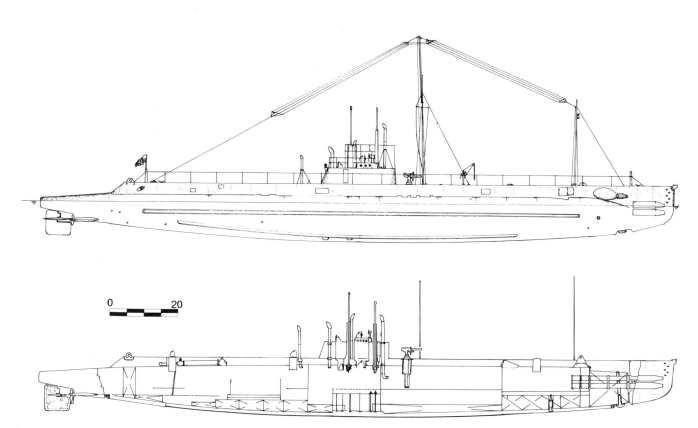

0   20

M-1 was Electric Boat's first U.S. double-hull submarine. The company had already designed a larger double-hull boat for Russia (EB 31A design, *Narval* class); M-1 had a similar stern, unlike those of standard Electric Boat single-hull submarines, with a single rudder and propellers well below the axis of the hull. Unlike Lake's stern, the stern on M-1 had a *vertical* chisel shape, much like contemporary cruiser sterns (but not raked forward). The 3-in/23 gun is shown set up on deck. A World War I British observer, Stanley Goodall (later Director of Naval Construction Sir Stanley) found crew accomodation particularly comfortable, with cots (bunks) three high, light and easily stowed. The boat was heated and had an ice tank (i.e., refrigerator), but she seemed crowded. Early in 1918 the existing Gould batteries had already been found unsatisfactory, and were being replaced by thin-plate Exides. (Jim Christley)

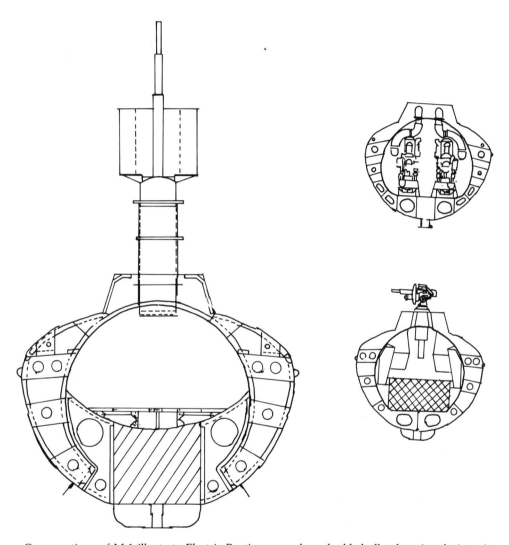

Cross sections of M-1 illustrate Electric Boat's approach to double-hull submarine design. At left is a structural drawing of the boat's midships cross section, with the safety tank shaded in. At right are cross sections at the engine room (top) and at the crew's quarters (below, where the battery is crosshatched).

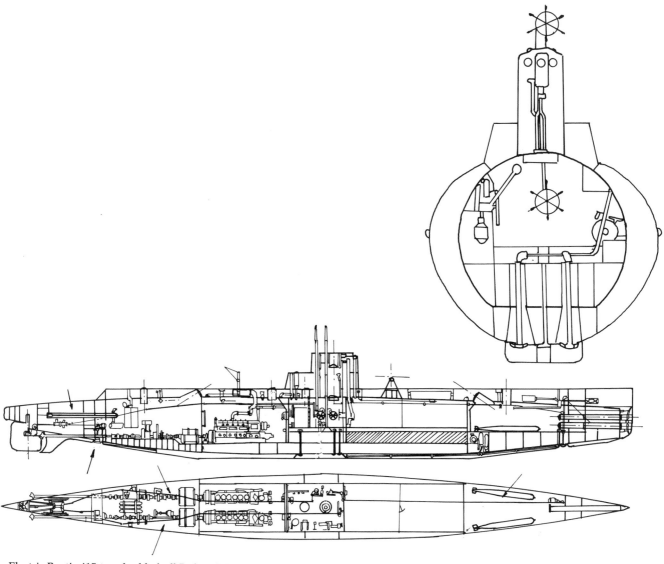

Electric Boat's 415-ton double-hull B class (EB 406B, for Norway) illustrates the company's standard design practices. This boat was essentially a stretched two-tube boat with two more tubes projecting out from her stern. Like Electric Boat's single hull craft, this one had a duct keel draining through Kingstons amidships, below (and controlled from) the control room. Planes and rudders were all controlled by rods leading from the wheels (the rod lines are indicated by arrows). The boat had the usual mushroom anchor forward and a Fessenden oscillator aft.

The enlarged cross section shows the unusual flat-floored pressure hull form, otherwise circular, and a pair of Kingstons, with their controls. Six boats were ordered in 1915, but material could not be delivered in wartime, so they were not completed (by Horten Navy Yard) until 1923–30. Characteristics: 420/545 tons, 51.00 × 5.33 × 3.50 m (167 ft 4 in × 17 ft 6 in × 11 ft 6 in), 2 Sulzer diesels, 450 BHP each, two 350 HP motors (14/11 kt). As completed they were armed with four 45 cm (18 in) torpedo tubes and a 76 mm antiaircraft gun (indicated here by dashed lines), although the gun seems not to have been included in the original design. Two escaped to Britain in 1940; the Germans put two others into service as UC 1 and UC 2.

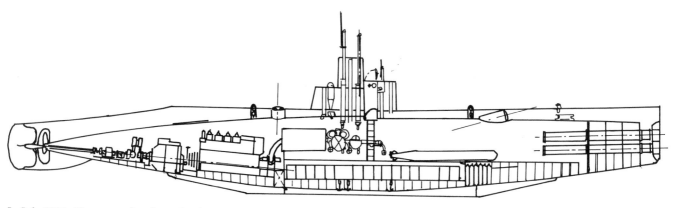

In July 1916, Norway ordered a pair of 220-ton, two-tube C-boats (EB 407A), but they were canceled.

Electric Boat's N-2 was used for training at New London in the early 1920s. She is shown loading a torpedo warhead.

Lake's N-5 is shown at the end of World War I, with standard sound gear (Y tube and SC tube) on her foredeck. This design was considered obsolete; the boat's engines were removed in 1922 for installation in an Electric Boat L-boat.

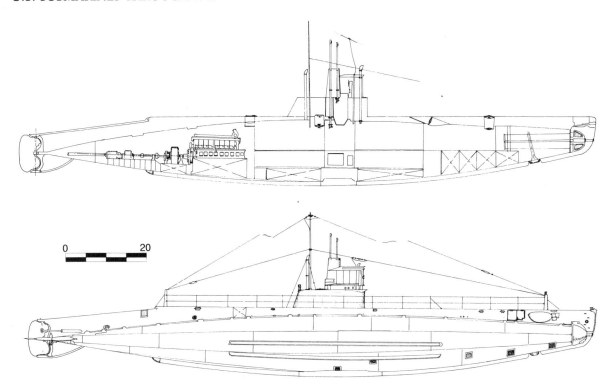

N-1 was intended for harbor defense; she was very nearly a modernized H-boat. Experience with N-boats was cited when the U.S. Navy rejected Electric Boat's proposal to mass-produce H-boats to fill a 1918 gap in submarine production. After World War I, these boats were used for training at New London. (Jim Christley)

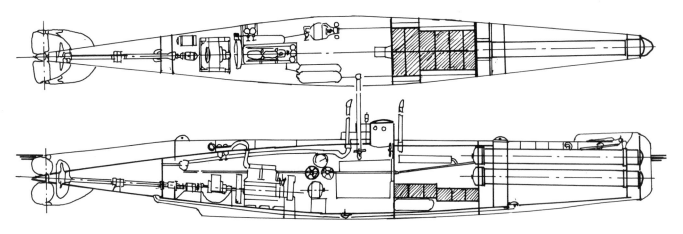

Electric Boat designed even smaller submarines for foreign customers. This is EB 27B, the midget built for the Russian army for Black Sea coast defense. At a length of 20.5 m (67 ft 4 in), EB 27B was only slightly longer than an A-boat. Three of these midgets were built by the Nevski Yard at St. Petersburg; they received numbers rather than names. The plan view does not show the bow plane. The batteries are shaded for clarity.

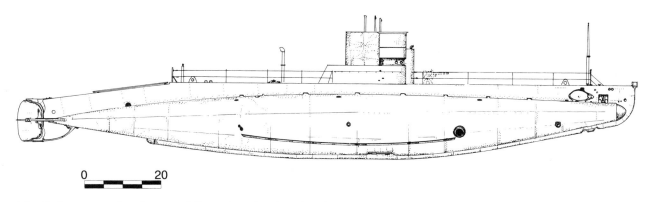

The O class reverted to the sort of dimensions developed in the K-boats and L-boats. Electric Boat's O-1 is shown; note that, like the K-boats (but not the L-boats), she has a bow cap for her torpedo tubes. (Jim Christley)

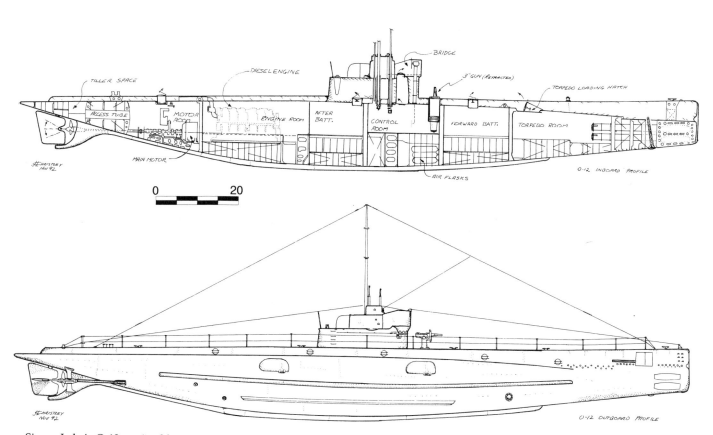

Simon Lake's O-12 retained his trademark stern and amidships planes (shown folded down in the outboard view). Note the separate flooding ports in the watertight superstructure. (Jim Christley)

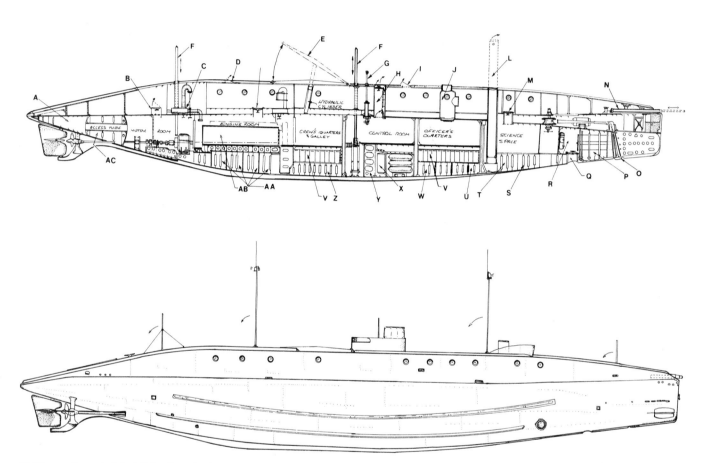

O-12 was discarded in 1930 to be rebuilt by Lake and Danenhower, Inc., of Bridgeport, Connecticut, for the Wilkins Arctic expedition. Lake had long thought about submarine operation under ice; in 1903, he built a trestle atop his *Protector* and deliberately operated her in iced waters. The *Nautilus* conversion, shown here, was far more sophisticated. Key: A, tiller room; B, hatch into superstructure; C, engine exhaust; D, hatch to topside; E, under-ice skid with roller; F, pneumatic ice-cutting tubes; G, periscope; H, topside access trunk; I, topside access trunk; J, escape trunk; L, telescoping escape trunk; M, superstructure access hatch; N, hydraulic bumper ram; O, mushroom anchor; P, forward trim tank; Q, diver's hatch; R, diver's chamber; S, freshwater tank; T, fuel oil tank; U, ballast tank; V, battery; W, ballast tank; X, adjusting tank; Y, store room; Z, ballast tank; AA, fuel and lubricating oil tanks; AB, diesel engine; AC, after trim tank. (Jim Christley)

O-10 and O-4 are shown at Boston Navy Yard, 28 September 1922. Note the big insulating fitting at the bow, which terminates the forward radio loop antenna.

In dry dock at Portsmouth, New Hampshire, 5 September 1918, O-1 displays the standard Holland (Electric Boat) stern, nearly symmetrical around the long axis of the hull, with identical rudders top and bottom and with propellers set in line with the axis of the hull. Note the massive skeg along the top of the hull, aft.

The O-boats were the oldest U.S. submarines retained for use during World War II. O-8 is shown here. The most obvious modification was the addition of a small platform for a light anti-aircraft gun abaft the bridge. Like other Electric Boat ("Holland") O-, R-, and S-boats, O-8 was modified for greater safety: its skeg superstructure was cut down aft to clear a new escape hatch in her motor room. The object right aft is an escape hatch. Note the JK passive sonar transducer forward.

Electric Boat's L class had performed well on wartime anti-submarine warfare (ASW) patrol, but the engines were worn out. Lake's L-boats had good engines in entirely obsolete hulls; they would be described in 1924 as "of no military value whatsoever, their surface and submerged performances unreliable." M-1 had totally unreliable engines. The N class, as small as the H-boats, had little or no military value. BuEng believed that, by combining good engines with useful hulls, it could salvage 7 good boats from among the D, E, L, and M classes.

OpNav was mindful of recent war experience: boats could not be sent overseas with green crews. It therefore wanted to keep old boats for the next few years to provide training in a war emergency, when seagoing boats could not be spared. OpNav wanted to retain the H-boats and K-boats for coastal defense. Except for 4 L-boats, the General Board wanted the boats of this class scrapped as the S-boats entered service. Later coastal boats (8 N-boats, the 8 Electric Boat O-boats, and all 27 R-boats [see chapter 7]) would be modernized and retained.

Secretary Denby decided to retain the H-, K-, and L-boats and to scrap M-1 (she was considered for retention as an experimental boat, with new engines). He ordered the satisfactory Busch-Sulzer engines of the 4 Lake N-boats removed and installed in 4 Electric Boat L-boats (the other 3 were sold in 1922). Most officers agreed that it was pointless to lay up submarines; they would deteriorate so badly that they would be difficult to recommission. By 1923, money was so short that there was no alternative. That July, all H-, K-, and L-boats were out of commission at Hampton Roads, Virginia, and Bremerton, Washington. With limited armament and somewhat antiquated periscopes, they were earmarked for wartime training. The H- and K-boats were well prepared for reserve, but money was too scarce to do much for the L-boats. The re-engined L-boats were retained until 1930; however, the 4 Lake L-boats, considered of no military value and with unreliable surface and submerged performances, were sold in December 1925.

The 3 Electric Boat N-boats were assigned to New London for training. They served until 1926.

The 6 Lake O-boats were laid up at Philadelphia in 1924 and stricken in 1930. O-12 of this class was drastically modified in 1930 at the Philadelphia Navy Yard (as *Nautilus*) for the Wilkins/Ellsworth Arctic Expedition. The longer-ranged Electric Boat O-boats were still considered useful at Pearl Harbor and in the Canal Zone; they were not laid up until 1931. Except for O-1 (stricken in 1938) and O-5 (sunk in the Canal Zone in 1923), they were recommissioned in 1941 to train WW II submariners.[31]

6

Fleet Submarines

A NOVEMBER 1911 article in the British magazine *Engineering* about Electric Boat submarines includes a sketch of a 17-kt, 950-ton submarine reportedly under construction for Russia, presumably the type to which Electric Boat had referred in 1910.[1] An official C&R sketch shows a 212-ft × 21-ft × 12-ft oval-section, single-hull submarine (650/950 tons) capable of 17 kt surfaced (on two 1,000-BHP 8- cylinder engines) and 11 kt submerged; she was credited with a 5,000-nm surface radius and a 140-nm radius submerged. Armament was eight torpedo tubes: two forward, two aft, and two twin trainable deck tubes. Two periscopes were let into the operating compartment. Unlike many earlier Electric Boat submarines, this one had bow planes. The 1911 article pointed out that the oval hull needed more strengthening than the usual circular-section hull, so diving depth was reduced from 200 ft to 125 ft.

This article seemed to confirm what submariners feared: the U.S. Navy had lost its lead. The January 1912 Submarine Flotilla Board (see chapter 5) wanted a thousand-tonner that was as fast as a battleship (about 21 kt), hence able to fight in a major fleet action. Submarine cruising speed already slightly exceeded battleship cruising speed, thanks to the characteristics of submarine diesels. As in many performance calculations of the period, this one did not take sea state into account. The submarine should be at least as fast submerged (2-hr rate) as on the surface; if existing motors were not powerful enough, they could be installed in tandem, as in Lake's G-1 and Laurenti's G-4. C&R pointed out that to achieve high surface speed, the submarine would need a ship-form outer hull unsuited to high submerged speed. A spindle-form submarine could gain about a knot in underwater speed by adopting heavier motors and using shorter-lived batteries. The board wanted to match the Russian boat's reported cruising radius of 5,000 nm (U.S. battleships could make 8,000 nm at 10 kt). The fleet submarine would be much larger, hence much less easily handled, than existing coastal types. She would dive more slowly: 15 min from light condition, 5 min (to 15 ft) from awash condition. Test depth would be the 200 ft of earlier U.S. submarines.

The board wanted 21-inch tubes: the usual four in the bow and also a pair of trainable tubes on the centerline; as in the Russian boat, torpedoes could not yet be angled in the tubes. BuOrd argued that the existing 18-in Mk VII would disable a modern battleship; visibility limited effective range to about 4,000 yd (the torpedo could reach 6,000 yd). Any increase in submarine tonnage should go into more torpedoes.

Because no member understood the technical trade-offs of submarine design, the board's report greatly underestimated the problems to be overcome. Existing diesels could not come close to supplying enough power. BuEng considered 900 BHP a practical limit.[2] The bureau anticipated what would become the German WW I combination of an auxiliary diesel generator (wired for diesel-electric propulsion) and big diesels for high surface speed (see chapter 5).

C&R suggested that the size of foreign boats had been exaggerated because the standard measurement was submerged displacement. Double-hull foreign boats had larger ballast tanks, hence they had a greater displacement submerged for a given surfaced displacement. C&R considered surfaced displacement a better measure of the volume of the submarine's pressure hull.

If it could be built, the fleet submarine would offer the commander of a surface fleet some new possibilities; the Naval War College worked these out in games during the fall of 1912.[3] It was most interested in whether fleet submarines could neutralize the battlecruiser, another new type of warship then in service abroad and being considered for the U.S. Navy. The college deliberately exaggerated submarine speed: its notional boat could run awash at 30 kt (submerged speed was only 5 kt, with a submerged radius of 35 nm). It would take 21 min to go from light to awash condition and another 6 min to submerge altogether. Armament was eight torpedo tubes (one reload each), firing 6,000-yd weapons, three of which were needed to sink a ship. Each submarine also carried five dummy periscopes and five dummy mines.

Off Provincetown on 8 September 1919, AA-1 (later T-1) shows the opening for a pair of deck torpedo tubes abaft her bridge fairwater. At this time she had not yet been fitted with a 4-in deck gun. (*Submarine Force Museum and Library*)

AA-1 fires a torpedo from her trainable deck tube. (*Submarine Force Museum and Library*)

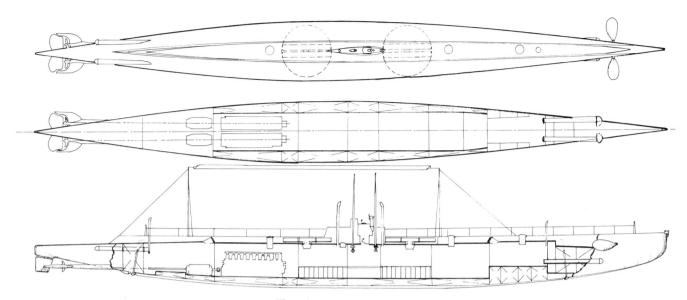

Electric Boat's Russian cruiser submarine (design EB 31A, built in modified form as *Narval*) inspired the U.S. fleet submarine program. EB 31A introduced the company's vertical-chisel (cruiser) stern (which it used in double-hull designs), and she had deck and stern torpedo tubes. Featured in a November 1911 issue of the British magazine *Engineering*, she convinced U.S. submariners that the U.S. Navy could have a long-range fleet submarine. AA-1 was essentially a stretched EB 31A. Oddly enough, the 1911 article described the submarine as single-hulled, with an elliptical cross section supported by "special construction." As the drawing shows, EB 31A was double-hulled amidships. The three *Narval*s were built at Nikolayev under the Russian 1911 program for the Black Sea Fleet. The planned deck torpedo tubes shown here were replaced by Drzwieki drop-collars. (Jim Christley)

Fleet submarines had to be at least as fast as battleships so that they could run ahead of the main fleet to get into position to attack the head of the enemy main column. In effect, they formed a mobile mine field that could be laid ahead of the enemy. This threat could affect enemy movements, as Adm. Sir John Jellicoe would be affected at Jutland in 1916 by fear that he was being drawn over U-boats. During the war games, an opposing fleet commander disregarded the submarine threat and lost one capital ship; two other ships were crippled. The threat forced battleships to steam farther apart, and it was more difficult to concentrate their gunfire. By reducing the mobility of the enemy's battlecruisers, the fleet submarines greatly reduced their value. Neither the War College nor the submariners pressing for a fleet submarine offered any solution to the serious problem of distinguishing friend from foe. For example, if both sides deployed fleet submarines, surface sailors might well consider all submarines as hostile. Also, the submariners apparently assumed that they could distinguish between friendly and enemy surface ships. Submarine bells would help, but they might well be disregarded in battle.

Because these problems have never really been solved, "direct support," the modern equivalent of the 1912 fleet submarine concept, is less than popular. Even so, direct submarine support offered a surface fleet so much (and still does) that the idea has never completely died. For example, it was a major consideration in the design of the modern U.S. *Los Angeles* class.

When surfaced, foreign double-hull, ship-form submarines were already believed to be much faster than their U.S. counterparts. A standard reference, *Clowes' Naval*

Pocket Book (1910) credited the French steam-driven *Gustave Zede* (800 tons) with a surface speed of 20 kt (in fact, she made 17.57 kt on trials), so the U.S. submariners' 21 seemed to be in sight. Because the fleet submarine would be so different from the coastal craft designed by Electric Boat, the War College suggested that C&R develop sketch designs, at least to help estimate the cost of the new type. Surface speeds would be 20, 25, and 30 kt (underwater speed not less than 5 kt), with a surface endurance of 2,000 nm at 14 kt, and armament would consist of four torpedo tubes (one reload each).

The General Board was told incorrectly that England, France, Germany, and Russia were all working on fleet submarines, with the ultimate object of achieving destroyer speed and thus displacing the destroyer as a type.[4] A fast submarine could deliver torpedo attacks by day and night, whereas a destroyer could attack only by night; however, the bureaus would not guarantee better than 16 kt. Spear of Electric Boat saved the fleet submarine by offering an apparently practical design, which he included in the company's 1913 bids for FY 14 submarines. In addition to the smaller types (described in chapter 5), Electric Boat offered two large boats, each more than twice as expensive as a coast defense submarine ($1.3 million, compared with about $600,000 for a follow-on M-1): EB 42C (254 ft 3 in × 22 ft 2 in, 854/1,148 tons) and EB 49B (264 ft 9 in × 22 ft 10 in, 960/1,280 tons). EB 42C was armed with eight torpedo tubes (four bow with one reload each, two twin deck tubes). EB 49B added two stern tubes. Each also had a single deck gun with 30 rounds. EB 42C was powered by two 1,150-BHP 6-cylinder engines (18 kt for 80 hr, 6,000 nm at 11 kt). EB 49B added sufficient length

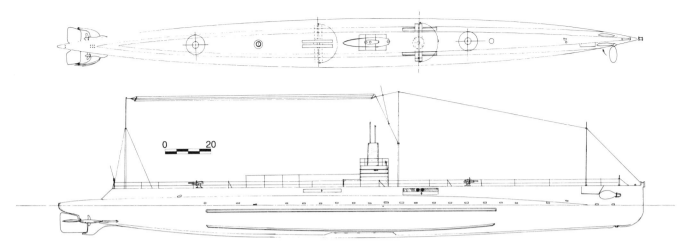

AA-1 (later T-1), as designed, had single 3-in/23 guns fore and aft on disappearing mounts and pairs of twin trainable torpedo tubes fore and aft of the bridge structure. The 3-in guns apparently were never installed; by 1920 the ship had a 4-in/50. (Jim Christley)

for two smaller engines on each shaft (total 3,560 BHP, 890 BHP each: 20 kt for 60 hr, 6,600 nm at 11 kt). In effect, this pair of designs served to prove that the 20-kt submarine could be built.

In July 1913, the Board proposed, and the secretary of the navy and Congress accepted (act of 30 June 1914), that the FY 15 program include a prototype fleet submarine capable of at least 20 kt on the surface. Money appropriated in 1913 for a wrecking pontoon was reprogrammed to help pay for the FY 15 submarines.

Spear eventually offered to combine two 8-cylinder, 1,000-BHP engines in tandem on each shaft; BuEng doubted that all 32 cylinders could be kept running for long. At the time of contract, he planned to use 2-cycle double-acting engines, the first such in U.S. submarines. Then Electric Boat had to revert to conventional 4-cycle single-acting engines. Because these engines were considerably longer, the submarine had to be lengthened (redesign took about 8–10 mo).[5] For the first time in a U.S. submarine design, Spear provided an auxiliary diesel generator (60 BHP). It was not wired to the motors for diesel-electric propulsion.[6] To pay for added weight of the power plant, Spear cut hull strength: test depth was 150 ft, rather than the usual 200 ft, which conformed more to European than to U.S. practice. The General Board initially wanted 10 tubes: 4 bow tubes, 2 twin deck tubes that were trainable underwater (U.S. submarines could not yet fire angled shots), and 2 stern tubes. As in 1913, C&R and the submariners argued against stern tubes, and they were omitted from the design. Like recent coastal defense submarines, the fleet boat has a single 3-in/23 gun.

The guaranteed surface speed of 20 kt sold the project. Spear quite reasonably argued that the new design was little more than an elaboration of the Russian 17-kt design, but with four instead of two engines. Unfortunately, neither he nor the technical bureaus realized that tandem diesels would be crippled by torsional vibration, not to mention the problem of aligning both diesels on each shaft.

The fleet submarine was distinguished by being named

USS *Schley*, as well as numbered, AA-1 (SS 52), later T-1.[7]

For FY 16, the General Board asked for three more fleet submarines to complete a division; Congress approved two (T-2 and T-3, SS 60 and 61). In line with the General Board's characteristics, the act specified that the FY 16 boats make at least 25 kt on the surface. This speed was predicated on increasing battleship speeds, which were expected to rise from 21 kt to 23 kt. The characteristics also called for endurance of at least 3,000 nm at 14 kt surfaced and 120 nm at 5 kt submerged. Armament would comprise two guns (capable of AA fire) and eight torpedo tubes: one of the twin deck tubes of the 1915 boat was to be replaced by a pair of stern tubes. Probably for the first time, a radio (daylight range of 100 nm) was specified.

Diesel power seemed to impose a limit of about 22 kt; in the fall of 1915, the bureaus sketched a big steam submarine. A C&R drawing (Scheme B) shows a double-hull boat, 316 ft × 24 ft 7 in × 13 ft 4 in, with a single funnel (diameter, 4 ft 6 in; 10 ft of its height taken down when the boat submerged); displacement of about 1,370 tons surfaced; armed with two disappearing 3-in guns (as in the contemporary L-boats), four bow tubes (12 reloads), and two twin trainable tubes abaft the conning tower. Unlike contemporary coastal submarines, she showed three periscopes, all with eyepieces in the operating compartment (in large coastal submarines designed the following year, one would be moved up into a large conning tower). Inner hull diameter was 16 ft.

BuEng sketched a 10,000-SHP steam plant: two 185-psi Express-type water tube superheater boilers back to back (so they could use a single funnel) driving two turbines side by side in one engine room, with double reduction gears. Because the boilers completely filled the hull, sponsons would have been built into the ballast tanks for narrow passages (18–24 in wide, 5 ft 9 in high) past them. Below 12 kt, one shaft would be turned by its motor, using electricity generated by the other turbine and supplied through the batteries. For compactness, there were no

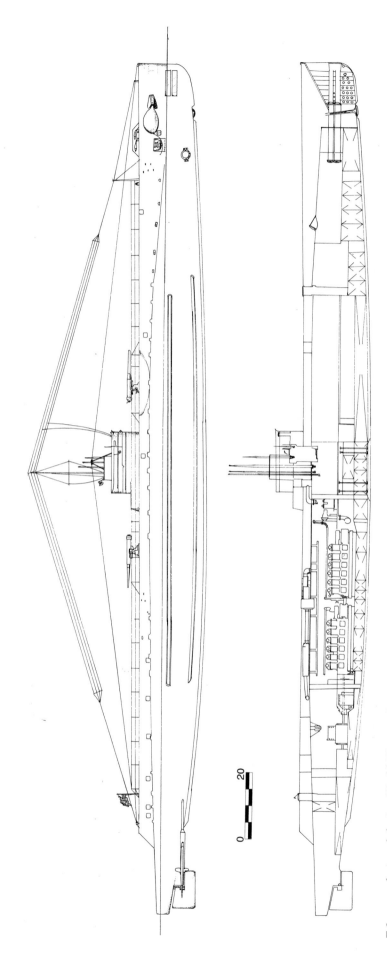

T-2 was redesigned during World War I with a pair of 4-in/50 deck guns, but only the forward gun was ever installed. Note the circular plate of a Fessenden oscillator below her waterline, and the Y-tube on deck. The inboard profile shows the unfortunate tandem diesel power plant. (Jim Christley)

20

0

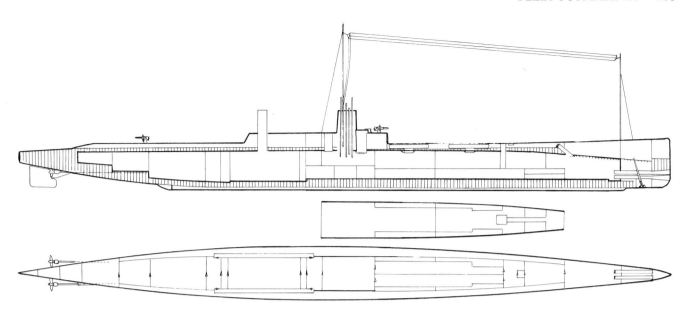

C&R's 1915 Scheme B design for a steam-powered fleet submarine is shown. Note the two trainable tubes on deck forward of the bridge and the special outboard passageways to allow access around the boiler room, which was just large enough to accommodate the boilers needed to generate 10,000 SHP. The hot boiler room was flanked fore and aft by cofferdams to insulate it from the rest of the hull when the submarine was submerged. Dimensions were 316 ft × 24 ft 7 in × 13 ft 4 in, for a normal displacement of 1,330 tons. The stern form was similar to that of M-1. The torpedo room forward accommodated four ready-use weapons, with another eight on the lower deck just abaft it under the officers' quarters. (Jim Christley)

reverse turbine stages; the boat would back down on its motors. Raising steam would probably take about twice as long (at least 7 min) as to start up a diesel. For a given fuel load, endurance would be about half as much as on diesels. Diving would be slow (the proposed contract allowed up to 12 min to pass from 18 kt surfaced to 18 kt submerged). It would be difficult to confine the steam plant's heat.[8]

The Naval War College considered all this an enormous sacrifice to gain only 3–5 kt. The General Board agreed; so did the builders. When bids were opened on 16 February 1916, none offered a Class 1 bid (to build the C&R/BuEng design). New York Shipbuilding did discuss a steam plant with the Talbot Boiler Co., but it decided not to bid. Lake's bid was rejected as too high. Electric Boat offered a repeat *Schley*. Three weeks before bids were opened, the secretary had already agreed with the General Board that SS 60 and 61 should be diesel submarines of maximum speed, partly because he feared war was imminent. Within a few months, the 1915 act was amended so that the navy could accept 19-kt boats. The new boats were ordered as near-repeat *Schley*s (T-1s, design EB 63C, rather than EB 63A).

By the time the T-boats were completed in 1920, their design was quite obsolete. The engines were never successful. For example, between December 1920 and Decem-

The T-boats were conceived as fleet submarines. Although their hulls were considered successful, they failed utterly because their complex power plants were unreliable. T-2 is shown here. During World War I she was modified (while under construction) with a big 4 in/50 gun.

ber 1921, T-3 completed only 4 of 13 full-power trials. One of the 4 very nearly failed; the piston on No. 3 cylinder of No. 2 engine seized up a few minutes after the 4-hr run ended. During the period of 4 January to 12 May 1921, T-3 was unavailable 49 percent of the time (63 days). During a later 2-mo period, she was unavailable 55 percent of the time, again because of engine trouble. BuEng considered derating the T-boats to 16 or 17 kt (18 kt full power maximum).[9] They could not cruise with the fleet (and its tankers) and they lacked sufficient range to operate independently. Although nominal radius, based on fuel oil capacity (using optimistic trial data), was 5,540 nm at 14 kt, lubricating oil sufficed for far less.[10]

Like other pre–WW I submarines, the T-boats dived very slowly. On trials, quick dives (from ahead 18 kt to submerged at periscope depth at 8 kt) took from 4 min 12 sec to 6 min 14 sec; the contemporary S-48 easily dived in 64 sec. By 1922, T-boat commanders estimated that they could dive in 2 min 20 sec to 2 min 50 sec by flooding some tanks beforehand, but even that was far too long. C&R's New Design Section considered the pressure hull only about half as strong as that of an S-boat designed to operate at 200 ft. Although 100-ft depth might be adequate for fleet work, it would be fatal in independent operations.[11]

The torpedo battery was no longer particularly impressive. In August 1918, a 4-in/50 gun was chosen to replace the 3-in/23 deck gun; the forward trainable tubes had to be landed as weight compensation. T-2 and T-3 were redesigned with a second 4-in/50 gun in place of the after set, although only one was ever installed. Operators could never be sure whether torpedoes launched from the trainable tube were running hot or cold (or, indeed, running hot in the tube). Torpedoes fired underwater were often deflected by water passing over them. In 1922, T-1's CO asked that the tubes be removed, but the General Board decided to retain them for experiments. Although the T-boats were redesigned in wartime with 21-in, rather than 18-in, tubes, the change was never carried out. Contract plans showed only a pair of periscopes. Like other WW I boats, the T-boats were redesigned to carry three retractable periscopes, one in the conning tower.[12]

The T-boats were soon laid up.[13] T-3 was taken from reserve in December 1924 to test the new 3,000-BHP BuEng/MAN engine. She was recommissioned on 1 October 1925 and went to sea in January 1926; she was again decommissioned on 14 July 1927. All three T-boats were discussed under the London Treaty of 1980.

The big 1916 (FY 17–19) program authorized nine more fleet submarines. They were all designated the V class; the earlier fleet submarines had become the T class, and U obviously had to be avoided. With the outbreak of WW I, the fleet submarine program was put off to FY 18 and then to FY 19.

Fleet Submarine 1917 was expected to duplicate the FY 16 design, except that fixed broadside tubes replaced the remaining twin revolving mount. BuOrd liked neither broadside tubes (later also considered for the S class) nor

stern tubes. Neither had really been tested, at least not in the U.S. Navy. A submarine finding her targets astern or off her beam might not be able to turn in time to bring her bow tubes to bear. U.S. torpedoes already could be set to turn through large angles after leaving their tubes, however, so a boat with only bow tubes should be able to attack targets abeam or even nearly astern. BuOrd was willing to revive stern tubes only to strew floating mines in the path of an approaching enemy fleet (fleet mine-laying destroyers, which appeared a few years later, had much this role). Underwater speed was set at 12 kt.

No fleet submarines were brought in FY 17. In November 1916, the General Board proposed new characteristics for FY 18. BuEng estimated that a balanced-design 1,200-tonner would make only 16.9 kt surfaced (12.5 kt submerged), a 1,600-tonner might make 17.8 kt surfaced (13 kt submerged; surface endurance, 5,375 nm at 12 kt or 3,580 nm at 14 kt), and 2,000 tons would buy a surface speed of 19 kt (submerged speed of 13.5 kt, 11.5, for 3 hr, 6.25 kt for 20 hr). C&R later challenged BuEng's idea of what constituted an apapropriate balance.[14]

The General Board adopted BuEng's figures for a "balanced" 1,600-tonner: 18 kt (originally 16 kt) surfaced and 13 kt submerged (10.5 kt at the 3-hr battery rate, which BuEng now thought should be included in the characteristics). The 1915 studies of a 25-kt fleet boat had shown that the same weight needed to buy 1 kt underwater (in motors and batteries) would buy about 3 kt on the surface (at 18 kt). C&R argued that BuEng had taken no account of tactical issues. In January 1917, the General Board restored the 20-kt surface speed, with 18 kt as a minimum. Maximum underwater speed would be reduced to compensate. Required endurance was still the prewar 3,000 nm at 14 kt, and test depth was still 150 ft. The General Board retained the broadside tubes (one reload each; two reloads [one quick] per bow tube). U.S. entry into WW I precluded building fleet submarines in FY 18.

By early 1917, the Office of Naval Intelligence (ONI) knew that the Royal Navy had a true fleet submarine, the 25 kt K-steam-powered boat. Her high speed did entail large size (ONI estimated 1,500–1,600 tons surfaced) and very limited underwater endurance (estimated at 70 nm, with a maximum underwater speed of 9 kt). Because it took time to shut down or start up the steam plant (before submerging or after surfacing), the designers provided a small auxiliary diesel. Initially, it was to have driven a third propeller shaft. As built, however, it drove a diesel generator that charged the battery (the turbines produced far too much power for that purpose). Directly connected to the motors on the propeller shafts, it could provide long surface endurance at low speed. These craft inspired the characteristics drawn up by the General Board in September 1917 for Submarine 1919.[15]

Submarine 1919 reverted to steam: 25 kt on the surface, with an auxiliary (cruising) diesel for 11 kt. Submerged speed would be at least 8 kt, with the usual required endurance of at least 20 hr at 5 kt. The British K-boats actually managed only 21–23 kt surfaced (9 kt on the auxil-

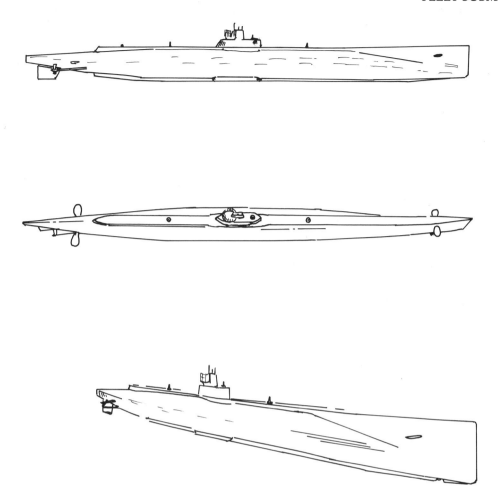

These sketches of Fleet Submarine 1918 are based on photographs of tank-testing Model 2034, dated 26 May 1917. The three vertical poles on deck (fore and aft of the conning tower fairwater, and on a sort of cigarette deck) are 3-in/23 Mk 9 guns on disappearing mounts. By February 1918 they had been replaced by 4-in guns, with 200 rounds per gun. This probably represents Scheme A-3 (320 × 26 × 15 ft, 1625 tons). The boat was designed to stow 12 (possibly 16) torpedoes. This model was tested at speeds corresponding to full-scale speeds of up to 25 kts surfaced, and up to 15 kts submerged. Tests showed that at 2.9 kts model speed (corresponding to 15 kts submerged), the conning tower and equipment added 71 percent to the resistance of the bare hull. Other contributions (as percentages of bare hull resistance) were: the two guns, 5 percent; the planes, 11 percent; the rudder, shafts, and struts, 8 percent; and the centerline keel and fairwater around the Kingstons, 11 percent. Tank tests showed 6265 EHP at 24 kts on the surface, and 2200 EHP at 13 kts submerged. Models of this type had to show the entire submarine because they were towed submerged (a surface ship towing-tank model generally shows only the shape of the hull, and sometimes only the below-water hull). Fleet submarine Scheme B-1 was also tested at about the same time. The other major series of World War I submarine models tested alternative ASW submarine designs. Three models were made during 1918: 2129 (the British R-boat), 2130 (the Electric Boat proposal), and 2131 (the C&R proposal). They were tested at depths equivalent to 5, 10, 20, and 35 ft (C&R assumed that at 35 ft depth the boat would not be affected by interaction with the surface) and at submerged speeds corresponding to full-scale speeds of up to 16 kts (and at surfaced speeds corresponding to up to 12 kts). Tests during the summer of 1918 showed that the Electric Boat hull (which showed a housing periscope for streamlining) was poorly shaped, and that bow tube recesses would add considerable resistance to the C&R hull (which had no bilge or duct keels, but which did have an exposed gun and a non-housing periscope). Design speeds were 7.5–9/15 kts for the Electric Boat design, and 10/15 kts for the C&R design.

iary diesel, and 8–9 kt submerged). Model basin tests of a 1,500-ton submarine (1,900 tons submerged) convinced BuEng that Submarine 1919 would have to displace at least 2,000 tons surfaced, about twice the size of a T-boat. The General Board wanted a normal radius of at least 6,000 nm at 11 kt (10,000 nm if ballast tanks carried fuel). Stores would be provided for 45 days at sea. Designed for the North Sea, the K-boats did not approach such figures. As in the British boat, the U.S. fleet submarine's four 21-in bow tubes (12 torpedoes) were supplemented by one broadside tube on each side (2 torpedoes each). Also, it would be armed with two battleship-type high-velocity 5-in guns, one 3-in AA gun, and two machine guns. Complement would be at least five officers and 50 enlisted men. Test depth was still 150 ft.

The British commander in chief, Adm. Sir David Beatty,

clearly valued the K-boats, not as conventional submarines, but as submersible destroyers used primarily for
torpedo attack, although they did carry a few depth
charges. They promised to help solve the tactical problem
that had frustrated the Grand Fleet at Jutland: they could
ambush a retreating German high seas fleet. The K-boats
sortied in the rear of the Grand Fleet's advanced scouting
line. This deployment was based largely on exercises, considered by some British officers to be unrealistic, in which
it was assumed that both sides were anxious to come to
battle. That made it relatively easy for the submarines to
take up position, whereas at Jutland the weaker Germans
had tried to avoid battle altogether. Without submarines
nearly as fast as the K-boats, the U.S. Navy would eventually decide to deploy supporting submarines well ahead
of its battle fleet. Ideally, the enemy fleet would be enticed
into the gap between the U.S. fleet and submarines falling
back toward it.

Steam power and sheer size drastically slowed diving.
Reportedly, K-boats normally took 5–9 min to dive (a reported 3-min dive was treated with great skepticism). The
K-boats had to be dived slowly and carefully to avoid
crashing their long hulls through their rather shallow test
depth.[16] The British argued that, safe from surprise, the K-
boats had time enough to dive when action was imminent.
They had only to get underwater before enemy lookouts
spotted them; surely, they would spot the enemy's masts
first. The argument was reminiscent of U.S. prewar thinking. BuEng was skeptical: they might not be spotted by
surface lookouts, but they could be spotted from aircraft
and balloons. No submarine could afford to dive slowly.[17]

Capt. C. J. Little, K-boat flotilla commander, admitted
their poor diving qualities but emphasized their high surface speed and good sea-keeping. Other officers at the
British fleet base at Scapa Flow, Scotland, did not match
his enthusiasm. For example, a destroyer skipper thought
them "awful failures and dangerous to operate, but I
would not dare to tell Little that because he is so wrapped
up in them and in their future that it would hurt his
feelings."

The General Board formally requested sketch plans on
6 February 1918. Electric Boat and Lake were not asked
for design proposals. The earliest surviving sketch design,
Scheme A-3 (1 March 1918), had the usual four bow tubes,
with stowage for 12 (possibly 16) torpedoes, and two
4-in guns. C&R worked out power requirements on the
basis of dimensions of 320 ft × 26 ft × 15 ft (1,625 tons
surfaced). To propel the submarine at 16 kt would take
1,525 effective horsepower (EHP), and 18 kt (13 kt submerged) would require 2,200 EHP, but it would take 6,765
EHP to attain 24 kt. Installed power (SHP or BHP) would
be about twice EHP, so 24 kt would require about 13,530
SHP. Even for 21 kt, the nominal battleship speed, the
submarine would have to produce 3,365 EHP (about 6,730
SHP or BHP). A modest submerged speed, such as 9 kt,
required only 815 EHP. The battery would be split into
two units, each probably of 120 cells.

This submarine could not accommodate the sort of

power plant it needed. Lengthening the hull would reduce
the power needed to achieve a given surface speed. The
next try, Scheme B-1 (9 March 1918), was enlarged to 1,900
tons (360 ft × 28 ft 6 in × 15 ft), with more reserve
buoyancy for better surface performance (31 percent compared with 22.9 percent). The submarine would have six
bow tubes (12 torpedoes; 16 in emergency conditions) and
could carry two 4-in or 5-in guns. Power estimates were
carried up to 23.13 kt surfaced (4,898 EHP) and 12.85 kt
submerged (1,836 EHP). A surface speed of 16.86 kt required 2,096 EHP; just half of that would drive the submarine at 10.54 kt submerged. A sketch design showed two
engine rooms in tandem; the storage battery probably
would be split into three groups, 60 cells each. The two
forward periscopes extended down into the control room;
the third was for the conning tower.

These designs offered little more firepower than a contemporary 800-ton S-boat (see chapter 7). In April 1918,
the preliminary designers tried for something more impressive (Scheme C-1): two 6-in guns, 10 tubes (21-inch;
6 forward, 2 aft, 2 broadside), surface speed of 20 (later
18) kt, and submerged speed of 12 kt. The initial estimate
was 3,000 tons (410 ft × 32 ft × 16.5 ft; reserve buoyancy
31.5 percent). The model tests conducted for Scheme
A-3 suggested that 4,500 EHP would be required to attain
19.93 kt and 5,975 EHP for 22.15 kt. Based on the percentage usually assigned to batteries, the large hull would
accommodate 360 cells. Work stopped about August 1918,
partly because C&R hoped to exploit captured German
information.

In December 1918, BuEng pointed out that only with
steam machinery could a submarine achieve 24–25 kt or
probably even exceed 20 kt, but submerged speed and
endurance would fall drastically with steam power. A
diesel-powered 1,200-ton submarine could make 18–20
kts, with submerged speed and endurance that would be
quite satisfactory. The Submarine Design Board (representing the submariners and chaired by Capt. T. C. Hart)
argued that not even 24 or 25 kt would suffice; future
battleships (the main targets) would be much faster (HMS
Hood was widely perceived as the prototype of future fast
battleships). Also, to maintain 25 kt in rough water, a
submarine needed so much buoyancy and a hull form
so shiplike that it would have little chance of survival
underwater. The submariners' board much preferred diesels; it wanted Steam Engineering to begin work on a two-
shaft 4,000 BHP plant for a T-class hull.

The General Board still wanted a fast fleet submarine.
All tonnage authorized by the 1916 act had to be laid down
by 1 July 1919. In theory, there was no time to develop
alternatives to the modified T-boat that the board seemed
to have in mind. As late as January 1919, however, no
plans, even preliminary ones, existed; C&R awaited the
return of naval constructor Land, who was examining
operational British craft and captured German U-boats.
Secretary of the Navy Daniels asked the General Board
to rewrite its characteristics in view of new information
becoming available.

The submariners, represented before the Board by Captain Hart and by Lt. Comdr. Chester Nimitz, argued that slow, long-endurance submarines sent out well ahead of the main body could be effective fighting scouts. They could operate, singly or in groups, independent of the fleet in enemy waters. They might not be able to cover a given area as easily as faster submarines, but more of them could be built and coordinated by the new high-frequency (HF) radio. Hart and Nimitz wanted to base this type of submarine on German cruiser submarines.

The General Board resisted; it was still interested primarily in direct fleet support. It argued that the navy could not risk breaking its agreement with Congress to build nine fast fleet submarines. The submariners and OpNav Plans Division replied that this deal, if it actually had been struck in 1916, surely should be reviewed, given all that had happened since. Why lock the navy into prewar thinking (albeit using wartime or postwar technology)? The General Board promised to build the submariners' scout in FY 20.

By late 1918, BuEng was aware that the Germans had developed an alternative diesel power plant configuration. They had decided that long underwater endurance at low speed, to escape hunters, was more important than burst speed. Large U-boats laid down from 1916 on had one or more small auxiliary diesels specifically for battery charging. Therefore, they could charge batteries while using the big main diesels to run at maximum surface speed. Directly coupled to the electric motors on the propeller shafts (i.e., running in diesel-electric configuration), the battery-charging diesel could drive the submarine at low speed. Because this small engine would be running at maximum (most efficient) power, the U-boat would enjoy very long endurance at low speed (a more conventional arrangement would have been very inefficient at low power). Motors no longer had to be scaled to the output of the diesels designed for maximum surface speed.[18]

BuEng still had no 2,000-BHP diesel, but it could use two of the new 900–1,000-BHP Busch-Sulzer diesels (as in S-boats) to drive generators, and two more to drive propellers directly. About 5 ft longer than the tandem-diesel plant in the T class, this arrangement was much more likely to work. Busch-Sulzer was said to be willing to build the next size up, a 1,300-BHP (1,400-BHP overload rating), 6-cylinder, 2-cycle diesel. A single such engine would suffice as a generator. C&R estimated that a three-engine submarine would require 85 ft of engine room, compared with 75 ft for four smaller engines. For a short time, NELSECO'S 700-BHP S-boat engine and 1,000-BHP T-boat engine were still considered viable alternatives to Busch-Sulzer vs diesels.

In February 1919, work began on Scheme O, a 1,700–2,000-ton, four-engine boat no more than 300 ft long and arranged generally as a T-boat.[19] The battery would be 120 cells of the type used in S-1. The broadside tubes were finally abandoned. Inspired by wartime German experience, the designers provided one or two stern tubes, with one reload per tube. Reserve buoyancy was reduced to about 25 percent. C&R hoped to exceed 22 kt, but the submarine turned out larger than expected (330 ft × 24 ft 8 in, 1,609 tons surfaced). By May, model tests had shown that it would suffer excessive resistance in the crucial speed range of 18–20 kt.

BuEng still preferred steam turbines. At first, it hoped that 1,700 tons would suffice, but a series of 1,700–2,000-ton sketch designs for 25-kt submarines (February 1919, for the FY 20 program) showed that only those at the larger end of the scale would work. Typical dimensions were 335 ft × 27.5 ft × 16.3 ft (1,960 tons); such a submarine could make 21.04 kt on 3,785 EHP. Like Scheme D, this study showed that a fleet submarine would have to be quite large. The General Board later decided that steam was altogether impractical.

On 13 March 1919, the General Board proposed characteristics for Fleet Submarine 1919. As in 1917, it wanted a sustained (at least 24-hr) surface speed of 18 kt; this implied a rather higher trial speed (desired maximum surface speed of 21 kt). Maximum submerged speed (1-hr rate) was set at 9 kt. In addition to four bow and two stern 21-in tubes, the former for the longest torpedoes and the latter preferably also for long torpedoes, there would be a 5-in high-powered wet gun (5-in/51) forward and two machine guns for air defense. Hart's suggestion that provision be made for a second 5-in wet gun aft was rejected.

Endurance would be 6,000 nm at 11 kt (10,000 nm with fuel in the main ballast tanks). Submerged endurance would be at least 10 hr at 5 kt and 36 hr at lowest possible RPM at which the submarine could be controlled at periscope depth. Test depth was increased from 150 ft to 200 ft to match the submarine standard. Length was not to exceed 330 ft. Complement was set at five officers and 50 enlisted men, with provisions for 45 days.

The preliminary designers tried to shave just enough wave-making resistance to make the required speed. A new body plan (Scheme E) showed horizontal, rather than vertical, oval hull sections, but this was not good enough. Some designers wanted to reduce speed, even to 18 kt, because they could not reach the goal of 23–24 kt in smooth water with any internal combusion power plant. The weight saved could go into greater surface endurance and underwater speed, as in OpNav's cruiser concept.

By this time Busch-Sulzer had designed a 2,000-BHP diesel. Two of them could be combined with a 900-BHP generator engine for a total of about 4,800 SHP. The Germans (MAN) had already developed 2,000- and 3,000-BHP engines, but BuEng was unwilling to use them; it had only begun to work on its version of the MAN 900-BHP engine. The navy could not afford to wait—better to rely for now on Busch-Sulzer.[20] The preliminary designers developed a new design series using Sulzer engines.

Scheme K was the smallest possible hull wrapped around the available machinery and a battery, with little regard to form. Minimum dimensions turned out to be too large (337 ft 4 in × 25 ft 6 in × 14 ft). Resistance was even worse than in Scheme D because the forefoot was cut away and the body was quite full. A slimmer hull

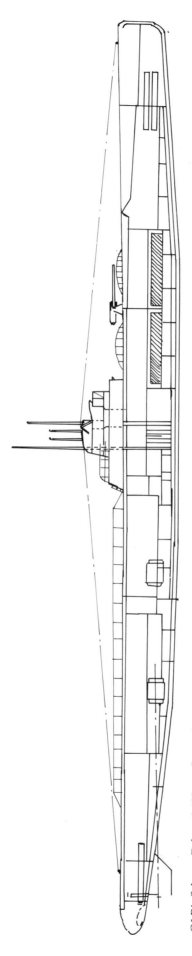

C&R's Scheme D for a 1,600-ton fleet submarine (May 1919) resembles an enlarged government S-boat, with all her storage batteries concentrated forward, under the crew's quarters abaft her forward torpedo room, but with an additional engine compartment for a pair of diesel generators inserted aft, between the control room and the after engine room. As in the S-boat, pumps were placed under the control room floor. All four 10-cylinder engines were identical, almost certainly Busch-Sulzers. Designed speed was 18 kt. Unlike later versions of the design, this one shows a vertical bow (as in an S-boat) and a very un-streamlined bridge structure. Dimensions: 330 ft 24 ft 5 in 14 ft 5 in.

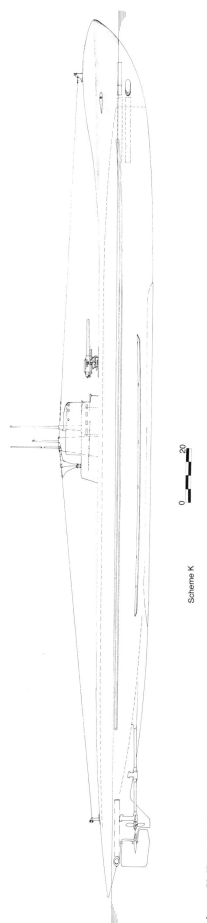

Scheme K

0   20

Scheme K (June 1919) was an approach to the V-1 design. Surface displacement would have been 1,881 tons; dimensions were 337 ft 4 in (overall) 25 ft 6 in molded 13 ft 2 in. The gun is a 5-in/51. Note the three periscopes, one emerging from the conning tower and two from the control room abaft it. (Jim Christley)

would have been better, but it could not have accommodated engines, batteries, main motors, and even torpedo tubes.

Now C&R tried to reduce wave making resistance by applying its standard surface ship solution, a bulbous bow (Scheme L, 324 ft × 25.5 ft × 13.8 ft). The torpedo tube muzzles would occupy the bulb. Carrying the tubes farther forward and lower down in the hull would reduce crowding in the pressure hull. Scheme L also had a flared clipper bow for sea-keeping and a slightly narrower stern (the broad stern introduced in Scheme E pulled eddies). The preliminary design hydrodynamicist doubted that the bulbous bow was worthwhile. October 1919 tests showed that on the same power, however, Scheme L would be 1.4 kt faster than Scheme K in the critical range of 19–20.

By this time, fleet submarine advocates had won out; on 2 August, Land authorized the designers to emphasize high surface speed. Papers in the preliminary design file suggest that he was much impressed by the 20.3-kt average speed attained on the few successful T-1 trial runs. He accepted the bulbous bow and flat stern, although he still hoped to hold displacement down to about 1,770 tons.

Lines could not be really optimized for surface performance. Aft, the hull cross section was fixed by battery capacity, main motors, and the size of the steering gear. Lines forward were determined by the size of the bulb needed to accommodate the torpedo tubes. Little attention had been paid to the shape of the above-water hull apart from topsides immediately abaft the bow, which were

shaped to keep the bow wave from breaking over the deck.

Weight calculations soon showed that surface displacement would be about 1,825–1,850 tons. The 6,950–7,000 BHP now needed to attain 20 kt or more could be provided by two 3,000-BHP MAN engines plus one 950-BHP Busch-Sulzer generator, but BuEng was unenthusiastic. It preferred to cut required power by cutting weight. For example, one of the two stern tubes could be eliminated, or normal fuel oil could be cut from 200 tons to 160 tons. Increasing frame spacing from 18 in to 24 in would save 60 tons. An alternative lengthened and further slimmed Scheme M was rejected because the lightened Scheme L offered much better internal arrangements. Captain Hart pushed hard for a 300-ft boat, which he felt would dive better in a heavy sea, but Chief Constructor David W. Taylor held out for the longer hull needed to maintain speed.

The power plant was reviewed again. BuEng suggested using four engines (two 2,000- or 2,200-BHP direct-drive, two 900-BHP generators) to save about 76 tons. The four engines offered a better longitudinal balance. C&R's preliminary design, based on Scheme L-3, was submitted on 9 January 1920.[21] The designers had to exceed the 330-ft limit (by 10 ft), but they also relied heavily on the somewhat controversial bulbous bow. Critics charged that C&R was ignoring sea-keeping; it turned out that, in service, the bulb pulled a submarine's bow down in waves.

The design showed foundations fore and aft of the

Fleet submarines had to be far larger than their predecessors to reach higher speeds and to run greater distances. *Bass* (V-2) lies alongside S-46 at the submarine base at Coco Solo in the Canal Zone. In the background is the minesweeper *Swan*. Note the big telescopic masts fore and aft, intended to raise the submarine's radio antennas and thus to increase her radio range.

conning tower, although only one 5-in/51 gun was to be carried. Gun location was quite controversial; providing for both alternatives avoided a difficult decision. Land, then in Europe, guessed that although only the forward 5-in/51 would be mounted in peacetime, a second gun would be mounted aft in wartime. He still wondered whether 5-in caliber was enough.[22]

The OpNav submariners were less than enthusiastic. The two generator engines filled much of the hull forward of the control room, and extra engineers (who would be difficult to accommodate) would be needed to service them. Eliminating one engine would save about 50 tons at a cost of about 0.75 kt in surface speed. There was some concern that C&R's S-boat battery would be too small for

the much larger V-boat. A roomier boat might be more reliable. C&R pointed out that increasing surface displacement to 2,150 tons would buy two more bow torpedo tubes, a more powerful gun (6-in/53 with 100 rounds), and about 10 percent more normal fuel oil capacity, at a cost of about 2 kt.

The new fleet submarine was redesigned in February 1920. To simplify maintenance, BuEng wanted to use auxiliary engines as similar as possible to the 2,200-BHP, 6-cylinder Busch-Sulzer main engines. Bush-Sulzer offered a 1,450-BHP, 4-cylinder version, not too much less powerful than two 900-BHP generator engines. Reducing total power from about 5,680 to 5,575 SHP (counting electric losses in each case) would cost a quarter knot (20.75 kt

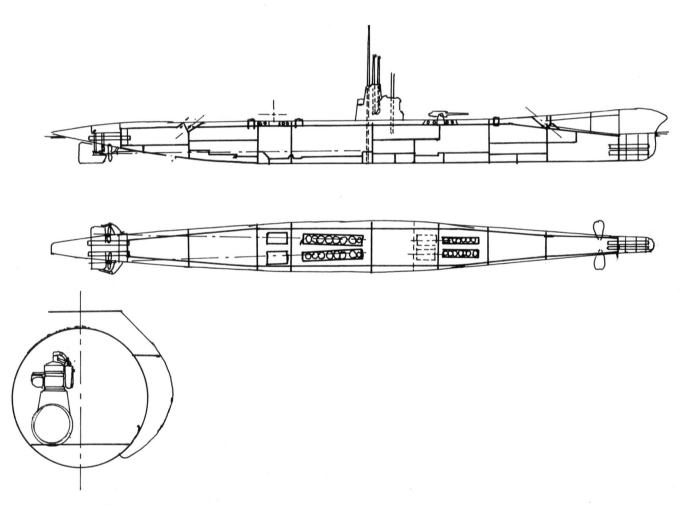

This "spring style," dated 6 January 1920, shows Fleet Submarine 1919, which became V-1. This design is taken from C&R Sketch 005561. Note that, although the 5-in/51 gun is shown forward, provision has been made for mounting it aft (the foundation is shown; the dashed lines indicate the gun). This version already shows the clipper bow and bulbous underwater form of the ship actually built. The crew is accommodated in the space built out above the forward torpedo room and the forward battery; abaft these spaces is the generator room, housing a pair of 900-BHP engines. The officers' quarters and control room are built out into the upper portion of this space. Below are auxiliaries. Some crew's quarters are also abaft the main motors, above the after battery. Of the three periscopes, one is let into the control room; the eyepieces of the other two are in the conning tower (not shown). There is also a tall radio mast, extending to 60 ft above designed waterline when erected. This submarine would have displaced 1,900 tons surfaced (325 ft LWL × 24 ft 8 in); she would have made at least 21 kt surfaced (the two main engines were Busch-Sulzers, each 2,000 BHP), with an endurance of 6,000 nm at 11 kt on 160 tons of fuel (11,750 nm with maximum fuel load, 320 tons). Submerged displacement would have been 2,572 tons. Designed complement was 5 officers and 50 enlisted men. Armament was six torpedo tubes (one spare per tube), one 5-in/51 wet gun, and two machine guns.

In dry dock in the 1930s, *Bass* shows her bulbous forefoot (carrying her bow torpedo tubes) and her clipper stem and flared deck. As in many surface ships, the bulbous bow was intended to reduce wavemaking resistance and thus to improve the submarine's surface speed; the unusual bow was expected to make the deck drier.

Bass underway. Note the unusual raised deck section around and abaft the bridge fairwater. Once U.S. submarines were named, the classes were designated by the initials of those names. Thus, the V-1 class became the B-class.

vice 21 kt). The submarine would make 19.25 kt on main engines alone. On the generator engine, the boat would make 11.5 kt (endurance, 8,200 nm on normal fuel and 16,400 nm on maximum fuel, compared with 3,210/6,420 nm on main engines). Although that had not been a major goal in the design, C&R was well aware of the need for a long cruising radius in the new Pacific war scenarios.

By December 1920, estimated displacement had increased to 2,079 tons surfaced and 2,460 tons submerged. C&R considered the pressure hull the strongest yet designed, good for at least 400-ft depth. Because it was not quite circular in section, the designers could not cut weight by dishing the internal watertight bulkheads; they would distort and break as the hull compressed with water pressure. Stability was so limited that the big main engines could not be raised to straighten shaft lines.

The three FY 19 fleet submarines (V-1–V-3, SS 163–165) were ordered from Portsmouth. In hopes that the other six would be approved in FY 21, the design was sent to Electric Boat and Lake in 1920 as a basis for bids. Lake much preferred a four-engine plant, using the 900-BHP or 1,450-BHP Busch-Sulzer generator. The BuEng decision was reversed, and the earlier four-engine plant, now using 2,250-BHP and 1,000-BHP engines, was revived, with an estimated speed of 20.4 kt.[23] The generators occupied their own engine room forward out the control room. The other important late change was reinstatement of two bow buoyancy tanks that had been eliminated earlier; it required some thicker bow plating. V-4 and later units were deferred beyond FY 21.

This class continued the wartime emphasis on big conning towers (these were the last boats with towers in the form of upright cylinders), with one periscope in the conning tower and two passing through it to the operating compartment below.

These boats turned out much heavier than planned. By 1929, C&R and BuEng were proposing drastic weight reductions. Those approved included replacement of the 5-in/51 gun by a 3-in/50. The design even then was not particularly successful, mainly because of poor seakeeping and unreliable engines. The V-1s (renamed the *Barracuda* class in 1931) were decommissioned in 1937. With their main engines removed (leaving their generator engines to propel them), they were recommissioned in 1940 and as cargo carriers in 1943. They were rated entirely unsuccessful in this role.

The steam submarine idea persisted. In May 1920, preliminary designers produced two new design studies (Table 6–1). Column 2 was a development to meet existing requirements for increased submerged performance and armament. Column 3 was an attempt to meet all the fleet submarine requirements, including high surface speed. The 1916 design was rejected because of excessive fuel consumption at all speeds, limited operating depth, and inferior armament. Column 2 showed excessive fuel consumption, but it was the least expensive option. Column 3 was superior to V-1, but it was too expensive. In June 1920, preliminary designers prepared a sketch design us-

Table 6–1. Steam Submarine Studies, May 1920

	1916 Design	(2)	(3)	V-1
Length overall (ft)	314	325	346	335
Length on waterline (ft)	314	325	340	325
Beamon waterline (ft)	23.76	23.5	23.5	24.7
Draft (ft)	13.72	14.25	15.5	14.5
Surfaced displacement (tons)	1,385	1,775	1,950	1,900
Guns (number/ diameter)	2/3 in	1/5 in	1/5 in	1/5 in
Bow tubes (number/ diameter)	4/18 in	6/21 in	6/21 in	6/21 in
Deck tubes (number/ diameter)	4/18 in	—	—	—
Fuel oil (normal) (tons)	130	285	200	160
SHP	10,000	10,000	12,000	6,600
Surface speed (nm)	25	23.5	23.5	21
Submerged speed	12	9	9	9
Radius/maximum speed (nm)	620	1,250	730	1,900 (20% allowance)
Weight (tons):				
Hull	555	720	810	770
Hull fittings	75	105	130	123
Machinery				
Steam	152	156	180	—
Electric	231	231	240	560
Diesel	—	—	80	—
Reserve feed water	15	15	18	—
Armament	18	30	30	30
Ammunition	17	28	28	28
Equipment	33	45	64	61
Outfit, stores	21	25	33	31
Fuel oil	130	285	200	160
Lubrication oil	15	15	15	21
Water	20	20	25	22
Margin	98	100	97	94
Total weight	1,380	1,775	1,950	1,900
Length of machinery spaces (ft):				
Battery room	61	60	56	30
Generator/ Generator engine	—	—	—	42
Cofferdams	9	9	(2)4	—
Boiler room	34.5	34	38	—
Main engine room	27	27	28	48
Motor room	18	18	46	26
After battery	—	—	—	32
Cost (million)	$2.091	$2.499	$3.184	$3.502

ing double-reduction geared turbines and a diesel driving through single reduction gearing. BuEng disliked the cramped engine room (Preliminiary Design wanted to limit pressure hull diameter to 18 ft) but offered 12,000-SHP turbines, a 1-000 BHP diesel, and a 1,000-HP motor.

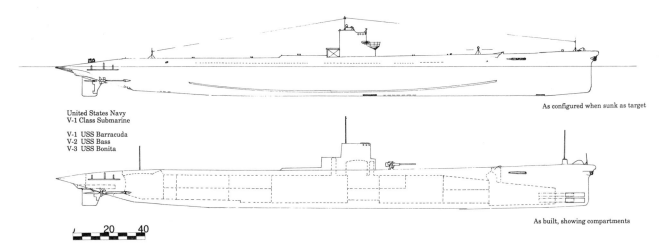

United States Navy
V-1 Class Submarine

V-1 USS Barracuda
V-2 USS Bass
V-3 USS Bonita

As configured when sunk as target

As built, showing compartments

20   40

Bass (V-2) is shown as built (bottom) and as stripped for sinking as a target (top) after having served unsuccessfully as a cargo submarine. The big compartments fore and aft of the control room (below the conning tower) were the forward and after engine rooms, respectively; the former accommodated the battery-charging engine. Compartments abaft the main engine room were, forward to aft: the maneuvering room above the motor room, crew's quarters above the aft battery, crew's mess, the after torpedo room, and the steering gear room. Additional crewmen were accommodated in the small upper-deck compartment above the forward engine room. Forward of it were officers' quarters above the forward battery, and then the forward torpedo room. As in the earlier submarines, the conning tower was a vertical cylinder. Conversion to a cargo carrier entailed removal of the main engines, so that the after engine room could be used for cargo. The forward and after torpedo rooms were also used for cargo stowage. (Jim Christley)

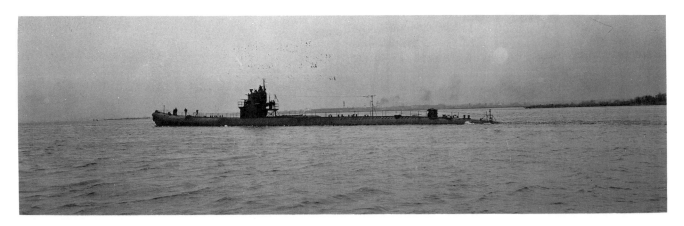

Bass is shown here, newly converted to a cargo submarine, off the Philadelphia Navy Yard on 30 March 1943. Conversion was relatively simple because she had a pair of battery-charging engines in addition to the main engines that drove her propellers directly. The battery chargers could drive her electrically (by being connected to her motors), with the main engines disconnected. Thus, the main engines could easily be removed to leave space for cargo. Similar flexibility made it relatively easy to remove one or two engines from a much later generation of diesel-electric *Gato*- or *Balao*- class submarines after World War II. Foreign navies, whose submarines were generally directly driven by their diesels, enjoyed no such flexibility.

By July, the steam idea had been dropped, to be revived briefly in January 1924.[24] The preliminary designers considered a fast submarine with the 1915 power plant (10,000 SHP), to achieve 25 kt on the surface and 9 kt submerged; it would be armed with one 6-in/53 gun and tubes and torpedoes in a V-boat. Pressure hull diameter probably would be about 20 ft, and the designers hoped to improve on V-1's freeboard and buoyancy. Radius would be 9,000–10,000 nm. This was the last gasp of the fast fleet submarine, although the name "fleet boat" survived.

The S-boats were almost an alternative to fleet boats, capable of great range (by pre–World War I standards), though not of high surface speed. S-33 was typical of the first series (S-18 through S-41) of Electric Boat–built "Holland" S-boats. Redesigned during construction to mount powerful 4in/50 guns instead of the planned 3in/23s, they had prominent gun sponsons. They could be distinguished from the second series of "Holland" boats by the small ammunition-passing trunks at the fore end of their conning tower fairwaters (covered by the second "3" in "S 33"); the later boats had much larger gun crew access hatch trunks. The prominent skeg aft (the sloping continuation of the upper deck) was typical of Electric Boat designs. (Lower photograph courtesy of Bethlehem Steel)

7177-43
PLAN VIEW, AMIDSHIPS LOOKING FORW'D
SAN FRANCISCO, CAL. 17 OCTOBER

The S-Boats

THE SUBMARINERS DISLIKED the General Board's two-type policy. They considered coast defense submarines too small to steam, without refueling, the length of the Atlantic coast and the Caribbean to the Panama Canal on the Atlantic coast, and from Puget Sound to the canal on the Pacific. They would have to operate 300–500 mi offshore for weeks at a time. For example, in the 18–25 May 1915 Atlantic Fleet maneuvers, submarines were formed into a mobile mine field as far out as 67 degrees W, to be moved north or south by radio command of the commander in chief (CinC). They had to run for shelter when a northeast gale approached, whereas the surface fleet easily rode it out. The Atlantic Submarine Flotilla hoped that the coming K-boats could weather an Atlantic gale; the submariners were disturbed by the reversion to a smaller size in the N class.

The flotilla wanted something much larger, yet not quite a fleet submarine: 800–1,000 tons submerged; length about 250 ft (draft, no greater than $12\frac{1}{2}$ ft; height from keel to top of periscope, 38 ft); surface speed 18–20 kt (radius 5,000 nm); submerged speed, 14 kt for 1 hr and 10 kt for 3 hr (200 nm or 40 hr at 5–6 kt); four bow tubes (two reloads each); three periscopes; radio aerials that did not require unrigging before diving (to allow quick dives). Surface speed might be traded off against submerged speed (i.e., the submarine might make 18/14 kt or 20/11.5 kt. These characteristics seem to have been inspired by those reported for contemporary 800-ton German U-boats. German 800-tonners managed sustained operations around the British Isles, well beyond what U.S. coastal craft could accomplish. In 1916, U-53, a standard German attack submarine, had visited Newport, Rhode Island (although she could not spend much time on patrol in American waters). Her transatlantic voyage seemed to confirm the submariners' belief that an 800-tonner would be a true Atlantic boat, capable of carrying war into the home waters of any possible European enemy. In 1915, Fleet CinC Adm. F. F. Fletcher supported the flotilla; coastal submarines, which he called intermediate, were not worth buying.

The flotilla seemed to expect something very close to fleet submarine performance on little more than half as much tonnage. C&R doubted that the flotilla's demands could be met. For example, 2 kt less of surface speed would hardly buy 2.5 kt of submerged speed; the 18–14-kt submarine would be far larger than one capable of 20–11.5 kt. Any 800-tonner would cost between $800,000 and $1 million. C&R also suggested that size had been much confused by the use of submerged displacement; surface displacement (without ballast) was the appropriate figure.

The General Board resisted the submariners' demands. The cost of the 800-tonner would be necessarily subtracted from the money needed for the battle fleet. In the end, the wartime naval budget grew to include both additional capital ships and the larger submarines. Thus, Submarine 1917 characteristics, issued on 13 August 1915, essentially duplicated those of Submarine 1916, except that the internal bulkheads could withstand water pressure at 60 ft and the radio set was expected to have a daylight range of 50 nm.

Emory S. Land, the first naval constructor assigned to submarines, argued that larger submarines were needed even for coast defense. During 1915, Land went to sea on board all the submarine types in the Atlantic, C through K classes. His longest cruise was 7 days on K 2 during the fall war game, of which he said that "conditions were as bad as have ever been experienced by our Submarine Flotilla." Their paper characteristics hardly matched reality; the nominally 14-kt Ks and Ls were really good for no more than 12 kt on a sustained basis, and they could not keep the sea for more than 10 days (2 wk in an emergency). German 800-tonners routinely stayed at sea off Ireland for 21 days.

A U.S. submarine would surely operate in at least 2-day zones from the coast (e.g., a 36-hr run out to her patrol area at 12 kt, 432 nm offshore). Operating radius would have to be at least 600 nm, preferably 1,000. Counting dives, it might take a week to go out to a patrol station

Designed during World War I, the S-boats survived to fight in World War II. S-45 is shown after a San Francisco refit, 17 October 1943. The new pole mast at the after end of the bridge fairwater carries an SD air warning radar (the smaller radar forward is SJ, for surface search). The bridge structure was redesigned to provide a platform forward for a 20-mm anti-aircraft gun, not visible here. Other S-boats had a gun platform added abaft their fairwaters.

and return. The submarine would need several weeks' endurance to make her mission worthwhile.

The Atlantic Submarine Flotilla pressed hard for a fast (18–20 kt) 800-tonner in the mistaken belief that foreign navies were already building such submarines in large numbers as a good compromise between small prewar craft and outsized fleet boats. Unconvinced by the bureaus' disclaimers, the submariners repeated their underwater speed requirements: 14 kt for 30 min, with an endurance of 6 hr at 8.5 kt; it was assumed that the battery sufficient for this endurance would give a radius of action of more than 100 nm at 5 kt. Engines had to be able to charge the battery in 4 hr. It did not seem to be understood that the surface ship hull form advocated by the flotilla for high surface speed would have precluded high underwater speed.

Surface radius of action would be 4,000 nm at 12 kt, not quite sufficient for transatlantic operations but not too far off. Stores endurance would be at least 30 days. Armament would be four bow torpedo tubes (two reloads each, total 12 torpedoes) and one 3-in gun (200 rounds). Submariners already knew about quick wartime dives: they wanted to dive in 3 min from light condition and 1 min from awash condition. Desired surface radio range was 100 nm.[1]

By early 1916, the L-boats, with their small conning towers, were nearly in service. The submariners clearly did not like this feature. They demanded a bigger conning tower (accommodating four men), with a housing periscope, as the CO's battle station; another housing instrument was to be placed abaft it for the operating compartment below. All facilities for underwater control would be concentrated in the operating compartment.[2] C&R's 22 September 1916 sketch design for an 800-tonner showed the conning tower periscope (plus two operating compartment periscopes). In Electric Boat's February 1917 EB 73A design, the 800-tonner was similarly equipped. Electric Boat's O-boat and R-boat (see below) were redesigned with large conning towers carrying periscopes. In each case, two instruments were retained in the operating compartment. Although Lake could not redesign his O-boat to include an additional periscope, he did redesign his R-boat. This new configuration was supported by the March 1918 report of the 1917–18 Submarine Standardization Board. The conning tower (large enough for three men) was confirmed as the CO's battle station and steering station. It would accommodate one (attack) periscope, magnetic compass, gyro repeater, steering stand, engine and motor telegraph, RPM indicators, depth and trim indicators, general alarm gong switch, torpedo firing key and selection switches, and torpedo tube indicators. As the CO's battle station when surfaced, it also needed eye ports. Plotting would be done below. The board justified the second periscope below because the CO would stand there most of the time. R-boat and S-boat conning tower periscopes were ordered eliminated in 1926 because they were rarely used; they were effective only at low speeds.

The submariners also made headway in their old demand for 21-in torpedoes. Torpedo caliber was reconsid-

ered in 1915 in light of wartime developments. In June, BuOrd argued that the O-boats might have to be armed with 21-in weapons to get any appreciable increase in warhead weight. It asked C&R whether 5-m × 21-in weapons could easily be substituted for the standard 5.2-m × 18-in torpedoes. C&R considered such a change impracticable at this late stage (the submarine bow would have to be far broader), but planned to switch in the next class and to take up the 21-in tube as a possible contract change in the O-boats. As a result, the 1916 proposals for R-boats and S-boats showed 21-in tubes, and they were so armed. They fired a short (5.2-m) Mk X torpedo to 5,000 yd at 30 kt (it was later rated at 3,600 yd at 36 kt) and had the heaviest available warhead (500 lb). The T-boats were redesigned to take 21-in tubes, but they were not installed.

In May 1916, the General Board rejected the Atlantic flotilla commander's view that U-boats were the proper model for U.S. submarines because it felt that they would conduct quite different operations. The submariners, however, had an important ally in Land, who apparently convinced C&R that its first venture into submarine design should be an 800-tonner. It is not clear to what extent Land shaped the Atlantic flotilla's requirements or whether he simply agreed that a major step-up in size was needed and that characteristics should follow the determination of size. C&R was particularly unhappy that the submariners associated a specific size with specific performance requirements. Surely, the requirements had to come first, with the size resulting from a design process. There was some fear that the submariners (now the Atlantic Submarine Force) might usurp the design function.

Unfortunately, submarine performance did not grow very rapidly with displacement: on paper, an 800-tonner did not appear that much better than a coastal submarine. It was not much faster (typically 16 versus 14 kt and did not demonstrate a great increase in underwater endurance or range, as expressed in hours of steaming time. It did carry twice as many reload torpedoes, but the vital differences, the ones instinctively grasped by the submariners, were its habitability, ruggedness, and operational endurance. Because these could not be measured mathematically, they were not readily expressed in terms normally used by the General Board.

At least some details of the argument about the 800-tonner had been made public. By July 1916, it seemed likely that Congress would explicitly include it in the new naval program. The General Board therefore laid out characteristics. It regarded the 800-tonner as a coastal submarine. In the event that Congress specified one, the board wanted increased displacement to go into more reliable machinery (diesels and battery), increased surface speed, and increased submerged radius but not speed. The board accepted that existing diesels were reliable only at less than full power: the maximum speeds of all coastal submarines had been overstated. It therefore called for a reliable 14 kt (maximum 16). Underwater speed (1-hr rate) would not be increased above 11 kt, and submerged radius would be 100 nm at 5 kt. The board endorsed the submariners' call for four bow tubes, with a total of 12 torpedoes. C&R's

proposed broadside tubes were rejected as too complicated.

Congress now clearly wanted to build three competing 800-tonners, one to a navy design in a navy yard and the others to designs by Electric Boat and Lake. To give each designer a free hand, the General Board tried to make the characteristics as general as possible. These submarines became the S class.

For the first time, C&R and BuEng made the sort of trade-off studies previously conducted only by Electric Boat and Lake. BuEng tried to balance submerged and surface performances (see details in chapter 6). Maximum submerged speed was a function of the motor-propeller combination, whereas radius was largely determined by the battery. It would be better, for example, to demand 12 kt for maximum speed and perhaps 10 kt for 3 hr (to fix battery capacity) than to call for a particular 1-hr speed and 20 hr at 5 kt.[3] BuEng suggested that one engine be powerful enough to charge the batteries in 6 hr (3 hr on two engines; the submariners wanted 4 hr on one engine) after a 10-hr discharge. BuEng also considered existing battery capacity, based on the requirement for a single attack, inadequate. The Submarine Force argued that even the demands of the single attack had been understated.[4]

BuEng estimated that a 560-ton submarine (costing about $700,000) could achieve 16 kt (4-hr-run) on the surface, with an endurance (48-hr) speed of 14 kt and a normal surface radius of 3,500 nm at 12 kt, not too far from what was required. Maximum submerged speed would be 11.5 kt (9.5 kt for 3 hr). As it happened, the battery capacity for the 3-hr run would suffice for 20 hr at 5 kt, the usual requirement. Similarly, a 16-kt 800-tonner would have a radius of 4,000 nm at 12 kt (2,480 nm at 14 kt) and a submerged speed of 12 kt (10 kt for 3 hr, 6 kt for 20 hr). These figures presumably drove the General Board's characteristics. In particular, it seemed impractical to meet the submariners' desire for either an 18-kt surface speed or a 13-kt submerged speed on 800 tons—better to accept the balanced figures of 16 kt surfaced and 12 kt submerged. These figures were based on test curves for a model of the C&R 800-ton submarine then being designed; the bureaus did not have access to Electric Boat's power-speed curves.

Work on the new naval bill had begun in December 1915. The secretary's proposed 5-year plan included 15 fleet and 85 coastal submarines. On 29 August 1916, Congress passed the General Board's smaller 3-year program (9 fleet and 58 coastal boats, FY 17–19). The 58 coastal submarines (SS 78–135) included both true coastal boats and three 800-ton prototypes. The coastal units were designated the R class, presumably to avoid using the letters P and Q, which could have been confused with the British P-class coastal patrol craft and their ASW decoys (Q-ships). The 800-tonners became the S class. This act also authorized a Neff submarine (SS 108), to be paid for only if its power plant proved effective. It was to displace about 150 tons and to approximate the C class in armament.

Characteristics for Coast Submarine 1917 submitted on 2 October 1916 generally duplicated those for Coast Submarine 1916 (the O-boat) but called for 30 days' stores. Normal radius would be not less than 3,150 nm at 11 kt, maximum not less than 5,600 nm at 11 kt. Speeds matched those of earlier coastal submarines. These characteristics mentioned, perhaps for the first time, that all torpedo tubes were to be fitted for angled fire. Engines matched those of the Electric Boat and Lake O-boats.

Electric Boat, Lake, California Shipbuilding, and Schneider (which built Laubeuf designs) all bid. CALSHIP's offer to build Lake boats on the West Coast was rejected because of its complex contract terms. Schneider was rejected because of the urgent war situation: there would not be enough time to develop the necessary diesels under license. Because Lake's reorganized company had yet to deliver a single submarine, the bureaus were unwilling to give him much of the program. They did not want to shut him out, however, so the R class was split between Electric Boat (R-1–R-20) and Lake (R-21–R-27).[5]

Lake's R-boats were the last submarines built in quantity to his design. They were also probably his best. In 1921, OpNav's submarine branch reported that the Lake O-boats and R-boats were no better, on the whole, than Electric Boat's; their engines were better but their electrical installations were worse. Lake finally abandoned his distinctive hydroplane in this design.

Coastal submarines had come a long way. The R-boat was about 50 percent larger than the H-boat, with substantial growth margin to meet war conditions: 21-in tubes, 3-in guns, radios $\frac{1}{2}$–2 kw), two gyrocompasses, chariot bridges, and air purifier. On paper, the R was no faster than the H, but, according to Land, they "will have good engines, while the H boats never did have." The R-boat was large enough to have a separate auxiliary room for the motors and machine tools, and it had a machine shop for emergency repairs. "Both as to quality and quantity their storage of air is considerably greater," Land said. Compared with the O-boat, the R "is also better for its crew. Each man has a bunk . . . the men that go to sea in submarines have a darned hard time. I think they are entitled to a place to sleep and a little convenience with regard to stowing clothes and storing food, so that every little bit of space you can give them will help. They have little fresh water and no sign of a place to bathe. This is certainly not the way you gentlemen train men to live."[6]

All of Lake's R-boats were laid up in 1924–25 and discarded in 1930. Like other Lake boats, they were slow (80-sec) divers. They also suffered from weak engine foundations. The Electric Boat craft were either laid up in the early 1930s or used for training; they served through WW II. R-6 had the distinction of testing the first U.S. experimental snorkel, a folding unit, in 1945.

S-boat characteristics were scaled up from those of the coastal submarine. Required endurance far exceeded previous figures: 3,400 nm at 14 kt, 5,400 nm at 11 kt (8,400 nm at 11 kt with ballast tanks used for fuel). This submarine would cross the Atlantic to fight. As in the past, Electric Boat offered a single-hull design, essentially an enlarged R-boat. Lake and Portsmouth Navy Yard used

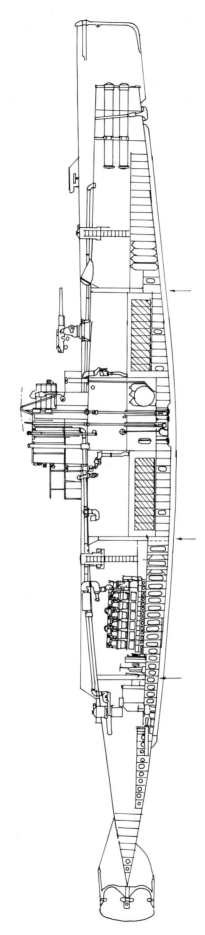

R-2 is shown as in April 1933, modified for safety, but not yet fitted with marker buoys. The arrows indicate bulkheads reinforced to full hull strength. Batteries are shaded, for clarity.

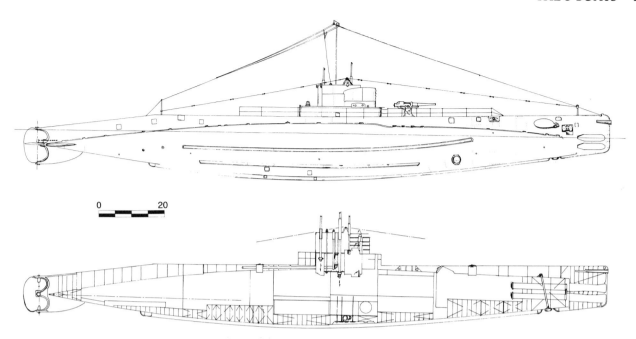

Electric Boat's R-1 is shown as completed, with three housing periscopes (conning tower, control room, and after battery compartment, the later extemporized during World War I) and a 3-in/50 deck gun. The only sound gear shown is the circular plate of the Fessenden oscillator. As in other Electric Boat designs, she has her battery fore and aft of the control room. (Jim Christley)

double hulls. Three prototypes were built under the FY 17 program: Electric Boat's S-1 (SS 105), Lake's S-2 (SS 106), and Portsmouth's S-3 (SS 107).

Electric Boat units suffered from the defects of all of its earlier single-hull submarines: they were wet (hence, poor gun platforms), the after part of their thin superstructures tore off in heavy seas and endangered propellers, and their stern planes were too weak to take the pounding aft.

Lake's S-2 was a slow diver, as might have been ex-

pected. She and the later Lake-built (Portsmouth-designed) boats (S-14 through S-17) needed larger motors for their diving planes and for their main ballast and bow buoyancy tank valves in order to achieve faster operation.

Portsmouth's S-3 design was unusual in having separate upper and main ballast tanks that were separately flooded. The upper tanks were a survival of prewar practice, in which a submarine would run light rather than in crash-dive configuration. Because these tanks had their flood valves above the waterline, they could not begin to

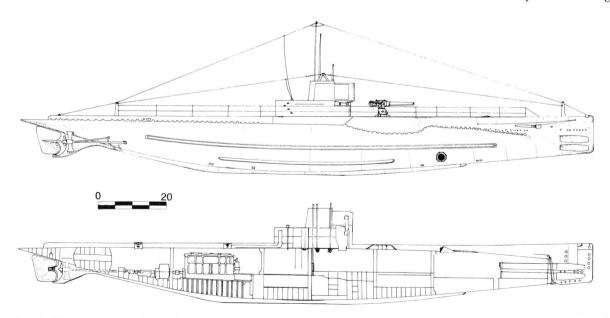

Lake's R-boats were the last of his designs to be built in any numbers. He abandoned amidships diving planes in this class, but his characteristic stern remained. The horizontal tube aft is an access tube connecting the motor room to the tiller room aft. (Jim Christley)

R-boats were, in effect, coastal equivalents to the S-boats. R-19 is shown here, with her telescoping radio mast raised.

flood until a submarine was well down in the water. They barred quick dives (Portsmouth's boats were credited with 100 sec instead of the 60 sec desired).[7] S-3 and then her sisters were later modified with a free-flooding superstructure and additional side Kingstons. She also got a bow buoyancy tank. The entire S class (but particularly the Portsmouth-designed S-3–S-13) had such large submerged turning circles that the boats could not make a quick reverse attack. S-48 through S-51 had tactical diame-

ters 40 percent over the contract figure. The S-boats were equipped with evaporators, heated by engine exhaust, that proved to have insufficient capacity. This class had the first U.S. submarine refrigeration and cold storage units. Wartime pressure for quick production precluded attention to defects in the Portsmouth design. In November 1918, Portsmouth developed new designs for the last boats of the class, S-10–S-13 and S-48–S-51.

The Navy's S-3 was designed to make 15 kt surfaced

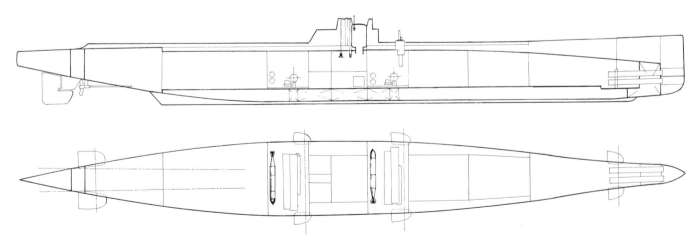

C&R's Scheme F for Submarine 1917 (the 800-tonner) was double-hulled, with a vertical-chisel (cruiser) stern similar to that of M-1. Dimensions were 221 ft × 23 ft 6 in × 12 ft 6 in, for a normal displacement of 830 tons. C&R's sketch shows a pair of British-style athwartships tubes, which BuOrd disliked. Like surface ship broadside tubes, the athwartships tubes would have been loaded from the side through a lengthwise flap. The British adopted them in their E class because their submariners believed that the boats were growing too large to maneuver quickly into bow-on firing position. They rejected contemporary foreign (presumably including U.S.) experiments with gyro-setting for angled fire. This sketch was not dated, but the requirement for three periscopes seems to have originated about early 1917. (Jim Christley)

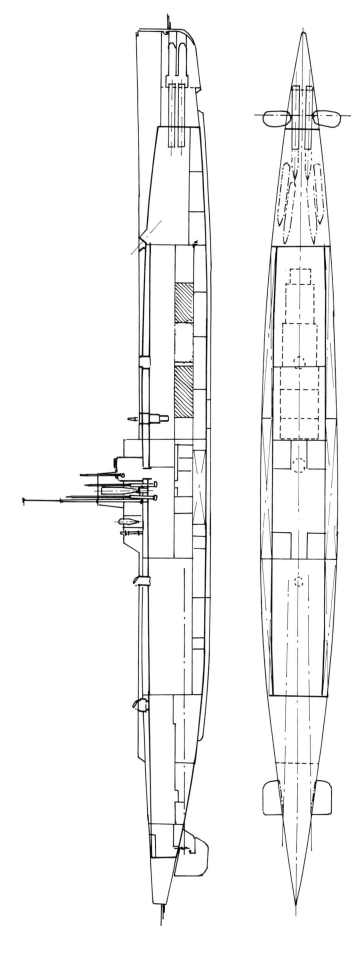

C&R's Scheme I for the 800-ton 1917 submarine was dated 20 September 1916. It was the basis for the bureau's design, which was generally called the government type. Note that the batteries were concentrated forward, under the crew's quarters abaft the torpedo room. Officers were concentrated in the space between crew's quarters and the control room. Under the control room were, fore to aft, auxiliary tank, adjusting tank, refrigerated stores, air flasks, Kingstons, and magazines. Just abaft the control room were the galley and radio room (note the radio tube, with the binnacle forward of it, just above them), with the engine/motor room abaft them. Note also that the stern form matches that of M-1. The pressure hull had a circular cross section, surrounded by tankage. Dimensions: 235 ft (overall) × 29 ft 9 in × 12 ft 8 in (800 / 1,055 tons).

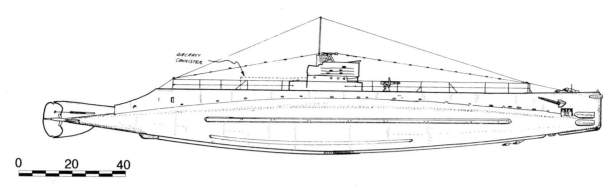

Electric Boat designed and built S-1. The dashed lines show the aircraft canister experimentally installed after World War I. Note also the disappearing 3-in/23 gun forward of the bridge and the Y-tubes on deck and under the keel. The company's output, S-18 through S-47, dominated the class; contracts for higher-numbered boats were canceled at the end of World War I. Although John Holland had long ago left Electric Boat, these craft were all called Holland S-boats. (Jim Christley)

(14 kt for 48 hr) and 11 kt submerged (for 2 hr) or 105 nm at 5.25 kt submerged (49.5 nm at 8.25 kt). Estimated endurance was 3,500 nm at 14 kt (5,500 nm at 11 kt, 10,000 nm using ballast tanks for fuel). Electric Boat could not offer as much: 14.5 kt surfaced, 11 kt submerged, 40 nm at 8 kt submerged, 3,400 nm at 11 kt surfaced (7,600 nm if ballast tanks were used as fuel). Lake claimed that he could do better: 16 kt surfaced, 11 kt submerged, 3,150/5,500 nm at 11 kt.

For follow-on boats, C&R based the circular of requirements on estimated S-3 performance. Electric Boat argued successfully that its estimates were based on experience; the bureaus had been overly optimistic. Its fuel arrangement allowed it to put in over 16 percent more battery capacity than S-3. A more realistic estimate of S-3 surface endurance, according to Electric Boat, would be 5,250/9,600 nm. The company suggested that No. 2 main ballast tank could be arranged to carry either fuel (for 5,750 nm) or ballast (2,900 nm). It offered to guarantee the same surface speed and underwater speed and endurance as S-3. Electric Boat refused to build boats to the government's design because, the company argued, it might well fail to make the unrealistically estimated performance on trials. It was the only U.S. firm placed to build enough boats within a short time period, so it received the largest S-boat contract.

Lake offered to build either to his own design or to C&R's, but with 2-cycle Busch-Sulzer diesels, rather than Electric Boat's 4-cycle engines. Unfortunately, in the spring of 1917, when designs were being chosen for production, Lake's reorganized company still had not delivered any boats (L-5 was running trials); his distinctive design features were still unproved. The bureaus refused to buy any more of Lake's designs, but he was offered a contract for the bureau design with 4-cycle engines; he used Busch-Sulzers. Other boats of this type were ordered from Portsmouth Navy Yard. This was a fortunate decision, since the S-2 design turned out to be badly flawed. Some of its problems could be traced to measures Lake took to evade Electric Boat patents.[8]

Early in 1917, the Senate began work on the FY 18 appropriation. The General Board objected to the proposed program of 20 fleet and 80 coastal submarines. An emergency program to deal with the possibility of war with Germany should have concentrated on conventional ASW craft. Because there were already quite enough coastal boats (albeit many not yet complete), the board wanted any new funds to be used for 20 fleet submarines. Instead, the act of 4 March 1917 provided 18 S-boats (SS 109–126); a special naval emergency fund bought 20 more (SS 127–146). Six H-boats (SS 147–152), built for Russia but undeliverable because of the revolution, were bought for the U.S. Navy under an emergency act of 6 October 1917.

On 29 August 1917, the General Board asked for 30 fleet boats for FY 19. The submariners wanted 60 S-boats, the estimated capacity of Fore River, Lake, and Portsmouth beyond the 12 already ordered from each yard. They got 24 (SS 153–176). Electric Boat's SS 159–168 and Lake's SS 173–176 were canceled on 4 December 1918.

The navy built S-4–S-13 (SS 109–118). Lake built S-14–S-17 (SS 119–122) and S-48–S-51 (SS 159–162) to the navy design (S-10–S-13 and S-48–S-51 were redesigned). Electric Boat built S-18–S-47 (SS 123–146, 153–158), of which S-42–S-47 were built to a modified design. They were the heaviest, and probably the best, S-boats.[9] S-48–S-51 were originally to have been SS 169–172. Canceled numbers, beginning with SS 163, were used for postwar submarines.

R-boats and S-boats were modified to accord with WW I experience (see chapter 8). That generally meant adding permanent structures, such as a chariot bridge and larger guns, hence drag. In a streamlined L-boat, appendages accounted for 46 percent of total underwater resistance at 11 kt. The conning tower and periscopes accounted for 21.6 percent of the total and bow planes, 11.4 percent. Tests of a model of the C&R 800-tonner showed that the proposed pair of antiaircraft guns would increase underwater resistance (at 11 kt) by 57 percent and reduce submerged speed to 8.5 kt. Without the guns, that much more power would add about 1.5 kt.

Short 3-in guns on disappearing mounts provided too

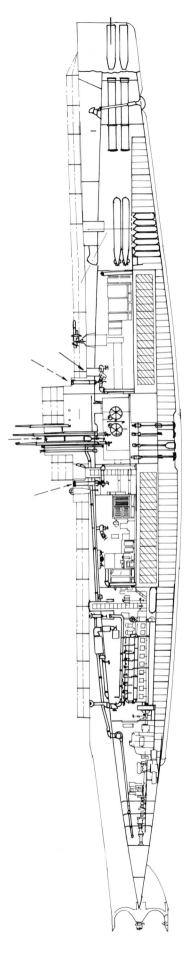

This inboard profile shows Electric Boat's S-1 as designed; it was drawn from the boat's contract plans, dated February 1917. Note the gun access hatch (arrowed) forward of the conning tower. When a big 4in/50 gun replaced the small 3in/23 shown, the access hatch had to be abandoned in favor of a smaller ammunition-passing scuttle. Dashed arrows indicate the usual three ventilators grouped around the conning tower fairwater. Batteries are shaded, for clarity.

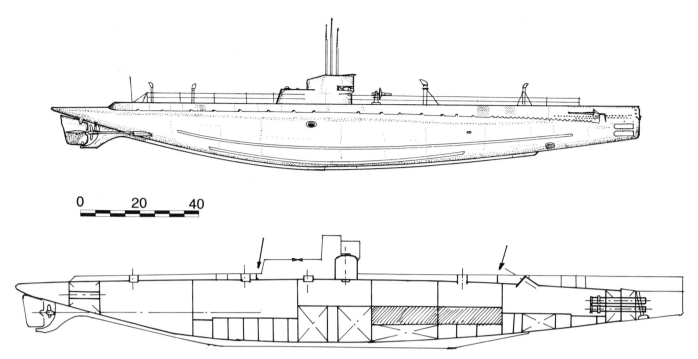

Simon Lake's S-2 was his last submarine design for the U.S. Navy. His other S-boats were built to C&R's design characteristics. In the inboard profile, the batteries are shaded. Major ballast tanks are indicated amidships, with trim tanks at the end; note the access tube connecting the motor room to the tiller room through the after trim tank. The arrows indicate the ends of the watertight part of the superstructure. Of the three main ballast tanks, the after one could be used for reserve fuel oil. Fuel was also stowed under the forward battery and under the engine room, with the forward two tanks there used for lubricating oil. Between the middle and aft main ballast tanks was an auxiliary ballast tank. Officers' and crew's quarters were in the space immediately abaft the torpedo room, with crew's quarters and the galley in the next space aft. (External view, Jim Christley)

little firepower. By May 1917, the Germans were reportedly carrying heavy gun batteries, that is, one 5-in forward and one 4-in aft (presumably, actual calibers were 4.1 in and 3.5 in because the Germans had nothing close to a 5-in gun); three boats, each armed with three wet (submersible) 5.9-in guns, were ready for service. As C&R had guessed, such heavy batteries (also used by other foreign navies) cut submerged speed to about 8 kt. To develop reasonably

high muzzle velocity, guns had to be too long to house in a submarine's deck; they had to add considerable drag underwater. The General Board, accepting the loss in underwater speed, approved a battery of two or three 3-in or 4-in guns for the S-boats.

There was space for only a single gun; the maximum possible caliber, 4-in/50, was chosen. The single mount could be easily removed at a navy yard to cut drag should

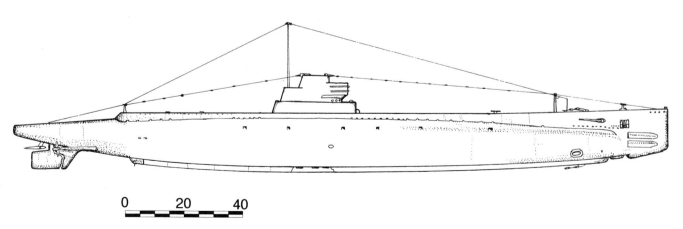

S-3 was C&R's (generally called the government's) version of the S-boat. Note that her stern was similar to that of M-1. Government S-boats could be identified by the prominent structures forward of their fairwaters, which held ready-use ammunition for the 4-in guns. (Jim Christley)

S-6 was a C&R–designed submarine built at Puget Sound.

higher underwater performance be wanted. Similar reasoning applied to the 3-in/50 adopted for the R class. The O class was so far along that the original 3-in/23s were never replaced by 3-in/50s.[10] BuOrd also wanted 0.30-caliber machine guns; in June, the secretary of the navy approved one for each submarine.

As the war continued, the Submarine Force became more interested in higher-powered deck guns. Submarines on patrol might encounter surfaced U-boats armed with 5.9-in guns. Considered, but rejected, were 5-in guns for the S-18 class. BuOrd had developed nonrecoil Davis guns for aircraft; they were light enough to mount on a submarine's bridge, from which they could fire even when her main deck was awash. BuOrd offered 4-in and 5-in Davis guns (muzzle velocities 2,700 and 2,300 ft/sec). The project ended with WW I.

Captain Hart urged a shift back from four 21-in to six 18-in tubes. Because tubes could not be reloaded quickly, only the torpedoes already in them could be fired in quick succession at targets encountered. Unfortunately, six 18-in tubes would weigh 280.8 lb more than the four 21-in tubes, and the basic S-boat design had already completely exhausted its weight margin. Hart's idea was rejected. The General Board suggested that any extra 21-in tubes be mounted aft or on the broadside.

After the war, U.S. officers were much impressed with the Germans' stern torpedo tubes. S-10–S-13 and S-48–S-51 were redesigned with single stern tubes. This version began with modifications requested by C&R: a mine defense bulkhead abaft the torpedo tubes (later abandoned); an evaporator plant; 200, rather than 80, rounds of 4-in ammunition; a chariot bridge; Hart's six 18-in tubes instead of four 21-in, with six torpedo impulse tubes forward; an 18-in tube aft; and 14 torpedoes (5.5 m) instead of 12 (21-in, 5 m).

Portsmouth first tried to gain the margin it needed (20 tons plus 20 tons of lead) through lengthening the hull by 7.5 ft (five frames); displacement increased to 911 tons. The extra length amounted to one frame in the torpedo compartment to gain space for the mine defense bulkhead, one in the battery compartment, one in the central operating compartment, one in the engine room, and one in the motor room. The battery could now be rearranged in two rectangular tanks (much simplified), with its center of gravity further aft. The wardroom and radio room in the central operating compartment were enlarged. Moving the main engines forward one frame space left more space for the main clutches and bearings. The motors were moved away from the bulkhead (S-3s had been too cramped). The extra weight bought the desired stern tube

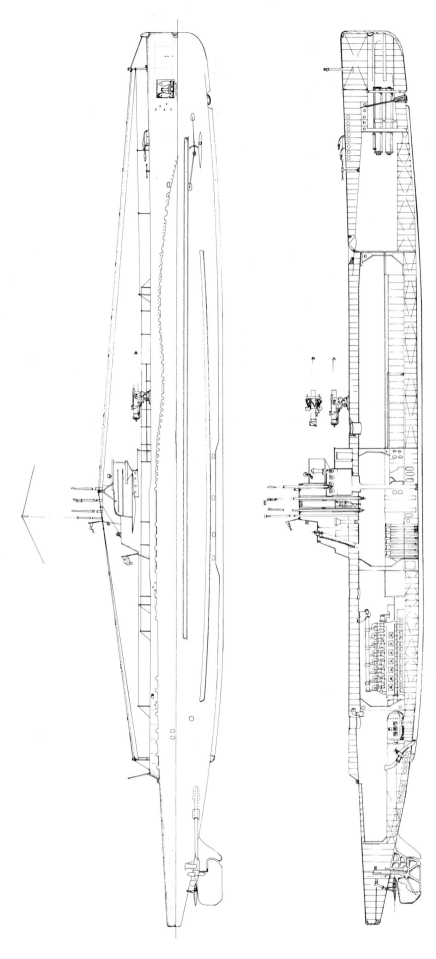

S-8, shown in April 1921, was a C&R-type boat (similar to S-4 through S-9 and S-14 through S-17) built at Portsmouth Navy Yard. Of the three periscopes, No. 2 is an alti-periscope. Submarines sometimes flew the small metal flag atop it to warn surface craft of their presence in the hope of avoiding collisions. Abaft the three periscopes is the telescoping mast. On deck are her Y-tube (3 rats) and SC-tube. Unlike an Electric Boat design, this one shows all batteries concentrated forward under the crews' and officers' quarters, all of which were abaft the torpedo room. The vertical tube forward of the conning tower accommodates 4-in ready-service rounds. Compared with the Holland version, these S-boats were much more heavily framed and more subdivided, with heavy bulkheads shown between the forward torpedo room, the control room, the engine room, and the motor room. Note the pipe aft, leading into the keel. In these boats something approaching an Electric Boat-style duct keel was provided, with Kingstons under the control room and a main bilge pump (not shown) at the upper end of the curved pipe. The combination of pressure-proof bulkheads and escape hatches forward and aft made it unnecessary to modify them very heavily after the S-4 disaster. (Jim Christley)

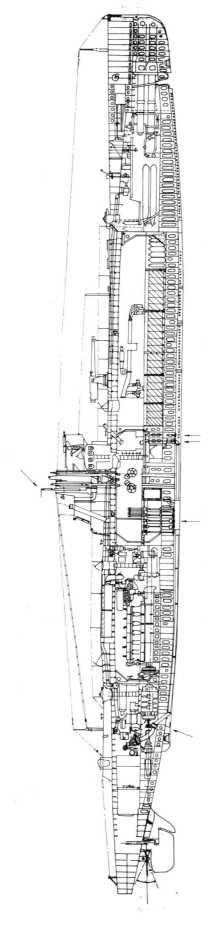

S-17 is shown in December 1942, after a refit. She has been fitted with SD air-search radar (arrowed, on top of the conning tower). She was one of four boats (S-14 through S-17) re-engined in 1925 with MAN diesels. A drain (equivalent to Electric Boat's duct keel) installed in her box keel was connected to the large low-pressure ballast pump shown aft (arrow). Kingstons were installed amidships, under the control room, and two remotely controlled Kingstons were fitted to No. 1 Main Ballast Tank, one connected to the drain and a larger one communicating directly with the sea. The objects atop the chariot bridge are a venturi, to limit wind, and the ship's whistle, with the navigator's chair inboard. The inclined tube rising just abaft the gun breech is an ammunition scuttle. Batteries are shaded, for clarity.

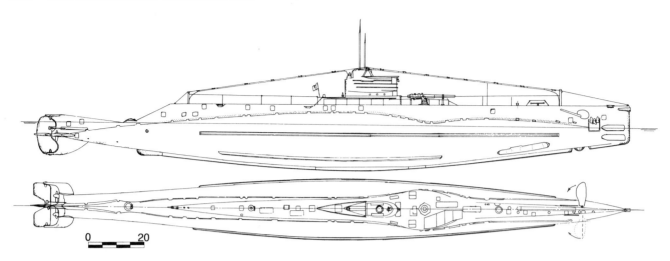

Electric Boat's S-26, shown in the early 1930s, was one of the company's first series (S-18 through S-41). She had been modified for greater safety, with an escape hatch installed in her motor room aft and her skeg cut away to clear it. Some S-boats were not so modified until they were reconditioned in 1941. The underwater blister visible forward contained a passive array (MV-tube) that replaced the earlier Y-tube. The SC-tube, with its guard, is visible on deck. About 1935, JK, in a round housing, began to be installed atop the SC. This arrangement was standard by 1941. The conning tower periscope was removed in the mid-1920s. The heavy cables suspended from the deck and from the A-shears atop the conning tower fairwater comprise the loop radio antenna. At the outbreak of war in 1941, S-26 was assigned to Coco Solo in the Canal Zone; she was rammed accidentally on 24 January 1942. (Jim Christley)

(21-in) but not extra torpedoes. The 200 rounds of gun ammunition had to be pared to 125 rounds. Portsmouth had to omit the mine defense bulkhead.

This design inspired further modifications. An alternative Scheme B merged the upper ballast tanks with the main ballast tanks. The double hull was shortened, and the battery compartment (too large in the first revised design) was somewhat reduced by lengthening the torpedo compartments. The hull structure was somewhat heavier, so less ballast was needed, and the hull was shortened by five frames (four at the bow, one at the stern). Estimated surface displacement, including the 20-ton margin and 20 tons of lead, was 926 tons. This version also incorporated the single stern tube and extra ammunition.

C&R much preferred Scheme B, but still wanted the hull lengthened. It doubted that eliminating the separate upper ballast tanks would increase diving speed. Experience abroad (Laurenti, Laubeuf, early Krupp, and British boats) suggested that any main ballast tanks with much volume above the waterline would materially slow down diving. Instead of extending their ballast tanks over the top of the pressure hull, foreign designers made such structures free-flooding and control-vented. C&R could see considerable virtue in one such tank, a bow buoyancy tank for better sea-keeping. C&R generally liked the idea of shortening the double-hull part of the submarine but

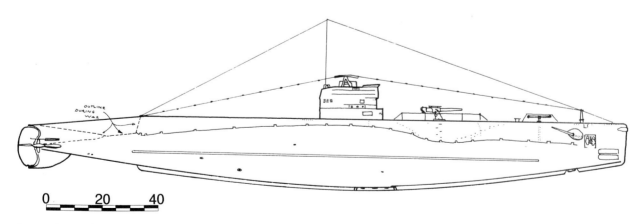

S-42, a Quincy-built S-boat, was the first of Electric Boat's second production series (S-42 through S-47). These boats could be recognized by the prominent gun access trunks at the forward ends of their conning tower fairwaters (the S-18 series had much smaller ammunition scuttles there). Other modifications, such as revised ballast arrangements, were more subtle. The dashed line indicates the way the skeg was cut away for the submarine safety improvement program; the boats of this series were modified during the early 1930s. All were modernized during World War II. (Jim Christley)

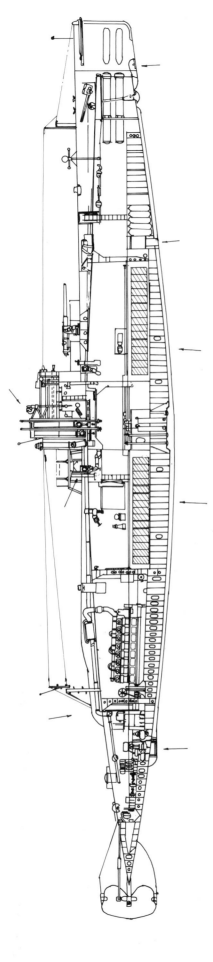

S-35 typified first-generation Holland S-boats modernized during World War II. The two most visible changes were the platform for a 20-mm gun and the installation of an SJ radar (its range indicator is the shaded box in the conning tower). A new keel sonar was installed (indicated by an arrow). An underwater signal ejector is shown under the 20-mm platform (arrow), with an internal platform for its operator. The two Fessenden oscillators have been removed (their cavities are arrowed). The boat's marker buoys were removed (note her stern contour) because they could become loose during depth charging. The boat was also air-conditioned (the air conditioner is indicated near the refrigerator abaft the control room, indicated by the arrow under the keel near amidships) and a Kleinschmidt still installed.

Other arrows indicate the motor generator forward (under the gun), presumably needed for the radar; the radar antenna itself (forward of the two periscopes); and the new signal ejector tube (under the 20-mm gun platform. (Note the ladder installed to reach its breech.) S-35 and her sisters all exchanged their 4-in/50s for 3-in/50s from newer submarines. This type of modernization applied to most surviving first-generation Holland S-boats: S-23 (summer 1943 at San Diego, probably including radar and keel sonar); S-28 (San Diego: 26 October–13 November 1942, including installation of SJ radar and Kleinschmidt still; superstructure modified at Puget Sound April–June 1943); S-30 (San Diego: October 1942–February 1943, including radar, possibly replacing an earlier set); S-31 (San Diego: January–February 1943); S-32 (San Diego: 11 November–21 December 1942, including radar and keel sonar); S-33 (San Diego: February–March 1943, including radar and keel sonar); S-34 (San Diego: January–April 1943, including radar and air conditioning); S-35 (Puget Sound: 29 January–20 May 1943); S-37 (San Diego: winter 1943); S-38 (San Diego: 6 November 1942–13 April 1943, including radar and air conditioning; radar may have been fitted earlier; completion was delayed by late arrival of equipment); S-41 (San Diego: 29 October 1942–April 1943). Modernization generally included installation of an echo fathometer, which replaced the earlier wire-weight sounding machine. Several boats, probably including S-32, received radar in one major refit, and had to wait for a 20-mm gun and its platform. It is not clear whether all boats were air-conditioned, and whether all were fitted with Kleinschmidt stills. S-18 and S-23 received their big refits just before being relegated to training, and they may not have been refitted as completely as sisters which went back into combat. In April 1945 S-18 had an Army-type single 40-mm gun in place of her 3-in/50.

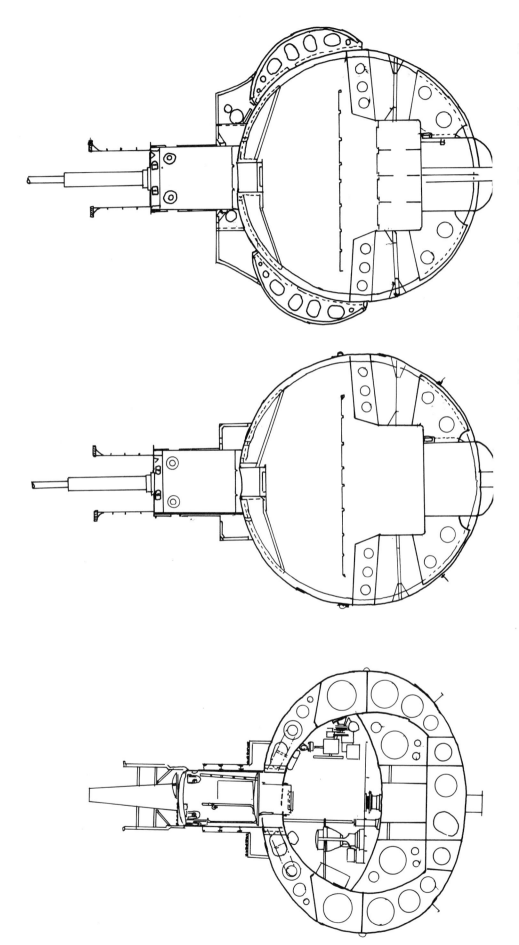

Comparative S-boat cross sections show the differences between C&R and Electric Boat designs. C&R's S-11, at left, has only limited internal space, partly because the bureau could not use Electric Boat's patented U-tank. In the middle is a standard Electric Boat S-boat midsection, showing the U-tank (under the floor plates) and the duct keel. At right, S-20 modified with blisters.

S-45 was an Electric Boat S-boat built at the Fore River Shipyard. She is shown here at Guantánamo Bay, April 1927. Note the small frame protecting her deck-mounted SC tube, forward.

wanted it lengthened forward, if possible to the forward torpedo room bulkhead, to improve protection against depth charging.

Redesign delayed the last navy-built bureau boats (S-10–S-13) long enough for them to be further modified to incorporate typical German features: flapper Kingstons for the main ballast tanks, a low-pressure turbo blower to blow the main ballast tanks, and German pumps and air compressors. They were powered by the BuEng copy of the 1,200-BHP MAN diesel (derated to 1,000 BHP). The resulting S-boats were considered far superior to their original sister ships, S-4–S-9. Lake's S-48 through S-51 also had the additional stern torpedo tube. Unlike the S-10 series, they were lengthened to include a separate maneuvering room. S-14–S-17 were re-engined with 1,200-BHP, German-built MAN diesels in 1926 (maximum speed increased to 15¼ kt); the result was considered a vast improvement.

The Electric Boat S-boats had to be rebuilt. To keep the submarine industrial base alive, the navy awarded contracts to both Electric Boat and Lake. In 1924, however, it reluctantly allowed Lake to go out of business, apparently because Lake's yard could not be expanded to build the new generation of fleet boats.[11]

Designed for the Atlantic, the S-boats entered service just as U.S. naval attention turned to the far vaster Pacific. Despite their poor wartime workmanship and obsolescent designs, they were the only existing U.S. submarines likely to be useful to a Pacific battlefleet. Most were completed just as U.S. naval funding collapsed after the Washington treaty, so many of their deficiencies were not even addressed. What effort could be spared went into their engines. For example, in October 1924, Submarine Commander Pacific (SubPac) was particularly concerned with unreliable engine air compressors; the solution was to install heavier moving parts.

Tropical waters, which were becoming the U.S. Navy's primary operating areas, were quite different from the colder water for which its submarines had been designed.[12] About 1920, all submarines retained in service were modified with ventilation systems supplying air to all compartments.[13] A study of the R-boats showed that, unmodified, they could probably operate continuously for 2 wk in tropical waters, with a 2-wk rest between patrols. Suggested solutions to the problems of heat and humidity were much better ventilation and limited air conditioning. The main capacity of the vertical supply blowers in

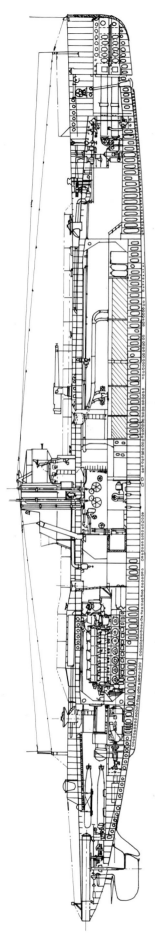

S-11, shown about 1941, was one of four government S-boats redesigned by Portsmouth Navy Yard to carry a torpedo tube aft. Structural detail has been included in this drawing to suggest the complexity of the C&R design, which made it extremely difficult to maintain. The V-1 class had similar complex structures.

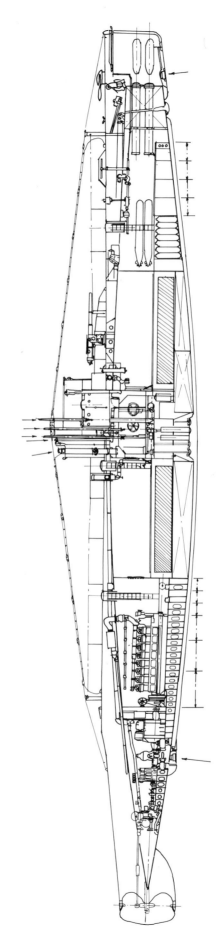

The S-boat was the culmination of Electric Boat single-hull designs for the U.S. Navy. This is a typical unit of the S-30 to S-41 group, as completed. Ballast tanks are indicated. Lines below the hull show the locations of the fuel tanks forward and aft (the foremost two tanks of the after group are the lubricating oil tank and the sump tank). Arrows indicate the two Fessenden oscillators under the boat's keel, fore and aft. Arrows in the bridge structure indicate the three periscopes (one in the conning tower, soon removed), the telescoping radio mast, and the radio tube leading down into the radio room.

In the control room the wheels controlling the planes were on the port side; the three levers for the Kingston valves were on the opposite (starboard) side, abaft the chart table. The radio room (below the radio tube, into which the antenna leads ran) was set into the after port side of the control room. Abaft the main motors were auxiliaries: the low-pressure main ballast pump on the centerline, the high-pressure main ballast pump on the starboard shaft, the motor for the Fessenden oscillator on the port shaft. Further aft were the air compressors, with coolers outboard. A lathe was mounted between the thrust blocks. A circulating water pump was mounted forward of each engine. The original drawing shows that the Y-tube forward was omitted on S-35 through S-41 (another drawing shows that it was omitted on S-26 through S-29).

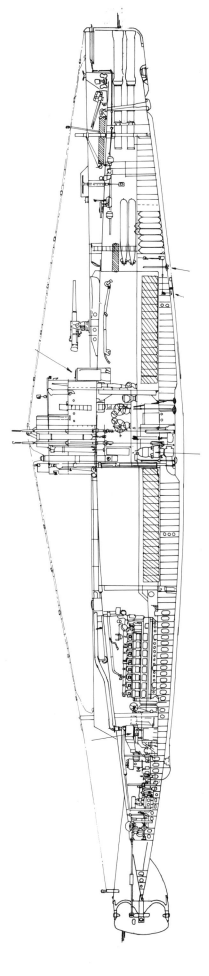

Typical of the last Electric Boat S-boats (S-42 through S-47), S-43 is shown as in 1924 or 1925 (the date of final changes to the original plan is illegible). These boats were part of a second, redesigned, series. They were lengthened enough to accomodate both the new 4in / 50 gun and the gun access hatch shown (arrowed) forward of the conning tower fairwater (it is the main visual difference between these and earlier Electric Boat units). Double lines seem to indicate strengthened bulkheads, presumably inspired by those in the C&R S-boats. Unlike earlier Electric Boat S-boats, this one (and her entire group) has her low-pressure ballast pump (arrowed) under the control room, in a location previously used only for Kingstons. The watertight duct keel terminates just forward of a small remotely-controlled Kingston (arrowed) serving No. 1 Main Ballast Tank; this tank can also drain via a much larger Kingston (also arrowed) connected to the non-watertight keel, i.e., directly to the sea. This new feature (for Electric Boat) would probably have made for faster diving, a major concern in S-boat operation. The arrow aft indicates an air cooler serving the main motors, an important feature for a boat intended to operate in the tropics. A smaller air cooler treated air coming from the compressor, drying it. This drawing does not show changes in ballast tankage, including fuel stowage in No. 4 Main Ballast Tank. By 1925 S-43's skeg had been cut down. She may well have been unique in this respect, although reportedly skegs rusted and worked loose, so C&R allowed individual COs to order them cut away. Eventually they were all cut down as part of the big safety modification program. Batteries are shaded for clarity. The torpedo impulse tanks above the torpedo room forward have also been shaded in.

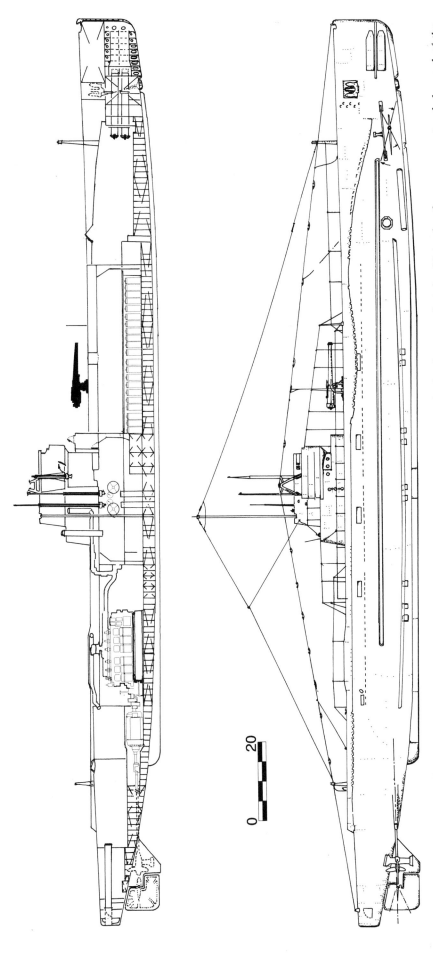

S-49 was a Lake-built, government-type S-boat, modified while under construction to incorporate a single after torpedo tube. Note also the gun access trunk forward of the conning tower fairwater, which replaced the ready ammunition stowage of the first series of "government" S-boats. She was lengthened to 240 ft to provide both a maneuvering room and a torpedo room aft. Displacement increased from 876 tons (surfaced) / 1092 tons (submerged) to 903 / 1230 tons. Note the blister of the passive MV system forward, just under the circular patch of her Fessenden oscillator. Also note the separate maneuvering room inserted between the engine room and the after torpedo room, above the motors. The entire battery is forward, under the space between the forward torpedo room and the control room. Note the kinked (discontinuous) pressure hull, with larger-diameter sections at the ends, which require heavier and more elaborate structure to support it. (Jim Christley)

0   20

the torpedo room could be nearly doubled (from 1,600 to 3,000 cu ft/min) and overhead fans installed in compartments for better circulation. The main intakes for the ventilation system could be raised sufficiently to gain free access to outside air (the intakes might need cowls for rough weather). Air in the hull soon became so saturated with humidity that the difference between the outside water temperature and the temperature inside the boat was insufficient to carry off heat quickly enough. The suggested solution was cooling and drying equipment in the forward and after battery compartments, the forerunner of WW II air conditioning.[14]

Main motor ventilation was a major problem. Lake supplied open motors to his O-boats and R-boats. The other classes had closed motors, some of them separately ventilated. According to a 1923 report, all of them were soon permeated with oil from the oily air of the motor room, which very quickly caused their insulation to break down and the motors to heat up. They had to be removed, baked out, and sometimes reinsulated.[15]

The S-boats were too slow to keep up with a fleet cruising at 12 kt. Fleet cruising was much more difficult than an independent run, during which a boat could stop briefly for minor repairs. In 1923, a slow-speed squadron run from San Pedro to Panama was considered 25–50 percent more difficult than the same trip undertaken independently. The S-18 class was credited with an endurance of 5,000 nm at 11 kt with the fleet or 7,600 nm independently, or a period of 1 mo with the fleet or 6 mo independently. These figures were rather less than nominal endurance as then estimated. In the summer of 1923, the rules for engineering competition allowed fuel consumption of $3\frac{3}{4}$ gal/mi, so a boat's fuel capacity of about 35,000 gal equated, in theory, to 9,400 nm at 7 kt. Allowing for battery charging while running, that might be reduced to 8,000 nm, or about 50 days at 7 kt. In reality, endurance was far shorter. Leakage contaminated many tanks with seawater. Until the tanks could be sealed effectively, moreover, a boat tended to leave a continuous visible oil slick.

S-20 was modified, with a raised bow (for better seakeeping) and external blisters to carry more fuel oil (total capacity of 33,089 gal versus 27,200 gal of her near-sisters). She was apparently not successful enough to be worth duplicating; she was cited as an example in opposition to the 1926 modernization proposal described in this chapter. In 1931, S-20 became an engineering experimental ship: her starboard diesel was replaced by a high-speed (600-BHP, 700-RPM) MAN diesel geared to the propeller shaft. In 1932, that was replaced by a higher-speed 16-cylinder MAN diesel-generator (built by Electric Boat) driving a high-speed motor geared to the shaft. In each case, the port engine was unchanged.

Post-1918 attack tactics made full use of the gyro-setting feature of U.S. torpedoes. Electric Boat's S-boats and their tubes, however, had been designed earlier: torpedo gyros could not be set in the tubes. Gyros could not be set quickly enough (before loading a torpedo) to be useful in an attack. Torpedo tube gyro setters were authorized, but SubPac complained in October 1924 that neither they nor the approved quick-opening vents had been installed. Government and Lake-built S-boats did have provision for tube setting. The situation was further complicated because the interior communications (visuals) needed to transmit gyro sets from conning tower to tubes were unsatisfactory. The authorized recognition signal ejectors, essential if the boats were to cooperate with surface forces, had not yet been fitted.

The S-boats all lacked sufficient range for Pacific operations, and postwar exercises often overtaxed them. To achieve their rated endurance, they had to stow fuel oil in their ballast tanks. They left oil slicks every time they submerged until the tanks were washed clean. In February 1925, C&R suggested that a submarine tanker accompany groups of S-boats to the Western Pacific. Wartime reports of U-boats supporting this solution had never been substantiated, but Allied submarines in the Sea of Marmora did fuel each other. The Germans would build and use U-tankers ("milch cows") during WW II.

S-20 was modified with increased bow buoyancy and blisters for increased oil capacity. She is shown, slightly further modified, on 2 February 1944 off the Philadelphia Navy Yard.

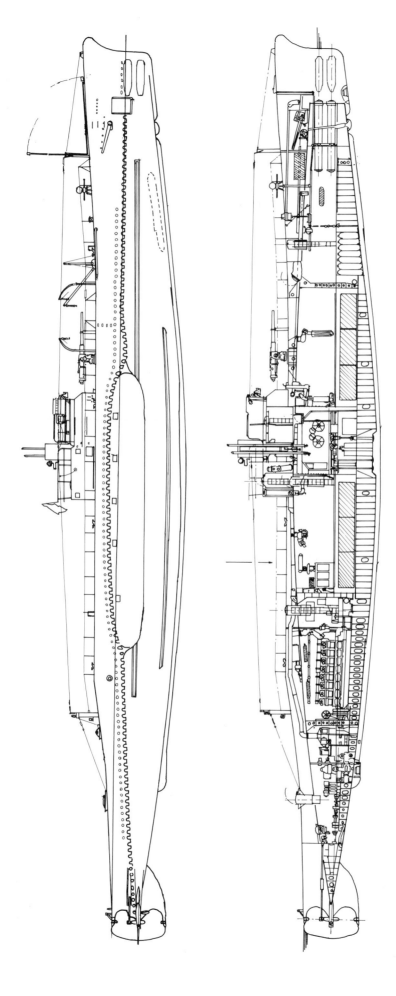

S-20 is shown as in February 1944, little changed during wartime. She had completed her safety refit in February 1932 (note the new escape hatch right aft). Unlike other boats modified for greater safety, she did not have her skeg cut all the way down. Modifications made at this time included: installation of salvage air connections in the superstructure; removal of the conning tower periscope; installation of a gyro repeater on the chariot bridge. She had already been drastically modified, between March 1924 and February 1925, with a new raked bow (something like that of the V-1 class) and shoulder blisters. The latter were similar in shape and placement to those the Germans later adopted for U-boats such as Type VII. Length increased to 222 ft 5$\frac{1}{4}$ in (displacement increased to 987.5/1,165 tons). Diving time increased from 90 to 106 seconds). The dashed lines forward indicate the former location of the MV passive sonar blister, removed in wartime. By February 1944, S-20 had been air-conditioned. Note too the venturi added to her bridge to shield personnel on it from the wind.

C&R estimated that one tanker the size of a cruiser submarine (V-5, described in chapter 9) could support three Portsmouth-type attack S-boats (radius of about 6,000 nm). After their transit together to the patrol area, the tanker would fuel them; the 6,000 nm radius would equate to 6–8 weeks on patrol. Afterward, the tanker would fuel them again for the long voyage home. The tanker would be about as fast as an S-boat (12 kt maximum, 9 kt sustained on the surface). C&R estimated that she would cost half as much as a cruiser submarine, about $1.6 million.[16]

The War Plans Division thought that the new tanker would be a valuable surprise weapon. An existing tanker, however, could not be kept secret in peacetime. The division therefore suggested that plans be drawn up but not implemented until an emergency arose. War Plans did fear that submarines would be unable to return home from the Western Pacific if their tanker was destroyed. This was prophetic: German U-boat operations in distant waters were badly disrupted when the "milch cows" were sunk.[17]

The following year (April 1926, the General Board rejected the tanker idea altogether. It preferred to lengthen the navy's design of double-hull S-boats (S-3–S-17, S-48–S-51) by 22 ft 6 in (later increased to 26 ft.)[18] This would add fuel stowage (for a radius of action of 10,000–11,000 nm) and, at the same time, provide the earlier units (S-3–S-9, S-14–S-17) with stern tubes. Modified bows would make them better sea boats. All but the MAN-engined S-10 through S-13 would be re-engined. The boats also would be repaired and modernized throughout. Displacement would increase to about 1,250 tons; greater length would so reduce wave-making resistance that little or no surface speed would be lost. Submerged speed and radius would suffer somewhat. C&R promised a new rudder that would prevent any increase in the already excessive turning circle. The estimated cost per boat, without re-engining, was $375,000–$500,000, compared with a price of about $2.5 million for a new 1,250-tonner. The single-hull S-boats were not worth modifying.

S-48 grounded, flooded, and suffered a battery fire in January 1925. Authorized repairs and alterations made her the General Board's prototype. Work began in February 1927 but was stopped by a lack of funds; it resumed in 1928, and she was recommissioned on 8 December 1928. She was lengthened by 25 ft 6 in, MAN engines were installed, and her displacement was increased to 1,165 tons.

The suspension of reconstruction work gave the Submarine Officers Conference a chance to comment on the General Board program. By this time (October 1927), the conference had already developed characteristics for a new generation of submarines. The General Board program competed with its plan to build really satisfactory boats. It seemed unlikely that reconstruction would cure the manifestly unsatisfactory S-boats; by then, each S-boat would be 7–10 years old. Remaining life would be little more than 2–5 years. Moreover, in the fall of 1927, it

seemed likely that rebuilding S-48 would cost at least $1,080,000; each rebuilt S-boat would cost up to half as much as a new submarine.

The submariners won. The General Board's failure to transform the short-range U.S. submarine fleet into a useful instrument for Pacific warfare led directly to construction of a new generation of relatively small submarines suitable for wartime mass production. The first of these was USS *Dolphin* (V-7).

S-4 was rammed on 17 December 1927 by the ex-destroyer (Coast Guard cutter) *Paulding* while surfacing from a submerged run off Provincetown, Cape Cod, Massachusetts. Divers heard signals from six men trapped in her forward torpedo room, but severe weather precluded their rescue. This disaster inspired a major inquiry and then a series of modifications to existing Holland (Electric Boat) S-boats. The most visible modification was an additional escape hatch in the motor room aft, to clear which the skeg had to be cut away. The safety modifications seem to have been applied to nearly all S-boats. However, plans to modify Electric Boat's O-boats and R-boats, seem to have been curtailed as boats were laid up and the Great Depression cut available funds. Many boats were modified only when they were recommissioned in 1940–41.[19]

From 1930 on, the London Naval Treaty forced the U.S. Navy to discard S-boats. The choices made at the time reflect preferences for the different types. Quoted in the FY 30 report of the C-in-C U.S. Fleet, the fleet submarine force commander commented that the "Holland" (Electric Boat) S-boats were limited in surface performance by their several critical speed ranges. After several months out of dock, engine RPM had to be cut materially to avoid exceeding safe engine cylinder pressures Weight growth was also a serious problem, particularly after the safety modifications had been made. For example, it turned out that an increase of 135 lb per cell (a total of 16,200 lb) in a new battery installed in S-26 limited her ability to dive in some circumstances. The safety modification program also badly disrupted a new operating schedule (which increased time between overhauls from 12 to 18 mo).

The following year, the submarine commander praised the double-hulled S-boats for their good MAN engines, their very reliable main motors, and their good seakeeping qualities. However, he had to admit that underwater they were very inferior to the "Holland" type, and that their hulls and superstructures were difficult to maintain. They were also troubled by chattering clutches, although BuEng thought that it had a modification which would solve that problem. The submarine commander rated doubled-hulled boats without MAN engines (the S-3 series) below O- and R-boats in military value.

In February 1930, with a 52,700 ton limit in sight, plans called for retaining all the Electric Boat S-boats, S-10 through S-17, and the rebuilt S-48. Lake's S-2 and the early C&R boats (S-3, S-6 through S-9) would all be stricken. Once the treaty was signed, S-2 and S-49 through S-51 were immediately stricken; the latter seem to have been particularly disliked. S-49, her valves welded shut so

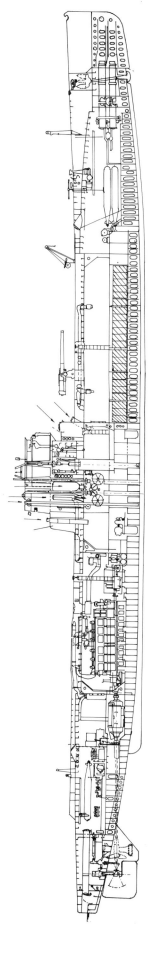

S-48 is shown as in 1922. Like the last series of Electric Boat S-boats, the last C&R boats, S-48 through S-51, were long enough to provide gun access hatches (arrowed; note the sloping tube of the ammunition scuttle crossing behind the hatch). From aft to forward (left to right), the arrowed tubes in the conning tower fairwater are the tube for the radio ratlines, the retractable mast, the main air exhaust, and the main air induction (between the periscopes). The batteries are shaded.

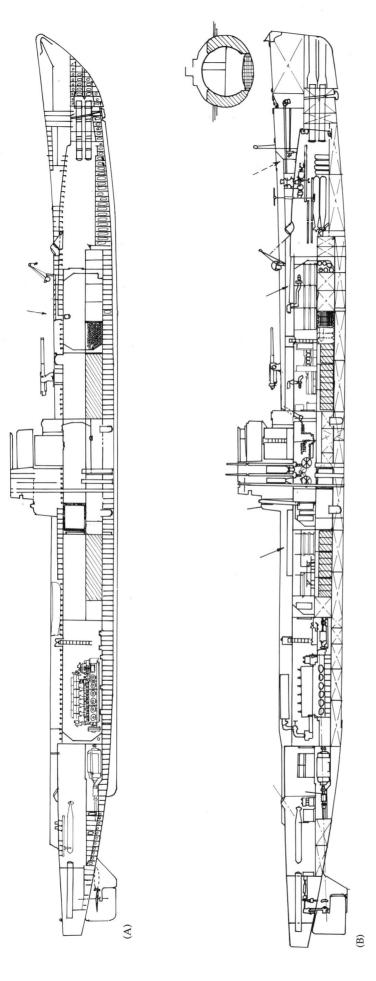

(A)

(B)

S-48 was completely rebuilt and rearranged. (A) shows the alterations planned in 1926, including a new sharply raked bow. Note that her battery has been rearranged, divided fore and aft. A new superstructure deck was planned to cover, for example, new boat stowage aft (the boat is shown). Small circles fill the 4-in magazine forward. The radio room (shown insulated) was abaft the control room, with crew's quarters abaft it, as well as forward of the officers' quarters forward of the control room. (B) shows her as reconditioned, with a less sharply raked bow. Reconstruction included redistribution of the battery (shaded for clarity), fore and aft of the control room, as in later submarines. Permanent buoyancy tanks were installed fore and aft (indicated by arrows) above the crew's quarters and just abaft the control room. The pump room was placed under the head just abaft the control room. Note that there was no separate maneuvering room aft, just a motor/engine room forward of the after torpedo room. Plans show a bulwark on either side forward, abaft a break in the deck, indicated by the dashed arrow. These drawings do not show the "down express" tank which so impressed fleet submarine skippers in the 1930s. S-48 was also air-conditioned during her big refit. The midships cross section (inset) shows the ballast tanks (shaded) and the fuel oil tank in the double bottom (cross-hatched). Above the main deck is the radio room opposite the crew's head. During World War II S-48 tested a passive triangulation sonar, among other equipment.

S-48 was the prototype for an abortive reconstruction of the "government" (C&R) double-hulled S-boats.

that she could not dive, survived at least until 1940 as an exhibition ship, initially at the 1933 Chicago World's Fair.

An August 1934 evaluation showed the S-1 group as equal to or better than S-14 in all qualities except radius. The later Electric Boat series (S-42 group), the newest of the S-boats, was considered equal to or superior to the S-1 series. Of the C&R boats, the S-10 series was criticized for its speed, radius, habitability, and poor maneuverability. The S-14 group had better surface radius. S-48 was disappointing; it was considered less valuable than S-14, despite its extra torpedo tube. The evaluation stated: "characteristics were not compatible with the large displacement." Inspections of double-hull C&R boats were beginning to show serious corrosion problems, particularly in narrow compartments toward the ends, which were not accessible in ordinary overhauls. Keeping them in service would require expensive refits; money was tight, so these boats had to be taken out of service. A list of boats in order of decommissioning showed S-48 first, then the S-14 and S-10 groups, and only then the Electric Boat (Holland) S-boats. Later that year the CNO moved up S-1 to be decommissioned with the first series of C&R boats, presumably because of her advanced age.[20] C&R developed a 5-year life-extension refit for the single-hull boats that had to be retained somewhat beyond their statutory age as the result of a lagging new-construction program.

O, R, and S class submarines recommissioned and reconditioned, mainly at Philadelphia, in 1940, had the safety modifications completed where that had not already been done. All boats that did not already have them re-

ceived two messenger buoys, fore and aft. Many boats had JK high-frequency passive sonars placed atop their old SC-tubes forward, to form a combination low- and high-frequency passive set.

Not surprisingly, only the Electric Boat S-boats were considered suitable for overseas work when war broke out. In August 1941 the British asked specifically for 18 of them; they rated the R-boats next and the government S-boats last.[21]

The Electric Boat S-boats often fought over ranges longer than their designers had envisaged. Of this group only the experimental S-20 remained in U.S. waters throughout the war. At the outbreak of war, six Electric Boat craft (S-36–S41), were serving with the Asiatic Fleet. As the Japanese overran the Philippines, they ran south and joined the six boats of SubDiv 53 (S-42–S-47) to form TF 42, assigned to attack Japanese shipping trying to pass south through the Bismarck Archipelago. Other S-boats (S-18, S-23, S-27, S-28, S-31–S-35) served in the Aleutians and the North Pacific, surely one of the war's worst submarine operating areas. Typically, the S-boats ran war patrols with fuel oil in their main ballast tanks and reserve lubricating oil in certain fuel tanks, for a total of about 42,000 gal of fuel and 3,000 gal of lubricating oil (maximum cruising range of about 7,000 nm compared with 2600 nm using normal tankage). By 1944, reserve fuel oil tanks were badly corroded, and reserve lubricating oil tanks were developing numerous leaks. Senior officers complained that continued use of ballast tanks for fuel oil would make it practically impossible to stop their leaks, nor could fuel oil be prevented from leaking into reserve lubricating oil tanks. By this time, the surviving S-boats had been largely

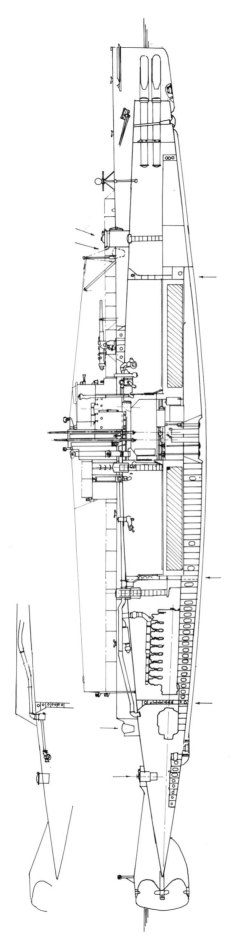

S-22 is shown after a refit at Philadelphia, June 1941. She had already been modified for greater safety (completed at Portsmouth in November 1929), with special escape hatches fore and aft, and with two marker buoys (the forward buoy, nearly abeam the forward escape hatch, is shown in dashed lines). The scrap view shows the after end of S-34 as it was in April 1932, after her safety refit. Boats differed slightly in the way their skegs were cut down aft. On deck forward note that a JK passive sonar was installed on top of the older SC; many boats had this modification either during the late 1930s or as refitted for war service. Many, but not all, "Holland" S-boats were refitted for increased safety from 1929 on. Other boats were refitted in 1940–41, many at Philadelphia.

Photographed in May 1942, R-12 shows few changes since completion. On deck she shows a high-frequency JK atop her original low-frequency SC tube, a common prewar and wartime combination in old submarines. The original flat JK transducer could not operate above about 5 kts. NRL developed the 19-in spherical cover (shown here) to reduce turbulence, roughly doubling maximum sonar speed. The acoustic window was a new substance, Rho-C rubber. Many submarines had QB and JK back to back in the same spherical dome: JK was used for initial (passive) detection, QB for localizing the target with a single ping to determine range. Many submarines later had QC instead of QB back-to-back with JK (others had QC back-to-back with QB). Wartime tests of experimental JPs (sonic rather than supersonic passive sonars) in six R-boats showed that they were superior to JKs. JPs were also added to JK/QB in several S-boats. The platform abaft the bridge was soon enlarged to take a 20-mm gun. The 4 in/50 deck guns were later removed.

S-45 is shown in San Francisco harbor, 21 October 1943.

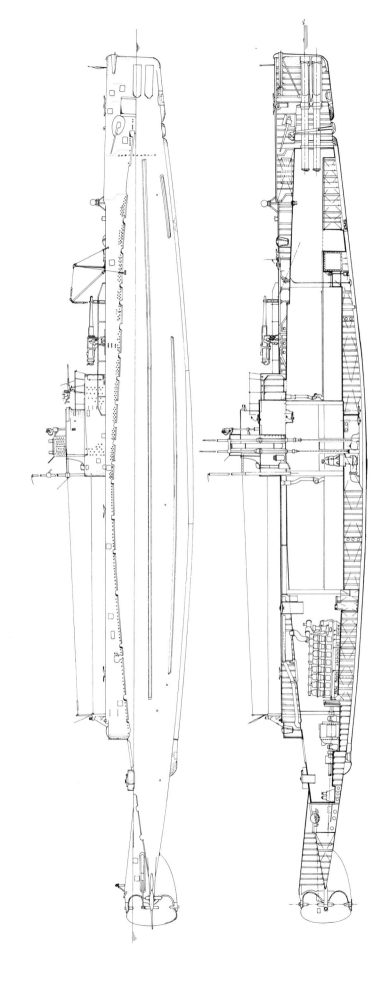

S-44 was one of six Electric Boat S-boats extensively modernized during World War II. The refit included installation of air conditioning, with the unit installed in the crew space abaft the control room, alongside the refrigerator. S-44 was fitted with radar (SJ forward, SD abaft the bridge), a loop antenna built into the periscope shears for underwater reception, and a free-flooding structure carrying a 20-mm antiaircraft gun, with a box for 4-in ready-service ammunition below it. A JK passive sonar, probably installed at Philadelphia during a refit between November and December 1941, was located on the forward deck. On the keel below it was a pair of echo oscillators. Although the plan from which this drawing was made shows the strip of an MV sonic array, the inboard part of this equipment apparently did not survive into World War II; the only inboard equipment shown is a JK control in the torpedo room. Marker buoys were emplaced in the deck forward (just abaft the JK) and aft (at the end of her cut-down superstructure). A new radio transmitting/receiving wire antenna was rigged from the bridge to a flag staff aft. All of the last group of Electric Boat S-boats were modernized: S-42 at Philadelphia, March–June 1943; S-43 at Mare Island, September 1943–February 1944; S-44 at Philadelphia Navy Yard, April–June 1943; S-45 at Mare Island, June–November 1943; S-46 at Philadelphia, April–June 1943; and S-47 at Philadelphia Navy Yard, May–September 1943). All but S-44, which was lost in October 1943, were rearmed with 3-in/50 dual-purpose guns in place of their 4-inchers (S-43 and S-47 were probably completed with 3-in/50s). S-42 and S-46 were equipped with Mk 14 torpedo directors, a modification also extended to many R-boats. (Jim Christley)

8

World War I

WORLD WAR I shocked U.S. submariners. Before the United States entered the war in April 1917, the U.S. Navy generally had considered itself quite up to date. It then learned that it had no idea of just how much naval warfare had changed since 1914. The surface fleet was far behind the Royal Navy in gunnery. Submariners discovered how little they knew about attacking surface ships. A submariner reported, however, that "in general knowledge of the boat, and handling thereof submerged, [the British] are our inferiors. Our enlisted personnel is superior to the British in natural ability and in training."[1]

Particularly in European waters, submariners found a radically different environment, in which they were the hunted as well as the hunters. A submarine was constantly at risk from patrolling ships, aircraft, and other submarines. Nominally friendly forces were sufficiently trigger-happy to attack any submarine they saw. Mines, nets, and other obstacles easily snared such projections as the fixed (nonhousing) periscopes of prewar U.S. submarines. Submarines had to be fitted with jumper cables to push nets and, to some extent, mine cables over such fixed and essential obstructions as bridges and deck guns.

Prewar submariners had imagined that, except quite near their targets, submarines would enjoy a benign environment and run mainly on the surface, day and night. Now, a submarine might encounter ASW forces anywhere. She still had to run on the surface to make good distance; if anything, surface sea-keeping had become more important. It was no longer worth sacrificing to high submerged speed. The greatest surprise was that a submarine always had to be ready to submerge instantly (crash-dive) upon the appearance either of ASW forces or of her targets. The prewar collapsible bridge and streamlined fairwater gave way to a permanent chariot bridge, despite its increased underwater resistance. Collapsible ventila-

tors and lifelines had to be made permanent, whatever their cost in underwater drag.

In prewar U.S. peacetime cruising (light) condition, all ballast tanks were empty and the collapsible cruising bridge, which took at least 20 min to stow, was rigged. Prewar expectations were that, in wartime, submarines would run awash. The fore and aft trim tanks and two smaller tanks (auxiliary and adjusting) were filled with just enough ballast to place the boat in diving trim when the main tanks were filled. The conning tower hatch was open and the radio rigged. It would take 5 min to trim the boat to submerged condition (ready to dive, but with a small reserve of buoyancy). Even then, K-boats averaged 1 min 48 sec and L-boats, 2 min 23 sec.

Now it was generally accepted that boats had to crash-dive in less than a minute; they always ran virtually rigged to dive. The U.S. Navy adopted the British and German practice of "riding the vents": the main ballast tank Kingstons were left open and the tanks kept empty only by the air in them. When the air vents at their tops were opened, the air left and the tanks quickly filled. Crash-diving also required more vent (limber) holes in the floodable superstructure to let air out quickly as the boat dived. Like the chariot bridge, they added underwater resistance. Even quick (not crash) diving from normal cruising condition required that the main ballast tank Kingstons be large enough to flood the tanks in half a minute. It turned out that ballast tanks sometimes trapped air and thus could not be flooded quickly enough, no matter how large the Kingstons were.

U.S. submarines were too thinly manned to crash-dive.[2] They needed a klaxon or hooter. The CO of K-4, operating in home waters, reported that he often crash-dived to 100 ft, the limit of the sea pressure gauge. Sailors became nervous as the gauge reached its limit; the CO wanted gauges calibrated well beyond test depth, so that

During World War I, the U.S. Navy conducted a highly successful crash program to develop passive sonars. The upper photograph shows the three rubber rats of a Y tube; the lower, the paired rubber bulbs of an SC tube. The rubber-diaphragm rats, so named for their appearance, could house a variety of sensors. Because they were not tuned to a narrow resonant frequency, they could sense signal details useful for target classification (contemporary British hydrophones were narrowly tuned).

Both the SC tube and rats were devised in 1917. Rats were also used in the first towed line array, the U-3 Eel (24 rats with carbon-button microphones). In 1918 it was used in conjunction with an MV hull array for triangulation ranging. Work on steered passive arrays ended in 1923 with a decision to concentrate on active high-frequency ("supersonic") sonar, although an electro-acoustic version of the SC-tube did appear in 1928 (but it did not enter production).

These photographs were taken aboard H-5 at San Pedro, California, about 1919.

a crash dive would not cause the gauge to reach more than halfway. The gauge had sufficed prewar, when typical operating depth was about 60 ft.

Long underwater endurance at low speed was increasingly important. Much of the battery capacity had to be saved for escape from the inevitable counterattack *after* firing torpedoes. A submarine might escape after dark to recharge batteries only after waiting out a depth charge attack. The prewar U.S. Navy had seen little need for minimum speed/maximum endurance. It did test each submarine's two batteries (banks of cells) both in series (for maximum power) and in parallel (for endurance). The British went one step further. About 1905–06, they introduced a "half-switch," by means of which they could switch half of each battery (one-quarter of the total number of cells) from series to parallel, for even lower power and longer endurance. The standard WW I British submarine type, the E-boat, had four separate batteries, which could be wired in series or grouped in parallel in pairs or fours. Apparently, the U.S. Navy first became aware of the idea when its officers observed the H-boats being built for Britain; they had been modified in accord with Admiralty practice. U.S. submarine batteries, however, were never wired in British fashion. In U.S. parlance, a half-switch was used to switch auxiliaries from series to parallel. It does seem significant that, during WW I, U.S. submarine characteristics changed to call specifically for long sub-

merged endurance at low speed. The S-boats needed what would later be considered excessive battery capacity to achieve reasonable endurance at what amounted to high minimum underwater speed. Their successors, more efficient at low speed, could make do with smaller battery capacity.[3]

Submerged, a boat was nearly as much at risk from a small surface craft carrying a depth charge as from a much larger destroyer, whose weapon was the same type of depth charge (and which, until 1917, did not even carry more of them). It might be better to surface and shoot it out with a small sub-chaser, which made guns useful in a way completely unsuspected before the war. Postwar guns were associated with attacks on merchant ships; surprise torpedoing in U-boat style was considered illegal under international law.

Wartime experience confirmed the submariners' prewar suspicions that U.S. submarines were far too small. C&R considered the H-boat an object lesson in insufficient size. It was already at the weight limit before wartime necessities, such as a chariot bridge, ventilation for the torpedo room, oscillator, and gyrocompass, had been installed. In 1918, unfortunately, it seemed that the H-boat, already in series production, was the only type the U.S. Navy could obtain within a reasonable time. Advocates claimed that the British liked their H-boats, but U.S. submariners suggested that they were only making the best

World War I taught the U.S. Navy to order submarine priorities differently. At Berehaven, Ireland, in 1918 L-1 displays her disappearing-mount 3 in/23 gun. The battleship *Nevada* is in the background.

of what they had.[4] The H-boat was not unique; Lake's L-boats were overloaded before they had been in commission for a month.

War experience thus justified the jump to the S-boat, the only type with sufficient space and weight margin to provide current necessities and to allow for future (meaning, in wartime, near-term) growth. Emory S. Land, C&R's submarine expert, felt that the 800-tonner was further vindicated by the sizes of typical British and German submarines. For example, not only had the Germans gone to 800 tons in their oceangoing U-boats, but their smaller UB-boats and UC-boats, although designed for the North Sea, had grown to about 800 tons during the war.[5]

It was finally possible to compare the Lake and Electric Boat designs. Prior to the R class, Lake's submarines had midships hydroplanes. A 1918 official report described them as an unnecessary complication, less effective than bow planes, which quickly shoved the bow up or down; also, they could not be powered.[6] Lake had not appreciated the vital wartime need for crash dives and quick depth changes; his emphasis on safety through even-keel diving was no longer appropriate. His other trademark feature, a watertight superstructure, added too much top weight and thus cost too much stability. It flooded too slowly for quick dives. Submarines did need more buoyancy for surface running, but Lake provided it in the wrong place, amidships instead of forward. Postwar Lake O-boats and R-boats dived too slowly (typically in 90 sec, rather than the desired 60 sec). Their open motors were too low in the bilges and thus became oil- and water-soaked too easily; their armatures were too weak. The R-boats had weak engine foundations.[7]

The war demonstrated strategic roles and modes of operation that the U.S. Navy had not previously explored. To the interwar U.S. Navy, probably the most interesting strategy was pre-positioning of submarines off an enemy base. British submarines were stationed in the North Sea to report German fleet movements; they were forbidden to attack outbound warships before they had reported by radio but could attack inbound ships at once.[8] The Germans were more interested in attacks in support of their fleet, which they tried before and after Jutland and in connection with their unsuccessful sortie in August 1916.[9]

After the war, U.S. submariners considered forward submarine operations far more valuable than direct support of the battle fleet. The General Board disagreed; in 1919–20, the planners (now in OpNav) and the OpNav submarine officers led by Captain Hart fought what they saw as the General Board's Atlantic-oriented fleet submarine, which was optimized for surface speed at the expense of range and torpedo armament. Subsequent "fleet" boats were the forward-operations types favored by the submariners and by the OpNav Plans Division. Speed was desirable but somewhat optional; long range was vital. The roots of this shift are to be found in the perceived experience of WW I.

A second vivid wartime experience was unrestricted submarine warfare against trade. As understood in 1914, the rules of war required a blockading warship to stop a merchant ship, search her for contraband, and then either seize her or place her passengers and crew in a place of safety before sinking her. The British countered blockading U-boats with Q-ships, warships masquerading as merchant ships, which could sink a surfaced U-boat. As the Germans became more desperate, attacks on Allied seaborne trade seemed more and more attractive. In February 1917, they began an "unrestricted" submarine campaign, in which U-boats, mainly submerged, attacked without warning. This soon caused a crisis in Britain, but it also helped to bring the United States, perhaps the deciding factor, into the war.[10]

The postwar U.S. Navy knew that Japan, the most likely future enemy, depended quite as much as Britain on its overseas trade. In 1919–20, some U.S. submariners argued that the wartime German submarine campaign had been far less destructive and potentially far more decisive than the horrible land war. Because the U.S. government had entered the war partly because of revulsion against that unrestricted submarine campaign, it could not adopt this same policy.[11] American officers wondered whether Germany's campaign had been a fatal error. Would a U.S. unrestricted campaign against Japan bring a neutral Britain, her merchant ships prominent among the targets, into a future war? Some argued that convoys had defeated the German trade offensive and would similarly defeat any U.S. offensive.

The U.S. Navy was impressed by the sheer size of the Allied force tied down by the U-boats. A few long-range U-cruisers operating off the U.S. East Coast in 1918 had forced the Allies to provide convoy escorts far outside the U-boats' normal European operating area. The U.S. Navy found it difficult to transfer all of its ASW craft, including submarines, to European waters. Long operating range and endurance were the keys. By the spring of 1915, a U-boat had traveled to Constantinople, Turkey, from Wilhelmshaven, Germany, a distance of 3,450 nm. A year later, U-53 made it all the way to Newport, Rhode Island, and back, about 7000 nm, but she could not spend any time on the U.S. coast. After the war, the Germans claimed that their first U-cruiser, U-139, made one cruise lasting 6 mo.

Allied submarines hunted U-boats. From 1915 on, British submarines were sent into German-controlled waters to intercept U-boats transiting on the surface to their patrol areas. Late in 1916, British submarine strategy changed. The Admiralty sent submarines into the North Sea on U-boat patrol.[12] They also patrolled the English Channel, the west coast of France, and the Irish Sea; eventually, the southwest coast of Ireland and the southern entrance to the Irish Sea were left to U.S. submarines. Code breaking and radio direction finding indicated current areas of U-boat operation; by early 1917, the Admiralty knew that its patrols were forcing the U-boats to move. Submarines were assigned patrol lines, each about 30 nm long, in these areas. Around southern Ireland and in the Irish Sea, these lines typically ran from inshore to about 100 nm offshore.[13]

At the end of the war, British submarines were credited with sinking 19 or 20 U-boats. In June 1917, a U.S. officer reported that submarines had cut a U-boat's average daily advance from 200 nm to about 5 nm in patrolled areas. Because total days at sea were limited, the effectiveness of the U-boats was much reduced. Postwar, U-boat commander Adm. Andreas Michelsen considered submarine attack the most unsettling Allied ASW measure. It could occur at any time, whether or not the U-boat was attacking targets. The work was dangerous on both sides: British destroyers were specifically instructed not to try to distinguish friendly from enemy submarines before attacking.

In May 1917, Lt. L. D. Causey, CO of SubDiv 4 (K-boats), made the first U.S. proposal for ASW submarine operations. Rejected as unrealistic, his blockade of U-boat bases opened the issue. By the end of June 1917, there was considerable interest in sending submarines to operate along the Irish Coast. After consulting British Admirals Jellicoe and Beatty, Adm. William S. Sims (CinC of U.S. Naval Forces in European Waters) asked that a second submarine division be based in the Azores.[14] On 2 July, CinC Atlantic Fleet was ordered to designate 12 submarines for European service; they would sail on 15 August.

Admiral Grant (SubLant) wanted submarines assigned to European waters to have housing periscopes and oscillators for communication. They should be able to crash-dive in a minute or less. Ideally, they also would have guns. Reliable and economical engines were necessary; the submarines had to cross the ocean on their own power and carry their own fuel supply because they could not fuel at sea. No U.S. submarines were completely qualified (none could dive fast enough). None of the boats' periscopes housed. Only the L-boats had guns (L-9 and above; guns were then being installed at Philadelphia in the first 4 Electric Boat L-boats. Both classes were powered by unreliable 2-cycle diesels. The other diesel boats, F and H classes, were all in the Pacific. The D-boats and E-1 were training submariners (who would be needed for new boats) at New London. L-11 was running important sound (detection) tests off Nahant, Massachusetts. Grant wanted to wait for the much better O-boats, but the war situation was far too urgent. On 15 August, the Navy Department formally decided to send a submarine flotilla to Europe (10 K-boats and L-boats; E-1 and L-11 were added on 1 September): SubDiv 4 (*Tonopah*, K-1, K-2, K-5, K-6, E-1) and SubDiv 5 (*Bushnell*, L-1, L-2, L-3, L-4, L-9, L-10, L-11). SubDiv 4 would operate from the Azores (with the monitor *Tonopah* providing local defense with her heavy guns); SubDiv 5 would patrol the Irish Sea from Bantry Bay. The submarines would be towed across the Atlantic to spare their machinery, so they would be ready to operate on arrival.

Bushnell, K-2, K-5, and K-6 left Philadelphia for New London on 7 October, 1917. K-5's engines broke down 3 mi out, and she had to be taken in tow. K-1 joined from New York Navy Yard on 9 October; her engines had been hurriedly rebuilt. By the end of the long voyage, she was considered the least reliable of the group. At Provincetown, Massachusetts, the group met the old cruiser *Chicago*, flagship of the Submarine Force. She and

Bushnell each took two K-boats in tow for the run to Halifax, Nova Scotia. Towing proved difficult, but boats trying to proceed on their own experienced severe engine problems. For example, a scavenger-receiver explosion knocked out one of K-2's engines for 3 days. K-1 arrived at Halifax with both engines disabled after a 520-mi run. Hardly equipped for European conditions and partly stripped (four torpedoes were taken from K-2), the K-boats were already badly overweight when full of fuel and oil. SubDiv 4 had a quiet war in the Azores, partly because, as Grant had suspected, the K-boats were quite unreliable. Admiral Sims soon wanted them replaced.

The next group (the L-boats and E-1 towed by *Bushnell* and two tugs) left Newport on 4 December for Ponta Delgada in the Azores. It hit a hurricane and had to make for Bermuda. Submarine gyrocompasses, always unreliable in a storm, gave the wrong headings. No one could remain on the bridges; all hands had to go below and trust that the boats would not collide. *Bushnell*, one tug, and two submarines made Bermuda 48 hours after the storm passed. Another boat arrived the next day. Several days later, one tug and one submarine arrived in Boston, and one tug and four submarines arrived in the Azores, but only after some had again met heavy weather. *Bushnell*, with one tug and six submarines, left the Azores for Queenstown, Ireland, on 19 January and met another gale; one submarine returned to the Azores. On 27 January, *Bushnell*, a tug, and four submarines arrived at Queenstown. One submarine arrived separately at Bantry Bay. By this time, another group was en route from the United States.

SubDiv 5's L-boats were renamed AL-boats to distinguish them from the altogether unrelated British L class.[15] The first two U.S. submarines left for patrol on 5 March and the British soon left Bantry Bay entirely to the U.S. force. Three of the seven U.S. submarines were sent out to patrol billets (patrol lines) every 8 days, allowing one a double rest for repairs.[16] A boat generally patrolled a billet with her periscope raised. If weather was so rough that she could not maintain periscope depth, she cruised at 60 ft, stopping occasionally to listen and sometimes porpoising to the surface to sweep with her periscope. Whenever propellers were heard, the boat prepared to fire and came to periscope depth. SubLant ordered all submarines to carry four ready torpedoes in their tubes, three set for 8 ft (i.e., for a surfaced U-boat) and one for 18 ft (i.e., for a U-boat at periscope depth).

Battery capacity sufficed for submerged runs on the longest summer days, but air became quite stale. Air purifiers (fans blowing air over chemicals, which had not existed in the prewar navy) had to be turned on, and sometimes oxygen had to be released. The water outside was cool enough to condense moisture; a SubDiv 5 war diarist recalled a gentle internal rain that fell into soup plates and men's eyes after about 4 hr submerged. Although allowed, smoking was unpopular because tobacco became sticky and there was not enough oxygen to support full combustion. The U.S. Navy lacked two essentials for prolonged navigation underwater: a good gyrocompass and

A row of L-boats in Irish waters displays the most important war modifications: the permanent open chariot bridge and retractable (housing) periscopes. Note also the deck recognition markings on L-4 and L-10 (all of the boats were marked in an AL series to distinguish them from the British L-class). L-10 shows three fixed-spot hydrophones forward, presumably comprising a K tube.

a depth sounder; the British had both. Nor did its heads work at depth; the British ones did.

Although SubDiv 5 spotted several U-boats, it sank none. AL-11 fired two torpedoes in rapid succession at a surfaced U-boat, but one exploded prematurely 100 yd short and apparently damaged the other. It seemed that she would have done better to fire a full four-torpedo salvo. On the other hand, AL-1 missed ahead by 1–2 yd with her first half-salvo, then also missed with the other half-salvo fired slightly later. On their first contacts with U-boats, AL-1, AL-4, and AL-11 all failed to fire full spreads, presumably because of torpedo tube problems.

AL-4 once spotted a U-boat in the mist. It crash-dived and immediately put up a periscope to take a shot. AL-4 also crash-dived and the crew heard the whine of a torpedo passing overhead. Near the Fastnet, a lookout aboard AL-2 spotted a periscope on the port bow, and a torpedo (set deep) was prepared for firing. Suddenly, there was a large violent explosion about 80 yd on the starboard quarter, with 5 ft of periscope visible. AL-2 crash-dived. When submerged and stopped level, she heard submarine propellers spinning rapidly and the call letters J-U-B on the typical German underwater signal set (from another direction). The propellers were interpreted as a damaged submarine trying to drive herself to the surface. It appeared that a single U-boat, trying to torpedo AL-2, had torpedoed herself, but it was also possible that the U-boat had been mined. The underwater signal had suggested that two U-boats were present. After a time, AL-2 tried to simulate the German oscillator signal and got no reply. UB-65 was lost about there that day.

By the end of the war, each SubDiv 5 boat had been attacked at least twice by destroyers and patrol craft.[17] Recognition (IFF) signals and even displaying the flag did not help at all. Presumably, the general view that the U-boats were pirates outside the normal laws of warfare contributed to such attitudes.

Wartime expansion of the submarine force presented real dangers. Running at 25 ft on 18 May 1918, AL-4 became slightly heavy, either because of a change in water density or leakage. The officer of the watch decided to blow (rather than pump) 1,000 lb from the adjusting tank. Unfortunately, the man at the valve had been assigned to AL-4 for only a few days; this was his third dive.[18] He opened the Kingston of the similarly named auxiliary tank. The officer of the watch decided to speed up (to increase the effect of the planes). Only then did the man at the planes call out that the boat was settling fast, having reached 75 ft. The officer of the watch tried to use the planes to recover, but the boat already had too much momentum. She stuck on the soft bottom at 284 ft (keel at 294 ft), well below test depth.

Hearing the motors speed up, the CO entered the operating compartment. By the time he had arrived, AL-4 was already on the bottom. Working against the water pressure, the main pumps kept blowing their fuses. An unsuccessful attempt to blow the adjusting tank wasted much of the compressed air. The stern glands and then the main circulating valves began to leak; water eventually rose to within 4 in of the motors. The crew tried going ahead with the rudder hard over, but the boat would not swing more than 3 degrees either way. Finally, all hands

Prewar U.S. submarine bridges were very small to limit underwater drag. With her enlarged chariot bridge, L-3 contrasts with the more streamlined L-9 (which was less suited to protracted surface runs). (*Burnell Poole Collection*)

were mustered aft, the motors were started ahead, and air pressure was put on the bow ballast tank. AL-4 had been resting at a slight up angle (about 2½ degrees). Her bow began to rise, but she did not break free until she reached about 6 degrees. Then she started up quickly at an up angle of about 50 degrees. She reached the surface after having been down 1 hr 10 min.

Her CO was impressed with how well AL-4 had stood up to severe punishment. The after bulkhead of the main ballast tanks, which was also the forward bulkhead of the forward battery tank, was designed to take 90 lb of pressure but stood 140 lb. Had it leaked, the battery would have failed and the boat could not have made it off the bottom. The CO wanted at least one pump usable against 150 lb of pressure.[19] He considered the bow ballast tank too small and wanted it blowable against substantial pressure. With that, he could have raised the bow instantly and quickly brought AL-4 off the bottom, or even counteracted the downward momentum in the first place.

In the spring of 1918, Admiral Sims urged that U.S. submarines be deployed to counter U-cruisers now operating along the U.S. Atlantic Coast. Unlike U-boats in European waters, U-cruisers could not afford to expend a torpedo on each ship they attacked because they were so far from home and reloads. When they surfaced to use their guns, they exposed themselves to counterattack. In June 1918, the commander of SubDiv 8 suggested that his submarines be assigned to ocean escort duty, either with

convoys or with individual ships; O-4 was the first submarine so assigned. Convoy work was abandoned after a merchant ship in convoy and later the destroyer *Paul Jones* fired at O-6.

The U.S. Navy then tried Q-ships, including schooners accompanied by one or two submarines.[20] As of 1 September 1918, three schooners, *Charles Whittemore* (SP-3232), *Helvetia* (SP-3096), and *Arabia* (SP-3434), were assigned to SubDiv 7 and one, *Robert H. McCurdy* (SP-3157), to SubDiv 8. *Whittemore* was later transferred to SubDiv 6. *Arabia* operated with N 1. While patrolling once with E-2 (L-5 operated independently), *Helvetia* very nearly caught U-117, but her lookouts did not react in time; her CO was relieved for this failure. She made a second patrol with N-6 and a third with E-2. *McCurdy* made two patrols, one with O-3 and O-5, one with O-3 and O-8. *Whittemore* patrolled with N-5 (N-6 was also to have gone, but her steering gear jammed and N-5 rammed her) and then with L-6. She was later assigned to Ponta Delgaga in company with L-8, but the war ended before she could go. *Helvetia*, M-1, and K-5 were to have operated from Bermuda.

These operations demonstrated the very limited endurance of the coastal submarines. In theory, patrols were limited only by the schooner's capacity for battery water (140 gal, 35 days in the case of *McCurdy*) and submarine fuel (7,100 gal). Submarines were towed both surfaced and submerged, the latter at 2.5–5.0 kt with their bows light to compensate for the weight of the towline. The schooner transferred fresh and battery water, but it did not fuel the submarines and submarine crew members could not transfer to the schooner to rest.

All East Coast submarines conducted ASW patrols.[21]

The wartime U.S. submarine force learned most of its lessons through SubDiv 5, which operated very closely with the Royal Navy. The British taught an entirely new way of operating. The CO had to be free to concentrate on the attack. Many early dummy attacks (approaches) by AL-boats in Bantry Bay failed because COs were at the diving gauge "juggling water," rather than at the periscope. In the Royal Navy, the CO concentrated on bringing the boat into firing position without being discovered. The navigator assisted him in plotting bearings, picking out deflections, and so on. A diving officer, usually the "sub" or executive officer (XO), maintained depth at the speed set by the CO. He was responsible for the readiness of the tubes. Postwar U.S. submariners adopted the division of responsibility between CO and XO.

The British taught the AL-boat crews a simpler way of underwater control: the planesmen worked independently except in crash dives or surfacings. The bow planesman controlled depth (observing the needle on the depth gauge). The stern man controlled the angle of the boat (observing the bubble that indicated angle). This technique eliminated that previously all-important diving rudder (i.e., plane) "expert." The separation of the planesmen's roles became a standard U.S. postwar practice.

The British taught the U.S. Navy attack tactics. They had perfected the Attack Teacher to train students and to analyze the elements of an attack. Immediately copied by the U.S. Navy, this system uses a periscope and small movable model ships. The models move as actual ships would seem to move when seen from a submarine following the student's course orders. The student's course is automatically plotted with that of the ships represented by the models. The success or failure of torpedo attacks ordered by the student is immediately evident. British students typically spent 3–4 wk (about 75 attacks) at the Attack Teacher.[22]

At the beginning of an approach, a submarine ran in to determine her bearing on the target's bow and also which bow she was on. She might find herself very nearly dead ahead of the target (very fine on the target's bow), in which case the target's bearing was very nearly its course. Otherwise, the submarine took up an approach course about 90 degrees from the target bearing. Students soon learned to estimate the angle on the bow (the angle between the target course and the observer's line of sight) from the appearance of the models in the Attack Teacher. The smaller (sharper) the angle, the easier it was to estimate (students typically overestimated at first). The British developed the Nasmith Director to help estimate the target's course; the U.S. Navy called it a course finder.[23]

A single periscope observation gave a bearing and estimates of target course (based on angle on the bow), range, and speed (based on the size of the bow wave). No submarine would keep the periscope up very long, so the approach and attack had to be based on a series of brief observations. (The prewar U.S. Navy assumed that it could keep the periscope up continuously for much of the approach.) Given very approximate data, the submarine CO had to lead the target to allow for the relatively low speed of the torpedo compared with that of the target. The Attack Teacher showed how to do so.

The way bearing changed over time (constant, closing, opening) indicated the relative speeds and courses of target and submarine. A constant bearing indicated a collision course: the submarine could slow to avoid coming too close. If the bearing did not then begin to open, the submarine was too close and had to turn onto a parallel course. If the bearing was opening, the submarine had to speed up; if it was closing, she had to slow down. If the submarine had been running parallel, turned on to the expected firing course, and found the bearing opening, she had to turn toward the target to get the appropriate deflection (lead angle).

The British learned to concentrate on the track angle, the angle between the target's bow and the course of a torpedo successfully fired at it (the Germans developed the same idea independently). Unlike deflection angle (the angle between submarine and target course), track angle did not change over the course of the attack.[24] Given the appropriate track angle, the submarine CO could work out the proper deflection and course. A track angle about 20 degrees abaft the target beam (110 degrees) was best if target speed, but not course, was known. When course and speed were both only approximately known, 100 degrees was best. Firing from abaft the beam minimized the target's chance of detecting the submarine. Targets found it most difficult to evade torpedoes fired from nearly abeam. Prewar U.S. submariners expecting fast targets preferred advancing shots (track angle, 50–70 degrees). They compensated best for errors in estimating target speed and allowed the submarine to fire earlier, hence reducing her chance of discovery. The tighter the track angle, however, the greater the chance of counterattack. War experience showed that less than 70 degrees was quite dangerous. Retiring shots (at broad [greater than 90 degrees] track angles, i.e., from abaft the beam) gave the target less chance to ram, better compensated for errors in estimating target course (and for target evasive maneuvers), and made escape easier. The British favored them for ASW, but Captain Hart suspected that to attack fast targets they would have been forced to use advancing shots.

The British used an elaborately calculated, but essentially static, set-up for each attack. The CO had to get into attack position in order to fire. Any last-minute maneuver by the target (e.g., a zigzag) would spoil the attack. The U.S. Navy enjoyed some additional flexibility. By 1918, its torpedoes could be angled; the submarine did not have to turn all the way toward her target. The firing solution had to take into account the torpedo's relatively slow turn: it advanced about 150 yd along the submarine's track before completing its turn toward the target. British torpedoes could not be angled.[25]

U.S. submariners considered British torpedoes more reliable than their own. They could be set either for the usual short-range, high-speed run or for long range at lower speed.[26] It seemed unlikely that U.S. turbine torpedoes could be designed for more than one setting (BuOrd solved this problem postwar). The advent of the British 21-in submarine torpedo in 1917 (44.5 kt to 2,500 yd or 35 kt to 4,200 yd) helped support the submariners' demand that the United States switch from an 18-in torpedo to the larger caliber.

Perhaps the most important wartime Allied innovation in submarine technology was listening gear (passive low-frequency sonar). In April 1917, only the British and French had it; however, the U.S. government conducted a very successful crash program. The Submarine Signal Co. (now a division of Raytheon Corp.) already made underwater bells and oscillators for signaling. Along with General Electric and Western Electric, the company established a joint experimental station at Nahant; later, the Navy established a laboratory (now Naval Undersea Systems) at New London. Work initially focused on the new 110-ft subchasers, but it was soon discovered that a submarine was a better acoustic platform.

Nahant developed the Coolidge tube (C-tube) a pair of 3-in rubber spheres at each end of a 5-ft T-pipe, which could be turned until both received the same level of sound. Later, it was made more sensitive by replacing each of the single spheres with up to six spheres. The C-tube was credited with a range of 1,000–8,000 yd based on 90 sec of listening; it could measure target bearing to within 5 degrees. C-tubes were mounted outboard, clamped to a ship's side. The improved SC-tube was mounted inboard, protruding from a ship's keel or a submarine's deck.

Handicapped by poor periscopes, the AL-boats had to rely largely on their SC-tubes. A U.S. officer surprised his British hosts (on board HMS *E 29*) "when I told them that on my last patrol . . . we had not only been able to anticipate by our SC tube all vessels sighted, but also had been able to determine their bearing within a few degrees, the character of the vessel and, if more than one, how many there were."[14]

New London developed a more elaborate trainable receiver, MB. Two rows of short pipes in the form of Ts were connected by the uprights of the Ts to larger pipes, and these larger ones to the central hearing tubes. MB used the interference effect between the arms of the T. Its longer arm was turned toward the sound and the shorter one away from it. When in line with the sound, both arms received the sound wave, but for the sound to come through the away-facing arm it had to travel the length of the arm facing toward it, hit the nipple on the away tube, and travel back. The length of the arms was such that, at a particular sonic frequency, signals from both arms would positively reinforce most strongly if the

device was pointing directly at the sound source. New London claimed that the device would eliminate much surrounding interference by, in effect, putting it out of focus.

The next step was a fixed array, the K-tube. Three microphones were arranged in a triangle, two being used simultaneously. Air lines compensated for the difference in time of arrival of sound at the two microphones; when the two earphones matched, the operator could read off the bearing of the sound. U.S. submarines used the Y-tube, a K-tube consisting of three rubber fish or "rats" (each containing a microphone) spaced 4 ft apart at the vertices of an equilateral triangle. G-1 tested a triple K-tube on a spar overhanging her bow on 27 and 29 March 1918, and the Y-tube was adopted a month later. Submarines typically had deck and keel outfits (the latter for listening while surfaced), with one compensator that could be connected to either. General Electric produced 80 complete sets and 25 limited to deck installation (for use only when submerged).

New London's MV-series employed lines of 12 button microphones, along each side of a ship's keel, feeding a compensator that turned the beam electrically by changing the effective length of the line to each microphone. In WW I this technique was applied only to surface ships, but it was adapted to submarines postwar. The U.S. Navy abandoned it in shifting to supersonic sound in the 1930s. It was much the technique used by the Germans in their later array devices, however, and the U.S. Navy adopted it after 1945 as BQR-2 and -4.

By mid-1918, the British preferred the U.S. K-, SC-, and C-tubes to their own; many British submarines tended not to use their sound gear at all. U.S. submariners were impressed with the British fixed hydrophones (directional plates) inspired by the prewar Submarine Signal hydrophones, in which the vessel's hull insulated the port from the starboard plate. In June 1918, a U.S. officer suggested that new U.S. O-boats and R-boats be fitted experimentally with British hydrophones, but the war ended before that could be done.

To exploit their listening gear, U.S. submariners had to learn to stop underwater for an extended period, which they had never practiced in peacetime. Because the submarine was never exactly neutrally buoyant and also because the Irish Sea lacked density layers on which to float underwater, she could never stop completely for as long as desired. It proved easy to come very close to neutral buoyancy, however, by pumping in and out periodically to keep from rising or sinking too much. By 1918, the submariners considered noteworthy the fact that AL-1 had remained for 6 hr at 65–80 ft with motors started for only 2 min (she used her ballast pump every 2–3 min).

In the early 1920s, the standard submarine outfit was an SC-tube and a Y-5 tube.[27] Because of its hydrophone superiority, the postwar navy developed a pure listening attack. An S-boat would approach her target at slow speed (to avoid self-noise) at about 60 ft, listening with her Y-5 tube, and occasionally stopping or drifting. When nearer, the submarine could complete her approach using the more accurate fix from her SC-tube. She had to raise her periscope, if at all, only when ready to fire. In April 1923, a submarine officer told the Asiatic Fleet War College that, during a listening attack made the previous year, a submarine took 27 bearings with an average error of only $1\frac{3}{32}$ degrees (maximum 4 degrees).[28] Listening attacks were largely discarded during the 1930s because they did not provide accurate range data. They reemerged late in the decade (in conjunction with single-ping sonars) as a way of avoiding air attack.

Wartime experience was reflected in a series of proposed building programs. In April 1917, the General Board developed a 5-year plan designed to deal with a potential future German-Japanese alliance, which had just been suggested by the "Zimmermann telegram". The board estimated that, by 1920, Germany would have 200 submarines (many of them fleet types); Japan would have 22, and the United States would have only 114. The plan included 9 fleet submarines (2 each in FY 17–20, 1 in FY 21) and 58 S-boats (20 in FY 17, 10 each in FY 18–20, 8 in FY 21). In August, the board asked for 30 fleet submarines in addition to those authorized in 1916 (see chapter 6).

Responding to a fall 1917 request by the Navy Department, Admiral Sims's London Plans Section wanted to look beyond boats needed for the European war, such as specialist ASW boats. If the war went badly (a very real possibility at the time), submarines would be needed to defend the United States against a transatlantic assault. In the event that the United States had to face Germany alone, it would be wise to build 54 long-range (scout) submarines. This was probably the first approach to the cruiser type (described in chapter 9). The planners wanted prototypes of one submarine minelayer and one fleet boat.

In March and April 1918, the General Board framed its own new submarine program (Table 8–1). In March 1918, the board wanted a total of 198 coastal submarines. It then added 24 to protect the Gulf Coast and 72 more to provide a mobile force to act far from bases, to allow for boats under repair, and to use for experimentation. All 107 small submarines (A through R classes) would ultimately be replaced by S-boats. Based on these figures, the board's request of 15 June 1918 included 125 new S-boats, 33 fleet submarines, 42 minelayers, and 24 ASW submarines. The war ended before anything could be done.

Through early 1918, the submariners argued that convoying by surface ships would not work and that what now could be called offensive ASW would be far more efficient. For example, listening devices were most efficiently deployed aboard submarines. It followed that submarines should take priority over destroyers in the emergency program. The submariners wanted plans drawn up for one minelayer (to correspond as closely as possible to an S-boat) and a fleet submarine. The minelayer could be built at a navy yard to avoid contractual problems with Lake or Electric Boat.

A destroyer often literally displaced a submarine. Electric Boat used two important destroyer yards, Fore River

Table 8–1. General Board Submarine Program, 20 April 1918

Location	Types			
	AA	Coastal	ASW	SSM
Atlantic Fleet	24			
Pacific Fleet	9			
Atlantic and Gulf coasts		144		12
Caribbean Sea		30		6
Pacific Coast		66		12
Hawaii		18		6
Guam		12		
Philippines		24		6
North Sea and adjacent			24	
Totals	33	294	24	42

Note: AA, fleet submarines; SSM, minelayers.

and Union Iron Works. It fabricated H-boat parts (to be erected elsewhere) at its Newark plant. Lake had his own yard but was relatively slow. According to Electric Boat, other bottlenecks were periscopes, batteries, engines, and crankshafts, the last probably most serious.

Because building time did not much depend on size, the program could not be accelerated by shifting to smaller and much less satisfactory submarines (Electric Boat's proposal to build more H-boats was rejected). Before the war, the usual contract time was 22–30 mo; by 1918, Union Iron Works was completing R-boats in about a year, but the British were doing far better. Vickers built a prototype slightly modified repeat E-class boat in 8 mo. It completed the lead L-class boat, including preparation of detailed plans, in 18 mo. Its R class prototype (including planning) was done in 8 mo.[29]

The wartime General Board saw fleet submarines as potential submarine cruisers capable of working independently far from their bases. Presumably, it was inspired by German U-cruiser operations off the U.S. East Coast. Coastal submarines (S-boats), according to the General Board, should be capable of operating far from their bases "in the ocean lanes of commerce; to reinforce threatened areas at a distance; to meet the armed merchantmen and larger submarines of the enemy, and to act with the fleet if necessary." These oceanic (Atlantic) patrol submarines were hardly the prewar coast defense craft.

The board wanted minelayers even before the war. They would be particularly valuable should an enemy establish bases in the Western Hemisphere. On 1 December 1916, the General Board asked for a design study of a boat capable of laying 20 mines while submerged and also armed with two bow tubes (two reloads each) and a 3-in gun. Board members seemed to be thinking in terms of a cruiser submarine hull because they asked for surface speed of 18 kt (endurance 3,000–4,000 nm normal and

5,000–6,000 nm maximum, using the ballast tanks for fuel) and submerged speed of 8 kt for 5 hr. No such submarine was ordered in wartime, but the submarine minelayer was revived postwar.

In December 1917, the General Board suggested that, as soon as yard capacity became available, the ASW submarine should have first priority among submarine types. The U.S. Navy became aware of the British R class about October 1917, soon after it had been ordered. It was designed for high underwater speed, to close with a U-boat spotted at a distance or detected by its elaborate hydrophone array. The boat would attack mainly submerged and fire a full six-torpedo salvo in hopes of gaining at least one hit on its small target. The concentration on speed recalled U.S. prewar practice. Designed speed was 15 kt submerged (1-hr rate), using two large electric motors in tandem. The single 240-BHP diesel (half an H-boat power plant) sufficed for 9 kt. Tank tests showed that resistance surfaced and submerged would be about the same; on the surface, the R-boat could be expected to make about 15 kt on its motors. Its very limited size, 160 ft × 15 ft (360/450 tons), was presumably acceptable in a submarine limited to the North Sea (i.e., to harbor work, in U.S. terms).

Admiral Sims found the idea very interesting; the General Board drew up tentative characteristics for a U.S. equivalent. It wanted to match the reported performance of the British boat (15 kt submerged, 9 kt surfaced) and added the usual 20 hr at 5 kt submerged. Because the

boat would be based in European waters, limited surface cruising endurance (2,500 nm normally, 4,000 nm maximum with fuel oil in ballast tanks) was acceptable. In December 1917, the characteristics were circulated to the two private yards; C&R began its own alternative design.

C&R argued that the United States could not duplicate a British R-boat because none of its torpedoes was small enough to be carried in sufficient numbers by a small boat. In February 1918, C&R suggested instead modifying and cleaning up an S-boat and adding more bow tubes. The bureau lacked the manpower to develop an entirely new design. Too, the British had supplied sketch plans but no hull lines. In March, with hull lines promised, the General Board ordered C&R to compare the British boat with the bureau's suggested modified S-boat. Because the ASW submarine was seen as a special type suited only to WW I conditions, it died at the end of the war. Apparently, neither C&R nor Electric Boat had made much progress.

With the end of the war, the U.S. government seriously considered trying to abolish submarines altogether (the London planners helped save them). Development work was suspended, work on boats already under construction was slowed, and 14 S-boats, on which little had been done, were canceled. On the other hand, the General Board certainly still valued submarines. In September 1919, in calling for 12 new ones (all to be completed by the end of FY 25) as part of a large program designed to exploit wartime expansion of the U.S. shipbuilding industry, the board stated, "The country will never again be in so favorable

Two L-boats lie alongside their tender at Berehaven, Ireland. (*Burnell Poole Collection*)

a position to carry out the large naval program that will render us reasonably secure for the future." Meanwhile, two mobile divisions were kept intact, one in the West Indies and the other (10 O-boats) attached to the fleet for its first postwar winter maneuvers, largely to test the concept of direct cooperation.

The end of WW I brought a new shock. The U-boats proved far superior to both British and U.S. submarines. The British allowed U.S. officers to inspect captured U-boats before any other foreigners. In December 1918, a special U.S. board selected several U-boats for detailed examination: U-53, a general-purpose submarine famous for its 1916 visit to Newport and also for sinking the U.S. destroyer *Jacob Jones*; UC-105, a small minelayer; UB-149, a coastal submarine; U-164, an ocean submarine of late-war design; U-124, a minelayer; and U-140, a new 2,500-ton U-cruiser. U-140 was inspected in a drydock at Kiel where she was refitting after a cruise to the U.S. East Coast (the French took over U-139 and the British U-141 of this class). By this time, U.S. official sentiment was much in favor of abolishing submarines altogether, and the Navy Department refused to take any U-boats. They could be inspected (and briefly test run), but that was all.[30]

The special Submarine Inspection Board decided to borrow UC-105, UB-149, U-164, and U-124 and take them from Harwich to Portland, England. This would relieve congestion at Harwich and also allow the board to take advantage of the services of USS *Bushnell* at Portland. The U-boats were taken to Portland on 12 December and returned to Harwich on 31 December. The boats's inspection resulted in four major conclusions: (1) the U-boat diesels were superior to any other submarine diesels in the world, (2) U-boat periscopes were at least as good as any others, (3) radius of action was greater than that obtained by any other nation on similar displacement, and (4) German double-hull construction was probably superior to other types as protection against depth charging. Clearly, the boats were worth further examination in the United States.

Then someone, probably Captain Hart, had a clever idea. The U-boats would be taken to the United States specifically to support the Victory Bond drive by charging the price of a bond ($50 or $100) as admission. The U.S. Navy had destroyed more U-boats than any other navy except the British. Surely, the U.S. public had a right to see some that still existed. Custody would be transferred only temporarily, the submarines would not operate as part of the U.S. Navy, and their fate would be decided by the Peace Conference. The U.S. official position was not compromised. Six boats were selected: U-111 (which replaced the badly sabotaged U-164), U-117, U-140, UB-88, UB-148, and UC-97; all but U-140 (towed by a collier) crossed the Atlantic in March 1919 under their own power.[31] U-111 and UB-148 were selected to run standardization trials, submerged trials, torpedo firing trials, tactical (turning circle) trials, and miscellaneous trials, including depth test for hull strength. Equipment, such as compressors and pumps, was tested.

U-111 operated extensively under service conditions. About the size of an S-boat, she could be directly compared with this craft. Because she was ready somewhat later than the others, she had to cruise alone directly from Portsmouth, England, to New York (7–19 April 1919). To make up time lost and, as it turned out, to avoid running out of fuel, she took the northern great circle route and encountered very rough weather. The crew could go on deck only one day. Her performance was impressive, particularly in view of the inexperience of her crew: 14 of the 35 enlisted men had never been on board a submarine before. After her arrival in the United States, U-111, operating with S-3 and S-4, visited New London; Dry Tortugas and Pensacola, Florida; and Havana, Cuba. During trials at Provincetown after a 2-wk engine overhaul and docking, she made 17.08 kt, although her German rating was 16.4 kt. She was decommissioned in April 1920.

Lt. Comdr. F. A. Daubin, the U-111's CO, was impressed by the German system of ventilation. Fresh, dry air made up for cramped quarters; he said, "In our submarines the men can stand almost anything except damp, foul air." The engines' air suction constantly renewed the air in the boat. There was no evidence of sweating (condensation). Daubin was sure that nonsubmariners could not have stood up to a similar voyage in a contemporary U.S. submarine. She also had much better toilet facilities than an S-boat. On the other hand, U-111 had no cold storage for fresh provisions and no means of cooling the drinking water, both of which might be important for extended Pacific operations. Nor did the Germans provide enough bunks for the entire crew.

Despite her low silhouette, U-111 was considered a very good seaboat. She could turn sharply, thanks to her big rudder and her sharply cut-away stern. Her commander for the U.S. trials (then Lt. Comdr. Sherwood Picking), later recalled that her seagoing behavior was quite comparable to the big V-boat he then commanded. She rode up over waves and had an easy roll (probably because of a small metacentric weight [GM]). Her steering was excellent; she handled more like a destroyer capable of submerging than like a U.S. submarine, which was awkward on the surface. The excellent surface sea-keeping of the larger German submarines was traced to their double-hull design, although the "dory" bow was probably more significant than the double hull per se.[32]

The U-111 diesels were far more reliable than their U.S. equivalents. They were so quiet that Daubin awoke several times at night during the Atlantic passage, sure that they had stopped. Both during and after the passage, Daubin never had to use his motors to maneuver (i.e., they always reversed reliably).

The Germans had learned to crash-dive; on U.S. trials, U-111 dived in 40 sec and her CO thought she would have done even better with a more experienced crew. Instead of Kingstons, the Germans used large flap valves on the bottoms of their main ballast tanks that worked easily through a system of universal joints and toggle gear from the interior of the boat. Later, C&R would be bitterly criticized for its slow-diving submarines. It would retort that the S-boats had Kingstons (with central control valves) at the direct demand of the submarine force. The captured boats thus symbolized the difference between the prewar U.S. submarine force and wartime reality. S-class characteristics (1916) required that they dive within 3 min (in 1921, the navy-designed S 3 was credited with 2 min 15 sec). Riding her vents, UB-148 could crash-dive in only 27 sec.[33]

The Germans were well aware that the floodable superstructure needed for good sea-keeping could trap air and thus slow diving. Numerous holes in U-111's flat wooden deck drained seas coming on board when she was on the surface, so that the water did not roll aft, and let out air when she submerged. Like the main ballast tanks, the bow buoyancy tank relied on its vents to retain air and keep water out when the submarine was on the surface. Opening the vents allowed it to flood quickly to bring the bow down when diving. The radio masts were counterbalanced so that they could fold quickly as the boat dived.

Flooding, pumping, and venting arrangements were all centralized so that a few men could operate the boat from the control room. Unlike a U.S. submarine, U-111 needed no one in the torpedo room to operate valves for trimming. The Germans decentralized emergency blowing, so that the boat could continue to operate even if a compartment had to be abandoned; tanks could be blown from the conning tower or from either the forward or after torpedo room. Bilges could be pumped from the control room or from either torpedo room. German design was also compact: most air bottles were in the superstructure, thus saving space in the pressure hull.

Daubin was quite impressed by the overall finish and workmanship of the submarine, despite its wartime construction. For example, cooking and washing spaces were tiled. Torpedo tube shutters fit so well that an Electric Boat draftsman thought each must have been specially made. As an example of attention to detail, Daubin recalled the steering gear, which made for easy hand steering even from the bridge. Each of the numerous brackets supporting the steering lines had ball bearings with forced lubrication, as well as universal joints on either side of the bracket. All manholes had removable knife edges for easy replacement.

Clearly, U-111 was enormously superior to S-3 and S-4, with two guns to their one and six torpedo tubes to their four. She dived much more quickly and was much faster on the surface. She was also far more habitable. C&R could claim only a longer radius (perhaps only on paper) and higher submerged speed.[34]

Displacing 510 tons surfaced, UB-88 (commanded by Lt. Comdr. J. L. Nielsen) was broadly comparable to an L-boat. Unlike the U.S. submarine, she had saddle tanks. With the tanks buoyant, she rode over seas through which U.S. boats (steered from the control room, rather than from a wet bridge) would have plowed. Completed in January 1918, UB-88 crossed the Atlantic in 1919 in convoy

with three other U-boats. She visited U.S. ports on the east coast south of Savannah, Georgia; on the Gulf coast; and up the Mississippi River, for a total of about 16,000 nm over a 9-mo period—the longest trip made by any captured U-boat. When Nielsen got her at Harwich, she had been in dock for several months and was badly neglected, with her battery empty. No one else, not even the Japanese, wanted her. After a 2-wk preparation, she completed the long voyage without any machinery casualties, and without any spares on board except for a few engine valve springs. This sort of performance was unimaginable for contemporary U.S. boats. On the other hand, ventilation was terrible.

The somewhat smaller UC-97 (commanded by Lt. Comdr. C. A. Lockwood, later ComSubPac during WW II) toured the Great Lakes after her Atlantic passage, for a total of about 9 mo in commission (ending in September 1919). Lockwood considered her better in a head sea than a much larger R-boat or S-boat because of her high sharp bow and broad deck. Crossing the Atlantic in the trough of the sea, she behaved much like larger U.S. submarines. UC-97, like UB-88, had very limited habitability. She could bunk only a third of her crew and carried little fresh water. There were almost no cooking facilities, no messing facilities (only a folding table for the wardroom), and no washing or bathing facilities (only a hand basin in the wardroom). Although ventilation was better than on K-boats, it was not up to that on S-boats.

U.S. officers who served on the U-boats were impressed by the logic of their design. Officers' quarters were partitioned off. To keep crews efficient, they were given comfortable quarters, which were over the battery. To make this space available, the Germans had designed batteries that evaporated water more slowly than their U.S. counterparts, hence did not have to be as accessible. The batteries could be watered quickly and efficiently without disturbing living arrangements. The crews' very poor messing arrangements were attributed more to the social gulf between German officers and enlisted men than to any fundamental design flaw. The Germans used electric pressure cookers to avoid spreading cooking odors through a boat during a long submerged run. U.S. submariners felt that BuEng and C&R loaded their boats with unreliable equipment, much of it apparently an afterthought, whereas the Germans carefully avoided anything that was unnecessary.

Even basic hull structure was different. U.S. and British submarines, which shared a common design ancestry, used relatively light pressure hull plating and relied mainly on framing for strength. The Germans used much heavier plating but lighter and more widely spaced framing; for example, U-140, a U-cruiser, had lighter framing than would have been used in a U.S. 400-ton design. In 1920, Captain Hart suggested that the choice might have been made to resist depth charge explosions or, alternatively, for quicker and easier construction.[35]

U.S. submariners who had seen the U-boats doubted that either C&R or BuEng had really appreciated their merits, but this opinion was not altogether fair. C&R did obtain plans, and the internal arrangement of V-boats probably owes something to German ideas. BuEng copied the MAN diesel and distributed samples of German equipment to U.S. companies. The submariners, frustrated by having to operate a basically prewar-designed submarine (S class), demanded in 1927 that bureau designs be abandoned altogether in favor of a direct copy of U-135 (an improved U-111).

Because the war had ended with an armistice, the Germans felt no compulsion (as they would in 1945) to provide the Allies with accounts of their tactics or with their own insights. They may have been somewhat more willing to share their views with U.S. than with British naval officers. Some German officers suggested that depth charges had not been nearly as effective as advertised, particularly against an experienced commander.

The Germans felt that, whatever the state of development of Allied listening gear, U-boats had been most often caught in daylight because their torpedoes left a visible wake and the act of firing produced a quite visible disturbance in the water. Therefore, they had worked on a wakeless (electric) torpedo that was ready in spring 1918, but too late for the war, and a bubbleless firing mechanism. BuOrd pursued both projects between wars. In 1941, it began to install poppet valves that were supposed to eliminate the firing bubble. Its electric torpedo lagged; the WW II Mk 18 was virtually a copy of the contemporary German electric torpedo, presumably directly descended from the 1918 weapon.

In February 1919, an experienced CO of four U-boats, including U-90 and U-164, discussed his experiences with a U.S. officer on the Armistice Commission.[36] He claimed that most Allied depth charges were set too deep, so that a calm CO could survive by deliberately *not* going deep. He tended to dive to 30 ft, go ahead full speed with small rudder for about 20 min, then put up his periscope to decide what to do next. The former CO claimed that he once sat out a 164-charge attack. Inexperienced U-boat commanders were in the greatest danger because they tended to go deep. Later U-boats often dived steeply (at 13 degrees), so a panicky CO could quickly dive too deep. On the other hand, in May 1922, the U.S. naval attaché in Berlin reported precisely the opposite, that depth charges although not necessarily effective, were always feared. In deep water, U-boats could dive to 60 m or more to ensure that depth charges exploded well above them.

The Germans used silent low speed ("creep") drives to evade Allied hydrophones. The former U-boat CO recalled that no German submarine had managed more than 4 kt at silent speed and even that under only ideal conditions. He thought experiments were in hand at the end of the war to increase silent speed. The CO considered the later U-boats quite unstable early in a cruise, when fully loaded and the upper tanks filled with oil. To improve stability, they were modified with additional tanks in the superstructure, presumably to reduce the free surface effect in any individual tank. They steered badly in a heavy sea. The CO felt that his boat dived too slowly; he could never be sure of getting to 20 ft in less than 45 sec and it often

took him 1 min. Nor did he like his torpedoes; he considered them useless beyond 600 yd and always tried to get within 300 yd of the target. The grass is always greener elsewhere: he thought that U.S. submarines were superior, they invariably dived quicker than U-boats, and their torpedoes were much better. On one occasion, probably in August 1918, he was attacked by a U.S. submarine off the west coast of Ireland. Her two torpedoes came very close, one missing by not more than 2 ft.

The U-boat CO showed little respect for Allied ASW measures, but the U.S. officer put that down at least partly to bravado. He naturally hoped that the Germans had been impressed by the big U.S.-laid Northern mine barrage, but the German showed little respect for mines. His talk about "buoys the motion of which exploded the mines" showed that he had no idea of the mine mechanism. An explosion in a mine field started a battery fire in his boat, but he reached port on the surface on his diesels.[37]

For submarine designers, the great question was how effective a depth charge could be. Although not shockproof in any way, some AL-boats had survived depth charges. The obsolete G-1 was selected for June 1921 tests. She was moored at a 60-ft depth. Eight attacks closed in from 300 ft to 178 ft. All but the last charge (at 80 ft) were at 60 ft. The last charge was most effective because so much less of its energy went into throwing up a column of water. A charge exploding under a submarine seemed most effective, as the greatest part of the blast was directed upward. A submarine under attack should try to dive below the charges. Shock and other depth-charge effects might jam her planes and drive her down, so she should level out as soon as possible.

Depth-charge damage tended to be cumulative. Hatches were a particular danger because they could be sprung; their numbers had to be reduced. Chain-driven gear, particularly subject to shock, had to be eliminated. Every compartment had to be provided with at least two shock-resistant carbon filament lamps.

Beyond a range of 275 ft, it appeared that the standard depth charge had no effect. At 275 ft, lamp filaments shattered. At 225 ft, periscopes, eyeports, and breakables were damaged. Paint and red lead shivered off one side of the boat at 200 ft, and the hatches were damaged. At 180 ft, particularly with the boat diving, she could be disabled temporarily by disarrangement of the steering gear clutches, diving gear, and other components. Some piping broke, some seams opened, and hatches were badly damaged at 175 ft, and the boat could be sunk.

G-1 was obsolete and unmanned; a more modern submarine might be tougher and her crew might be able to reduce the effect of damage. One conclusion was that new submarines should be made stronger than required for the 200-ft test depth. At 175 ft, a depth charge produced a 1,400-lb impact, compared with a depth pressure of only 35 psi at 200 ft. All outboard piping or fittings, whose rupture would allow water into the submarine, had to be strengthened against depth bombing. Outboard shafting had to be strong enough to withstand explosions.

9

Submarines for a Pacific War

AFTER WORLD WAR I, U.S. naval attention turned to the enormous spaces of the Pacific.[1] In mid-1920, for example, the OpNav War Plans Division estimated the number of submarines (based at Manila in the Philippines and on Guam) required to blockade Japan.[2] Patrol stations (8) along the east and south coasts of Japan averaged 1,300 nm from Guam; stations (15) in the East China and Yellow seas averaged 1,300 nm from Manila. The Sea of Japan itself (4 stations, summer only) was 2,000 nm from Manila. Shorter-range submarines could operate in the China Sea and in the Formosa Straits; they could also protect Guam and Luzon. Even to cover these stations, which the planners considered would damage but not defeat Japan, astronomical numbers of S-class submarines would be needed: 124 based on Guam and at Manila or 144 if Manila were lost. Moreover, Guam could not possibly support enough submarines.

S-boats had range but no endurance. They were credited with 24 days at sea for every 36 days in port. The new fleet submarine V-1 could keep the sea for 40 days but had to spend 60 days in port between sorties. A new cruiser would have twice its cruising radius, spending 90 days at sea for 15 days in port.[3] In theory, 55 cruisers could prosecute a war from Manila and Guam or 63 from Guam alone. Although still a large number, it was conceivable. S-boats could fill some roles: with 51 S-boats on hand or building, the blockade would require 32 cruisers. The 1920 OpNav planners also wanted 12 long-range minelayers and 18 fleet submarines.

The Washington Treaty (1922) outlawed German-style submarine blockades. Submarines near Japan were still invaluable, however, because only submarines could lie off Japanese ports and bases to warn of a sortie. That required both long endurance and effective long-hull radio. Scouting encouraged interest in providing each submarine with its own small airplane, as the Germans had tried during WW I. By killing off the nascent U.S. battlecruiser program, the treaty made submarine tactical scouting in direct support of the fleet very important. Battlecruisers had been the only surface scouts likely to fight through an enemy's screen to observe its battle line

during the run-up to a fleet action. Although aircraft carriers eventually solved the problem, their potential was far from obvious in 1922. Direct support required sufficient speed to keep up with the fleet; a strategic scout needed range but not high speed. Submarines in forward areas could also attack Japanese warships, particularly capital ships, and they might lay mines.

By outlawing fortification of the Western Pacific, the treaty made it most unlikely that either Manila or Guam would be long available in a war against Japan. American submarines would have to cross the Pacific. It was argued that the United States could build the large expensive submarines needed for fleet support and strategic scouting precisely because she did not need the numbers associated with antishipping warfare. Yet, after Pearl Harbor, it turned out that the characteristics developed for fleet support were exactly those required to attack Japanese shipping.

Once blockade had been abandoned, OpNav was willing to halve the cruiser figure: fleet submarines were cut to 16, but minelayers were not affected in a December 1921 calculation. The General Board wanted 24 cruisers (strategic scouts), 24 fleet submarines, and 16 long-range minelayers. There were already more than enough short-range (then called general service) submarines; until the R-boats and S-boats began to wear out, new construction meant big long-range submarines.

In December 1919, the General Board asked that the remaining 6 V-boats be built under the FY 21 program: 2 cruisers, 2 minelayers, and 2 general purpose submarines (800–1,000-ton prototypes, 200–260 ft long, based on S-boats, T-boats, and U-111).[4] Congress refused. The following year (September 1920), the board asked for 6 boats in each of FY 22–24; it substituted 2 more minelayers for the 2 general purpose boats of the FY 21 plan. The board was silent in 1921 because the United States had convened the Washington Conference.

The resulting treaty did not limit submarine fleets, but from about 1926 on the General Board sought to apply its 5:5:3 fleet tonnage ratio (intended for battleships and aircraft carriers) to submarines. In May 1922, the board

Cuttlefish was one of the last two V-boats, a link between the big cruisers and the much smaller submarines that the London Treaty of 1930 forced the U.S. Navy to accept. Although externally she was much like the later "fleet submarines," internally she was quite different, with vastly different propulsion.

renewed its call for a 6-boat annual program (for FY 23–25; this time for 3 cruisers and 3 minelayers each year). Congress balked. These numbers were dwarfed by a reported Japanese 46-submarine program; in April 1923, the board asked for 6 cruisers and 6 minelayers in FY 25. Congress bought only 1 minelayer, V-4. In April 1924, the board asked for the same program in FY 26 as part of a much larger plan. Congress bought 2 cruisers (V-5 and V-6).

Now the General Board argued that although the U.S. Navy had the largest submarine fleet in the world, it was far behind Britain and Japan in modern submarines. In January 1928, the United States had 94,000 tons of submarines, compared with Britain's 65,000 tons and Japan's 76,000 tons, but it had only about 38,000 tons of modern long-range boats, compared with 55,000 British tons and 73,000 Japanese tons. Britain and Japan had already scrapped submarines equivalent to those the United States was counting as first-line submarines (only in 1929 did the secretary of the navy order obsolete submarines scrapped). The board could choose between a program to maintain parity (5:5) with Britain or a considerably larger one to maintain superiority (5:3) over Japan. It offered a 20-year program (FY 28–47) in December 1926. Both versions began with 5 submarines in FY 28. To maintain the treaty ratio over Japan would require 4 submarines each year in FY 29–32 (parity with Britain required 3 in each of FY 29 and 30, then 2 each year in FY 31–33). This plan was formally approved for long-range budgeting.

In 1927, however, Britain announced that it would build 6 fleet boats each year between 1927 and 1929 and seemed likely to continue this pace. To maintain parity, the United States would have to build 7 submarines each year through 1933, then 6 per year. If Japan built at the British rate (accurate data were not available), the 5:3 ratio would demand 12 U.S. submarines per year. In September, the secretary of the navy asked for a 5-year plan based on the FY 28–47 plan. The General Board wanted to use this plan to remedy U.S. deficiencies, such as the lack of long-range submarines; then, during the following 15 years, it could schedule replacements, based on the statutory ages of ships. A 20-year program, proposed in January 1928, called for 7 submarines per year in FY 29–34, then 6 per year in FY 35–48.

About this time, the OpNav War Plans Division estimated that 35 cruisers would be needed: 20 to work with the fleet and 15 for strategic scouting. In the fall of 1927, after the failure of the Geneva disarmament conference (also convened by the United States), the division proposed a 5-year, 71-ship program, including 32 new submarines plus completion of the last 3 V-boats. Congress bought the 3 V-boats (V 7–9) in FY 29 but no more submarines. In April 1929, the General Board revived its 5-year plan of 1927 for FY 31–35.

With the onset of the depression, governments became more interested in limiting naval spending by treaty. At London in 1930, unlike Washington in 1921–22, submarines were included. A draft proposal allowed the United States up to 90,000 tons of submarines, but the treaty cut that to 52,700 tons (and offered Japan parity). Because successful operations required a considerable number of submarines, the treaty forced down the unit size of U.S. boats. There were no limitations on small coastal submarines (up to 600 tons), however, and many O-boats and R-boats were not scrapped.

Submarines could be replaced after age 13 (replacements could be laid down 2 years before the submarines became overage), a submarine lifetime that the General Board accepted about 1926. When the London Treaty expired on 31 December 1936, the United States would still have 9 underage V-boats and 11 underage S-boats. This left 25,800 tons to replace during the interim. To obtain sufficient numbers, unit tonnage would have to be cut to about 1,200. The depression intervened; no submarines at all were authorized in FY 32. In 1931, the board planned 6 boats in FY 33, but the depression also precluded that. In December 1931, the General Board drew up alternative 10-year and 15-year programs to bring the submarine force to full modern treaty strength. The board much preferred the 10-year plan (6 boats per year).

In March 1933, the C-NO promulgated a 7-year plan (FY 34–40), to meet "the Navy's needs," that would fully modernize the submarine fleet by FY 40. The first 4 new submarines were built under special depression relief legislation (FY 34 program).The earlier desired figure of 6 submarines per year was reached in FY 35. In March 1934, the Vinson Act made it U.S. law to maintain an underage treaty-level fleet, without requiring the disposal of overage units. It authorized a steady program that built a wartime mobilization base (the London Treaty force would not have sufficed to fight Japan). The needs of the steady program, in turn, caused the navy to turn back to Electric Boat to supplement Portsmouth and Mare Island Navy Yards.

At the beginning of FY 36, modernization still required 27,550 tons of submarines, including 15,100 tons of replacements due in FY 37–39. The FY 36 and FY 37 programs continued at a steady 6 submarines per year. When the FY 38 program was being drawn up in mid-1936, 12,862 tons were left to lay down before the end of 1940 (i.e., FY 38 – 39): something over 8 of the current 1,450-ton submarines. The General Board decided to ask for half of this tonnage (4 submarines) (4) in each of FY 38 and FY 39 (more tonnage would become available in FY 40).

The 1930 treaty included an "escalator clause": a signatory threatened by other powers could retain overage tonnage or build new ships after notifying the other powers (who would then be free to match that step). Retaliating for Japanese escalation, the United States added 15,698 tons of submarines late in 1936.[5] That year, a new London Treaty dropped the tonnage limits altogether, largely because Japan had renounced the treaty structure in 1934 (effective in 1936). They survived in the Vinson Act. A supplemental Vinson-Trammell Act of 17 May 1938 increased authorized underage submarine tonnage to 81,956 tons (i.e., 20 percent over the total of the 1930 figure and the escalator figure). Given this extra tonnage, the annual 6-boat program was restored in FY 39 (the War Plans Division had wanted 8 submarines as compensation for the FY 38 cut to 4).

Early in May 1938, with the Vinson-Trammell Act pending, the last of the smaller old submarines become overage. The General Board therefore wanted to buy prototype 1,200-tonners (S-boat replacements) and 650-tonners (R-boat or O-boat replacements) in the FY 40 program (it expected to buy 5 large submarines, but 6 were bought). That July, the General Board drew up a new 10-year plan (FY 39–48): 6 submarines in FY 41, 4 per year in FY 42–47, and 5 in FY 48 (in FY 46–48, all would be replacements, Vinson-Trammell tonnage having been exhausted). Production would shift to 1,250-tonners in FY 42, then to 850-tonners in FY 43–46; the FY 47–48 replacements would be 1,300-tonners. On 24 August, the secretary of the navy approved the General Board plan as a basis for budgeting.

The outbreak of WW II, of course, threw out all of these calculations. In October 1939, OpNav suggested that the navy be increased by about a third (174,115 tons), of which 72,000 tons might be devoted to 45 submarines. By November, the proposed increase had grown to 400,000 tons, which might add 28 submarines to the 14 available under existing authorization (total 62,700 tons), and the secretary of the navy approved this. Then France collapsed. In mid-June, CNO Adm. Harold R. Stark asked what forces the United States would need if both France and Britain collapsed. A quick General Board study showed that 120 modern fleet submarines would be needed. Authorized modern submarine strength increased by 21,000 tons on 14 June and then by another 70,000 on 19 July 1940 (equivalent to a total of about 47 boats). These increases created the "two-ocean navy," so called because the force required to face Japan had to be supplemented by a force to be used in the event the British lost control of the Atlantic. Once the United States entered the war, overall authorized tonnage increased again, but the submarine fraction was not spelled out.

The post-1922 prohibition on trade attack focused U.S. naval attention back on the prewar mission of attacks on the enemy fleet. Four 21-in torpedoes were considered necessary to sink or disable a modern capital ship. A submarine was expected to run ahead of the target on the surface, outside visual range, and estimate target course by observing smoke and masttops. During the late 1920s, U.S. torpedo attack doctrine favored stern shots toward a zigzagging ship. Stern tubes were retained even after submarine size had been severely limited by treaty.

Many submarines believed that a fleet submarine might have to fire "browning shots" (somewhat random shots "into the brown," i.e., into a group of ships) from outside a destroyer screen, beyond the range of the standard Mk X. Shortly after WW I, BuOrd had developed a multi-speed turbine drive using a gear shift. Its Mk XI (tested in 1926) was intended for both surface ships and submarines: 15,000 yd at low speed (27 kt), medium range at medium speed (10,000 yd at 34 kt), or short range at high speed (6,000 yd at 46 kt). Its greater length (6.8 m, rather than 5.2 m, i.e., nominally 268 in versus 205 in) cost about 200

tons in a V-boat.[6] To meet demands for smaller submarines, BuOrd had developed a special short (246-in), two-speed submarine torpedo, Mk XIV, with a range of 4,500–5,000 yd at 45 kt and 9,000 yd at 32 kt.[7] Lacking the gear shift, it was inefficient at anything but its optimal speed; hence, it could reach long range only at very low speed, but it was expected to be more rugged and more reliable. Development was completed about 1931, and Mk XIV entered service about 1938.

Then, short ranges became more important. By the late 1930s, it was estimated that a target could evade easily at 1,800 yd and probably at 1,000 yd, but at 750 yd (30-sec warning) the target could do nothing at all. U.S. submariners had already almost abandoned browning shots in favor of aimed (rifle) shots. In 1937 battle torpedo practices, fleet submarines made only 23 percent hits (none at all at ranges beyond 3,000 yd). *Dolphin* got two hits and two misses at 900 yd and about the same at 1,200 yd, but the target evaded the whole spread at 1,800 yd. In 1938 BuOrd proposed a new single-speed weapon (50 kt to 5,000 yd), but it never entered service. The wartime single-speed Mk 23 was a more basic Mk 14 introduced to simplify production.[8]

A submarine attacking the enemy's fleet faced patrolling aircraft. They could appear even when the submarine was not inviting attention during attacks. For example, pilots might always spot a periscope's feather, hence the intense prewar interest in attacks based on sound alone. Pilots could easily spot a submarine's oil slicks. Although a submarine could extend her range by storing fuel in the main ballast tanks, leaky tanks unfortunately left an oil slick. Even after the oil had been exhausted, it left a film on the inside of the tank that produced a new slick every time seawater ran out of the tank. Oil was caught in pockets, and it stuck to the tank sides and to the inside of the superstructure. Oil attacked the preservative with which fuel ballast tanks were painted to form a mixture that gummed up fuel lines. Dual purpose tanks were eliminated in the FY 36 submarines. In 1935, however, Subron (Submarine Squadron) 6 had reported that oil slicks could be avoided by repeatedly filling and blowing while on the surface. Dual tankage was too attractive to be foregone; it was restored in later classes.

The submarines' air defenses were generally four 0.50- or 0.30-caliber machine guns. Because they were stowed below to be set up on deck or atop the bridge, their fire was delayed after the boat broke the surface. Wet versions were not developed.

The new strategic scouts needed long-range radios. WW I boats had flat-top antennas supported by pairs of collapsible masts, which took time to erect or take down. BuEng substituted pairs of cables extending from bow and stern to a T-topped mast telescoping from the periscope shears, forming fore and aft loops. A boat could transmit at periscope depth by using a short antenna fixed to a periscope. In February 1930, an S-boat used the new antennas and the associated new radio to contact a station 7,900 nm away. The submarine could make contact at 2,000 nm by using 3 ft of vertical antenna pushed up

A fleet boat returning from patrol displays a major drawback of pre–World War II U.S. submarine design: light anti-aircraft guns had to be taken out and set up before they could be used. A water-cooled 0.50, the standard prewar weapon, is shown on deck forward of the bridge. This boat may be *Trigger*, whose commanding officer originated the practice (very visible here) of drilling holes at the turn of the deck to let out the air in the superstructure more quickly so as to speed diving.

through the water. Low-frequency signals (less than 100 kHz) could be received at depths up to 64 ft.

Even the loops took time to rig, and they blocked machine-gun arcs of fire. By the fall of 1935, the Submarine Force wanted a pair of wires (wing antennas) strung directly from the deck to the periscope shears above the bridge fairwater. The loops and the telescoping mast could be abandoned. With the top of the bridge fairwater nearly clear, machine guns on the bridge enjoyed much better arcs of fire. The periscope-depth antenna still had its own mast and therefore made its own feather. The Submarine Force wanted, but did not get, a radio mast incorporated into the periscope itself.

Habitability drove up the size of the new generation of submarines. Crews would live aboard for protracted periods. Sacrifices acceptable in wartime could not be expected of an all-volunteer peacetime force. For example, hot-bunking (providing fewer berths than crewmen) had to be avoided. Living compartments needed much better ventilation (ultimately, air conditioning), preferably a system that was separate from ventilation in engine and mo-

tor rooms. Submarines needed better toilet and bathing facilities.

The U.S. naval planners in London during WW I probably made the first formal proposal for a cruiser (19 August 1918) (see chapter 8). The proposal called for a radius of action of 10,000 nm at 10 kt, with reliable diesels good for 16 kt surfaced (9 kt submerged; less would be accepted, if necessary, to achieve the surface speed). This submarine would be armed with four bow and two stern tubes, with a total of 24 torpedoes (i.e., 1 in each tube plus 3 reloads), as well as one 6 in gun and one 3-in AA gun. The design would emphasize crew comfort during long-endurance voyages. Daytime radio transmission range would be 500 nm.

Despite its strong preference for fleet submarines, the General Board included rough characteristics of a cruiser based on wartime German U-cruisers (about 2,000 tons, 300 ft long) in the 1919 Navy Department annual report: moderate surface speed (about 14 kt), very long endurance (including submerged endurance), four bow and two stern

During World War II, aircraft fulfilled their prewar promise as anti-submarine weapons. At Mare Island on 17 July 1945, *Sunfish* shows a variety of counters, including new single 40-mm and 20-mm guns (only the mount for the latter is visible, abaft the periscope shears). This photograph also shows two more subtle measures. The long-wire radio antenna has been moved from the centerline (strung between fairwater and stern) to short poles alongside the fairwater, on each side. Note too the holes drilled into the superstructure, near the turn of the deck. They were first suggested by the commanding officer of USS *Trigger*. Like additional limber holes cut into the side of the superstructure, they made for quicker diving.

tubes (15 long torpedoes), two 6-in guns, and one antiaircraft gun. Scouting would require the longest practical radio-sending range.

Late in December 1919, C&R's design section suggested that the cruiser could be a modified 1919 fleet submarine, shortened to 310 ft (the minimum length to accommodate everything wanted) and widenend (to increase capacity). C&R planned to use three 1,000-BHP diesels, two for direct drive (14 kt) and one driving a generator. Because it occupied much less beam than the pair planned for the fleet submarine, the single generator could be moved forward and interchanged with the forward storage battery of the fleet submarine. The would leave enough volume to double the number of battery cells. An enlarged lower hull could provide 275 tons of tankage for 6,000 nm (19,000 nm by storing 610 tons of fuel oil in ballast tanks).

Early in 1920, it was unclear just which submarines would be built under the V-class appropriation. A February 1920 conference of OpNav Planning Division and OpNav submarine officers proposed that only the three boats already funded be completed as fleet submarines; the others should be cruisers. One submarine officer suggested that the nine V-boats be divided among six cruisers, one fleet boat (V-1 type), one minelayer, and one really fast steam submarine. The General Board maintained that its 1916 bargain with Congress specified true fleet submarines.

The Washington submarine officers had started to developed characteristics for the long-range cruiser they wanted in January 1920. In February, the OpNav submarine section, led by Captain Hart, suggested the two alternatives shown in Table 9–1, much the same except for

O-6 shows a typical post–World War I radio-receiving antenna, comprising insulated loops running fore and aft of her bridge. The antennas were supported by the clearing lines intended to keep obstacles such as mine cables from fouling the deck. The loop antennas were first demonstrated. In 1918, when a submarine at a 21-ft depth off New London received European radio stations (29 to 30 kHz). The fore-and-aft loops were directional and generally supplemented by a pair of small pancake loops in sealed wooden containers in the bridge wings. The post forward of the bridge fairwater is actually the barrel of a 3 in/23 gun on a disappearing mount.

Table 9–1. Cruiser Submarine Proposals, February 1920

	A	B
Dimensions (ft)	326 × 29	310 × 28.75
Displacement (tons)	2,150	2,000
Nominal speed (kt)	18	17
Main engines (BHP)	2 × 2,200 Busch-Sulzer	2 × 1,750 MAN
Charging engines (BHP)	1 × 1,000 Busch-Sulzer	1 × 1,200 MAN
Motors (HP)	2 × 1,000	2 × 1,000
Main engines (kt)	17.6	17.5
All engines (kt)	18.5	18.1
Trials: 48-hr (kt)	16.75	16.4
Diesel-electric (kt)	9.5	9.7
Submerged speed (kt)	9.5	9.5
Fuel oil (tons)	475	425

surface speed (opinions varied from 15–18 kt). The submarine had to be fast enough to get into position to attack reasonably fast merchant ships and to escape armed merchant cruisers on the surface. Cruising operation required twice the stores endurance of the fleet boat (90 days versus 45 days for a complement of six officers and 64 crewmen) and a radius of 20,000 nm at 9 kt. Two S-3 batteries or their equivalent would drive the submarine at 5 kt for 20 hr. Only folding masts offered the required radio transmitting range of at least 2,000 nm (the limit for permanent masts was probably 500 nm).

The officers wanted six long 21-in bow tubes (10 torpedoes) for a quick second salvo, either to reattack an evading target or to hit a second target appearing immediately after the first (it took about 10 min to reload four tubes). Long torpedoes would help overcome a target's speed advantage in a bow shot. There would be two short 21-in stern tubes (10 torpedoes): a stern shot would be at shorter range, and long stern tubes probably would be difficult to install. The submarine would also have a 6-in/53 cruiser gun forward and a 5-in/25 AA gun aft, with two machine guns on the bridge.

It was not clear whether the submarine would be controlled from the conning tower or the control room. One officer wanted two bifocal periscopes, one long and one short, in the control room and a firing (attack) and twilight periscope in the conning tower.

C&R agreed that it might be wise to build at least two types of submarines. Lt. Comdr. H. L. Abbott, C&R's representative to the General Board, prepared modified cruiser characteristics after a discussion with board members. He suggested all long torpedoes (two reloads per tube, six tubes forward and two aft) plus one 8-in/50 or 6-in/53 gun forward and one 3-in/23 AA gun aft. Surface speed would be 16 kt and submerged maximum speed, 9 kt for 1½ hr, rather than the 1 hr usually de-

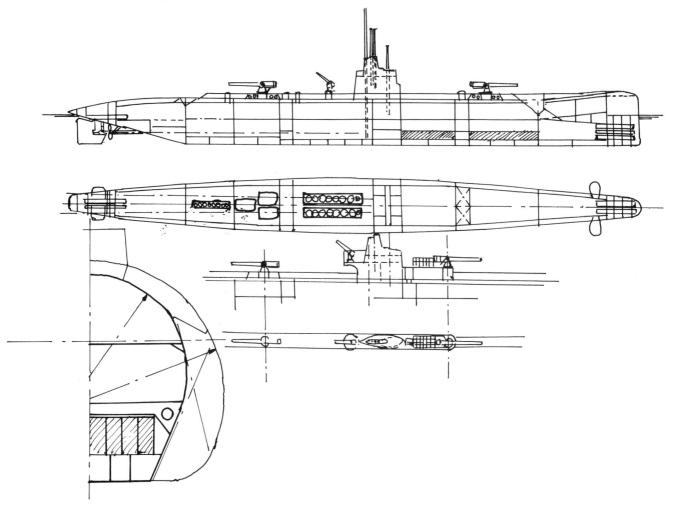

Cruiser Submarine 1920 was a first design step toward a viable long-range submarine. This drawing, based on C&R sketch 005687 of 9 April 1920, shows a 2,680-ton boat (325 ft × 27 ft 7¼ in) armed with eight torpedo tubes (six bow and two stern, with two reloads each), plus two 6-in/50 guns and one 3-in/23 antiaircraft gun. Had the submarine been built, the heavy guns would have been 6-in/53s, as in the big cruisers. The power plant would have been a pair of 2,300-BHP Busch-Sulzer diesels in the main engine room, plus a single 1,100-BHP Busch-Sulzer generator diesel further aft. An additional generator (900 BHP) would share a space with the main motors. Each of two batteries (shaded) would contain 120 S-1 cells. Estimated performance was 17 kt surfaced and 10.5 kt submerged; radius would be 20,000 nm at 11 kt with maximum fuel oil. Complement was 6 officers and 70 enlisted men. The scrap views (bottom) show an alternative gun battery arrangement. A midships cross section at lower left shows an unusual flat bottom. The two radius lines indicate the centers of the circular parts of the pressure hull (radius, 11 ft) and the outer hull (radius, 15 ft 3 in). Another unusual feature was two usable decks, with the upper one at about the waterline (as shown). Below the lower deck were batteries (shaded) and, below them, oil fuel. Both decks would contain quarters, the crew on the forward upper and lower levels and the officers on the after upper level. The spaces between the quarters forward and between the main engine room and the motor room aft would be occupied by 6-in magazines, with fresh water tankage below the forward magazine. Aft, electrical auxiliaries and a switchboard would occupy the space over the motor/generator room. The diesel generator would have an unusual placement abaft the main engines, which would require long shafts. Other sketch studies of this period show a 6-in/50 or 8-in/50 gun forward and a 5-in antiaircraft gun aft. The undated 8-in gun design shows three sets of battery cells (60 cells each). The entire series was designated Long Radius Submarine 1919 (Design 222 in the Preliminary Design group series). Another study, Low-Speed (Small Displacement) Submarine 1919 (Design 225), suggested that surfaced displacement could be cut to about 1,700 tons, but nothing approaching a spring style was developed.

manded. Normal endurance would be 10,000 nm at 11 kt (20,000 nm using some main ballast tanks for fuel). C&R offered a test depth of 300 ft, presumably appropriate to a much longer submarine. It suggested a submerged endurance of at least 15 hr at 5 kt and at least 36 hr at the minimum speed at which the submarine could be controlled. Requiring a fixed endurance at minimum speed, a new idea, was adopted for subsequent classes. As in OpNav's proposal, the cruiser would have an endurance of 90 days (complement of six officers and 70 crew).

Based on these characteristics, C&R developed a spring style for what it called Long-Radius Submarine 1919 (submitted on 9 April 1920), in time for the FY 21 program (Table 9–2). Congress did not approve further submarine construction, so work on this project ceased. That June, however, OpNav Submarine Section presented new proposals (Table 9–3) incorporating the 300-ft test depth and 90-day endurance. They formed the basis for the cruiser submarines actually built.

At first the General Board held its ground; it would ask for fleet submarines in FY 20 and cruisers in FY 21. OpNav revived its argument in June 1920; whatever the General Board's fears, Congress had shown no interest in actually

paying for more than the first three boats. The treaty prohibition on fortifying U.S. Pacific bases changed the General Board's mind. No existing U.S. submarine could scout from the remaining secure base in Hawaii. In October 1922, (FY 22 report), the General Board called for development of a scout (cruiser) and a minelayer. The scout would have much greater endurance than the earlier V-1 class fleet submarine (17,000 nm versus 6,000 nm, 90 days versus 45 days) and a heavier gun battery (two 6-in/53 guns versus one 5-in/51 gun); it would also carry more torpedoes (30 versus 12) because it would have to operate independently for a long period. Radio range would be at least twice that of a fleet submarine. The similar minelayer would carry fewer torpedoes and tubes.

Much more exotic ideas were also considered. About June 1920, Lt. Comdr. F. S. Craven pointed out that a true strategic scout might have to fight for her information; he wanted a submersible cruiser or battlecruiser, with a surface speed of 25 kt (i.e., with steam power), armored against 8-in shell fire (at 8,000 yd), and armed with four or six 12-inch guns in watertight rotating turrets. Craven knew that he was asking for a very large submarine. Pressure hull diameter was limited. He suggested wrapping an outer hull around several parallel tubular pressure hulls. This may have been the first such proposal; the Soviet Typhoon is the only current submarine of this type.

C&R and BuEng sketched a Craven-type submarine scout in August 1920 but argued that it was too risky and too expensive to build.[9] With the conventional cruiser apparently dead, however, the idea of a very large submarine scout remained attractive. On 5 October, Chief Constructor Rear Adm. David W. Taylor ordered studies of long-range armored submarines capable of carrying scout aircraft and 8-in guns (he suggested eight in twin turrets). Unlike Craven, Taylor did not require high speed. To accommodate fairly large airplanes, the proposed airplane compartment (tank) was 16 ft in diameter (see Table 9–4). A small airplane was later tested aboard S 1.[10]

The unprotected Taylor cruiser (type 1, 20 October 1920) could not dive safely if its hangar tubes were damaged and therefore floodable. Type 2 (23 October) added armor (a 90-lb deck) against gunfire but lacked protection against torpedo hits. Type 3 added battleship-type layered torpedo protection. All of this cost too much speed: 11.75 kt (type 3) was far too slow; foreign submarines might soon be as fast submerged and able to keep up without risking exposure to her guns. She needed at least 15 kt (17 kt, preferably). Speed was expensive: to make 17 kt, she would have displaced about 16,000 tons (length 460 ft), with steam power. Unprotected and with reduced gun power, Type 4 tested the effect of increasing speed to 18 kt. It had wet seaplane stowage (the upper parts of the hangars could be flooded).

Type 5 showed that 20 kt would have required 18,500 tons surfaced and a length of 500 ft. This version was reported to Taylor and to the chief of preliminary design, Capt. Robert Stocker. By late 1920, steam power no longer seemed attractive, so early in November work began on

Table 9–2. C&R Sketch Designs for Long-Radius Submarine, 1919

	4 February 1920 Proposed Long-Radius	9 April 1920 Long-Radius
Displacement (tons)	2,150	2,680
Dimensions (ft)*	305 × 29 × 15.5	325 × 30.5 × 15-7¼
Main ballast tank capacity (tons)	——	About 500
Reserve buoyancy	——	About 20%
Speed (kt)	18.4/——	17/10.5
Main engines (BHP)	2 × 1,750	2 × 2,300
Charging engines (BHP)	1 × 1,200	1 × 900
Motors (HP)	2 × 600	2 × 1,100
Batteries	2 × S-3	2 × S-1
Radius, normal (nm/kt)	——	6000/11
Radius, maximum (nm/kt)	——	20,000/11
Submerged radius	——	13.5/9, 75/5
Torpedo tubes (bow/stern)	6 long/2 short	6 long/2 short (16)
Guns	1 × 6-in, 1 × 5-in AA	2 × 6-in, 1 × 3-in AA
Complement	——	6/70
Test depth (ft)	300	——

* Length might refer to overall (LAO), on waterline (LWL), or between perpendiculars (LPB) (draft in diving trim).

Table 9–3.   Cruiser Submarine Proposals, June 1920

	Scheme A	Scheme B	Scheme C	Scheme D
Dimensions (ft)	310 × 29.5	340 × 32	245 × 21.5	230 × 20.5
Displacement (tons)	2,100	2,800	1,000	800
Nominal speed (kt)	16.5	17.5	15	16
Main engines (BHP)	2 × 1,750 MAN	2 × 3,000 MAN	2 × 1,200 MAN	2 × 1,200 MAN
Charging engines (BHP)	1 × 1,200 MAN	1 × 1,200 MAN	——	——
Trials: 4 hr (kt)	16.75	18.0	15.5	16.0
48 hr (kt)	15.0	16.25	14.0	14.5
Motors (HP)	2 × 1,000	2 × 1,250	2 × 700	2 × 700
Batteries	2 × S-2	2 × S-3	S-3	S-3
Submerged speed (kt)	9	8.5	9.5	10
Torpedo tubes	6 long/2 short	6 long/2 long	4 long/2 long	6 long/2 short
Guns	1 × 6-in/53 1 × 5-in/25	1 × 8-in high-powered 1 × 5-in/25	1 × 4-in/50 forward 1 × 3-in AA aft	—— 1 × 5-in/25 AA aft
Complement	6/64	6/64	4/33	4/33
Fuel oil (tons)	425	500	85	85
Radius (nm/kt)	20,000/8	25,000/7	5,000/11	5,000/11

Note: Schemes C and D were described as austere medium general purpose submarines (e.g., without a sounding machine or machine tools, and with short-range [250-nm] radio). Scheme D had 18-in tubes (16 torpedoes, compared with 12 in Scheme C). Alternative Scheme B machinery was two 2,200-BHP and one 900-BHP Busch-Sulzer engines (17.5/15.75 kt). Alternative Schemes C and D machinery was two 900-BHP Busch-Suzler engines.

Table 9–4.   C&R Cruiser Submarines, 1920

	20 October 1920 Type 1	Type 2	Type 3	23 October 1920 Type 4	Type 5
Displacement (tons)	10,000	13,500	13,500	8,750	18,500
Dimensions (ft)	400 × 48 × 33.25	490 × 60 × 29	425 × 71 × 26	550 × 42 × 27	500 × 72 × 29
Speed (kt)	14/——	15.5/——	11.75/——	18/——	20/——
Surface power (BHP)	5,600	8,800	4,400	13,250	26,000
Power plant	Diesel-electric	Diesel-electric	Diesel-electric	Diesel-electric	Steam-electric
Motors (HP)	4 × 1,400	8,800	4,400	13,250	8,800
Battery (cells)	480	480	240	720	480
Normal oil (tons)	1,000	1,350	1,350	750	1,600
Surface radius (nm/kt)	16,000/10	20,000/10	18,000/10	9000/10	11,500/10
Torpedo tubes	6/2	6/2	6/2	6/2	6/2
Guns	8 × 8-in, 2 × 4-in AA	8 × 8-in, 2 × 4-in AA	4 × 8-in, 2 × 4-in	2 × 8-in, 2 × 4-in AA	8 × 8-in, 2 × 4-in AA
Airplanes	4	4	6	3	8
Test depth (ft)	400	——	——	——	——
Protection for conning tower (in)	——	6/3	6/3	——	6/3
Turret port/roof/side (in)	——	6/3/2	6/3/2	——	6/3/2
Deck protection (lb)	——	90	90–120	——	90–120
Torpedo protection	——	——	Yes	——	Yes

Note: Type 2 had a vertical hangar; all others were horizontal (with elevators in types 3, 4, and 5).

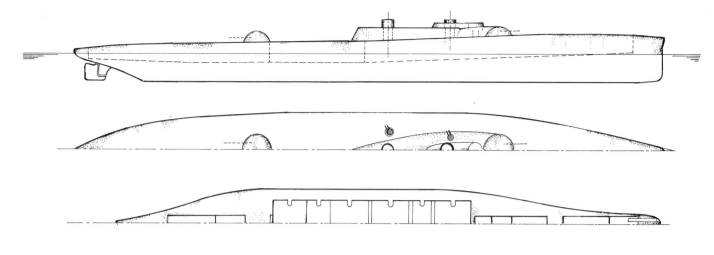

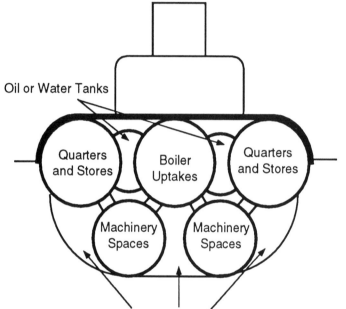

20,000 ton submarine proposed in 1920

Particulars

Length: 625' on waterline
Beam: 72' on waterline

Speed, Knots 25

Cruising Range at 10 kts, 20,000 miles
HP at 25 knots, 52,500

Propulsion: Steam Turbines, Diesel and Electric
4 Boilers Rooms, 2 Boilers in each

Main Battery, (4) 12"/50 cal guns
    (10) 21" torpedo tubes, bow
    (4) 21" torpedo tubes, stern

Armor: 6" maximum on sides, 6" on turrets,
    6" on conning tower

C&R's Preliminary Design Section developed a design series of large submarine scouts in 1920. This 20,000-tonner, with four 12-in/50 guns in hemispherical turrets (to resist water pressure) and four 4-in/50 antiaircraft guns, was typical. She would have 10 bow and 4 stern torpedo tubes; armor protection would amount to a 2-in deck and 3- to 6 in side armor extending 3 ft below the waterline. Dimensions were 625 ft (wl) × 72 ft 10 in × 30 ft. Despite the submarine's huge size, the power plant was limited to 52,500 SHP, for a surface speed of 25 kt, and consisted of eight boilers in four boiler rooms. Practicable pressure hull diameter was limited to 22 ft for machinery spaces and 20 ft for boiler spaces, so the designers used multiple parallel pressure hulls to obtain sufficient internal space. One advantage of this scheme was that boiler heat could be isolated when the craft submerged. This series of designs might have been the first to utilize multiple pressure hulls. The idea was reinvented, probably independently, by a Free Dutch naval constructor, M. F. Gunning, during World War II. After failing to interest British and American submarine designers, he convinced the Royal Netherlands Navy to use his concept in its *Potvis* class. One of Gunning's arguments was that, if post-1945 submarines were to be powered by closed-cycle steam plants, a multiple-hull design would isolate their heat and dangerous oxidants (e.g., hydrogen peroxide) from vital spaces in the main pressure hull. The Soviets used a multihull configuration for their Typhoon-class missile submarine, probably because they could not get sufficient diameter in any single cylinder. (Jim Christley)

a diesel type 6. The final version (early 1921) could make 17 kt (530 ft × 79 ft × 31 ft, 21,100 tons). By that time, the project was clearly academic.

Without congressional action on submarines in FY 21 and FY 22, Taylor could not justify further design effort. Looking toward the FY 23 or FY 24 program, C&R resumed

work in February 1922 on a cruiser submarine based on the 1920 concepts. It had already worked out many design problems of large submarines in developing the V-1 class, and the BuEng version of the MAN diesel was now available. The new design was based on the 1919 characteristics, with two 6-in guns; four (rather than six) bow and two stern tubes, all for long (6.8-m) torpedoes (total of 24); and a battery-charging engine. The first design, SC I (19 May 1922), had two 1,600-BHP, 10-cylinder BuEng diesels plus a 550-BHP charging engine (with a pair of 1,200-HP V-1 main motors). The designers considered placing the entire battery forward, in the lower part of a figure-eight hull. (This arrangement was never used in a U.S. submarine, but it would be adopted by the Germans in their high–battery-capacity Types XXI and XXIII during WW II.)

Because the layout was not particularly attractive, the control room was moved forward in SC II (20 May) and half the battery put abaft the motor room (as in V-1). The hull was too cramped; in SC III, the designers omitted the charging engine altogether, in the hope (not fulfilled) that the main engines could be throttled down to apply the small finishing charge to the battery. The battery was again moved forward, with its two halves separated by the forward 6-in magazine.

SC IV (October 1922) was the first serious approach to a long-range submarine cruiser (see Table 9–5). It of-fered only 15.5 kt (14 kt sustained). SC V was still slower: 1,400-BHP engines, 15 kt. That seemed slow: C&R developed a higher-powered SC VI (2,350-BHP main engines, 2,465 tons, 332 ft on the waterline, maximum 17 kt). The General Board still wanted substantial power and speed, so SC VI was selected for further development. BuOrd suggested that one or two 8-in guns be substituted for the single 6-in/53s, but they would have added too much top weight. C&R found that improved hull lines so cut resistance that a fast 2,465-tonner needed no more power than SC IV.

About the end of 1922 a pressure-proof tank for a 2,000-lb airplane was placed abaft the conning tower. BuAer wanted a 60-ft Mk 1 catapult, but, after much discussion, the preliminary designers provided only the tank and left launching arrangements for later.

The hull was enlarged (20-ft versus 19-ft pressure hull) and divided into sleeping, messing, and other crew spaces, as on a surface ship. Officers' quarters were concentrated in the forward torpedo room to gain space, as in the contemporary V 1 design (Febraury 1923). Officers

Table 9–5.   C&R Cruiser Submarines, 1922

	13 October 1922 SC IV	13 October 1922 SC VI	22 December 1922 SC VII	13 March 1923 SC VIII
Surfaced displacement (tons)	2,330	2,465	2,575	2,530-2,600
Dimensions (ft)	320 × 29.3 × 15	332 × 31 × 15	332 × 31.6 × 16	336 (LWL)/348 (LOA) × 34 × 16
Main ballast tank capacity (tons)	602	——	——	——
Reserve buoyancy	About 26%	——	——	——
Speed (kt)	15.5/8.0	17.0/8.0	17/8.0	17/8.0
Engines (BHP)	2 × 1,600 MAN	2 × 3,000, 1 × 550 MAN	2 × 2,350, 1 × 550 BuEng	2 × 2,350, 1 × 550 BuEng
Motors (HP)	2 × 1,200	2 × 1,200	2 × 1,200	2 × 1,200
Battery	V-1	V-1	V-1	V 1 (120 cells)
Normal radius (nm/kt)	6,000/10	6,000/10	6,000/10	6,000/10
Maximum radius (nm/kt)	17,000/10	20,000/10	20,000/10	20,000/10
Submerged endurance (hr)	36	36	36	36 (2.5 kt)
Torpedo tubes (bow/stern)	4/2 long	4/2 long	4/2 long	4/2 long
Torpedoes	24	24	24	24
Guns	2 × 6-in/53 wet 200 rpg	2 × 6-in/53 wet 200 rpg	2 × 6-in/53 wet 200 rgp	2 × 6-in/53 wet 200 rpg
Surface endurance (days)	90	90	——	90
Complement	6/64	6/64	6/64	6/64
Time to dive (min)	1	——	1	——
Test depth (ft)	300	300	300	300
Airplane	1	1	1 × 2,000 lb	——

Note: SC VIII was to have at least 10 percent reserve buoyancy when fully loaded with reserve fuel. This design incorporated four 60-ft masts in pairs, hinged to fold aft; main antenna span was 186 ft.

were provided with their own hatch for use in port. An emergency cabin was provided amidships, with a wide passageway through the entire boat. The crew's mess was moved to the after battery room, just forward of the control room. As in V-1, electrical control gear had to be moved from the control room to a separate maneuvering room.

In April 1923, the General Board issued characteristics for a cruiser and a minelayer for FY 25; both were based on the evolved SC VI (SC VIII). As the U.S. Navy had no experience with submarine minelaying, it looked to German ideas. It wanted dry stowage to avoid damage to mines during a long Pacific crossing or patrol. Comdr. H. E. Saunders (then head of submarine hull design at C&R) suggested a horizontal rotating structure (cage). The Preliminary Design Section combined three German-style double tracks (port and starboard) for stowage and fore-aft movement (using worm gears) with revolving cages to shift mines between tracks and into the two 40-in mine-launching tubes (each of which carried four mines, moved aft by worm gears toward the opening through which they dropped). Plans initially called for stowing the mines

in upper and lower tracks, the main transverse bulkhead separating the mine rooms from the battery room. Because the mines were quite light, the tracks ended up on one level with a watertight flat separating them from the after batteries below (the crew was immediately forward of the mines). Mine stowage was divided into two rooms aft (two tracks forward, one aft), so that no single compartment was so large that flooding it would sink the boat. Eight mines were stowed in a mine-compensating tank. The entire system was controlled by numerous hydraulic motors. Rated surface speed was cut from 17 kt to 15 kt (engine power was cut to 1,400 BHP to reduce engine room volume), and complement was increased to seven officers and 66 enlisted men.

Maximum surface radius for both types was set at 18,000 nm. Daytime radio range would be at least 2,000 nm. If critical speeds could not be avoided altogether, the General Board hoped that they could be pushed above fleet cruising speed (10 kt) to 11–13 kts. In July 1924, however, the General Board complicated design: fleet cruising speed might be increased to 12 kt, so vibration had to be minimized between 9 kt and 13 kt.

Before being launched in November 1927, *Argonaut* shows her stern minelaying tubes. (*San Francisco Maritime Museum*)

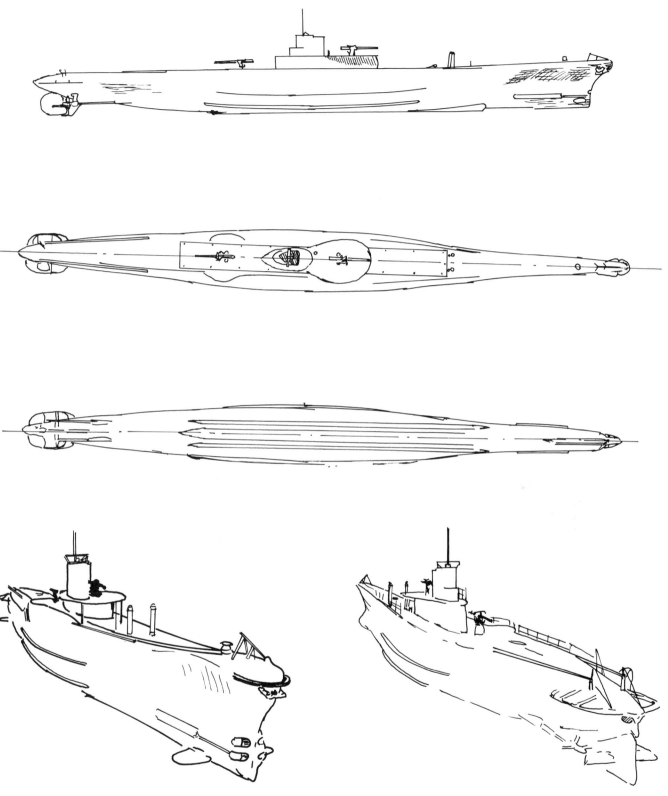

Model 2519 was made in July 1923 to test a Preliminary Design Section cruiser design. These sketches, made from photographs of the model, show the deck view and the underbody view. Note the docking keels. The guns are 6-in/53s. The long thin rods on deck are folded-down radio masts. There is no airplane hangar, and the bow is the bulbous type used on the V-1 class. This was one of the last designs developed before the airplane hangar was added abaft the bridge. It is probably a version of SC VII, which was powered by a pair of Bureau-type (BuEng-built engines to the copied MAN design) 2,350-BHP, 10-cylinder diesels, plus a 550-BHP charging engine, with a V-1 battery (120 cells) and a pair of 1,200-HP motors of the V-1 type. Overall length was probably about 332 ft (displacement 2,330 tons surfaced).

The FY 25 program (act of 28 May 1924) included only the minelayer, V-4 (later renamed *Argonaut*).

Late in 1923, the design showed a V-1–style bulbous/clipper bow. Officers familiar with the U-boats much favored their dory-type bows with long overhang, as well as their broad flat decks with substantial sheer forward. In November, Comdr. H. S. Howard, preliminary design chief, suggested that the German bow be considered. It was better for net cutting and for surface sea-keeping but worse for accommodating torpedo tubes, and it required a longer hull for the same speed (e.g., 350 ft × 31 ft × 15 ft 9 in, versus 340 ft × 33 ft × 15 ft, for 2,670 tons). It was slightly better at 10–15 kt. Either minelayer hull form would be better than V-1 (model tests showed it likely to be wet under nearly all conditions, partly because its deck was cut away forward for quick diving). Howard found little observable difference in behavior in the model basin. He adopted the German dory bow because seagoing officers were so firm; it was used in later U.S. submarines.[11]

By March 1924, displacement was 2,700 tons; overall length was 381 ft. The mines left space for only 110 tons of fuel (60 tons had to be carried in the main ballast tanks to make the normal endurance). When the requirement to carry an airplane was abandoned, internal tankage was rearranged; all 166 tons needed for the normal operating radius were carried internally. The mines also squeezed berthing; C&R could promise habitability equal only to that of later S-boats and the V-1 class.

The Control Force questioned the value of both the airplane and the 6-in/53 gun. Because it required a pressure-proof tank, the airplane could not be easily added to a mature submarine design.[12] The tank's buoyancy had to be taken into account in the design of the remaining tankage. Even the small tank for a 2,000-lb observation plane caused considerable trouble in the design.

Tests of a 2,000-lb scout on board the older submarine S-1 were disappointing. Any submarine carrying it would have been endangered because several hours were required to assemble or disassemble the plane. It seemed improbable that an airplane of this size could ever develop the requisite 200-nm range to reconnoiter enemy bases, such as those on the Japanese Inland Sea, that were 60–90 nm from the closest likely submarine position. An acceptable seaplane would carry a radio to relay its observations before higher-performance enemy aircraft could shoot it down, and it ought to be operable in 3–4 ft seas. Even if these requirements could be met, a returning airplane would surely lead enemy forces to the submarine. A submerged submarine would have to expose a radio antenna to receive the scouting report.

The General Board was far from sure that a better airplane, which had been designed (but not built) for V-4, would be worth the trouble. The airplane tank would considerably enlarge the submarine's silhouette on the surface, and it would make for sluggish behavior submerged. The large (11-ft) door closing the tank might be sprung by depth charging or the tank holed on the surface. Either would make submerged control difficult. The board

decided that V-4 would not carry an airplane, but that the question would remain open for future scouts, depending on whether an appropriate airplane could be developed.

The board preferred the 6-in gun to the alternative 5-in/51 because its shell had twice the destructive power, and also because it shot straighter (i.e., could be controlled at greater range). Its shells required power hoists. C&R initially planned to use rotating gun platforms, then shifted to a fixed gun table extending about 4 ft beyond the rails.

V-4 had twice the battery volume of the S-boats—240 cells, rather than 120, in two banks. They could be connected either singly or in parallel but not in series; the wiring could not take all 240 cells discharging in series. Operating voltage was doubled from 120 to 240 (the standard for later U.S. submarines). That made for smaller motors.

V-4's conning tower, longer than V-1's in order to accommodate two periscopes (rather than the usual one), was a cylinder on its side, as in all later U.S. submarines. One of these periscopes had a retractable fairing to reduce vibration resulting from the wave formed by the periscope. The second periscope was an experimental hydraulic type in a pressure-proof casing (it was soon removed).

The submariners disliked so large a submarine, and V-4 was not altogether satisfactory. For several years, the navy sought funds for modernization, including re-engining; they were finally included in the FY 40 budget. The Submarine Officers Conference wanted V-4 converted to a conventional submarine that laid mines (if at all) through her torpedo tubes. The General Board retorted that conversion would take 6 mo and cost about $225,000 for two stern tubes, or $300,000 for four. She might then carry 61 Mk 10 torpedo tube mines instead of 68 Mk 11s. The Board considered Mk 11 much superior, and the two mines were so different that a combination would much complicate minesweeping.[13]

The approach of war delayed work, but *Argonaut* was modernized at Mare Island between Febraury and July 1942. Her two BuEng engines were replaced by four 1,200-BHP GM 12-258S 4-cycle diesels (then being installed in the *Cachalots* [see below]) driving through hydraulic couplings and reduction gears; the auxiliary diesel was replaced by one 300 kw GM 8-268A and one 150 kW GM 4-268A. Other improvements were air conditioning; a torpedo data computer (TDC); new electronics, including SD and SJ radar; new long periscopes; and a negative tank. Two aft external tubes were operated from the mine room, and two external stowage tubes were added aft. The minelaying tubes remained. En route to the Pacific, *Argonaut* was converted to a transport (APS-1) by stripping out her mine gear at Pearl Harbor to carry 120 Marines to the raid on the Central Pacific island of Makin.[14]

The 1924 appropriations act required that plans of both a scout submarine and a fleet submarine be prepared for a possible FY 26 program, but by then the terms were interchangeable. Although the General Board had sought

For a time the U.S. Navy hoped to carry aircraft on board its cruiser submarines. The concept was tested on board S-1, as shown here (the submarine trimmed down to either launch or recover the airplane).

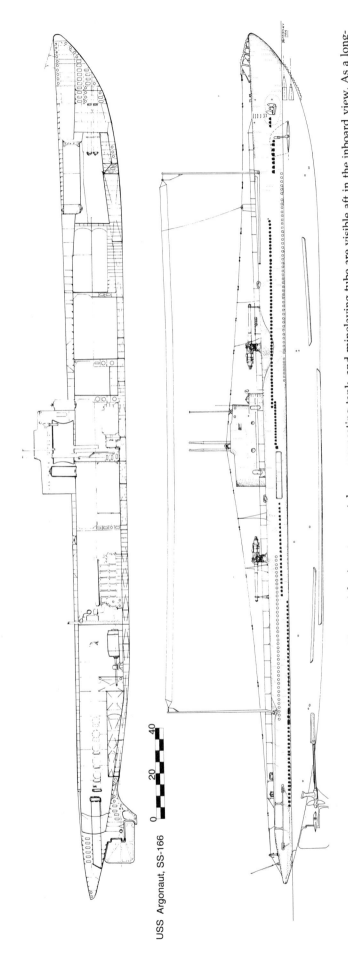

USS Argonaut, SS-166

0 20 40

Argonaut (SS 166) was built specifically as a minelayer. Her special mine stowage tube, compensating tank, and minelaying tube are visible aft in the inboard view. As a long-range cruiser, she had special habitability features: just abaft the torpedo room forward was a large crew's mess, with refrigerated stowage below it. Abaft those spaces were officers' quarters above a 6-in magazine. Below the control room (directly below the conning tower) were pumps and forward (battery-charging) engine rooms. Abaft them were CPO quarters and the maneuvering room above the after battery and the after 6-in magazine. Mines were stowed above and abaft the motors. The space above the torpedo room was a windlass room. This was the first U.S. submarine design to have a horizontal cylindrical conning tower; this type later became standard. (Jim Christley)

three scouts and two minelayers (to complete the 1916 program), only two scout/cruisers, V-5 and V-6 (later renamed *Narwhal* and *Nautilus*), were authorized for FY 26. They were initially designated SC, to distinguish them from fleet submarines (SF) and general purpose submarines (SS). The cruiser design was submitted on 24 November 1924. The board would have preferred a dual-purpose scout/minelayer, as fast as a scout/cruiser (17 kt) but armed as a minelayer with four torpedo tubes, 16 torpedoes, and 40 (not 60) mines (mine capacity being traded for larger engines). A quick study had shown that it would be too large, at 2,880 tons, and far too expensive.[15] BuOrd was already working on a mine that could be fired out of a standard torpedo tube.

By March 1925, C&R had lengthened its cruiser 9 ft to 360 ft (and added 296 tons to the 2,600 tons originally envisaged) to make it easier to achieve 17 kt on the surface.[16] That moved the forward torpedo room too far forward; blowing ballast tanks aft could no longer compensate if it was flooded. That was not acceptable: grounding or collision might well rupture a forward torpedo room (and torpedo rooms were specially vulnerable to flooding through the tubes). Adding watertight, pressure-proof

bulkheads cost too much length and tonnage. The hull was shortened to 345 ft by cutting fuel stowage inside the pressure hull to 62 tons (470 tons were in main ballast tanks), and the airplane (already deleted from V-4) was eliminated. The gun atop the airplane tank was brought down to the main deck (later the platform under both 6-in guns was raised). By July, the length had been cut another 2 ft, and the ballast tanks rearranged so that they could compensate for flooding of either torpedo room.

To avoid the wider critical speed range, machinery had to be considerably lengthened. Early in July 1925, BuEng asked for rearranged machinery.[17] Even a modest rearrangement demanded completely new calculations, which would take 3–4 wk. There was no dedicated submarine design section; the drafting room force had to be shifted to work on a new light cruiser. New outline sketch plans for the V-5 class were not submitted until 22 October.

Displacement rose from 2,869 tons to 2,996 tons, and length increased from 343 ft to 355 ft. That bought a second charging engine, which BuEng liked in view of the heavy estimated auxiliary power load and the difficulty it expected in charging the batteries with the main engines. The two charging engines would drive the submarine at

Narwhal was one of two cruiser submarines inspired by the German U-cruisers of World War I, armed with 6 in/53 guns. Her high freeboard reflects great reserve buoyancy.

The big cruiser *Nautilus* shows the stern form, similar to Lake's, that the U.S. Navy adopted after World War I. (*Donald R. McPherson via the Naval Historical Center*)

9 kt, within the range of critical speeds defined by the main engines. The secretary of the navy approved this design on 16 November 1925.

The submariners considered this cruiser too large, and some said it was too slow. Control Force thought that, at the least, two more bow torpedo tubes could be added for a total of six, as in the earlier proposed characteristics. In May 1926, C&R showed that was possible, but the General Board considered four tubes a sufficient salvo; an extra two would crowd out other essential features. In service, the two *Narwhals* were slow divers, sluggish underwater, and their speed slower than designed.

In 1939, *Nautilus* was modified to refuel seaplanes and carry 19,320 gal of aviation gasoline in converted fuel tanks. Reconstruction money became available in the FY 40 budget (for 1940 and 1941 overhauls). Each *Narwhal* would get four diesels, like those being installed in the *Cachalot*s (GM 16-258S), paired to each shaft through hydraulic clutches and gearing. *Nautilus* was modernized at Mare Island (July 1941–April 1942). Her charging diesels were replaced by two 300-kW GM 8-268s. Other improvements included air conditioning, new electronics (SD and SJ radar), a TDC, and four external torpedo tubes (two forward and two aft). The deck tubes proved weak; at

Midway, a Japanese depth charge set off a torpedo stowed in one (it made a "hot" run). The bow external tubes were moved closer to the bow in 1943. *Narwahl* was refitted at Mare Island between 15 September 1942 and 4 April 1943. Her engines were replaced by four 2-cycle GM 16-278As (as in the later fleet boats) for diesel-electric drive (the 16-258 was used for direct drive) and her auxiliaries by two 300-kW GM 8-268As. Compared with *Nautilus,* her external tubes were closer to her ends.

These submarines were roomy enough to accommodate troops. Upon completion of her big refit, *Narwhal* had her torpedoes and torpedo handling gear removed at San Diego, California; 120 wooden bunks were installed to accommodate an army scout unit for the invasion of the Aleutians. *Nautilus* also served as a transport (e.g., at Makin).

The FY 27 appropriations act required plans to be drawn up for possible FY 28 boats. In April 1926, the General Board proposed one repeat V-5 and two repeat V-4s. The Preliminary Design Section argued that a conventional minelayer would need too much lead ballast because it had to carry too much weight (mines) too high. In the fall of 1926, two designers (James L. Bates and George Sieker) offered a figure-eight solution (Bates had proposed the 1922 figure-eight design, SCI, described above). The less valuable space at the sides of the submarine would be eliminated, and underwater stability improved by moving the center of volume (buoyancy) farther above the center of gravity. Surface hydrodynamics also might be better because a fat circular-section hull made for a blunter bow with a worse curve of sectional areas (as a result of the cutaway forefoot of the dory bow). The figure eight could be arranged so that its narrowest section was at the waterline. The figure-eight hull would be viable only for submarine displacement above about 2,000 tons: otherwise, there would not be enough headroom for the engines. To test the idea, two alternative designs were put through preliminary design.

These ideas went nowhere because the big cruisers died. The submariners argued that it would take forever to build enough V-boats. They pressed for markedly smaller submarines that were much better suited to wartime production. Prototypes had to be built at once because production required fully worked-out designs, to the point of preparing viable working drawings and actually testing boats. Congress would never buy both cruisers and mobilization prototypes. Many submarine officers believed that C&R had unnecessarily complicated the big V-boats.

OpNav formally asked the new Submarine Officers Conference to recommend characteristics for new submarines. Through the fall of 1926, Comdr. J. H. Hoover, conference secretary, collected glowing accounts of the U-boats taken over in 1919. The conference wanted virtually to duplicate the ultimate U-boat of WW I, U-135, with a trial displacement of 1,000–1,400 tons on the surface (in diving trim), surface speed of 16 kt (8 kt submerged), and endurance of 10,000 nm at 9 kt (submerged, 36 hr at 3 kt). The V-boat's four bow and two stern tubes would

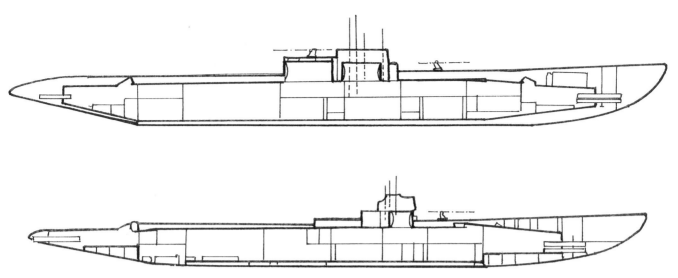

Depicted are designs for two generations of cruisers. A 14 November 1924 cruiser design (top) was sent to the secretary of the navy on 1 December for approval. Note the hangar under the after 6-in/53 gun. The submarine was designed to carry four 21-in torpedoes per tube. Dimensions were 360 ft (wl) × 34 ft (wl) × 16 ft, with surfaced displacement of 2,460 tons (3,365 tons when fully loaded with emergency oil fuel). Pressure hull diameter was 20 ft 5 in. Speed was 17 kt surfaced and 8 kt submerged. Estimated cruising radius at 10 kt was 6,000 nm with normal oil supply and 18,000 nm with emergency oil. Expected patrol duration was 90 days. Submerged endurance at minimum speed (1½–2½ kt) was 36 hr. The power plant, consisting of two 2,350-BHP, 10-cylinder Bureau diesels driving directly and one 450-BHP, 6-cylinder Bureau diesel driving a generator, was in a single engine room abaft the bridge structure. There were two 120-cell (UL 37-cell) batteries; underwater propulsion was by two 1,200-HP motors. Complement was 7 officers and 66 enlisted men. The conning tower and airplane room were armored (30-lb STS), as were the upper strakes of the pressure hull (50-lb STS). The internal arrangement was elaborate, with a wardroom and officers' quarters immediately abaft the forward torpedo room, then CPO quarters, the crew's mess, and the galley. Abaft the galley were the control room, radio room (important for a cruiser on strategic scouting duty), and then crew's quarters split fore and aft of the single machinery space. Magazines for the 6-in guns were under the galley and the radio room. The cruiser was C&R Design 318; this is Sketch 08094 in the C&R Preliminary Design series. Even at this stage, the design had to be worked out in considerable detail because weights and volumes had to match precisely, hence the elaborate assignment of such spaces as wardrooms and galleys. Submarine preliminary sketch designs have always entailed far more calculation than their surface ship counterparts, for which details are typically developed at a later stage. The big cruiser eventually became V-5 and V-6 (*Nautilus* and *Narwhal*).

V-7 (bottom) is the more austere successor cruiser, as conceived in July 1930 (Sketch 10673). The design shows a generator room just forward of the engine room; however, the crew space and washroom have been moved from just abaft the torpedo room to abaft the control room. The battery is now split between a forward battery under the officers' quarters and an after battery under the crew's quarters. CPO quarters are just forward of the after torpedo room. Total complement is 5 officers and 52 crewmen, of whom 36 are accommodated in the main crew's quarters, another 10 in the after torpedo room, and 8 in a space alongside the CPO quarters and maneuvering room (with space available for 2 additional crewmen). The earlier vertical cylinder conning tower has been replaced by the horizontal cylinder actually used, but the bridge fairwater has not yet been streamlined. The space abaft the conning tower is for vents, such as the main induction. The raised area abaft the fairwater is marked for ship's boats, but it was later used for torpedo stowage. Dimensions are 309 ft 9 in × 27 ft 10¼ in × 14 ft ⅞ in (1,687.55/1,979.01 tons). This design was built in somewhat different form as USS *Dolphin*. (Jim Christley)

be retained but with torpedo stowage halved (12 versus 24), and there would be one deck gun. Test depth would be reduced to 250 ft. A complement of about 60 should suffice. The conference officers thought that these figures were attainable because they expressed U-135 performance. The officers suggested duplicating her machinery and hull design (lines, framing, plating, tankage). They hoped to discipline C&R to accept the efficient design practices that they all associated with the wartime U-boats.[18] Memories of Electric Boat's perfidy had cooled: some thought a private constructor would be able to go to Europe for the lighter-weight machinery suited to a German-type submarine.

C&R could not agree. U-135 had far exceeded the performance of contemporary U.S. submarines, but she was hardly suited to a lengthy partrol in the western Pacific. For example, she lacked the oil coolers needed to operate in hot seas and the necessary space for stores (she had no cold storage at all). Although more comfortable than an S-boat, she lacked berths for one third of her crew, which would be unacceptable in peacetime. Wartime practices, such as accepting poor accessibility, would not do in a U.S. submarine intended for extended service, particularly independent operations far from home. The torpedo rooms were too short; German torpedoes (shorter than their U.S. counterparts) could not be handled with their

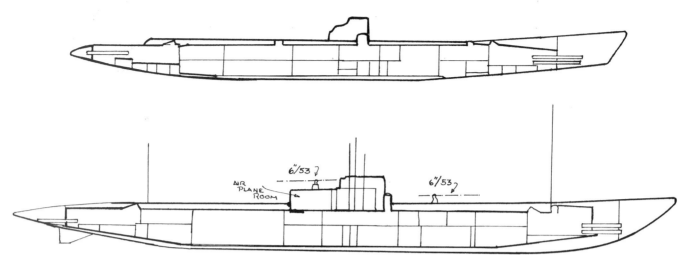

In accordance with C&R's attempt to pare cruiser submarine displacement, a 1,550-ton design (top) was submitted on 11 June 1929 (Sketch 010101: Scheme A for Design 356). This was C&R's first approach to the small cruiser submarine that eventually became V-7 (*Dolphin*). The arrangement was radically revised from that of V-5 and V-6. The generator engines (two 450-BHP) were in a separate auxiliary engine room forward, and the two direct-drive, 1,750-BHP diesels were in the big machinery space aft. Underwater propulsion was by two 750-HP motors. The crew was in the space immediately abaft the forward torpedo room, with the crew's mess abaft the auxiliary engine room and its galley abaft that. Officers were accommodated abaft the small control room, with CPOs and the maneuvering room abaft their quarters. Some of the crew was accommodated in the after torpedo room. Note that the conning tower is a small vertical cylinder, rather than the big horizontal one of V-5 and V-6. In contrast to the big V-boats, there were three torpedoes per tube. Dimensions were 308 ft 6 in × 26 ft 7 in × 14 ft 4 in (1,550 tons standard, 1,945 tons with emergency fuel). Rated speed of 17 kt (14 kt sustained) matched that of a big cruiser; submerged speed was 8 kt. Cruising radius with maximum oil supply was 11,000 nm at 10 kt or 16,000 nm at 7 kt. Submerged endurance at minimum speed (1.5 kt) was 36 hr. For this design, underwater endurance was calculated at 1- and 8-hr battery discharge rates, rather than 1- and 10-hr rates, as quoted for V-5. The battery was 240 R cells. The gun was a 4-in/50, as in an S-boat. It was provided with 100 rounds, compared with 200 rounds per 6-in/53 gun in the big V-cruisers. Test depth was cut from 300 ft to 250 ft, and pressure hull plating was 22 lb, rather than 30 lb. Patrol duration was cut from 90 to 75 days. Complement was 5 officers and 52 enlisted men.

For comparison, a more developed version of Sketch 08094 (which evolved into V-5 and V-6), dated 8 April 1925, is shown (bottom). Dimensions have been cut to 345 ft × 34 ft 4 in × 15 ft 8 in (2,896/3,332 tons). Pressure hull diameter was cut to 20 ft 2 in. Note the dishing of the two big pressure-proof compartments above the pressure hull, the conning tower, and the hangar. Accommodation has been rearranged, with crew's quarters alongside CPO quarters abaft the officers' quarters forward and no separate crew's mess. (Jim Christley)

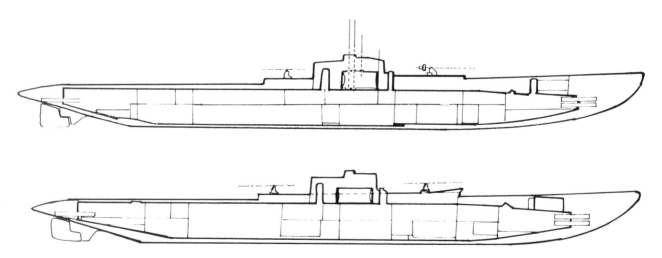

In these sketches, C&R reaches the V-5 design. At top is the step (5 June 1925: Design 325, sketch 08359) in which C&R eliminated the hangar. That cut dimensions to 343 ft × 31 ft × 16 ft 8 in (2,869/3,302 tons). Pressure hull diameter was increased to 20 ft 6 in. Quarters were rearranged again. A crew space was immediately abaft the forward torpedo room, with officers' quarters abaft it. Between the officers' quarters and the control room were the galley and a much smaller radio room; abaft the control room were crew and CPO quarters. A maneuvering room was cut into the after crew quarters above the motors. The 16 October 1925 sketch (bottom) was a late stage in the design. Complement grew to 8 officers and 80 enlisted men. Dimensions were increased to 355 ft × 31 ft × 16 ft 8 in (2,996/3,441 tons) pressure hull diameter to 20 ft 4 in. (Jim Christley)

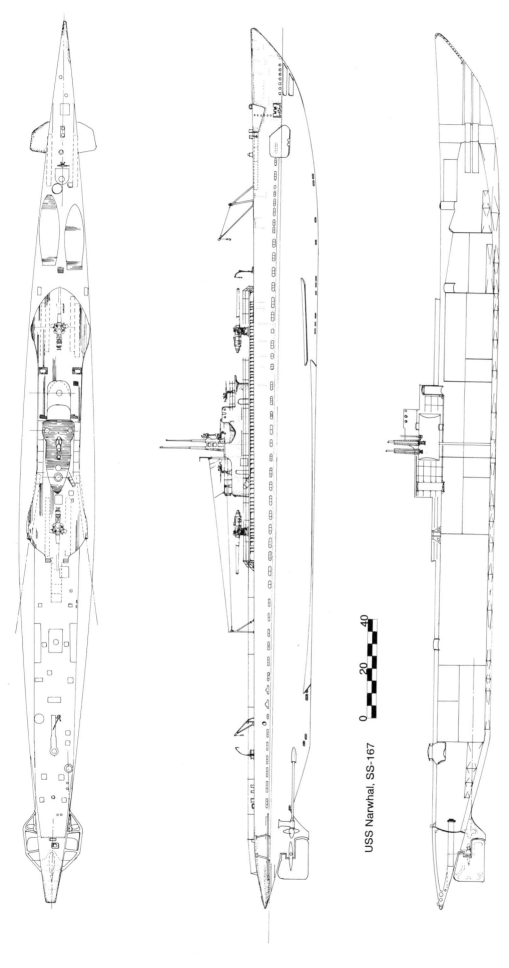

USS Narwhal, SS-167

0   20   40

Narwhal was, in effect, a cruiser version of *Argonaut* but without the special mine tubes. She is shown, as modified during World War II, with superstructure platforms for 20-mm guns and wartime-type open periscope shears. Note how her ship's boats were recessed into the deck forward of her 6-in guns. The added torpedo tubes under the gun deck are indicated in the plan view. As in *Argonaut*, pumps and the forward (battery-charging) engines occupied the space below the control room, which had a galley at its fore end. Abaft the control room were the crew's mess and CPO quarters above the after battery and the after 6-in magazine. Officers' quarters were above the forward battery and the forward 6-in magazine. In contrast to *Argonaut*, the maneuvering room was moved aft, above the motor room, which was abaft the big engine room. The small space abaft it, forward of the after torpedo room, was crew's quarters. The crew was also accommodated in the space between the forward torpedo room and the officers' quarters. (Jim Christley)

Narwhal, as modified, shown here on 3 April 1943 off Mare Island Navy Yard. Her SD radar mast is raised. Note the external tubes forward and right aft.

warheads attached. The submarine's outer shell plating was so light that C&R believed that oil leaks would develop.

With all these sacrifices, U-135 was about 40 tons overweight; C&R estimated that she needed 30–40 tons of ballast and had no margin for future growth. She lacked underwater stability (the British had reported in 1919 that she was difficult to control while submerged). C&R estimated that, to make her satisfactory, she should have grown by 70–80 tons or have had a complete generator set (or equivalent weight) removed in order to carry ballast and compensating water. On the widely held assumption that U.S. machinery and workmanship were inferior to Germany's, a U.S. copy of U-135 would be much more overweight. The submarine officers were therefore interested in buying as much equipment as possible in Europe, where they believed it could be built to something more like wartime German specifications. BuEng and C&R disagreed. To save weight, C&R accepted that a shorter submarine could have her test depth reduced from the V-boats' 300 ft to 250 ft (an increase back to 300 ft would cost about 75 tons in the C&R sketch designs).[19]

The General Board accepted that the new submarine must be a mobilization prototype. It submitted characteristics for the 1,500-ton Cruiser Submarine 1929 in September 1927. Cruising radius would be 6,000 nm at 10 kt (not less than 16,000 nm at 7 kt); stores endurance was cut from 90 to 75 days. Reliable speed would be 17 kt/4 hr and 14 kt/20 hr, using two main and two generator engines. Submerged maximum speed would be at least 8 kt (endurance at least 10 hr at 5 kt or 36 hr at minimum controllable speed, as in the larger submarines). Torpedo stowage was cut from 24 to 18 and the gun battery to one 4-in/50 gun, which needed no ammunition hoist (the alternative 5-in/

51 did), forward of the conning tower, plus four machine guns. Like the earlier V-boats, the new submarine would have to dive in less than a minute. Complement would be five officers and 52 enlisted men. The characteristics were formally approved on 22 May 1928.

Meanwhile, Electric Boat had offered an alternative "general purpose" submarine of roughly U-135 dimensions in January 1928. She was criticized for her light structure, but her key feature was a new-generation lightweight diesel. C&R and BuEng rejected the engine as experimental, hence unsuited to an operational submarine. Almost certainly, Electric Boat's proposal drove C&R to more aggressive weight reduction measures than it would otherwise have accepted.

C&R submitted three sketch designs on 8 May 1928 (see Table 9–6). The largest design used two direct-connected 1,750-BHP diesels and two 450-BHP generators (for diesel-electric drive); maximum surface speed was 17.25 kt (16.75 kt sustained). Three identical engines could fit a smaller-diameter hull: two 1,200-BHP direct-drive and one 1,000-BHP generator (derated) for 17.0/16.5 kt. The simplest and lightest plant consisted of two 1,750-BHP direct-drive engines (16.5/16.0 kt). This was least economical at low speed and the most risky because the boat would lose half of her power if one engine failed.[20]

Although the proposed characteristics included the usual normal and maximum endurance figures, C&R argued that only the maximum endurance, which included fuel stowed in main ballast tanks, was worth specifying. Internal tankage for the required normal endurance would cost about 260 tons. The General Board warned specifically of the danger of oil slicks. Size also could be cut by substituting short (195-in) for long (272-in) torpedoes.

C&R cautioned that any attempt to cut overall size dras-

Narwhal (*facing page*) shows war modifications in these Mare Island photographs taken on 28 March 1943. Circled changes include two external tubes forward, several 20-mm antiaircraft guns, and masts for SJ (forward) and SD (aft) radars. The ship was also fitted with external stern tubes right aft (her sister *Nautilus* had her after external tubes under the raised gun platform amidships).

Nautilus (as modified) is shown off Mare Island Navy Yard on 3 August 1943. She had already received external torpedo tubes during a Mare Island refit, July 1941–April 1942. One of them, firing aft, is visible under her gun deck. Another pair was fitted under the gun deck firing forward. During the 1943 refit, they were relocated to positions nearer the bow, as shown here. Also visible is torpedo stowage added under the gun deck. The weapons in deck tubes turned out to be vulnerable; during the Battle of Midway in June 1942, for instance, a Japanese depth charge started a torpedo in one tube. That was potentially extremely dangerous: the torpedo armed after making a fixed number of propeller revolutions, and the external tube was not accessible unless the submarine surfaced. Presumably, *Narwhal* had her after external tubes moved right aft, beyond the after end of the pressure hull, to reduce this danger.

tically might cost habitability and even reliability (engines would be less accessible); it would take about 1,600 tons to get better habitability than an S-boat or V-1. Simplifying machinery could cut manning; the most complex design required 54 enlisted men, rather than the 52 included in the General Board characteristics.

Table 9–6. C&R Schemes for V-7, 8 May 1928

	1	2	3
Standard displacement (tons)	1,431	1,160	1,317
Length on waterline (ft)	285	285	265
Beam on waterline (ft)	27.5	24.5	27.5
Draft (ft)	14	12.75	14
Surfaced displacement (tons)	1,575	1,275	1,450
Speed (kt)	17.25/8	17/8	16.75/8
Radius (nm/kt)	16,400/7	14,800/7	16,200/7
Main engines (BHP)	1,750 twin	1,200 twin	1,750 twin (6-cylinder)
Charging engines (BHP)	450 twin	1,000 single	——
Motors (HP)	2 × 900	2 × 800	2 × 900
Battery (cells)	240 R-type	240 short	240 R-type
Torpedo tubes (bow/stern)	4/2	4/2	4/2
Torpedoes (21 in × 17 ft) per tube	4	3	4
Test depth (ft)	250	250	250
Complement	5/54	5/48	5/54

In July, Rear Adm. Ridley McLean, commanding Battle Force submarines, complained that too little emphasis had been placed on the sustained ability of each submarine to operate far from home: on what he called reliability, accessibility (for repairs), and flexibility. Because no existing diesel could operate nearly continuously for 75 or 90 days, the submarine should have three or more engines and be able to run with one shut down for overhaul. McLean wanted at least 15 kt on two of three engines; he considered this maximum fleet cruising speed. On all three engines, the submarine could make 17–18 kt, which the fleet would rarely exceed. Admiral McLean contrasted solitary cruisers with fleet submarines that could rely on tenders. He liked the flexibility of all-electric drive for a fleet submarine but believed that it would be too unreliable for a cruiser.

The General Board agreed that the new submarine should have at least three engines. C&R submitted three new preliminary designs on 29 June (see Table 9–7). The board chose the four-engine option, designated (by blueprint number) 010101, which displaced 1,550 tons (rather than the 1,500 specified). As in a V-cruiser, the generator room was forward of the control room, at the opposite end of the submarine from the main engines. Although that probably made for better survivability, it added length. The board wanted something slightly smaller. C&R moved the generator room aft (just forward of the engine room). The two storage battery compartments then had to be moved forward. That moved the center of gravity forward; lines (distribution of buoyancy) had to be changed. The net result was heavier but shorter and beamier (010160A). Using emergency fuel oil stowage, the boat would run 11,000 nm at 10 kt (16,000 nm at 7 kt).

Table 9–7.   V-7 Design Alternatives, June and August 1929

	Blueprint Number/Date		
	010101 11 June	010160 14 August	010160A 14 August
Standard Displacement (tons)	1,550	1,570	1,570
Length on waterline (ft)	308.5	301	301
Beam (ft-in)	26-7	27-8	27-8
Draft (ft-in)	14-4	14-0	14-0
Ready to dive (tons)	1,676	1,695	1,695
Ballast (tons)	494	525	525
Emergency load (tons)	1,945	2,000	2,000
Speed (kt)	17/8	17/8	17/——
Endurance (nm/kt)	11,000/10 and 16,000/7 for all designs		
Submerged speed	8 kt/1 hr	8 kt/1 hr	4.3 kt/10 hr
Crawl	1.5 nm/ 36 hr	34.5 nm/ 8 hr	34.4 nm/ 8 hr
Drive (BHP)	2 × 1,750	2 × 1,750	To be determined
Generators (BHP)	2 × 450	2 × 450	To be determined
Motors (HP)	2 × 750	2 × 750	To be determined
Cells	240 R-cells in all designs		
Sustained speed	14 kt in all designs		
Armament			
Gun	1 × 4-in/50 (100 rpg) in all designs		
Torpedo tubes (bow/stern)	4/2 (3 torpedoes/tube) in all designs		
Machine guns	4	4	4
Test depth (ft)	250	250	250
Endurance (days)	75	75	75
Complement	5/52	5/52	5/52

Estimated surface speed was 17 kt. Submerged speed was 8 kt (endurance speed, 1.5 kt at the 36-hr rate).

This design was approved in August 1929. Sacrifices for compactness included a small conning tower modeled on that of an S-boat but enlarged to 7-ft diameter to accommodate instruments, a steering station, signal flags, and access to the gun. C&R tried to keep the torpedo tube shutters short (which entailed a blunt bow) yet make the entrance as fine as possible to maintain good speed. It also needed as much bow buoyancy as possible for good sea-keeping. The resulting bow form, which differed from that so successful in V-4, was criticized.

There was now clear evidence that the British and the Japanese were installing six bow tubes. In December 1929, the Control Force asked why U.S. submarines were limtied to four. C&R found that two more bow tubes would probably cost about $\frac{1}{2}$ kt (the design was already marginal for the required 17 kt) and 1,000 nm in endurance. If no more reloads were carried, about 20 tons would be added to the fore end of the submarine; access to the bow tubes would be somewhat worse. Installation would not be difficult, but it would delay the ship by 6 mo and cost $90,000–$180,000. The General Board, which had rejected the idea in 1928, did so again in May 1930.

One submarine officer, Comdr. Holbrook Gibson, remarked that because the torpedo firing manual described a stern shot as the easiest and the best of all, a balanced battery of four tubes forward and four aft might be far more desirable than six forward and two aft. Adding two stern tubes would move the steering gear down into an inaccessible and undesirable location. The changed stern contour would cost about $\frac{1}{4}$ kt submerged; the after torpedo room would be badly cramped.

Only V-7 (*Dolphin*) was built to this design. Too old to be worth modernizing, she made three war patrols, then served as a training boat at Pearl Harbor and later at New London. Before the end of 1929 (well before V-7 had been laid down), it was clear that the Untied States would be agreeing to a drastic cut in total submarine tonnage in the approaching London Treaty (1930). V-7 was now too large.

Dolphin was an attempt to prune back submarine size. She would have had at least two sister ships but for the London Treaty of 1930, which cut size even further.

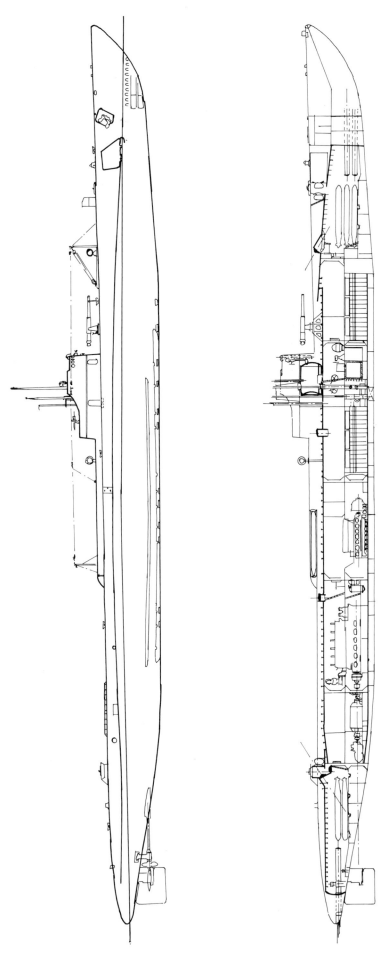

Dolphin (V-7), shown about 1943, is little modified from her peacetime appearance. She was then being used to train submariners at Pearl Harbor. After an inspection revealed considerable corrosion in her tanks, she was sent back to New London for less demanding training work. Torpedoes were stowed, as shown, in the external tubes abaft the bridge fairwater. Designed torpedo capacity was initially 18; in 1933, the General Board ordered that 3 more torpedoes be stowed externally, as shown, in a space originally planned for boat stowage. Note the separate generator engine in its compartment forward of the engine room. The officers lived forward, between the forward torpedo room and the radio room (which was forward of the control room); the main crew's quarters were abaft the control room, between it and the generator room. The maneuvering room was above the motor room, with CPO quarters abaft it. An unusual feature (not visible) was a third electric (25-HP creep) motor supplementing the usual two. Although common in German submarines, creep motors did not become standard in the U.S. Navy.

A new lightweight MAN diesel might make an even smaller cruiser practical. Enthusiasm for the 1,200-ton U-135, which seemd to promise what was wanted (albeit with shorter torpedoes and a 185-ft test depth), was revived. The General Board decided that V-8 and V-9 should approach V-7 characteristics as closely as possible within a new limit of 1,200 tons. The secretary of the navy approved this proposal on 12 August 1930.

This result was not preordained. Many favored going over to small defensive submarines (U.S. national policy limited the armed forces to defense). The Naval War College successfully defended the logic of Pacific warfare. All U.S. submarines should remain on patrol in the theater of operations, most likely to be the western Pacific, for as long as possible. If U.S. bases beyond Hawaii were lost, the submarines might need 3 wk to reach their patrol areas, so 75 days' endurance (the General Board standard) equated to 33 days in the war zone. Although 90 days (48 on station) would be much better, they were attainable only in a much larger (hence unacceptable) submarine. The longer the patrol time, the more targets the submarine might encounter. The War College wanted more torpedoes, rather than more tubes, but it wanted six bow tubes, if possible. Some torpedoes might be stowed in watertight containers (coffins) on deck (a total of 18 internally and 6 externally). This idea had not yet been tested.

Speed was set by the primary mission: to attack the enemy's main body, probably as it steamed toward its forward base prior to offering battle. At this time, the U.S. war plan called for the fleet to cruise toward an advanced base (either already in U.S. hands or on a largely uninhabited island) in convoy with its train (which would be deposited at the base as the fleet steamed out to seek battle). It was assumed that the Japanese fleet would have to act similarly, presumably, in part, because Japan had not been permitted to fortify its own Pacific island possessions. Tactical studies suggested that the submarine needed a 25 percent edge. It was unlikely that a cruising force (including a fleet train) could exceed 12 kt, so a sustained speed of 15 kt (maximum 17 kt) seemed sufficient. Speed might also be set by the need to operate with the fleet. Clearly, many submarines would not do so, but at least some would. Game board and full-scale exercises clearly demonstrated that submarines could contribute greatly to the success of a fleet action. The United States would never have enough submarines to guarantee that specialized units would be available when needed; all submarines should be capable of both cruiser and fleet support roles. This drive toward a single, general purpose submarine was characteristic of U.S. submarine development, both before and after WW II.

Speed and endurance equated to steaming radius: at

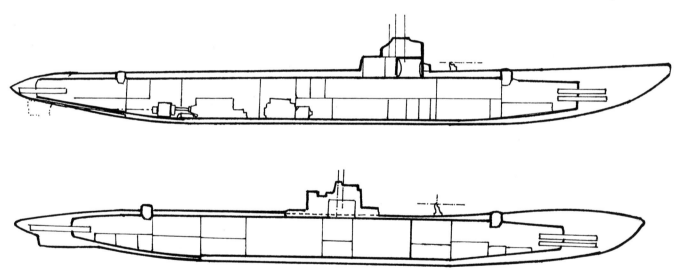

Scheme A (top) for *Cuttlefish* (Sketch 010721 of 9 November 1930) was essentially an Americanized U-135, with a German-style full double hull instead of the partial double hull of the V-7 design. Like earlier V-boats and the German submarine, she had a pair of diesel generators (in this case, 450 BHP each), in addition to a pair of 1,750-BHP direct-drive engines. In comparison with V-7 (*Dolphin*), the auxiliary engine room was moved forward, with the battery concentrated under the crew's and officers' quarters forward of it; the crew was just abaft the forward torpedo room. The complement was cut to 4 officers and 45 enlisted men; to save space, enlisted men were to be accommodated in the forward torpedo room (4 men), as well as in the usual forward (8 men) and after (12 men) crew's quarters and the after torpedo room (6 men). Berths were two high in most spaces and three high in the after torpedo room. With an insufficient number of berths for the crew, hot-bunking would be necessary. Although this design had the same six torpedo tubes as *Dolphin*, torpedo capacity was cut to 16. Dimensions were 268 ft 6 in × 26 ft 2 in × 13 ft 9½ in (1,326 tons surfaced). Battery cells totaled 360.

The later Scheme A-2 (bottom) used lightweight German 1,400-HP main engines and 600-HP generator engines in an attempt to make Scheme A acceptable. The generator engines were moved aft. There were now sufficient berths: 36 in the main crew's quarters, 8 abeam the maneuvering room (with 3 CPOs abaft the maneuvering room), and 6 in the after torpedo room. Complement was 5 officers and 48 enlisted men. Dimensions were length, 278 ft; draft, 14 ft; displacement, 1,375 tons standard, 1,489 tons surfaced, and 1,936 tons submerged. Estimated endurance was 9,900 nm at 10 kt. (Jim Christley)

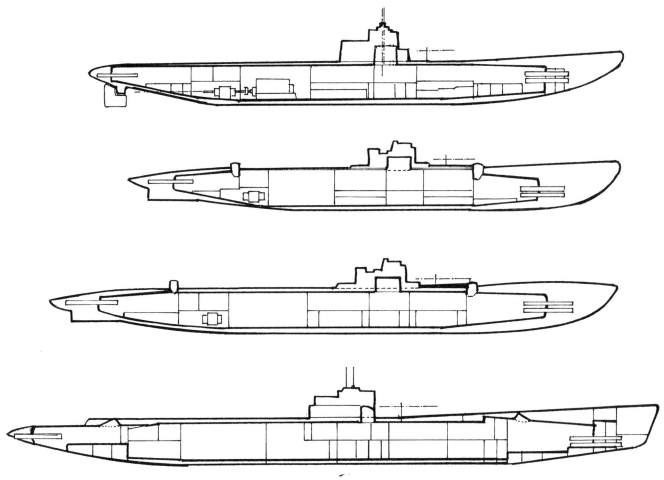

At top is Scheme C-2, which was developed into the *Cachalot* class. The other drawings show earlier stages in its development. C-2 was Scheme C (below); redesigned with new lightweight German 1,400-BHP diesels. Length was 250 ft 6 in; draft, 13 ft 6 in; displacement, 1,050 tons standard, 1,140.5 tons surfaced, 1,480.5 tons submerged. Estimated surface speed was 16.5 kt, and endurance was 8,400 nm at 10 kt. Complement was 5 officers and 39 enlisted men. All crew accommodation was in triple berths: 21 men in the main crew space, 9 abeam the maneuvering room (plus 3 CPOs abaft the maneuvering room), and 6 in the after torpedo room. The gun was described as 3.5-in caliber, a nonexistent size in the U.S. Navy (but equivalent to the standard German 88-mm U-boat gun).

The very light 1,400-BHP engines replaced lightweight German 1,750-BHP diesels in Scheme C (second drawing) which applied U.S. design practices (albeit with a U-135 underbody) to an earlier and larger Scheme B (below it): 241 ft × 24 ft 6 in × 13 ft 3 in (1,065 tons surfaced, 1,385 tons submerged). With the same power as Scheme B, she would have made 17.2 kt surfaced and 8.8 kt submerged. Complement would have been 4 officers and 33 enlisted men, the latter accommodated in the forward torpedo room (4 men), a crew compartment abaft amidships (18), abeam the maneuvering room (6), and in the after torpedo room (6), with space left over for 1 extra man.

Scheme B (C&R Sketch 010722: 1,276 tons surfaced, 1,656 tons submerged, 267 ft × 26 ft × 13 ft 7 in, third drawing) was an attempt to cut submarine size simply by eliminating generator engines. That cut the enlisted crew to 37. The 240-cell battery was now split between the space under the officers' quarters forward of the control room and the space under the crew's quarters abaft it. There were now 4 berths in the forward torpedo room, 24 in the main crew's quarters, 8 abeam the maneuvering room (with space for 3 CPOs abaft the maneuvering room), and 6 in the after torpedo room, for a total of 3 CPOs and 42 enlisted men. Estimated surface speed was 17 kt (8.4 kt submerged at the 1-hr rate). Enough space was saved for this design to accommodate long (i.e., long-range) torpedoes without paying any unacceptable tonnage penalty.

The drawing at the bottom shows what C&R wanted to avoid, a version of the 1,570-ton (standard displacement; 1,695 tons surfaced, 2,000 tons with emergency fuel oil; 301-ft × 27-ft × 14-ft), four-engine *Dolphin* design (this particular one is Scheme B, C&R Sketch 010160 of 14 August 1929). In this version of the design, the diesel generators were placed abaft the control room. Merely eliminating them would clearly save considerable length. The officers and radio room were moved forward (to abaft the crew's quarters), with the after battery below them (so that the entire battery was concentrated forward). An alternative Scheme C (C&R Sketch 010160A of 14 August 1929) used four generator engines for the kind of full diesel-electric drive adopted a few years later in the *Porpoise* class and proved successful during World War II in the Pacific. No calculations were made at this time; engines were not yet specified. The former auxiliary engine room had to be enlarged to accommodate larger engines, at the expense of the former main engine room, and the maneuvering room set into the after engine room, rather than being placed above the motor room, as in the contemporary Scheme B shown. (Jim Christley)

least 12,000 nm at economical speed (18,000 nm, as in V-7, seemed preferable). The War College suggested using the standard battery, which could provide 4 kt for 12 hr.

The War College estimated optimal unit displacement to maintain the maximum number of potential torpedo hits and the maximum service of information (i.e., the maximum number of deployed submarines) in an operating area assumed to be 3,900 nm from a base, within the allowed total tonnage. Similar techniques had been used to determine the optimal type of submarine within a given total outlay (e.g., $100 million in 1924).

A boat would run out to the patrol area (round trip of 33 days), operate there at two-thirds fuel rate, return home, and turn around in 20 days (an optimistic figure). Thus, a 1,062-ton submarine, with a nominal radius of 7,000 nm, would spend 11 days of every 64 (17 percent) on station. Treaty tonnage equated to 49 such submarines. Table 9–8 shows figures developed by the Naval War College for the General Board. Presumably, performance figures were scaled from one of the C&R designs. All of the candidate submarines had the same torpedo battery, but the logic strongly favored a submarine with more tubes (bow or stern) if they did not cost much in displacement (i.e., in total numbers). The War College's optimum treaty submarine was a 1,140-tonner with a radius of action of 12,500 nm at 10 kt (matching the 75-day stores endurance; the usual 11,000 nm at 10 kt was mismatched to 75 days). This estimate explains the General Board's belief that something between 1,100 and 1,200 tons would suffice.

Table 9–8. Number of Submarines on Station, 1930

Standard Displacement (tons)	Radius/ 10 kt	Days on Station	% of Time on Station	Submarines Continuously on Station
1,062	9,000	11	17	8 (of 49)
1,075	10,000	20	27	13 (of 49)
1,095	11,000	29	35	17 (of 48)
1,130	12,000	38	42	20 (of 47)
1,140	12,500	42	45	21 (of 47)
1,200	13,000	47	47	20 (of 44)

C&R submitted three sketch designs in September (Table 9–9). All had German-style double hulls; V-7 had used double-hull construction amidships but single-hull ends. Scheme A was a developed U-135, powered by BuEng engines, with inner hull diameter increased to get satisfactory submerged stability with moderate lead ballast. Additional weight might have been saved by using the new lightweight MAN diesel, but the engine's center of gravity was below that of the submarine. Any reduction in engine weight would decrease underwater stability and so would require added lead. Scheme B was a U-135-type hull with a lighter machinery arrangement of two direct-drive diesels. Unlike A and C, she would use long torpedoes. Scheme B still incorporated the features considered

The new *Cachalot* is shown at Portsmouth Navy Yard on 9 July 1934. Note the loop antenna (a pair of insulated lines) extending from the frame forward to stubs atop the bridge, as well as the flat top lines extending up to the telescoping mast. Part of the after loop is also visible. These radio antennas severely limited machine gun arcs of fire for submarine air defense.

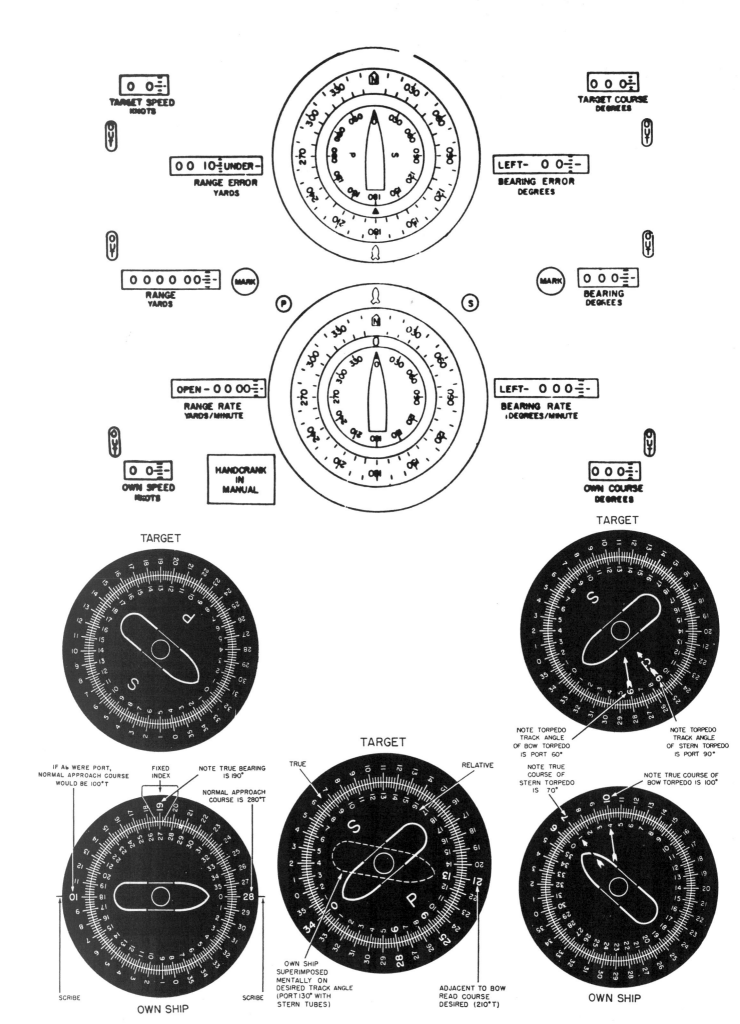

TARGET SPEED
KNOTS

TARGET COURSE
DEGREES

0 0 10 UNDER-
RANGE ERROR
YARDS

LEFT- 0 0
BEARING ERROR
DEGREES

0 0 0 0 0 0
RANGE
YARDS

MARK

MARK

0 0 0
BEARING
DEGREES

OPEN - 0 0 00
RANGE RATE
YARDS / MINUTE

LEFT- 0 0 0
BEARING RATE
DEGREES/MINUTE

0 0
OWN SPEED
KNOTS

HANDCRANK
IN
MANUAL

0 0 0
OWN COURSE
DEGREES

TARGET

TARGET

NOTE TORPEDO
TRACK ANGLE
OF BOW TORPEDO
IS PORT 60°

NOTE TORPEDO
TRACK ANGLE
OF STERN TORPEDO
IS PORT 90°

NOTE TRUE
COURSE OF
STERN TORPEDO
IS 70°

NOTE TRUE COURSE OF
BOW TORPEDO IS 100°

IF AÞ WERE PORT,
NORMAL APPROACH COURSE
WOULD BE 100°T

FIXED
INDEX

NOTE TRUE BEARING
IS 190°

NORMAL APPROACH
COURSE IS 280°T

TARGET

TRUE

RELATIVE

SCRIBE

OWN SHIP

SCRIBE

OWN SHIP SUPERIMPOSED
MENTALLY ON
DESIRED TRACK ANGLE
(PORT 130° WITH
STERN TUBES)

ADJACENT TO BOW
READ COURSE
DESIRED (210°T)

OWN SHIP

10

Submarines for Mobilization

THREE TECHNOLOGIES SHAPED the new submarine fleet that succeeded the V-boats: (1) a new approach to torpedo fire control, (2) sonar, and (3) new lightweight, high-speed diesels.

By the end of WW I, U.S. torpedoes could be gyro-set to turn as much as 90 degrees after firing. A submarine running parallel to her target could, in effect, fire all of her tubes as a broadside.[1] The Naval War College strongly espoused such tactics, although many submarines continued to think mainly of bow shots. Gyro shots were cumbersome. Settings had to be worked out in advance for a particular combination of submarine and target course and speed. Angles could not be recalculated quickly enough to deal with unexpected target maneuvers or for a submarine's need to evade escorts. Nor could orders be transmitted (by voice tube or telephone) or torpedoes quickly reset.

The two key dials of the position-keeper section of a torpedo data computer (TDC) are shown. They model the approach and attack situation. The upper dial shows the target, the lower the submarine; the line between represents the line of sight from submarine to target (postwar systems designed for attacks on submarines called this the line of sound). Outer rings show true bearing; inner ones are relative bearing. The submarine image is aligned to show the angle between the line of sight and the submarine heading; the target shows the angle on the bow, i.e., the angle between the line of sight and the target's course. The submarine attack officer steered according to true (compass) bearing, but the progress of the approach was reflected in the changing relative bearings of target and submarine, as American submariners learned from the British during World War I.

The small symbol below the target ship symbol represents a torpedo; it shows the track angle, i.e., the angle at which a torpedo fired to hit will approach the target. The similar symbol on the bottom dial shows the corresponding torpedo gyro angle, the angle through which the TDC turns the torpedo to approach the target. The approaching submarine commander sought to minimize gyro angle while obtaining the broadest possible track angle (closest to 90 deg) to make up for possible errors in target course and speed. Data—target course, target speed, relative target bearing, and range—were entered by hand using cranks. Own-ship data were entered automatically. The odometer dials shown here were added during World War II to existing TDCs as a field change.

The TDC contained separate angle-solver sections. Power switches could energize either the position keeper or the angle solver or both. Typically the angle solver was turned on only after a valid enemy course had been computed by the position keeper. Angle-solver dials showed the ordered gyro angle (at top) and the desired spread; the expected torpedo run was shown. Buttons could be pressed to indicate to the angle solver that the solution in the position keeper was correct.

A real TDC would have white numbers and symbols on a black background, but this version of the display is more legible.

No other navy developed a comparable instrument. The Germans and Japanese used angle solvers without position keepers (at least in the Japanese case, the device also had a timer that allowed it to dead reckon target position for indirect fire through smoke or mist). Probably because the Japanese had no TDC, they abandoned stern torpedo tubes in their later cruiser and fleet submarines on the grounds that they would require excessive gyro angles (Top). (U.S. Navy via Capt. James Patton, USN, Ret.)

These U.S. Navy diagrams show how the TDC was to have been used. At left is the pair of own- and target-course dials, showing the target and the submarine. The officer making the approach had to work out the course needed to obtain a given track angle. If the two dials were mentally superimposed (as at center), they showed the angle between the courses of the submarine and the target. For a stern shot, the necessary course angle appeared opposite the angle on the bow corresponding to the desired track angle. For a bow shot, the necessary course angle was read off 180 deg from the angle on the bow. True (as well as relative) bearings were shown on these dials because they corresponded to directions actually steered. (U.S. Navy via Terry Lindell)

Arrows on the TDC indicated torpedo course and gyro angle, as shown at right (solid arrow for bow tubes, broken arrow for stern tubes). The arrows on the target dial indicated present track angle, the angle at which the torpedo would hit if it were fired at any given moment (i.e., how good a shot was likely to be). Present track angle for a straight shot could be read off the dials by transposing the number on the outer ring opposite the submarine's disengaged axis to the target outer ring, then reading the corresponding inner number. In this example, submarine and target are on converging courses. (U.S. Navy via Terry Lindell)

Too, 90 degrees limited the submarine to targets exactly abeam. (The later Mk XIV could angle to 135 degrees.)

The submariners sought quick positive transmission and gyro-setting. The V-boats had visual indicators of desired gyro-settings in 15-degree increments. Because they were not connected to the gyro-setters, the repeat-back (set at the torpedo tubes) did not ensure proper setting. Neither intermediate angle orders nor orders for individual tubes (e.g., to attack two targets or to arrange a spread) could be sent. In 1930, the Submarine Officers Conference rejected power (i.e., remote) gyro-setting as excessively complicated; there was no point in being able to reset gyros rapidly to match a rapidly changing situation when calculations could not be made quickly enough.

That position changed after BuOrd developed a torpedo data computer (TDC) analogous to surface ship gun fire-control systems. The submarine system had to use far less precise initial target data, however, and had to make do with more intermittent observations of the target. Its operator input initial estimates of target range, course, and speed. On that basis, the TDC position keeper automatically projected ahead (generated) target position, course, and speed. Submarine course and speed were automatically input so that the TDC could keep track of own-ship position. At any moment, then, it could display relative range and bearing, which could be checked against a quick periscope observation. The operator could then correct assumed target course and speed to come closer to accurate figures. Once the data seemed to match (i.e., once it appeared that the target track was correct), the TDC operator passed it to an angle solver, a torpedo ballistic computer, that remotely set torpedoes through power gyro-setters at the tubes. As the submarine maneuvered, her torpedoes were kept properly aimed: a submarine evading escorts could still expect to hit a target. With two angle solvers, the system could fire any two tubes (one from each nest) simultaneously and all of the tubes in rapid succession.

Work on the TDC began during the winter of 1932–33, and the first specification (to apply to *Dolphin* and later submarines) was issued in February 1935. The prototype TDC was completed in the spring of 1938. The Mk 1 TDC included a plotter showing submarine and target courses and positions (e.g., as an aid to detecting the target's zigzag pattern). Each of two stations would be at a periscope: a main station (with the plotter) in the control room and a remote station in the conning tower. Mk 1 proved unduly complicated, but before that became obvious it had been ordered for all submarines through SS 197 (*Seawolf*). BuOrd then ordered competitive simplified systems from Arma (which had designed Mk 1) and from Ford Instrument (which provided most fire control systems). Arma's Mk 3 was selected in preference to Ford's Mk 2. Mk 2 was to have been installed in the 800-ton submarines *Marlin* and *Mackerel*, but it appears that they (and all WW II submarines) received versions of Mk 3.[2]

The original TDC limits were own-ship speed up to 12 kt and target speed up to 36 kt; torpedo speed could vary within 2 kt of nominal (with ballistics for torpedoes Mk XII, used only on board *Dolphin*, and Mk XIV). Torpedo gyro angle could be up to 135 degrees, for a track angle of up to 180 degrees. Generated present range had to be accurate to 10 yd/min of time, and generated bearing to within 60 min of arc/min of time at 300 yd, or 10 min of arc/min of time at 1,600 yd and beyond.

Mk 3 carried two dials on its face, one carrying a symbol representing the target and the other, below it, showing the submarine. The dials modeled the tactical situation: they showed the relative courses of target and attacker. The line between the two dials represented the submarine's line of sight to the target. An officer could easily see whether the estimated target angle (to the line of sight) matched what he saw through the periscope. As in WW I, bearings (shown on the two dials) were a guide to the appropriate approach tactic.[3]

The *Tambors* (SS 198 class) were designed as TDC Mk 1 matured. Clearly, it was so bulky that it had to be placed in the control room. Because sonar was an alternative source of TDC data, the sound gear was to have been moved from its usual location in the forward torpedo room (near the sound heads) into a combined radio/sound room in the control room, near the TDC. The CO normally

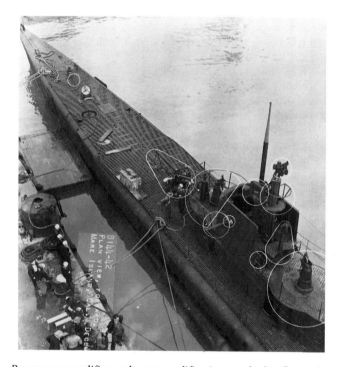

Pompano exemplifies early war modifications to the big fleet submarines in this 24 December 1942 Mare Island photograph. Changes have been circled. Her old streamlined bridge fairwater has been cut away, leaving a small open bridge. Forward of it is a new platform for a 20-mm gun (the gun itself is not atop its mount) and the retractable mast of her SD air-warning radar. The 3 in/50 gun has been moved forward of the fairwater. Atop the bridge are a square loop antenna (to receive HF radio signals at periscope depth) and the mast of a new SJ surface-search radar. The after end of the fairwater supports a second 20-mm mount. Note also the strut built out from the fairwater to support a long-wire radio antenna for use when surfaced.

conducted attacks from the conning tower above the control room. It was soon obvious that a remote indicator would not do: a CO would want to see (and to affect) the evolving solution. Generations of experience had shown that placing the CO in the control room caused congestion and confusion.

The TDC had to go up into an enlarged conning tower to be near its primary sensor, the CO's attack periscope. Sonar controls then had to be moved nearby.[4] Many COs liked to see what the sound operators were doing, rather than depend on delayed transmission of information describing a rapidly changing tactical situation. Moving both the TDC and the sound gear to the conning tower would eliminate the control room as a potential secondary battle station. Concentrating all fire control in the conning tower would also greatly simplify wiring and shrink the TDC switchboard by two-thirds. The conning tower had to be enlarged to accommodate seven men: CO, XO (at the chart desk), communications officer (at the TDC), steersman, two sound operators, and BOT (battle order telephone) operator (talker).

On the other hand, with everything concentrated in the conning tower, the submarine might be left defenseless if the conning tower were lost. To protect against that, emergency fire-control equipment (a loudspeaker and simple instruments) was placed in the forward torpedo room. One of two 40-ft periscopes was kept in the control room. It allowed the diving officer there to act as officer of the deck (OOD). Otherwise, a second officer would have been required in the conning tower at all times when the submarine ran submerged, an excessive burden for a boat with only five officers.

In theory, the TDC could transform tactics. Instead of maneuvering the submarine into attacking position, a CO using his TDC could maneuver his torpedoes. The location of the tubes might become almost irrelevant. Stern tubes should have become more important; however, after WW II, they were generally dismissed as not having been worth their cost. Apparently, many officers so distrusted the Mk XIV torpedo that they were hardly willing to risk shots requiring large gyro angles; these were generally used in desperation shots at targets that had gotten by a confused submarine in an awkward position. The TDC did help to sell the six-tube bow in 1939 by eliminating any delay in gyro-setting that might have been associated with additional tubes.

Sonar changed submarine tactics. Compared with its WW I ancestor, it operated at much higher frequency ("supersonic," i.e., above sonic frequency, typically above 15 or 16 kHz) and therefore at much shorter wavelength. Small trainable transducers produced beams narrow enough (typically 15 degrees wide) for fire control. The narrow operating frequency range could be set to exclude most natural sea noise, and the narrowness of the beam also excluded much interference. Although outside the human hearing range, sonar signals could be detected and amplified electronically, using the new technology of vacuum tubes. Ships' propellers produced supersonic, as well as sonic, noises (before WW II, it was argued that propeller sounds at supersonic frequency would be stronger than those at lower frequency).[5]

Prewar and wartime sonars were searchlights looking in one direction at a time. When a sonar was pinging, the operator waited long enough to receive the reflected echo before trying another bearing. Search was inefficient; active surface ship sonars turned out to be mainly a means of keeping contact with a submarine that had exposed itself (e.g., by firing a torpedo), but this fact was not immediately obvious. In January 1936, for example, a board of Subron 6 officers wrote that "destroyers equipped with echo ranging gear . . . can locate and follow a submarine with alarming regularity and at the present time with impunity." The board's proposal for a countermeasure foreshadowed wartime interest in antiescort homing torpedoes.

Mainly, submarines used their sonars to detect the continuous sound emitted by the target's propeller. The sonar had to be trained in one direction only long enough for the operator to recognize that sound. Unlike a periscope, passive sonar could continuously track target bearing. Its operator could estimate speed from the propeller blade rate. A single ping could establish target range. Combining these data gave target course. By 1938, it seemed that a submarine might attack on the basis of sonar alone and never have to expose her periscope. In wartime, that turned out to be far more difficult than expected.

The Naval Research Laboratory (NRL) was responsible for all interwar U.S. sonars, which were made by the Washington Navy Yard and by the Submarine Signal Co. S-49 and S-50 ran the first at-sea tests in January and February 1927. The projector (4-in thick quartz sandwiched between steel disks, 16-in diameter) was driven by a modified HF radio transmitter; the quarter-second echoes (pings) were picked up by a modified radio receiver, located in the radio room, that fed earphones and a range indicator. The projector extended through the bottom; the head of the housing trunk and the rotating shaft extended up into the control room. Only about 20 watts of power went into the water. Bottomed in 70 ft of water, the submarine could detect vessels drawing 18–20 ft at 1,500–1,800 yd and those drawing 10–12 ft at 1,000–1,200 yd. Bearings were accurate to within 2 degrees. Under less favorable conditions, range was often no more than a few hundred feet. Given its low power, the sonar was limited by flow noise to operation at 3–4 kt. The installation was massive (6,500 lb).

BuEng wanted a division of S-boats for further tests (only the S-18–S-41 class could accommodate the equipment). Commander in Chief, U.S. Fleet (CinCUS) feared that supersonic gear could not detect or give bearings on propeller noises and that it would greatly reduce signaling range, as well as the range over which bearings could be obtained. Nor could it be used (with submarine bells) for navigation. The CNO argued that this immature technology should not displace more useful equipment on board active boats. BuEng retorted that the existing sonic sets were ineffective. It claimed that supersonic echoes were independent of water depth, of the speed of the target ship, and, within limits, of the speed of the listener. They offered very accurate bearings and uniform range performance under all depth conditions. Four boats (S-18 and S-21–S-23) were fitted (weight was cut to 3,500 lb).

By 1929, NRL had produced a passive JK sonar to replace submarines' SC-tubes. It was the first one to use the new Rochelle Salt crystal transducer (more sensitive than quartz or steel). JK was soon provided with a small pinger for communications, and a few were modified for voice communications). For some years, it was the only sonar aboard U.S. submarines. In February 1935, JK was credited with an effective range of up to 6,000 yd in a moderate sea and a bearing error of less than 3 degrees. BuEng thought that this would suffice to bring a submarine within active sonar range (3,000–4,000 yd, error $\frac{1}{2}$ degree). During 1940–41, NRL and Submarine Signal converted the current JK-9 to the echo-ranging QBE Sonar by adding a Rochelle Salt projector. It was carried by some submarines and by most small wartime ASW craft.

The step following JK (1931) was a Rochelle Salt–active sonar, QB. The submarine versions, QBA and QBB, each had an active-passive keel unit and a passive-only deck unit. QBA required a separate supersonic echo-sounder; QBB incorporated one. By 1935, Washington Navy Yard was making about 60 JKs and Submarine Signal had begun work on about 30 QBs.

The next step up in transducer power was magnetostriction (QC series: a small electromagnet in a $\frac{3}{8}$-in × 5-in tube surrounded by coils of wire elongated or contracted as the current pulsed). BuEng had designed QC in 1934; Submarine Signal later produced six for submarines and six for destroyers each year. QCC (1937), equivalent to QBA, worked with a magnetostriction echosounder (NM-4). Because a Rochelle Salt transducer was more sensitive, it was retained for the topside listening element. BuEng abandoned QB in favor of the much better QC in 1938.

In March 1937, the Submarine Force recommended that new submarines have separate keel-mounted QB and topside QC-JK. Some submarines had combination sonar-sounders (W series). Meanwhile, the existing sonic communication oscillators were discarded: In January 1937 their installation in SS 182–187 was suspended; they were canceled for SS 186–193. The submariners wanted nondirectional supersonic gear, largely unaffected by own-propeller noise and thus effective at up to one-third speed. As pingers, they would be all-round underwater lookouts and collision alarms.

Tests in 1938 showed that a keel sonar performed far better than one on deck, so BuEng suggested that submarines be limited to a single QC-JK (redesignated QCD) in a keel sea chest. That left no means of listening when bottomed. Five listening transducer were therefore installed around the conning tower; the modified systems were QCG and QCH (modified to QCM with a remote-controlled, power-trained transducer).

The ultimate prewar sonar, WBA (designed in 1940), combined listening, ranging, and sounding for the new 800-ton coastal submarines. One Rochelle Salt transducer was used for listening and ranging, the other for sounding. During 1941–42, it was modified as WCA and WDA for fleet submarines. Each had a sounder and port and starboard ranging and listening transducers using both magnetostriction and Rochelle Salt, magnetostriction alone, and Rochelle Salt alone.

Sonar had definite limits. It was soon discovered that the layers in the water bent its beams. Flow noise made JK and QB ineffective above about 5 kt. Later, NRL's 19-in rubber spherical cover raised maximum listening speed to 10 kt. Only in 1940–41 did the U.S. Navy encounter British thin-steel domes, which made it possible to operate at about 15 kt.

BuEng continued to work on sonic devices that it believed would be more effective in shallow water, particularly when a submarine was running slowly or lying on the bottom. Hence, BuEng developed a hull-mounted directional sonic magnetophone, JL.

By 1941, modern submarines typically had JK-4 or -5; JL-4 or -5; QC-1 or -7, QCD, or QCG; and NM-4, -8, or -10. *Dolphin* had JG, JK-2, QC-2, and NM-4. *Argonaut* and *Nautilus* had JK and QCD-1 (*Narwhal* had QCH) plus sounders (NG, NM-4, NM-10, respectively). The V-1s had the combination WBA only. The surviving older submarines had JK-8, JK-2, or JK; S 27 and S 28 also had QC-4. In addition, the large submarines had K-series transmitters (KC, KD, KD-1, and KE-4) for underwater communications.[6]

The first four post–V-class submarines were included in the National Industrial Recovery Act (public works act) of 16 June 1993, a depression measure to revive U.S. industry. (It included the two *Yorktown*-class carriers.) Both C&R and BuEng rejected any repeat V-8 as impossibly cramped.

C&R called a series of conferences with submarine officers and also with designers from Electric Boat, which would be part of any future building program. New draft characteristics were drawn up at the final meeting on 23 May 1933. The General Board's desire for all-electric drive (see Appendix A) now would be met, with four 1,250-BHP engine-generators in two engine rooms (each no more than 40 ft long) in a 305-ft hull, for a maximum surface speed as high as 19 kt (C&R promised 18.0, compared with 16.5 kt for *Cachalot*). The new submarine would have the small conning tower of the earlier submarine. She would broadly match her predecessor, with 75 days' endurance and a radius of action of 11,000 nm at 10 kt. To run the more complex power plant, complement rose to five officers and 45 enlisted men. The General Board adopted these characteristics. It accepted increased tonnage (which cut the allowable number of submarines within the total tonnage limit from 35 to 31) because it expected overall treaty limits to change drastically when the London Treaty was reviewed in 1935.

The *Porpoise* class (SS 172–175 of FY 1934) was the precursor of the U.S. WW II "fleet" submarines of the *Gato* and *Balao* classes. *Porpoise* was much more scout/cruiser than fleet submarine. High maximum speed (19 kt rated)

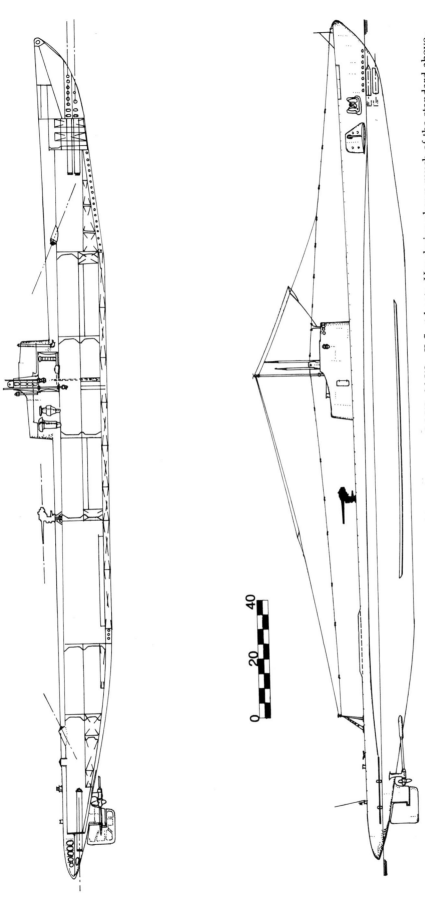

Porpoise was the first of the new generation of submarines that developed into the successful World War II fleet boats. Her design shows much of the standard above-water configuration for U.S. submarines completed through 1942. Many features of her internal arrangement were adopted in *Dolphin* (V-7): officers' quarters above the forward battery, control room below the conning tower and above the pump room, crew's quarters above the after battery, the engine room, and a maneuvering room above the motor room. *Dolphin* differed in having a large galley above an auxiliary (battery-charging) machinery room abaft the crew's mess / after battery and forward of the main engine room. In *Porpoise*, a small galley and washroom, with storeroom below, was worked in at the after end of the control room. (Jim Christley)

40

20

0

was mainly due to the demand for reliability (adequate speed on less than full power). The main power plant of four 1,150-BHP Winton diesels was supplemented by three 100-kW auxiliary (nonpropulsion) diesel generators (two 75-kW units had been originally planned). The auxiliary diesels were intended to avoid draining the battery while running surfaced (full power load 105–150 kW) or in port (load 50–60 kW), thus reducing the number of annual battery cycles from about 150 in *Dolphin* (V-7) to about 30, which would greatly prolong battery life. They were also valued for their ability to put a finishing charge on the battery. Removal of the third auxiliary diesel set was considered but rejected. These submarines used the new high-speed geared electric motors tested on S-20: two 1,075-BHP (1,300 RPM) motors on each shaft (one for running submerged, both for surface runs), on forward outboard and one aft and inboard in a separate motor compartment abaft the single engine room.

Electric Boat offered a modified design, with single ends and welded, rather than riveted, construction, to displace 1,310 tons, rather than the 1,300 tons of the C&R design. At first, Electric Boat was offered only one boat, but it eventually built two (the General Board approved a C&R proposal that contractors be allowed up to 1,317 tons). The other two submarines were built by Portsmouth Navy Yard, in accordance with the original C&R double-hull riveted design.

It turned out that much of the tank space near the ends of the fully double-hulled boats was inaccessible for maintenance; all later U.S. submarines had single-hull ends (the only fully double-hulled U.S. submarines after WW I were the very large V-4 through V-6, V-8, and V-9 [*Cachalots*] and the *Porpoises*).

At this time there was intense interest in welding. Portsmouth had built several welded barges; about 1934, the yard built a caisson, half-welded and half-riveted, and tested it against a depth charge. The steel tore between the narrow supports provided by I-beam framing behind it. Portsmouth concluded that riveting was best. Some time later, however, a second series of caisson tests was run, using separate welded and riveted caissons. This time the welded unit did far better, and C&R adopted welding.[7]

The forward torpedo room was too cramped: it had shrunk from 40 ft 3 in for *Dolphin* to 34 ft 11.5 in for *Cachalot* (which introduced the short torpedo); it was 36 ft long in Electric Boat's FY 34 submarines. The after torpedo room was not a problem: 45 ft 6 in for *Dolphin* and 46 ft 7 in for *Cachalot*. Torpedoes could not be easily pulled from their tubes for servicing, and reloading was cumbersome. Later classes grew to provide larger torpedo rooms.

The FY 35 characteristics (*Perch* class, SS 176–181), which repeated those for FY 34, were formally approved by the secretary of the navy on 18 April 1934. These six boats were powered by the new Winton, FM, and HOR diesels. The three 100-kW diesel generators of the *Porpoises* were replaced by two 235-kW units, which crowded the engine room. This class was unique in having eight, rather than four, main propulsion motors (*Pompano* reverted to four). It was the first class to incorporate air conditioning

(mainly dehumidification, actually,) as standard equipment (air conditioners had been tested aboard *Cuttlefish*).[8] The three navy-built boats were still being riveted and Electric Boat used welding. All six boats were built according to Electric Boat's partial double-hull layout. A BuShips design summary, written just before WW II, describes the *Perch* class as "perhaps unknowingly, [the] first step towards [the] all-purpose submarine" represented by the later "fleet boats." Many submariners argued that it was time to begin replacing the old S-boats: no single type could be satisfactory.

In framing its characteristics, the General Board needed some way to estimate an appropriate balance between surface speed underwater speed, and underwater endurance. It particularly wanted specific examples of the tactical value of surface speed. The new British *Thames* class made 22 kt, but submariners admitted that a longer-range U.S. boat could not make more than 19 kt on trials. A submarine capable of reliably sustaining 17 kt could keep up with the fleet cruising at 15 kt. Yet, recent tactical exercises certainly had shown that fast submarines could counter an enemy's unpredictable movements. For example, USS *Nautilus*, representing a division of fleet submarines, was ordered to attack an enemy landing force 28 nm from her current position. To get there soon enough, she ran in on the surface for 2½ hr, until she was within enemy air reconnaissance range. She had to run the rest of the distance submerged (which took 3 hr). Had she been a bit faster, *Nautilus* would have arrived in time to sink an enemy battleship. In the same exercise, *Bonita* tried to reach the landing zone from 55 nm away by running in on the surface. Had she been a knot or two faster, she would have arrived in time for her attack and doubled the force opposing the landing. Exercises also had shown that submarines of roughly fleet speed (15 kt) could not quickly respond to changes of fleet course (moving across the front of the fleet), whereas 20-kt submarines would have experienced no such problems. Although submarine surface speed probably could not be raised very much, it should not be reduced.

Many submariners wanted six bow tubes to overcome the improved underwater protection of foreign battleships.[9] C&R claimed that adding a pair of bow tubes would cost far too much displacement. Operating officers thought space was already available in the FY 34 design. A December 1933 Electric Boat sketch design showed that two more bow tubes could be added for only about 35 tons. The following month, the company proposed adding two external bow tubes and two external stern tubes. Pressed again by the submariners, C&R estimated that six bow tubes might cost as little as 20 tons (1,330 tons standard). Once that was accepted, a little more tonnage might well be worthwhile, for example, to buy space both in the torpedo room, to pull weapons for maintenance, and in the engine room, for better maintainance (1,352 tons for 2 ft more in the engine room or 1,364 tons for 2 ft more in the engine room and 4 ft in the torpedo room).

In December 1934, the Submarine Officers Conference met to recommend characteristics for the next (FY 36)

Porpoise was still in much her prewar form when this photograph was taken on 13 October 1942. *Porpoise* shows the flat stern introduced in the big V-boats. By this time, two external tubes had been added forward, and a fixed loop radio antenna is visible atop the bridge fairwater. Little changed since the boat was completed except for a 20-mm gun platform.

submarines, the six *Salmon* class (SS 182–187). The prospect of the TDC made after torpedo tubes much more valuable; the officers called for an additional pair aft, at a cost of about 30 tons, $\frac{1}{8}$ kt in submerged speed (nothing in surfaced speed), and some maneuverability. Aside from broadside fire, the extra tubes were attractive because, in theory, they allowed a submarine to engage two capital ships simultaneously, with four shots each. The submariners were also becoming more interested in approaching their targets from ahead and firing stern tubes as they passed. This fast approach gave escorts much less time to deal with the submarine. The chief of the Pacific Submarine Force found bow approaches particularly attractive for sound firing below periscope depth, "which is rapidly becoming almost a necessity against air-screened targets."

Many submariners were still leery of the congestion in a six-tube forward nest. At the short ranges then favored,

all of a given salvo would either hit or miss; surely, it would be better to miss with four torpedoes than with six. To avoid mutual interference, torpedoes had to be fired at least 5 sec apart. That so spread the torpedoes that two of six might well miss. Providing extra tubes might lead captains to wasteful ("shotgun") rather than aimed ("rifle") tactics. The extra weight involved might make a submarine firing a salvo of six more difficult to control. Others revived the argument that six tubes offered two salvos of three shots each without reloading. The crucial (and erroneous) argument at the 1935 Submarine Officers' Conference, however, was that extra bow tubes would push displacement up to 1,750 tons.

At their 1934 conference, the submarine officers asked for (and got) more torpedoes: one per tube, two reloads forward, one aft, plus one reload for each after tube carried externally under the superstructure. This was a total of

Thresher (SS 200) was typical of the big submarines prior to World War II, with her streamlined bridge fairwater and periscope shears and her 3 in/50 gun abaft the fairwater. The substantial masts fore and aft supported radio antenna cables.

Sealion shows the new stern form introduced to accommodate four rather than two after tubes. She is shown, newly completed, off Provincetown, Massachusetts, on 6 October 1939.

24, the same number carried by the big V-boats, rather than the 16 of earlier classes.[10] By this time, BuOrd had developed a mine launchable from torpedo tubes. The short torpedo skids of earlier fleet submarines could accommodate only one mine, but the long skids in the new class could each accommodate two mines. Their after tubes were adapted to launch mines; 16 could be carried aft in place of torpedoes.[11] The submariners wanted the tubes lengthened about $2\frac{1}{2}$ in order to fire long torpedoes if reserves of the short submarine torpedo proved inadequate in wartime. A longer tube might also fire without a telltale bubble.[12]

Characteristics were issued in February 1935. Because oil no longer would be stowed in main ballast tanks, a distinction between normal endurance (using fuel in oil tanks) and maximum endurance (using oil in ballast tanks) was not needed. Required sea speed was still 17 kt, but now it had to be maintained at deeper displacement (maximum fuel load), with enough reserve power to recharge the main batteries in 8 hr (an increased load given increased battery capacity). This apparently trivial change entailed a major increase in power. Similarly, the 11,000-nm cruising radius now took into account a 30 percent reserve for battery charging. Reserve buoyancy (for sea-keeping) was calculated on the basis of full (formerly "emergency"), rather than normal, load. On this basis, for example, the 36 percent reserve buoyancy of the *Porpoises* fell to 14.5 percent. Corresponding figures for the *Salmon* class were 34.2 percent and 18.2 percent. It was generally agreed that a long-range submarine needed 20–25 percent reserve buoyancy. BuShips later said that this FY 36 submarine (Salmon class [SS 182]) was designed really to accompany the fleet.

Battery capacity increased to maintain minimum submerged speed (2.5 kt) for 48 hr, rather than 36 hr; the threat of an air attack might force a submarine to stay

down much longer. Maximum submerged speed was set at 8.75 kt. Instead of enlarging individual cells, the number of cells per group was increased from 120 to 126. The 235-kw generators of the previous class were replaced by 330-kw units, powerful enough to make a real contribution to propulsion if one engine was down for overhaul or for battery charge. Clearly the engine room was now quite crowded.

The FY 36 displacement limit originally had been set at 1,360 tons, including 30 tons for the two extra stern tubes. The new design grew more, however, first to 1,400 tons and then to about 1,450 tons, partly because of the tacit requirements for higher speed and longer submerged endurance. These *Salmons* were of all-welded construction.

BuEng found it particularly difficult to charge batteries in 8 hr while the submarine maintained high speed in the open sea. In February 1935, it estimated that merely to maintain 17 kt with a foul bottom would add 2,000 BHP to the 2,600 BHP needed for a clean bottom in smooth weather (using more efficient geared drive would cut this to about 4,230 BHP). Another 2,120 BHP would be needed when charging began, for a total of at least 6,720 BHP. The usual quartet of engines supplied about 5,200 BHP. Two engines could be devoted to battery charging (usable for diesel-electric drive) and four others geared to the shafts, for a total of 7,800 BHP. Together, the six engines might drive a boat at 22.3 kt. Any submarine built around this power plant would be far too large.

Existing engines could be enlarged. Larger cylinders would boost the Winton (16-248, rather than 16-201A) to 1,535 BHP. Adding a cylinder would boost the HOR to 1,600 BHP (later 1,535 BHP). An all-electric plant (two engines with nine cylinders and two with eight cylinders) could charge the battery in 9–10 hr. If lower speed was accepted for the first 4 hr of battery charging, three of the

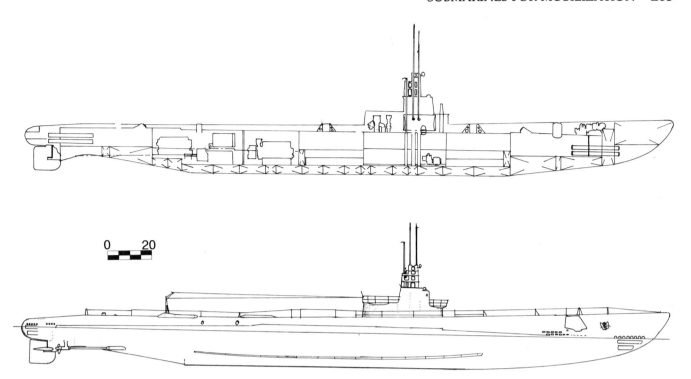

Salmon (SS 182) is shown as modified during World War II, with her bridge fairwater considerably cut down. Note the division into two separate engine rooms (to accommodate composite drive, the after engines being geared to the shafts) and the propulsion control cubicle in the after engine room; there was no separate maneuvering room. Portsmouth boats differed slightly from this Electric Boat unit. Their conning towers had the forward face dished out instead of in. Also slightly different were the hatch locations over the crew's quarters/after battery and the forward engine room; they were located in the middle of each compartment, rather than at the fore end of one and the after end of the other, as shown here (the engine room hatch is not shown). Both periscopes were let into the conning tower. The inboard profile shows gun mount foundations installed both fore and aft; boats normally carried only a single gun on one or the other. *Salmon* introduced a modified stern that accommodated four, rather than two, torpedo tubes. The after mast carried an SD air-search radar. For clarity, guns have been omitted in the sketch. (Jim Christley)

four engines could then be devoted to surface propulsion. Unfortunately, a submarine had to charge her batteries during darkness, which in some areas might not last even 8 hr. A boat needed sustained nighttime speed to get into a useful tactical position (relative, for instance, to a battle fleet) at dawn.

Four diesels came so close that marginal improvements might suffice. BuEng proposed a composite power plant, with two diesels driving the generators and two driving directly. Although it might seem that halving the charging plant would cut the charging rate, the limiting factor was the battery's ability to absorb energy. The other diesels were geared to the shafts through hydraulic clutches, which isolated the propeller shafts from engine vibration. To simplify maintenance, all four diesels would be identical enlarged engines (9-cylinder HORs or 16-248s). Two 500-BHP auxiliary generators could be equated to nearly two-thirds of a third diesel generator. The greater efficiency of the hydraulic clutch/gearing combination gained 0.4 kt (5,652 SHP versus 5,380 SHP) over the key speed range of 17–20 kt.[13]

In April 1935, BuEng calculated that a submarine could make 8.5 kt on one auxiliary diesel, 10.8 kt on two, 13.8 kt on one main generator, 17.3 kt on two main generators, 16.3 kt on pure diesel-hydraulic drive, 19.3 kt on

hydraulic plus one diesel-generator, and 21.5 kt on all six diesels. One main generator and the two auxiliaries could charge the battery in 8 hr while the submarine ran at 19.3 kt (assuming a smooth bottom under trial condition). Subtracting 1–1.5 kt for a foul bottom, BuEng estimated that the submarine could make 17.3 kt under war load while charging her batteries.

The composite power plant was lighter (by about 36,000 lb, total 322,000 lb) and more compact than its diesel-electric predecessor; it saved about 200 sq ft in *Salmon*. Machinery was more accessible. For example, all generators except one auxiliary unit had free space above them and thus were relatively easy to remove. In the earlier classes, the main generators were buried under heavy equipment. On the other hand, the plant was more complicated and less flexible. The auxiliary generators made so great a contribution that it was not at all clear that the complexity was needed. Like direct drive, geared/hydraulic drive required that shaft lines lead to the diesels (they could be more efficiently arranged in a diesel-electric submarine). For example, they could not run parallel to the centerline of the boat. Smaller propelling motors could be used in an all–diesel-electric boat (up to four per shaft), but that was impractical in composite drive.

By the fall of 1936, BuEng badly wanted to revert to

diesel-electric drive. The General Board agreed (for the FY 38 submarines). Opinion was hardly unanimous, partly because of teething problems with the early diesel-electric submarines. Adm. T. C. Hart, the only experienced submariner on the General Board, argued that any full diesel-electric plant could be disabled by flooding. Early in 1939, BuEng had to formally justify its position. The only alternative was to use two direct-drive diesels, with all their torsional vibration problems. It was impractical to gear two diesels to each shaft, and no existing hydraulic clutch, which would buffer the propeller shaft from engine vibration, could transmit half the power a submarine needed, say 2,000 BHP.

Foreign navies found direct or geared drive acceptable. It was not completely certain that U.S. submarines intended for work with the battlefleet could avoid critical speed ranges, so direct drive was much less palatable. No suitable U.S. 2,000-BHP engine existed because BuEng had been pursuing smaller lightweight, high-speed engines. They were far lighter than foreign diesels; for example, the 16-cylinder Sulzers used by Britain and France were at least 9.7 lb/SHP heavier than their U.S. counterparts. To meet General Board characteristics, U.S. boats required lightweight machinery. BuEng had already reduced *Dolphin's* 105 lb per BHP to 62 lb in modern submarines (e.g., *Plunger*), a difference equivalent to 79.5 tons in the earlier submarine.

The six FY 37 submarines (*Sargo* class, SS 188–193) generally repeated the FY 36 design. Inspired by the Submarine Officers Conference, the General Board required that the submarine maintain its sustained sea speed (17 kt) on three engines (i.e., with one down for repairs). It required 25 percent reserve buoyancy. Some officers associated the 17-kt requirement with the new standard auxiliary ship speed of 16.5 kt (like submarines, major auxiliaries were expected to cruise to the western Pacific with the main fleet). The conference wanted sea speed maintained with sufficient reserve to recharge the storage batteries with 2,000 BHP (a figure deleted by the General Board) or in minimum time within permissible battery limits. This change from previous language much simplified BuEng's problem. Dual-purpose (fuel-ballast) tanks were again prohibited.

Maximum submerged speed would be 8.75 kt. The boat had to sustain at least 2 kt submerged, with air conditioning and other auxiliaries running for 48 hr. The new standard BuEng battery (henceforth a *Sargo* battery) replaced the earlier commercial type bought from Exide and Gould. This and the next class had pairs of 250-kW auxiliary diesel generators. Such generators, however, were becoming less attractive. They could top off a battery charge and could carry the auxiliary load, but they tended to carbon up and smoke when carrying only the light port load. The FY 39 boats therefore had two generators of different power, one for the full-service load and one for the light port load.

The Portsmouth-built *Sculpin* and *Squalus* came out badly overweight, and portions of superstructure framing had to be cut away. Similar weight problems afflicted con-temporary destroyers, especially those built in navy yards. Submarine overweight was particularly serious because the weight and volume of a submarine have to match precisely for her to submerge properly. Portsmouth began an aggressive program to save weight through simplification. It built up margin for later additions and ultimately for the 1941 redesign.

By late 1936, C&R knew that two bow tubes could be added at a direct cost of only 15 tons (perhaps 35 altogether) and an extra 100 HP to maintain speed.[14] The forces afloat and the General Board clearly favored the change. Repeating the FY 37 design, however, would save at least 6 mo. In March 1937, Admiral Hart suggested that only the two contract-built FY 38 boats repeat the previous class because, in their case, the navy would have to pay for postcontract design changes. This technique of redesigning only the navy yard units of a class already had been used in the cruiser program. On 31 March, the secretary of the navy approved a General Board recommendation that the FY 38 submarines (SS 194–197) repeat the FY 37 design. The last FY 37 boat (*Swordfish*) was designed to revert to full diesel-electric drive; the FY 38 ships followed suit.

Extra tubes waited for the next class, the *Tambors* (SS 198–203 of FY 39). The four externally stowed torpedoes of earlier classes were moved into the hull. Both torpedo rooms could now lay mines (total stowage was 40; some of the bow racks could not carry two mines each). Hull lines were optimized for 17 kt. BuEng rerated the main diesels for 1,600 BHP (without any physical change) so that the submarine could make her required speed on her rated power. There were two auxiliary generators, a 300-kW and a 120-kW. The double hull was extended back to the after end of the motor room (leaving an 8-in bump in way of the motors). Frame spacing in this section was doubled (from 15 in to 30 in), partly to save weight. Tankage and piping were simplified and the torpedo rooms enlarged. An autopilot ("automatic steersman") was installed when the boats were completed but removed before the outbreak of war. Oil fuel once again could be stowed in certain main ballast tanks (two thirds were carried in main fuel tanks).

These boats could exceed 18 kt while one engine charged batteries or was repaired. Operating with the fleet, they could change stations at night in preparation for a dawn battle without running down batteries. The *Tambors* had much the same designed power as the big V-boats of the previous decade (5,400 BHP versus 5,495 for *Nautilus*) in less than half the volume (14,100 cu ft, rather than 31,100 cu ft) and in considerably less weight (61 lb/SHP versus 105 lb/SHP, counting engines, motors, gears, and controls).

This class was armed with a single 3-in/50 gun abaft the conning tower, as in its predecessors, but the foundation was strengthened to take a 5-in/51 gun. Many still feared that providing a powerful gun would tempt COs into suicidal gun battles. In January 1936, Subron 6 (in the Philippines) argued that it would be foolish to foreclose an option that could be bought merely by providing a

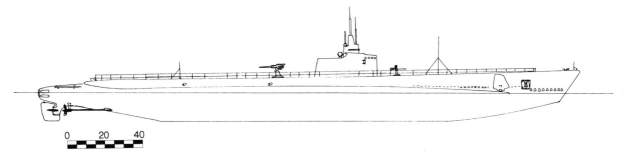

Triton (SS 202) is shown in prewar configuration. A 0.50-caliber machine gun was set up forward of her bridge. The gun could not be permanently mounted, nor could it be located atop the bridge because of its interference with radio antennas. Submariners disliked this arrangement. It entailed delay, which meant that a submarine often could not defend herself against a surprise attack. (Jim Christley)

stronger gun foundation, which would be difficult to install later. In January 1938, the Submarine Officers Conference voted in favor of the 3-in/50 gun on a 5-in foundation. CinCUS disagreed. The General Board on 18 January 1939, formally approved the heavy mounting and, the following November, recommended procuring 12 wet 5-in/51 guns for possible installation. Only then did it learn that no wet 5-in/51s were available; BuOrd was concentrating on the wet 3-in/50.

Some doubted that such large boats could dive quickly enough. A 5-ton "down express" tank below the torpedo tube breeches helped the S 48s dive quickly (35 sec). It pulled the bow down, and was blown (for safety) as soon as the bow went under. A 5- to 8-ton tank just forward of amidships was expected to get the big submarine to 100 ft about 15 sec faster and greatly improve depth control, including rapid changes of depth. Fitted with a 7.5-ton negative (quick dive) tank, *Stingray* (SS 186) was tested in November 1938. With a considerable sea running and the tank flooded, she reached 40 ft (at 11 kt) in 35 sec. When the tank was flooded at periscope depth, she dove to 100 ft (3-degree down angle at 5.5 kt) in 59 sec. These times were somewhat disappointing. The CO suggested that the tank be located farther forward to get a down angle more quickly; these submarines tended to hang up at 26 ft for about 10–15 sec until they reached a down angle of 2 or 3 degrees. The bow buoyancy that kept them relatively dry in a seaway also slowed their dives.[15] The down express tank was added to the *Tambor* design and installed in all earlier fleet submarines.

The FY 40 program was six large submarines (*Gar* class, SS 206–211) and two 800-ton coastal boats (see Chapter 11). On 17 December 1938, the secretary of the navy decided that the large submarines would duplicate the FY 39 boats. Designed test depth was still 250 ft, but collapse depth increased to 500 ft. It turned out that another 50 ft would buy a great deal. Because existing sonars could not measure depth, depth charge barrages had to allow for the full range of possible submarine depths. Tests against the new *Tambor* suggested that, whereas two depth charges could cover the depth range to 250 ft, a third would be needed to deal with a deeper-diving submarine. The number of charges in a barrage was fixed by the number of tracks and throwers, so the extra 50 ft, in effect,

cut the number at the right setting from one-half to one-third. The General Board wanted FY 40 boats strengthened for 300 ft if that could be done without delay. It wanted 300 ft in the next class, if that could be done without changing the rated collapse depth.[16] C&R believed that existing submarines could safely operate at 300 ft but wanted to test numerous fittings, systems, and other components to ensure against weak points.

Tests of the *Tambor* series began on 20 December 1940 off Portsmouth, with the submarine under way at periscope depth in 110–125 ft of water. A charge at 60 ft, 510 yd from the submarine, produced a sensation similar to a slammed watertight door or the flapping of a Kingston valve—a sharp but not very intense jolt. The only damage was a dislocated microswitch on No. 6 main ballast tank vent (the vent showed red incorrectly). A shot at 340 yd produced a sensation described as three times as intense (theory had predicted only twice as intense). The boat was shoved sideways and noticeably shaken. One electric light bulb filament broke, and the 200-lb blow line (diver's connection) in the conning tower opened slightly and started to bleed air. A third shot at 275 yd, not quite doubling the intensity of the earlier ones, did real damage. For example: the No. 4 battery ventilation blower developed a slight knock, apparently as the result of a loose stuffing box on the fan and no packing; the No. 3 main engine outboard exhaust valve began to leak, a potentially dangerous matter; the main vent valve of a fuel-ballast tank leaked, to form the beginning of a tell-tale oil slick; six or seven bulb filaments broke; and a fuse burned out. For the short-range shots, at 100 yd or less, the crew was removed and the submarine moored underwater. The last in the series was at 100 ft.

Depth charges were far less lethal than had been imagined; allowances on surface ships were increased and heavier (600 lb vice 300 lb) charges standardized. By the end of the war, it was assumed that a 300-lb depth charge had to explode within 14 ft to have a reasonable chance of breaking the pressure hull. At twice that distance, it would probably disable the submarine. Within 60 ft, it would tend to demoralize the crew, but that could be minimized by training, discipline, and morale.

Detail improvements inspired by these tests included a shock-mounted main propulsion control cubicle and watertight electric cabling, which otherwise would have acted as hosing and admitted water.[17]

FY 41 (*Gato* class, SS 212–214 and 228–230) was the last peacetime program. On 6 April 1940, C&R (about to merge with BuEng to form BuShips) suggested modest growth (to 1,523 tons and, by 4 ft 6 in, to 311 ft 8 in) to accommodate more powerful engines and improve stability and subdivision. The big engine room was divided in half by a pressure-proof bulkhead. The auxiliary ballast tanks were finally enlarged to compensate for the weight of 24 torpedoes or 40 mines. The General Board approved the new characteristics on 25 April 1940. It appeared that the new engines, providing as much as 2,000 BHP in the same space and weight, would be available for the FY 42 program. The generators were enlarged to match, but engine design was frozen in order to increase wartime production.

Submarines were among the types of craft whose production was accelerated after the shocks of the spring and summer of 1940, as France fell and Germany seized most of Western Europe. It was impractical to build anything other than the current *Gato* class. On 20 May 1940, OpNav directed an 11 percent naval expansion, including 22 submarines (SS 215–21, 231–39, and 253–58). OpNav ordered a 70 percent expansion program (43 submarines) on 16 August (SS 222–227, 240–252, and 259–282); included were the first units to be built by Manitowoc Shipbuilding Company of Manitowoc, Wisconsin. Thus, the FY 41 program as a whole included 71 submarines (SS 212–282). Two more boats included in the previously authorized total tonnage (SS 283–284) were ordered from Mare Island on 29 April 1941.[18]

President Franklin D. Roosevelt wanted available building slips filled but would approve no more submarines until those under construction were completed. Excluding Mare Island, the 25 submarine slips could accommodate 23 new submarine keels (SS 285–307) during 1942. They were formally approved on 1 Janurary 1942. Submarines enjoyed a very high priority because they were the only U.S. warships likely to penetrate Japanese waters while the rest of the fleet was on the strategic defensive.

The Navy Department's war program, dated 1 December and released 17 December, called for 30 submarines per year to replace war losses (estimated as 1.3 submarines per month, based on British experience) and to increase overall strength. By mid-February, the 1942 figure had been increased to 30 submarines, including 5 at Portsmouth (SS 308–312) and 2 at Electric Boat (SS 313–314, the company's first thick-hull submarines). Directives for this construction were issued on 31 March and 11 April 1942, respectively.

The president was soon convinced that submarines deserved a higher priority. A 13 May 1942 directive called for 120 submarines for FY 43 (SS 315–434), to be ordered in advance (in fact, in June 1942). Portsmouth gained a fifth building slip in 1942, and a basin for side-by-side construction was completed in March 1943. A month later, the yard's graving dock was used for side-by-side construction. The yard's best wartime record was 56 days from keel laying to launch (*Cisco*, 1942). Four boats were assigned to Boston Navy Yard in 1944. In 1940, new owners had reopened the large old Cramp yard (closed since 1926). It was not particularly successful, and several boats had to be completed at Portsmouth.[19] Wartime Mare Island capacity was limited because it was needed so badly for refits.

In September 1940, money was provided to add 3 slips to the original 4 at Electric Boat's North Yard; a new South Yard had 4 slips and an erection shed. All facilities were in use by July 1941. The navy later bought the former Groton Iron Works and converted it into the 10-slip Victory Yard, which Electric Boat operated. It laid down the first boat in July 1942. Fully operational by March 1943, the Victory Yard brought Electric Boat slips to a total of 21. Also in September 1940, Manitowoc Shipbuilding agreed to build Electric Boat submarines under license. The Navy Department had rejected the company's proposal to build destroyers. Manitowoc launched its submarines sideways and floated them down to the Gulf of Mexico on barges via the Illinois Waterway and the Mississippi River. It had five launching positions.

This expansion was expected to increase capacity to 40–50 new keels in 1943 (perhaps 70 in 1944), but the yards

---

Gato (SS 212) (*facing page*) (top), the prototype of all wartime U.S. submarines, is shown as completed late in 1941, with a 3-in/50 gun abaft the bridge fairwater. Two views (middle and bottom) of a typical *Balao*-class submarine demonstrate her appearance at the end of World War II, with a 5-in/25 wet mount on deck abaft the sharply cut-down conning tower fairwater. Abaft the forward torpedo room were officers' quarters above the forward battery (126 cells). Amidships, below the conning tower, was the control room, with the pump room below it. Immediately abaft the control room was the crew's mess, opening aft into the crew's quarters above the after battery (126 cells). The small space between the pump room and the after battery contained the magazine for the main gun, pyrotechnics, and the small arms (machine gun) magazine. Abaft the after battery and crew's quarters were two main engine rooms (two diesel generators each) and the maneuvering room above the motor room, from which the shaft line leads. Abaft that was the after torpedo room. Crew members were also berthed in the forward and after torpedo rooms (14 and 15 berths respectively, with 36 in the crew's quarters). Officers' quarters housed both commissioned (4 berths) and petty (4 berths) officers, for a total of 73 berths. The large structure in the after end of the fairwater was the mushroom valve of the main induction, which fed the engines with air. When boats were fitted with snorkels postwar, their air intakes were connected to these valves. The inboard profile shows a *Gato* with a telescoping mast passing through the conning tower. This was replaced by a separate radar mast, carrying an SD air warning radar, that did not detract from conning tower space (as shown in the outboard profile). Note, too, the ship's wheel at the fore end of the conning tower that corresponded and connected to a similar wheel in the control room below it. (Jim Christley)

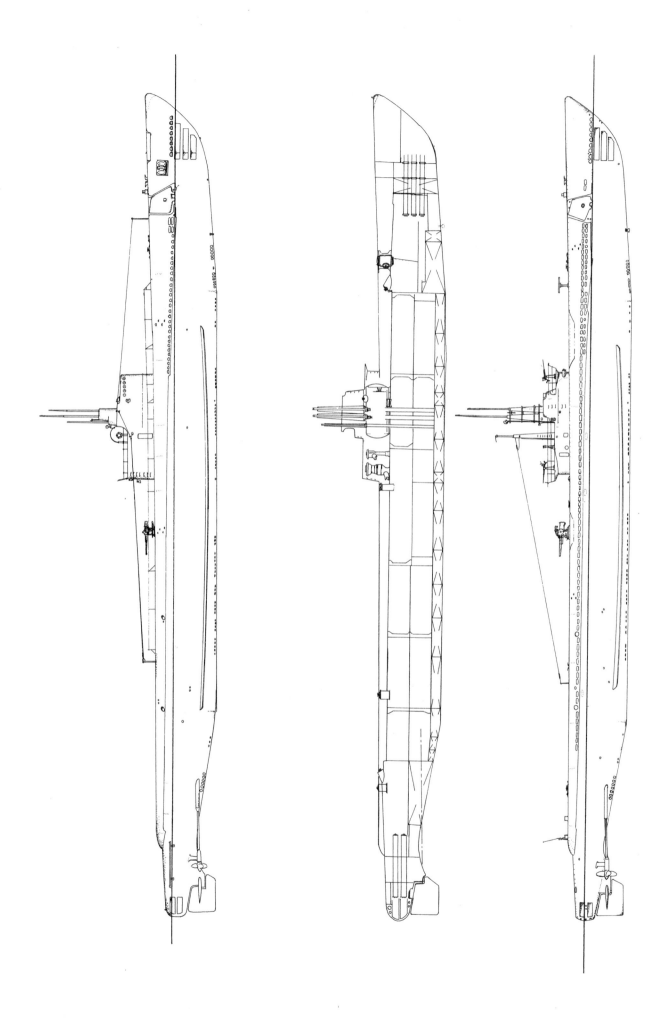

did much better. The FY 44 program (1945 Combatant Building Program), to use up the remaining authorized tonnage, included 110 boats (SS 435–544 ordered under a 28 May 1943 VCNO directive).

Through mid-1943, submarines clearly demonstrated their potential despite torpedo problems. Once those problems had been solved, smaller numbers of submarines seemed sufficient and submarine industrial effort, such as diesel engine production, was shifted to landing craft. On 30 June 1944, CNO/Cominch Adm. Ernest J. King ordered BuShips to cut submarine production as quickly as possible to 7 per month (84 per year, still far beyond the dreams of 1942). On 4 July 1944, SS 356–360, 379–380, 429–474, 517–521, and 526–544 were canceled. On 23 October 1944, SS 353–355 were canceled and SS 435–437 reinstated. President Roosevelt rejected a final wartime program (SS 546–562) on 22 March 1945. SS 491–494 were canceled on 12 August, as the war was coming to a close.

On 25 July 1944, Admiral King proposed that only the two main prewar yards, Portsmouth and Electric Boat,

continue to build submarines postwar. SubPac and Commander in Chief, Pacific (CinCPac), suggested that Mare Island build one boat per year to preserve its submarine capability. Admiral King also ordered the O, R, and S classes and the obsolete *Barracuda*s (V-1s) scrapped. The useful *Narwhal* and *Nautilus* would be retained as long as their condition permitted (and as long as *Nautilus* did not have to be re-engined).

Late in 1941, the two leading navy submarine designers, Andrew McKee (Portsmouth) and Armand F. Morgan (BuShips in Washington) met to consider redesign for deeper diving, mainly to evade depth charging.[20] The available weight margin could buy a thicker hull (35-lb plate versus 27.5-lb in earlier boats, i.e., 7/8 in, rather than 9/16 in, thick), sufficient to increase collapse depth to 650 ft. Adopting a stronger material, high-tensile steel (HTS), would increase collapse depth to 900 ft.[21] Some in the submarine force feared that the thick skin would rupture more easily under depth charging, but that did not happen. McKee and Morgan proposed that operating depth be increased to 450 ft. Quite aside from hull strength, pene-

Later war-built boats were designed with low bridges. *Pampanito* is shown after a Hunters Point refit, 23 July 1945, with a new SV air-search radar on her separate radar mast and new periscope shears with a DF loop between the periscopes and an SJ mast abaft them. The object forward of the bridge fairwater is a 20-mm mount.

trations, such as propeller shaft glands, had to survive increased pressure. The most critical component was the trim pump, whose design was based on German WW I practice. It could not be redesigned and tested in time, so the chief of BuShips, Rear Adm. E. L. Cochrane (a former submarine designer), set test depth at 400 ft. In any case, the trim pump had to be replaced because it was noisy. The Gould centrifugal type, adopted in 1944, could pump 35 gal/min at 600 ft; using it, fleet submarines could finally fully exploit their thicker skins.

The change to thicker skin could be made relatively easily in Navy Yards; by mid-December 1941, Portsmouth had redesigned the FY 42 boat. Its design also applied to boats built at Mare Island and to those planned for Cramp. At first, it seemed unlikely that Electric Boat could switch before FY 43, but, in March 1942, BuShips suggested that two of the FY 42 Electric Boat units be redesigned, so that material could be ordered and jigs and templates prepared. BuShips had informally suggested this change before the outbreak of war, and the company had sufficient drafting capacity. Electric Boat initially offered 400-ft operating depth (at least 675-ft collapse depth) but hoped ultimately to get 900-ft collapse depth using 35-lb HTS steel. The modified Electric Boat design also applied to boats built at Manitowoc. Boats beginning with *Balao*

(SS 285) had the thick HTS skin, except for Manitowoc's SS 361–364, which were built to Electric Boat's earlier design.

In 1943, Portsmouth completed a second redesign that became the *Tench* (SS 417) class. The revised tank layout eliminated risers (weak points) through the torpedo rooms. The inadequate fuel capacity was increased by a "variable fuel tank." Because salt water is about 18 percent heavier than fuel, a submarine would gain weight if she pumped salt water into the fuel tank as she burned oil. Because the tank would be partly empty (i.e., variable), it had to be able to withstand water pressure. No. 4 main ballast tank was converted to a variable fuel ballast tank, which increased rated capacity from about 94,000 gal to 113,510 gal. Rated endurance increased from 12,000 nm to 16,000 nm at 10 kt.[22] Water ballast was reduced to compensate for the added weight.

The electric motors were geared to the propeller shafts; gear whine was a major noise source. The BuShips electrical division, headed by Capt. H. G. Rickover, completed work on a direct-drive motor early in 1944, and the first two were installed on board *Sea Owl*, commissioned in July 1944. The slow-speed motor had to fit the space provided for two compact high-speed motors and their reduction gears. The solution was a double-armature motor. BuShips developed a two-unit ("split") propulsion control

The Manitowoc-built *Mero* is shown running trials with her SV air-search radar retracted. As in *Pampanito*, the bridge is as low as possible, without the frames characteristic of the *Gato*s.

so that a boat would not lose power on both shafts if one shorted out (however, this did not solve the fire and flooding problems that had concerned Admiral Hart before the war). Many submarines were converted to direct (electric) drive in wartime, and others postwar.[23]

The addition of 4 reload torpedoes brought total torpedoes to 28. In 1941, average diving time was 50 sec (minimum, 40 sec). By 1945, the average was 40 sec; some boats could get underwater in 30 sec. Flood valves were removed from main ballast tanks and flood openings in the tank bottoms enlarged (cutting diving time by about one-third). Modified diving planes could be rigged out and in with a dive angle. The negative (down express) tank was enlarged. Extra limber holes in the superstructure let out air more quickly. Diving procedure changed. The negative tank was kept flooded in wartime even when the submarine was surfaced. Kingstons (flood valves) were omitted altogether, about at SS 220 (*Barb*). Hand-operated Kingstons had replaced the earlier hydraulic ones in the *Gar* (SS 206) class. This was the ultimate consequence of "riding the vents." Kingstons were opened when the submarine was "rigged to dive." That was a deliberate procedure, not the beginning of a crash dive. Because it would never be done hurriedly, there was little point in powering the valves. In wartime, it was clear that boats would leave port rigged to dive, so there was even less point in having Kingstons at all. They were 10 percent tin, a metal in short supply, so were eliminated early in the war program.

Two external bow tubes were to have been added to all of the pre–WW II boats, with only four internal bow tubes. That was done on all boats of the six-tube *Porpoise/Shark* class (except *Shark*, lost before she could be refitted), as well as *Pickerel* and *Permit* of the following *Perch* class (the others did not receive extra tubes). Of the eight-tube boats, for which extra bow tubes were presumably less important, only *Stingray* was refitted, at Mare Island in 1942 (the tubes were removed at her next refit in 1943). No maintenance work could be done on the torpedoes

inside the external tubes at sea. In a simulated war patrol, the unmaintained torpedoes proved useless, and the program was stopped.[24]

Because submarines often attacked at night on the surface, their silhouettes had to be reduced. Through 1942–43, conning tower fairwaters were cut down. First, the after portion was cut away to form a "cigarette deck," on which a light machine gun could be mounted. Then, the enclosed bridge steering station was eliminated, leaving a second open deck forward of the periscope shears. A very small open bridge remained.[25] Exhaust sparks could reveal a submarine. Originally, many COs chose to trim their boats by the stern, thus immersing their mufflers. In December 1942, wet mufflers, which could not spark, were approved for all new boats; all operational submarines had them by the fall of 1943.

Depth charges could spring hatches and doors, so the forward engine room hatch and the conning tower door were both eliminated. Early in 1944, Portsmouth designed a protective blanking plate (with a manhole in it) that could close off a hatch from below to protect the submarine if the main hatch opened under attack.

The prewar three-bladed propellers were replaced by four-bladed ones with different pitch (presumably more efficient at cruising speed). This change, plus increased wartime loads, reduced effective maximum speed from 20.5 kt to 19–19.5 kt. The smaller of the two auxiliary diesels (100-kW) was ordered removed on 1 January 1942, although many *Gato*s were completed with it.[26]

Maneuverability was still a sore point. In 1942, the mean diameter of the surface turning circle was given as 370 yd and the submerged turning circle as 300 yd. The 1946 edition of *Submarine Warfare Instructions* (USF 9), which reflected wartime experience, however, gave the surface tactical diameter as 500 yd at 15 kt and the submerged diameter as 450 yd at 6 kt. The rudder could not be enlarged (to reduce surface turning circle) because it already consumed full hydraulic power in the worst case, in which

Stingray shows her two new external bow tubes in this photograph taken on 2 October 1942 off Mare Island Navy Yard. Her bridge fairwater had not yet been cut down, but she had been fitted with radar (SJ forward of the periscope shears, SD on the telescoping mast abaft them), and the fairing around the periscope shears had been cut away. Although she had a loop antenna for underwater radio reception (visible just below the SD antenna), she still retained the cumbersome long loop radio antenna strung between the tripods fore and aft and the bridge fairwater itself. *Stingray* was the only eight-tube boat to have external bow tubes added, and they were removed during her next (1943) refit.

Details of early war modifications to *Porpoise* are shown here. The new mast carries an SD air-warning radar. Circled just abaft it are a radio-receiving loop antenna and, above it, an SJ surface-search radar antenna. Abaft both are the boat's two periscopes: the tall one with its eyepiece in the conning tower, the short one with an eyepiece in the control room. Further aft is a 20-mm mount, the gun for which has not been mounted. The submarine still has her prewar-type covered bridge with glassed-in eye ports.

Sturgeon shows typical further wartime modifications. (The overall view is dated 3 May 1943, the detailed view, 23 April 1943. Both were taken at Hunters Point, California.) A platform has been built out forward of the old bridge fairwater to take a 20-mm cannon, and two gun access trunks have been built into it to serve the 3 in/50 mount moved forward. The top of the old enclosed bridge has been removed and a venturi added atop it to shield a new open bridge. The fairing around the periscope shears has been removed. SD and SJ radars are circled in the detail view. The modifications aft are covers for new mufflers.

Photographed off the U.S. coast on 5 April 1945, *Snapper* shows prominent raised casings above her engine rooms. They accommodate the new mufflers installed in wartime. The *Gato*s had raised after decks and slightly smaller mufflers, so they showed no such bulges. The gun is a 4 in/50 salvaged from an old S-boat.

Off Mare Island on 8 May 1943, *Spearfish* shows humps above her two engine rooms. They accommodate her new mufflers.

Tambor was fitted with a 5 in/51 gun. She is shown off San Francisco after a refit, 6 December 1943. Note the double row of additional limber holes.

the boat ran full astern on the surface. Because the rudder felt less torque submerged than on the surface, rudder area could be added if it acted only when the submarine was submerged. In July 1945, *Gato*'s CO suggested just that: an auxiliary (topside) rudder to reduce the submerged turning circle. OpNav forwarded the idea to BuShips the following January. SubPac considered the auxiliary rudder justified if it could reduce submerged tactical diameter by 25 percent or reduce the time for a 90-degree submerged turn at 4 kt by 20 percent. It seemed likely that a topside area with half the area of the main rudder would do. *Amberjack* was the test boat; a few other fleet boats were similarly fitted.

Guns proved far more important than had been imagined prewar. The Japanese deployed many small ASW and other picket craft. Also, by late in the war, large targets worth torpedoing were quite rare, yet the numerous small targets remaining were important because, together, they still carried substantial cargoes of vital materials. Subma-

rines began the war with a single 3-in/50 gun abaft the conning tower, one or more 0.50-caliber machine guns, and two to four 0.30s. Reflecting service opinion, the Submarine Officers Conference, in February 1942, unanimously urged that the gun be moved forward of the conning tower. Access would then be through the conning tower hatch, rather than the conning tower door, which had always been considered a weak point. Ammunition could be passed through the hatch. Locating the gun forward of the bridge simplified control and added little to the boat's silhouette. The gun crew could get below decks more quickly in the event of a crash dive, and men would not be lost overboard when running aft to the gun. This change was approved early in 1942 (if the CO wanted it). The 3-in/50 gun was not nearly powerful enough, so COs who wanted them got 4-in/50s from S-boats withdrawn from patrol duty.

Captain Lockwood was responsible for the prewar decision to provide boats with foundations strong enough for a 5-in gun. In July 1942, as commander of submarines in

Photographed off Mare Island on 22 November 1943 after a refit, *Gar* shows her new 5 in/51 gun on its oversized sponson.

By the end of the war, submarine commanders could elect to carry two 5 in/25 guns. *Pargo* is shown from above on 21 May 1945; note the sponson built out around her after gun. *Aspro* is shown on 24 May 1945 after a refit at Hunters Point. Each of the boats shown has a single 40-mm gun forward of the bridge and a twin 20 mm abaft it. *Aspro* clearly shows the wire loop antenna running from the stub mast near the bow to struts built out from her bridge.

Heavy gun batteries were of somewhat limited value because they lacked fire controls. The next step, then, was to add a surface-ship type fire control system: an Mk 6 stable element, and an Mk 6 computer driving gun-order repeaters at the guns. The most striking change was internal: a gun plot was installed in the forward crew quarters. *Sea Cat*, shown here, was the prototype. She also had a pair of single 40-mm guns. The cylindrical object on her foreback is a dome covering her new WFA "integrated" sonar, which (in theory) would replace both the older WCA and JT. In fact, JT was retained because its long line array gave more precise bearings than the small array inside the radome. Note too that the usual wartime SD air warning radar has been replaced by the big antenna of the late-war SV, on the auxiliary mast abaft the periscope shears and conning tower. Six other submarines (SS 229, 340, 401, 406, 407, and 408) were also converted to "gunboats."

OFFICIAL PHOTOGRAPH
NOT TO BE RELEASED
FOR PUBLICATION
NAVY YARD MARE ISLAND, CALIF.

RESTRICTED

Shown on 23 and 29 November 1944 (overall view), *Gato* was typical of submarines in mid-war. Her open bridge was cut to a minimum. Numerous extra limber holes were cut into her superstructure for faster diving. Patterns varied from boat to boat. The bridge fairwater accommodates a 20-mm gun forward and a single 40-mm aft. The deck gun is a 4 in/50 taken from an S-boat. Modifications made at the refit she had just completed included installation of a new freestanding mast for her SD radar and relocation of her SJ to a new mast supported by her periscope shears. In some boats the new SJ mast was mounted forward of the periscope shears. The three girders supporting the shears are the only remnants of the prewar enclosed bridge; their height indicates how far the fairwater has been cut down. Note also the ammunition-passing scuttle let into the deck abaft the bridge fairwater.

NOT TO BE RELEASED
FOR PUBLICATION
MARE ISLAND NAVAL SHIPYARD
MARE ISLAND, CALIFORNIA
RESTRICTED

Grouper (SS 214) typifies the Gato class at the end of World War II. The overall photograph was taken at Mare Island on 17 July 1945, after a refit. It shows 40-mm guns fore and aft, a new 5 in/25 deck gun forward, and a twin 20-mm mount aft in a space into which a second 5 in/25 could fit (submarines normally carried one gun in either location). The detailed view was taken at Mare Island on 15 May 1950 when the submarine was being prepared for conversion for ASW. By this time all guns had been landed. The new SS radar had replaced the earlier SJ; the big antenna was for the wartime SV air-search set. Note the venturi at the fore end of the bridge. By this time the DF loop for underwater HF reception was generally mounted between the two periscopes.

the Southwest Pacific, he convinced BuOrd to authorize installation of 5-in/51s. Initially, one was removed from *Bonita* and mounted on board *Thresher* (SS 200). Six boats had been modified by mid-1943: SS 198–200, 203, 206, and 209. Early in 1943, four more conversions were authorized (to be ready by June 1944). Development of a submarine version of the existing 5-in/25 and of new 4-in ammunition was approved. Ready by August 1944, the 5-in/25 became the standard late-war U.S. submarine gun. It was first mounted on board *Spadefish* (SS 411).

Late-war submarines typically had two 5-in gun foundations; the single gun could be mounted fore or aft. The first submarine with two 5-in/25 (and two 40 mm guns) was *Sennet* (SS 408); her first patrol was in January 1945. She then operated in a wolf pack with two similarly armed boats, *Haddock* (231) and *Legato* (371). They were so successful that OpNav authorized this battery for any submarine whose CO wanted it. By September 1945, the approved battery was two 5-in/25s (of which one was normally carried). A major early postwar submarine force goal was to buy enough 5-in guns to provide two for all active and reserve boats.

These weapons lacked effective fire controls. In February 1945, SubPac asked BuOrd to devise a surface ship–style fire-control system, in which a plotting room (in the forward port quarter of the crew's sleeping compartment) continuously computed and transmitted gun train and elevation to indicators at the guns.[26] *Sea Cat*, the first such "gunboat" submarine, completed her training on 30 July 1945. Target bearing was measured by the target bearing transmitter (TBT) on the bridge or by periscope; range was measured by ST or SJ radar. These, target course, and own-ship data were input by hand to an Mk 6 computer (a modernized "Baby Ford" range keeper),

Some boats (*above and facing page*) never did have their bridges completely cut down. This is *Gurnard* at Mare Island on 23 July 1945. Note her gun access trunks fore and aft, to serve 5 in/25 guns in either position. Her port forward gun access trunk has been blanked off. The circled alteration on the periscope presumably indicates installation of the ST range-only radar there.

which computed advance (projected) range, sight angle, and sight deflection. An associated Mk 6 stable element corrected for the submarine's roll and pitch. Six more gunboats (SS 229, 340, 401, 406, 407, 408) were available by September 1945.

Launchers for 5-in finned rockets were adapted to attack small surface craft and shore targets. The first submarine so fitted, *Barb* (SS 220), made her first attack on 27 June 1945 and two more before the war was over. By the end of the war, *Requin* (481), *Chivo* (341), and *Chopper* (342) each had six Mk 51 launchers (12 rockets each). Baseplates were welded to the boat's deck, the launchers being emplaced after she surfaced. Abortive plans called for at least one Mk 102 director-controlled rocket launcher (as in an LSMR) on each submarine.

Although BuOrd never developed a wet 20-mm gun, it turned out that dry 20s would survive submergence if their barrels were changed often enough. Initially, single 20s were mounted fore and aft of the small open bridge. Submariners hoped that more powerful guns would allow them to beat off initial air attacks and give them time to dive. A triple 20-mm developed by Pearl Harbor was not adopted, but many single 20s were replaced by the new twin mounts. Single 40-mm guns, tried early in 1944, were so successful that, in the fall of 1944, OpNav ordered 30 boats so armed. Late in the war, submarines typically mounted a single or twin 20-mm forward of the bridge and a single 40-mm aft, plus a pair of 0.50-caliber machine guns. By September 1945, the approved battery was two 40-mm Mk 3 and four 0.50-caliber Mk 32 machine guns. BuOrd was working on a twin 40-mm dry (enclosed) mount (Mk 7) and a twin 37-mm wet mount; it was studying a 35-mm/55 (2,800 ft/sec). These projects were soon abandoned.

Detour: The Return to Limited Dimensions

DESPITE THE DEVELOPMENT of the big fleet boats, it could be argued that the old O-boats and R-boats still had to be replaced, preferably with submarines of about the same size. The General Board saw them as mobilization prototypes, on the theory (ultimately proved incorrect) that big fleet boats never could be mass-produced. Asked what could be done on 650 tons, C&R produced rough characteristics on 2 March 1934 for a single-hull local defense submarine, based on comparisons with existing ships.[1] This idea eventually led to two 800-tonners, the only excursions from what became the standard U.S. prewar and wartime type of submarine.

Electric Boat's modified R-boats for Peru were about the same size, so in March 1934 the company offered a pair of sketch designs: EB 191A and EB 191B. EB 191A abandoned BuEng's complex electric drive for the much simpler direct drive. Electric Boat claimed that using 6-cylinder engines would limit torsional vibration and that its crosshead engine design would allow for a large-diameter (i.e., vibration damping) crankshaft. The electric-drive EB 191B had four engines, rather than two. They added 4 ft and 18 tons, and a boat built to this design was expected to make 1/4 kt more. Neither version had a deck gun.

Nothing more happened until Admiral Hart joined the General Board in June 1936. Hoping to go back to something like a *Cachalot*, he ordered two studies of simplified fleet submarines. The all-electric No. 1 would use two 1,535-BHP main engines and two 330-kW (500-BHP) auxiliaries. No. 2 would use two direct-drive, 1,600-BHP, 4-cycle Wintons (16-258, then being installed in the *Cachalots*). Hart thought this engine could be supercharged to the 2,000 BHP needed (no existing U.S. engine was powerful enough). There would be two 250-kw auxiliary diesels.

Shorter machinery space would make No. 1 shorter by 10 ft than the first modern fleet boat, *Perch* (some saved space went into habitability). The current *Sargo* would be 0.5 kt faster at full load and somewhat faster when charging batteries, but no faster at normal load. At 1,325 tons, No. 1 would have less wetted surface, hence less underwa-

ter resistance, than *Sargo*, so she would be faster submerged. Normal fuel load (60,000 gal; 90,000 gal. with fuel in ballast tanks) would give only two thirds of the fuel radius of *Sargo*, but Hart argued that "when a crew has burned 60,000 gallons on a war mission they have done about all they can." She would have six bow and two stern tubes (20 torpedoes). Hart expected No. 1 to require about six fewer crewmen because she had two fewer diesels.

The smaller No. 2 would be about midway between *Cachalot* and *Perch* (250–265 ft long, 1,200–1,250 tons). Normal fuel load would be 50,000 gal (maximum 80,000 gal). Armament would be four or six bow and two stern tubes (16 or 18 torpedoes). Surfaced, she would be slower than *Sargo* (by 1.25 kt at full load, 0.75 kt at normal load). With seven-eighths battery capacity of *Sargo* on four-fifths displacement, however, she would probably do much better underwater. She would also be more habitable because she would house a crew of only about 40 in the same space as a *Perch*.

In Hart's view, minor sacrifices in surface speed and in miles made good while charging batteries would buy easier maintenance, simpler operation, and smaller crews. He convinced some, but not enough, members of the Submarine Officers Conference to vote for smaller submarines in the FY 39 program. At least one, Comdr. R. W. Christie, voted for six austere Hart submarines (which he called the *Turtle* class) and two prototype coastal craft (600–800 tons).

Adm. J. R. DeFrees, the Submarine Force commander, was unimpressed. To keep station on a fleet, submarines had to sustain 15 (preferably 16–17) kt while charging batteries at normal rate (8–10 hr) in a moderate sea (wind 3–4) with normal fouling (3–4 mo out of dock) at war load (in diving trim) and without exceeding 80 percent pressure rating on the diesels. The all-electric submarine might be too vulnerable, but No. 2 would be crippled if either of its main engines failed. Big, heavy engines required larger engine rooms. Nor would four lighter-weight engines necessarily require more men: *Dolphin* needed 20 engine room ratings for her two diesels, compared with 15 for the four

Photographed off Portsmouth on 19 May 1943, *Marlin* shows war alterations, most importantly the 20-mm gun platform abaft her bridge, the wire loop for underwater HF reception, and an SD air-warning radar. Another 20-mm gun was mounted forward of her bridge.

engines in *Porpoise*. DeFrees liked BuEng's composite power plant, although inevitably it would be cramped.

Both of Hart's proposed designs cut torpedo stowage by a greater proportion than displacement. For example, *Sargo* could accommodate 28 torpedoes by removing some crew bunks. DeFrees considered the new balanced armament, four bow and four stern tubes, the minimum acceptable: "Equal power in bow and stern simplifies the approach and goes a long way to prevent getting caught in a bad position." Nor did he want to go back to using main ballast tanks for fuel, as Hart's designs did.

Hart persevered. At the 1937 Submarine Officers Conference, he argued that development had been incremental mainly to speed procurement, not because the big fleet boats were particularly desirable; that judgment had yet to be made. Unit size should be cut back, he said, "because most think some kind of limitation [presumably on total tonnage] will return." In September 1937, Hart circulated a personal paper that was not formally approved by the General Board. He saw no immediate point in building a coastal submarine; however, a lower-performance but simpler prototype might be justified after the FY 39 program (32 fleet submarines had been bought in FY 34–39). Diesels were so reliable that fewer main engines were now acceptable. Hart wrote: "Defensive qualities decrease with size; [probably] a return to more moderate dimensions will soon be due." By this time, No. 1 had gained a third main diesel, so it was clearly less attractive. Hart preferred No. 2.[2] (Final versions of both are described in Table 11–1.) Neither was built: these simplified boats were not different enough from the fleet boats. Not reliable enough for fleet cruising, they depended on a new diesel; the existing ones had not yet been wrung out.

At their January 1938 conference, many submarine officers argued that peacetime construction should concentrate on fleet boats because they took too long to build (30 mo in peacetime, an [incorrectly] estimated 20 mo in wartime) to be included in any wartime mobilization. They were also just the type most useful in the early phases of a Pacific war. Once war began, a smaller mass-production boat might replace existing R-boats and S-boats. The submarine school at New London also might need smaller submarines for better maneuvering around its finger piers. Existing school boats would have to be replaced beginning in FY 45. Because no mass production submarine could be developed without building one or more prototypes in order to solve detail design problems, the conference recommended two coastal submarines for the FY 40 program.

Hart was not alone. For example, on 18 March 1938, Capt. C. A. Lockwood sent Hart tentative characteristics for a "patrol-type submarine" midway between an R-boat and S-boat. Distrusting large gyro angle shots, Lockwood wanted two stern tubes (with 4 torpedoes, for straight shots), space for which surely could be provided by modern compact diesels and a smaller battery. There also would be four bow tubes (10 torpedoes forward, 4 in the superstructure, total 18; or 16 mines in place of the after torpedoes), a 4-in/50 gun (as in an S-boat), and two 0.50-caliber machine guns. The main sacrifices were in speed

Table 11–1. Small Submarines for Admiral Hart, 12 October 1937

	Sargo	No. 1	No. 2	*Perch*
Length overall (ft-in)	310-6	290-7	278-6	300-7
Displacement (tons)	1,450	1,335	1,275	1,335
Machinery space (ft-in)	70-2	62-6	50-6	72-6
Normal fuel (gal)	93,000	60,000	52,000	34,000
Reserve fuel (gal)	93,000	92,000	80,000	89,000
Reserve buoyancy:				
Normal (%)	24.5	27.5	29.0	34.0
Fully loaded (%)	——	17.5	19.3	20.3
Torpedo tubes	4/4	6/2	6/2	4/2
Torpedoes	24	20	18–20	16
Battery (amp-hr; 3-hr rate)	16,200	14,280	14,280	14,280
Main engines (BHP)	4 × 1,535	3 × 1,535	2 × 2,000	4 × 1,300
Drive (ED, electric; DD, direct)	2 ED, 2 DD	3 ED	2 DD	4 ED
SHP	5,500	4,050	3,860	4,300
Auxiliary engines (kW)	2 × 258	2 × 330	2 × 258	2 × 200
SHP	620	800	620*	†
Maximum speed (kt)	19.2	19.0	18.6	18.6‡
Miles (nm)	166	157	127	135§

* Usable only to hold main engines up to maximum RPM in all conditions.
† Cannot be used for propulsion as now installed.
‡ Diving trim, 6 mo out of dock, normal fuel.
§ Miles made good while charging empty battery.

(10–12 kt surfaced and charging batteries, not over 7–8 kt submerged) and in radius (5,000 nm at 10–12 kt, enough to patrol Midway from Pearl Harbor). Lockwood's submarine would operate at 250 ft; it would use a "down express" tank to dive in 40 sec or less. Equipment would be simplified, with the underwater sound outfit limited to sonics for bearings only.

Hart embraced the project as a vehicle to press for the simple boat he wanted. He personally knew L. Y. Spear of Electric Boat; the company could design his austere submarine. On 18 March, he asked Spear to develop a sketch design, as it "seems likely that in future the Department will be building coastal boats." It had to be simple and inexpensive, using readily obtainable machinery, operated by a minimum crew. Armament would be four bow tubes (plus four reloads) and two 0.50-caliber machine guns, at least one on the bridge. Spear suggested that service radius (at sufficient buoyancy for sea-keeping) should be set by the longest passage the boat would make, for example, San Diego to the Canal Zone, 2,715 nm, at 9–10 kt, with due allowance for unfavorable seas and a foul bottom. He also suggested that the boat be self-sustaining for at least 2 wk, preferably 3. Spear was probably aware of Lockwood's tentative characteristics.

Hart wanted a bit more for offensive operations. A small boat might be risked more freely than a fleet boat, a theme to which he would later return. A few days later (25 March) he wrote Spear that he feared the boat would become too complex. Adding stern tubes would enlarge the crew, and many captains would demand the new TDC; Hart thought they would be willing to rely on older, simpler methods if they had only bow tubes. Any offensive submarine would probably need a full sound outfit.

Electric Boat submitted Design EB 231A on 5 May. Hart hoped for a 650-tonner (but expected something more like 700 tons), partly because he still hoped that it would have a larger consort, a 1,200-tonner to replace the standard fleet boat. Electric Boat started with 700 tons but ended up with 807. EB-231A was partially double hulled, like a fleet boat; Hart wondered whether the older single-hull designs would have been better. Spear already had just that in the form of EB 191 A and EB 191B (except for modern bows, EB 191A/B had the hull forms of old R- or S-boats). EB 231A's modern hull would provide enough reserve buoyancy for good sea-keeping. The shallow propellers of the older hull would come out of the water too often in rough weather, costing speed and radius of action. EB 231A could be operated from the bridge under much worse sea conditions than EB 191B; she also had more tubes and torpedoes (see Table 11–2).

In keeping with Hart's desire for simplicity, Spear used his conning tower as the access trunk to the open chariot bridge but not as a fire-control station. His simple sound outfit included an old-style multispot receiver and a JK. Length was fixed by machinery requirements. Although Hart had specified no deck gun, length sufficed for a 3-in/50 with a 75-round magazine.

The bureaus reviewed EB 231A at the end of May. They suggested that ballast tanks be concentrated at the ends

Table 11–2. Electric Boat Designs for Small Submarines, 1934 and 1938

Hull	EB-191A	EB-191B	EB-231A
	Single	Single	Partial double hull
Length overall (ft-in)	212-0	229-0	236-6
Beam (ft-in)	——	——	20-6
Draft (ft-in)	——	——	13-1
Standard displacement (tons)	632	707	738
Normal displacement (tons)	694	769	807
Deep displacement (tons)	737	819	849
Buoyancy (%)	13.0	14.5	21.3
Normal fuel (gal)	37,000	38,500	40,400
Maximum fuel (gal)	70,000	73,300	75,700
Torpedo tubes	4/0	4/0	6/2
Torpedoes	8	8	10
Auxiliary general sets	0	2	2
Engines (total HP)	950	1,280	1,280
Surface speed (kt)	13.6	14.9	14.8
At Deep Load	——	——	14.3
Normal radius, 2 engines (nm/kt)	3,300/10	3,350/10	3,350/10
Maximum radius, 2 engines (nm/kt)	6,120/10	6,180/10	5,975/10
Endurance (days)	——	——	45
Submerged speed (kt)	9.25	9.25	9.0
Endurance At 5 kt (submerged) (hr)	11.6	11.6	11.0
Test depth (ft)	——	——	250
Complement	4/26	4/29	4/33

Note: Normal and maximum radii were based on a 77 percent fuel load. These figures differ slightly from those presented in 1934 for EB-191A and EB-191B. At that time, EB-191A (two 4-cycle Electric Boat six-cylinder in-line engines, 685 BHP at 450 RPM) was credited with a surface speed of 15 kt and a submerged speed of 9.75 kt; radius was given as 8,500 nm at 10 kt. EB-191B used four Electric Boat eight-cylinder vee engines (470 BHP each); propeller RPM was reduced to 300. Surface speed and endurance matched that of EB-191A; submerged speed was 10 kt. EB-231A was powered by 4-cycle, six-cylinder, single-acting, low-speed engines (for direct drive), each rated at 640 BHP at 450 RPM ($13\frac{3}{4}$-in × 16-in cylinders). EB-231A could cruise at 10.5 kt (normal) or 10.35 kt (deep) on one engine (3,450/6,200 nm at 10 kt).

(to provide surface buoyancy for sea-keeping) and fuel tanks moved from the ends to amidships. They wanted normal fuel capacity to be a larger fraction (preferably two thirds) of full capacity, to avoid undue reliance on ballast fuel tanks. Finally, they wanted a fleet boat–style conning tower and semiclosed bridge: the boat might often operate in narrow waters where access to a dry chart table would be important.

The Submarine Officers Conference seems to have used Lockwood's patrol submarine as a basis for formal characteristics it proposed on 23 May. It also had before it a copy of the Electric Boat proposal. The Conference rejected Lockwood's externally stowed torpedoes (it settled for a total of 12) and substituted Spear's 3-in/50 gun for Lockwood's 4-in/50. It strongly agreed that the boat should be designed to operate continuously at 250 ft, "without heating of stern bearings and other evidence of hull distortion which sometimes occurs on deep submergence." Deeper diving surely would become more important as a counter to depth charging. Like a fleet boat, the small one would have to dive within 60 sec. Sustained surface speed (4 mo out of dock) would be 12 kt, and an auxiliary charging engine would be installed, if possible. Submerged speed (with wartime battery fluid) would be 9 kt and minimum acceptable surfaced range, 6,000 nm.

The General Board met to set characteristics for a medium or small boat for the FY 40 program. There was some fear that the small boats would displace fleet boats, but Adm. W. G. duBose of C&R said that each of the two design yards (Portsmouth and Electric Boat) could build two fleet submarines while building one experimental boat (Mare Island would build the other two fleet boats of the usual six-boat program. The Deficiency Bill then before Congress would expand Portsmouth, and Electric Boat could already build three or four boats simultaneously.

There were still not enough full-sized boats to execute the war plans. A large submarine could do what a small one could do but not vice versa. Although many people imagined that a 1,450-tonner was large and unwieldy, in fact, she was more maneuverable than an S-boat. From one officer: "Any of us that have had experience in war games in the Pacific area, especially those that handled submarines, have been struck with the vast distances . . ."

Hart offered the improved *Cachalot*, his study No. 2; Spear's EB 231A; and a 600-ton, single-hull boat. He admitted that re-engining *Cachalot* as planned probably would sufficiently test the idea of the larger austere boat. Lockwood pointed out that 1,200 tons was little better than 800 tons; it just bought a bit more speed and sea-keeping. The single-hull alternative died because caisson experiments suggested that a double hull would stand up much better to depth charging. Too, 750 tons might be a very real lower limit. S-boats were considered quite punishing; crews lost their edge after 4 or 5 days submerged. An officer felt that surely the small submarine could do better than 12 kt surfaced.

The CNO and secretary of the navy agreed with Admiral duBose's idea of adding two small mobilization prototypes to the usual six-boat program. The General Board submitted characteristics for two 800-ton prototype submarines on 21 June 1938. On 12 July, the General Board asked C&R and BuEng to develop a sketch design to help fix formal characteristics. It could be as large as 900 tons, but the board hoped it would not exceed 800 tons. This partial double-hull boat would operate at 250 ft (preferably 300) and dive in about 45 sec. Armament would be one 3-in/50 gun, two machine guns, and four bow and two stern torpedo tubes for Mk 14s, with at least 10 torpedoes on board, including 4 spares in the forward torpedo room; if practicable, 2 more spares would be carried aft. The power plant would be two direct-drive diesels for simplicity, durability, and economy of personnel. An auxiliary diesel was optional. The boat would make about 14.5 kt on the surface under trial conditions (i.e., with a clean bottom, at diving trim with normal fuel). Minimum radius was set at 6,000 nm, with two thirds of fuel in normal tanks. Stores would be provided for 30 days. Submerged speed would be 9 kt, with 48-hr endurance at minimum controllable speed. The boat would be controlled from a conning tower with two 34-ft periscopes.

These characteristics very nearly described EB 231A. Electric Boat had just submitted a revised design with more powerful engines (800 BHP, rather than 620, for a trial speed of 15.5 kt), a bigger conning tower, and spare torpedoes; normal displacement rose to 940–950 tons. The larger engines would be slightly harder to produce, an important consideration in a mobilization design. Spear knew of the desire to go to 300 ft (crush depth 525 ft with the usual 1.75 safety factor). C&R strongly preferred a safety factor of 2.0. A 250-ft boat designed to crush at 500 ft could operate at 300 ft with a safety factor of 1.7.

Hart wrote Spear that the next program would probably include two 750- to 800-tonners, one probably to be built by a navy yard. The navy designers had not gone nearly so far as Electric Boat. Hart imagined that they would use 800-BHP engines.

Through August 1938, Electric Boat's design grew: Spear had to add 10 tons for more fuel, 3 tons for two more torpedoes, 0.8 ton for a larger conning tower, and 5.4 tons for shockproof steel battery cells—a total of at least 19.2 tons. The boat grew by about 2 tons for every ton directly added, so that the original 807 tons (surface displacement) would go to 850. Imposing the new safety factor (2.0) would bring it to about 935 tons. Spear wanted displacement limited so that the new submarine could be powered by Electric Boat's new crosshead supercharged engine. Whether the engine also powered the C&R-designed boat depended largely on pressure hull diameter.[3] Hart deeply distrusted electric drive: Spear offered direct drive using Electric Boat's own flexible friction coupling to damp partly the torsional vibration.

Growth was excessive. Electric Boat submitted EB 231C on 16 January 1939. It cut pressure hull weight by reducing diameter from 14 ft 5 in to 13 ft 10 in. The boat was slightly lengthened (to 238 ft × 21 ft 6 in × 13 ft 10 in). Displacement was given as 815 to 820 tons *standard*, rather than surfaced in diving trim. Now the conning tower was a horizontal cylinder, like that of a fleet boat. Electric Boat hoped its engines would develop 800 BHP at 450 RPM. It accepted the new safety factor of 2.0. The bureaus liked this design. The Germans had just revealed a 712-ton U-boat, U-25, quite close to the U.S. design except a bit faster (18 kt) and with a slightly larger crew (40, rather than 39, men).[4] The bureaus agreed that it would be unwise to demand a more complex engine to boost the speed of the

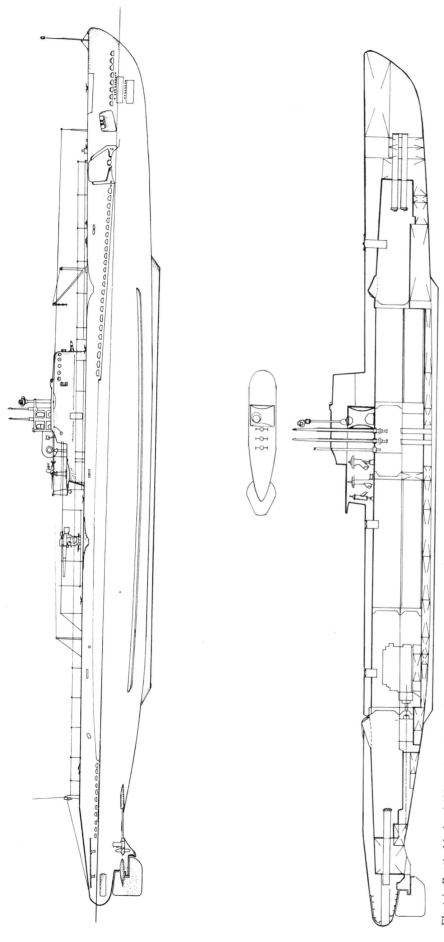

Electric Boat's *Mackerel* (SS 204) is shown in December 1942. The bridge fairwater was never rebuilt. The periscope shears have been cut away and a 20-mm gun mounted abaft the bridge. Aft was a 3-in/50 gun. Plans originally called for a 0.50-caliber machine gun in the bridge position, with another atop the bridge itself. Radars (SJ forward, SD aft) were added. Unlike a contemporary fleet boat, she had direct-drive diesels (the auxiliary generator was mounted just forward of the starboard engine), and she had no separate maneuvering room or control cubicle (these controls were in the main crew berthing area). The objects inside the bridge fairwater, from forward to aft, were the main induction (and ship's air supply valve), the ship's air supply valve, and the battery exhaust valve; the first two are big mushrooms. This drawing does not show *Mackerel*'s sonar, originally a JK (probably QB/JK by 1942) that could be lowered from a keel trunk just abaft the well for the antenna (SD) mast. Although complement was listed as 4 officers and 38 enlisted men, the plans show only 32 enlisted and 4 petty officer berths: 10 enlisted berths in the forward torpedo room, 20 in the crew's quarters abaft the control room and galley, and 2 adjacent to officers' berths. The plans do not show any berths in the after torpedo room. The petty officers were accommodated just forward of the officers' berths. (Jim Christley)

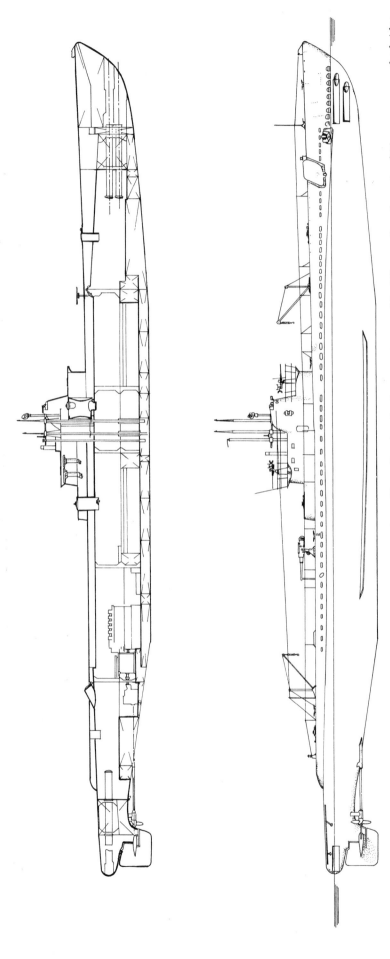

Portsmouth's *Marlin* (SS 205) is shown in February 1944; her bridge was cut down like a fleet boat's. Armament was a 3-in/50 gun aft and a pair of 20-mm guns on the bridge fairwater. Radar had been added: a surface-search SJ forward of the periscopes and an air search SD on the vertical antenna mast abaft the periscopes. On deck, just abaft the forward boat/torpedo derrick, is a JP sonar. There was also a keel sonar (presumably QB/JK) in a trunk just abaft the well for the SD mast. Unlike a fleet boat, she had a very small conning tower; both periscopes were let into the control room below it; the control room also housed the torpedo data computer at its after end, port side. *Marlin*, unlike a contemporary *Gato*, had direct-drive diesels. Her motors were controlled from a console at the forward end of the machinery space. Most of the crew was accommodated in the big crew space abaft the control room (24 berths), but there was also accommodation in the forward (8 berths) and after (6 berths) torpedo rooms. Complement was 4 officers and 38 enlisted men. (Jim Christley)

U.S. submarine. They did want a small TDC, and Hart soon accepted the simplified Mk 2.

General Board Characteristics were formally approved by the secretary of the navy on 27 January 1939.

Portsmouth submitted its own design that May. Like Electric Boat, it used direct diesel drive rather than the diesel-electric drive of the larger fleet submarine. In keeping with the mobilization concept, Portsmouth adopted a standard 850-BHP ALCO (American Locomotive Co.) M-6 (540) engine. Otherwise, the design was very similar to the Electric Boat proposal; both included 60-kw auxiliary diesel generators. Hart suggested that the two designs were similar because both had been limited to about 800 tons (standard). It is probably fairer to suggest that the characteristics to which C&R worked were written around EB 231.

One of each design was built: Electric Boat's *Mackerel* (SS 204) and Portsmouth's *Marlin* (SS 205). Electric Boat used its own 840-BHP engine (see Table 11–3).

It seemed likely that many more would be built. In March 1938, the Submarine Officers Conference estimated that, in addition to 44 fleet submarines, the future fleet required 30 small ones: 6 at New London, 6 at Coco Solo, and 18 at Pearl Harbor (presumably for a combination of local defense and Midway patrols). When he left the General Board in May 1939, Hart left a memorandum:

Table 11–3. Small Submarine Designs, 1939

	Portsmouth 12 May	Electric Boat 16 January
Length overall (ft-in)	235-4	238-0
Standard displacement (tons)	800	815–820
Normal displacement (tons)	899 (including trim)	897 (including trim)
Fuel oil (normal/full load [tons])	57/83	54/83
Radius, 2 engines (nm/kt)	6,000/11 (maximum fuel)	6,800/10 (maximum fuel)
Total SHP	1,700–1,800	1,600
Normal surfaced (kt)	——	15.9
Motors (HP at 9 kt)	1,300	1,300
Battery (amp-hr; 1-hr rate)	7,000	5,700
Endurance (hr at 5 kt)	10	11
Auxiliary diesel	1 × 60 kW	2 × 75 kW
Compartment lengths (ft-in):		
Forward torpedo room	33-3	36-0
Control room	20-0	22-6
Engine room	30-6	27-6
Length inside (ft-in)	175-6	178-0
Pressure hull diameter inside (ft-in)	13-9	13-9
High-pressure air, cu ft/hr	40	40
Low-pressure air, cu ft/hr	900	1,800

Table 11–4. Portsmouth's Proposed Redesign of *Marlin*, 1941

	Marlin	Proposed
Standard displacement (tons)	800	835
Diving trim (full load) (tons)	912	973
Emergency diving trim (tons)	950	1,012
Submerged displacement (tons)	1,163	1,193
Length overall (ft-in)	238-11	238-11
Length on waterline (ft-in)	234-9	234-9
Beam molded (ft-in)	21-7¼	21-7¼
Mean draft at full load (ft-in)	13-0¼	13-8
Fuel oil (normal) (tons)	59.00	87.35
Fuel oil (emergency) (tons)	89.92	118.93
Tubes	6	10
Torpedoes	12	20

"Tell [Adm. J. W. Greenslade, his successor] I hope he will foster the little submarines. They are my pet babies."

Unfortunately, by the time *Mackerel*, the first of the pair, had been completed in 1941, the United States was mobilizing. Only tested designs could be selected for mass production. That squeezed out the small submarine, despite considerable support within the submarine community. Too, the engines of both small submarines were unique and not used for anything else in the navy.

The Board of Inspection and Survey liked Electric Boat's *Mackerel*. Because *Marlin* was so similar, BuShips expected her to be similarly satisfactory. Portsmouth suggested that a bit more tonnage would buy a great deal more. In June 1941, it offered to design a modified *Marlin* with 10, rather than six, torpedo tubes on only 850 tons. Having received formal approval on 22 July, Portsmouth submitted the revised design (see Table 11–4) on 26 December 1941. Most of the changes came out of the 104 tons of lead ballast in *Marlin* (reduced to 40 tons in the new design). The forward torpedo room would have been increased in height to take 2 more tubes (total of 6) and two more reload torpedoes. Two more tubes and two more reloads were added aft; the rudder and stern planes were moved aft. The conning tower was changed to a vertical cylinder to reduce its silhouette, and the bridge steering station was replaced by one inside the conning tower. Raised periscope supports could accommodate 40-ft periscopes like those in the fleet boats. The two single-armature motor on each shaft were replaced by a single double-armature motor. As in larger contemporary submarines, collapse depth was increased to 625 ft for a test depth of 400 ft. Portsmouth estimated that its 850-tonner would take about two thirds of the work required to build a 1,500-tonner. Shifting to smaller submarines would require a lead time of 6 mo.

Admiral Hart returned to the General Board in 1942. Although not formally a member until August, he contributed a March memorandum that supported construction of small submarines. Hart's views had considerable impact

Newly completed, *Mackerel* runs trials in 1941.

because his Asiatic Fleet included both fleet boats and S-boats. As proof of the value of small submarines, he argued that the S-boats were in as great demand in Asiatic waters as their younger and larger brethren. They were simple, they seemed to get results, and they were sent on attack missions into waters where bigger boats could not be risked. He could offer no evidence, however, that they had accomplished more.

No other major navy in the world had given up building small submarines. Hart said, "If we run counter to all other professional opinion I submit that we should be able to present an airtight case for the all-big idea." Capt. James Fife, Hart's submarine commander, disagreed. He liked small submarines, but so far they had not been used for, or accomplished, anything that was impossible for the 1,500-tonners. The larger boats had proved far more valuable—to date. Later in the war, the United States might gain advanced bases, from which small boats could reach enemy waters. If *Mackerels* could indeed be built in much greater numbers, they would then be quite useful.

Admiral King largely rejected Hart's logic. The U.S. naval problem was so different from that of other navies that their choices were largely irrelevant. The small submarine lacked offensive capability because it lacked a full TDC and good sonars. Nor was it clear that small size in itself bought less visibility, quicker diving, and better submerged handling. Certainly mobility, fuel radius, sea endurance, and habitability all favored the larger submarine. Even so, King was willing to accept any small submarine program that did not interfere with building the large fleet boats.

Submarine officers were more sympathetic. A few days after King's rejection, the Submarine Officers Conference voted unanimously for building as many small submarines as possible, if that could be done without cutting production of larger ones. The submariners expected the smaller boats to be more effective on a ton-for-ton basis, as long as they could get within range of enemy shipping. VCNO Adm. F. J. Horne, who supervised warship production, interpreted noninterference to mean that the small submarines would be built in yards that could not build the larger type. That effectively killed the project because no yard was incapable of building the larger submarines.

The submariners must have been affected by reports of very successful operations by small U-boats off the U.S. East Coast. Reportedly, they were 517- and 750-ton Types VII and IX, but actually tonnages were somewhat larger. Many senior submarine officers remembered the arguments of the 1920s. Once again, the Germans seemed to be packing much more into a small U-boat than the bureaus could pack into one twice as large. ONI reported that the Germans credited a 500-tonner (actually rather larger) with a cruising endurance of 10 to 65 days; it could patrol the East Coast for 4 wk. German official data showed a raange of 4,050 nm at 16 kt, 7,900 nm at 10 kt, or 11,000 nm at 7 kt. Based on examination of the captured log of U-651, such a submarine normally cruised at 12–14 kt, making 5,000 nm at 13 kt (16 days) at half power.

While the debate raged in Washington, the Atlantic Fleet tested the two small submarines. Both operated successfully at 15–16 kt, but at such high speeds fuel consumption limited them to an effective range of about 4,000 nm. Neither submarine could much exceed 8 kt in heavy weather. *Marlin* enjoyed 10–16 percent better fuel economy than her half-sister. Both far exceeded the old S-boats in endurance. Early in April 1942, Submarine Commander Atlantic (SubLant) formally supported a further program of one Portsmouth boat and one updated single-hull boat from Electric Boat.

Some SubLant officers visited the captured U-570, a Type VIIC that might have been considered broadly comparable to the two small U.S. boats. On 19 January 1942, SubLant appointed a special board to compare the two U.S. designs and also to compare both of them with U-570. No reader of the previous chapters will be surprised that the board blamed the U.S. designers' excessive interest in habitability for making the 800-tonners too large. Any successor should be substantially smaller, yet faster with longer range. The U-boat was so strongly built that the board thought it could surely cruise at a 400-ft depth. It dived quickly, was very maneuverable, and had good sound equipment, a simple means of eliminating the torpedo impulse bubble, a good magnetic compass, an excellent gyrocompass, an excellent attack periscope, and a small, simple TDC. The board admitted that U-570 had comparatively poor habitability, but the Germans clearly considered it adequate for long periods at sea. The board considered both U.S. submarines too slow surfaced, with too little cruising radius, too few reloads, and too much silhouette. They dived too slowly and not deep enough. A detailed comparison showed that the BuShips design was superior to Electric Boat's design (see Table 11–5). CinCLant endorsed the board report: he wanted future small submarines to have 10 tubes (as in fleet boats), to make 18 kt on the surface (and sustain 15 kt), to be more maneuverable, and to dive more deeply.

Postwar analysis suggested that the Germans achieved more on a given tonnage, thanks to three factors: (1) lighter (short-life) batteries, (2) lighter engines, and (3) some improvement in hull structure.[5]

In June, BuShips designer Captain Morgan commented sarcastically that apparently those who had seen U-570 believed that no other submarine was good "and only those who saw [her] are fully informed." It turned out that U-570 did not dive as quickly as advertised, partly because of inherent safety problems. Her best time was 28.2 sec from low buoyancy condition to periscope depth starting at 12 kt and diving at about 5.25 kt. Without the Q (quick dive) tank (which had no indicator), she dived about 6 sec slower. This was equivalent to the U.S. awash condition, with the submarine riding on her safety tank.

U.S. submarines, with their long periscopes, projected much farther out of the water. A U-boat was completely underwater at a keel depth at which U.S. masts would be still exposed. BuShips pointed out that U-570 took 60 sec to reach a depth of 42 ft 9 in. U.S. *fleet* submarines had to get to 48 ft in that time (and did it in 49–53 sec). *Mackerel* completely submerged at 35 ft in 41 sec (U-570 submerged at 30 ft in 50 sec). *Mackerel's* dive started at 10 kt, compared with 12 kt for U-570.

The General Board kept the small submarine idea alive for a few more months. It announced characteristics on 7 April and revised them on 1 June 1942. They described the Portsmouth design in perhaps inappropriate detail: about 950 tons in diving trim, overall dimensions about 240 ft × 22 ft × 14 ft. Operating depth would be 400 ft, and diving time was specified as 40 sec. Complement would be four officers and 43 enlisted men, with provisions for 30 days (rather than 75, as in a fleet boat). The small submarine could afford less reserve buoyancy than a fleet boat because she would often operate at less than full fuel load. The board therefore accepted 15 percent buoyancy at two-thirds fuel load (i.e., with normal fuel tanks full). She would have six short bow and two short stern tubes (12 torpedoes forward and 8 aft, originally 8 forward and 4 aft) controlled by a simple TDC, plus two 20-mm guns with provision for a 3-in gun. Surface speed would be 16 kt in diving trim (corresponding to a conservative rating of 1,600 BHP), the diesels driving directly through flexible couplings (i.e., not electrically—probably a provision resulting from Hart's influence). Maximum submerged speed would be 9 kt on 1,300-SHP motors. Endurance was listed as 6,000 nm at 10 kt (8,000 nm with Nos. 3 and 4 main ballast tanks filled with oil fuel). Submerged endurance would be the usual 48 hr at 2 kt.

Clearly, BuShips was working on a design because these figures were modified on 10 June to allow for 1,000 tons in diving trim and 8 kt submerged; gun armament was now one 3-in and one 20-mm. It seemed likely that the boat would dive in 45 sec, and main ballast tanks were to be blown, as in a U-boat, by engine exhaust. The board suggested building 12 units to develop the design and expand yard capacity.

A version issued on 18 June changed diving time to 30 sec (presumably because of reported U-570 performance), and the boat was to operate for 45 days with 45 enlisted men. Armament increased to one 4-in gun and one 20-mm gun, and the torpedo tubes were to be adapted to piston ejection (if that was available in time). The General Board now wanted plans developed, after which "a number to be determined later dependent on the develop-

Table 11–5. SubLant's Comparison of *Mackerel* and *Marlin* Designs, 1942

Superiority	
Mackerel	*Marlin*
Control room arrangement	General arrangement
Location of radio and sound	Power and lighting voltage control
Equipment in control room (radio room, in which the sound gear is located, is at the after end of the control room; in the *Marlin*, the sound gear is actually in the control room)	Hydraulic control of vents
	Hydraulic clutches
	Main engines
	Magnetic compass
	Bow plane operating gear
Galley and mess space	

Mackerel shows her war modifications in this 16 December 1942 photograph: an SJ radar forward of her two periscopes; an SD abaft them; and a 20-mm gun abaft her bridge fairwater. Note the paired radio antennas extending to her bridge.

ment of the design and the availability of building facilities" would be built.

BuShips warned that every increase in capability added tonnage; by 24 June, it doubted that it could stay within 875 tons. It was also most skeptical that it could design a submarine to dive in 30 sec; "conditions under which other navies do that well are not known." War experience had already shown that two engines were not enough. Patrol reports showed that *Cachalot*'s CO had not relished the risk of being caught with only one operable engine. Four small engines might use some form of composite drive. No suitable short 4-in gun existed; it was best to revert to the 3-in/50. The bureau also rejected short torpedo tubes: submarines might have to fire surface ship torpedoes.

The last set of characteristics was issued on 3 July. The General Board still wanted a quick diver: it asked for

Marlin as modified, 19 May 1943, showing SJ and SD (circled) radars. She retained her old bridge face, with its windows, but had the roof removed to provide an open bridge, with a venturi to protect it.

30 sec but would accept 40. It also wanted accommodation for two more officers in an emergency. Not much else was changed, but the General Board file copy shows 18 kt penciled in. Maximum endurance was set at 12,000 nm at 10 kt, with 25 percent allowance for battery charging and the use of emergency (fuel ballast) tanks.

This was terribly close to what a full fleet boat could do.

No more small submarines were built for the U.S. Navy. Their only real successors were four postwar submarines, based on the *Mackerel* design, that Electric Boat built for Peru. More streamlined than their predecessors, they were slightly faster underwater (10 kt), and they were powered by standard 1,200-BHP GM 12-278A diesels. Unlike their predecessors, each had a single 5-in/25 deck gun.

The small submarines were conceived as successors to World War I–built R- and S-boats. Four first-generation ''Holland'' S-boats are shown, with their radio masts raised.

12

World War II

THE BIG SUBMARINES triumphed in the Pacific War. As Admiral (then Captain) Hart and the London planners had predicted so many years before, Japan was uniquely vulnerable to submarine attack. Its newly conquered resources all had to be brought home by sea, so their initial advances made the Japanese more vulnerable. Although demands on their shipping increased, the conquests added few merchant ships and the Japanese merchant fleet was badly stretched before sinkings even began. Japan never developed the sort of emergency construction program used by the United States and Britain to help overcome the German submarine campaign.

To the prewar U.S. Navy, international law made submarine commerce raiding (though not convoy warfare against troop transports) impractical.[1] By late 1939, however, both Germany and Britain were engaging in WW I–style unrestricted submarine warfare. When war began in the Pacific, U.S. submarines were ordered to follow suit. They were stunningly successful.[2] They were also quite effective against major Japanese warships. Their speed disadvantage was more than balanced by a major advantage: their supporting intelligence system often cued them into position ahead of targets.[3]

As had been expected, surface speed mattered. A U.S. submarine approaching a convoy generally tried to get ahead of it and dive only just before reaching visual range.[4] There she could usually maneuver to counter zigzag in order to reach a good firing position with a broad track angle. If a firing position could be attained for a bow shot, one salvo (typically three torpedoes) would be fired at one target and, as quickly as possible, a second salvo fired at a second target. Shifting from bow to stern tubes or vice versa required a course change of about 140 degrees and therefore a somewhat longer delay, but this was usually attempted unless the escorts prevented it. Very few COs

angled their torpedoes to combine bow and stern shots against the same target. When possible, the submarine withdrew, surfaced, reloaded, and reattacked. If time was short, she might approach directly from the beam or quarter.

Concentration on attacking merchant ships may have skewed wartime attacks toward longer-range shots; they were less likely than warships to evade because their lookouts were less alert.[5] Merchant ships spotted submarine wakes and evaded in only about 8 percent of incidents. Quite contrary to prewar thinking, effectiveness of torpedo attacks fell off rapidly *below* 1,500 yd because fire-control errors became more serious: target bearing changed more rapidly. Optimal range turned out to be slightly below 1,500 yd. About 80–85 percent of steam torpedo attacks between 1,500 and 3,000 yd succeeded. Accuracy dropped off quite sharply beyond about 3,000 yd. The risks of shorter-range attacks were significant. From 1 January 1944 to the end of the war, of ships attacked at up to 2,500 yd, 32 percent counterattacked (compared with 26 percent of ships attacked from beyond 2,500 yd). The closer the submarine, the better the chance that a counterattack would succeed; 31 percent of counterattack shots fired within a distance of 1,500 yd found their marks. That figure fell to 24 percent for attacks executed at 1,500–2,500 yd and to only 17 percent for attacks beyond 2,500 yd.

Most attacks were near the 90-degree track angle favored by doctrine, where errors in estimating target speed were most significant—and, it turned out, most likely. The steady increase of error with track angle, discovered postwar, was completely unexpected. A 1945 analysis of attacks against medium-sized (2,000–10,000 GRT) merchant ships however, shows that beam shots were generally the most likely to hit:

During World War II, U.S. submarines sank the Japanese merchant fleet, starving the Japanese empire. Lt. Comdr. Dudley W. ("Mush") Mortons's *Wahoo* returns victorious to Pearl Harbor early in 1943, flying the traditional broom from her attack periscope. The flags indicate that she claims two Japanese warships and six merchant ships. Morton was lost when *Wahoo* was sunk on 11 October 1943.

Sector	Track Angle (degrees)	Range		
		0–1 kyd	1–2 kyd	2–3 kyd
From astern	180–120	45 (16%)	197 (23%)	158 (30%)
From abeam	120–60	221 (39%)	842 (38%)	557 (33%)
From ahead	60–0	34 (47%)	130 (32%)	37 (35%)

In columns 3, 4, and 5, the first number refers to total torpedoes launched; the number in parentheses indicates the percentage of hits. The 16, 47, and 35 percent cases represent too few attacks to justify statistical conclusion.

The average hitting rate, about 33 percent, was much lower than had been assumed. The last prewar edition of the submarine handbook, *Current Submarine Doctrine*, USF 25, assumed that submarines would make 75 percent of hits (50 percent if forced to resort to spreads). The 1944 handbook edition assumed no better than 50 percent. Table 12–1 shows prewar and 1944 estimates of the number of torpedoes required to attack various classes.

A faster torpedo got to the target more quickly; it was less affected by errors in estimating target course and speed. For example, data from the latter half of 1944 showed that a salvo of 46-kt Mk 14/23 was 14 percent likelier to hit than the 29-kt Mk 18 against merchant ships and was twice as effective against destroyers, escorts, and patrol craft (for single hits, superiority was 17 percent and 150 percent, respectively).

Because most targets were not heavily defended fleet units, much of the prewar concern with exposure to aircraft dissipated. The Japanese did not even form a special convoy-defense ASW air unit until the end of 1943.[6] Fear of sound detection also had little effect on basic tactics. Submarines tried to go quietly in the later stages of an attack, avoid presenting a beam target to sonar, and side-step escorts.

By late 1944, U.S. submariners preferred to remain on the surface in the face of escorts unless they definitely had contact because a surfaced submarine was hard to see and also faster and more maneuverable than when submerged. Being faster than her targets, she could also

Table 12–1. Torpedo Firing Doctrine: Hits Required

Type of Ship	1939	1944
Battleship or battlecruiser	7.0 (9.3)	7 (14)
Large carrier	5.0 (6.7)	5 (10)
Small carrier	2.7 (3.6)	3 (6)
Large cruiser	1.5 (2.0)	2 (4)
Seaplane tender, large auxiliary, or medium light cruiser	1.3 (1.7)	2 (3 or 4)
Merchant ship, small cruiser, or small auxiliary	1.0 (1.3)	1 (2)
Destroyer	0.5 (0.7)	1 (3)
Submarine	0.3 (0.4)	1 (3)

Note: In each case, the first number is the number of hits required to sink the ship; in the prewar (1939) column, the figures are taken from Naval War College game rules. Numbers in parentheses refer to total number of torpedoes that a submarine should fire to get the requisite number of hits. The 1944 edition of *Current Submarine Doctrine* used whole numbers only. It also assigned only a 33 percent hit probability against an evasive target, such as a destroyer or submarine.

more easily reattack. This was much like the U-boats' situation in the Atlantic before Allied escorts were given good centimetric (surface-search) radars (which the Japanese never had). According to a postwar Pacific Fleet history of Japanese ASW, late in the war, submarines sometimes refused to dive at night "even under fire from escorts."[7] By that time, radar had made it about as attractive to approach at night as in the daytime. At night, minimum surfaced range was determined by visibility, sometimes above 6,000 yd but so poor at other times that a submarine could attack surfaced.

Postwar analysis showed that U.S. submarines attacked about one-third of all merchant ships they saw; three-fourths of those attacked were hit, and two-thirds of those hit were sunk. Although only 17 percent of large warships sighted were attacked, 66 percent were hit and 35 percent of those hit were sunk. For smaller warships, it was not clear what percentage of those seen were attacked. Of those attacked, 49 percent were hit and 72 percent of ships that were hit sank. Overall, about two-thirds of all attack opportunities were taken. Many ships were passed up because the submarine could not close in (or because the targets were not worthwhile); hence the intense interest, late in the war, in higher surface speed.

The U.S. submarine force entered WW II far better prepared than in 1917. Early contact with a Royal Navy already at war provided few surprises. The British did pass on an important discovery: even submerged, a radio direction-finder loop could receive low-frequency signals (reported in November 1940). A loop 10 ft or more below the surface could receive at 425 nm in daylight. S 50 used a DQ loop for February 1941 tests. Loops were soon adopted; they also solved the antiaircraft sky arc problem. By 1944, a submarine with her loop antenna 15–20 ft below the surface could expect good low-frequency reception at range of 2,000–3,000 nm.

As in WW I, the United States established special research centers. During WW II, they were often associated with major universities. The civilian effort was coordinated by the National Defense Research Committee (NDRC) set up in 1940. Particularly significant for submarine sonar were the Columbia University Divison of War Research and the University of California Division of War Research. Harvard University Underwater Sound Laboratory developed the QH series of scanning sonars. Massachusetts Institute of Technology (MIT) was mainly responsible for microwave radar (it formed the Radiation Laboratory). Woods Hole Oceanographic Institution formally raised the importance of studying ocean thermal structure in August 1940, having developed the first bathythermograph (BT). Funded that September, this work led to submarine BTs and to tactics exploiting the layering structure of the ocean. The Submarine Operational Research Group (SORG) analyzed the effects of particular tactics and weapons; its conclusions influenced postwar thinking.

With war apparently imminent in the spring of 1941, work began on war modifications. The new magnetic mines made degaussing important. Many submarines were not air conditioned, yet it seemed likely that the navy would concentrate in the South Pacific. SubLant particularly emphasized silencing, partly on the theory that a surfaced submarine might well use sound to detect an approaching ship. Submarines that could not yet listen while surfaced (O, R, and S classes) might tow hydrophones at slow speed. The Germans were demonstrating just how effective night surface attacks could be, so SubLant wanted simple bridge directors. Priority would go to ships not fitted with TDCs: the O, R, S, and V-1 (*Barracuda*) classes.

The last important prewar technical development was SD, the first submarine-borne radar. It used a whip antenna in the periscope to warn a submarine to dive before an airplane could reach her.[8] OpNav ordered SD into production in August 1941. From 1943 on, U.S. submariners

suspected that the Japanese were picking them up on the basis of their own radar emissions, particularly SD's omnidirectional ones.[9]

During 1940, the British provided the United States with the magnetrons that made centimetric (highly directional) radar practicable. Western Electric soon developed SJ for surface search. The postwar official naval research and development (R&D) history credits SJ with the dramatic shift from day to night submarine attacks. Because Japanese surface radars were ineffective, a U.S. submarine could operate freely on the surface at night, even in the face of escorts (few of which had radar before September 1944). Using SJ, she could confidently attack at night after spending the day trailing her target at or just beyond the horizon. In 1942, when only a few submarines had SJs, 30 percent of attacks were conducted at night. In 1944, that figure rose to 57 percent. By the end of the war,

Radar revolutionized submarine tactics. At Mare Island on 20 April 1945, *Lapon* shows the vertical antenna of her ST range-only radar (the strip under the window of her forward periscope). Her new radar mast, aft, shows an SD air-warning antenna, soon to be replaced by SV. Note also the revised forward end of her bridge fairwater, with a single gun access trunk.

according to the R&D history, many COs passed up daylight opportunities to take advantage of better conditions at night. *Haddock* made the first SJ attack on 22 August 1942. A transport ran off after having been hit. *Haddock* surfaced and pursued. Because it was a moonless night, she had to use her SJ. She detected the target at 13,000 yd and then tracked it continuously. *Haddock* fired at 1,300 yd and sank the transport. During the summer of 1942, SJ was modified (as SJ-a) to drive a plan-position indicator (PPI), and its training mechanism was altered to turn at variable speed (10 RPM down to $\frac{1}{20}$ RPM or less) or manually, and in both directions. Range and bearing data could be fed automatically into the TDC. Initially, the limited height of the antenna (33 ft) gave a typical maximum range of only 5 nm. In the summer of 1943, power was increased by 50 percent and a new slotted parabolic antenna was fitted. This SJ-1 could detect a battleship at 12 nm, a surfaced submarine at 5 nm, and a bomber (altitude of 500 ft) at 5 nm. Because SJ was larger and more complex than SD, it could not fit as easily into WW I–built submarines. It was not installed in boats relegated to training duty.

The next step was X-band (3-cm, rather than 10-cm,

wavelength). SS, a much smaller replacement for SJ, was conceived as a combination surface search and torpedo fire-control radar. Surface ranges were comparable to those achieved by SJ-1, but SS could detect a bomber at 10 nm. In addition to the usual A-scope and PPI, it had a B-scope, an expanded type of sector PPI usually associated with fire control. Production began in 1945, too late for war service; SS became a standard postwar radar.

ST, the other new X-band radar, was a range-only set for the head of the night periscope. Developed in 1943–44, it became operational late in 1944.[10] Roughly contemporary with SS and ST was Bell Laboratories' SV, an S-band air search radar to replace SD. Its telescopic mast could be raised and used by a boat at shallow depth. First installed about August 1945, SV used the SJ radar scopes. The postwar SV-1 used the SS scopes. Such multiplexing was essential because conning tower space was so limited.

During the summer and fall of 1944, ships and submarines in the Pacific were fitted with a standard electronic intelligence (ELINT) suit, an APR-1 receiver with an APA-6 pulse analyzer.[11] Although their antennas had to be specially pressure-proofed, submarines were particularly valued because they could approach Japanese-held islands

Crevalle (above and facing page) shows her new ST periscope (the forward one) and her new air-search radar mast in these 27 January 1945 photographs taken at Mare Island. The sonars are the JT line array and WCA.

At Mare Island on 1 August 1945, *Bashaw* (*above and facing page*) shows final wartime radar and other modifications, all indicated: ST on her night (Type 4) periscope; SJ and SV search radars; and a whip radio antenna (for HF communication without fouling the sky arcs of her anti-aircraft guns).

unseen. The same intercept equipment could also detect Japanese airborne radar before airplanes carrying it came within attack range. USS *Batfish* once sank three Japanese ships detected by ELINT.

The standard sonars at the outbreak of war were WCA (18–24 kHz) and WDA, combined passive and active sonars and depth sounders.[12] Using the BDI (bearing deviation indicator) introduced during the war, submarines could track a target automatically. The sonar beam was split; the sounds or echoes in the two adjacent beams were equal only when the sonar pointed directly at its target. Late in the war, the standard sets were modified for torpedo and mine detection: TDM (torpedo detection modification), OL (object locator), and MATD (mine and torpedo detection).[13]

As before the war, doctrine called for using sonar to obtain accurate ranges on surface targets during submerged approaches. To use the main alternative, the periscope stadimeter (see Appendix B), the submarine CO had to know a vertical distance on board the target. A single accurate range at 2,500–3,000 yd could calibrate the stadimeter (in effect measuring masthead height), making further periscope ranges (as the submarine closed in) accurate.[14] Otherwise, sonar range generally would be more accurate than periscope range, albeit perhaps more dangerous to take.

The first major new sonar development was to add deck units (ordered by VCNO on 22 September 1942), which were needed particularly by submarines bottoming, as in the Southwest Pacific. Probably inspired by the Ger-

OFFICIAL PHOTOGRAPH
NOT TO BE RELEASED
FOR PUBLICATION
NAVY YARD MARE ISLAND, CALIF.

RESTRICTED

mans, VCNO asked that the deck gear cover sonic, as well as supersonic, frequencies. A proposal to add a toroidal transducer (as in small-boat sonic listening gear) to the existing supersonic JK was rejected in favor of a small-boat passive sonar (JP, covering 70 Hz to 12 kHz).

Beginning in mid-1945, JP was superseded by the specially designed JT, a rotating 5-ft line hydrophone working at 100 Hz to 12 kHz (later extended up to 60 kHz). It could scan continuously, or it could track a single target. For tracking, it had a right-left indicator (RLI) that showed directly how far off the target it was trained. The JT bearing was repeated to the TDC to check the bearing projected (generated) by the fire-control solution and to the sonar stack to simplify single-ping ranging. The TDC could also drive the JT. That simplified rate control because the RLI meter indicated whether the target was leading or lagging the generated bearing. In 1945, JT was standard for all

submarines; 165 were made. BQR-3 was a postwar version.

JT could determine bearing so precisely that two of them, in theory, could measure range directly by triangulation. In 1944, the NDRC mounted two JTs at the ends of a submarine (S-48). A mechanical solver automatically converted their bearings into range, up to 4000 yd. OpNav and Commander-in-Chief, U.S. Fleet (Cominch), representatives were so impressed that, in November, USS *Conger* was ordered fitted with this triangulation listening ranging (TLR) set, and a contract for five pre-production models was let. TLR promised reversion to the prewar concept of sound-only attacks. The basic idea, quite differently implemented, resurfaced postwar as PUFFS, (passive underwater fire control feasibility) and then WAA (wide aperture array).[15]

WFA, the last wartime operational sonar, was intended

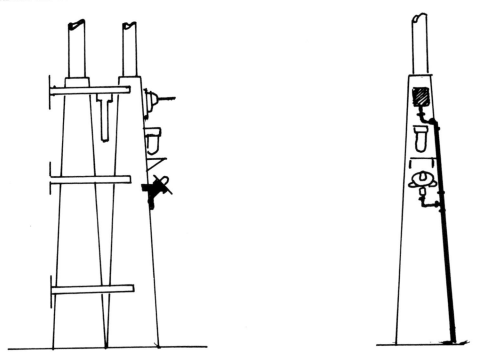

By late 1944, many submarines had limited radar detector installations called radar countermeasures (RCM), although they never included jammers. These sketches show the typical installation consisting of an aircraft-type APR stub (top) and an AS-44 antenna (bottom). The stub served an APR-1 or SPR-1 (shipboard version of the APR-1 designed for aircraft), which could detect low-frequency radar signals (80–1,000 MHz). AS-44 detected microwave (S-band) signals at 1,000–3,500 MHz, serving an APR-5AX or SPR-2. Both antennas were omnidirectional, and both could be connected to a pulse analyzer (SPA-1), from which the signal's pulse repetition rate and pulse width could be read. If the radar was a known type, these figures could identify it.

to replace all the wartime sonars. Its transducers were split for BDI (bearing deviation indication). It incorporated MTB (maintenance of true bearing; i.e., its bearings compensated for submarine maneuvers, so that it could more easily detect target course and speed). For its two range scales, 1,500 yd and 3,750 yd, it used 75-msec and 187.5-msec pulses, respectively. For mine detection, the short scale was used with a special short pulse (10 msec) and the chemical recorder stylus was set to fly back at 600 yd.

WFA used a bottom side projector (ranging and listening at 22–32 kHz) and a three-part topside projector (in a cylindrical dome): (1) high frequency (to detect small objects, ranging at 40–46 kHz; listening at 35–100 kHz), (2) intermediate frequency (ranging at 20–28 kHz, listening at 17–35 kHz), and (3) sonic (listening only at 110 Hz–15 kHz, less precise bearing data than the larger JT). WFA fed two sonar stacks, one in the conning tower and one in the forward torpedo room. Each contained a chemical recorder, a listening amplifier (with sonic and supersonic units), an echo-ranging receiver amplified with a dial indicator, and a unit to train the transducers. The transmitter (ranging) driver, thyratron training control, BDI amplifier, and fathometer driver were all in the forward torpedo room. The transducers used a new adenosine diphosphate (ADP) crystal, which could withstand greater temperatures and shocks than the Rochelle Salt of the earlier WCA and WDA.

WFA was first installed on board SS 435–437 and SS 477, completed in 1945. At the end of the war, OpNav ordered that it and the improved WFA-1 replace WCA and WDA on all the fleet boats, from *Gato* (SS 212) onward. In 1945, a total of 100 sonars were ordered, 90 for the planned active postwar boats plus 10 for training (110 were made). Some earlier boats had domes installed.

The most important late-war sonar development was scanning sonar, using a fixed transducer and a rapidly spinning commutator. As it spun, the commutator sampled sound from all directions; turning quickly enough, it covered the whole space around the sonar almost continuously. The idea had two quite different applications. Long-range QH sonars had high search rates; QHBs were installed aboard many submarines postwar. QLA enjoyed high resolution, albeit at short range. Modified searchlight sonars, such as WCA and WFA, could detect mines, but it took the scanning sonar QLA to search quickly enough to guide a submarine through a minefield. QLA guided U.S. submarines into the closed Sea of Japan in 1945.[16]

In 1944, the Arma Corp. (which had developed TDC Mk 3) and the New York Navy Yard developed TDC Mk 4 to exploit the new sensors, which resulted in virtual elimination of oral reports (Table 12–2 gives typical sensor ranges). TDC Mk 4 carried four sets of repeaters: (1) optical (No. 1 periscope and forward or after TBT), (2) radar (SJ bearing), (3) range (SJ or ST range), and

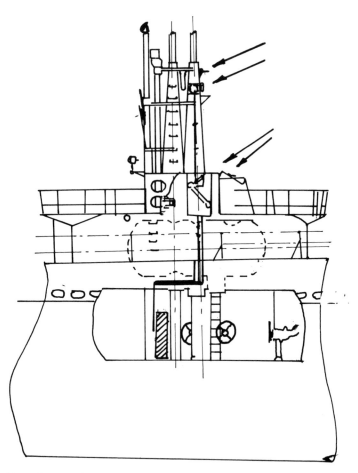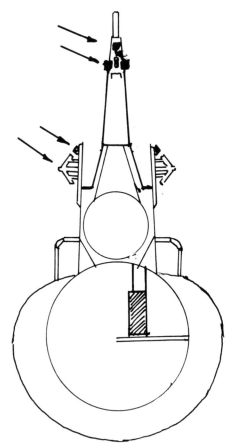

By mid-1945, plans called for adding directional RCM antennas. Arrows on the profile drawing (left) indicate the antennas. The APR stub (top) would remain for early warning and for use at radar depth. Below it were three pairs of directional antennas, one pair on each side of the periscope shears. DBV (XCV), a directional replacement for AS-44, was mounted on each side of the shears just below the APR stub. DBU (also called XCV or 66AJO) was a directional APR-1 antenna consisting of a pair of antennas on the sides of the bridge fairwater: small high-band units (800–1,000 MHz) and larger low-band units (80–300 MHz). The antennas could indicate whether a signal came from port or starboard; to get anything more precise, however, the submarine had to swing back and forth. Note the location of the inboard electronics in the control room below the conning tower.

(4) sound (JT or QB-JK sound bearings).[17] Each readout could be compared with the relative range or bearing calculated (generated) by the TDC. Actual input was manual, as in TDC Mk 3. Generated bearing and range could be transmitted automatically to the JT and SJ, with corrections

Table 12–2. Average Detection Ranges for Submarine Sensors, 1945 (kyd, 50 percent detections)

	QB/JK	JP	Enemy Sonar	Periscope	SJ-1
Independent merchant ship	7	10	17	12.5	17
Convoy	10	15	17	17	19
Independent combatant	7	10	17	10	10.5
Escorted combatant	15	20	17	17	25

Source: *Submarine Warfare Instructions*, USF 9, 1946.

fed back to the TDC. The key quantities were the *rates* at which range and bearing were changing. Now they could be measured almost directly. For example, the JT operator could estimate the rate at which a target's bearing was changing. He could set JT to turn at that rate; if it stayed on the target, the estimate was correct. The measured bearing rate could be fed back to the TDC. Mk 4 could handle more torpedo range and speed settings than its predecessor. Maximum tracking range was up to 30,000 yd, and target speed was to 40 kt. Maximum torpedo gyro angle was 150 degrees. The postwar Mk 106 submarine fire-control system was based on Mk 4.

By 1945, the NRL representative at Pearl Harbor thought the main postwar problem would be to integrate the numerous new electronic systems to gain space. As an interim step, *Corsair* (SS 435) was completed with a 5-ft longer conning tower, to accommodate a separate combat information center (CIC). Surface warships already had CICs separate from their bridges; the submarine CIC would contain the TDC, DRT (dead-reckoning tracer),

Submarines also sprouted radar detectors. *Hake* is shown at the end of a Mare Island refit, 30 May 1945. Several short ESM whip antennas are visible: one facing forward on the periscope shears; one facing up among the shears; one angled aft alongside the bridge structure; and another mounted on the rail forwod of the twin 20-mm cannon. New ammunition-passing scuttles have been cut to serve the forward 5 in/25 gun, and the deck has been sponsoned out aft for a second such weapon. As in many other submarines at this time, a new mast has been provided for the SD air search radar. It cleared the conning tower, thus considerably reducing congestion within.

communications facilities, torpedo-firing facilities, radio remote control, and ECM. The rest of the conning tower would become more like a bridge. In September 1945, as part of a critique of the new submarine design, submarine officers asked that CIC be moved down into the pressure hull adjacent to the control room, so as to shrink the conning tower drastically and thus reduce silhouette. Modern U.S. submarines have attack centers next to their control spaces.

By that time, BuOrd expected its new Mk 31 computer to replace the TDC. Its large console would occupy much of the CIC. An automatic plot on its 20-in CRT (cathode-ray tube) would show three targets simultaneously. Five or six operators would man radar, sonar, angle solver, position keeper, and plot. Mk 31 would be at least partly electronic in order to minimize solution time. It would automatically position radar and sonar beams and automatically track targets (by rate-aided or other techniques). Salvo devices would automatically fire selected tubes at appropriate intervals after the key was closed. To control

the new very–long-range Mk 16 torpedo, tracking range would exceed that of TDC Mk 4. Mk 31 would include a ballistic and predicting section for 5-in gun control. Using its auxiliary control system, a submarine could fire her 40-mm and 5-in guns at one target and her torpedoes at another. The Mk 31 project included an associated K-band (1-cm) radar and an IR bearing indicator in a periscope (effective to 8,000 yd).[18] Mk 31 evolved into the postwar Mk 101.

In 1941, BuOrd believed it had provided submarines with a revolutionary weapon: the Mk XIV torpedo, with a Mk VI magnetic pistol (exploder) intended to trigger the warhead as it passed under a target. The resultant rising and pulsating sphere of gas might break the target's keel; in any case it would vitiate the classic side protection of a capital ship. Unfortunately, to maintain its secret, BuOrd had tested the magnetic pistol only once, and that was in Narragansett Bay.[19] Magnetic conditions in the Pacific Ocean were different enough to make the device ineffec-

OFFICIAL PHOTOGRAPH
NOT TO BE RELEASED
FOR PUBLICATION
NAVY YARD MARE ISLAND, CALIF

RESTRICTED

At Mare Island on 20 June 1945, *Hoe* displays two typical main late-war submarine sonars: the JT line array (left) and a topside WCA in its spherical dome (right). At the end of the war, both were being replaced by the vertical cylindrical dome of the new WFA integrated sonar.

tive. The backup contact exploder failed when the torpedo struck its target at nearly right angles (i.e., when shots were best); it worked better at oblique angles. The torpedo ran deeper than set. Its prominent wake alerted targets. In at least one case (possibly as many as five), it ran circular and sank the firing submarine. There is also evidence that many Mk XIVs exploded prematurely.[20]

Submarine officers began reporting torpedo failures very early in the war, but BuOrd refused either to believe them or to sanction tests. Submariners were infuriated. The first controlled depth test (at the Fremantle advanced base, 20 June 1942) showed that, on average, torpedoes ran 11 ft deep. Many COs set their torpedoes to run shallow, but torpedoes still failed because their exploders did not work. In mid-1943, test firings against a cliff in Hawaii showed that the weak exploder mechanism was crushed in a perfect shot. Pearl Harbor developed a replacement, but Mk XIV (14) did not work as designed until the fall of 1943. U.S. submarines fired 14,277 torpedoes against Japanese targets, mostly between January 1943 and April 1945. Postwar analysis showed that straight-running tor-

pedoes (Mks 14, 18, 23) made 4,794 hits, or 33.5 percent; of 4732 salvos, 2,716 were successful (57.5 percent). Attacks averaged 3 torpedoes per salvo.

Two new wakeless types of torpedoes had been in prospect by 1941: slow electric torpedoes and fast hydrogen peroxide (Navol) weapons. Work on an electric torpedo had been under way since 1915.[21] In 1942, Westinghouse Electric Co. was ordered to copy the German G7e recovered from the captured U-570. The first G7e was acquired in January 1942, and the Mk 18 (4,000 yd at 29 kt) prototype appeared 15 mo later. The first six production torpedoes were delivered 6 mo after contract award; 9,000 torpedoes were made. Wartime COs preferred to fire wakeless electric torpedoes for longer-range shots because they did not alert their targets. A mid-1945 study showed that the average range for electric torpedoes was 2,660 yd surfaced and 2,150 yd submerged, compared with 2,350 yd and 2,020 yd respectively, for steam. In 1944, 30 percent of all torpedoes fired in combat were Mk 18s, but that figure increased to 65 percent in 1945.

Mk 18 used the air-powered controls of its steam-air

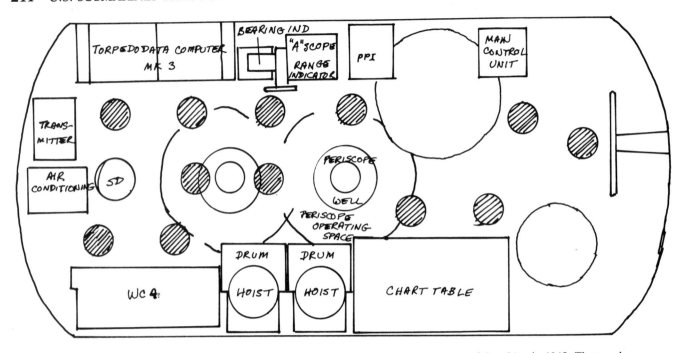

By the end of World War II, conning towers were badly crowded. This drawing shows that of *Sea Lion* in 1945. The two large open circles on the right are the hatches, up from the pressure hull (above) and up to the open bridge (below). Wartime additions included the third mast (for SD) passing through the conning tower to the left, and the radar scopes to the right of the torpedo data computer. The shaded circles indicate the location of the crew in the conning tower.

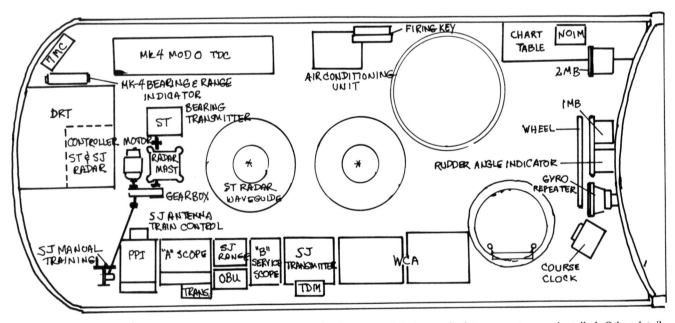

Haddo's conning tower is shown after her last wartime overhaul, when a new Mk 4 torpedo data computer was installed. Other details include the course clock near the wheel, for systematic zigzagging to avoid Japanese submarine torpedoes; and the ST and SJ radars (SD had been moved outside the conning tower). SJ was provided with manual train so that the antenna could be pointed at a target before the radar was turned on; sweeping the radar beam might be quite dangerous. Other indications are: 1 MB, engine order telegraph; 2 MB, motor order telegraph; and 7 MC, maneuvering intercom that connects the bridge, conning tower, maneuvering room, control room, wardroom, and torpedo rooms.

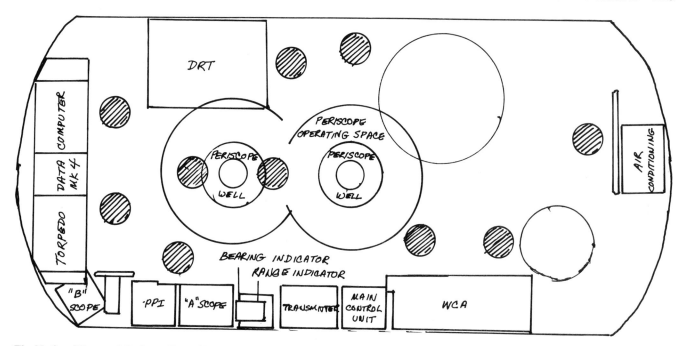

The National Research Defense Council, using the time and motion techniques developed prewar for major companies, studied submarine internal arrangement. This sketch shows its proposal for a rearranged conning tower, with the SD radar and its hoists removed; SD was moved to a new radar mast abaft the conning tower. The council's concept was adopted for new and refitted submarines. Note that two men were removed from the crowded conning tower. Although not evident here, presumably it would have been possible to move ESM equipment into the space thus freed up in order to provide the CO with more immediate attack information.

predecessors. Mk 19 was a MK 18 with electric controls. It was canceled (in favor of Mk 26) after only 10 had been made. Development of Mk 20, BuOrd's alternative to Westinghouse's Mk 18/19, was completed in 1945, too late for war service. It could reach 3,500 yd at 33 kt, but it was not considered sufficiently better than Mk 18 to be worth producing in quantity; only 20 were made. Mk 26 was conceived as the next step in electric torpedo performance; it used a primary seawater-activated battery in place of the secondary (storage) batteries of Mk 18/19 and Mk 20. Predicted performance, 6,000 yd at 40 kt, was nearly that of contemporary steam torpedoes. After 25 were made, it was abandoned in 1945 because the new hydrogen peroxide Mk 16 offered much higher performance without leaving much more of a wake than an electric torpedo. Mk 26 was the first torpedo to use an explosive impulse start gyro and electric on-off ("bang-bang") steering and depth controls.

BuOrd and Westinghouse experimented unsuccessfully with chemical fuels from 1915 through late 1926. The project was then transferred to NRL, which suggested an oxygen torpedo. Work began in 1929; the torpedo ran successfully in 1931. In 1934, NRL chose to substitute Navol (hydrogen peroxide). In September 1937, a Navol Mk 10 reached 9,500 yd, 275 percent beyond its usual range. About 1940, a Navol Mk 14 made 16,500 yd at 46 kt. Interrupted by the war, work resumed in 1943. The Mk 16 Navol torpedo was issued postwar. Mod 1 ran

11,000 yd at 46 kt. Later versions had a circular pattern run feature.[22]

By 1945, a distinction had been drawn between offensive (anti-ship) and defensive (anti-escort) torpedoes, the latter a homing torpedo fired as a submarine dived to evade attack. Defensive weapons came first: electric torpedoes were inherently so quiet that they could be adapted to acoustic homing. The first, NDRC's air-launched passive acoustic anti-submarine homing torpedo, Mk 24 (Fido) appeared in 1943. Late in 1944, a submarine-launched version, Mk 27 (Cutie: 19 in × 90 in, 720 lb, 5,000 yd at 12 kt), entered service. Unlike conventional steam torpedoes, it started in the tube without fire-control set-up and swam out under its own power in 8–10 sec.[23] This was a major innovation. Prewar doctrine was to maneuver radically to evade depth charges. A few COs managed to fire torpedoes "down the throats" of approaching Japanese destroyers, but that was considered quite tricky.

The analogous homing offensive version of Mk 18 was Mk 28 (21 in × 246 in, 2,800 lb, 4,000 yd at 20 k, followed a preset course for the first 1,000 yd). Production continued until 1952; Mk 28 was not replaced (by Mk 37) until 1960.[24] Mine Mk 27, a modified electric torpedo, was the first U.S. submarine-launched standoff mine. Submarine minelaying was always hazardous. The submarine often had to penetrate enemy defensive fields, and she could not safely reseed fields laid earlier. The slow-running Mk 27 could be fired into the area to be mined.

The combination of radar, sonar, and the torpedo data computer was extremely effective. This is a mocked-up conning tower (No. 4 attack teacher) at the submarine school at New London. The torpedo data computer is at the left, the display behind the glass window showing target and own-ship headings and range. The sonar stack is on the right, the handwheel directing the sonar beam. The large dial shows bearing relative to the submarine. The CO stands at the periscope; another officer reads off stadimeter ranges and other data. In a real submarine another periscope would rise out of the well in the foreground.

Three projects died at the end of the war. Mk 22 was a full-length active acoustic anti-ship homing torpedo with much the same performance as Mk 18/19. Active homing was attractive—the returning ping could be heard against background noise because of faster water flow. Mk 22 was probably dropped in favor of the projected dual-purpose Mk 35. Mk 30 was a wake-follower using an optical wake sensor developed in cooperation with the Royal Australian Navy. The basic idea had been conceived about 1944 by the Germans. By 1946, work on a torpedo had been superseded by a more general wake research program. Wake-following was never adopted by the U.S. Navy, but it eventually became standard in the Soviet Navy.

A third idea never received a formal Mark number: SOB, a combined evasion decoy and weapon. It would loiter while simulating submarine noise and returning es-

cort sonar pings. An influence exploder fired when the escort made a run on the weapon. SOB was little more than a concept; by 1947, it had been abandoned.

The submariners' desired characteristics for postwar submarine torpedoes reflected their wartime experience.[25] The greatest lesson of all, taught so painfully by the magnetic exploder disaster, was that torpedoes had to be tested thoroughly in peacetime. Torpedoes had to be more rugged. Depth charging could start them in the tube; at least one hot-running electric torpedo melted its explosive. Delicate exploders limited firing rate; a torpedo running close to another might be countermined. A reliable anticircular run device was needed, particularly for homing torpedoes. Finally, the standard U.S. (and foreign) practice of having torpedoes explode at the end of the run gave away the presence of an otherwise undetected submarine.

Nothing could be done to expand submarine weapon stowage to accommodate the new variety of weapons. In 1945, the submariners wanted to cut back to two standard types. A very fast (65-kt or more) nearly wakeless offensive homer should have a range of at least 10,000 yd. A shorter-range defensive (anti-escort) wakeless homer would have a range of at least 3,000 yd and speed of more than 20 kt and carry at least 500 lb of explosive. Hopefully, it would be short enough to stow two per rack and would be launchable at maximum submarine operating depth (i.e., as the submarine was evading pursuit). Both torpedoes needed an effective influence exploder. By September 1945, BuOrd's future development program showed three types: a very fast straight-runner (Mk 36, ultimately abortive), an offensive homer (Mk 35), and a small defensive homer (Mk 37).

The Japanese used both active and passive (often sonic) sonar. A postwar U.S. report considered their listening gear (at the outbreak of war) "every bit as good as ours" but their active sonar no more than fair. However, "early in the war they repeatedly demonstrated facility in locating a submerged submarine by using sonar and in this respect their ASW craft appeared to be about on a par with ours."[26] Hydrophones could detect a U.S. submarine at about 5,000 m while running at about 5 kt; active sonar had a maximum range of about 3,000 m for a ship running at 12 kt.

U.S. submarines were therefore silenced. Those tested in the fall of 1944 were about 20 dB quieter than those tested in the spring of 1942, a 99 percent reduction in sound intensity that reduced average sonobuoy detection range from 160 yd to 50 yd. Under similar conditions, a U-boat could be detected at 1,600 yd.[27] Beginning in April 1945, U.S. submarines had noise level monitors (NLM, using 4 hull hydrophones reading out at the JP amplifier) that allowed COs better to evaluate their "acoustic housekeeping." A submarine typically ran her NLM 15 min a day, and 30 min once a week for a more thorough check.

Woods Hole's on-board bathythermograph (BT) allowed wartime U.S. submarines to take greater advantage of their environment, particularly the layering of water, which refracted and reflected sound. The BT measured the temperature (hence, generally, the sound velocity) at the submarine's depth. Each day, a submarine dove deep to take a full temperature profile (automatically filling out a BT card) as a guide to later evasion. The BT was first tested for submarine use in 1942.

A submarine decoy program began in April 1943.[28] Evolved from ASW training aids (echo repeaters) that the University of California Division of War Research (UCDWR) began to develop in 1942, decoys could be released from a submarine's 3-in signal ejector tube and from her torpedo tubes. NAC was a barrage jammer with only limited output at any one frequency band. After tests on board an S-boat in February 1944, 450 NACs were ordered in June 1944; that increased to 5,450 in August.

Another 5,000 NAC-1s were ordered in June 1945. A total of 4,308 were supplied to the submarine force during the war (contracts were cut back drastically at the end of the war). NAC proved only partially effective against experienced sonar operators. Its successor, NAH, used a high-velocity tape or disk recorder to pick up the sonar ping, then retransmitted it for 15 sec, beginning 0.10 sec after it arrived. It worked over the 10–30 kHz band. Development began in May 1945.

NAC did not move through the water like a real submarine. Work on a self-propelled NAD began in May 1943. The 3-in NAD-3 simulated a submarine running at periscope depth at 120 turns. It could not accommodate a sonar repeater. A 6-in (diameter) decoy ejector was proposed; beginning in December 1943, an enlarged NAD-6 (6 in × 48 in) incorporating a repeater was designed to fit it. The new ejector was then canceled, and NAD would have to be fired from a torpedo tube. UCDWR enlarged NAD again (the 10-in NAD-10 was made from an M30 mine body). The first NAD-6, carrying a sonar repeater, was completed in August 1944. BuShips demanded a simulator; a redesigned NAD-6 was tested in October 1944. Contracts for 500 NAD-6s and 500 NAD-10s were let late in 1944 and doubled in 1945; at the end of the war they were cut back to 500 each. These decoys held a straight course within 2 degrees so that the launching submarine could know where they were and evade away from them; gyro angle was present to within plus or minus 90 degrees. NAD-3 ran at 5 kt at a depth of 50 ft and slowed to 3 kt to begin noisemaking at a present distance. NAD-6 ran out of a torpedo tube at 4 kt; noisemaking began after 35 sec, and lasted 30–35 min. NAD-10 ran out at 7 kt, then slowed to 3.75 kt after 1 min; it lasted an hour. At least some NADs were in fleet service in the summer of 1945.

David Taylor Model Basin began work in 1944 on NAE, a mechanical noisemaker derived from the towed FXR and effective above 6 kHz. Mk 1, a wideband masker, was field-tested in October 1944 and operational in the spring of 1945. Mk 2, introduced in the summer of 1945, differed from Mk 1 in that it could be launched down to 400 ft and its supporting balloon hovered below the surface of the water so that it was not visible from the air. Mks 3 and 4 were high-frequency maskers and jammers. NAE was considered effective at high sonic and supersonic frequencies and could even jam some sonars, but it was less effective at lower sonic frequencies. Postwar, it was developed mainly as a rocket-fired noisemaker (acoustic torpedo countermeasure) for use by surface ASW ships.

UCDWR and David Taylor conceived NAG in 1943 as a lower-frequency companion to NAC to counter hydrophones in the 0.1–10 kHz range. A second sound head was later added, so that it could also operate at supersonic frequencies. NAG was under test at the end of the war. There were also false target shells (FTSs) and false target cans (FTCs). MIT designed pepper signals (Mk 14 and Mk 20) to mask submarine self-noise at sonic frequencies in shallow water. Reverberation would add its own masking;

in deeper water, sonar operators could maintain contact between explosions.

A combined-use doctrine was quickly worked out. If the submarine was not sure that the enemy had gained contact, she launched an NAD or ejected FTSs and FTCs. If the enemy had contact, quantities of NACs and NAEs could jam receivers, confuse an attack, and break contact; then FTSs and FTCs would be ejected to add to the confusion. Once contact was clearly broken, an NAD emerging from the masked area would attract attention. The submarine had to choose her evasive course so that the NAD emerged before she did. Decoys always had to be ejected in rapid succession to avoid forming a trail that pointed to the submarine. These ideas and decoy categories (static noise beacon, mobile submarine simulator) have persisted ever since. Analogous radar beacons were developed to decoy radar-directed ASW aircraft. Hopes of an antisonar coating were not realized.

Once a submarine was detected and attacked, the typical evasive maneuver, a radical course change coupled with a dive, was intended to keep the enemy astern so that the submarine could slip away. Submarines could often dive under layers (literally, under the depth at which the BT trace broke). It turned out that neither the Japanese *nor* the U.S. submariners realized just how deep a fleet submarine could dive. The Japanese often set their bombs and depth charges shallow, although late in the war they learned to do better.[29]

An evading CO wanted to know where the attackers were and to gauge the intensity of their attack. Knowing where the depth charges were exploding might indicate an appropriate evasive course. The idea of a depth charge direction indicator (DCDI) probably predated the war; early in February 1942, the Submarine Officers Conference had formally rejected one recently developed on the ground that the best way to avoid attack was to use standard sound gear to locate the attacking vessel. Although it might not take up much space, DCDI was considered merely another piece of equipment needing upkeep and repair.

War experience suggested otherwise. Columbia University developed both DCDI and DCRE (depth charge range estimator). DCDI work began in January 1944; the first unit was delivered in July 1945. After 5 prototypes and 10 pre-production models (one of which went to the Royal Navy) had been delivered, DCDI was adopted as standard; 256 were ordered. DCRE was formally requested in January 1944. The first of 4 experimental units was delivered that August and production orders for 115 units followed in April 1945. By that time, a project was under way to add a range meter to DCDI in order to combine DCRE and DCDI functions.

The last U.S. submarine design of WW II, although never built, expressed wartime lessons. It originated with the mid-1944 decision to wind down fleet submarine production. Late in July, Admiral King asked the senior operational submarine commanders in the Atlantic and Pacific to comment on the postwar plan and also to suggest characteristics for postwar combatant, cargo, and tanker submarines. By the fall of 1944, characteristics for a new submarine had been drawn up, and BuShips was working on a design.

The submariners wanted higher surface speed (typically stated as 25 kt), much greater test depth (typically doubled, to 800 ft), and much better maneuverability (both surfaced and submerged). Only a very fast submarine could overtake enemy formations running at 21–22 kt, attack and reattack, and then escape escorts on the surface (and thus avoid being driven down and depth charged). The cost of additional surface speed could be reduced by lengthening the hull, but that added wetted surface (hence underwater resistance). Also length would probably cost underwater maneuverability—an important factor in survival.[30] The ideal solution would be a new, more compact power plant. ComSubPac Admiral Lockwood suggested a gas turbine, provided that it could be made quiet enough.

Both SubPac and SubLant wanted higher submerged speed, 12–15 kt. Theory suggested that the probability of a successful depth charge attack was about inversely proportional to the square of submarine speed.[31] Adding 2 kt to the existing 9.5-kt submarine would improve her chance of survival by about 46 percent. Maximum underwater speed was set by battery capacity (because it was 1-hr speed), so either battery volume, hence weight, had to grow in a larger hull or the battery rating had to increase at the cost of battery life.

Many submariners had survived depth charging because their fleet boats could dive below design test depths. They had learned to hide beneath the layer.[32] They also believed that the strength associated with greater test depth would help a submarine operating at a shallower depth to survive a depth charge explosion. Greater diving depth was quite expensive, in terms of overall submarine size, unless some new pressure hull material was used. BuShips argued for a 500-ft test depth; it claimed that layers had not been observed below about 400 ft and that, for theoretical reasons, they were extremely unlikely below 450 ft. Postwar, however, a layer depth of about 600 ft was commonly attributed to the North Atlantic in winter.

The simplest way to improve underwater maneuverability was to add a topside rudder (see chapter 10); submariners were generally satisfied with surface maneuverability.

ComSubPac also wanted much heavier armament: two more stern tubes, with two reloads for each forward tube and one for each after tube, a total of 30 torpedoes. Lockwood favored a new heavy 24-in torpedo to match the Japanese "Long Lance," but SubLant was less enthusiastic. Many submariners were more interested in bubbleless firing; presumably, poppet valves had not solved the bubble problem. Piston ejection cost too much volume: the tube had to be enlarged to 25-in diameter and a second cylinder added above it. Fortunately (given postwar requirements), the alternative of hydraulic firing was suitable for greater depths than previously had been required.

Lockwood also wanted "special weapons" (defensive torpedoes). His submarine would have two 5-in/25 wet guns (SubLant asked for only one), plus automatic weapons at bridge level that were remotely controlled and thus could be fired as the submarine dived to escape air attack. To cut silhouette, both Lockwood and Sublant wanted the electronic equipment moved into a separate CIC, as in the new *Corsair* (see above). Everyone knew all this would cost something in overall size. Admiral Lockwood wanted growth limited to 320 ft and 2,000 tons. BuShips found this totally unrealistic.

BuShips and the submariners collided in several Submarine Officers Conferences in Washington during September and October 1944. The previous summer, BuShips had begun development of its first entirely new fleet submarine design since the late 1930s. First, it simply offered to boost the standard fleet boat diesels (to 1,750 BHP each), while increasing hull strength to reach a collapse depth of 1,000 ft (operating depth 660 ft). Scheme 1 (5 August 1944: 340 ft × 28.7 ft × 15 ft 6 in, 2,418 tons, 16-ft pressure hull) added a pair of hull plugs (17 ft 6 in) for buoyancy. Surface speed would have been a disappointing 21.95 kt.[33]

The next step was to add another pair of engines in a third engine room. That increased overall length (Scheme 2) to 352 ft (2,447 tons; pressure hull diameter, 17 ft 3 in). Speed would have increased to 24 kt, but the boat would have been unwieldy underwater. The alternative (Scheme 4, 7 October 1944) was to reduce pressure hull weight and length by cutting collapse depth (to 750 ft: 500-ft operating depth) and by placing the engines three abreast in wider engine rooms. Calculated surface speed fell to 23.8 kt (the shorter 332-ft hull suffered more wave-making resistance). This configuration was soon abandoned, as three diesels in one engine room were considered objectionable. A shorter hull was still attractive, so in Scheme 7 (27 October 1944) the designers tried making the after pair of diesels drive hydraulically, rather than diesel-electrically. They thought the shorter (332-ft) hull could be designed to collapse at 1,000 ft, and they increased pressure hull diameter to 17 ft 3 in to add buoyancy. Under ideal conditions, they hoped to achieve 23.6 kt. The alternative (Scheme 9, 21 November 1944) was to return to the long hull (352 ft) but to cut pressure hull weight (800-ft collapse depth). Maximum surface speed would have been 24.5 kt (23.4 kt on 9,000 BHP, the sustained output). This 2,424-tonner barely would have made the required 16,000-nm endurance at 16 kt (it offered 28,000 nm at 10 kt). Scheme 11 (358 ft, 2,832/3,667 tons), the last gasp of the six-engine series, used a new GM "W" engine (1,760 BHP, 2,125-BHP emergency overload). It was by no means clear that any of these ideas would be practical because there might be insufficient tip clearance for propellers capable of absorbing 50 percent more power.

Scheme 9 offered, probably for the first time in the series, a much more powerful armament: six stern tubes (total of 30 torpedoes, 21 in × 246 in, plus two triple deck tubes for homing torpedoes (21 in × 198 in, total of 10 on board).

Given this experience, the BuShips designers succeeded in impressing the facts of life on the heretofore recalcitrant submariners. The 500-ft limit (800-ft collapse depth) was accepted. The designers had to abandon six-engine layouts; they could hope only to uprate existing diesels and add engine room length to accommodate them.

Existing diesels often ran for long periods at somewhat higher power. The 1,600-BHP (720 RPM), 10-cylinder Fairbanks-Morse (FM) diesel was typically rated at 1,800 BHP in surface ships. BuShips offered to uprate it to 2,000 BHP (850 RPM) and to add 2 more cylinders to reach 2,400 BHP, a 50 percent improvement. Two-stage supercharging might add another 400 BHP, for a net 75 percent improvement at the cost of only 3 ft of extra length per engine room. There was also the new GM "W" engine.

Scheme 10A was the first of a new series of four-engine designs using more powerful engines (331 ft 5 in × 31 ft 9 in extreme [beam] × 16 ft 5.5 in, 2,580 tons: 21.6 kt under ideal conditions [7,040 BHP], 22.3 kt emergency [8,500 BHP], endurance 18,000 nm at 15 kt or 30,000 nm at 10 kt). Scheme 14 (17 January 1945) used 2,900-BHP FM engines. Length was cut to 320 ft, and estimated sustained speed was 23.1 kt, not too far from a six-engine boat. This design was too tight; the engines needed more space plus a plenum chamber (possibly for a snorkel). Scheme 15 (March 1945) seems to have introduced 19 in Mk 27 torpedoes in place of the 21-in weapons of Scheme 9; they would be in fixed tubes, pointed athwartships, in the superstructure. The 30 big torpedoes all would be long. The series ended with Scheme 17, May 1945. In addition to torpedoes, the submarine would have carried one 5-in/25, two 40-mm, and two 0.50-caliber guns. The diesels would have been either 12-cylinder FMs or 24-cylinder GMs (presumably "W" engines). Estimated continuous surface speed (9,500 SHP) was a disappointing 22.5 kt.

The possibilities for submerged speed were dismal. Radar antennas and deck guns could not be faired to reduce resistance. Improvements in battery capacity would buy very little. For example, 10 percent more battery capacity (at the cost of 10 ft more in length) would buy only about $\frac{1}{2}$ kt underwater. Higher maximum rating (but shorter life) would buy only about $\frac{1}{2}$ kt. The new short-life cells were adopted postwar (together with rigorous streamlining) in the Guppies.

New General Board characteristics reflected the BuShips limits: 500-ft operating depth, higher speed (23 kt on the surface, 10 kt submerged), 12 torpedo tubes (21-in, rather than 24-in, with 18 reloads (2 per tube forward, 1 aft), plus 6 anti-escort weapons (19-in diameter, 128-in length). Torpedo racks would each accommodate 1 long (21-in) or 2 short torpedoes. In a departure from previous practice, all tubes would be the same length (formerly the after tubes had been longer) to accommodate the new Mk 16 peroxide torpedoes. Deck armament would be one 5-in/25 wet deck gun and two free-swinging machine guns.

The General Board specified machinery suitable for "fitting of engine air supply and exhaust trunk, if developed" (i.e., for a snorkel, which the Germans were then introducing); this was clearly required if the submarine was to operate in the face of enemy aircraft. The new submarine would snorkel at 6 kt,[34] but she still would be a submersible surface ship as reflected in her heavy deck armament and limited underwater performance.

BuShips submitted its first tentative design study (A in Table 12–3) early in February 1945. Adding 19 ft (primarily for engines, but including 2 ft for the longer forward torpedo tubes) bought a bit more surface speed. New characteristics (12 March), based on this design, called for about 22.5 kt during surface trials and sufficient power to sustain 20.5 kt in the open sea, with adequate reserve power for battery charging at the maximum permissible rate. Submerged speed was set at 9.25 kt (1 hr rate). The board had to retreat on underwater endurance, to 48 hr at 2 kt.

More careful calculation showed that BuShips had been too optimistic. Weights had been underestimated, so the center of gravity was higher than expected. The submarine had to be enlarged, lengthened (at the cost of $\frac{1}{4}$ kt underwater), and given greater pressure hull diameter; 160 tons were added, but their effect on surfaced speed was balanced by the greater length. Design B was submitted on 9 May.

This submarine still had only one deck gun. The submariners wanted a second, with both remotely controlled. Shortly after the war, it was estimated that this would cost about 25.5 tons, including 100 rounds of ammunition per gun, plus weight of four 0.50-caliber machine guns and a desired 8,000 rounds of ammunition. These weights were so high in the ship that BuShips estimated that each added ton of armament would cost 2 tons in displacement (1 ton for ballast). The submarine would probably grow to 2,000 tons.

This seemed far too small an improvement over the existing (and, after all, successful) fleet submarine. For all BuShips protests, senior officers continued to demand deeper diving, as in a mid-March comment on the characteristics by Chief of Naval Personnel (and future CNO) Adm. L. E. Denfeld. On 10 May 1945, Secretary of the Navy James V. Forrestal proposed a program of postwar prototypes to embody wartime lessons. It included three attack submarines, to be armed with 24-in torpedo tubes.

Late in May, Admiral King complained that only 2 kt (in surface speed) had been gained at a disproportionate cost in power and in vulnerability caused by more induction piping. A 24-in torpedo surely would have greater destructive power, but it would like the submarine much larger, hence slower and less maneuverable. The larger torpedo was killed in August 1945.[35] In September, the Submarine Officers Conference reviewed Design B (which it called the "General Board" design). As might have been expected, the officers disliked the increased size required to achieve 22.5 kt. Nor did they like the two fixed external nests of 19-in tubes. They did want the longer bow tubes, even though that would lengthen a submarine by about

Table 12–3. Submarine Characteristics, May 1945

	SS 475	Design A	Design B
Length overall (ft-in)	311-9	323-6/330-0	336-0
Length between perpendiculars (ft-in)	307-0	320-0/326-0	331-0
Length on waterline (ft-in)	305-0	320-0/326-0	331-0
Beam molded extreme (ft-in)	27-2	29-0	29-2
Displacement standard (tons)	1,570	1,800	1,960
Displacement full load (tons)	1,860	2,100	2,300
Displacement, emergency (tons)	2,000	2,300	2,475
Displacement, submerged (tons)	2,430	2,700	2,990
Radius (nm at approximately 10 kt)	19,000	19,000	19,000
SHP, surfaced	5,400	9,500*	9,500*
Full load SHP, submerged	2,740	2,740	2,740
Speed trial, surfaced, full load (kt)	20.5†	22.5*	22.5*
Speed trial, submerged (kt)	9.5	9.25	9.0
Pressure hull diameter (ft-in)	16-0	16-6	17-0
Plating (high-tensile steel) (lb)	35.0	40.8	40.8
Collapse depth (ft), yield of 39,150 psi	750	800	800
Operating Depth (ft)	450	500	500
Internal bulkhead depth (ft)	450	450	450
Battery (cells)	252	252	252
Armament: Torpedo tubes (bow/stern) (21 in)	6/4	6/6	6/6
Deck tubes (19 in × 128 in)	——	6 × 128-in	6 × 128-in
Torpedoes	28 × 246 in	30 × 271 in 6 × 19 in × 123 in	30 × 271 in 6 × 19 in × 123 in
Guns	1 × 5-in/25 2 × 20-mm	1 × 5-in/25 2 × 40-mm	1 × 5-in/25 2 × 40-mm
Rudder	1	2 (upper and lower)	2 (upper and lower)

* Estimated, with two-stage supercharging; without, about 22 kt.
† Based on analysis of standardization trials of several submarines.
Note: In design A, the first length figure is without superchargers.

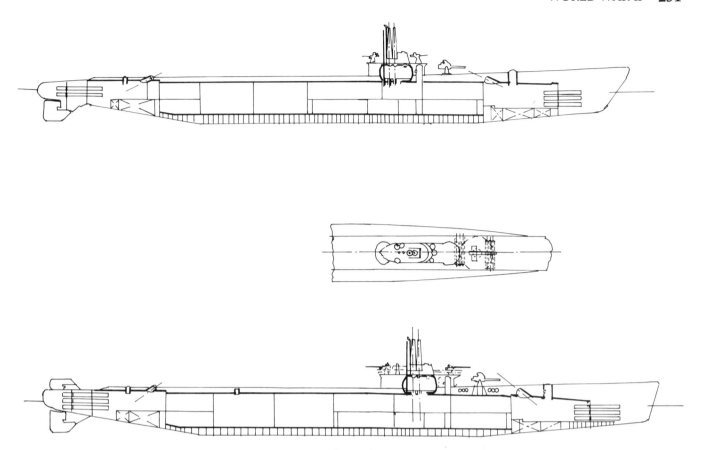

These sketches compare a standard 1945 *Tench* (top) with the fleet submarine presented to the General Board in May 1945 (bottom). The scrap view shows the proposed sextet of 19-inch external fixed anti-escort torpedo tubes, three firing to either side. Other major improvements were the topside rudder, for better maneuverability underwater to escape depth charging, and the additional pair of torpedo tubes aft. Less obvious differences are the longer engine rooms, 30 ft (versus 26 ft 4½ in) in the 1945 design, and the somewhat larger bridge fairwater to accommodate the two 40-mm guns (shown) in place of the 20-mm guns in the standard boat. Standard boats were later fitted with pairs of single 40-mm guns in just these positions.

By 1945, many American submarines carried 5 in/25 guns fore and aft of their bridge fairwaters. *Archerfish* is shown off Hunters Point, 5 June 1945.

for Chile but taken over by Canada at the outset of WW I).

With the failure of these engines, NELSECO reverted to the 4-cycle, 8-cylinder type for the N class (240V8FS: 240 BHP, 350 or 375 RPM).[22] The U.S. H-boats and K-boats were refitted with pairs of these engines, which also powered the export H-boats. They were derived from NELSECO commercial engines that probably harked back to the original Vickers design. The British quite liked these engines but never ran them at full speed.[23] The L-boats retained (and suffered with) their 2-cycle engines during WW I, but 4-cycle engines from the N class were installed in L 1–3 postwar. Many 240V8FS engines were also made for commercial purposes. The smaller 180-BHP version (350-RPM, 180V6FS) powered the Russian *Narval* class (Electric Boat design 31A, in tandem pairs on each shaft). Smaller 120-V4FS (120-BHP, 350-RPM) diesels re-engined the U.S. C-class and D-class gasoline-engined boats. These engines were exported to Russia, probably for the *Bars* class.

NELSECO produced a more powerful 4-cycle, 6-cylinder engine, 6-EB-14 (440 BHP, 400 RPM), for the O and R classes (first completed in 1917); the same engine powered the four submarines built for Peru by Electric Boat in the 1920s. The prototype of this reliable engine was probably the 550-BHP 8-EB-14 completed in mid-1916 for the Spanish *Isaac Peral* (Electric Boat design 903A). Like the smaller engines, these units performed very well in service.[24] S-1, the prototype Electric Boat S-class submarine, had 600-BHP (380-RPM), 8-cylinder engines, developed by adding two cylinders to the O/R-class diesel. This exhausted the design's growth potential.

For its later S-boats, NELSECO scaled up the 240-BHP, 8-cylinder engine (75, rather than 30, BHP/cylinder) as 8-EB-15 (700 BHP, 410 RPM, later derated to 600 BHP at 380 RPM).[25] The rival U.S. Navy prototype (S-3) was powered by 8-EB-16s (700 BHP, 350 RPM), which used larger cylinders than the S-1 engine. Navy-built S-boats (S-4 through S-9) used a navy-built version of this engine (700 BHP, 350 RPM). The new crankshaft was ligher than that in the far less powerful R class. BuEng later claimed that shop tests showed no vibration only because the test engine was bolted down to very heavy machinery. It is probably fairer to say that resonant frequencies were determined not only by the details of the engine, but also by the size and weight of the attached propeller shaft and by propeller characteristics. Unless it included the shaft and a propeller in a water brake, no shop test could have duplicated seagoing conditions. The U.S. Navy first met torsional vibration in the S-3 engine. The S-1 engine broke its crankshaft on trials. Electric Boat eventually agreed to install heavier crankshafts (New York Navy Yard proposed a friction vibration damper). The new shaft stood up better and moved the dangerous major critical speed above the range of the engine.[26] Electric Boat supplied 8-EB-15s for the Spanish ''B'' class submarines it designed (the company's Spanish ''C'' class had Vickers diesels).

The three AA-class (later T-class) fleet submarines were powered by tandem pairs of 1,000-BHP, 6-cylinder 6-EB-

19 engines on each shaft. The first such engines were completed in 1918 for AA 1. These very unsuccessful engines pushed pre-1914 U.S. diesel technology much too far.

Busch-Sulzer offered an American-made alternative to NELSECO. Adolphus Busch, the Milwaukee brewing magnate, bought American rights to Diesel's patents in 1897, imported and exhibited a single-cylinder engine in 1898, and formed the American Diesel Co. to sell American rights. In 1911, Busch bought a license to build Sulzer 2-cycle engines; he opened a plant in 1912 (his old company was reorganized as Busch-Sulzer). Simon Lake obtained an exclusive contract for them, ordering his first for G-3 in January 1911.[27] The 2-cycle Busch-Sulzer diesels in Lake's L- and N-class submarines were generally successful. Because Lake built submarines so slowly, however, these boats did not run trials before engines had been chosen for Lake's O-boats and R-boats. The failure of NELSECO 2-cycle engines led the navy to order Lake to install 6-cylinder, 4-cycle Busch-Sulzer engines.

Lake used 6-cylinder, 2-cycle 900-BHP Busch-Sulzers in his S-class prototype (S-2) but had to use less powerful 6-cylinder, 4-cycle Busch-Sulzers (as in his R-boats) in his first series of production boats (S-14 through S-17). Lake's last boats (S-48 through S-51) reverted to the big Busch-Sulzer 2-cycle engine. S-boats with the 4-cycle engines were considered underpowered.

By the end of WW I, the navy considered Busch-Sulzer the equal of any foreign manufacturer, but few American submarines would be built in the near term. Without any other U.S. domestic market for compact high-speed diesels, there was no reason for Busch-Sulzer to invest in their development.[28] NELSECO was ruled out by the failure of its new S-boat diesels and, probably, by the bad odor of its earlier 2-cycle failures.

The German MAN diesels in the six U-boats brought to the United States after the war made a tremendous impression. BuEng copied a range of war-developed MAN 4-cycle diesels and derated them to compensate for less exacting U.S. workmanship and to make them more reliable[29] (see Table A-2). The first ''bureau'' engines (6 cylinders, 4 cycles, 1,000 BHP at 400 RPM) were installed in the last navy-built S-boats, S-10 through S-13. Made at the New York Navy Yard, they were about 10 percent heavier than their German prototypes. By the mid-1920s, BuEng considered them quite reliable despite lingering problems. They still suffered excessive piston wear and valve breakage. Air injection compressors consumed about 7 percent of their power and were considered tempermental.

Unfortunately, the Germans never put the prototype of the largest ''bureau'' engine (10 cylinders, 3,000 BHP), which powered the big post–WW I fleet submarines, into wartime service. Its torsional problems, unanticipated by its designers, could not be easily cured.[30]

BuEng developed mathematical methods to predict the critical speeds of particular engine-shaft combinations. Machinery could be arranged (e.g., by choice of the length and weight of the shaft connecting the diesel to its clutch) to keep critical speeds away from likely operating speeds.[31]

Table A–2.   Comparison of BuEng and German MAN Engines, 1928

BHP Rating		Cylinders	Bore × Stroke (in)	RPM	
German	BuEng			German	BuEng
3,000	2,350	10	20 $\frac{7}{8}$ × 20 $\frac{7}{8}$	380–390	345
1,750	1,400	6	20 $\frac{7}{8}$ × 20 $\frac{7}{8}$	380–390	345
1,200	1,000	6	17 $\frac{3}{4}$ × 16 $\frac{9}{16}$	450	425
550	550	6	13 $\frac{3}{4}$ × 13 $\frac{3}{4}$	450	——
450	450	6	13 $\frac{3}{4}$ × 13 $\frac{3}{4}$	——	425

Note: Bureau ratings were reduced because it was felt that German nameplate ratings were equivalent to the U.S. maximum. Of the last two, figures indicate the same engine rated down for continuous load. The V-1 class had Busch-Sulzer main engines but BuEng 1,000-BHP charging engines. Subsequent V-class submarines had BuEng engines. In 1919, the MAN engines were described as having a lower stroke-to-bore ratio than usual (and very high piston speeds, 1,323 ft/min), probably to save head room in cramped submarines. Fuel consumption was about 0.44 lb/BHP-hr, about 15 percent more than contemporary British engines.
From A. Rich, "War Developments in Warship Propelling Machinery," *Brassey's Naval Annual* (1919).

By 1928, BuEng espoused diesel-electric drive, an extension of its earlier use of separate diesels for battery charging, to solve the torsional problem. Instead of driving the propeller directly when on the surface, the diesel always drove a generator, which might either charge the battery or directly drive the motor. Motor speed was independent of diesel speed; the diesel could always run at optimum (noncritical) speed. Diesel-electric drive also offered reliability, by which operators meant the ability to shut down one or more engines for overhaul while still running at a useful speed.[32] Electric drive demanded a new approach to electrical (generator and motor) control because the submarine always would be operating on her motors. Controls were concentrated in a new center, the control cubicle, located in a new compartment called the maneuvering room.

Diesel-electric drive was heavier and bulkier than direct drive: no other navy adopted it before 1945, although many foreign submarines are often mistakenly called diesel-electric. To make it practical, BuEng needed a lightweight engine that did not yet exist. Because the engine would not be connected directly to the propeller shafts, several alternative types of engine could be installed in a single class of submarine: BuEng could benefit from competition. By avoiding critical speeds altogether, a diesel-electric plant could save considerably on such components as flywheels and drive shafts, but no diesel-electric power plant could be justified below about 1,200 tons. The treaty-limited *Cachalot* class reverted to direct drive (this time with gearing).

By early 1929, BuEng wanted to use four identical engines all driving generators; the submarine could run on any combination from one-quarter to full diesel power. It also believed that composite drive (two diesel-electric, for 10–12 kt, and two direct-drive engines) would make the most efficient use of space in two engine rooms. Impressed by the bureau's arguments, the General Board hoped that one of the three V-7s (1929 design) would be all–diesel-electric. The single boat built had composite drive (direct-drive main engines and separate small generator engines).

BuEng thought diesel-electric drive would cure the unreliability of the S-boats. In 1928, it tested the idea by running some of them on the surface on their electric motors.[33] That year, the bureau began to canvass U.S. diesel manufacturers. In March 1929, the secretary of the navy approved diesel-electric drive for S-3, S-6, and S-7, both to test the basic concept and to decide whether to modify the other S-boats. The bureau chief, Rear Adm. H. E. Yarnell, saw this as the opportunity to buy prototype lightweight (15–30 lb/BHP, compared with 60-lb or more for MAN) high-speed diesel-generator sets suited to new submarines.

No suitable engine yet existed, nor was there a U.S. commercial market for one except, perhaps, for railroad locomotives. Unfortunately, apart from switching service and single self-propelled cars, the railroads showed no enthusiasm whatever for large-scale use of diesel locomotives. The main exception was the Canadian National Railroad, which had just placed a diesel locomotive in service. Westinghouse produced the power plant, using a British Beardmore diesel.

Nordberg, a highly respected firm in Milwaukee, had secured a FIAT license (it had already built French-designed Carels engines). It offered an aluminum-framed 8-cylinder, 2-cycle engine (13 in × 14 in, 600 RPM, 1,200 BHP), with an estimated output of 27.5 lb/BHP. BuEng also liked Busch-Sulzer, but the company was unwilling to bet its own money on a competition; $300,000 to $500,000 was believed necessary for research and development. The other big U.S. builder was McIntosh & Seymour, which was building large marine engines and 4-cycle locomotive engines. It proposed a 6-cylinder, 4-cycle engine (16 in × 16 in, 600 RPM, 1,200 BHP), which would be rather expensive. Winton (Cleveland) was a small company that had been making small high-speed diesels (e.g., for yachts and tugboats) for about a decade. Its best engine offered 45 BHP per cylinder (8 in × 10 in, 750 RPM) in 4-, 6-, and 8-cylinder in-line versions. Winton proposed a V-16 version (boosted to 1,000 RPM for 1,200 BHP). BuEng was skeptical. It disliked so many cylinders; as a rule of thumb, maintenance effort was proportional to the number of cylinders and, in this engine, they would be inaccessible. The bureau doubted that the company's small design staff could build so complex an engine, capable of standing up to its excess rating in RPM and pressure. Westinghouse offered its Beardmore V-12 4-cycle locomotive engine (12 in × 12 in, 800 RPM, 1,340 BHP, 30 lb/BHP), but it was still effectively experimental. Another high-speed V-12 experimental engine was offered by Trieber: 12.25 × 13 in, 600 RPM, 1350 BHP.

BuEng found Busch-Sulzer, McIntosh & Seymour, and

The old and the new. The engine room of S-20, shown in 1932 at Mare Island, reveals the existing MAN engine and the space cleared for a new test engine to port. S-20 tested diesel-electric propulsion, perhaps the most important U.S. interwar submarine design innovation. The U.S. Navy was alone in adopting diesel-electric power plants; all other navies continued to use direct-drive, accepting that their submarines would be unable to operate at fixed critical speeds.

In a few cases, such as that of the Imperial Japanese Navy, separate generating diesels were used for low speed or for battery charging, but these did not constitute diesel-electric power plants. Only after 1945 did other navies adopt diesel-electric arrangements: the Royal Navy, because it made for better silencing (the diesels could be sound isolated, and their sound could not travel down the propeller shafts); and then the French navy, in its *Arethuse* class. The Germans also adopted this system in their postwar submarines because it allowed several diesels to be associated with a single (hence, most efficient) propeller. So did the Italians and the Swedes. Not until much later did the Russians follow suit, with their Kilo (Project 877) class.

Nordberg the most attractive; each had the experience and engineering staff such a project demanded. Westinghouse was rejected because its diesel knowledge all resided in England. Its multicylinder vee engine offered too little access and was considered too complex. Much the same mechanical problems afflicted Trieber, although an in-line alternative was interesting.

Above all, the bureau had no hope of choosing one or another on the basis of paper evaluation. It had to test prototypes. Therefore, Yarnell asked the Bureau of the Budget for $2.31 million (FY 29) for S-boat diesel-generator sets and also wanted the usual requirement for competitive bidding set aside. Yarnell hoped that this seed money would pay for design and development work. That August, the Bureau of the Budget refused to buy sets for S-6 and S-7. The S-class was approaching the age at which major investment was no longer worthwhile. Diesel-electric power was tried on only one of the two shafts of S-20.[34]

BuEng was unable to provide experimental engines for the new FY 29 submarines. It considered its existing engines as good as any (General Board comments that the engines were obsolescent stung), but it wanted to go to a new generation.[35] Without either a railroad market or

Yarnell's seed money, no U.S. manufacturer would take a chance on developing an appropriate engine. In Germany, however, heavily-subsidized MAN had just developed a modernized version of its wartime engine (MVu series, 38 lb/BHP compared with 60 lb/BHP for BuEng diesels) and had designed a much more compact, faster-running lightweight series (WV, 20 lb/BHP).[36] In 1930, the bureau decided to license-produce the new engines (1,500-BHP WV 28/38 and 2,000-BHP MV 40/46).[37] U.S.-built MV 40/46s were installed on board the two *Cachalots* (V-8 and V-9). Electric Boat championed Sulzer's alternative 2-cycle technology. In 1931, BuEng planned to buy a 9-cylinder Sulzer diesel (about 1,550 BHP) to compare with the MAN engines; it was never adopted. Because any new lightweight diesel might have to be geared down to propeller speed, BuEng's initial diesel development program (1931) included a test of the noise such a geared reduction drive would transmit into the water, where it might be picked up by an enemy's hydrophone. (See Table A–3.)

R Adm. Samuel M. Robinson relieved Yarnell on 29 May 1931. He shared his predecessor's determination to bring lightweight diesels into service[38] and was personally responsible for adopting diesel-electric drive in the next generation of submarines. In 1931, Robinson tried to get a $3 million appropriation to buy experimental engines in Europe and the United States, but Congress balked; it wanted no European engines at all. BuEng was permitted to buy the MAN license, apparently with the understanding that the bureau would shift to American engines as soon as they became available. Limited to U.S. manufacturers, the diesel competition bill passed in 1932.

Looking back early in 1939, BuEng rationalized. It argued that the United States had to shift to domestic manufacturers. Tension was steadily increasing; surely, foreign manufacturers would find it more difficult to provide full details of improvements to engines with such important military applications.[39] Even the lightweight MAN diesel was too big and heavy. By stopping new submarine construction, the depression gave BuEng time to find a new engine. The bureau estimated that it needed 6–8 years.

In 1932, BuEng still saw fast railroad locomotives as the most likely civilian market for the kind of diesel it wanted. Existing builders were concerned mainly with slower locomotives, such as switchers, that could tolerate heavier engines. In 1930, however, General Motors' chief of research, Charles Kettering, had convinced his management that diesels were the coming technology. Kettering argued that the automobile market was already saturated (partly because of the depression) but that fast locomotives and then trucks and buses would offer new markets. Railroads bought custom-designed steam locomotives, often assembled in their own workshops. Kettering envisaged something more like the truck market. General Motors would offer a standard locomotive. In 1930, it had bought Winton, which was then just beginning to invest in a new high-pressure fuel injector. Kettering ordered a shift to a 2-cycle design. General Motors, in effect, changed Winton from a small specialist company into a powerhouse whose resources dwarfed those available to the established diesel locomotive builders (ALCO, which had absorbed McIntosh & Seymour; Baldwin Locomotive Co.; General Electric; and Westinghouse). The depression forced other locomotive companies out of the market before they could make the transition from slow switchers to fast passenger locomotives.

As before, BuEng doubted that it could obtain a new diesel without seed money. The depression made companies even more reluctant to invest in research. General Motors was a major exception. In theory, the railroad market offered BuEng an enormous return. It would be far larger than the submarine market; if the navy adopted a locomotive diesel it would gain the benefits of large-scale development and production. Fast locomotives were almost certain to be diesel-electric (a generator that powered motors at the wheels), and they needed compact diesels.[40]

In March 1932, BuEng invited all U.S. diesel and gasoline engine makers to bid for a new generation of lightweight (27.5 lb/BHP, Nordberg's 1929 figure) diesels suited to mass production. Except for General Motors,

no railroad engine builder responded. By December, five companies had offered engines:

1. Winton Engine Corp. (later the Cleveland Diesel Engine Division of General Motors): a 12-cylinder, 950-BHP 2-cycle vee, Model 201, with exhaust valves in the cylinder head for uniflow scavenging (i.e., for the scavenging air to flow one way, up the cylinder, rather than across and down, as in a Sulzer). Its unit fuel injectors combined the functions of fuel injection valve and fuel injection pump into one unit in each cylinder, operated by a single cam; and it was the first to use a welded-steel housing. Preliminary tests of a single cylinder encouraged the company to accept an order for two 8-cylinder in-line engines for the 1933 Chicago World's Fair.[41] The Winton ran successfully at the Naval Engineering Test Station (BuEng's Annapolis laboratory); BuEng ordered 16 of the 16-cylinder Model 201-As (16-201A) for the 1933 program and another 12 for 1934. The 1,535-BHP 16-248 used larger cylinders at a sharper V-angle, with a stronger crankcase and more reliable

Table A–3.   Lightweight Diesels

Type	Cylinders	Rating (BHP)	RPM	Bore × Stroke
MAN (*Cachalot*)	9	1,550	480	15.75 × 18.11
GM 16-258, *Cachalot* re-engined*	V-16	1,535	900	9.5 × 12.0
GM 12-258S, *Argonaut* re-engined*	V-12	1,500	900	9.5 × 12.0
GM 16-258, *Nautilus* re-engined*	V-16	2,000	900	9.5 × 12.0
Winton, prototype	V-12	950	720	8.0 × 10.0
Stearns, prototype	Diamond-4	321	1,300	5.25 × 8.5
Sun Ship, prototype	6	685	620	6.25 × 9.75
Continental, prototype	Radial-10	635	1,400	6.5 × 7.5
Electric Boat, prototype	V-16	635	1,150	7.0 × 8.25
Winton 201A *Porpoise* as built	V-16	1,300	750	8.0 × 10.0
GM 16-248 *Tambor* and later fleet boats	V-16	1,600	750	8.5 × 10.5
GM 16-278A, SS 313 and later fleet boats; *Narwhal*, SS 182–184, 188–190, 194, 253–264 re-engined; 1,200-BHP V-12 version in 172, 173, 175, re-engined	V-16	1,600	750	8.5 × 10.5
GM 16-338, 16-cylinder pancake in postwar submarines	Pancake	1,000	1,600	6.0 × 6.5
Fairbanks-Morse 38A8, *Plunger-Pollack*	8	1,300	720	8.0 × 10.0
Fairbanks-Morse 38D8-⅛, 179–180 re-engined, SS 201, and later	9	1,600	720	8.5 × 10.0
Fairbanks-Morse 38A6-¾, postwar lightweight version of Fairbanks-Morse engine	8	1,000	1,335	6.75 × 8.0
HOR-MAN, *Pompano*	8	1,300	700	9.056 × 13.38
Electric Boat, 1933 engine for S-20: 16VM1		635	1,175	6.25 × 8.25
Electric Boat, *Mackerel*: 65MIR145*	6	850	460	14.0 × 14.5
ALCO, *Marlin**	6	900	900	12.5 × 13.0

* Indicates 4-cycle engines. Except as noted, engines are in-line.
Data are from E. C. Magdeburger, "Diesel Engines in the United States Navy," *ASNE Journal* (April 1949), 45–93 (early engines), from a BuShips data sheet (ca 1942), and from J. D. Alden, *The Fleet Submarine in the U.S. Navy* (Annapolis, Md.: Naval Institute Press, 1979), Appendix I, and from BuShips submarine handbooks.

pistons and rings. It was superseded by the 1,600-BHP 16-278 (aluminum pistons) and then 16-278A (steel pistons).

2. Stearns Mechanical Laboratories of Cleveland: 2-cycle, 8-piston ''diamond'' engine (two vees merged, with common combustion spaces for each pair of cylinders). As the first to respond to the circular, Stearns encouraged other companies to compete. This engine presented too many problems; it wrecked itself soon after being accepted at Annapolis.

3. Sun Shipbuilding and Dry Dock: 6-cylinder, 2-cycle in-line, opposed-piston, 685-BHP engine with two crankshafts (top and bottom), similar to contemporary German Junkers aircraft diesels. The critical speed was much lower than expected, so it had to be down-rated to 650 BHP. This engine had a remarkably low fuel consumption (0.354 lb/BHP/hr); it was installed on board the experimental submarine S-20. Its aircraft parentage showed in its aluminum

frame, which was, however, rather difficult to machine; five partly machined castings had to be rejected. Although this engine was never adopted, Fairbanks-Morse later successfully offered much the same configuration.

4. Electric Boat: 4-cycle, 635-BHP vee-16 engine with a lightweight aluminum frame. The floating bushing over its crank pin was intended to allow higher crank pin pressures and therefore shorter distance between cylinders and lighter weight; it had a special Lanova combustion chamber to maintain high cylinder pressure and a geared supercharger blower. BuEng complained that Electric Boat assigned its engine a very low priority. Eventually, it decided that the engine could not be adopted for submarines. Thus Electric Boat, which had probably done more than any other firm to push BuEng toward a new generation of submarine diesels, lost out entirely.[42]

5. Continental Motors Corp., an aircraft engine builder: commissioned to develop a radial 10-

Diesel intakes (induction) are visible on board the incomplete *Ulua* (SS 428), at left, at the Cramp shipyard, 2 July 1945. They trunk up into the main induction just abaft the conning tower pressure vessel. The starboard branch feeds the forward engines; the port branch, whose 22-in pipe is visible under the flat boards, feeds the after engines. When snorkels were installed postwar, their intakes connected to the main induction visible here. Exhaust piping is also visible. At right, slightly more advanced, is *Trumpetfish* (SS 425). *Ulua* was never completed.

cylinder, 2-cycle 635-BHP diesel mounted directly above a bell-shaped generator housing. This engine had to be derated to 480 BHP (1,100 RPM) to pass its acceptance tests.

BuEng did not particularly like Winton's effective monopoly on the new generation of U.S. submarine engines. Fortunately, two other companies competed in the second year of the program:

1. Fairbanks Morse: 8-cylinder, 2-cycle, opposed-piston diesel (based on the German Junkers Jumo), similar in configuration to Sun's. Although Fairbanks Morse was not then building locomotives, this engine was apparently selected as part of a wider company program. It had a one-piece welded steel frame. A silent chain transmitted power from the upper to the lower crankshaft (later engines used gearing). Because scavenging ports were in the upper cylinder, only about 30 percent of total output went into the upper crankshaft, which also drove the scavenging blower: only about one quarter of total output went through the chain. BuEng ordered eight Fairbanks-Morse engines for two 1934 submarines. Early engines developed cracks in their welded cylinder blocks that threw them out of alignment; the frames and blocks had to be redesigned. The 8-cylinder 38A8 was superseded by a 1,365-BHP, 8-cylinder 38D-⅛ and then by a 9-cylinder, 1,535-BHP 38D8-⅛; wartime submarines (from SS 381 on) used a 10-cylinder, 1,600-BHP 38D8-⅛.
2. Hooven, Owens, Rentschler (HOR), the postwar MAN licensee: 1,300-BHP, 2-cycle, double-acting engine, identical to that in the German cruiser *Leipzig* except that it had 8 cylinders (the main parts of the test engine were imported from Germany). HOR was the only firm to offer a double-acting engine. It used a one-piece welded steel frame. BuEng ordered four engines for one FY 34 submarine. This engine excited interest because it offered more power than either General Motors or Fairbanks Morse (in a tight double-action package), but it soon gained a reputation for gross unreliability.[43] The HOR was noisy, and it needed 40 percent more air than the other two engines. HOR engines, however, were adopted for WW II surface craft.

General Motors and Fairbanks Morse engines powered most of the new submarines. Wartime versions weighed about 18.5 lb/BHP, somewhat below what MAN had promised in 1930. All used solid (airless) injection. Their small cylinders needed far less cooling water. Fresh water was circulated through a heat exchanger (radiator), rather than salt water from the sea; this eliminated the scale that salt water deposited on the cooling surfaces of a bureau engine. Fast-circulating water was very efficient: these engines typically ran at no more than 500°F, compared with 750–1,000°F for bureau engines. Because all the moving

parts (except the crankshaft) were small, they could be removed quickly (in 1935, the Winton plant pulled a piston in 16 minutes), often without chain falls.

Supercharging could increase engine output without enlarging or multiplying cylinders. Sulzer's Buchi turbocharger (developed in 1910–16) was successfully tested on board S 19 in 1933. The first of many wartime 4-cycle installations was on the small modern submarine *Marlin* in August 1941. Supercharging a 2-cycle engine was inherently more difficult because it needed so much more air flow. In 1945, 2-cycle supercharging was still in the development stage. It was proposed for the 1944–45 fleet submarine, which badly needed additional power.

The decision to adopt commercial types of engines proved fortunate. As ship production accelerated in 1941, steam turbines, almost universally used formerly, could not be produced fast enough. Nor could their large reduction gears be cut quickly enough. Many destroyer escorts and fast auxiliaries (such as small seaplane tenders) therefore had submarine-type diesel-electric power trains. Later in the war, submarine-type diesels powered many ships; these diesels often used smaller-diameter gearing whose production did not interfere with that of high-powered steam turbine ships.

Just as the internal combustion engine was the key to successful submarine surface propulsion, the rechargable storage battery was essential to cruising underwater. Although it was invented in 1859, the storage battery did not become really useful until 1881, when a Frenchman, Faure, applied a thick layer of red lead "paste" to the plates. Before that, some submarine inventors tried to store energy in the form of compressed air.

In almost all storage batteries, metal plates (usually lead, sometimes silver in modern high-capacity units) are bathed in an acid electrolyte.[44] The basic chemistry of such batteries has not changed since Holland's day. The batteries in submarines described in this book generally used lead plates suspended in a water-sulfuric acid solution. The lead-acid combination determines the voltage a single cell (i.e., a single combination of positive and negative plates) produces, nominally 2.6 volts in a modern storage battery.[45] Battery energy capacity is measured in ampere-hours. It varies with the rate of discharge; the faster the battery is discharged, the less energy it can supply.[46]

By 1917, the two competing forms of lead-acid battery used Planté and paste construction. In the Planté process, a cast lead grate is converted electrically to either a positive or a negative plate. The alternative, which won out, was to compress a pasty mass of lead and antimony into a lead grid (in each case the active material itself is too weak to support itself without the grid). Then each plate is processed electrically to the appropriate type. Because the spongy pasted material has a greater surface area, a pasted battery has about 30 percent more capacity than a Planté, for a given space and weight. However, it has about half the lifetime of the Planté battery.[47]

Typically the positive plate in a modern battery is lead dioxide; the negative plate is pure lead. Capacity depends in part on how much plate surface area is exposed to the electrolyte. Modern positive plates consist of a lead grid with lead dioxide pressed into the spaces; negative plates consist of similar grids with sponge lead pressed into them. Special measures must be taken to keep the positive and negative plates from moving and thus touching (shorting out the battery) as the submarine moves in the water.

As the cell discharges, sulfate from the electrolyte is deposited on its plates. The specific gravity of the electrolyte decreases. Concentrated sulfuric acid has a specific gravity of 1.800; the electrolyte in a fully charged battery typically has a specific gravity of 1.260. Voltage is proportional to specific gravity, starting at about 2.75 volts at 1.260. A fully discharged cell (1.060) is down to 1.06 volts.

Because the character of the cell determines its voltage output, higher voltage can be attained only by adding cells. By WW II, the U.S. standard was 126, for a nominal voltage of 260 (range from 210 to 350 volts). These figures in turn set the voltage characteristics of all auxiliary equipment on board a submarine.

Not all the cells of a battery discharge at the same rate; some that discharge faster get so far down that their polarity reverses. If the battery continues to discharge, such a cell will begin to charge uncontrollably as electricity flows through it, gassing heavily. The reversed cell might have to be disconnected. The entire battery must be charged.

Capacity (energy per unit weight or volume) depends on the acidity of the electrolyte (its specific gravity). Before WW II, for example, U.S. submarine batteries had rated peacetime (long battery life) and wartime specific gravities. The prewar specific gravity, 1.210, was increased to 1.280 in 1940 for increased capacity. Batteries overheated and gassed, and took too long to charge, so 1.250 was adopted. It gave 25 percent more capacity than 1.210, 9,300 amp-hr.

Battery charging must begin with sufficient voltage to break up the sulfate crust and drive it back into solution. In pre–WW II U.S. submarines, the voltage was then turned down (typically halved) to keep the battery from gassing excessively and breaking down the plates. Ideally, it should be turned well down for a "finishing" charge. A battery charged at high rate also loses capacity. These considerations explain the desire for low-powered charging engines in several classes of submarines.

Modern practice (probably at least since WW II) is different. Excess current breaks down water, thus creating hydrogen gas. The charging rate has to be controlled to avoid creating too much gas. The optimum charging voltage (depending on sulfate reduction versus gassing) also depends on temperature (it is called TVG, for temperature, voltage, gassing). The voltage applied to the battery is turned up until it reaches TVG, then maintained. As the battery charges, its resistance increases, so the charging current decreases. At some point, then, the charging current is maintained constant (at a low enough level to avoid gassing) and the voltage is allowed to rise.

On each charge-discharge cycle, the battery loses a little of its lead structure. Small particles of lead and lead sulfate

form a sediment on the bottom of the cell. The lead also forms crystals, which grow up from the plates, that reach across the cell (and ultimately short it out). Battery lifetime is measured in cycles. Each cycle is normally a fixed number of amp-hr, typically 4,000 to 5,000 (5,000 for the post–WW II MLB-27 and TLX-39 in Guppies, 8,200 for *Sargo II*). Each charge is between half and one cycle. Early batteries managed 150–200 cycles; later ones were good for 300–500 cycles. Typically, a diesel-electric submarine runs through 10 cycles per month, so her battery must be replaced every 18 mo to 2 years. It takes a well-trained team about 10–14 days to replace a battery. After WW II, the U.S. Navy retired its ex-German Type XXI U-boats when they needed new batteries (the navy had run out of spare ex-German batteries).

As the battery discharges, the specific gravity of the electrolyte falls, but not evenly. Instead, liquid of lower specific gravity settles at the top of the cell. Lower portions of each plate, bathed in electrolyte of a higher specific gravity, wear out more quickly, so the cell must be scrapped before its plates have worn evenly. In the 1950s, U.S. batteries were equipped with "air lift pumps" that pushed the heavier electrolyte to the top of the cell to equalize specific gravity.

Batteries also have heating problems. Electric current passing through the cell plate end connectors and the plate header bus bars heats them. Heating can limit output. In post–WW II Guppy submarines, battery water cooling had to be installed; the water passed through the cell terminals. In turn, the heated water was cooled by seawater in a heat exchanger.

As it discharges, a battery produces a mixture of hydrogen, hydrogen sulfide, and water/acid vapor. Hydrogen can explode in air when its concentration rises above 7 percent; a 4–7 percent mixture burns. Eventually a safe limit of 2.5 percent was imposed; special measures were taken to siphon off the gas. With its distinctive rotten egg smell, hydrogen sulfide irritates eyes, nasal passages, and lungs. Water/acid attacks organic substances, including skin. To prevent fire or explosion, the battery is ventilated.

Initially, ventilation was by natural air circulation within the submarine. Then forced ventilation was introduced—fans took air from the battery well and delivered it to the vicinity of the engine intakes. Hydrogen is produced at a high rate when charging and at a lower rate when the battery is providing power (discharging). The higher the discharge rate, the higher the gassing rate. When charging, the running engine can burn the hydrogen gas. Fleet submarines (and many of their predecessors) used ducts to each cell, a system called closed-cell ventilation.

One consequence was that water evaporated very rapidly from each cell. In warm weather, distilled water had to be added to each cell every 2–4 days; loss of distilled water capacity would end a patrol. A simpler alternative, open-cell ventilation, was used in Guppies. It required some way of venting the hydrogen produced by each cell, without allowing sparks or fire flash into the cell. On the other hand, it ended the need for so much distilled water.

Ventilation does not always work. For example, on 2 February 1910, USS *Snapper* suffered a battery explosion while charging: the battery covers were lifted powerfully enough to shatter the wooden hatches.

If salt or salt water leaks into the cells, the battery produces poisonous chlorine gas. That was a particular problem in early submarines, whose batteries were open-topped in a battery tank directly under the conning tower hatch. In later submarines, the problem was greatly reduced by closing the cells, sealing the well, and reducing seawater leakage into the battery. Even so, chlorine is so deadly that American submariners are not allowed to use chlorine bleach for fear that its odor will cover the tell-tale smell of chlorine gas.

Gas emerging from a battery appears in bubbles covered in acid electrolyte, which can corrode hull and machinery. Acid can also leak out of a battery. F-4 (*Skate*) sank on 23 March 1915 because acid had weakened her hull. Other likely losses to acid damage were O-9 off Portsmouth, 23 October 1941, and S-28 off Hawaii, 4 July 1944. Bubbles could be spread through a boat by her ventilation system and injure crewmen as they breathed in the gas.

Early cells were steel boxes with $\frac{1}{16}$-in to $\frac{1}{8}$-in walls, with their inner and outer surfaces covered in hard rubber. The rubber insulated and kept the acid from eating away the steel, but acid leakage was a problem. Cells were generally open at the top, except for a rubber cover, and thus could let in dirt and water. To avoid leakage, the steel box was replaced by hard rubber. Although it was structurally less sound, rubber was lighter and tended not to leak (the acid could not eat it away). About 1941, however, it was discovered that hard rubber could break under stress (e.g., depth charging). The solution, suggested by Lt. E. E. Yeomans, the first commander of the new *Sargo*, was to place a thin layer of soft rubber between the two layers of hard rubber; it would catch acid spilling through a crack in the thicker layers.[48] *Sargo* cells became standard in the U.S. submarine force.

With its proprietary connection to storage battery production, Electric Boat installed Exide (Electric Storage Battery Co.) "pasted" plate batteries. The A class used 13.5-in × 19-in × 33.5-in cells (288 lb each, including electrolyte) with "Manchester"-type positive plates (lead dioxide was inserted into holes in the lead-antimony plate in the form of a $\frac{3}{8}$-in wide strip wrapped in a spiral).

When *Moccasin* (A-4) grounded in December 1903, her battery was ruined and had to be replaced. BuEq saw an opportunity to promote alternative battery manufacturers.[49] Although the *Moccasin* replacement battery was bought from Electric Boat, that for her sister *Adder* (A-2) was bought from Gould. By 1911, Exide batteries descended from these early ones were credited with a lifetime of 250 cycles (for the positive plate; 450 cycles for the negative). Electric Boat's single-hull submarines typically used the wall of the battery tank as the U-shaped wall of an internal main ballast tank, a practice that could be extremely unsafe if the wall broke.

Lake used the competing Gould Planté battery. A typical cell was 19 in × 17 in × 35.5 in (1,200 lb). Early 60-cell batteries had a capacity of 1,120 amp-hr. Lead-lined cells were wedged into their compartment with wooden wedges and battens, and the intercell spaces were filled with asphaltum cement. Plates were separated by rubber tubes and separated from side walls by glass plates. The top was lead with a rubber gasket. Lake considered his cell arrangement superior to Electric Boat's for efficiency, but against that it seriously limited head room in the submarine.

Gould later adopted paste batteries; its verison first appeared in the K-boats. About 1911, Exide introduced a new "ironclad" battery with a cylindrical positive plate to increase battery capacity and lifetime. It was first installed in L-8, and then in Lake's O-11–O-16. Exide and Gould shared the U.S. submarine battery market. All of these batteries used lead plates in a sulfuric acid electrolyte.

Thomas Edison tried to eliminate the dangers of lead-acid batteries by using a nickel hydrate positive plate and an iron oxide negative plate. The electrolyte was alkaline, rather than acid: potassium hydrate in place of sulfuric acid. Edison claimed that his cells were more robust, as well as more compact, than the alternatives. BuEng tested Edison's battery in E-2. Unfortunately, hydrate batteries produce both hydrogen and oxygen in quantity, whereas lead-acid batteries produce only hydrogen in quantity. E-2 suffered a severe battery explosion in 1916. Lead-acid survived.[50]

After WW I, submarine officers perceived a tendency to reduce storage battery size. *Barracuda* (V-1 class) and *Dolphin* (V-7) might find it difficult to remain down throughout the day, including a submerged daylight attack. BuEng increased the ratio of amp-hours to submarine tonnage from 6.80 in *Barracuda* to 7.25 in *Dolphin*, 8.45 in *Cachalot*, and 9.22 in *Porpoise*; the latter had 8 percent more battery capacity than her predecessors.

From the C class on, cells were split between two batteries. They could be connected in series (for maximum power) or in parallel (for maximum time). The S-boats were the first to have motors with double armatures, which could be connected in series or in parallel (the series arrangement was for the 1-hour overload rafting). Later boats had double motors, which could be similarly connected. Doubling up also limited motor diameter. The later diesel-electric boats used a pair of high-speed motors geared to the shaft. Both were used to supply high power on the surface, but only one submerged (boats converted to Guppies postwar used both motors submerged).

Submarines had two 60-cell batteries until the *Argonaut*, which would have needed excessively large cells. Instead, she had two 120-cell batteries. Each provided so much voltage that they were no longer connectable in series (either or both batteries could run the motors; to allow for series operation would have required new motor designs). Each battery was enlarged to 126 cells in the *Sargo* class. *Sargo II* batteries, widely used postwar, had thinner plates for greater capacity per cell. Many postwar submarines had thin-plate Guppy cells, which were smaller than *Sargo*s (46 in × 14 in × 18 in versus 54 in × 21 in × 21 in) but had about 90 percent of their capacity at a lesser weight (1,008 lb versus 1,650 lb filled).

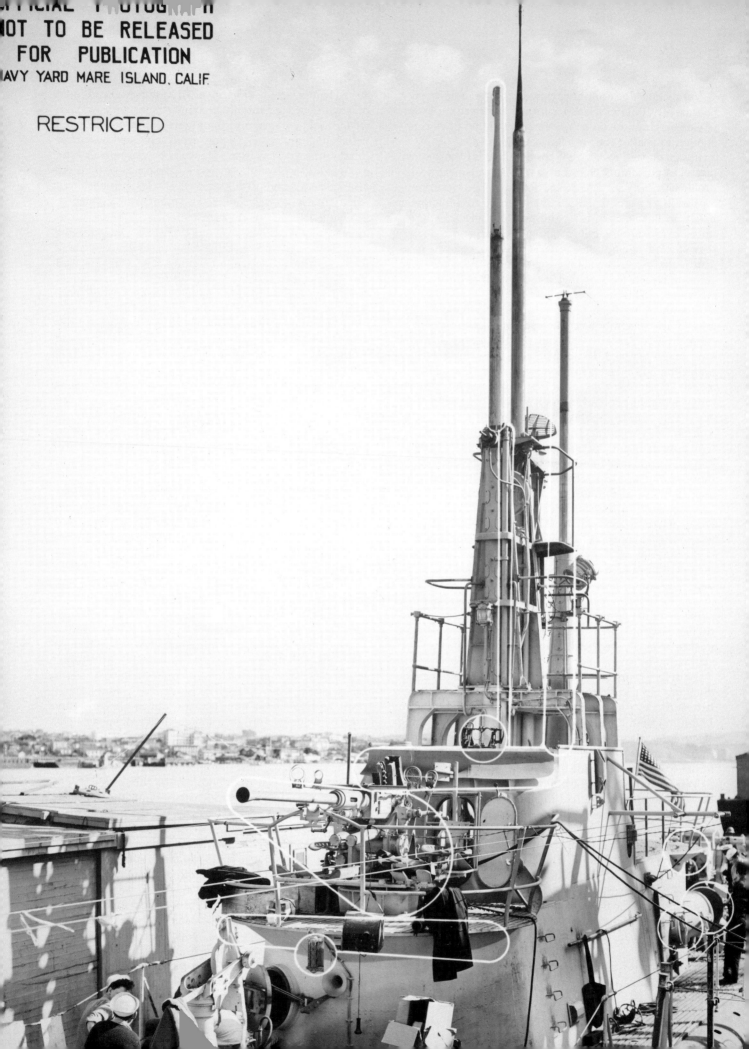

Appendix B

Periscopes

C&R WAS RESPONSIBLE for U.S. submarine periscopes.[1] They were generally bought as part of a new submarine; thus, Electric Boat was the main periscope maker. BuOrd bought periscopes for major ships (as fire-control devices, projecting out of their turrets and conning towers). As a consequence, during WW I, submarine periscopes were often inspected by ordnance inspectors, rather than by C&R. During the war, BuOrd tried (but failed) to take control of all U.S. periscope manufacture. BuOrd did supply some or all of the WW I instruments in U.S. Navy Attack Teachers, presumably because such devices did not need the special nonmagnetic watertight construction of submarine periscopes (and because submarine periscopes were in terribly short supply).

Submarine periscopes presented some very difficult design problems; many of them were not completely solved until well after WW I. The chief design factors are tube length and diameter, size of field, magnification, and illumination (brightness of image: how much light the periscope transmits). The longer the tube, the deeper the submarine hull at periscope depth, hence the safer the boat is from broaching and from accidental collision. A long, slender unsupported tube, however, will vibrate as the submarine moves through the water. A larger-diameter tube will be more rigid: in 1918, C&R estimated that a 5-in periscope could be up to 26 ft long and a 6-in periscope more than 30 ft (postwar periscopes were 34 ft long). After WW I, a shift to 7.5 in ultimately made it possible to extend periscopes to the standard 40-ft length of WW II. A larger tube, however, will also be more visible (and it may make a more prominent wake, or feather). Much also depended on the speed at which the periscope was to be used. Before 1917, U.S. submariners expected to approach their targets at relatively high speeds. It took a 6-in diameter to provide enough strength to keep 8–10 ft of periscope rigid at 9.5 kt. In modern periscopes, an inner tube revolves within a rigid fixed outer tube.

Ideally, periscope tubes had to be nonmagnetic (e.g., brass) to avoid interference with compasses, but it was difficult to make rigid tubes long enough in this mate-

rial. During WW I, Electric Boat secured permission to use steel tubes, which could be made in the requisite lengths.

For navigation or search, the periscope had to present the widest possible field of view when pointed in any one direction. Experience showed that about 40–45 degrees was best. Above that, the image was too small to be usable; below it, too little was seen in any one direction. Simon Lake developed a panoramic "omniscope" using prisms to form a 360-degree view, but it was too massive and seems not to have gained any favor.

It might be imagined that a magnification of 1.0 would produce lifelike images, but experiments showed that $1.5\times$, which became standard after WW I, was required.[2] Higher power was needed for fire control. By the end of WW I, $6\times$ was standard. Although in theory a submarine could operate with one low- and one high-powered instrument, in fact it was much preferable to be able to switch between two powers in one bifocal periscope. Bifocal operation added a new complication in the form of the focus-shifting mechanism. Its handle or control penetrated the periscope tube and thus became an additional source of moisture. Too, it was essential that the instrument point in almost exactly the same direction after shifting back and forth between magnifications. For these reasons, the U.S. Navy seems to have gone back largely to single-power periscopes about 1914.

The simplest type of periscope consists of a pair of mirrors or prisms at top and bottom, to turn the image seen at the top twice so that it is visible in the eyepiece. Such a periscope has only a very limited field of view because the image formed on the upper mirror is the one seen on the lower.

To get the desired large field of view in the eyepiece at the bottom of the periscope, sets of lenses must alternately reduce and enlarge the image. Any simpler arrangement cannot accomodate a wide image in a narrow tube. Early Electric Boat periscopes used series of lenses spaced down the tube to form a single optical system. All of them had to be in the appropriate focus to form any sort of image at

The Type 2 needle-nose periscope was the culmination of a quarter-century of development. *Cod* (SS 224) shows a Type 2 abaft the broader head of a Type 3 in this photograph taken at Mare Island on 14 February 1945. The big mast farther aft supports an SD air-warning radar. The smaller radar is SJ-1, for surface search.

A view looking aft through the operating compartment of E-2 shows the dual eyepieces of her two periscopes, each with a handwheel nearby. The wheels controlling the planes, each with its own depth gauge, are to the right. Note the belt connecting the stern plane wheel to the control rod running along the overhead. In the background is the ship's wheel, in a yoke suspended from the overhead. The ladder abaft the foreground periscope leads up to the conning tower. (*Submarine Force Museum and Library*)

the bottom. The window (objective lens) and the eyepiece were typically part of the single integrated system, whose optics were bent by prisms at top and bottom. Early Electric Boat walk-around periscopes had long horizontal sections at the eyepiece end.

For the E class, the U.S. Navy asked for bifocal operation by substituting a higher-powered eyepiece section for the usual lower-powered one. This arrangement apparently did not work, so Electric Boat developed a two-window bifocal periscope, in which the lenses in the windows helped in determining magnification. There was a mirror behind each window. With the lower mirror flipped up out of the way, light passed through the upper (lower-powered) lens directly to the rest of the periscope (the light from the lower window was not reflected down). When the lower mirror was flipped into place, light from the upper lens was blocked. The combination worked, but it required a very large (hence visible) periscope head. One peculiarity of the two-lens arrangement was that there was no particular relationship between high and low

power (the ratings were 1.2× and 3×, with 40- and 16-degree fields of view). This type of periscope probably first appeared in the H class (1913). Periscopes of this configuration were also made by Keuffel & Esser, as replacements for Electric Boat instruments. Typically, boats had two periscopes, the head of the after one slightly higher than the head of the forward one (No. 1 scope) to look forward over it.

Electric Boat's configuration proved useful during WW I, when the navy demanded periscopes looking directly up. The upper (high-powered) lens was simply replaced by a glass dome looking directly up. When the mirror was flipped down, light traveled directly down the periscope tube. When it was flipped up, the periscope functioned as a conventional unifocal instrument. This alti-periscope provided the desired overhead view, but at a very low magnification (typically about 0.8×, with a 100-degree field of view) because the optical path did not include the usual lens (the effect of the lens plus the optics in the tubes was to obtain a net magnification of 1.2×).

About 1911 Dr. Frederick O. Kollmorgen, then of Keuffel & Esser, suggested an alternative: a pair of independent telescopes at the top and bottom of the periscope. The telescope in the upper part of the periscope reduces the image, which is received by the enlarging telescope at the bottom of the tube. The net magnification of the periscope is the product of the reduction of the upper tube and the magnification of the lower. This configuration is now universal. In modern periscopes, then, the upper window is plain glass; the eyepiece does not magnify. The combination of telescopes is designed to achieve the high-magnification setting ($6\times$ in most modern instruments); the low-magnification setting ($1.5\times$) is obtained by flipping a quarter-power telescope into place above the upper periscope. Magnification shift is called power shift (for the shift in magnification power). This arrangement has several advantages. Since the window is no longer a lens, it need not be very large; the periscope head can be made far smaller so as to be far less visible. Too, because no intermediate lenses are needed to transmit the image down the tube, the same optical parts can work with a variety of overall tube lengths. The two-telescope arrangement is probably also less affected by vibration, since slight movement of the image from the upper telescope over the lens of the lower one will not throw the image in the eyepiece out of focus.

By 1917, both the British and the Germans had modern-type two-telescope periscopes that shifted magnification by shifting lenses internally. U.S. manufacturers began work on such instruments during WW I, and they were standard postwar. The modern configuration makes for a much smaller head. The head mirror or, more commonly, prism can easily elevate and depress the line of sight for both magnifications. British periscopes typically elevated to $+20$ degrees and depressed to -10 degrees so that an operator could keep the horizon in sight as the submarine pitched or rolled. Some special periscopes had high-angle prisms that allowed a view to the zenith. The standard German periscope elevated to $+45$ degrees, so at low power (with a field of view of about 40 degrees), it could come close to the zenith. A single such standard instrument could function both as periscope and as altiperiscope. By December 1917, C&R was demanding this type of performance, which became standard postwar.

Writers of the WW I period tended to emphasize the need to keep the upper window clear, but C&R documents show that moisture entering the periscope tube was a major problem. Many designs required multiple openings (e.g., for cranks to move mirrors or lenses) and thus could not be properly sealed. Tubes themselves were difficult to make in a single piece, and their joints leaked. Much effort went into arrangements for keeping the tube dry, including air pumps.

Effective fire control requires some means of estimating the range to the target. Some time well before WW I, the U.S. Navy adopted telemeter scales, markings showing the size of the target in angular terms.[3] An observer could estimate range by counting the number of markings filled by a known distance, such as the height of a mast. The telemeter scale itself always had to be in focus, so it was generally marked on a glass inserted in the focal plane, near the top of the periscope (so that it would move with the periscope head). After the end of the war, the U.S. Navy adopted an alternative, the *stadimeter*, a kind of reverse coincidence range finder, measuring the angle subtended by two points on the target.[4] A 1912 attempt to produce a vertical coincidence rangefinder failed.[5]

Initially, C&R did not supervise periscope design or construction in any detail, although it did include periscope specifications in general information for bidders and also in specifications for construction of individual submarines. Electric Boat and Lake initially made their own periscopes. In 1909 C&R bought its first foreign periscopes, two German-made Goerz walk-around units for *Viper* (B-1) and *Cuttlefish* (B-2), Registry numbers 11 and 13. They replaced a pair of Electric Boat walk-around periscopes (which were installed on board *Adder* and *Moccasin*).[6] Beginning about 1912, Keuffel & Esser (K&E, well known to earlier generations of engineers and scientists for its drawing instruments and slide rules) of Hoboken, New Jersey, became C&R's independent source of periscopes.[7] K&E periscopes seem to have replaced Lake's periscopes almost immediately, probably in his G-2. Electric Boat continued to manufacture periscopes through the early part of WW I, its last being installed in its N-boats. Electric Boat periscopes, however, were generally considered unsatisfactory, and C&R began a replacement program in 1915, mainly with K&E instruments. By 1915, Bausch & Lomb (B&L) of Rochester, New York, was also making submarine periscopes.[8] One of K&E's young engineers, Dr. Frederick O. Kollmorgen, left in 1916 to form his own firm, Kollmorgen Corp., which became dominant.[9] Beginning with its O-boats, Electric Boat gave up producing periscopes and subcontracted most of them to Kollmorgen.

In all, Electric Boat probably made 89 periscopes. K&E probably sold C&R its first periscope about 1910 for a B-boat, for comparison with the two Goerz prototypes. In 1912, a K&E periscope was installed in D-3. K&E supplied periscopes for Cramp's G-4 (after the instruments originally supplied by a Philadelphia firm, the Queen-Gray Co., proved unsatisfactory) and probably also for Lake's G-2 and G-3. It supplied the periscopes for the Lake L-boats and housing periscopes that replaced the original Electric Boats units in M-1.

K&E's first replacement periscopes were for K-6, followed by D-2 and then hull periscopes for the A class. B&L apparently joined the program with replacements for L-11 but produced few periscopes before the United States entered WW I. K&E replacement production before the wartime production classes (O and later types) probably amounted to about 55 periscopes. At the same time, K&E made about 16 periscopes directly for Lake.

The first B&L periscope production contract apparently dates from May 1915 and amounted to 2 L-class and 2 D-class periscopes. Prior to the O-boats, this company probably received contracts for about another 5 instruments.

Kollmorgen's first major contract was for three periscopes for each of the 10 Electric Boat O-boats. This new company also received contracts for the Electric Boat AA class (T-boats) and then for Electric Boat's R-boats and S-boats, as well as for some replacement K-boat periscopes.

As an indication of the size of the program, the C&R Periscope Registry stood at 187 instruments before the instruments for the O class were ordered in 1916. They equipped a total of 58 submarines (2 periscopes each). The war program brought the Registry total to 510, including numerous spares. Typical early U.S. periscopes are described in Table B–1.

Early in the century, the major foreign periscope makers were Howard Grubb of Ireland (who made most British periscopes), Goerz and Carl Zeiss in Germany, and Galileo in Italy (which now makes electro-optical fire-control systems). Grubb supplied the British A-boat periscopes and apparently was connected with Vickers; he might have designed some or all of the earliest Electric Boat periscopes. By WW I, the British also bought periscopes from Kelvin, Bottomley, & Baird, Ltd. of Glasgow. Barr & Stroud, well known for its rangefinders, was just becoming interested in periscopes at this time; after WW I, it dominated the British domestic and export markets. C&R bought instruments from all of these companies (see Table B–2).

The first U.S. Navy periscope was a British-type fixed unit (altiscope) temporarily rigged through the forward ventilator of *Adder* (A-2) for trials in November 1902. The trials board was impressed, but it wanted improvements: a wider field of view (the original altiscope offered only 30 deg); capability to rotate to give an all-round view; a marked arc around the instrument's tube to indicate bearings; and an indication of the fore-and-aft line in the objective lens. The board also suggested that two periscope lengths be compared. Electric Boat argued convincingly that rotation would be unnecessary, so C&R ordered two fixed altiscopes (as were then being used in the Royal Navy) for comparative trials aboard *Adder* (8 ft tube) and *Moccasin* (14 ft tube).[10] The results were unimpressive; in September 1903 the CO of the two boats said that he preferred Lake's device (then called a multiscope), which provided an all-round view. C&R asked Lake for plans and prices, but Lake demurred; he was unwilling to sell anything short of a complete submarine (and he thought he had a very good chance of selling his new *Protector*). C&R therefore went back to Electric Boat, asking for a rotatable periscope.

Electric Boat soon worked out a means of rotating the periscope, while keeping the eyepiece fixed.[11] In April 1904, Electric Boat offered the navy both an 8-ft motor-rotated periscope with fixed eyepiece, specifically to be fitted to a submarine's conning tower, and a long (15-ft or 18-ft) power or hand unit to pass into a submarine's hull.[12] The short periscope was tested on board *Plunger*.[13]

The two alternative long (hull-penetrating) periscopes

Table B–1.   Some Typical U.S. Periscopes, Pre-1919*

Registry Number	Maker	Remarks
26–31	Electric Boat	D class: 4-in diameter, two fixed (D-1 and D-2) or one fixed and one walk-around (D-3); 1×, FoV about 30 degrees.
32–35	Electric Boat	E class: 4-in diameter walk-arounds with hand control only.
49–56	Electric Boat	F class: 4-in diameter walk arounds with hand control only.
61–66	Electric Boat	First EB bifocals, for H-boats (1.2/3.0×, 13 ft ¼ in and 22 ft 2½ in long); 4.5-in diameter Replacements: 147–152
69–84	Electric Boat	K-boat bifocals: 12 ft 4 in and 22 ft 4 in long (5-in diameter)
89–96	Electric Boat	L-boat bifocals (1.2/3.0×), 21 ft ¼ in and 22 ft 11 in × 5 in; also 114–119 Keuffel & Esser replacements for L-11: 120–121
97–98	Keuffel & Esser	Replacements for K-6: 1.2/3.0×, 12 ft and 22 ft 7¾ in × 5 in
99–104	Keuffel & Esser	Lake L-boats (L5–7), 1.2/3.0×, 18 ft 3 in × 5 in
144–145	Kollmorgen	Replacements for K-1: both 1.4× unifocals 146: Keuffel & Esser unifocal (1.2×) for E-1
163–166	Keuffel & Esser	F-class replacements, both unifocal: 1.2×, 20 ft 5 in and 21 ft 5 in × 5 in; also 186–187
182–183	Bausch & Lomb	Replacements for L-9; both unifocal (1.3×); one is 20 ft 11¾ in × 5 in
188–217	Kollmorgen	For Electric Boat O-boats; 18 ft 2 in × 5 ft ¹³⁄₁₆ in 1.2×, 41° FoV No. 3 scopes removed in 1924 as obsolete Alti-periscope: 0.72/1.23×, 19 ft 10½ in × 5-¹⁵⁄₁₆ in Bifocal: 1.2/3.0×, 21 ft × 5 ft ¹³⁄₁₆ in
273–332	Kollmorgen	For Electric Boat R class; No. 3 periscopes, removed 1924, were unifocal: 6×, 8° FoV, 18 ft 10⅜ in × 6 in; low-power: 1.25×, 38° FoV, 23 ft 6 in × 5 in; also alti-periscopes

* Where two lengths are given, the first is for No. 1 periscopes.
Note: FoV is field of view.

Table B–2.   Foreign Periscopes Bought by C&R Through 1927

Registry Number	Maker	Remarks
11	Goerz	B-1(1)
13	Goerz	B-2(1)
36	Goerz	Bifocal: D-1(1)
37	Goerz	Unifocal: E-1(1), stationary eyepiece with erect image
38	Galileo	Unifocal: C-1(1)
39	Galileo	Unifocal:C-3(1)
40	Galileo	Bifocal: C-4(1), used ground glass screen at eyepiece end
45	Goerz	Bifocal: 1.5/6×, for G-1(2)
511–520	Grubb	512 in L-10, 513 in L-11, 514 in L-1, 515 assigned R-4 1919, 519 in K-1(1), 520 in K-5(2) 511: unifocal, 24 ft $3\frac{11}{16}$ in long 512: bifocal, 24 ft $6\frac{1}{2}$ in long (both $5\frac{19}{32}$-in diameter) 513: bifocal altiperiscope 514: bifocal altiperiscope, 24 ft $6\frac{1}{2}$ in × $5\frac{19}{32}$ in, 1.5/6×, 40°/10° FoVs, 4 in head 515 and 516: bifocal 11 ft 9 in × 6 in, 1.5/6×, 3.75 in head 517 and 518: unifocal, 21 ft × 6 in, 1.5×, 1.75 in head 519 and 520: bifocal altiscopes, 18 ft $10\frac{1}{2}$ in × 6 in 1.5/6×, 4 in head
521	Barr & Stroud	Vertical-base coincidence range finder, tested 1918 and 1928 (failed both times, image too dim); 30 ft $6\frac{1}{2}$ in × 5.906 in
522–526	Kelvin	10DA-30 (see Table B–3)
527–531	Kelvin	10DA-25 (see Table B–3)
595H	Zeiss	UB-148(1), to K-6(2): bifocal altiscope, 20 ft × 5.9 in 1.54/6.0×, 40°/9.4° $2\frac{3}{16}$-in head, steel
596H	Goerz	UB-143(2), to K-4(2): 20 ft × 5.9 in, 1.5/6×, 38.5°/9.5°, $2\frac{3}{16}$-in head, steel
597H	Goerz	UB-88(1): bifocal altiscope, 20 ft 6 in × 5.9 in, 1.49/6.05×, steel
598H	N/A	UB-88(2), to L-7(2)
599H	Zeiss	UC-97(1): bifocal altiscope, 20 ft $4\frac{1}{2}$ in long, 1.5/5.65×, 41°/10° FoVs
600H	Zeiss	UC-97(2): bifocal altiscope, 1.52/5.94×, 40.6°/9.7° FoVs
601H	Goerz	U-117(1): 20 ft 5 in, tilt 0° to 80°, 1.5/6.0×, FoVs 39.67°/9.5°
602H	Goerz	U-117(2), to K-8(2): tilt −10° to +20°; 1.5/6.0×, FoVs 42.33°/9.75°
603H	Goerz	U-117(3), to K-7(2): 1.5/6×, 40.5°/9.5° FoVs
604H	Goerz	U-111(1): 20 ft 4 in × $5\frac{13}{16}$ in, 1.5/6×
605H		U-111(2): 20 ft 4 in × $5\frac{13}{16}$ in, 1.5/6×
606H		U-111(3): 20 ft 4 in × $5\frac{13}{16}$ in, 1.5/6×
X632	Goerz	23 ft × 6 in, 1.43/5.75×, 39.75°/9.33° FoVs, $2\frac{3}{16}$-in head
X633	Zeiss	$2\frac{5}{16}$-in head

Note: Source is a table compiled by C&R in 1927 (C&R correspondence file, RG 19, NARS). The number in parentheses is the position of the periscope on board the submarine; for example, (2) is the No. 2 periscope, and (1) is the forward or No. 1 periscope. This list is probably complete because it was compiled to support C&R's claim that it had indeed been attentive to foreign developments. FoV is field of view.

were installed on board *Shark* and *Porpoise* in July 1904 for comparative trials. Each extended $148\frac{1}{2}$ in (12 ft $4\frac{1}{2}$ in) above the hull, and thus its total length was probably about 16 ft. The periscope in *Shark* was a walk-around unit turned by a hand wheel and gearing; *Porpoise* had a power-trained periscope with a fixed eyepiece. These units had an outside diameter of 3.5 in. The remaining four *Adder*s initially received only the long units, penetrating their hulls abaft the conning tower.[14]

Electric Boat liked the fixed-eyepiece type because its eyepiece could be let into the conning tower at the level of the helmsman's eyes. He could use it to sweep the horizon or to steer toward a target. Once it had been

perfected (ca 1905), it was incorporated in the B-, C-, and D-boats. Unfortunately, as the barrel rotated, the image in the eyepiece also rotated; it was upside down when the window atop the periscope pointed dead astern. This problem killed off the fixed-eyepiece periscopes.[15] About 1904, Goerz found that a prism turning at half the speed of the barrel could keep the image erect. The U.S. Navy tried a Goerz erecting periscope in 1912 (in E-1) but did not decide to adopt it as standard.[16] Too, to keep the joint between the rotating barrel and the fixed lower end dry, the rotating joint had to be quite tight, ultimately often too tight for the instrument to turn.[17]

Electric Boat tried one other type of periscope. In 1907 it proposed a fixed-eyepiece instrument with all-round vision, obtained by replacing the usual single window with an array of windows. The observer would have seen a kind of fish-eye image, with objects abaft turned upside down. No such periscope was ever bought, but this "ring lens" design appeared in several later popular books on submarine design and was seriously considered in 1917.[18]

Unlike modern periscopes, these instruments could not retract (house). To bring them up out of the water or down into it, a submarine had to porpoise, a difficult maneuver even in a handy Holland boat. Too, the periscopes were a source of drag underwater, a serious consideration to a navy very interested in relatively high speeds to attack fast surface ships. In 1909, therefore, C&R's specifications for building the E-boats and F-boats included a requirement that their two walk-around periscopes (4-in diameter) partly house.[19] Periscopes would retract when the submarine was at rest or at low speed. The following year,

the specification for the H-class called for quick-acting retraction, with a travel of about 5 ft 3 in. The 4.5-in diameter periscopes would house at moderate speed and would be kept housed at high underwater speed, presumably to reduce drag. A similar requirement was apparently levied on the K-boats; an August 1911 Electric Boat K-class (EB 32) drawing shows a travel of 5 ft 8 in, slightly more than the distance down to the deck. The two E-boats were completed with housing periscopes, but they failed in service.[20] Both boats were refitted with fixed periscopes, and the F-boats and H-boats were modified at government expense. When the question arose again in 1915, all U.S. submarines had nonhousing periscopes (European navies felt differently).

Lake developed a very different kind of periscope, which he called an omniscope. His G-1 had two conning towers ("turrets"), one for the helmsman and one for the CO, each equipped with a periscope. The helmsman's simple periscope (3 in × 9 ft, slightly over 1× magnifica-

The eyepiece of D-3's hull periscope is shown. The nearby handwheel was geared to turn the barrel of the periscope against the strong resisting forces of the sea and of the packing that kept the barrel's penetration through the hull watertight. Above the handwheel the ring gear attached to the periscope barrel is clearly visible. Note also that the plane wheel visible at lower right is connected by belt to the rod in the overhead that actually controls the plane, as in earlier Electric Boat submarines. (*Submarine Force Museum and Library*)

tion, field of view 17 degrees) housed and could partially rotate. The big omniscope (diameter, $8\frac{5}{8}$ in, outer tube, 9 ft 1 in) consisted of two concentric tubes. The inner was a conventional periscope (3 in × 17 ft $3\frac{1}{2}$ in, magnification about 1.25×, field of view 17 degrees), which could house over a 4-ft travel. The outer tube used eight prisms to provide eight individual views. When the periscope was trained dead ahead, two looked ahead, two astern, and one on each quarter. Of the ahead or astern views, one was telescopic (about 8× over a 3-degree field); the other was pictorial (1.25×, 11 degrees). The beam views were "finders" (65-degree field of view at slightly below 1× magnification). The ahead view was upright, the side views were on edge, and the aft view was inverted. The whole instrument could turn, and there was a range-finder (presumably telemeter) slide for the telescopic viewer.[21] The trials board was less impressed (it considered the view dim), and it seems most unlikely that later Lake G-boats had Lake periscopes.

Experience with Electric Boat's instruments convinced C&R that it could do better. To evaluate possible competitive bids from alternative U.S. makers, the bureau had to write a detailed specification, which it wanted to base on the best (i.e., foreign) practice.[22] By December 1910 the Navy Department approved C&R requisitions for six foreign periscopes for comparison with existing U.S. types, three from the Optische Anstalt C.P. Goerz Aktiengesellshaft and three from Societa Anonima Officine Galileo of Italy. Presumably these instruments were delivered in 1911. They were initially intended for installation in the D- and E-classes. However, the three Galileo instruments (Registry numbers 38, 39, and 40) were installed (as auxiliary periscopes) in C-1, C-3, and C-4. D-1 had a Goerz bifocal periscope (Registry number 36), and E-2 had a Goerz erecting-image fixed-eyepiece periscope (Registry number 37). The third Goerz periscope (Registry number 45) was installed on board Lake's G-1. Meanwhile C&R began to buy U.S.-made periscopes. Registry number 41 was a U.S.-made K&E periscope (No. 1 in D-3), probably the company's first for a submarine.[23] This series also included B&L's unsuccessful vertical range-finder. The detailed C&R periscope specification was issued in 1912.

In March 1915, C&R asked the Bureau of Standards to compare number 41 and K&E's new Registry number 98 (bought for K-6), with a German-made Goerz periscope. To C&R's delight, the bureau said that its periscopes were practically equal to the Goerz in size of field, magnification, and size of exit pupil; however, its reply begged such questions as illumination and dryness. In 1915, C&R began to order replacements, mainly from K&E, for earlier unsatisfactory periscopes, beginning with the A class. By that September, replacement A-class instruments were being installed, and contracts had been let for the C and D classes. New periscopes were being, or had been, bought for the E through L classes.[24] Early reports on the A-class periscopes were quite encouraging. In February 1916, C&R stated that, with one exception, the B-class submarines all had good periscopes, and new ones were going into

the C class. New periscopes would be delivered shortly for the D class and for E-2. They were being bought for the H-boats (whose Electric Boat periscopes had been acknowledged by C&R as bad) and for some K-boats (whose original instruments had been installed only in 1914–15).

The replacement program was quite large. It was complicated because periscopes were not standardized from class to class, either by length or by diameter. Thus, small specialized contracts were the rule. Unfortunately, C&R's hopes were not realized. A special Periscope Board, convened at the New London submarine base in May 1917, was unhappy with new periscopes installed on board the D-boats, K-6, and L-11. It wanted to limit new periscopes to walk-around types, stationary eyepiece types with very limited arcs of train, and "ring lenses," which might give panoramic views (but were never bought). The board rejected bifocal periscopes in favor of simpler fixed-focus types (1.2× or 4×, with 40- or 12-degree field of view). Hopefully, handles (now so familiar) could replace the existing training wheel and gearing in walk-around instruments.

In some cases, several periscopes were bought in quick succession for the same submarine. Periscope delivery took about a year after a contract was let, presumably because all of these units were hand made. Then WW I brought large new submarine programs. Electric Boat could not cope. In 1916, it sublet the replacement periscopes for K-1 (Registry numbers 144 and 145) to the new firm, Kollmorgen, which also received a direct U.S. Navy contract for two more (numbers 167 and 168; K&E received a parallel contract for 169 and 170).[25]

Periscopes became a major bottleneck in the submarine program. Tubes were difficult to make. For some of them, Electric Boat turned to a gun-making company, General Ordnance of Derby, Connecticut (which later tried unsuccessfully to market its own periscopes). Before the war, lens glass came from Europe. Kollmorgen managed to secure enough French optical glass to fill its wartime needs. K&E developed its own formulas, using American sand (whose chemical composition differed from that of European sand, so the same formulations could not be used). Electric Boat found itself buying heavily from Kollmorgen. In turn, Kollmorgen found the jump difficult from very limited to massive orders.[26] It was undercapitalized and had to turn to the navy for financing; by 1918, C&R had a production manager on the premises. The bureau considered this wartime arrangement quite satisfactory. By the end of the war, Kollmorgen was probably the dominant U.S. periscope maker.

C&R looked to England as a new source of supply, but it soon learned that the Royal Navy was using everything that could be made and that delivery time was about the same as in the United States.[27] C&R did obtain a few test periscopes from Britain in 1918. Even after the war, deliveries ran so short that C&R feared that new R-boats and S-boats would be completed without their periscopes. Submarines designed for three periscopes ran trials (and operated) with only two. Ironically, in 1924, it was accepted that the conning tower instruments in these boats were not needed, so they were removed.

War experience showed that it was essential to be able to retract periscopes. In September 1915, Chief Constructor David W. Taylor revived the idea of housing periscopes (which were used by all the European navies) and cited "information from abroad." It appears that U.S. officers were also impressed by the housing periscopes aboard the visiting U-53. Taylor asked the two submarine builders and the two periscope makers for ideas. Electric Boat had already developed a winch (block and tackle) for the modified H-boats that it exported to England. In October, K&E proposed a new type of periscope (in which the optics revolved inside a glass dome at the head, independent of the outer tube), and quoted a price for a housing version. C&R decided to buy four, a fixed pair for a K-boat and a housing pair for a K-boat and a housing pair for an L-boat, probably L-10 or L-11.[28]

Modifying a submarine, even one under construction, to house her periscopes was not a trivial affair. L-11 already had her fixed periscopes on board. They would have to be dismantled, some frames cut, and the ventilator removed. Her completion would be unacceptably delayed. C&R still wanted to try Electric Boat's "proven" technique; in March 1916, the company offered to deliver two periscopes, appropriately modified, to Boston Navy Yard. The project seems to have died because cost ran too high.

Too, U.S. periscopes all had large heads; they were all constant-diameter tubes. During WW I, periscope design changed in favor of less visible, small-head instruments, with tubes that tapered for several feet. For example, in March 1915, Electric Boat rejected a C&R request for tapered-head periscopes for the L and M classes on the ground that the instruments for these boats already were nearly complete. The need for smaller heads helps to explain the massive program of replacement instruments. By 1918, the accepted marks of a modern periscope were a small head (i.e., a tapered body) and hermetic sealing (self-contained operation) for dryness. Few U.S. WW I submariners apparently liked their periscopes. In March 1919, for instance, the CO of L-8 wrote that in wartime patrols he generally had stayed below 60 ft (off Nantucket Light) specifically for good listening.

In April 1917, C&R became aware of the new altiperiscope, used for warning a submarine that airplanes were overhead. This was a periscope from which the upper prism had been removed, giving a 100-degree field of view looking straight up.[29] Submarine Force Commander

Submarines preparing for war at Philadelphia Navy Yard, 18 July 1917, display typical prewar U.S. non-housing periscopes, with their single round windows (lenses) and large-diameter heads. The boat nearest the viewer is L-3; K-6 is in the background. The instruments are probably Keuffel & Esser bifocals. The small bottle probably contains alcohol to keep the upper window clear.

considered the alti-periscope useless; it was unlikely that it could pick up something as small as an airplane. The altiscope was placed in production, however, and the U.S. version could switch between looking directly up and conventional periscope operation at low power. By May 1917, the S-boat had been redesigned to show three periscopes: a conning tower unit; a low-power, long periscope; and an alti-periscope aft.

After two conferences (10 October and 19 November 1917), a special board to standardize periscopes proposed that all future submarines have three: (1) a bifocal short-housing (6 ft to 8 ft) unit in the conning tower (Submarine Force Commander wanted at least 1.5/6.0× magnification); (2) a single-power unit (housing, 6 ft to 10 ft) in the operating compartment (Submarine Force Commander wanted 3×); and (3) a combined altiscope or sweep-around altiscope (combining overhead and horizontal views) in the operating compartment, with maximum housing distance (to provide air warning at maximum depth), to be used (for observation only, not for firing torpedoes) completely extended at speeds up to 5–6 kt (Submarine Force Commander wanted 3×). C&R badly wanted the altiscope; it considered that aircraft soon would be a major threat, even to submarines running at moderate depth. Navy experts commented that "this armament has already been developed and perfected in this country and its adoption is only a question of time." Submarine Force Commander wanted a 40-degree field of view at low power and would accept 15 degrees at 3×. At this time, C&R believed that a short bifocal instrument could be hermetically sealed, but that a long one could not. Tests had shown that a submarine approaching her target at 8–11 kt could not operate a periscope with more than 6 ft to 8 ft 6 in unsupported.

U.S. naval officers visiting British submarines in the fall of 1917 discovered that the British had gone beyond the simple alti-periscope to instruments in which the line of sight could be elevated or depressed by moving a prism at the upper end. The British used moderate angles of elevation or depression (+20 degrees/−10 degrees) to keep the line of sight on the horizon as the submarine rolled and pitched. Special instruments with more extreme elevation limits were used for sky search. In December 1917, C&R ordered similar instruments, but they were not delivered before the war ended.

A U.S. visitor to HMS H-12 reported that she had a Grubb bifocal (1.5/6×) sky-search (tilting prism) housing periscope (with "excellent optics and mechanism"). Most British officers wanted sky-search, all considered the motor cable hoist best (the U.S. officer found it slow), and all considered walk-around periscopes best. Significantly for U.S. practice, the British considered single-power (low-power) periscopes extremely dangerous. Because boats so equipped were not allowed out of habor at Kingstown, Ireland, two patrol stations (billets) were left unfilled. The U.S. officer recalled that, on three separate occasions, he had picked up destroyers hull-up with high power, but that he could distinguish nothing at all when he switched to low power. At dusk, however, low power was valued, and it was always used for a quick search of the sky.

With U.S. entry into WW I, making periscopes house became a high priority. In September 1917, the Submarine Force Commander ordered all Atlantic Fleet submarines fitted with housing periscopes as soon as possible. COs of the D class hoped in vain that their boats would be modernized with diesels and housing periscopes. By May 1918, it was clear that the E-, F-, and H-boats had too little available weight margin and that, in any case, periscopes installed on board them would not house any great distance. The newer K-boat and L-boats, however, were suitable. The AL-boats in Ireland enjoyed a high priority; material for them was collected at Philadelphia between December 1917 and January 1918 and shipped in February; L-1 through L-4 and L-11 were modified at Queenstown Dockyard during 1918. The Lake L-boats (including Portsmouth's L-8) were modified while under construction. K-5 was ordered modified in May 1918 as a prototype for the K class. Electric Boat's M-1 was commissioned with two new Kollmorgen unifocal housing periscopes in place of the fixed Electric Boat units originally installed.[30] Electric Boat's N-boats had the last periscopes made by that company, and they housed pneumatically. The company's T-boats were completed with Kollmorgen periscopes.[31] Lake installed K&E pneumatic bifocal periscopes in its N-boats.[32]

It turned out to be much easier to modify Electric Boat submarines than Lake boats for housing. There were also other problems. The L-boats had bifocal periscopes. L-5 dislocated her periscope head, apparently when the crank for changing magnification hit a stop as the periscope descended. The upper inner tube turned about 10 degrees, making it impossible for the viewer at the bottom to be sure of the bearing of any target. Converted to house at Portsmouth Navy Yard, L-8's periscopes were not hermetically sealed and thus could not be kept dry and airtight (periscopes for L-5 through L-7, which were converted by the manufacturer, K&E, were properly sealed).

C&R wanted quick-housing periscopes, working at 1 ft/sec over 6–10 ft (in fact, most designs housed over shorter distances), so that total time to raise or lower a periscope would not exceed 20 sec. The Germans used a simple wire winch to house their periscopes. C&R developed a pneumatic piston, and a hydraulic piston was also suggested. K&E offered a screw thread technique, which C&R disliked. Submarine Force Commander liked wire best, but space had to be provided for taking up the wire as the periscope rose and descended. That made a pneumatic mechanism, adopted initially in the C&R-designed S-boats (S-3 class) attractive. When Portsmouth installed the pneumatic housing mechanism in its new L-8, however, it turned out that control was poor and that the periscope often stuck in its tube. Under water pressure, the stuffing box in the top of the cylinder always leaked telltale air bubbles. L-9 demonstrated a very successful winch.

Submarines under construction in 1917 all had been designed with two fixed periscopes. The typical diameter was 5-in (e.g., in K-boats and L-boats). New designs for the S-boats showed 6-in diameter, which C&R wanted to avoid. Kollmorgen pointed out that it was difficult to arrange the electric shift to the altiscope in so narrow a tube. Nor could it provide the fixed-eyepiece forward periscope then planned for S-1 in so small a diameter. The company argued that a 6-in periscope would be at least twice as efficient as a 5-in instrument. It would be much more rigid and could accommodate much more substantial lens mounts that would protect the lenses from being deformed or injured by bending or straining of the outer tube. In a smaller-diameter periscope, heavy lens mountings would block too much of the light. Finally, Kollmorgen argued, the Germans used 6-in periscopes and managed to avoid vibration. Even U.S. 6-in bronze periscopes, 22 ft long, vibrated a little (with their $\frac{3}{8}$-in walls); 5 in would be too flimsy. C&R approved, and 6 in became standard in the new generation of Electric Boat submarines.

Electric Boat's O-boats soon had their No. 1 bifocal periscopes replaced by alti-periscopes. Later, probably in 1917, a third periscope was added in the conning tower (a low-powered instrument).[33] All of these $5\frac{13}{16}$-in instruments were made by Kollmorgen. Lake's boats had two 5-in K&E pneumatic unifocal periscopes, one high-powered and one low-powered.[34]

Through WW I, C&R sought longer and longer periscopes, initially 27-footers and then 30-footers. The latter were not ready until well after the war. For example, B&L's prototype 30-ft periscope (10BA-30) was not delivered until February 1920. Comparable Kollmorgen and K&E instruments appeared about the same time.

In September 1917, Electric Boat proposed what looked like a simple way of adding a third periscope to its R-1–R-20: it could replace the access hatch just abaft the midships compartment. The depth of the hull there would accept a long-travel periscope, which could be extended at low speed. C&R agreed, but both it and the builder became less enthusiastic as they realized the delay that the change would impose. C&R soon decided that the third periscope would be installed, if at all, only after delivery of the R-boats. Thus, the boats were delivered with two 6-in Kollmorgen periscopes raised by windlass: a short alti-periscope (11 ft 9 in, $0.7\times$ as altiscope and $1.2\times$ as periscope, with 96-degree and 40-degree fields of view) in the conning tower and a 21-ft, low-power instrument ($1.2\times$, 38.5-degree field of view). Later, a long, high-power instrument was added (18 ft $10\frac{1}{2}$ in). In 1924, the short periscope was eliminated. The standard installation was then two 27-footers (e.g., 45KA27 and 90KA27s).

Lake R-boats used pneumatic periscopes, all in the operating compartment: 5-in B&L in R-21–R-24 ($1.32\times$ alti-periscope, 17 ft 8 in long; $1.2\times$ periscope 18 ft 4 in long; and $1.2/3.6\times$ bifocal, 23 ft 6 in long, with only the latter housing in a well). Lake's R-25–R-27 were designed for 5-in K&E pneumatic periscopes ($0.7\times/1.2\times$ alti-periscope, 18 ft 8 in long; $1.2\times/3.0\times$ bifocal, 19 ft 4 in long; and $1.2\times$ unifocal, 23 ft 6 in long). In May

1918, C&R ordered changes, but R-21–24 were too far along to change. Periscopes for R-25–R-27 were reordered as single-power units with small heads: a $1.5\times$ alti-periscope, 18 ft 4 in long, with a narrow end and projecting 12 in above the periscope shears when housed; a high-power periscope (5–$6\times$), 19 ft 4 in long, with a 4 ft taper and projecting 12 in when housed), and a unifocal, 23 ft 6 in long, upgraded to $1.5\times$ and flush when housed.

C&R much disliked Electric Boat's original proposal for the S-boat periscope arrangement, particularly that the periscope heads were exposed when the periscopes were housed. It wanted the proposed alti-periscope replaced with an alti-azimuth periscope (an instrument capable of functioning as a conventional periscope or an altiscope). The company retorted that any change at all (in this case, moving the amidships periscope back on the centerline) would require considerable drafting effort. Nothing could be done with S-1, but S-18–S-41 could be redesigned. The after periscope could be lengthened by 10 ft by eliminating the adjusting tank and making relatively minor changes. It would take 2 mo to make the required new drawings, but Electric Boat thought that would be acceptable, given other delays (such as those at Union Iron Works as a result of the higher priority assigned to destroyers).

Electric Boat particularly objected to C&R's demand for a short instrument for the conning tower. The boat had a large conning tower specifically to provide an isolated underwater station for the CO. The short periscope would be used only for a high-speed underwater approach. Approaches would normally be at slow speed, when a long periscope would be appropriate. Placing the two long periscopes in the body of the boat would amount to moving the CO there.

In June 1918, Kollmorgen received a contract for all 72 periscopes for Electric Boat's S class (S-18–S-41).[35] All were windlass types, $5\frac{13}{16}$-in diameter: a unifocal alti-periscope ($1.25\times$, 22 ft 9.5 in long) in the conning tower and a bifocal periscope ($1.5/3.75\times$, with fields of view of 33 and 13 degrees, 22 ft 3 in long) and a low-power periscope ($1.5\times$, 33-degree field of view, 23 ft long) in the control room. C&R considered the powers offered too low; it demanded $5\times$ or $6\times$ in the bifocal periscope and $1.5\times$ to $1.75\times$ in the altiscope. In November 1918, C&R asked that Nos. 2 and 3 periscopes be lengthened to 27 ft and both made bifocal ($1.5/6X$). The bureau wanted all three periscopes to be the same height, but that could not be done with the altiscope (it was, however, increased in power to $1.75X$). Kollmorgen agreed to lengthen the periscopes but could not make No. 3 bifocal (too much of it already had been manufactured). In January 1919, the contact was changed to lengthen No.2 periscope to 26 ft 3 in and No. 3 to 27 ft. In October 1919, C&R shipped three 27-ft unifocal periscopes to Portsmouth for experimental installation in S-boat (S-4, S-5) conning towers in place of the short alti-periscopes in hopes that the S class could standardize on 27-footers.

C&R wanted still longer periscopes. In November, it

asked for 30-footers for S-42–S-65 and, if possible, for S-18–S41 as well. To accommodate such long instruments, 27-in wells would have to be sunk in the auxiliary tank and No.2 ballast tank; this would block water flow to the Kingstons. The company argued that any such change would delay completion. Instead, it offered to rearrange S-42–S-57 amidships.

By May 1918, Lake's S-2 was assigned three 5-in K&E pneumatic periscopes: (1) bifocal ($1.5 \times -1.75 \times /5 \times -6 \times$), 24 ft 9 in long, retracting 10 ft), (2) bifocal ($1.5 \times$), 12 ft 4 in long (with 17 in diameter head) in the conning tower and (3) alti-periscope ($1.5 \times$) 20 ft 7 in long.

C&R's early revision of its S-boat design (S-3) allowed for only very limited housing distances: as of 4 April 1917, 3 ft 6 in forward, 5 ft aft. Submarine Force Commander considered these distances grossly inadequate; they would make little difference to a submarine trying to stay well below the surface in rough weather. Submarine Force Commander wanted the head of the conning tower instrument to be at least 25 ft above the roof of the conning tower when raised, with a shorter instrument (let into the hull) forward of it. The May 1917 board wanted all periscopes to house at least 12 ft. To get such distances, the submarine would have to be redesigned with wells into which periscopes could retract.

As designed, the Navy S-3–S-13 used Kollmorgen bifocal periscopes (10 ft 6 in long) in their conning towers and B&L instruments in their operating compartments (alti-periscope, 23 ft 6.5 in long, and 19 ft 7 in high-power periscope, 19 ft 7 in long; both 6-in diameter). Because her assigned conning tower periscope was not yet ready, S-3 was completed with a very short (10 ft 6 in) Kollmorgen bifocal alti-periscope in her conning tower. By November 1920, she had much longer instruments in her control room, a Kollmorgen bifocal alti-periscope (29 ft 5.5 in long) and a 30-ft British Kelvin DA-1 bifocal alti-periscope, for trials. Later boats all had long periscopes in their conning towers, but, given shortages of modern instruments, few had all three assigned periscopes. Experiments with S-4 showed that it was impractical to install a 30-footer in the conning tower (27 ft was the maximum there).

The Lake-built S-14–S-17 were to have been similar except that all three of their periscopes were by B&L (the 19 ft 7 in was a low-power instrument). As completed, however, these boats had much longer standard Kollmorgen periscopes (types 20KS-23, 10BA-25, or 10EA-25 in the conning tower; types 10KL-27, 40KA-27, and 50KA-30 in the control room). In January 1921, for example, C&R ordered S-14–S-17 fitted with a 27-ft bifocal alti-periscope in No. 1 position and a 30-ft bifocal alti-periscope in No. 2, with No. 3 blanked off pending availability of enough long periscopes. In 1923, S-12 had 30-ft periscopes (10BA-30 and 70 EA-30) in her conning tower and control room. C&R also bought a pair of British Kelvin, Bottomley, & Baird 30-ft periscopes (Registry numbers 524 and 525) for experimental installation in this group of boats.

Even a 30-ft length was not enough; in 1921 C&R was considering a 34-ft periscope (type 60KA-34 or 80KA-34) for one of the two control room periscopes.

By 1925, the standard S-boat installation was a 23- or 27-footer in No. 1 position, a 30- or 34-footer in No. 2, and a 27-, 30-, or 34-footer in No. 3. Within a few years, the No. 1 periscopes (conning tower installations) had all been landed, as they were little used in service.

The most important lesson of wartime production was that periscopes had to be standardized. In November 1918, C&R decided that it wanted all periscopes in each class to be the same length, so that instruments could be easily interchanged. In 1919, C&R estimated that no fewer than 20 distinct types were in service, though some differed mainly in length. Older submarines used a wide variety of 5-in instruments; the wartime O-, R-, and S-boats used 6-in periscopes. It was difficult even to be sure of how many types there were, because there were no type designations; instruments were indicated either by their Registry numbers or by vague indications of planned use (e.g., "replacement for K-4, -5, -6, -7, -8," which might never be used for that purpose).

In mid-1919, C&R convened a standardization conference. One of its recommendations, adopted that fall, was for standard designations, to consist of a sequence number, a manufacturer letter, a function letter, and the optical length to the nearest foot. If periscope diameter were other than 6 in, the length was preceded by a 0 to indicate 5 in and by 00 to indicate $5\frac{5}{16}$ in. Periscopes made by each manufacturer were to be numbered separately, by tens (intermediate numbers would indicate minor variations). Related periscopes were given the same sequence number. This system applied only to new instruments; the old ones, which probably would be soon discarded, were not designated. Manufacturer letters were B for B&L, E for K&E, and K for Kollmorgen, to which were eventually added D for Kelvin, Bottomley, & Baird; G for Naval Gun Factory; N for Nedinsco (Nederlandische Instrumentin Cie., a Dutch manufacturer); S for Barr & Stroud; and Z for Zeiss. Function letters were A for bifocal alti-periscope (i.e., with tilting line of sight), B for bifocal, H for high-power unifocal, L for low-power unifocal, N for night or low visibility, and S for a low-power full altiscope.

Early designations are listed in Table B–3. Within a few years, the system had collapsed. In the mid-1920s, all periscopes were collected into a single system, with numbers beginning at 75. Then a new type of periscope was numbered 71, and the series began again (see below for details).

By the early 1920s, with only O-, R-, and S-boats in service, the U.S. Navy had standardized on what it called Type A: 6-in periscopes with two magnifications ($1.5 \times$ and $6 \times$; fields of view, 32 degrees and 8 degrees), with prisms tilting between $+45$ degrees and -10 degrees, for a combination of stabilization and limited sky search. Standard lengths were 27, 30, and 34 ft. For example, an S-boat typically had a 23-ft or 27-ft periscope in No. 1 position, a 30-footer in No. 2 or 3, and sometimes a 34-footer in No. 3. O-boats and R-boats had only one Type

Table B–3.   Standard Periscopes, Post-1919

Designation	Number Made	Remarks
10BA-30	32	S-4–S-17: 1.5/6×, 33.5°/8.4° FoVs, tilt +45°/−15°, light transmission 17% LP, 23% HP. Left handle for elevation. Ordered December 1917.
20BA-30	1	Special type ordered December 1917; 1.56/6×, 34° 10′/8° 38′ FoVs, tilt +45°/−10°; transmission 17% LP, 25% HP.
78BA-30	10	Probably 1925 contract.
10DA-25	5	1.49/5.9×, 40°/10° FoVs head 3.25 in, transmission 12.4%–13.6%
10DA-30	5	1.5/6× 40°/10° FoVs, tilt +55°/−10°, head diameter 3.25 in, transmission 12.9%–11.3%; used as No. 3 scope in S-48, S-49, S-50.
10EL-015	4	K-3, K-4, K-7, K-8 (No. 1); C&R wanted tilt 20° to 45°, settled for 20°.
10EA-25	4	K-3, K-4, K-8 (No. 2): 1.5/6× FoVs, 32°/8° FoVs.
20EA-025	6	O-class replacements: 1.5/6×, 32°/8° FoVs.
70EA-30	29	1.5/6×, 32°/8° FoVs, tilt +45°/−10°.
75EA-30	10	2.5-in head. 1.5/6×, FoVs 32°/8° (i.e., 48° divided by magnification. Light transmission: 26% HP, 20.5% LP). *Note:* registry numbers for these periscopes come *before* those for 70EA-30.
76EA-30	1	No data.
83EA-30	2	Last Keuffel & Esser periscope; 7.5-in type with integral stadimeter.
10GA-23	1	Prototype Naval Gun Factory steel-tube periscope, 1924 (Mk XI in BuOrd series): 1.43/5.75× (34°7′ and 8°43′). Tested as No. 1 periscope in S-4.
10KA-0015	2	AA-2, AA-3 (No. 1 periscope).
10KL-27	17	S-18–S-41 (No. 3 periscope).
10KS-0026	2	AA-2, AA-3 (No. 3 periscope).
20KA-0026	2	AA-2, AA-3 (No. 2 periscope).
20KS-23	20	S-18–S-41 (No. 2 periscope): 1.75× at 28° FoV, tilt +88°, so complete field is 116°.
25KA-23	4	1.5/6×, 32°/8°, tilt +45/−10°.
30KA-15		R spare (No. 1 periscope).
30KA-30	14	1.5/6×, 32°/8° FoV, tilt +45°/−10°.
40KA-27	24	S-18–S-41 (No. 2 periscope): 1.5/6×, 32°/8° FoV, tilt +20/−10°.
45KA-27	24	1.5/6×, 32°/8° FoV, tilt +45°/−10°.
50KA-30	11	S-3–S-13 (No. 1 periscope): 1.5/6×, 32°/8°, tilt +20°/−10°.
60KA-25	5	M-class and O-class spares.
60KA-34	18	1.5/6×, 32°/8° FoVs, tilt +45°/−10°.
70KA-30	1	Tilt +20°/−10°.
71KA-30	10	First Kollmorgen with integral stadimeter, ordered 1931.
77KA-30	10	Probably 1924 contract.
79KA-30	10	December 1926 contract.
80KA-34	10	1.5/6×, FoV 32°/8°, tilt +45°/−10°.
81KA-30	10	First 7.5-in with stadimeter.
82KA-30	1	7.5-in diameter.
84KA-30	2	7.5-in diameter.
85KA-34	5	6-in diameter.
86KA-34	48	Standard 34-ft type, 7.5-in diameter.
87KA-40	11	Type 1 periscope of late fleet boats, progenitor of Type 2 high-angle periscope.
90KA-27	24	1.5/6×, 32°/8° FoV, tilt +45°/−10°.
100KA-30	3	"Anyheight" type for V-1 class; 3 101KA-30 almost identical: 1.5/6×, 32°/8° FoVs, tilt +45°/−10°.
73NA-30	5	Zeiss (Nedinsco) 6-in bought for trials; 3 modified as 103ZA-30.
72SA-30	5	6-in Barr & Stroud bought for trials.
74SA-30	3	7.5-in Barr & Stroud bought for trials.

Note: FoV, field of view; LP, low power; HP, high power.

A periscope. These periscopes looked like modern ones, with folding handles on each side of the eyepiece, one for the power shift and the opposite one controlling the tilt of the head prism. The main suppliers were K&E and Kollmorgen.

C&R was very impressed with the U-boat periscopes it obtained in 1919. Most boats had two periscopes with eyepieces in the conning tower, and many also had an emergency periscope let into the central (operating) compartment, offset and abeam the fore end of the conning tower fairwater. The Germans had virtually standardized on two optical lengths, 20 ft 4 in and 23 ft, with one length in each boat. Virtually all were tilting-prism altiscopes with 38–42 degree fields of view at low power (1.5×). For range-finding, a stadimeter could be attached to the periscope eyepiece.

The most radical development was an "any-height" configuration, which kept the eyepiece at a constant height while the periscope head moved up and down. Any-height was attractive because it allowed for a shorter unsupported extension when the boat ran at high speed (to limit vibration) and also for fine adjustment when the boat ran at steady depth. It was achieved by placing a mirror at the bottom of the periscope barrel. The double path down the barrel and then back up to the observer was constant as the head rose and fell.

C&R and BuOrd developed a stadimeter attachment for periscope eyepieces. By about 1924, they were up to Mk VI, but none of these devices was produced in great numbers. Stadimeters were originally used only as rangefinders, to measure the angle subtended by the known height of the target's mast. Once that range was known, the stadimeter could be turned on its side to measure the angle subtended by the target's length (in practice, by an easily observed part of the length, such as the distance between masts). Because the target normally would not be exactly perpendicular to the line of sight, the target would appear somewhat foreshortened: its observed length would give the target angle. This feature was called course angle finding. C&R probably first encountered it in a Zeiss proposal presented in 1924 or 1925 by B&L (see below). Prototype Zeiss combination stadimeter–course angle finders gave good results in service. By 1930, C&R had requested proposals for six combined stadimeter–course angle finders for attachment to periscopes. This effort was overtaken by the development of new periscopes (see below).

A new periscope specification issued in October 1920 reflected war experience and U.S. studies of British and German periscopes. For example, new periscopes were made of corrosion-resistant steel for stiffness (compared with bronze or brass). The new program (90KA-27, 30KA-30, 70EA-30, 75EA-30, 80KA-34) amounted to 87 periscopes (including a single 76EA-30). By way of contrast, C&R considered 20KS-23 and 10BA-30 obsolescent wartime designs, built too urgently to incorporate war experience. The only other periscopes ordered at this time were by K&E: four sets for K-boats (10EL-0015 and 10EA-25 for

each boat) and replacements for the No. 2 periscopes of the Lake O-boats (20EA-025).

The first post–WW I submarines, the V-1 class, continued the wartime policy of three periscopes. The 27-ft forward periscope, let into the hull, was intended as an emergency instrument if the conning tower (with Nos. 2 and 3 periscopes) were carried away. (The forward periscope could not be a 34-footer because too much of its length would be unsupported.) No. 2 periscope was a 34-footer with a deep well. When it was extended, the top of the boat's hull would be 38 ft below the surface, reasonably safe from collision. No. 3 was an any-height periscope (100KA-30) developed by Kollmorgen at C&R request. In theory, the combination of the long and adjustable periscopes covered the range of approach speeds. The any-height periscope had a 7.5-in diameter (the others were standard 6-in types). V-4–V-6 were similarly equipped (their any-height periscopes were designated 101KA-30). By about 1930, all six periscopes had been condemned and scrapped; large (7.5-in) wells were left in the big V-boats.

C&R reviewed the periscope situation in 1923. By this time, conning tower periscopes were proving fairly useless, so the bureau recommended that they be eliminated (the secretary of the navy agreed in January 1924). That left two periscopes for each submarine except the V-boats. A census of Type A periscopes showed that there was generally a spare for every 5 instruments, but that there were too few 30-footers; in theory, 14 more 30-ft periscopes were needed. The reserve of spares was fortuitous because of a combination of 1918 cancellations and orders for longer periscopes to displace shorter ones. In the past, periscopes had been ordered only for specific installations; however, C&R reasonably pointed out that many submarines had suffered periscope casualties.

An order for new 30-footers would be a great opportunity to improve U.S. periscope design. Beginning about 1924, C&R ran annual programs of 10 such periscopes each (77KA-30, 78BA-30, 79KA-30, the last made under a contract awarded 31 December 1926). Then new procurement ended until 1930. For these programs, B&L offered Zeiss designs in October 1924 and again in October 1925. Both used tilting prisms (+40/−10-degree limits) and had relatively small heads (2.16 in and 2.36 in, respectively). The 1925 version transmitted 22 percent of available light at low power (1.5×) and 25 percent at high (6×). Zeiss offered a constant-bearing indicator that allowed a fairly accurate estimate of target speed. It also offered a periscope camera. In theory, its photographs might be developed in a few seconds, then used for rangefinding. K&E gained no contracts; it was effectively out of the market.

Meanwhile, American submariners in the Asiatic Fleet encountered modern British and Dutch periscopes in submarines operating in Chinese waters. In April 1927, Lt. Comdr. E. R. Morrisey, CO of S-40, wrote to C&R that a British periscope head he saw off Hong Kong looked like a broomstick compared with the massive U.S. No. 2 periscope. The tiny head of the Dutch Nedinsco periscope seemed to admit quite as much light as his Kollmorgen, and its detachable (stadimeter) rangefinder seemed far more accurate than his telemeter. He also liked the reliable tilt-prism mechanism of the Dutch periscope, which could be used to take pictures. A British officer was "certain" that Japan, the likely future enemy, had bought many Nedinsco periscopes. The same officer commented on the large size of U.S. periscope heads. British submarines had two periscopes, with 1¼-in and 2½-in heads; U.S. officers felt that the 2½-in heads of their periscopes produced an excessive wash. They considered the Kollmorgen better for ruggedness and for light transition, and far superior for concealment; the narrow part of the B&L periscope was so large that concealment near a target was no more than a matter of luck.

The comments on Dutch periscopes were significant because Nedinsco was a subsidiary of the German Zeiss company, which had made so many wartime U-boat instruments.

Morrisey was detached to the United States to report directly to C&R. Meeting at Tsingtao, China, the Asiatic Fleet submarine commanders agreed that they wanted one bifocal periscope with minimum-diameter head and one low-power unifocal periscope. The bifocal would be used for approach, the unifocal for attack in daylight in a smooth sea. Any significant wave action would so hide the bifocal head that it could be used for attack. In October 1927, the Control Force urged that some foreign periscopes be bought for comparison. Even if U.S. optical designs were as good as foreign ones, the Europeans might well have better optical glass and better workmanship. It was well known that, late in WW I, U-boats had repeatedly attacked successfully in twilight, which implied good light transmission.

Not all officers agreed that U.S. periscope heads were too large. SubDiv 19 (S-42–S-47) doubted that reducing head size would eliminate the periscope's feather (C&R later investigated a proposed float for that purpose). Light transmission was clearly paramount. Too, in torpedo practice off Perlas Island in the Bay of Panama, the division made 72 approaches without being detected, and 100 training approaches with few detections. None of its submarines was ever spotted on a record run (i.e., on a run used to keep score). SubDiv 9 of the Asiatic Fleet agreed: "About 10 or 12 years ago, periscope heads were of such diameter that they might possibly be mistaken for moving piles or broken ends of submerged masts. This condition no longer exists." It was more important to train officers to avoid making a wake or feather. Very few periscopes had been spotted during Battle Practice "C" the previous year at Lahaina Roads, Hawaii; the periscope's wake was always spotted first.

C&R considered its own periscopes as good as anyone else's; it condemned Morrisey's criticism as destructive. CNO Adm. E. W. Eberle disagreed; C&R had lost sight of the fleet's point of view. Although independent of the CNO, C&R felt that it had to reconsider. On 3 October,

the bureau's submarine expert, Comdr. (later Rear Adm.) C. B. Momsen, proposed ordering eight periscopes from Holland, Germany, and England. Ten more would be bought as the spares proposed in 1923.

ONI was ordered to report on British, Dutch, and German periscopes; it also investigated Italian and French ones, but C&R had no interest in buying them. C&R did buy from Nedinsco and from Barr & Stroud in England. Of earlier suppliers, neither Grubb, Kelvin, nor Goerz any longer made periscopes.

Nedinsco offered both search and small-head attack periscopes. Like the wartime German periscopes (and contemporary U.S. ones), its periscopes could be fitted with external stadimeters for range-finding. Other fittings included a "triangle magnifier" to determine the appropriate lead angle (or gyro setting) for torpedo fire, and a "stabilized line in space." An observer who already knew the target's range and course angle could use the "line in space" to measure speed by observing how quickly the target passed through it.[36] Barr & Stroud offered a wide range of periscopes with internal range finders, course angle estimators, fixed lines in space, and integral torpedo directors (triangle solvers).[37]

To cover the foreign purchases, C&R developed a new periscope specification in June 1929. It wanted an internal stadimeter/course angle finder. The periscopes would be bifocal (1.5/6×, 48-degree field of view at low power) altiscopes (prism elevation +45/−10 degrees). C&R wanted to buy five 6-in × 30-ft periscopes from each of Nedinsco and Barr & Stroud (to test two on submarines on each coast and retain the fifth for study). Barr & Stroud, however, argued that 6-in diameter was too small; it preferred 7.5 in or even 8.5 in. Then special nonmagnetic bronze could be used instead of steel. Too, the company normally elevated the line of sight to 70 degrees (rather than the 45 degrees sought) to get the valuable view of the zenith. C&R found the larger diameter attractive, particularly because it did not have to rebuild any submarines to test it: the six V-boats already had 7.5-in wells for the abortive any-height periscopes, already removed. It therefore ordered three 7.5-in Barr & Strouds (74SA-30), alongside the five 6-in periscopes (72SA-30) originally planned (the Nedinsco periscopes were designated 73NA-30). When the big Barr & Strouds were delivered in 1932, one was assigned to *Dolphin*, not yet completed, and one each to *Narwhal* and *Nautilus*.

C&R therefore bought 5 Nedinsco and 8 Barr & Stroud periscopes. In January 1930, it called for bids for 10 U.S. periscopes, using the 1929 specification (bids were opened 14 February 1930). All three manufacturers bid. Kollmorgen won with its 71KA-30, incorporating the first built-in U.S. stadimeter/course angle finder. The first was installed on board S-21 on 6 October 1932. It proved far superior to the earlier external stadimeter.[38]

Kollmorgen developed and patented its own form of stadimeter; it used split objective lenses.[39] K&E copied Barr & Stroud's rotating annular wedges working in the parallel light rays between the upper and lower telescopes. By this time, B&L was no longer capable of designing new periscopes, although it could import Zeiss designs.

Impressed by Barr & Stroud's arguments, C&R decided to ask the U.S. manufacturers for prototype 7.5-in bifocal (the usual 1.5/6×) periscopes. A specification issued 1 December 1932 called for light transmission of at least 28 percent at 6×, 22.5 percent at 1.5×, with the power shift operated by turning the right training handle and prism tilt (+40/−10 degrees) by turning the left one. The eyepiece would carry a stable line, and the internal stadimeter would read on a dial on the outside of the periscope.[40] On 3 March 1933, C&R asked each maker for a prototype. Kollmorgen's became 81KA-30 (further developed versions were 82KA-30 and 84KA-30); K&E's became 83KA-30. B&L could not bid because navy regulations forbade it from sending the specification to Zeiss. C&R was unhappy; it saw B&L as a valuable wartime source of periscopes.

Meanwhile, the new generation of smaller submarines appeared. Beginning with *Dolphin* (V-7), the complement of periscopes was cut to one in the control room and one in the conning tower. Presumably, because only the three experimental Barr & Stroud 7.5-in instruments were available, *Dolphin* had one 7.5-in (81KA-30) and one 6-in (80KA-34) diameter periscope. *Cachalot* and *Cuttlefish* had the same arrangement. By 1938, their short 7.5 in periscopes had been replaced by long ones (86KA-34s, see below). *Dolphin* apparently retained her 7.5-in instrument.

The next step was a 7.5-in, 34-ft periscope. On 20 February 1935, C&R issued a specification calling for somewhat better light transmission (30 percent at 6×, 23.5 percent at 1.5×), a 48-degree field of view at 1.5×, and elevation limits of +45 degrees and −10 deg. As in existing periscopes, head diameter would be 2.5 in (with at least a 2-ft section at that diameter; as in existing instruments, the total reduced-length section would be 6 ft).

Kollmorgen produced 86KA-34, which offered easier

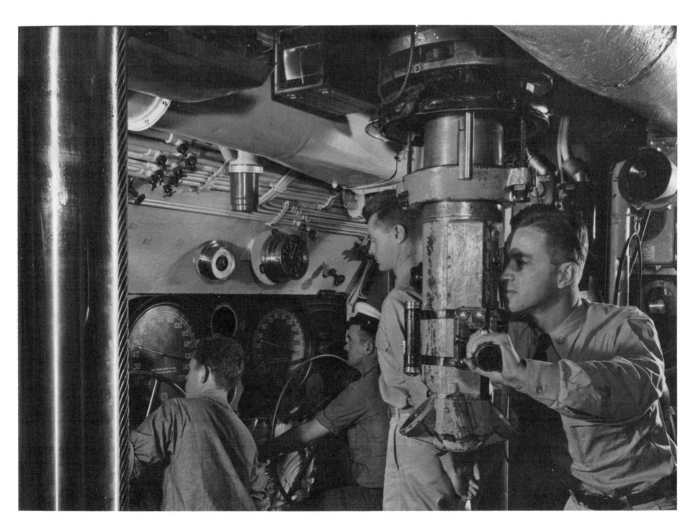

The lower end of a modern periscope is shown in the control room of USS *Marlin*, serving as a training submarine in 1943. The pair of angled dials below the handles are stadimeter readouts. One is provided opposite the observer to allow an assistant to take readings. The two planesmen are at the left.

and quicker stadimeter operation due to ball bearings, a higher gear ratio, and a better-located wheel. Using a duplicate stadimeter dial, an assistant could read off stadimeter range and course while the periscope observer kept his eye on the target. A new eyepiece allowed for increased eye distance (by about 12 mm), thus the full optical field could be seen much more easily.

These periscopes were first installed (as No. 2 periscopes) in the *Porpoise* (SS 172) class, which retained the 6-in No. 2 periscopes of earlier classes, so Kollmorgen manufactured a new 6-in instrument (its last), 85KA-34. In the *Salmon* (SS 182 class), both periscopes were 7.5-in 86KA-34s. About 1938, the *Perch*-class submarines were apparently modified to take 7.5-in periscopes in both positions.[41] In some cases, short 81 KA-30s were installed temporarily because the longer instruments were not yet available.

Kollmorgen was well aware of the controversy over periscope head size. On 10 February 1936, it proposed a special attack periscope using a small-diameter head (1.25 in) screwed onto a 7.5-in barrel. To keep diameter down, the periscope had to be drastically simplified, with only one magnification (1.5×, 30-degree field of view), limited prism tilt (sufficient to compensate for pitch and roll, plus or minus 10 degrees), and without a stadimeter. The image would be curved because all lenses had to be collective. The dry-air pipe could be carried only halfway up the taper. However, such a small head would make little or no feather at low speed and would be effectively invisible at any great distance.

A Periscope Board convened by Subron 6 was unenthusiastic; the sacrifices involved seemed excessive. With only low power, the periscope would be useless beyond 2,000 yd. Too, it seemed likely that it would vibrate badly when even a small part of its sharp taper was submerged and very badly as a submarine accelerated to fire torpedoes. It was clearly a step in the right direction, but it was not yet acceptable. The board wanted a 40-ft periscope with a small head but with all other standard features, including full dry-air circulation. Length meant good depth control in rough water and also safety: *Bonita*, the squadron flagship, had recently been run over by a screening destroyer. Comdr. R. S. Edwards, the squadron CO, badly wanted a zenith-search feature in at least one periscope to check for aircraft before surfacing.

In January 1936, Subron 6 reported that its submarines often risked broaching at periscope depth off the Philippines in moderate to heavy seas. Its most useful periscopes, carrying internal range finders and angle solvers, were only 30 ft long. A submarine trying to maintain shallow depth drained her batteries because she had to run. Even 34 ft did not seem sufficient; the squadron wanted 40.

By October 1936, C&R wanted a 40-ft periscope. Kollmorgen was then dominant and K&E had withdrawn entirely, so Kollmorgen's 87KA-40 was adopted. B&L was still interested; C&R was willing to provide its partner, Zeiss, with the specification, but it appears that noth-

ing came of this effort.[42] In the *Sargo* (SS 188) class, 40-ft periscopes were fitted as attack (conning tower) instruments. These submarines retained 34-footers (86KA-34) in their control rooms; however, by February 1939, plans called for 40-footers to replace the shorter instruments. That made the issue of 40-ft periscope design (described below) critical. The *Tambor* (SS 198) class was designed with two 40-ft periscopes (originally 87KA-40s).

Unfortunately, long tubes vibrated, sometimes at low speed (3.5 kt for the 34.5-ft conning tower periscopes in the *Porpoises*). C&R provided 2.5-ft longer periscope supports. In 1938, the Submarine Officers Conference suggested streamlined housing sleeves, which had been tried in the big V-boats. This idea was revived postwar. *Gato*-class characteristics (November 1939) called for periscopes usable at the highest speed, not less than 6 kt. The following year, there was an abortive attempt to increase that to 9 kt, but the submarine officers admitted that 6–7 kt would suffice (they wanted to use the search periscope at 8 kt).

By this time, the control room periscope was seen largely as insurance against the loss of the attack periscope. Shorter than the attack instrument, its eyepiece was so much deeper in the submarine that its upper window was only about 3½ ft above the shears of the 40-ft periscope. A submarine using it would have to run so shallow as to be visible from the air. Some submariners argued that the insurance periscope should be moved up to the conning tower, but then the OOD in the control room no longer would have any periscope.

Kollmorgen now revived the narrow-head attack periscope, which it called the needle periscope. In July 1938, it proposed a version of 87KA-40 with a narrow-diameter (1.95-in) head, practically without any change in optical characteristics. C&R decided to buy eight of these. In August, it suggested a 1.26-in (32-mm) head. C&R found the idea so attractive that it suspended purchases of periscopes for the *Tambor* (SS 198) class pending tests.

This time, the main question was whether the narrow head would transmit enough light. Kollmorgen argued that it would even transmit almost as much as the old periscopes of the O-boats and S-boats, which transmitted 22.5 percent at high power and 18 percent at low, yet were satisfactory in service. Compared with the 2.5-in periscopes then in service, the 1.26-in head would cut light transmission at high power from 29 percent to 18.5 percent and at low power from 24 percent to 14.5 percent. Fields of view would be 36/9 degrees, instead of the 32/8 degrees of existing instruments. The prism would be restricted to +30/−10 degrees compared with +45/−10 degrees. Kollmorgen offered to modify an 87KA-40 to transmit less light by replacing its 5-mm exit pupil with a 4-mm pupil. The project was urgent, because *Tambor*-class periscopes had to be ordered. C&R asked Kollmorgen to design the narrow-head section so that it could be replaced by a conventional 1.95-in head should tests be unsuccessful.

The submarine *Stingray* was selected; her 87KA-40 was

modified, and she was tested at the Washington Navy Yard on 3 October 1938. All observers were impressed. Loss of image flatness was no problem, although higher prism elevation was desired. All of them wanted the 1.26-in head. Work now proceeded on two prototypes, financed under the FY 39 budget, Registry number 807 and 808, which were designated Types A and B. Number 808 was designated 88KA-40/1.414, to indicate its head diameter (a second prototype was shipped in October 1939).

Both periscopes were tested in April–May 1939 on board the new submarine *Saury*. Number 807 was usable to about 3.5 kt with 1 ft of periscope exposed or up to about 4 kt with 4 ft exposed. Number 808 was usable to about 7 kt with 1 ft exposed and to above 8 kt with 4 ft exposed.[43] A conventional 87KA-40, number 792, was usable up to about 6 kt with 1 ft exposed and to 8 kt with 4 ft exposed (but usable only to see, and not sufficiently stable for range finding). The conclusion was that the needle-head was best for vibration and admitted adequate light. The trials board recommended that it be adopted for both periscope positions.

The needle periscope became Type 1 (89KA-40/1.414). Like the earlier instruments, its line of sight elevated to +45 degrees and depressed to −10 degrees. The first production instrument was shipped on 7 June 1940.[44] By this time, aircraft were a major threat, and the WW I call for a periscope capable of looking straight up was revived. Kollmorgen proposed a modified Type 1, which was designated Type 2 (89KA-40/1.414HA). The Type 3 designation was reserved for the earlier large-head periscope, 89KA-40/1.99 (the initial production version was 91 KA-40/1.99). All three incorporated the usual stadimeters.

Type 2 could elevate its line of sight to 74.5 degrees, so at low power (32-degree field of view) it could cover the entire sky (the upper edge of the field of view was at 90.5-degree elevation).[45] Kollmorgen shipped the prototype for tests in October 1940. Initial teething problems, with insufficient light transmission and with prism movement, were resolved in time for these instruments to equip FY 42 submarines.

Gatos and their successors generally had two periscopes; both let into the conning tower: a Type 2 and a Type 3 search periscope. The first Type 3s were shipped in December 1940. Later versions had smaller heads (92KA-40T/1.9 and the short Type 3A, 92KA-30/1.9).

During WW II, a night periscope, Type 4 (93KN-36; 4A was 94KN-36; 4B was 95KN-36), replaced Type 3. It had a much fatter head (to gather more light: 3.75-in diameter) and was shorter than the other instruments (to lose less light in its tube). Like the earlier periscopes, it elevated between −10 degees and +45 degrees. Type 4 incorporated an ST range-only radar for night attacks. The first production Type 4, Registry number 1456, was shipped 9 July 1944. From then on, this type superseded Types 2 and 3 in production, the final total being 243 such periscopes.

Very large numbers of periscopes were required in wartime. The first production Type 1 was Registry number 817. The last Type 4 was Registry number 1698, a Type 4A that shipped on 4 April 1946. (The next periscope, a Type 5, was not shipped until 26 Janaury 1951.) Wartime submarine cancellations eliminated numbers 1249–1281 and 1430–1455. Kollmorgen was the only producer. BuShips did seek a second source, however, and ordered (but canceled) a pilot run of 10 periscopes (Registry numbers 1282–1291), probably from Bausch & Lomb.[46]

Appendix C

U.S. Submarines Through 1945

FOR NAMED SUBMARINES later assigned numbers, the original name is listed in the right-hand column (Fate). SS 2–35 were all renamed 17 November 1911 (some had not yet been launched).

Building yards: The yard is listed on the second line of each entry. Refer to the following key.

BNY   Boston Navy Yard
CAL   California Shipbuilding Corp., Los Angeles, California
CR   William Cramp & Sons, later revived as Cramp Shipbuilding Co., Philadelphia, Pennsylvania
CRA   Craig Shipbuilding of Long Beach, California
CRE   Crescent Shipyard, Elizabethport, New Jersey (Lewis Nixon)
EB   Electric Boat (General Dynamics) (NOTE: H-boats listed as EB-built were built in sections, probably mainly at Newark, for Russia and assembled at Puget Sound Navy Yard)
FR   Fore River Shipbuilding Co., Quincy, Massachusetts (later Bethlehem Steel, Quincy, later General Dynamics, Quincy)
LTB   Lake Torpedo Boat Corp.
MA   Manitowoc Shipbuilding Co., Manitowoc, Wisconsin
MINY   Mare Island Navy Yard
MO   Moran Bros., Seattle, Washington
NN   Newport News Shipbuilding & Drydock Co., Newport News, Virginia
NY   New York Shipbuilding Corp., Camden, New Jersey
PNY   Portsmouth Navy Yard
PSNY   Puget Sound Navy Yard
UIW   Union Iron Works (later Bethlehem Steel, San Francisco)

Abbreviations used in column heads: LD, date laid down (appears on first line of each entry); Lch, date of launch (appears on second line of entry; Comm, date of first commissioning on first line with subsequent dates of recommissioning listed below in same column; Decomm, dates of decommissionings, in same order as commissionings.

Fate: This column includes reclassifications and conversions. Refer to the following key:

AGSS   Auxiliary submarine (e.g., test or at-sea ASW training)
AOSS   Oiler submarine
APSS   Transport submarine (designation replaced by LPSS)
ASSA   Cargo transport submarine (replaced SSA)
ASSP   Transport submarine (designation replaced by APSS)
BU   Broken up
Cpl   Completed
Del   Delivered incomplete
FS   Fleet Snorkel
G   Guppy (with numeral to indicate type)
ICIR   In commission in reserve (reduced status with crew, pre–WW II)
ISIR   In service in reserve (pierside trainer)
IXSS   Miscellaneous submarine designation
L   Loss
LPSS   Transport submarine (formerly APSS)
PT   Pierside trainer (with dates)
Ret   Returned; in some cases a boat was returned to U.S. custody and then sold back to a foreign nation for scrapping
S(C)   Sunk in collision
SS   Submarine (reversion to status)
SSA   Cargo submarine (replaced by ASSA)
SSAG   Auxiliary (AGSS retaining combat capability)
SSG   Missile submarine
SSK   ASW submarine
SSO   Oiler submarine
SSP   Transport submarine (designation replaced by ASSP)
SSR   Radar picket submarine
S(T)   Sunk as target
Str   Strike date
WL   War loss
WL(C)   Constructive war loss; damaged beyond repair

In constructing this list, the author has drawn upon Appendix 8 of J. D. Alden, *The Fleet Submarine in the U.S. Navy* (Annapolis, Md., Naval Institute Press, 1979); also, Jim Christley's unpublished list of U.S. submarines and their fates, as well as the ship biographies in the *Dictionary of American Naval Fighting Ships*, 8 vols. (Washington, D.C.: Naval Historical Center, 1959–81).

No.	Name/Yard	LD/Lch	Comm	Decomm	Fate
1	Holland CRE	17 May 97	12 Oct 00		Str 21 Nov 10, sold Nov. 10, reacquired, sold 18 Jun 13; on display in a park, Paterson, N.J., until sold for scrap, 1932
2	A-1 CRE	21 May 01 / 22 Jul 01	19 Sep 03 / 23 Feb 07	3 Nov 05	*Plunger*; Str 24 Feb 13, sold 26 Jan 22; was target
3	A-2 CRE	3 Oct 00 / 22 Jul 01	12 Jan 03 / 10 Feb 10	26 Jul 09 / 12 Dec 19	*Adder*; Str 16 Jan 22, S(T); modernized Norfolk Navy Yard 1907–9 [towed to Norfolk Dec 1903 (in Reserve Torpedo Fleet Jan 1904)]. Phillipines 1909–22
4	A-3 UIW	10 Oct 00 / 31 Jul 01	28 May 03 / 13 Jun 08 / 17 Apr 15	28 Nov 06 / 28 Jun 12 / 25 Jul 21	*Grampus*; Str 16 Jan 22, S(T); modernized MINY 1906–8. Phillipines 1915–22
5	A-4 CRE	8 Nov 00 / 20 Aug 01	17 Jan 03 / 10 Feb 10	26 Jul 09 / 12 Dec 19	*Moccasin*; Str 16 Jan 22, S(T); modernized Norfolk Navy Yard 1907–9 (laid up for repairs after grounding Dec 1903 while under tow to Norfolk; to Reserve Torpedo Fleet 15 Jun 1904). Phillipines 1909–22
6	A-5 UIW	10 Dec 00 / 14 Jan 03	28 May 03 / 8 Jun 08 / 17 Apr 15	28 Nov 06 / 28 Jun 12 / 25 Jul 21	*Pike*; Str 16 Jan 22, S(T); modernized MINY 1906–8; sunk by explosion 15 Apr 1917 (salvaged). Phillipines 1915–22
7	A-6 CRE	13 Dec 00 / 23 Sep 01	19 Sep 03 / 20 Nov 08	06 / 1 Dec 18	*Porpoise*; Str 16 Jan 22, S(T); had been turned over for sale 12 Dec 19, but use as target authorized Jul 21; modernized New York Navy Yard Sep 1904–Feb 1906 after bottoming at 127 ft, 18 Aug 1904 (arrived at Navy Yard 23 Sep 1904). Phillipines 1908–22
8	A-7 CRE	11 Jan 00 / 19 Oct 01	19 Sep 03 / 14 Aug 08	21 Apr 08 / 12 Dec 18	*Shark*; Str 16 Jan 22, S(T); had suffered gasoline explosion 24 Jul 17, in ordinary 1 Apr 18; modernized New York Navy Yard 1904–6. Phillipines 1908–22
9	C-1 FR	3 Aug 05 / 4 Oct 06	30 Jun 08 / 15 Apr 10	14 Feb 10 / 4 Aug 19	*Octopus*; sale list 26 Dec 19, sold 13 Apr 20
10	B-1 FR	3 Sep 05 / 30 Mar 07	18 Oct 07 / 15 Apr 10 / 17 Apr 15	30 Nov 09 / 1911 / 1 Dec 21	*Viper*; Str 16 Jan 22, S(T). Phillipines 1915–22
11	B-2 FR	30 Aug 05 / 1 Sep 06	18 Oct 07 / 15 Apr 10 / 2 Aug 13	30 Nov 09 / 4 Dec 12 / 12 Dec 19	*Cuttlefish*; Str 16 Jan 22, S(T). Phillipines 1913–22
12	B-3 FR	5 Sep 05 / 30 Mar 07	3 Dec 07 / 15 Apr 10 / 2 Sep 13	6 Nov 09 / 4 Dec 12 / 25 Jul 21	*Tarantula*; Str 16 Jan 22, S(T). Phillipines 1913–22
13	C-2 FR	4 Mar 08 / 8 Apr 09	23 Nov 09	23 Dec 19	*Stingray*; to sale list 26 Dec 19, sold 13 Apr 20 (laid up 22 Aug 19)
14	C-3 FR	17 Mar 08 / 8 Apr 09	23 Nov 09	23 Dec 19	*Tarpon*; to sale list 26 Dec 19, sold 13 Apr 20 (laid up 22 Aug 19)
15	C-4 FR	17 Mar 08 / 17 Jun 09	23 Nov 09	15 Aug 19	*Bonita*; to sale list 26 Dec 19, sold 13 Apr 20 (laid up 12 Nov 18)
16	C-5 FR	17 Mar 08 / 16 Jun 09	2 Feb 10	23 Dec 19	*Snapper*; to sale list 26 Dec 19, sold 13 Apr 20
17	D-1 FR	16 Apr 08 / 8 Apr 09	23 Nov 09	8 Feb 22	*Narwhal*; for sale 25 Mar 22, sold 5 Jun 22 (ICIR 9 Sep 19, in ordinary 15 Jul 21)
18	D-2 FR	16 Apr 08 / 16 Jun 09	23 Nov 09	18 Jan 22	*Grayling*; for sale 15 Dec 21, sold 5 Jun 22 (ICIR 9 Sep 19, in ordinary 15 Jul 21). Sank at dock 14 Sep 17 (salvaged).
19	D-3 FR	16 Apr 08 / 12 Mar 10	8 Sep 10	20 Mar 22	*Salmon*; for sale 18 Apr 22, sold 31 Jul 22 (ICIR 5 Sep 19, in ordinary 15 Jul 21)
19½	G-1 NN	2 Feb 09 / 8 Feb 11	28 Oct 12	6 Mar 20	*Seal*; S(T) 21 Jun 21 (designated target 19 Feb 20), Str 29 Aug 21
20	F-1 UIW	23 Aug 09 / 12 Mar 12	19 Jun 12		*Carp*, S(C) with F-3, 17 Dec 17
21	F-2 UIW	23 Aug 09 / 19 Mar 12	25 Jun 12	15 Mar 22	*Barracuda*; ordered sold Apr 22, sold 17 Aug 22 (in ordinary 15 Mar 16–13 Jun 17, ICIR 18 Sep 19 as trainer)
22	F-3 MO	17 Aug 09 / 6 Jan 12	5 Aug 12	15 Mar 22	*Pickerel*; ordered sold 22 Apr 22, sold 17 Aug 22 (in ordinary 15 Mar 16–13 Jun 17, training ship 1919–21)
23	F-4 MO	21 Aug 09 / 6 Jan 12	3 May 13		*Skate*; foundered, 25 Mar 15, raised 29 Aug 15, Str 31 Aug 15, buried as fill off Pearl Harbor 1940

No.	Name/Yard	LD/Lch	Comm	Decomm	Fate
24	E-1 FR	22 Dec 09 27 May 11	14 Feb 12	20 Oct 21	*Skipjack;* to sale list 22 Oct 21, sold 19 Apr 22 (ICIR 20 Mar 20; in ordinary 18 Jul 21)
25	E-2 FR	22 Dec 09 15 Jun 11	14 Feb 12 25 Mar 18	13 Mar 16 20 Oct 21	*Sturgeon;* to sale list 22 Oct 21, sold 19 Apr 22; had been decomm after battery explosion 15 Jun 16. In fall 1914 filled with chlorine gas due to saltwater reaching battery; accident led to revised battery linings, etc. in submarines
26	G-4 CR	9 Jul 10 15 Aug 12	22 Jan 14	5 Sep 19	*Thrasher;* finally accepted 7 Mar 16, sold 15 Apr 20; had been designated a depth charge target 6 Dec 19
27	G-2 NN	20 Oct 09 10 Jan 12	6 Feb 15	2 Apr 19	*Tuna;* extensive overhaul by New York Navy Yard and LTB 20 Mar 16–28 Jun 17; foundered awaiting depth charge tests 30 Jul 19, partially raised for scrapping 1962
28	H-1 UIW	22 Mar 11 6 May 13	1 Dec 13		*Seawolf;* grounded Magdalena Bay, Mexico, 12 Mar 20, sank 24 Mar, sold 25 Jun 20
29	H-2 UIW	23 Mar 11 4 Jun 13	1 Dec 13	23 Oct 22	*Nautilus;* Str 18 Dec 30, sold Sep 31
30	H-3 MO	3 Apr 11 3 Jul 13	16 Jan 14	23 Oct 22	*Garfish;* Str 18 Dec 30, sold 14 Sep 31; had survived major grounding 16 Dec 16
31	G-3 LTB	30 Mar 11 27 Dec 13	22 Mar 15	5 May 21	*Turbot;* ordered sold 9 Sep 21, sold 19 Apr 22
32	K-1 FR	20 Feb 12 3 Sep 13	17 Mar 14	7 Mar 23	*Haddock;* Str 18 Dec 30, sold 25 Jun 31
33	K-2 FR	20 Feb 12 4 Oct 13	31 Jan 14	9 Mar 23	*Cachalot;* Str 18 Dec 30, sold 3 Jun 31
34	K-3 UIW	15 Jan 12 14 Mar 14	30 Oct 14	20 Feb 23	*Orca;* Str 18 Dec 30, sold 3 Jun 31
35	K-4 MO	27 Jan 12 19 Mar 14	24 Oct 14	10 May 23	*Walrus;* Str 18 Dec 30, sold 3 Jun 31
36	K-5 FR	10 Jun 12 17 Mar 14	22 Aug 14	20 Feb 23	Str 18 Dec 30, sold 3 Jun 31
37	K-6 FR	19 Jun 12 26 Mar 14	9 Sep 14	21 May 23	Str 18 Dec 30, sold 3 Jun 31
38	K-7 UIW	10 May 12 10 Jun 14	1 Dec 14	12 Feb 23	Str 18 Dec 30, sold 3 Jun 31
39	K-8 UIW	10 May 12 11 Jul 14	1 Dec 14	24 Feb 23	Str 18 Dec 30, sold 25 Jun 31
40	L-1 FR	13 Apr 14 20 Jan 15	11 Apr 16	7 Apr 22	Ordered sold 6 Feb 22, sold 31 Jul 22
41	L-2 FR	19 Mar 14 11 Feb 15	29 Sep 16	4 May 23	Str 18 Dec 30, sold 28 Nov 33
42	L-3 FR	18 Apr 14 15 Mar 15	22 Apr 16	11 Jun 23	Str 18 Dec 30, sold 28 Nov 33 (had been re-engined with Busch-Sulzer diesels from N-4, 1923)
43	L-4 FR	23 Mar 14 3 Apr 15	4 May 16	14 Apr 22	Ordered sold 6 Feb 22, sold 31 Jul 22
44	L-5 LTB	14 May 14 1 May 16	17 Feb 18	5 Dec 22	Str 20 Mar 25, sold 21 Dec 25
45	L-6 CRA	27 May 14 31 Aug 16	7 Dec 17	25 Nov 22	Str 20 Mar 25, sold 21 Dec 25
46	L-7 CRA	2 Jun 14 28 Sep 16	7 Dec 17	15 Nov 22	Str 20 Mar 25, sold 21 Dec 25
47	M-1 FR	2 Jul 14 14 Sep 15	16 Feb 18	15 Mar 22	Ordered sold 5 Apr 22, sold 25 Sep 22
48	L-8 PNY	24 Feb 15 23 Apr 17	30 Aug 17	15 Nov 22	Str 20 Mar 25, sold 21 Dec 25
49	L-9 FR	2 Nov 14 27 Oct 15	4 Aug 16	4 May 23	Str 18 Dec 30, sold 28 Nov 33 (re-engined with Busch-Sulzer diesels from N-7, 1923)

No.	Name/Yard	LD/Lch	Comm	Decomm	Fate
50	L-10 FR	17 Feb 15 16 Mar 16	2 Aug 16	5 May 22	Ordered sold 6 Feb 22, sold 31 Jul 22
51	L-11 FR	17 Feb 15 16 May 16	15 Aug 16	28 Nov 23	Str 18 Dec 30, sold 28 Nov 23 (re-engined with Busch-Sulzer diesels from N-5, 1923)
52	T-1 FR	21 Jun 16 25 Jul 18	30 Jan 20	5 Dec 22	*Schley*; AA-1 24 Aug 17, to T-1 22 Sep 20, Str 19 Sep 30
53	N-1 MO	26 Jul 15 30 Dec 16	26 Sep 17	30 Apr 26	Str 18 Dec 30, sold for BU 1931
54	N-2 MO	29 Jul 15 16 Jan 17	26 Sep 17	30 Apr 26	Str 18 Dec 30, sold for BU 1931
55	N-3 MO	31 Jul 15 21 Feb 17	26 Sep 17	30 Apr 26	Str 18 Dec 30, sold for BU 1931
56	N-4 LTB	24 Mar 15 27 Nov 16	15 Jun 18	22 Apr 22	Ordered sold 5 Apr 22, sold 25 Sep 22
57	N-5 LTB	10 Apr 15 22 Mar 17	13 Jun 18	19 Apr 22	Ordered sold 5 Apr 22, sold 25 Sep 22
58	N-6 LTB	15 Apr 15 21 Apr 17	9 Jul 18	16 Feb 22	Ordered sold 5 Apr 22, sold 25 Sep 22
59	N-7 LTB	20 Apr 15 19 May 17	15 Jun 18	7 Feb 22	Ordered sold 5 Apr 22, sold 25 Sep 22
60	T-2 FR	31 May 17 6 Sep 19	7 Jan 22	16 Jul 23	AA-2; to T-2 22 Sep 20, Str 19 Sep 30
61	T-3 FR	21 May 17 24 May 19	7 Dec 20 1 Oct 25	11 Nov 22 14 Jul 27	AA-3; to T-3 22 Sep 20, Str 19 Sep 30
62	O-1 PNY	26 Mar 17 9 Jul 18	5 Nov 18	11 Jun 31	Experimental vessel 28 Dec 30, Str 18 May 38
63	O-2 PSNY	27 Jul 17 24 May 18	19 Oct 18 3 Feb 41	25 Jun 31 26 Jul 45	Str 13 Aug 45, sold 16 Nov 45
64	O-3 FR	2 Dec 16 29 Sep 17	13 Jun 18 3 Feb 41	6 Jun 31 11 Sep 45	Str 11 Oct 45, sold 4 Sep 46
65	O-4 FR	4 Dec 16 20 Oct 17	28 May 18 29 Jan 41	3 Jun 31 20 Sep 45	Str 11 Oct 45, sold 1 Feb 46
66	O-5 FR	5 Dec 16 11 Nov 17	8 Jun 18		S(C) Panama 28 Oct 23, raised Nov 23, sold for BU 12 Dec 24
67	O-6 FR	6 Dec 16 25 Nov 17	8 Jun 18 4 Feb 41	9 Jun 31 11 Sep 45	Str 11 Oct 45, sold 4 Sep 46
68	O-7 FR	14 Feb 17 16 Dec 17	4 Jul 18 12 Feb 41	1 Jul 31 2 Jul 45	Str 11 Jul 45, sold 22 Jan 46
69	O-8 FR	27 Feb 17 31 Dec 17	11 Jul 18 28 Apr 41	27 May 31 11 Sep 45	Str 11 Oct 45, sold 4 Sep 46
70	O-9 FR	15 Feb 17 27 Jan 18	27 Jul 18 14 Apr 41	25 Jun 31	Foundered off Isle of Shoals, Me., 20 Jun 41
71	O-10 FR	27 Feb 17 21 Feb 18	17 Aug 18 10 Mar 41	25 Jun 31 10 Sep 45	Str 11 Oct 45, sold 21 Aug 46
72	O-11 LTB	6 Mar 16 29 Oct 17	19 Oct 18	21 Jun 24	Str 9 May 30, sold Jul 30
73	O-12 LTB	6 Mar 16 29 Sep 17	19 Oct 18	17 Jun 24	To Shipping Board 29 Jul 30, Str 29 Jul 30 for Wilkes expedition as *Nautilus*, scuttled in Norway 20 Nov 31
74	O-13 LTB	6 Mar 16 27 Dec 17	27 Nov 18	11 Jun 24	Str 9 May 30, sold 30 Jul 30
75	O-14 CAL	6 Jul 16 6 May 18	1 Oct 18	17 Jun 24	Str 9 May 30, sold 30 Jul 30
76	O-15 CAL	21 Sep 16 12 Feb 18	27 Aug 18	11 Jun 24	Str 9 May 30, sold 30 Jul 30
77	O-16 CAL	7 Oct 16 9 Feb 18	1 Aug 18	21 Jun 24	Str 9 May 30, sold 30 Jul 30

No.	Name/Yard	LD/Lch	Comm	Decomm	Fate
78	R-1 FR	16 Oct 17 24 Aug 18	16 Dec 18 23 Sep 40	1 May 31 20 Sep 45	Str 11 Oct 45, sold 13 Mar 46. Connected for special ASW trials, Dec 44–26 Feb 45
79	R-2 FR	16 Oct 17 23 Sep 18	24 Jan 19	10 May 45	Str 2 Jun 45, sold 28 Oct 45
80	R-3 FR	11 Dec 17 18 Jan 19	17 Apr 19 19 Aug 40	10 Aug 34 4 Nov 41	To UK 4 Nov 41 (P-511), beached 12 Nov 47 en route to BU, BU 1948
81	R-4 FR	16 Oct 17 26 Oct 18	28 Mar 19	18 Jun 45	Str 11 Jul 45, sold 22 Jan 46
82	R-5 FR	16 Oct 17 24 Nov 18	15 Apr 19 19 Aug 40	30 Jun 32 14 Sep 45	Str 11 Oct 45, sold 22 Aug 46
83	R-6 FR	17 Dec 17 1 Mar 19	1 May 19 15 Nov 40	4 May 31 27 Sep 45	Str 11 Oct 45, sold 13 Mar 46. Snorkel test ship 45
84	R-7 FR	6 Dec 17 5 Apr 19	12 Jun 19 22 Jul 40	2 May 31 14 Sep 45	Str 11 Oct 45, sold 4 Sep 46
85	R-8 FR	4 Mar 18 17 Apr 19	21 Jul 19	2 May 31	Sank at moorings in Philadelphia reserve fleet 26 Feb 36, raised, Str 12 May 36, S(T) (bombing) 19 Aug 36
86	R-9 FR	6 Mar 18 24 May 19	30 Jul 19 14 Mar 41	2 May 31 25 Sep 45	Str 11 Oct 46, sold Feb 46
87	R-10 FR	21 Mar 18 28 Jun 19	20 Aug 19	18 Jun 45	Str 11 Jul 45, sold 22 Jan 46
88	R-11 FR	18 Mar 18 21 Jul 19	5 Sep 19	5 Sep 45	Str 11 Oct 45, sold 22 Jan 46
89	R-12 FR	28 Mar 18 15 Aug 19	23 Sep 19 1 Jul 40	7 Dec 32	Foundered Key West 12 Jun 43
90	R-13 FR	27 Mar 18 27 Aug 19	17 Oct 19	14 Sep 45	Str 11 Oct 45, sold 13 Mar 46
91	R-14 FR	6 Nov 18 10 Oct 19	24 Dec 19	7 May 45	Str 19 May 45, sold 28 Oct 45
92	R-15 UIW	30 Apr 17 10 Dec 17	27 Jul 18 1 Apr 41	7 May 31 17 Sep 45	Str 11 Oct 45, sold 13 Mar 46
93	R-16 UIW	26 Apr 17 15 Dec 17	5 Aug 18 1 Jul 40	12 May 31 16 Jul 45	Str 25 Jul 45, sold 22 Jan 46
94	R-17 UIW	5 May 17 24 Dec 17	17 Aug 18 25 Mar 41	15 May 31 9 Mar 42	To UK 9 Mar 42 (P-512), Ret 6 Sep 44, served as target, Str 22 Jun 45, sold 16 Nov 45
95	R-18 UIW	16 Jun 17 8 Jan 18	11 Sep 18 8 Jan 41	13 May 31 19 Sep 45	Str 11 Oct 45, sold 4 Sep 46
96	R-19 UIW	23 Jun 17 28 Jan 18	7 Oct 18 6 Jan 41	15 May 31 9 Mar 42	To UK 9 Mar 42 (P-514), S(C) 21 Jun 42
97	R-20 UIW	4 Jun 17 21 Jan 18	26 Oct 18 22 Jan 41	15 May 31 27 Sep 45	Str 11 Oct 45, sold 13 Mar 46
98	R-21 LTB	19 Apr 17 10 Jul 18	17 Jun 19	21 Jun 24	Str 9 May 30, BU 1930
99	R-22 LTB	19 Apr 17 23 Sep 18	1 Aug 19	29 Apr 25	Str 9 May 30, BU 1930
100	R-23 LTB	25 Apr 17 5 Nov 18	23 Oct 19	24 Apr 25	Str 9 May 30, BU 1930
101	R-24 LTB	9 May 17 21 Aug 18	21 Aug 18	11 Jun 25	Str 9 May 30, BU 1930
102	R-25 LTB	26 Apr 17 15 May 19	23 Oct 19	21 Jun 24	Str 9 May 30, BU 1930
103	R-26 LTB	26 Apr 17 18 Jun 19	23 Oct 19	12 Jun 25	Str 9 May 30, BU 1930
104	R-27 LTB	16 May 17 23 Sep 18	3 Sep 19	24 Apr 25	Str 9 May 30, BU 1930

No.	Name/Yard	LD/Lch	Comm	Decomm	Fate
105	S-1 FR	11 Dec 17 26 Oct 18	5 Jun 20 16 Oct 40	20 Oct 37 20 Apr 42	To UK 20 Apr 42 (P-552), sold 14 Sep 45
106	S-2 LTB	30 Jul 17 15 Feb 19	25 May 20	25 Nov 29	ICIR 1924–28; Str 26 Feb 31, sold 14 Sep 31
107	S-3 PNY	29 Aug 17 21 Dec 18	30 Jan 19	24 Mar 31	Str 25 Jan 37, BU
108	Assigned to abortive Neff submarine				
109	S-4 PNY	4 Dec 17 27 Aug 19	19 Nov 19 19 Mar 28	16 Oct 28	S(C) 17 Dec 27, raised 17 Mar 28, Str 15 Jan 36, scuttled 15 May 36
110	S-5 PNY	5 Dec 17 10 Nov 19	6 Mar 20	7 Apr 33	Foundered 1 Sep 20
111	S-6 PNY	29 Jan 18 23 Dec 19	17 May 20	10 Apr 31	Str 25 Jan 37, BU
112	S-7 PNY	29 Jan 18 5 Feb 20	1 Jul 20	3 Apr 31	Str 25 Jan 37, BU
113	S-8 PNY	9 Nov 18 21 Apr 20	1 Oct 20	11 Apr 31	Str 25 Jan 37, BU
114	S-9 PNY	20 Jan 19 17 Jun 20	21 Feb 21	15 Apr 31	Str 21 Jul 36, BU
115	S-10 PNY	11 Sep 19 9 Dec 20	21 Sep 22	17 Jul 36	Str 21 Jul 36, BU 1936
116	S-11 PNY	2 Dec 19 7 Feb 21	11 Jan 23 6 Sep 40	30 Sep 36 2 May 45	Str 19 May 45, sold 28 Oct 45
117	S-12 PNY	8 Jan 20 4 Aug 21	30 Apr 23 4 Nov 40	30 Sep 36 18 May 45	Str 22 Jun 45, sold 28 Oct 45
118	S-13 PNY	14 Feb 20 20 Oct 21	14 Jul 23 28 Oct 40	30 Sep 36 10 Apr 45	Str 19 May 45, sold 28 Oct 45
119	S-14 LTB	7 Dec 17 22 Oct 19	11 Feb 21 10 Dec 40	22 May 35 18 May 45	Str 22 Jun 45, sold 16 Nov 45
120	S-15 LTB	13 Dec 17 8 Mar 20	15 Jan 21 3 Jan 41	26 Apr 35 11 Jun 46	Str 3 Jul 46, sold 4 Dec 46
121	S-16 LTB	19 Mar 18 23 Dec 19	17 Dec 20 2 Dec 40	22 May 35 4 Oct 44	Str 13 Nov 44, S(T) 3 Apr 45
122	S-17 LTB	19 Mar 18 22 May 20	1 Mar 21 16 Dec 40	29 Mar 35 4 Oct 44	Str 13 Nov 44, S(T) 3 Apr 45
123	S-18 FR	15 Aug 18 29 Apr 20	3 Apr 24	29 Oct 45	Str 13 Nov 45, sold 9 Nov 46
124	S-19 FR	15 Aug 18 21 Jun 20	24 Aug 21	10 Feb 34	Str 12 Dec 36, S(T) 18 Dec 38
125	S-20 FR	15 Aug 18 9 Jun 20	22 Nov 22	16 Jul 45	Str 25 Jul 45, sold 22 Jan 46; was rebuilt PNY 1924
126	S-21 FR	19 Dec 18 18 Aug 20	24 Aug 21	14 Sep 45	ICIR 32–34, to UK 14 Sep 42 (P-553), Ret 11 Jul 44, sunk as sonar target 23 Mar 45
127	S-22 FR	6 Jan 19 15 Jul 20	23 Jun 24	19 Jun 42	To UK 19 Jun 42 (P-554), Ret 11 Jul 44, sonar target at New London and Minas Basin, N.S., Str Aug 45
128	S-23 FR	18 Jan 19 27 Oct 20	30 Oct 23	2 Nov 45	Str 16 Nov 45, sold 9 Nov 46
129	S-24 FR	1 Nov 18 27 Jun 22	24 Aug 23	10 Aug 45	To UK 10 Aug 42 (P-555), Ret at end of war, scuttled 25 Aug 47
130	S-25 FR	26 Oct 18 29 May 22	9 Jul 23	4 Nov 41	To UK 4 Nov 41 (P-551), then to Poland (*Jastrzab*), WL 2 May 42
131	S-26 FR	7 Nov 18 22 Aug 22	15 Oct 23		S(C) 24 Jan 42
132	S-27 FR	11 Apr 19 18 Oct 22	22 Jan 24		Grounded in Aleutians 19 Jun 42
133	S-28 FR	16 Apr 19 20 Sep 22	13 Dec 23		Foundered Hawaii 4 Jul 44

No.	Name/Yard	LD/Lch	Comm	Decomm	Fate
134	S-29 FR	17 Apr 19 9 Nov 22	22 May 24	5 Jun 42	To UK 5 Jun 42 (P-556), Ret 26 Jan 46, Str 1946; sold 24 Jan 47 but ran aground off Portsmouth, UK; hull still intact 1976, cut up and barged to Spain for BU 1986–87
135	S-30 UIW	1 Apr 18 21 Nov 18	29 Oct 20	9 Oct 45	Str 24 Oct 45, sold 5 Dec 46. Built at expense of Phillipine govt
136	S-31 UIW	13 Apr 18 28 Dec 18	11 May 22 18 Sep 40	7 Dec 37 19 Oct 45	Str 1 Nov 45, sold 6 Dec 46
137	S-32 UIW	12 Apr 18 11 Jan 19	15 Jun 22 18 Sep 40	7 Dec 37 19 Oct 45	Str 1 Nov 45, sold 19 Apr 46
138	S-33 UIW	14 Jun 18 5 Dec 18	18 Apr 22 16 Oct 40	1 Dec 37 23 Oct 45	Str 1 Nov 45, sold 5 Dec 46
139	S-34 UIW	28 May 18 13 Feb 19	12 Jul 22	23 Oct 45	Str 1 Nov 45, sold 23 Nov 46
140	S-35 UIW	14 Jun 18 27 Feb 19	17 Aug 22	19 Mar 45	Str 21 Feb 46, S(T) 4 Apr 46. After decomm, damage control hulk for new Fleet Damage Control School
141	S-36 UIW	10 Dec 18 3 Jun 19	4 Apr 23		Grounded in Makassar Strait, scuttled, 21 Jan 42
142	S-37 UIW	12 Dec 18 20 Jun 19	16 Jul 23	6 Feb 45	Str 20 Feb 45, S(T) 4 Apr 46
143	S-38 UIW	15 Jan 19 17 Jun 19	11 May 23	14 Dec 44	Str 20 Jan 45, S(T) 20 Feb 45
144	S-39 UIW	14 Jan 19 2 Jul 19	14 Sep 23		Grounded Rossel Is., 14 Aug 42
145	S-40 UIW	5 Mar 19 5 Jan 21	20 Nov 23	29 Oct 45	Str 13 Nov 45, sold 19 Nov 46
146	S-41 UIW	17 Apr 19 21 Feb 21	15 Jan 24	13 Feb 45	Str 25 Feb 46, sold 15 Nov 46
147	H-4 EB	12 May 18 9 Oct 18	24 Oct 18	25 Oct 22	Str 26 Feb 31, sold 14 Sep 31, used as oil barge, then area around her filled in (end of Sheldon St., Bremerton, Wash.)
148	H-5 EB	12 May 18 24 Sep 18	30 Sep 18	20 Oct 22	Str 26 Feb 31, sold 28 Nov 33
149	H-6	14 May 18 26 Aug 18	9 Sep 18	23 Oct 22	Str 26 Feb 31, sold 28 Nov 33
150	H-7	15 May 18 17 Oct 18	24 Oct 18	23 Oct 22	Str 26 Feb 31, sold 28 Nov 33
151	H-8	25 May 18 14 Nov 18	18 Nov 18	17 Nov 22	Str 26 Feb 31, sold 28 Nov 33
152	H-9 EB	1 Jun 18 23 Nov 18	25 Nov 18	3 Nov 22	Str 26 Feb 31, sold 28 Nov 33
153	S-42 FR	16 Dec 20 30 Apr 23	20 Nov 24	25 Oct 45	Str 13 Nov 45, sold 7 Dec 46
154	S-43 FR	13 Dec 20 31 Mar 23	31 Dec 24	10 Oct 45	Str 13 Nov 45, sold 7 Dec 46
155	S-44 FR	19 Feb 21 27 Oct 23	16 Feb 25		WL 7 Oct 43
156	S-45 FR	29 Dec 20 26 Jun 23	31 Mar 25	30 Oct 45	Str 13 Nov 45, sold 6 Dec 46
157	S-46 FR	23 Feb 21 11 Sep 23	5 Jun 25	2 Nov 45	Str 16 Nov 45, sold 19 Nov 46
158	S-47 FR	26 Feb 21 5 Jan 24	16 Sep 25	25 Oct 45	Str 13 Nov 45, sold 22 Nov 46
159	S-48 LTB	22 Oct 20 26 Feb 21	14 Oct 22 8 Dec 28 10 Dec 40	7 Jul 25 16 Sep 35 29 Aug 45	Str 17 Sep 45, sold 23 Jan 46, rebuilt PNY Feb 27–Dec 28
160	S-49 LTB	22 Oct 20 23 Apr 21	5 Jun 22	2 Aug 27	Str 21 Mar 31, sold 25 May 31, battery explosion 20 Apr 26; later reacquired for Naval Mine Warfare Proving Ground, Solomons, Md.

No.	Name/Yard	LD/Lch	Comm	Decomm	Fate
161	S-50 LTB	15 Mar 20 18 Jun 21	20 May 22	20 Aug 27	Str 21 Mar 31, BU 31, battery explosion 6 Feb 24
162	S-51 LTB	22 Dec 19 20 Aug 21	24 Jun 22		S(C) 25 Sep 25, raised 5 Jun 26, Str 27 Jan 30, sold 23 Jun 30
163	Barracuda PNY	20 Oct 21 17 Jul 24	1 Oct 24 5 Sep 40	14 May 37 3 Mar 45	V-1; cargo sub Mar 43, Str 10 Mar 45; sold for BU 16 Nov 45
164	Bass PNY	20 Oct 21 27 Dec 24	26 Sep 25 5 Sep 40	9 Jun 37 3 Mar 45	V-2; cargo sub 1943, Str 10 Mar 45; scuttled as sonar target 12 Mar 45
165	Bonita PNY	16 Nov 21 9 Jun 25	22 May 26 5 Sep 40	4 Jun 37 3 Mar 45	V-3; cargo sub Apr 43, Str 10 Mar 45; sold for BU 4 Oct 45
166	Argonaut PNY	1 May 25 10 Nov 27	2 Apr 28		V-4; WL 10 Jan 43
167	Narwhal PNY	10 May 27 17 Dec 28	15 May 30	23 Apr 45	V-5; transport 1942–45, Str 19 May 45; sold for BU 16 Nov 1945
168	Nautilus MINY	2 Aug 27 15 Mar 30	1 Jul 30	30 Jun 45	V-6; transport 1942–45, Str 25 Jul 45, sold for BU 16 Nov 45
169	Dolphin PNY	14 Jun 30 8 Mar 32	1 Jun 32	2 Oct 45	V-7; Str 24 Oct 45, sold for BU 26 Aug 46
170	Cachalot PNY	21 Oct 31 19 Oct 33	1 Dec 33	17 Oct 45	V-8; Str 8 Jul 46 (Str 1 Nov 45, reinstated 28 Nov), sold for BU 26 Jan 47
171	Cuttlefish EB	7 Oct 31 21 Nov 33	8 Jun 34	24 Oct 45	V-9; Str 3 Jul 46, sold for BU 12 Feb 47
172	Porpoise PNY	27 Oct 33 20 Jun 35	15 Aug 35 8 May 47 (ISIR)	15 Nov 45 Feb 56	PT Houston 1947–56, Str 13 Aug 56, sold for BU 14 May 57
173	Pike PNY	20 Dec 33 12 Sep 35	2 Dec 35 31 Jul 47 (ISIR)	15 Nov 45 17 Feb 56	PT Baltimore 1947–56, Str 17 Feb 56, sold for BU 14 Jan 57
174	Shark EB	24 Oct 33 21 May 35	25 Jan 36		WL 11 Feb 42
175	Tarpon EB	22 Dec 33 4 Sep 35	12 Mar 36 17 Apr 47 (ISIR)	15 Nov 45 5 Sep 56	PT New Orleans 1947–56, Str 5 Sep 56; sold for BU 8 Jun 57, foundered 26 Aug 57
176	Perch EB	25 Feb 35 9 May 36	19 Nov 36		WL 3 Mar 42
177	Pickerel EB	25 Mar 35 7 Jul 36	26 Jan 37		WL 3 Apr 43
178	Permit EB	6 Jun 35 5 Oct 36	17 Mar 37 24 Jan 47 (ISIR)	15 Nov 45 1956	PT Philadelphia 1947–56, Str 26 Jul 56, sold for BU 28 Jun 58
179	Plunger PNY	17 Jul 35 8 Jul 36	19 Nov 36 May 46 (ISIR)	15 Nov 45 Feb 54	PT Brooklyn 1946–52, Jacksonville 1952–54; Str 6 Jul 56, sold for BU 22 Apr 57
180	Pollack PNY	1 Oct 35 15 Sep 36	15 Jan 37	21 Sep 45	Str 11 Oct 45, reinstated 28 Nov, Str 29 Oct 46, sold for BU 2 Feb 47
181	Pompano MINY	14 Jan 36 11 Mar 37	12 Jun 37		WL Sep 43
182	Salmon EB	15 Apr 36 12 Jun 37	15 Mar 38	24 Sep 45	Str 11 Oct 45, WL(C), BU 1946
183	Seal EB	25 May 36 25 Aug 37	30 Apr 38 19 Jun 47 (ISIR)	15 Nov 45 1956	PT Boston 1947–56, Str 1 May 56, sold 6 May 57
184	Skipjack EB	22 Jul 36 23 Oct 37	30 Jun 38	28 Aug 46	Bikini target sunk 25 Jul 46, raised 2 Sep 46, S(T) 11 Aug 48
185	Snapper PNY	23 Jul 36 24 Aug 37	15 Dec 37	15 Nov 45	Str 30 Apr 48, sold 18 May 48

No.	Name/Yard	LD/Lch	Comm	Decomm	Fate
186	*Stingray* PNY	1 Oct 36 6 Oct 37	15 Mar 38	17 Oct 45	Str 1 Nov 45, reinstated 28 Nov, Str 3 Jul 46, sold 6 Jan 47
187	*Sturgeon* MINY	27 Oct 36 15 Mar 38	25 Jun 38	15 Nov 45	Str 30 Apr 48, sold 12 Jun 48
188	*Sargo* EB	12 May 37 6 Jun 38	7 Feb 39	22 Jun 46	Str 19 Jul 46, sold 19 May 47
189	*Saury* EB	28 Jun 37 20 Aug 38	3 Apr 39	22 Jun 46	Str 19 Jul 46, sold 19 May 47
190	*Spearfish* EB	9 Sep 37 29 Oct 38	19 Jul 39	22 Jun 46	Str 19 Jul 46, sold 19 May 47
191	*Sculpin* PNY	7 Sep 37 27 Jul 38	16 Jan 39		WL 19 Nov 43
192	*Squalus* PNY	18 Oct 37 14 Sep 38	1 Mar 39 15 May 40	15 Nov 39 27 Oct 45	Sunk on trials 23 May 39, raised 13 Sep 39, renamed *Sailfish* 9 Feb 40, Str 30 Apr 48, sold 18 Jun 48; conning tower is memorial, Portsmouth, N.H.
193	*Swordfish* MINY	27 Oct 37 1 Apr 39	22 Jul 39		WL 12 Jan 45
194	*Seadragon* EB	18 Apr 38 21 Apr 39	23 Oct 39 8 Feb 46	15 Nov 45 29 Oct 46	Str 30 Apr 48, sold 2 Jul 48; had been recommissioned 1946 to assist in inactivation and preservation of submarines, including U-boats, at Hingham, Mass.
195	*Sealion* EB	30 Jun 38 25 May 39	27 Nov 39		WL 25 Dec 41 (scuttled *Cavite*)
196	*Searaven* PNY	9 Aug 38 21 Jun 39	2 Oct 39	11 Dec 46	Bikini target Jul 46, S(T) 11 Sep 48
197	*Seawolf* PNY	27 Sep 38 15 Aug 39	1 Dec 39		WL 3 Oct 44
198	*Tambor* EB	16 Jan 39 20 Dec 39	3 Jun 40 2 Apr 47 (ISIR)	10 Dec 45 1 Sep 59	PT Detroit 1947–59, Str 1 Sep 59; sold 5 Dec 59
199	*Tautog* EB	1 Mar 39 27 Jan 40	3 Jul 40 Apr 47 (ISIR)	8 Dec 45 1 Sep 59	PT Milwaukee 1947–59, Str 1 Sep 59, sold 1 Jul 60
200	*Thresher* EB	27 Apr 39 27 Mar 40	27 Aug 40 6 Feb 46	13 Dec 45 12 Jul 46	Str 23 Dec 47, sold 18 Mar 48
201	*Triton* PNY	5 Jul 39 25 Mar 40	15 Aug 40		WL 15 Mar 43
202	*Trout* PNY	8 Aug 39 21 May 40	15 Nov 40		WL 29 Feb 44
203	*Tuna* MINY	19 Jul 39 2 Oct 40	2 Jan 41	11 Dec 46	Bikini target Jul 46, S(T) 24 Sep 48
204	*Mackerel* EB	6 Oct 39 28 Sep 40	31 Mar 41	9 Nov 45	Str 28 Nov 45, sold 24 Apr 47
205	*Marlin* PNY	23 May 40 29 Jan 41	1 Aug 41	9 Nov 45	Str 28 Nov 45, sold 29 Mar 46
206	*Gar* EB	27 Dec 39 7 Nov 40	14 Apr 41 Apr 47 (ISIR)	11 Dec 45 1 Aug 59	PT Cleveland 1947–59, Str 1 Aug 59, sold 11 Dec 59
207	*Grampus* EB	14 Feb 40 23 Dec 40	23 May 41		WL 5–6 Mar 43
208	*Grayback* EB	3 Apr 40 31 Jan 41	30 Jun 41		WL 26 Feb 44
209	*Grayling* PNY	15 Dec 39 29 Nov 40	1 Mar 41		WL 9–12 Sep 43
210	*Grenadier* PNY	2 Apr 40 29 Nov 40	1 May 41		WL 22 Apr 43

No.	Name/Yard	LD/Lch	Comm	Decomm	Fate
211	*Gudgeon* MINY	22 Nov 39 25 Jan 41	21 Apr 41		WL 12 May 44
212	*Gato* EB	5 Oct 40 21 Aug 41	31 Dec 41 1952 (ISIR)	16 Mar 46 1 Mar 60	PT 1952–56 Brooklyn, 1956–60 Baltimore, Str 1 Mar 60
213	*Greenling* EB	12 Nov 40 20 Sep 41	21 Jan 42 Dec 46 (ISIR)	16 Oct 46 1 Mar 60	PT 1946–60 Portsmouth, Str 1 Mar 60
214	*Grouper* EB	28 Dec 40 27 Oct 41	12 Feb 42	2 Dec 68	SSK Jan 51, AGSS 21 Jun 58, Str 2 Dec 68
215	*Growler* EB	10 Feb 41 22 Nov 41	20 Mar 42		WL 8 Nov 44
216	*Grunion* EB	1 Mar 41	11 Apr 42		WL 1 Aug 42
217	*Guardfish* EB	1 Apr 41 20 Jan 42	8 May 42 18 Jun 48 (ISIR)	25 May 46 1 Jun 60	PT 1948–60 New London, Str 1 Jun 60, S(T) 1 Oct 61
218	*Albacore* EB	21 Apr 41 17 Feb 42	1 Jun 42		WL 7 Nov 44
219	*Amberjack* EB	15 May 41	19 Jun 42		WL 16 Feb 43
220	*Barb* EB	7 Jun 41 2 Apr 42	8 Jul 42 3 Dec 51 3 Aug 54	12 Feb 47 5 Feb 54 13 Dec 54	G IB 1954 for Italy (*Enrico Tazzoli*), Ret, sold 15 Oct 72
221	*Blackfish* EB	1 Jul 41 18 Apr 42	22 Jul 42 5 May 49 (ISIR)	11 May 46 19 May 54	PT 1949–54, Str 1 Sep 58
222	*Bluefish* EB	5 Jun 42 21 Feb 53	24 May 43 7 Jan 52	12 Feb 47 20 Nov 53	Str 1 Sep 58
223	*Bonefish* EB	25 Jun 42 7 Mar 43	31 May 43		WL 18 Jun 45
224	*Cod* EB	21 Jul 42 21 Mar 43	21 Jun 43 1 May 60	22 Jun 46 15 Dec 71	PT 1960–71 Cleveland, AGSS 1 Dec 62, IXSS 30 Jun 71, Str 15 Dec 71, memorial Cleveland, Ohio
225	*Cero* EB	24 Aug 42 4 Apr 43	4 Jul 43 4 Feb 52 12 Sep 59 (ISIR)	8 Jun 46 23 Dec 53 30 Jun 67	PT 1959–67 Detroit, Str 30 Jun 67
226	*Corvina* EB	21 Sep 42 9 May 43	6 Aug 43		WL 16 Nov 43
227	*Darter* EB	20 Oct 42 6 Jun 43	7 Sep 43		WL 24 Oct 44
228	*Drum* PNY	11 Sep 40 12 May 41	1 Nov 41 18 Mar 47 (ISIR)	16 Feb 46 30 Jun 68	PT 1947–68 Washington, AGSS 1 Dec 62, Str 30 Jun 68, memorial at Mobile
229	*Flying Fish* PNY	6 Dec 40 9 Jul 41	10 Dec 41	28 May 54	AGSS 29 Nov 50, sonar tests; Str 1 Aug 58, sold 1 May 59
230	*Finback* PNY	5 Feb 41 25 Aug 41	31 Jan 42	21 Apr 50	Str 1 Sep 58, sold 15 Jul 59
231	*Haddock* PNY	31 Mar 41 20 Oct 41	14 Mar 42 Aug 48 (ISIR) Jun 56 (ISIR)	12 Feb 47 May 52 1960	PT 1948–52 Jacksonville, PT 1956–60 Boston, Str 1 Jun 60, sold 23 Aug 60
232	*Halibut* PNY	16 May 41 3 Dec 41	10 Apr 42	18 Jul 45	WL(C), Str 8 May 46, sold 9 Dec 46
233	*Herring* PNY	14 Jul 41 5 Jan 42	4 May 42		WL 1 Jun 44

No.	Name/Yard	LD/Lch	Comm	Decomm	Fate
234	Kingfish PNY	29 Aug 41 2 Mar 42	20 May 42 6 Oct 47 (ISIR)	9 Mar 46 1 Mar 60	PT 1947–60 Providence, Str 1 Mar 60, sold 6 Oct 60
235	Shad PNY	24 Oct 41 15 Apr 42	12 Jun 42 Oct 47 (ISIR)	1947 1 Apr 60	PT 1948 Beverly, Mass., PT 1948–60 Salem, Str 1 Apr 60, sold 11 Jul 60
236	Silversides MINY	4 Nov 40 26 Aug 41	15 Dec 41 15 Oct 47 (ISIR)	17 Apr 46 30 Jun 69	PT 1947–69 Chicago, AGSS 1 Dec 62, Str 30 Jun 69; memorial Muskegon, Ill.
237	Trigger MINY	1 Feb 41 22 Oct 41	31 Jan 42		WL 28 Mar 45
238	Wahoo MINY	28 Jun 41 14 Feb 42	15 May 42		WL 11 Oct 43
239	Whale MINY	28 Jun 41 14 Mar 42	1 Jun 42 22 Jan 57 (ISIR)	1 Jun 46 60	PT 1957–60 New Orleans, Str 1 Mar 60, sold 14 Oct 60
240	Angler EB	9 Nov 42 4 Jul 43	1 Oct 43 2 Apr 51 10 Sep 53 1 Apr 68 (ISIR)	2 Feb 47 10 Nov 52 1 Apr 68 15 Dec 71	SSK 18 Feb 53, SS 15 Aug 59, AGSS 1 Jul 63, IXSS 30 Jun 71, PT 1968–71 Philadelphia, Str 15 Dec 71, sold 1 Feb 74
241	Bashaw EB	4 Dec 42 25 Jul 43	25 Oct 43 3 Apr 51 28 Mar 53	29 Jun 49 10 May 52 13 Sep 69	SSK 18 Feb 53, SS 15 Aug 59, AGSS 1 Sep 62, Str 13 Sep 69, S(T) 13 Sep 69, sold 1 Jul 72
242	Bluegill EB	7 Dec 42 8 Aug 43	11 Nov 43 3 May 51 2 May 53	1 Mar 46 7 Jul 52 28 Jun 69	SSK 18 Feb 53, SS 15 Aug 59, AGSS 1 Apr 66, Str 28 Jun 69, salvage trainer, scuttled for training off Hawaii 3 Dec 70
243	Bream EB	5 Feb 43 17 Oct 43	24 Jan 44 5 Jun 51 20 Jun 53	31 Jan 46 10 Sep 52 28 Jun 69	SSK 18 Feb 53, SS 15 Aug 59, AGSS 15 Apr 65, Str 28 Jun 69, S(T) 7 Nov 69
244	Cavalla EB	4 Mar 43 14 Nov 43	29 Feb 44 10 Apr 51 15 Jul 53 30 Jun 68 (ISIR)	16 Mar 46 3 Sep 52 3 Jun 68 30 Dec 69	SSK 18 Feb 53, SS 15 Aug 59, AGSS 1 Jul 63, PT 1968–69 Houston, Str 30 Dec 69; memorial Galveston, Tex.
245	Cobia EB	17 Mar 43 28 Nov 43	29 Mar 44 6 Jul 51 12 Sep 59 (ISIR)	22 May 46 19 Mar 54 1 Jul 70	PT 1959–70, AGSS 1 Dec 62, Str 1 Jul 70; memorial Manitowoc, Wis.
246	Croaker EB	1 Apr 43 19 Dec 43	21 Apr 44 7 May 51 11 Dec 53 2 Apr 68 (ISIR)	15 Jun 46 18 Mar 53 2 Apr 68 20 Dec 71	SSK 9 Apr 53, SS 15 Aug 59, AGSS 1 May 67, IXSS 30 Jun 71, PT 1968–71 Portsmouth, Str 20 Dec 71; to Groton, Conn., Jun 76 as memorial, then to Buffalo, N.Y.
247	Dace EB	22 Jul 42 25 Apr 43	23 Jul 43 8 Aug 51 22 Oct 54	12 Feb 47 15 Jan 54 31 Jan 55	G IB 1955 for Italy (Leonardo da Vinci), Ret, sold 15 Oct 72
248	Dorado EB	27 Aug 42 23 May 43	28 Aug 43		WL 12 Oct 43 (probably by U.S. aircraft)
249	Flasher EB	30 Sep 42 20 Jun 43	25 Sep 43	16 Mar 46	Str 1 Jun 59, sold 8 Jun 63; conning tower is memorial at Groton, Conn.
250	Flier EB	30 Oct 42 11 Jun 43	18 Oct 43		WL 13 Aug 44
251	Flounder EB	5 Dec 42 22 Aug 43	29 Nov 43	12 Feb 47	Str 1 Jun 59, sold 2 Feb 60
252	Gabilan EB	5 Jan 43 19 Sep 43	28 Dec 43	23 Feb 46	Str 1 Jun 59, sold 11 Jan 60

No.	Name/Yard	LD/Lch	Comm	Decomm	Fate
253	*Gunnel* EB	21 Jul 41 17 May 42	20 Aug 42	18 May 46	Str 1 Sep 58, sold Dec 59
254	*Gurnard* EB	2 Sep 41 1 Jun 42	18 Sep 42 Apr 49 (ISIR)	27 Nov 45 Jun 60	PT 1949–53 Pearl Harbor, 1953–60 Tacoma; Str 1 May 61, sold 29 Oct 61
255	*Haddo* EB	1 Oct 41 21 Jun 42	9 Oct 42	16 Feb 46	Str 1 Aug 58, sold 4 May 59
256	*Hake* EB	1 Nov 41 17 Jul 42	30 Oct 42 15 Oct 56 (ISIR)	13 Jul 46 19 Apr 68	PT 1956–68 Philadelphia, AGSS 1 Dec 62, Str 19 Apr 68, salvage training hulk 1968–72, sold 5 Dec 72
257	*Harder* EB	1 Dec 41 19 Aug 42	2 Dec 42		WL 24 Aug 44
258	*Hoe* EB	2 Jan 42 17 Sep 42	16 Dec 42 Sep 56 (ISIR)	7 Aug 46 15 Apr 60	PT 1956–60 Brooklyn, Str 1 May 60, sold 10 Sep 60
259	*Jack* EB	2 Feb 42 16 Oct 42	6 Jan 43 20 Dec 57	8 Jun 46 21 Apr 58	FS 58 for Greece (*Amphitriti*), Ret, S(T) 1 Sep 68
260	*Lapon* EB	21 Feb 42 27 Oct 42	23 Jan 43 13 Apr 57	25 Jul 46 10 Aug 57	FS 57 for Greece (*Poseidon*), Ret, S(T) 73
261	*Mingo*	21 Mar 42 30 Nov 42	12 Feb 43 20 May 55	Jan 47 15 Aug 55	To Japan unmodified 15 Aug 55 (*Kuroshio*), Ret to U.S. control 31 Mar 66, sold to Japan 20 Feb 71
262	*Muskellunge* EB	7 Apr 42 13 Dec 42	15 Mar 43 31 Aug 56	29 Jan 47 18 Jan 57	To Brazil unmodified 18 Jan 57 (*Humaita*), Ret Mar 68, S(T) 9 Jul 68
263	*Paddle* EB	1 May 42 30 Dec 42	29 Mar 43 31 Aug 56	1 Feb 46 18 Jan 57	To Brazil unmodified 18 Jan 57 (*Riachuelo*), sunk about 30 Jun 68
264	*Pargo* EB	21 May 42 24 Jan 43	26 Apr 43 12 Jun 46 (ISIR)	12 Jun 46 1 Dec 60	PT 1946–60 Portland, Str 1 Dec 60, sold 16 May 61
265	*Peto* MA	15 Jun 41 30 Apr 42	21 Nov 42 Jan 43 Nov 56 (ISIR)	25 Dec 42 25 Jun 46 1 Aug 60	PT 1956–60 Houston, Str 1 Aug 60 (decomm for barge trip down Mississippi; only she and *Pogy* (266) were decomm this way in wartime), sold 29 Nov 60
266	*Pogy* MA	15 Sep 41 23 Jun 42	10 Jan 43 12 Feb 43	1 Feb 43 20 Jul 46	Str 1 Sep 58, sold 1 May 59
267	*Pompon* MA	26 Nov 41 15 Aug 42	17 Mar 43 15 Jun 53	11 May 46 1 Apr 60	SSR 11 Dec 51, Str 1 Apr 60, sold 22 Dec 60
268	*Puffer* MA	16 Feb 42 22 Nov 42	27 Apr 43 1946 (ISIR)	28 Jun 46 10 Jun 60	PT 1946–60 Seattle, Str 1 Jul 60, sold 3 Dec 60
269	*Rasher* MA	4 May 42 20 Dec 42	8 Jun 43 14 Dec 51 22 Jul 53	22 Jun 46 28 May 52 27 May 67	SSR 11 Dec 51, AGSS 1 Jul 60, IXSS 30 Jun 71, PT 1967–71 Portland, Str 20 Dec 71, sold 7 Aug 74
270	*Raton* MA	29 May 42 24 Jan 43	13 Jul 43 21 Sep 53	11 Mar 49 28 Jun 69	SSR 18 Jul 52, AGSS 1 Jul 60, Str 28 Jun 69, sold 12 Oct 73, but reported used as target
271	*Ray* MA	20 Jul 42 28 Feb 43	27 Jul 43 13 Aug 52	12 Feb 47 30 Sep 58	SSR 2 Jan 51, Str 1 Apr 60, sold 18 Dec 60
272	*Redfin* MA	3 Sep 42 4 Apr 43	31 Aug 43 9 Jan 53	1 Nov 46 15 May 67	SSR 2 Jan 51, SS 15 Aug 59, AGSS 28 Jun 63, PT 1967–70 Baltimore, Str 1 Jul 70, sold 31 Mar 71
273	*Robalo* MA	24 Oct 42 9 May 43	28 Sep 43		WL 26 Jul 44
274	*Rock* MA	23 Dec 42 20 Jun 43	26 Oct 43 12 Oct 53	1 May 46 13 Sep 69	SSR 18 Jul 52, AGSS 31 Dec 59, Str 13 Sep 69, sold 17 Aug 72, but reported used as target
275	*Runner* PNY	8 Dec 41 30 May 42	30 Jul 42		WL 1 Jul 43
276	*Sawfish* PNY	20 Jan 42 23 Jun 42	26 Aug 42 15 May 47 (ISIR)	20 Jun 46 1 Apr 60	PT 1947–60 San Pegro, Str 1 Apr 60, sold 2 Dec 60

No.	Name/Yard	LD/Lch	Comm	Decomm	Fate
277	*Scamp* PNY	6 Mar 42 20 Jul 42	18 Sep 42		WL 16 Nov 44
278	*Scorpion* PNY	20 Mar 42 20 Jul 42	1 Oct 42		WL 1 Feb 44
279	*Snook* PNY	17 Apr 42	24 Oct 42		WL 8 Apr 45
280	*Steelhead* PNY	1 Jun 42 11 Sep 42	7 Dec 42 12 Nov 47 (ISIR)	29 Jun 46 1 Apr 60	PT 1947–60 San Diego, Str 1 Apr 60, sold 21 Dec 60
281	*Sunfish* MINY	25 Sep 41 2 May 42	15 Jul 42 Apr 49 (ISIR)	26 Dec 45 1 May 60	PT 1949–60, Vallejo, Str 1 May 60, sold 15 Dec 60
282	*Tunny* MINY	10 Nov 41 30 Jun 42	1 Sep 42 25 Feb 52 6 Mar 53	12 Feb 46 30 Apr 52 28 Jun 69	SSG 18 Jul 52, SS 15 May 65, APSS 1 Oct 66, LPSS 1 Jan 69, Str 30 Jun 69, S(T) 19 Jun 70
283	*Tinosa* MINY	21 Feb 42 7 Oct 42	15 Jan 43 4 Jan 52	23 Jun 49 2 Dec 53	Str 1 Sep 58, scuttled Nov 60 after use as ASW target
284	*Tullibee* MINY	1 Apr 42 11 Nov 42	15 Feb 43		WL 26 Mar 44 (own torpedo)
285	*Balao* PNY	26 Jun 42 27 Oct 42	4 Feb 43 4 Mar 52	20 Aug 46 11 Jul 63	AGSS 1 Apr 60, Str 1 Aug 63, S(T) 4 Sep 63; conning tower memorial at Navy Memorial Museum Washington, D.C.
286	*Billfish* PNY	23 Jul 42 12 Nov 42	20 Apr 43 1 Jan 60 (ISIR)	1 Nov 46 1 Apr 68	PT 1960–68 Boston, AGSS 1 Dec 62, Str 1 Apr 68, sold 17 Mar 71
287	*Bowfin* PNY	23 Jul 42 7 Dec 42	1 May 43 27 Jul 51 10 Jan 60 (ISIR)	12 Feb 47 22 Apr 54 1 Dec 71	AGSS 1 Dec 62, IXSS 30 Jun 71, PT 1960–71 Seattle, Str 1 Dec 71; memorial Pearl Harbor
288	*Cabrilla* PNY	18 Aug 42 24 Dec 42	24 May 43 May 60 (ISIR)	7 Aug 46 30 Jun 68	PT 1960–68 Houston, AGSS 1 Dec 62, Str 30 Jun 68; to Galveston as memorial but returned 21 Jan 71, sold 18 Apr 72
289	*Capelin* PNY	14 Sep 42 20 Jan 43	4 Jun 43		WL 1 Dec 43
290	*Cisco* PNY	29 Oct 42 24 Dec 42	10 May 43		WL 28 Sep 43
291	*Crevalle* PNY	14 Nov 42 22 Feb 43	24 Jun 43 6 Sep 51 11 Apr 57	29 Jul 46 19 Aug 55 9 Mar 62	AGSS 1 Apr 60, PT 1962–68, Str 15 Apr 68, sold 17 Mar 71
292	*Devilfish* CR	31 Mar 42 30 May 43	1 Sep 44	30 Sep 46	AGSS 1 Dec 62, Str 1 Mar 67, S(T) 14 Aug 68
293	*Dragonet* CR	28 Apr 42 18 Apr 43	6 Mar 44	16 Apr 46	Str 1 Jun 61, S(T) 17 Sep 61 after explosives tests
294	*Escolar* CR	10 Jun 42 18 Apr 43	2 Jun 44		WL 1 Oct 44
295	*Hackleback* CR	15 Aug 42 30 May 43	7 Nov 44	20 Mar 46	AGSS 1 Dec 62, Str 1 Mar 67, sold 4 Dec 68
296	*Lancetfish* CR	30 Sep 42 15 Aug 43	12 Feb 45	24 Mar 45	Sank at pier, Boston 15 Mar 45, raised 23 Mar and laid up incomplete; Str 9 Jun 58, sold 20 Aug 59
297	*Ling* CR/BNY	2 Nov 42 15 Aug 43	8 Jun 45 Mar 60 (ISIR)	26 Oct 46 1 Dec 71	PT 1960–71 Brooklyn, AGSS 1 Dec 62, IXSS 30 Jun 71, Str 1 Dec 71; memorial at Hackensack, N.J.
298	*Lionfish* CR/PNY	15 Dec 42 7 Nov 43	1 Nov 44 31 Jan 51 1 Mar 60 (ISIR)	16 Jan 46 15 Dec 53 20 Dec 71	AGSS 1 Dec 62, IXSS 30 Jun 71, PT 1960–71 Providence, Str 20 Dec 71; memorial at Fall River, Mass.

No.	Name/Yard	LD/Lch	Comm	Decomm	Fate
299	*Manta* CR/PNY	15 Jan 43 7 Nov 43	18 Dec 44 2 Aug 49 Apr 60 (ISIR)	10 Jun 46 6 Dec 55 30 Jun 67	AGSS 16 Aug 49, target ship (converted at San Francisco) 1949–53, PT 1960–67 New London Str 30 Jun 67, hull tests Portsmouth 1967–69, S(T) 16 Jul 69
300	*Moray* CR	21 Apr 43 14 May 44	26 Jan 45 27 Mar 45	12 Apr 46 1 Jun 46	AGSS 1 Dec 62, Str 1 Apr 67, test hulk San Clemente, S(T) 18 Jun 70
301	*Roncador* CR	21 Apr 43 14 May 44	Feb 60 (ISIR)	1 Dec 71	PT 1960–71 San Pedro, AGSS 1 Dec 62, IXSS 30 Jun 71, Str 1 Dec 71, but conning tower barrel at Navy Memorial Museum, Washington, D.C.
302	*Sabalo* CR	5 Jun 43 4 Jun 44	19 Jun 45 Jun 51	7 Aug 46 1 Jul 71	FS 1952, Str 1 Jul 71, S(T) 15 Feb 73
303	*Sablefish* CR	5 Jun 43 4 Jun 44	18 Dec 45	1 Nov 69	FS 1951, AGSS 30 Jun 69, Str 1 Nov 69, sold 39 Jul 71
304	*Seahorse* MINY	1 Jul 42 9 Jan 43	31 Mar 43	2 Mar 46	AGSS 1 Dec 62, Str 1 Mar 67, sold 4 Dec 68
305	*Skate* MINY	1 Aug 42 4 Mar 43	15 Apr 43	11 Dec 46	Bikini target Jul 46, S(T) 5 Oct 48
306	*Tang* MINY	15 Jan 43 17 Aug 43	15 Oct 43		WL 24 Oct 44 (own torpedoes)
307	*Tilefish* MINY	10 Mar 43 25 Oct 43	15 Dec 43 30 Jan 60	12 Oct 59 4 May 60	FS 1960 for Venezuela (*Carite*)
308	*Apogon* PNY	9 Dec 42 10 Mar 43	16 Jul 43		Bikini target 25 Jul 46 (sunk)
309	*Aspro* PNY	27 Dec 42 7 Apr 43	31 Jul 43 23 Sep 51	30 Jan 46 30 Apr 54	AGSS 1 Jul 60, Str 1 Sep 62 S(T) 16 Nov 62
310	*Batfish* PNY	27 Dec 42 5 May 43	21 Aug 43 7 Mar 52 Jan 60 (ISIR)	6 Apr 46 Jan 60 1 Nov 69	AGSS 1 Dec 62, PT 1960–69 New Orleans, AGSS 1 Dec 62, Str 1 Nov 69; memorial Muskogee, Okla.
311	*Archerfish* PNY	22 Jan 43 28 May 43	4 Sep 43 7 Mar 52 1 Aug 57	12 Jun 46 21 Oct 55 1 May 68	AGSS 22 Feb 60, Str 1 May 68, S(T) 19 Oct 68
312	*Burrfish* PNY	24 Feb 43 18 Jun 43	13 Sep 43 2 Nov 48 17 Jan 61	10 Oct 46 17 Dec 56 11 May 61	SSR 1 Feb 49, SS 15 Jan 61; to Canada 11 May 61 (*Grilse*), S(T) 19 Nov 69
313	*Perch* EB	5 Jan 43 12 Sep 43	7 Jan 44 20 May 48 11 Nov 61	Jan 47 31 Mar 60 27 May 67	SSP 20 Jan 48, ASSP 31 Jan 50, APSS 24 Oct 56, LPSS 1 Jan 69, IXSS 30 Jun 71, PT 1967–71 San Diego, Str 1 Dec 71, sold 15 Jan 73
314	*Shark* EB	28 Jan 43 17 Oct 43	14 Feb 44		WL 24 Oct 44
315	*Sealion* EG	25 Feb 43 31 Oct 43	8 Mar 44 2 Nov 48 20 Oct 61	16 Feb 46 30 Jun 60 20 Feb 70	SSP 5 Apr 48, ASSP 31 Jan 50, APSS 24 Oct 56, LPSS 1 Jan 69, PT 1960–61 Portsmouth, Str 15 Mar 77, test hulk, S(T) 8 Jul 78
316	*Barbel* EB	11 Mar 43 14 Nov 43	3 Apr 44		WL 4 Feb 45
317	*Barbero* EB	25 Mar 43 12 Dec 43	29 Apr 44 28 Oct 55	30 Jun 50 30 Jun 64	SSA 5 Apr 48, ASSA 31 Jan 50, SSG 25 Oct 55, Str 1 Jul 64, S(T) 7 Oct 64
318	*Baya* EB	8 Apr 43 2 Jan 44	20 May 44 10 Feb 48	14 May 46 30 Oct 72	AGSS 16 Aug 49 (sonar tests), Str 30 Oct 72, sold 12 Oct 73
319	*Becuna* EB	29 Apr 43 30 Jan 44	27 May 44	7 Nov 69	G IA 1951, AGSS 1 Oct 69, SS 30 Jun 71, Str 15 Aug 73; memorial Philadelphia, Pa.
320	*Bergall* EB	13 May 43 16 Feb 44	12 Jun 44	18 Oct 58	FS 1952, to Turkey 18 Oct 58 (*Turgut Reis*), Ret (sold back) 15 Feb 73, barracks ship
321	*Besugo* EB	27 May 43 27 Feb 44	19 Jun 44	21 Mar 58	AGSS 1 Dec 62; to FS for Italy, transferred 31 May 66 (*Francesco Morosini*), Ret, sold 20 Jun 77
322	*Blackfin* EB	10 Jun 43 12 Mar 44	4 Jul 44 15 May 51	19 Nov 48 15 Sep 72	G IA 1951, Str 15 Sep 72, S(T)

No.	Name/Yard	LD/Lch	Comm	Decomm	Fate
323	*Caiman* EB	24 Jun 43 30 Mar 44	17 Jul 44	30 Jun 72	G IA 1951; to Turkey 30 Jun 72 (*Dumlupinar*)
324	*Blenny* EB	8 Jul 43 9 Apr 44	27 Jul 44	7 Nov 69	G IA 1951, AGSS 1 Oct 69, SS 30 Jun 71, Str 15 Aug 73, S(T) to form artificial reef at Ocean City N.J.
325	*Blower* EB	15 Jul 43 23 Apr 44	10 Aug 44	16 Nov 50	FS 1950 for Turkey (*Dumlupinar*), L 4 Apr 53
326	*Blueback* EB	29 Jul 43 7 May 44	28 Aug 44	32 May 48	To Turkey 23 May 48 (*Ikinic Inonu*); FS 1953
327	*Boarfish* EB	12 Aug 43 21 May 44	23 Sep 44	23 May 48	To Turkey 23 May 48 (*Sakarya*); FS 1953; Ret, sold 1974
328	*Charr* EB	26 Aug 43 28 May 44	23 Sep 44 28 Jun 69 (ISIR)	28 Jun 69 20 Dec 71	FS 1951, AGSS 1 Jul 66, IXSS 30 Jun 71, PT 1969–71 Alda, Str 20 Dec 71, sold 17 Aug 72
329	*Chub* EB	16 Sep 43 18 Jun 44	21 Oct 44	23 May 48	To Turkey 25 May 48 (*Gur*), FS 1953, Ret, sold 1974
330	*Brill* EB	23 Sep 43 25 Jun 44	26 Oct 44	23 May 48	To Turkey 25 May 48 (*Birinci Inonu*), FS 1953
331	*Bugara* EB	21 Oct 43 2 Jul 44	15 Nov 44	1 Oct 70	FS 1951, AGSS 30 Jun 69, SS 1 Oct, 69, Str 1 Oct 70, L under tow for target 1 Jun 71
332	*Bullhead* EB	21 Oct 43 16 Jul 44	4 Dec 44		WL 6 Aug 45
333	*Bumper* EB	4 Nov 43 6 Aug 44	9 Dec 44	16 Nov 50	FS 1950 for Turkey (*Canakkale*)
334	*Cabezon* EB	18 Nov 43 27 Aug 44	30 Dec 44 Apr 60 (ISIR)	24 Oct 53 15 May 70	AGSS 1 Dec 62, PT 1960–70, Tacoma, Str 15 May 70, sold 28 Dec 71
335	*Dentuda* EB	18 Nov 43 10 Sep 44	30 Dec 44 11 Dec 46 (ISIR)	11 Dec 46 30 Jun 67	Bikini target Jul 46, PT 1946–67 San Francisco AGSS 1 Dec 62, Str 30 Jun 67, sold 12 Feb 69
336	*Capitaine* EB	2 Dec 43 1 Oct 44	26 Jan 45 23 Feb 57	10 Feb 50 4 Mar 66	AGSS 1 Jul 60, FS 1966 for Italy (*Alfredo Cappellini*); sold to Italy 5 Dec 77
337	*Carbonero* EB	16 Dec 43 15 Oct 44	7 Feb 45	1 Dec 70	Missile launcher 1949, FS 1952, AGSS 30 Jun 69, SS 1 Oct 69, Str 1 Dec 70, S(T) 27 Apr 75
338	*Carp* EB	23 Dec 43 12 Nov 44	28 Feb 45 18 Mar 68 (ISIR)	18 Mar 68 20 Dec 71	FS 1952, AGSS 1 May 68, IXSS 30 Jun 71, PT 1968–71 Boston, Str 20 Dec 71, sold 26 Jul 73
339	*Catfish* EB	6 Jan 44 19 Nov 44	19 Mar 45	1 Jul 71	G II 1949; to Argentina 1 Jul 71 (*Santa Fe*), WL 25 Apr 82
340	*Entemedor* EB	3 Feb 44 17 Dec 44	6 Apr 45 24 Oct 50	10 Dec 48 31 Jul 72	G IIA 1952; to Turkey 31 Jul 72 (*Preveze*); sold to Turkey 1 Aug 73
341	*Chivo* EB	21 Feb 44 14 Jan 45	28 Apr 45	1 Jul 71	G IA 1951; to Argentina 1 Jul 71 (*Santiago Del Estero*)
342	*Chopper* EB	2 Mar 44 4 Feb 45	25 May 45	27 Aug 69	G IA 1951, AGSS 15 Sep 69, IXSS 30 Jun 71, PT 1969–71 New Orleans, Str 1 Oct 71, salvage and rescue hulk, sunk 21 Jul 76 while being rigged as tethered underwater target
343	*Clamagore* EB	16 Mar 44 25 Feb 45	28 Jun 45	12 Jun 73	G II 1948, G III 1972, Str 12 Jun 75; memorial Patriots' Point Charleston, S.C.
344	*Cobbler* EB	3 Apr 44 1 Apr 45	8 Aug 45	21 Nov 73	G II 1949, G III 1962; to Turkey 21 Nov 73 (*Canakkale*)
345	*Cochino* EB	13 Apr 44 20 Apr 45	25 Aug 45		G II 1949, L 26 Aug, 49 (battery fire)
346	*Corporal* EB	27 Apr 44 10 Jun 45	9 Nov 45	21 Nov 73	G II 1948, G III 1962; to Turkey 21 Nov 73 (*Birinci Inonu*)
347	*Cubera* EB	11 May 44 17 Jun 45	19 Dec 45	5 Jan 72	G II 1948; to Venezuela 5 Jan 72 (*Tiburon*)

No.	Name/Yard	LD/Lch	Comm	Decomm	Fate
348	Cusk EB	25 May 44 28 Jul 45	5 Feb 46	24 Sep 69	SSG 20 Jan 48, FS 1954, SS 1 Jul 54, AGSS 30 Jun 69, Str 24 Sep 69, sold 26 Jun 72
349	Diodon EB	1 Jun 44 10 Sep 45	18 Mar 46	15 Jan 71	G II 1948, Str 15 Jan 71, sold 12 May 72
350	Dogfish EB	22 Jun 44 27 Oct 45	29 Apr 46	28 Jul 72	G II 1948; to Brazil 28 Jul 72 (*Guanabara*)
351	Greenfish EB	29 Jun 44 21 Dec 45	7 Jun 46	19 Dec 73	G II 1948, G III 1961; to Brazil 19 Dec 73 (*Amazonas*)
352	Halfbeak EB	6 Jul 44 19 Feb 46	22 Jul 46	1 Jul 71	G II 1948, Str 1 Jul 71, sold 13 Jun 72
353	Dugong				Canceled 23 Oct 44
354	Eel				Canceled 23 Oct 44
355	Espada				Canceled 23 Oct 44
356	Jawfish, ex- Fanegal				Canceled 20 Jul 44
357	Ono, ex- Friar				Canceled 20 Jul 44
358	Garlopa				Canceled 20 Jul 44
359	Currupa				Canceled 20 Jul 44
360	Goldring				Canceled 20 Jul 44
361	Golet MA	27 Jan 43 1 Aug 43	30 Nov 43		WL 14 Jun 44
362	Guavina MA	3 Mar 43 29 Aug 43	23 Dec 43 1 Feb 50 Feb 60 (ISIR)	1946 27 Mar 59 30 Jun 67	SSO 16 Aug 48, AGSS 11 Dec 51, AOSS 22 June 57, PT 1960–67 Baltimore, Str 30 Jun 67, S(T) 14 Nov 67
363	Guitarro MA	7 Apr 43 26 Sep 43	26 Jan 44 6 Feb 52	6 Dec 45 22 Sep 53	FS 1954 for Turkey (*Preveze*); sold to Turkey 1 Jan 72
364	Hammerhead MA	5 May 43 24 Oct 43	1 Mar 44 6 Feb 52	9 Feb 46 21 Aug 5	FS 1954 for Turkey (*Cerbe*), sold to Turkey 1 Jan 72
365	Hardhead MA	7 Jul 43 12 Dec 43	18 Apr 44 6 Feb 52 24 Mar 53	10 May 46 22 May 52 26 Jul 72	G IIA 1953, to Greece 26 Jul 72 (*Papanikolis*)
366	Hawkbill MA	7 Aug 43 9 Jan 44	17 May 44 1953	20 Sep 46 21 Apr 53	G IB for Netherlands (*Zeeleuw*), sold to Netherlands 20 Feb 70
367	Icefish MA	4 Sep 43 20 Feb 44	10 Jun 44 5 May 52 10 Dec 52	21 Jun 46 29 Jul 52 21 Feb 53	G IB for Netherlands (*Walrus*); Ret, sold for BU 12 Nov 71
368	Jallao MA	29 Sep 43 12 Mar 44	8 Jul 44 4 Dec 53	30 Sep 46 26 Jun 74	G IIA 1954; sold to Spain 26 Jun 74 (*Narciso Monturiol*)
369	Kete MA	25 Oct 43 9 Apr 44	31 Jul 44		WL 20 Mar 45
370	Kraken MA	13 Dec 43 30 Apr 44	8 Sep 44 1959	4 May 48 24 Oct 59	FS 1959 for Spain (*Almirante Garcia De Los Reyes*), sold to Spain 1 Nov 74
371	Legarto MA	12 Jan 44 28 May 44	14 Oct 44		WL 4 May 45
372	Lamprey MA	22 Feb 44 18 Jun 44	17 Nov 44 1960	3 Jun 46 21 Aug 60	To Argentina unmodified (*Santiago Del Estero*), sold to Argentina 1 Sept 71
373	Lizardfish MA	14 Mar 44 16 Jul 44	30 Dec 44 1959	24 Jun 46 9 Jan 60	FS 1959 for Italy (*Evangelista Torricella*), Ret 15 Jul 78, sold to Italy 15 Jul 79
374	Loggerhead MA	1 Apr 44 13 Aug 44	9 Feb 45 1 Jun 60 (ISIR)	1946 30 Jun 67	PT 1960–67 Portland, AGSS 1 Dec 62 Str 30 Jun 67, sold 29 Aug 69
375	Macabi MA	1 May 44 19 Sep 44	29 Mar 45 6 May 60	16 Jun 46 11 Aug 60	To Argentina unmodified (*Santa Fe*), Ret, sold to Argentina 1 Sept 71
376	Mapiro MA	30 May 44 9 Nov 44	30 Apr 45 1960	16 Mar 46 18 Mar 60	FS 1960 for Turkey (*Piri Reis*), sold to Turkey 1 Aug 73

No.	Name/Yard	LD/Lch	Comm	Decomm	Fate
377	*Menhaden* MA	21 Jun 44 20 Dec 44	22 Jun 45 7 Aug 51 6 Mar 53	31 May 46 13 Aug 52 13 Aug 71	G IIA 1953, Str 15 Aug 73, tethered underwater target 1976, sold for BU 88
378	*Mero* MA	22 Jul 44 17 Jan 45	17 Aug 45 1960	15 Jun 46 20 Apr 60	FS 1960 for Turkey (*Hizir Reis*), sold to Turkey 1 Aug 73
379	*Needlefish*				Canceled 29 Jul 44
380	*Nerka*				Canceled 29 Jul 44
381	*Sand Lance* PNY	12 Mar 43 25 Jun 43	9 Oct 43 6 Apr 63	14 Feb 46 7 Sep 63	To Brazil unmodified (*Rio Grande do Sul*), Ret, sold to Brazil 12 Oct 72
382	*Picuda* PNY	15 Mar 43 12 Jul 43	16 Oct 43 19 Jun 53	25 Sep 46 1 Oct 72	G IIA 1953; to Spain 1 Oct 72 (*Cosme Garcia*); had been chosen for abortive minelayer conversion, FY 52, but canceled 1 Oct 52; Ret 1974, sold
383	*Pampanito* PNY	15 Mar 43 12 Jul 43	6 Nov 43 Apr 60 (ISIR)	15 Dec 45 20 Dec 71	PT 60-71 Vallejo, AGSS 1 Dec 62, IXSS 30 Jun 71, Str 20 Dec 71; memorial San Francisco, Calif.
384	*Parche* PNY	9 Apr 43 24 Jul 43	20 Nov 43 10 Feb 48 (ISIR)	11 Dec 46 8 Nov 69	Bikini target Jul 46, PT 1948–69 Alameda, AGSS 1 Dec 62, Str 8 Nov 69, sold 18 Jun 70
385	*Bang* PNY	30 Apr 43 30 Aug 43	4 Dec 43 1 Feb 51 4 Oct 52	12 Feb 47 15 May 52 1 Oct 72	G IIA 1952; to Spain 1 Oct 72 (*Cosme Garcia*), sold to Spain 1974
386	*Pilotfish* PNY	15 May 43 30 Aug 43	16 Dec 43	29 Aug 46	Sunk Bikini 25 Jul 46, raised, S(T) 16 Oct 48
387	*Pintado* PNY	7 May 43 15 Sep 43	1 Jan 44	6 Mar 46	AGSS 1 Dec 62, Str 1 mar 67, sold 19 Feb 69
388	*Pipefish* PNY	31 May 43 27 Oct 43	22 Jan 44	19 Mar 46	AGSS 1 Dec 62, Str 1 Mar 67, sold 4 Feb 69
389	*Piranha* PNY	21 Jun 43 27 Oct 43	5 Feb 44	31 May 46	AGSS 1 Dec 62, Str 1 Mar 67, sold 11 Aug 70
390	*Plaice* PNY	28 Jun 43 15 Nov 43	12 Feb 44 18 May 63	Nov 47 7 Sep 63	To Brazil unmodified (*Bahia*); memorial Santos
391	*Pomfret* PNY	14 Jul 43 27 Oct 43	19 Feb 44 5 Dec 52	Apr 52 1 Jul 71	G IIA 1953, to Turkey 1 Jul 71 (*Oruc Reis*), sold to Turkey 1 Aug 73
392	*Sterlet* PNY	14 Jul 43 27 Oct 43	4 Mar 44 26 Aug 50	18 Sep 48 30 Sep 68	FS 1952, BQR-4 fitted 1955; Str 1 Oct 68, S(T) 31 Jan 69
393	*Queenfish* PNY	27 Jul 43 30 Nov 43	11 Mar 44	1 Mar 63	AGSS 1 Jul 60, Str 1 Mar 63, S(T) 14 Aug 63
394	*Razorback* PNY	9 Sep 43 27 Jan 44	3 Apr 44 1954	Aug 52 30 Nov 70	G IIA 1954, to Turkey 30 Nov 70 (*Murat Reis*)
395	*Redfish* PNY	9 Sep 43 27 Jan 44	12 Apr 44	27 Jun 68	AGSS 1 Jul 60, Str 30 Jun 68, S(T) 6 Feb 69
396	*Ronquil* PNY	9 Sep 43 27 Jan 44	22 Apr 44 16 Jan 53	May 52 1 Jul 71	G IIA 1953, to Spain 1 Jul 71, (*Isaac Peral*)
397	*Scabbardfish* PNY	27 Sep 43 27 Jan 44	29 Apr 44 24 Oct 64	5 Jan 48 26 Feb 65	FS 65 for Greece (*Triaina*), sold for spare parts 31 Jan 76
398	*Segundo* PNY	14 Oct 43 5 Feb 44	9 May 44	1 Aug 70	FS 1951, Str 8 Aug 70, S(T) 8 Aug 70
399	*Sea Cat* PNY	30 Oct 43 21 Feb 44	16 May 44	2 Dec 68	AGSS 30 Sep 49, SS 11 Dec 51, FS 1952, AGSS 29 Jun 68, Str 2 Dec 68, test hulk 1968–72, sold 18 May 73
400	*Sea Devil* PNY	18 Nov 43 28 Feb 44	24 May 44 3 Mar 51 17 Aug 57	9 Sep 48 19 Feb 54 17 Feb 64	AGSS 1 Jul 60, Str 1 Apr 64, S(T) 24 Nov 64
401	*Sea Dog* PNY	1 Nov 43 28 Mar 44	3 Jun 44	27 Jun 56	AGSS 1 Dec 62, PT 1960–68 Salem, Str 2 Dec 68, S(T) 18 May 73
402	*Sea Fox* PNY	2 Nov 43 28 Mar 44	13 Jun 44 5 Jun 53	15 Oct 52 14 Dec 70	G IIA 1953, to Turkey 14 Dec 70 (*Burak Reis*)

No.	Name/Yard	LD/Lch	Comm	Decomm	Fate
403	*Atule* PNY	2 Dec 43 6 Mar 44	21 Jun 44 8 Mar 51	8 Sep 47 6 Apr 70	G IA 1951, AGSS 1 Oct 69, SS 30 Jun 71, Str 15 Aug 73; to Peru 31 Jul 74 (*Pacocha*), S(C) 90, then raised and cannibalized
404	*Spikefish* PNY	29 Jan 44 26 Apr 44	30 Jun 44	2 Apr 63	AGSS 1 Jul 62, Str 1 May 63, S(T) 4 Aug 64
405	*Sea Owl* PNY	7 Feb 44 7 May 44	17 Jul 44	15 Nov 69	FS 51, BQR-4 fitted 1955; AGSS 30 Jun 69, Str 15 Nov 69; sold 3 Jun 71
406	*Sea Poacher* PNY	23 Feb 44 20 May 44	31 Jul 44	15 Nov 69	G IA 1952, AGSS 1 Nov 69, SS 30 Jun 71, Str 15 Aug 73; to Peru 1 Jul 74
407	*Sea Robin* PNY	1 Mar 44 25 May 44	7 Aug 44	1 Oct 70	G IA 1951, Str 1 Oct 70 sold 3 Jun 71
408	*Sennet* PNY	8 Mar 44 6 Jun 44	22 Aug 44	2 Dec 68	FS 1952, Str 2 Dec 68, sold 15 Jun 73
409	*Piper* PNY	15 Mar 44 26 Jun 44	23 Aug 44	16 Jun 67	FS 1951, BQR-4 fitted 1955, AGSS 15 Jun 67, PT 1967–70 Detroit, Str 1 Jul 70, sold Jun 71
410	*Threadfin* PNY	18 Mar 44 26 Jun 44	30 Aug 44 7 Aug 53	10 Dec 52 18 Aug 72	G IIA 1953; to Turkey 18 Aug 72 (*Birinci Inonu*), sold to Turkey 1 Aug 73
411	*Spadefish* MINY	27 May 43 8 Jan 44	9 Mar 44	3 May 46	AGSS 1 Dec 62, Str 1 Apr 67, sold 17 Oct 69
412	*Trepang* MINY	25 Jun 43 23 Mar 44	22 May 44 Feb 60 (ISIR)	27 Jun 46 30 Jun 67	PT 1960–67 San Diego, AGSS 1 Dec 62, Str 30 Jun 67, S(T) 16 Sep 69
413	*Spot* MINY	24 Aug 43 19 May 44	3 Aug 44 19 Aug 61	19 Jun 46 12 Jan 62	To Chile unmodified (*Simpson*)
414	*Springer* MINY	30 Oct 43 3 Aug 44	18 Oct 44 24 Sep 60	Jan 47 23 Jan 61	To Chile unmodified (*Thomson*), Ret, sold 1 Sep 72
415	*Stickleback* MINY	1 Mar 44 1 Jan 45	29 Mar 45 6 Sep 51 26 Jun 53	26 Jun 46 14 Nov 52	G IIA 1953, L (rammed) 29 May 58
416	*Tiru* MINY	17 Apr 44 16 Sep 47	1 Sep 48	1 Jul 75	Completed as G II; G III 59, Str 1 Jul 75; last U.S. fleet submarine in service; planned for conversion to remote-control submersible target, S(T) 2 Oct 76
417	*Tench* PNY	1 Apr 44 7 Jul 44	6 Oct 44 Oct 50	Jan 47 8 May 70	G IA 1951, AGSS 1 Oct 69, SS 30 Jun 71, Str 15 Aug 73 (to Peru for spares 16 Sep 76)
418	*Thornback* PNY	5 Apr 44 7 Jul 44	13 Oct 44 2 Oct 53	6 Apr 46 1 Jul 71	G IIA 1953; to Turkey 1 Jul 71 (*Uluc Ali Reis*), sold to Turkey 1 Aug 73
419	*Tigrone* PNY	8 May 44 20 Jul 44	25 Oct 44 Jul 48 10 Mar 62	Jan 47 Oct 57 27 Jun 75	SSR 5 Apr 48, SS 1 Mar 61, AGSS 1 Dec 63, Str 27 Jun 75 S(T) 25 Oct 76
420	*Tirante* PNY	28 Apr 44 9 Aug 44	6 Nov 44 26 Nov 52	20 Jul 46 1 Oct 73	G IIA 1953, Str 1 Oct 73
421	*Trutta* PNY	22 May 44 18 Aug 44	16 Nov 44 1 Mar 51 2 Jan 53	1947 14 May 52 1 Jul 72	G IIA 1953; to Turkey 1 Jul 72 (*Cerbe*)
422	*Toro* PNY	27 May 44 23 Aug 44	8 Dec 44 13 May 47	2 Feb 46 11 Mar 63	AGSS 1 Jul 62, Str 1 Apr 63, sold Apr 65
423	*Torsk* PNY	7 Jun 44 6 Sep 44	16 Dec 44	4 Mar 68	FS 1952, AGSS 1 May 68, IXSS 30 Jun 71, PT 1968–71 Washington, Str 15 Dec 71; memorial Baltimore, Md.
424	*Quillback* PNY	27 Jun 44 1 Oct 44	29 Dec 44 27 Feb 53	Apr 52 23 Mar 73	GIIA 1953, Str 23 Mar 73, sold 21 Mar 74
425	*Trumpetfish* CR	23 Aug 43 13 May 45	29 Jan 46	15 Oct 73	G II 1948, G III 1962; to Brazil 15 Oct 73 (*Goias*)
426	*Tusk* CR	23 Aug 43 8 Jul 45	11 Apr 46	18 Oct 73	G II 1948; to Taiwan 18 Oct 73 (*Hai Pao*)
427	*Turbot* CR	13 Nov 43 12 Apr 46			Suspended 12 Aug 45, machinery test hulk Annapolis
428	*Ulua* CR	13 Nov 43 23 Apr 46			Suspended 12 Aug 45, underwater explosion test hulk Norfolk 1951–58, Str 12 Jun 58

No.	Name/Yard	LD/Lch	Comm	Decomm	Fate
429	Unicorn				Canceled 29 Jul 44
430	Vendace				Canceled 29 Jul 44
431	Walrus				Canceled 29 Jul 44
432	Whitefish				Canceled 29 Jul 44
433	Whiting				Canceled 29 Jul 44
434	Wolffish				Canceled 29 Jul 44
435	Corsair EB	1 Mar 45 3 May 46	8 Nov 46	1 Feb 63	AGSS 1 Apr 60, Str 1 Feb 63, sold 8 Nov 63
436	Unicorn EB	21 Jun 45 1 Aug 46			Suspended 30 Jan 46, Del 16 Sep 46, Str 9 Jun 58, sold 7 Oct 59
437	Walrus EB	21 Jun 45 20 Sep 46			Suspended 30 Jan 46, Del 2 Oct 46, Str 9 Jun 58, sold 7 Oct 59
438–474					Canceled 29 Jul 44
475	Argonaut PNY	28 Jun 44 1 Oct 44	15 Jan 45	2 Dec 68	FS 1952; to Canada 2 Dec 68 (*Rainbow*)
476	Runner PNY	10 Jul 45 17 Oct 44	6 Feb 45	29 Jun 70	FS 1952, AGSS 1 Feb 69, IXSS 30 Jun 71, PT 1970–71 Chicago, Str 15 Dec 71, sold 19 Jun 73
477	Conger PNY	11 Jul 44 17 Oct 44	14 Feb 45	29 Jul 63	AGSS 9 Mar 62, Str 1 Aug 63, sold 9 Jul 64
478	Cutlass PNY	22 Jul 44 5 Nov 44	17 Mar 45	12 Apr 75	G II 1948; to Taiwan 12 Apr 73 (*Hai Shih*)
479	Diablo PNY	11 Aug 44 1 Dec 44	31 Mar 45	1 Jun 64	AGSS 1 Jul 62, FS for Pakistan, transferred 1 Jun 64 (*Ghazi*), WL 4 Dec 71
480	Medregal PNY	21 Aug 44 15 Dec 44	14 Apr 45	1 Aug 70	FS 1952, AGSS 1 May 67, SS 1 Oct 69, Str 1 Aug 70, sold 13 Jun 72
481	Requin PNY	24 Aug 44 1 Jan 45	28 Apr 45	2 Dec 68	Picket 46 (SSR 20 Jan 48), SS 15 Aug 59, AGSS 29 Jun 68, IXSS 30 Jun 71, PT 1969–71 St. Petersburg, Str 20 Dec 71; memorial Pittsburgh, Pa.
482	Irex PNY	2 Oct 44 26 Jan 45	14 May 45	17 Nov 69	FS 1947 (prototype U.S. snorkel), AGSS 30 Jun 69, Str 17 Nov 69, sold 13 Sep 71
483	Sea Leopard PNY	7 Nov 44 2 Mar 45	11 Jun 45	27 Mar 73	G II 1949; to Brazil 27 Mar 73 (*Bahia*)
484	Odax PNY	4 Dec 44 10 Apr 45	11 Jul 45	8 Jul 72	G I 1947, G II 1951; to Brazil 8 Jul 72 (*Rio de Janiero*)
485	Sirago PNY	3 Jan 45 11 May 45	13 Aug 45	1 Jun 72	G II 1949, Str 1 Jun 72
486	Pomodon PNY	29 Jan 45 12 Jun 45	11 Sep 45 2 Jul 55	1 Apr 55 1 Aug 70	G I 1947, G II 1951, str 1 Aug 70, sold 26 Jan 72
487	Remora PNY	5 Mar 45 12 Jul 45	3 Jan 46	29 Oct 73	G II 1947, G III 1962; to Greece 29 Oct 73 (*Katsonis*)
488	Sarda PNY	12 Apr 45 24 Aug 45	19 Apr 46	1 Jun 64	AGSS 1 Jul 62, Str 1 Jun 64, sold 14 May 65
489	Spinax PNY	14 May 45 20 Nov 45	20 Sep 46	11 Oct 69	Cpl as picket (SSR 20 Jan 48), SS 15 Aug 59, AGSS 30 Jun 69, Str 11 Oct 69, sold 13 Jun 72
490	Volador PNY	15 Jun 45 21 May 48	1 Oct 48	18 Aug 72	Suspended 30 Jan 46, completed as G II, G III 1963; to Italy 18 Aug 72 (*Gianfranco Gazzana Priaroggia*), sold to Italy 5 Dec 77
491	Pompano PNY	16 Jul 45			Canceled 12 Aug 45, BU on slip
492	Grayling				Canceled 12 Aug 45
493	Needlefish				Canceled 12 Aug 45
494	Sculpin				Canceled 12 Aug 45
495–515					Canceled 29 Jul 44
516	Wahoo MINY	15 May 44			Canceled 7 Jan 46, BU on slip

No.	Name/Yard	LD/Lch	Comm	Decomm	Fate
517	MINY	29 Jun 44			Canceled 29 Jul 44, BU on slip
518–521					Canceled 29 Jul 44
522	*Amberjack* BNY	8 Feb 44 15 Dec 44	4 Mar 46	17 Oct 73	G II 1947; to Brazil 17 Oct 73 (*Ceara*)
523	*Grampus* BNY	8 Feb 44 15 Dec 44	26 Oct 49	13 May 72	Suspended 17 Jan 46, completed as G II; to Brazil 15 May 72 (*Rio Grande do Sul*)
524	*Pickerel* BNY	8 Feb 44 15 Dec 44	4 Apr 49	18 Aug 72	Suspended 17 Jan 46, completed as G II, G III 1962; to Italy 18 Aug 72 (*Primo Longobardo*)
525	*Grenadier* BNY	8 Feb 44 15 Dec 44	10 Feb 51	15 May 73	Suspended 17 Jan 46, completed as G II; to Venezuela 15 may 73 (*Picua*)
526	*Dorado*				Canceled 29 Jul 44
527	*Comber*				Canceled 29 Jul 44
528	*Sea Panther*				Canceled 29 Jul 44
529	*Tiburon*				Canceled 29 Jul 44
530–544					Canceled 29 Jul 44
545–547					Canceled 28 Mar 45
548–550					Canceled 27 Mar 45
554–562					Authorization canceled 26 Mar 45

H-5 was a typical Electric Boat submarine of pre-World War I design. This 1919 photograph shows her torpedo room. The mechanism between the tubes, with its lever and wheel, operated the bow cap that uncovered tube muzzles two at a time. Torpedo racks (with the upper ones empty), chain hoists, and loading rails (in the overhead) are all visible. (U.S. Navy photo by J. E. Hogg, Los Angeles)

Appendix D

Submarine Data

THE FOLLOWING TABLES of data for submarine designs give length as overall; beam is extreme (figures in parentheses are pressure hull diameters, which for double-hull boats are less than beam). Pressure hull thickness is given in pounds per square inch (lb/sq in; 1 in equals 40.8 lb). Complement is given as officers/enlisted men or as officers/chief petty officers/enlisted men. Where test depth is followed by an asterisk (*), the figure given is *collapse depth*. Surface engine power is in brake horsepower (BHP), submerged motors are in horsepower (HP), and auxiliary power plant is rated in kilowatts (kw). An engine rating followed by an asterisk is a continuous, rather than a peak, figure. Weights are in long tons (2,240 lb). Weights in parentheses are design figures. Where two fuel weights are given, they are normal/maximum capacity. Machinery weights include water. Engine weights include auxiliaries and shafts. In the entries for battery, the number is the number of cells (e.g., 2 × 126 means two 126-cell batteries). Battery types are: EP, Exide Paste; GP, Gould Paste; Ir, Ironclad; PP, Planté Paste; S, Sargo. In submarines carrying guns, asterisks indicate that armament and ammunition weights are limited to torpedo tubes and torpedoes. The entries for guns do not include automatic weapons (40-mm, 20-mm, .50 caliber, and .30 caliber).

Dashes indicate entries that *do not apply;* blanks indicate missing (but applicable) data.

Schemes I, II, and III (Table 4) were austere submarine designs developed for Adm. Thomas C. Hart. Weight data for *Mackerel* (Table 5) are design figures reported 24 September 1939. *Marlin* (Table 5) weight data are Bureau of Construction and Repair (C&R) estimates made before the design was sent to Portsmouth Navy Yard. *Balao* (Table 5) weight data are Portsmouth Navy Yard calculations, dated 9 February 1942, based on modifications to the *Gato* class.

Schemes 2 through 17 of 1945 (Table 5) were attempts to develop a successor to the wartime *Balao* and *Tench*. Scheme 17 armament included six fixed 19-in × 123-in torpedo tubes, plus two 40-mm guns and two 0.50-caliber machine guns. All of the main tubes were 276 in long. Designed radius was to have been equal to or better than that in the *Tench* class, but the design sheet gives no figures.

Table 1.

	Plunger	Holland SS 1	A-1 SS 2	B-1 SS 10	C-1 SS 9	D-1 SS 17	E-1 SS 24	F-1 SS 20	G-1 SS 19½	G-2 SS 27
Length (ft-in)	85-3	53-10	63-9⅞	82-5	105-3½	134-10	135-2¾	142-7	161-0	161-0
Beam (ft-in)	11-6	10-3	11-10½	12-5½	13-10½	13-10⅝	14-7	15-5	13-1	14-4
Draft (ft-in)	11-0	8-6	10-7	10-7	10-10¾	12-6	11-8	12-2	12-6	12-6
Pressure hull thickness (lb/sq in)	20	16	16			14–17.5		17.5		
Surfaced displacement (tons)	149	64	106.55	145	240	288	287	330	400	375
Submerged displacement (tons)	168	74	122.55	170	273	337	342	400	516	481
Complement	1/6	1/6	1/6	1/9	1/14	1/14	1/19	1/21	1/23	1/23
Surface plant	2×750 IHP	1×50 BHP	1×180 BHP	1×250 BHP	2×240 BHP	2×300 BHP	2×350 BHP	2×390 BHP	4×300 BHP	4×300 BHP
Submerged plant	70 HP	1×50 HP (136 HP overload)	1×70 HP	1×115 HP	2×115 HP	2×165 HP	2×265 HP	2×310 HP	2×375 HP	2×375 HP
Auxiliary plant	1×125 IHP									
Battery (cells)	48 PP	66 EP	60	60	120 EP	120 EP	120 PP	120 EP	120 PP	120 PP
Capacity (amp-hr)		1,400 (4-hr rate)	1,840 (4-hr rate)	1,840 (4-hr rate)	2,700 (3-hr rate) (3,500 for 35 hr)	2,970 (3-hr rate)	2,940 (4-hr rate)	3,060 (3-hr rate) 2,040 (1-hr rate)	3,840 (3-hr rate)	
Surface speed (kt)	15	6	8.5	9.2	11	13	13	14	14.706	14
Surface endurance (nm/kt)		200/6		600	776/8.13	1,179/9.6	2,090/10.17	2,500/11	3,500 nm	3,500 nm
Maximum (fuel in MBTs)	—	—	—	—	—	—	—	—	—	—
Submerged speed (kt)	8 (6-hr rate)	5.5	7.2	8.2	9	9.5	11	11.25	10.675	10.5
Submerged endurance (nm/kt)[1]	48/8	30/5.5	4 hr		24/8	24/8	27/9	25.5/8.5	24/8	25.5/8.5
Test depth (ft)	75	75	150	150	200	200	200	200	200	200
Tubes: bow	2×18 in	1×18 in	1×18 in	2×18 in	2×18 in	4×18 in	4×18 in	4×18 in	2×18 in	4×18 in
Tubes: stern	—	—	—	—	—	—	—	—	2 × 2 deck 18 in	2×18 in
Torpedoes	5	3	3	4	4	4	8	8	6	8
Guns	—	1 pneumatic (8.425 in)								
Weights (tons):										
Hull				65.78	97.33	108.48	112.1	145.18	255.95	191.2
Hull fittings				20.13	18.4	25.87	26.8	29.47		57.13
Machinery:			9.67 (w/o battery)	43.9	90.21	105.64	107.02	121.99	79.89	116.88
Engines		1.74	5.77	10.79	12.24	17.1	23.7	27.4		30.12
Battery		24.11	32.14	33.11	51.3	51.6	51.6	61.4	64	64
Motors		1.27			8.36	8.36	11.1	13		
Armament				2.08	2.44	7.72	6.64	6.94	16.02	10.03
Ammunition				2.75	2.68	2.98	2.61	2.62	1.49	1.49
Equipment and outfit				0.66	1.62	2.89	1.25	2.37		7.26
Stores and fresh water				0.31	2.12	2.25	3.53	3.56		
Complement				—						
MBT capacity		10	16	19.91	16.04	18.31	61.65	72.86	116	106
Lead ballast				8.46			4.7			
Standard displacement				144.13						
Fuel oil	3,425 gal (oil)	5		4.98	10.21	10.63/15.82	12.48/16.37	12.68/18.51	41	36
Lubricating oil							1			
Design displacement				169.02	241.13	288.13	339.76	403.5		

[1] Unless otherwise indicated.

Table 2.

	G-3 SS 31	G-4 SS 26	H-1 SS 28	K-1 SS 32	L-1 SS 40	L-5 SS 44	M-1 SS 47	N-1 SS 53	N-4 SS 56	O-1 SS 62	O-11 SS 72
Length (ft-in)	161-0	157-5¾	150-3½	153-6½	168-5⅝	165-0	197-0¼	147-3½	155-0	172-4	175-0
Beam (ft-in)	14-4	17-4⅜	15-9½	16-8⅜	17-4¾	14-9	19-⅜	15-9¼	14-6	18-0	16-7
Draft (ft-in)	12-0	11-5 3/16	12-5	13-1	13-7 light	13-3	11-0	12-6	12-4	14-5	13-11
Pressure hull thickness (lb/sq in)			14–17.5	15–17.5	15–17.5			15-6	14–17.5		14-17,5
Surfaced displacement (tons)	393	370	358	392	450	451	488	347	331	520	485
Submerged displacement (tons)	468	452	434	520	548	527	676	414	385	629	566
Complement	2/23	2/18	2/23	2/26	2/26	2/26	2/26	2/23	3/26	2/27	2/27
Surface plant	2×600 BHP	4×400 BHP (250*)	2×475 BHP	2×475 BHP	2×450 BHP	2×600 BHP	2×420 BHP	2×240 BHP	2×300 BHP	2×440 BHP	2×500 BHP
Submerged plant	2×300	2×660 (1 hr)* HP	2×170 HP	2×170 HP	2×170 HP	2×400 HP	2×170 HP	2×280 HP	2×150 HP	2×370 HP	2×400 HP
Auxiliary plant	—		—	—	—	—	—	—	—	—	—
Battery (cells)	120 GP	124	120 EP	2×60 GP	2×60 PP	120 EP	2×60 GP	2×60 PP	120 EP	2×60 PP	120 Ir
Capacity (amp-hr)		4,620 (3-hr rate) (3000 for 1 hr)			4,150	4,050 (3-hr rate) 3,000 (1-hr rate)	4,600	3,135 (3-hr rate) 2,325 (1-hr rate)			4,200 (3-hr rate) 3,000 (1-hr rate)
Surface speed (kt)	14.0	14.4	14	14	14	14	14	13	13	14	14
Surfaced endurance (nm/kt)		2,200/8	2,500	3,150/11	3,150/11	3,150/11	2,400/11	3,500/11			
Maximum (fuel in MBTs)		—	—	—	5,500/11		6,200/11				
Submerged speed (kt)	9.5	9.5	10.5	10.5	10.5	10.5	10.5	11	11	10.5	11
Submerged endurance (nm/kt)[1]		24/8	25.5/8.5	25.5/8.5	25.5/8.5	2 hr 42 min at 8.5 kt	25.5/8.5	30/5			
Test depth (ft)		200	200	200	200	200	200	200	200	200	200
Tubes: bow	4×18 in	2×18 in	4×18 in	4×18 in	4×18 in	4×18 in	4×18 in	4×18 in	4×18 in	4×18 in	4×18 in
Tubes: stern	2×18 in	2×18 in	—	—	—	—	—	—	—	—	—
Torpedoes	10	8	8	8	8	8	8	8	8	8	8
Guns	—	—	—	—	1×3 in/23	—	1×3 in	—	—	1×3 in/23	1×3 in/23
Weights (tons):											
Hull			148.8	161.13	198.69	32.48					
Hull fittings			34.23	35.97							
Machinery:			115.39	124.5	126.34						
Engines		22.75	34.7	31.2	33.3	46.2	44.2	34.8	34.89	45.6	52
Battery		65	56.7	54.3	60.2	64.3	54.3	49.1	53.5	80.4	59.3
Motors			11.1	13	13.1	13.4	16.95	11.6	10.27	16.8	
Armament		11	6.52	7.06	7*	7.1*	7*			7*	7*
Ammunition		2.98	2.22	5.27	5.56*	5.56*	5.56*	5.56	5.56	5.56*	5.56*
Equipment and outfit			4.72	4.17	4.43						
Stores and fresh water			3.05	3.53							
Complement											
MBT capacity	75	82	16.85	20.83	98	75	188	67	54	109	81
Lead ballast		87			31.47						
Standard Displacement											
Fuel oil	48.21	49.4	16.64	27.28	30.6	46.2	32.7	19.4	21	33.3	34.6
Lubricating oil		3.5			4.7	4	7	2.1	3	3.9	5.5
Design Displacement			350.47	390.55							

[1] Unless otherwise indicated.

Table 3.

	R-1 SS 78	R-21 SS 98	S-1 SS 105	S-2 SS 106	S-3 SS 107	S-10 SS 115	S-18 SS 123	S-20 rebuilt SS 125
Length (ft-in)	186-3¼	175-0	219-3	207-0	231-0	231-0	219-3	222-5½
Beam (ft-in)	18-¼	16-7¾	20-8	19-7	21-10 (14-6)	21-10¼	20-8	23-11¾
Draft (ft-in)	15-6	13-11	15-11	16-2	13-1	13-7	17-3	17-4⅜
Pressure hull thickness (lb/sq in)		17.5				17.5		
Surfaced displacement (tons)	574	497	854	800	875	930	930	987.5
Submerged displacement (tons)	685	652	1,062	977	1,088	1,138	1,094	1,165
Complement	4/3/26 (1939)	3/23	4/34	4/34	4/34	4/34	4/39 (1939)	4/39 (1939)
Surface plant	2 × 440 BHP	2 × 500	2 × 600 BHP	2 × 900 BHP	2 × 700 BHP	2 × 1,000 BHP	2 × 600 BHP	2 × 600 BHP
Submerged plant	2 × 467 HP	2 × 400	2 × 750 HP	2 × 600 HP	2 × 600 HP	2 × 600 HP	2 × 1,175 HP	2 × 1,175 HP
							(750 HP in S-30 to -41)	
Auxiliary plant	——	——		——	——	——	——	——
Battery (cells)	2 × 60	120	120	120	120	2 × 60 EP	2 × 60 EP	2 × 60 GP
Capacity (amp-hr)	4,700	4,500 (3-hr rate) 3,000 (1-hr rate)	9,500	7,590 (3-hr)	8,850 (3-hr) 6,250 (1-hr)		9,500	9,500
Surface speed (kt)	12.5 (1939)	14	14.5	15	15	14	13 (1939)	11.5 (1939)
Surface Endurance (nm/kt)	4,700/6.2	3,523/11				5,500/11	3,420/6.5	3,710/6.5
Maximum (fuel in MBTs)	7,000/6.2	6,499/11				7,121/9.6	8,950/9.5	7,900/6.5 (1939)
Submerged speed (kt)	9.3	11.46 (trial)	11	11	11	11	9	8.9
Submerged endurance (nm/kt)[1]			20 hr at 5 kt	20 hr at 5 kt	20 hr at 5 kt	20 hr at 5 kt	20 hr at 5 kt	20 hr at 5 kt
Test depth (ft)	200	200	200	200	200	200	200	200
Tubes: bow	4 × 21 in	4 × 21 in	4 × 21 in	4 × 21 in	4 × 21 in	4 × 21 in	4 × 21 in	4 × 21 in
Tubes: stern	——	——	——	——	——	1 × 21 in	——	——
Torpedoes	8	8	12	12	12	14	12	12
Guns	1 × 3 in/50	1 × 3 in/50	1 × 4 in/50	1 × 4 in/50	1 × 4 in/50	1 × 4 in	1 × 4 in	1 × 4 in
Weights (tons):								
Hull					(400.2)			
Hull fittings					(57.88)			
Machinery:								
Engines					(259.73)			
Battery					(59.63)			
Motors					(125.85)			
Armament					(11.85)			
Ammunition					(9.31)			
Equipment and outfit					(9.47)	10.85		
Stores and fresh water					(10.71)	16.08		
Complement					(3.48)			
MBT capacity	111		208	177	(229.43)	208	164	177.5
Lead ballast					(21.28)			
Standard displacement								
Fuel oil		64.00			(68.52)	67.41	53.93/97.14	55.5/118.17
Lubricating oil					(9.2)	7.04		
Design displacement					(1,089)			

Table 3. (cont'd.)

S-42 SS 153	S-48 SS 159	S-48 rebuilt SS 159	Schley (T-1) SS 52	Bass (V-2) SS 164	Argonaut (V-4) SS 166	Nautilus (V-6) SS 168	Dolphin (V-7) SS 169
225-4½	240-0	267-0	268-9⅜	341-6	381-0	371-5/16	319-3
20-11	21-11¾	21-6	22-7½	27-6⅝	33-9½	33-3¼	27-11
17-6	13-6¾	12-5	14-2	15-2	16-¼	16-11¼	
		17.5	10-20	22.5	30	30	24
963	903	1,180 (1945)	1,106	2,119	3,046 (1939)	2,730 (standard)	1,718 (normal)
1,135	1,230	1,460	1,487	2,506	4,164 (1939)	3,900	2,240
4/39 (1939)	4/34	5/46 (1945)	4/5/45	7/11/69	7/9/71	9/10/70	7/3/53
2 × 600 BHP	2 × 900 BHP	2 × 1,000 BHP	4 × 1,000 BHP	2 × 2,250 BHP	2 × 1,400 BHP	2 × 2,350 BHP	2 × 1,750 BHP
				2 × 1,000 BHP	1 × 450 BHP	2 × 450 BHP	2 × 450 BHP
2 × 750 HP	2 × 750 HP	2 × 750 HP	2 × 750 HP	2 × 1,200 HP	2 × 1,100 HP	2 × 800 HP	2 × 875 HP
——	——	——	1 × 50 HP/25 kw	——	——	——	——
2 × 60 EP	120	2 × 60 EP	2 × 60 GP	2 × 60	2 × 120	2 × 120	2 × 120
9,500	9,500				8,500	8,500	9,800
12.5 (1939)	14.8	14.2 (trial)	20	21	15	17	17
2,510/6.5	5,900/11		3,000/11	6,000/11	8,000/10	9,380/10	4,900/10
10,000/8.1		16,000/11		10,000/11	18,000/10	25,000/5.7	18,780/10
9.5	11	10.0	10.5-11.5	9	8 (trials 7.43)	8 (6.5 by 1939)	8 (8.7 in 1939)
20 hr at 5 kt	20 hr at 5 kt	20 hr at 5 kt	20 hr at 5 kt	10 hr at 5 kt	10 hr at 5 kt	10 hr at 5 kt	10 hr at 5 kt
200	200	200	150	200	300	300	300
4 × 21 in	4 × 21 in	4 × 21 in	4 × 18 in	4 × 21 in	4 × 21 in	4 × 21 in	4 × 21 in
——	1 × 21 in	1 × 21 in	2 deck 18 in	2 × 21 in	2 mine tubes	2 × 21 in	2 × 21 in
12	16	14	12		60 mines		18
1 × 4 in	1 × 4 in/50	1 × 4 in	1 × 4 in/50	1 × 5 in/51	2 × 6 in/53	2 × 6 in/53	1 × 4 in/50
	439			1,280.2 (828)	(1,290)	1,289	618.7 (660)
	121			396.2 (171)	(389)	350	162.6 (167)
	231			752.4 (610)	(524)	679	488.1 (506)
			173.5				
			117.9				
			29.5				
	44		12.6*	25.2 (29)	(45)	51	23.9 (24)
			11.2*	30.8 (26)	(107)	68	40.8 (29)
	28			67.8 (94)	(121)	115	57.5 (61)
	25			46.1 (27)	(55)	65	24
				9.2 (11)			
172	327	280	381	395.2 (358)		471	59
				48.8 (70)	(112)	92	
59.03/150.94	78	128.57/267.86	74.8	155 (159)	(153)	165	91
			8.2	(14)	(9)	17	7
	1,000			2,181.2 (2,119)	(2,878)	2,987	1,688

Table 4.

	Cachalot (V-8) SS 170	Porpoise SS 172	Shark SS 174	Perch SS 176	Salmon SS 182	Sargo SS 188	Seadragon SS 194	Scheme I 10 May 1937	Scheme II 14 June 1937	Scheme III 21 June 1937
Length (ft-in)	274¼	301-0	298-¾	300-6¾	308-0	310-6	310-6	282-6 (LWL)	285-0 (LWL)	273-0 (LWL)
Beam (ft-in)	24-1⅛	24-11¼	25-¾	25-⅞	26-1¼	26-10	26-10 (15-7)	(15-6)		(15-6)
Draft (ft-in)	13-10¼	13-10	15-1¼	15-0	15-8	16-7¼	16-8			
Pressure hull thickness (lb/sq in)	24	25	25	25	27.5	27.8	28			
Surfaced displacement (tons)	1,110 (standard)	1,310 (standard)	1,316 (standard)	1,350 (standard)	1,435 (standard)	1,450 (standard)	1,450 (standard)	1,547.58	1,553.1	1,447.8
Submerged displacement (tons)	1,650	1,934	1,968	1,997	2,198	2,350	2,350	1,975.83	1,980.2	1,846
Complement	6/39	5/49	5/49	5/49	5/54	5/54	5/54			
Surface plant	2×1,535 BHP	4×1,300 BHP	4×1,300 BHP	4×1,300 BHP	4×1,535 BHP	4×1,535 BHP	4×1,535 BHP	3×1,600	4,000 BHP	4,000 BHP
Submerged plant	2×800 HP	4×521 HP	4×521 HP	8×296 HP	4×665 HP	4×685 HP	4×685 HP			
Auxiliary plant	1×330 kw	3×100 kw	3×100 kw	2×200 kw	2×330 kw	2×258 kw	2×258 kw	2×330 kw	1×330 kw	1×300 kw
Battery (cells)	2×120	2×120	2×120	2×120	2×120	2×126 S	2×126 S			
Capacity (amp-hr)	8,500	2×5,600	2×5,600	2×5,900 (also given as 2×7,140)	2×6,200	2×8,100	2×8,100			
Surface speed (kt)	17	19	19.5	19.25	21	21	20.8	19.4 (normal)	19.5 (normal)	19.5 (normal)
Surface endurance (nm/kt)	6,000/10	6,000/10	6,000/10	11,000/10	11,000/10	11,000/10	11,000/10			
Maximum (fuel in MBTs)	14,000/10	22,000/8	21,000/10				——			
Submerged speed (kt)	8 (7 in 1939)	8	8.25	8.75	9	8.75	8.75			
Submerged endurance (nm/kt)[1]	10 hr at 5 kt	10 hr at 5 kt; 36 hr at minimum speed	10 hr at 5 kt; 36 hr at minimum speed	10 hr at 5 kt; 36 hr at minimum speed	48 hr at 2 kt	48 hr at 2 kt	48 hr at 2 kt			
Test depth (ft)	250	250	250	250	250	250	250			
Tubes: bow	4×21 in	4×21 in	4×21 in	4×21 in	4×21 in	4×21 in	4×21 in	4×21 in	4×21 in	4×21 in
Tubes: stern	2×21 in	2×21 in	2×21 in	2×21 in	4×21 in	4×21 in	4×21 in	2×21 in	2×21 in	2×21 in
Torpedoes	16	16	16	16	24	24	24			
Guns	1×3 in/50	1×3 in/50	1×3 in/50	1×3 in/50	1×3 in/50	1×3 in/50	1×3 in/50			
Weights (tons):										
Hull	475.3 (507)	563.6 (548)	526	544.7 (548)	544.0 (560)	673.2 (600)	653.7	538	543	519
Hull fittings	149.4 (144)	160.7 (148)	126	165.1 (173)	175.6 (60)	189.8 (170)	168.2	172.8	172.8	172.8
Machinery:	297.8 (329)	386 (435)	395.6	408.8 (424)	442.9	428.6 (465)	460.7	406.82	388.9	373.1
Engines					(175)					
Battery					(247)					
Motors										
Armament	20.7 (21)	20 (21)	22.8	22 (21)	32.6 (84)	31.6 (29)	38	21.29	21.3	21.3
Ammunition	26.8 (25)	27.4 (30)	25	25 (28)	32.6	39.5 (38)	33	28.29	28.3	28.3
Equipment and outfit	44.3 (46)	56.3 (57)	55.3	56.2 (55)	57.4 (111)	58 (57)	56	55.34	55.3	55.3
Stores and fresh water	43.1 (20)	47.1 (29)	37.5	37.5 (14)	49 (14)	64.5 (34)	49.4	27.15	27.2	26
Complement	4.8	5.8 (5)	5.8	5.8 (5)	5.9 (6)	6.8 (5)	6.3	5.39	5.4	4.5
MBT capacity	407.9	517.8	500.6	506.4	565.2	455.9	455.9	428.25	427.1	398.3
Lead ballast	98.3	123.7 (28)	123.7	107.5 (62)	93.9 (94)	74.3 (66)	64.8	62	92.7	49.3
Standard displacement	(1,130)	(1,291)	(1,316)	(1,330)	(1,449)	(1,464)	(1,450)	1,308.13	1,313.6	1,236.6
Fuel oil	79 (85)	86.1 (85)	104.4	112	126.5 (125)	292.1 (300)	309	193.6/298	193.6/298	161.3/258.1
Lubricating oil	5	(25)			(17)	(28)		12.29	12.3	12.3
Design displacement	1,239.5 (1,242)	1,448.7 (1,416)	(1,467)	1,484.6	1,610.4 (1,638)	1,858.4 (1,861)	1,838.1 (1,867)	1,547.58	1,553.1	1,447.8

[1] Unless otherwise indicated.

Table 5.

	Tambor SS 203	Mackerel SS 204	Marlin SS 205	Gato SS 212	Balao SS 285	Tench SS 417	Scheme 2 28 Aug. 1944	Scheme 3 27 Oct. 1944	Scheme 14 17 Jan. 1945	Scheme 17 May 1945
Length (ft-in)	307-2	243-1	238-11	311-9	311-9	311-8	352-0 (LWL)	332-0 (LWL)	320-0 (LWL)	331-0 (LWL)
Beam (ft-in)	27-3	22-1 (13-9)	21-7¼ (13-9)	27-3	27-3	27-3 (16-0)	30-2	30-2	(16-9)	(17-0)
Draft (ft-in)	14-7½	14-6	13-¼	15-3	15-3	15-3	15-6½	15-6½		
Pressure hull thickness (lb/sq in)	27.5			27.5	35–35.7	35–35.7			60	
Surfaced displacement (tons)	1,475 (standard)	825	800 (standard)	1,526 (standard)	1,525	1,570	2,447	2,414.67	2,111.69	2,286.05
Submerged displacement (tons)	2,370	1,190	1,165	2,410	2,415	2,415	3,247.9	3,293.04	2,734.96	2,988.81
Complement	6/54	4/33	4/34	6/54	10/70–71	10/71				
Surface plant	4×1,600 BHP	2×850 BHP	2×900 BHP	4×1,350 BHP	4×1,350 BHP	4×1,350 BHP	6×1,750 BHP	6×1,750 BHP	4×2,900 BHP	4×2,250 BHP*
Submerged plant	4×685 HP	2×750 HP	2×750 HP	4×685 HP	4×685 HP	2×1,370 HP				
Auxiliary plant	1×300 kw 1×100 kw	1×60 kw	1×60 kw	1×100 kw (most units: 1×300)	1×300 kw	1×300 kw				
Battery (cells)	2×126 S	2×60 S	2×60 S	2×126 S	2×126 S	2×126 S				
Capacity (amp-hr)	2×8,100			2×9,300 (war)	2×9,300 (war)	2×9,300 (war)				
Surface speed (kt)	20.4		14.5	21	20.25	20.25	24.0	23.6	23.1	22.5
Surface endurance (nm/kt) Maximum (fuel in MBTs)	11,000/10	6,500/10 (service)	7,400/10 (service)	11,000/10	11,000/10	11,000/10				
Submerged speed (kt)	8.75		9	9	8.75	8.75				
Submerged endurance (nm/kt)[1]	48 hr at 2 kt			48 hr at 2 kt	48 hr at 2 kt	48 hr at 2 kt				
Test depth (ft)	250	250	250	300	400	400	1,000*	1,000*	500	500
Tubes: bow	6×21 in	4×21 in	4×21 in	6×21 in	6×21 in	6×21 in				6×21 in
Tubes: stern	4×21 in	2×21 in	2×21 in	4×21 in	4×21 in	4×21 in				6×21 in
Torpedoes	24	12	12	24	24	28				30
Guns	1×3 in/50	1×3 in/50	1×3 in/50	1×3 in/50	1×5 in/25	1×5 in/25				1×5 in/25
Weights (tons):										
Hull	660.4	(356.4)	(339.5)		(697.06)	695.45	999.33	879.44	769.93	900.83
Hull fittings	179.1	(99.6)	(106.7)		(149.15)	139.52	155.97	158.27	140	159.3
Machinery:	455.3	(229.7)	(202.9)		(448.65)	455.9	594.15	590.55	554	557.9
Engines					(52.43 dry)					
Battery					(192)					
Motors					(24.30)					
Armament	38.4	(21.3)	(23.9)		(41.05)	47.3	47.3	76.61	73.65	75.18
Ammunition	38.5	(14.7)	(19)		(40.88)	47.57	39.85	62.64	58.6	58.98
Equipment and outfit	59.2	(30.1)	(29.5)		(54.19)	57.97	60.8	60.51	58	65.54
Stores and fresh water	55.8	(17.1)	(12.6)		(37.99)	39.95	43.57	46.34	39.86	42.95
Complement	6.5	(4)	(4.6)		(6.47)	8.33	8.93	9.53	8.33	8.81
MBT capacity	606.6	(225.3)			(615.72)	580.2	810.31	878.37	623.27	702.76
Lead ballast	75.3	(56.7)	(48.5)		(87)	82.48	90	100	92	104
Standard displacement	(1,475)		(796.4)		(1,545.29)	1565.28	2,036.42	1,966.91	1,779.17	1,959.96
Fuel oil	175/301.9	(57.3/95)	59/89 (58.2/84.14)	175/324.25	(175.94/300.91)	193.87/361.46	296.28/548.68	325.78/625	234.67/430.56	214.65/399.01
Lubricating oil		(3.8)			(19.33/22.63)	20.28	30.42	30.42	25.35	23.12
Design displacement	1,870.2	(916.7)	(895.2)		(1,804.1)	1,920	2,447.00	2,414.67	2,111.69	2,286.05

[1] Unless otherwise indicated.

Notes

Chapter 1

1. Until 1894, torpedo craft, including submarines, were the province of BuOrd; only then did C&R gain full authority over hull designs. BuOrd conducted the competitions that chose John P. Holland's submarine design. Until abolished in 1910, a separate Bureau of Equipment was responsible for electrical equipment, including submarine batteries and motors. During the 19th century, both constructors (C&R officers) and engineers (officers who operated propelling plants and were assigned to BuEng) were members of separate specially trained staff corps, rather than line officers. Constructors (naval architects) typically rotated between C&R in Washington, shipyards, and the fleet. In 1899, the Engineer Corps was amalgamated with the line, but the Construction Corps survived until C&R merged with BuEng in 1940. After the special corps were abolished, specially trained officers were designated EDO (engineering duty only). No special designations were applied to BuOrd's weapons experts. Unrestricted line officers served within each bureau, the hope being that they would carry the fleets's views and its experience to the specialists.

2. Before the creation of an Office of Operations (Office of the Chief of Naval Operations) in 1915, line officers sent comments and suggestions on submarine materiel through BuNav. Senior Officers in BuNav frequently endorsed important ideas. Examples cited below are the light detachable (flying) bridge and the second periscope. Much of the relevant correspondence is in NARS RG 19, Entry 92 (folded "E" correspondence), file 17693E. Later, the Bureau of Navigation became the Bureau of Naval Personnel, concerned mainly with personnel assignments, but at least before WW II it was often referred to as BuNav (now it is BuPers).

3. For details of this fight, see Norman Friedman, *U.S. Battleships: An Illustrated Design History* (Annapolis, Md.: Naval Institute Press, 1985), particularly 53–55, 79–82.

4. In particular, there was no generally accepted base of submarine design knowledge from which C&R could work. When he left the navy to join Electric Boat in 1902, naval constructor Lawrence Y. Spear quickly absorbed that company's base of experience, so that within a few years he was able to replace John Holland as a submarine designer. In the case of submarines, C&R eventually took over the concept, or preliminary design, role, in which basic features were set. For airplanes, the navy continued to buy complete designs. Eventually, however, its in-house aeronautical engineers developed their own preliminary or sketch designs on which to base the specifications submitted to the industry. In many cases, the same individuals became involved in both of the new technologies, submarines and aero-

nautics. For example, Emory S. Land, who became the first C&R submarine designer, joined the Bureau of Aeronautics after WW I and rose to assistant chief before returning to C&R as chief constructor (head of C&R). In England, Murray Sueter was one of the first submariners and later became a driving force in WW I British naval aviation.

5. Electric Boat's patents could prevent other designers from producing efficient submarines. For example, Simon Lake's S-2 was badly flawed largely because he had to use flat tank tops. U-shaped tank tops would have solved many of the design's problems, but that arrangement had been patented by Electric Boat, which used it. Electric Boat also apparently patented the characteristic stern form of its submarines, with its skegs.

6. Holland blamed the *Plunger* fiasco on features imposed on him by the navy. Contemporary minutes of the Board on Construction show the members' deep suspicion of Holland's work.

7. According to an unsigned mimeographed history of Electric Boat, 1899–1949 (located in the Rare Book room of the Navy Department Library, Washington, D.C.), the company also suffered other disasters. In 1917, its holding company, Submarine Boat Corp., established a freighter plant at Port Newark to build 150 steel 5350 DWT ships for the Emergency Fleet Corp. By the end of the war, 118 had been completed. Submarine Boat then decided to complete the other 32 ships for its own account, largely in hopes of selling at least 18, and possibly 28, to Italy. That did not happen, and the postwar commercial shipbuilding market crashed. Submarine Boat had little success in operating some of its freighters. Electric Boat had advanced $2.8 million to Submarine Boat; it had to reorganize in 1925. A new company, including NELSECO (diesels), Electro Dynamic (motors), and Elco (small boats), was incorporated in New Jersey on 2 June 1925. To survive, Electric Boat built small craft, marine diesels, and nonmarine industrial equipment (such as printing presses, paper folders, wire-spoke machines for carmakers, and metal stamping machines); it even repaired locomotives. Foreign royalties on the basic Holland patent (complete filling of ballast tanks when dived: about $4 million between 1916 and 1927) helped. Work on war program S-boats continued through 1925, and Peru ordered two submarines in 1924 and another pair in 1926. Then came the 1929 crash. (The Port Newark plant also prefabricated parts for H-class submarines during WW I; presumably that experience inspired the company's proposal to mass-produce freighters.)

A World War I British naval observer, naval constructor Stanley Goodall (later Director of Naval Construction Sir Stanley) was much impressed by Electric Boat prefabrication techniques. The company built mock-ups for all piping, wiring, etc. to get what Goodall considered extremely neat layouts. Early in 1918 it was considering adopting electric welding; it had tested welds to 190 psi, over twice the test requirement, but the U.S. Navy Department was still unwilling to chance either nonuniform welds or the effects of vibration. About fifteen years later Electric Boat would pioneer welded pressure hulls for U.S. submarines. Goodall's comments are in his letter 14 to the Admiralty, ADM 229/97 in the British PRO, Kew, England.

The issue of prefabrication came up in a 17 June 1918 letter from L. Y. Spear, then Vice President of Electric Boat, to the CNO, Admiral W. S. Benson. At this time the General Board was pressing for a 25-knot fleet submarine (capable of 11 kt on its auxiliary diesel), which Spear estimated would be about 400 ft long (2700 tons), and would have a 16,000 SHP powerplant. Benson had asked whether Electric Boat could place it in production. Spear's reaction was that this would have to be an experimental design, since it was so much larger than anything previously attempted in the United States, and thus that it could not be built by semi-skilled labor. Even if it were allowed to displace destroyers under construction, it could not be built quickly. Each such boat would cost at least 4 S-boats. Submarine construction was already hampered because the two main yards, Fore River and Union Iron Works, were also principal destroyer yards. No more submarines could be laid down until 1919, and then 20–30 per year could be built. Spear offered an alternative: parts could be prefabricated at Newark Bay, then assembled at a new plant (for which he had a suitable site in mind) at a rate of 70 to 100 S-boats per year. World War I ended before any such project could begin. Spear's letter is in NARS RG 19 correspondence, series 22-S.

8. While acting as BuNav submarine expert, Marsh commanded the transport USS *Yankee* from 1908 through 1911. He retired in 1913 after commanding the battleship *Ohio*, but was later recalled to duty in the OpNav Division of Naval Militia [i.e., reservist] Affairs (*Yankee* had been used largely to train the naval militia). Oddly, the navy press release issued at his death in 1933 made no mention of his connection with the submarine force, yet correspondence in the National Archives (RG 19 file 17693E) makes his significance clear. As a Lt. Comdr., Marsh served on the *Octopus* (C-1) trials board in 1907. It strongly advocated installing submarine bells (for underwater signalling) on board U.S. submarines. About a year later Marsh was responsible for the decision to actually install them. When changes to the D class were being considered in 1908, L. Y. Spear of Electric Boat wrote to Marsh to find out whether his proposals would be acceptable.

9. McLean was not actually a submariner but took the course at the Naval Torpedo School (October 1899–March 1900); he probably met Sims on board *Kentucky*. McLean was in charge of target practice in the North Atlantic Fleet and was later aide on the staff of the fleet commander for target practice (Sims was director of target practice, i.e., of operational gunnery). Just prior to serving on the General Board, McLean was aide to the fleet ordnance office. Sims later wanted McLean to command the Atlantic Fleet submarines (when Sims commanded the Atlantic Torpedo Fleet), but Yates Stirling served instead. In June 1927, McLean took command of the Submarine Divisions of the Battle Fleet; he had not commanded any submarines but had served mainly in battleships (he had been director of naval communications, 1924–27). The connection between gunnery and torpedo/submarine work was not altogether unusual. For example, Sims's British equivalent (and friend), Adm. Sir Percy Scott, came to believe, about 1914, that submarines and aircraft would soon displace battleships.

10. This is largely based on a letter from Adm. Thomas C. Hart to Comdr. James Fife, 25 April 1939.

11. Many modern submarines hover by taking water aboard or expelling it as they float up and down in the water.

Chapter 2

1. Alex Roland, *Underwater Warfare in the Age of Sail* (Bloomington: Indiana University Press, 1978), suggests that Bushnell built on an earlier submarine designed and built by Denis Papin (for the Landgrave of Hesse-Cassel, in Germany) at the end of the 17th century. Crude sketches of Papin's craft were widely reproduced during the 18th century, but they did not show how it was propelled.

2. This account is from the *Dictionary of American Naval Fighting Ships*, Vol. VII (Washington, D.C.: Naval Historical Center, 1981), 354–355; presumably, it reflects recent historical research. According to contemporary British records, however, HMS *Eagle* was not present in New York Harbor on the night of Sergeant Lee's attack, so it is not altogether clear whether he attacked at all. Intense exertion in the closed and unfamiliar confines of the boat would have generated enough carbon dioxide to intoxicate him. (Bushnell was probably grossly optimistic in estimating that his craft held enough air for 30 minutes.) Many writers have suggested that the attack failed because Sergeant Lee's auger (used to attach his mine) could not penetrate the copper sheathing of the British ship (and because the buoyancy of the *Turtle* did not press it hard enough against the target's bottom). After the three abortive sorties, Bushnell turned exclusively to mines. Depressed by his failure, Bushnell went to France at the end of the war. In 1787, he provided Thomas Jefferson, then U.S. minister to France, with full details of his *Turtle*. Bushnell seems to have influenced several French inventors of the 1790s. He might have communicated with (and thus influenced) Fulton; in some ways, Fulton's boat was a modified *Turtle*. When Bushnell returned to the United States some years later, he settled in Georgia under the assumed name of Dr. Bush. He disclosed his true name only in his will (he died in 1826 at the age of 90). In an 1875 lecture, "Submarine Boats and Their Application to Torpedo Operations," Lt. F. M. Barber (BuOrd) said that *Turtle* "seems, notwithstanding its failures, to have been the most perfect thing of its kind that has ever been constructed, either before or since the time of Bushnell."

Murray Sueter, *Evolution of the Submarine Boat, Mine and Torpedo—From the 16th Century to 1907* (Portsmouth, England; J. Griffin & Co., 1907), points out Bushnell's strengths: he understood the need for a strong hull to withstand depth; he understood that gunpowder could explode underwater (and thus in effect invented the mine); he understood that a ship's bottom is her most vulnerable point; and he saw that a conning tower directly above the center of gravity would help stability and permit vision when awash. Sueter was an important early British submarine exponent and WW I chief of the Royal Naval Air Service. Description is based on an October 1787 letter ("General Principles and Construction of a Sub-marine Vessel") from Bushnell to Thomas Jefferson, who was then U.S. minister to France, quoted in A. Preston, *The First Submarines* (London: Phoebus, special edition in *Purnell's History of the World Wars;* no date, probably about 1973), 6. Bushnell seems to have envisaged taking in just enough water to descend slowly: "When the skilful operator had obtained an equilibrium, he could row upward, or downward, or continue at any particular depth. . ."

3. William Hovgaard, *History of Modern Warships* (London: E. F. Spon, 1920), suggests that Fulton's hydroplane was less than successful because ultimately he had to add a bow haul-

down propeller. (Hovgaard had written a book on submarines in 1887.) Notes on early submarines are based in part on Lt. Col. C. Field, Royal Marine Light Infantry, *The Story of the Submarine, from the Earliest Ages to the Present Day* (London: Sampson Low, Marston & Co., 1908). Field describes virtually all the known 19th century attempts to build submarines. Fulton first proposed a submarine to the French Directory on 13 December 1797. According to Roland, *Underwater Warfare*, Fulton's first design was essentially a *Turtle* with an extended tail, a vertical rudder, and a sail. This first *Nautilus* was launched on the Seine near Rouen on 13 July 1800. A larger boat was completed at Paris in June 1801. Field mentions a 100-ft Fulton-type submarine built by a well-known smuggler named Johnson (who might have participated in Fulton's British experiments) to rescue Napoleon from St. Helena, but she was incomplete when Napoleon died. The boat had two folding masts for sails.

4. W. S. Hutcheon, Jr., *Robert Fulton: Pioneer of Undersea Warfare* (Annapolis, Md.: Naval Institute Press, 1981), suggests that Fulton became aware of Bushnell's ideas through his friendship with Joel Barlow, a Yale freshman when Bushnell was a senior. Barlow's brother-in-law, Abraham Baldwin, was a close friend of Bushnell's. Bushnell reportedly left France in 1795; Fulton arrived in 1797. On the other hand, W. B. Parsons, *Robert Fulton and the Submarine* (New York: Columbia University Press, 1922), claims that Bushnell offered the Directory his own submarine in 1797. Bushnell seems to have used a full Archimedes screw; Fulton might have been the first to realize that separate blades were more efficient. According to a contemporary French report, *Nautilus* was 6.48 m × 1.94 m (21 ft 3 in × 6 ft 4 in), with a hollow iron keel 0.52 m deep and running to within 1 m of the bow.

5. Hutcheon, *Robert Fulton: Pioneer*, 43–44.

6. Some of Fulton's plans might have survived in France; in 1809, Napoleon let a contract for a French submarine. According to a 20 September 1801 letter, Fulton considered that his success with *Nautilus* justified building much larger boats, 36 ft × 12 ft, large enough for eight men (with air for 8 hr) and capable of carrying 25 to 30 bombs (towed torpedoes) at a depth of 60 or 80 ft. Such a boat could sail at 5–7 kt according to Parsons, *Robert Fulton and the Submarine*.

7. The British plans came to light many years later. Fulton had left them with the U.S. consul in London, General Lyman, to be opened if he were lost at sea en route to the United States, so that his ideas would not die with him. The drawings were auctioned in England in 1870 but attracted no great attention. Parsons, *Robert Fulton and the Submarine*, published them. Although the full story of Fulton's dealings with the French government was unearthed from a French archive only in 1896, he apparently managed to publicize his submarines quite widely during his lifetime. Hence Fulton's prominence in this account. Parsons reprinted a British Admiralty secret circular (19 June 1803) describing Fulton's submarine as a considerable danger and claiming that Fulton had remained underwater for as much as 7 hr and made 2.5 kt underwater. Parsons believed that the British enticed Fulton to England specifically to neutralize this threat, not knowing that the French had already abandoned it. Fulton contributed to British interest by furnishing a friend, the Earl of Stanhope, with a complete description of his "system" of underwater warfare.

8. Fulton had had much the same idea: he tried to finance his experiments by payments per ship sunk.

9. Barber, "Submarine Boats," *Nile's Register*. Barber describes no sinkings. The August 1813 date and the association with Bushnell are from Sueter, *Evolution of Submarine Boat*.

10. Roland, *Underwater Warfare*, shows a sketch of a cigar-shaped one-man submarine found in Samuel Colt's papers. The operator drove the bow screw propeller with one hand and steered with the other. The sketch shows a ballast ("forcing") pump but no down-haul screw. The operator had a breathing tube. Presumably, he exited through a "water lock" in the keel to attach a limpet mine to the target. Colt's annotation is "lost in New London harbor in an effort to blow up a British 74 in 1814." Colt developed a controlled mine system that he called his "underwater battery."

11. Sueter, *Evolution of Submarine Boat*, reports that Bauer tried to sell his submarine to the U.S. Navy before going to Russia, where he launched one in 1855.

12. L.H. Bollander, "The *Alligator*, First Federal Submarine of the Civil War," *Proceedings of the U.S. Naval Institute*, June 1939. de Villeroi demonstrated his first submarine (10 ft × 3 ft) in France in 1832. Failing to sell a boat to the French Navy during the Crimean War, he then came to Philadelphia in 1859. There he built another submarine, financed by Stephen Girard, possibly in hopes of salvaging the treasure of the British warship *de Braak,* lost in 1780 off Lewes, Del. The submarine was propeller-driven, 33 ft × 4 ft (20 ft parallel midbody), and had a chemical air regenerator and an air lock for a diver. She remained underwater for 3 hr, diving to about 20 ft. In 1861, de Villeroi sought trials at the Philadelphia Navy Yard in hopes that he could patent his boat. Capt. Samuel F. duPont, then commandant of the yard, convened a three-officer board on 30 May to examine the boat. The officers were favorably impressed; Secretary of the Navy Gideon Welles ordered Comdr. Joseph Smith, chief of Bureau of Yards and Docks, to investigate further. Smith was interested but skeptical; the air regenerator had not been explained, it was not clear how de Villeroi dived and surfaced (he evaded the depth control problem by suspending his boat from two large buoys on the surface), and his boat was too small to test his ideas for war. He suggested that de Villeroi be paid to build a larger boat (cost not to exceed $14,000). de Villeroi proposed a contract to destroy the ships at Norfolk, particularly the *Merrimack*, for a set fee, with no payment in the event he failed. Reportedly, de Villeroi was ultimately offered a fee of $10,000, plus another $5,000 for each successful operation. A $14,000, 40-day building contract was let to Martin Thomas of Philadelphia on 1 November 1861; he subcontracted to Neafie & Levy. The cost of platinum-covered silver plates (the "secret" of the air purifier) was a major point of contention. de Villeroi could not be contacted; fittings whose design he alone could furnish could not be supplied. Work was therefore suspended until the navy took over the boat on 13 June 1862 (the boat was launched on 30 April 1862).

13. According to Rear Adm. T. O. Selfridge in his memoirs, Assistant Secretary of the Navy Gustavus Fox offered him command of *Alligator* in July 1862; he would be promoted to captain if he took the boat up the James River and destroyed the Confederate ironclad *Virginia II*. Selfridge initially demurred, then accepted. When he sought a crew on board the receiving ship *North Carolina* in New York, half the men on board volunteered. He selected 14. Early in August, *Alligator* successfully submerged and surfaced but then nearly sank while running awash (she began to trim by the bow as men ran forward to escape after the air supply gave out); Selfridge gave up on her.

14. For a summary, see P. Pry and R. Zeitlin, "Torpedo Boats: Secret Weapons of the South," *Warship International*, no. 4 (1984): 384–393. Pry and Zeitlin do not list Alstilt's submarine. For the 1861 submarine, see M. F. Perry, *Infernal Machines: The Story of Confederate Submarine and Mine Warfare* (Baton Rouge: Louisiana

State University Press, 1965), 92. Perry cites a report of a November 1861 test by a Pinkerton operative, a Mrs. E. H. Baker. The submarine towed a green rubber float, through which an air tube passed. Two or three men left her in diving suits to fasten a charge to the target ship. Mrs. Baker said that the relatively small test craft was demonstrating the principle of a much larger one under construction. A sketch in *Harper's Weekly* (2 November 1861) was strikingly similar to plans captured from a courier trying to cross the Mississippi River into Texas in November 1863. In an accompanying letter, a James Jones of Richmond claimed that he had designed the Richmond boat. Intelligence reported that Jones built another such boat at Houston, Texas, and four at Shreveport, Louisiana. They were never seen in combat and perhaps did not exist.

15. Found and raised about 1879, *Pioneer* was placed on display in New Orleans in 1907; she is currently in the Louisiana State Museum. She was built by McClintock, at his New Orleans machine shop, of quarter-inch plates cut from boilers. According to *Dictionary of American Naval Fighting Ships*, Vol.II (Washington, D.C.: Government Printing Office, 1969), 556–557, *Pioneer* was intended specifically to counter the U.S. steamers *New London* and *Calhoun* on Lake Pontchartrain. After the Civil War, McClintock claimed that she had made several dives in the lake and had destroyed a small schooner and several rafts in tests. The discrepancy between her measured length as raised (20 ft) and the length given in the letter of marque (34 ft) could indicate either that her spar torpedo is missing or that the boat raised was in fact another, otherwise unknown Confederate submarine. (McClintock claimed after the war that she was 30 ft long, with a 10-ft cylindrical midsection). Measured inside width was 3 ft 2 in, and measured depth was 6 ft. P. van Doren Stern, *The Confederate Navy: A Pictorial History* (Garden City, N.Y.: Doubleday, 1962), quotes a 1926 description by W. M. Robinson, Jr. He suspected that a 2-in opening at the bow was for forward vision, rather than for a spar torpedo; he had "little doubt" that the weapon was a towed charge.

16. P. C. Coker III, *Charleston's Maritime Heritage 1670–1865* (Charleston: CokerCraft Press, 1987. The new submarine's dimensions were 25 ft × 5 × 6 ft (depth). After the war, W. A. Alexander, a Confederate Army engineer of Company B, 21st Alabama Volunteers, claimed credit for her construction, assisted by George E. Dixon of the same unit, but McClintock was principal designer). McClintock invested heavily in an unsuccessful electric power plant, then substituted four-man cranks to turn the propeller. That gave insufficient speed to deal with Union ships blockading Mobile. In 1868, McClintock gave dimensions as 36 ft × 3 ft × 4 ft (12 ft of each end tapered). According to *Dictionary of American Naval Fighting Ships*, this was probably the submarine described on 26 February 1863 by a Confederate deserter. He claimed that the submarine had left Fort Morgan to come up at Sand Island, get the range and bearing of the nearest Union ship, then dive and attach a clockwork mine to her. On emerging, however, they found themselves too far out and the current too strong, so they cut the mine loose and tried to get back.

17. Coker, *Charleston's Maritime Heritage*, differs from other authors in claiming that the eight men were the full complement: six crankers, the commander, and his assistant (who sometimes joined the crankers, but otherwise was responsible for air supply and for the tanks aft). The captain, who had a small conning tower, steered and handled the boat forward. Like *Pioneer*, she was built under the supervision of Alexander and Dixon from plans supplied mainly by McClintock. Alexander was second in command, but he was detached before the fatal last patrol. From memory rather than contemporary notes, he later wrote that the towed charge worked in tests at Mobile but not in the rougher water at Charleston, hence the 22-ft downward-pointing spar with its fixed charge. His article claimed that the full complement was nine: the captain, his assistant, and seven crankers. See W. A. Alexander, "Thrilling Chapter in the History of the Confederate States Navy. Work of Submarine Boats," in *Southern Historical Society Papers* XXX (1902), 165.

18. These dimensions were provided by a Confederate deserter in 1864; *Hunley* was never raised, hence not measured postwar. According to Alexander, "Thrilling Chapter," *Hunley* was a 25 ft × 4-ft cylindrical boiler cut lengthwise, with two 12-in iron strips inserted between top and bottom and the ends tapered. Coker, *Charleston's Maritime Heritage*, estimates her dimensions as 35 ft × 4 ft × 5 ft, but he notes that some contemporaries (including witnesses on board *Housatonic*) claimed that she was as little as 20 ft long and that the only contemporary painting suggests a length of about 40 ft. In a letter to Matthew F. Maury, (1868), McClintock gave 40 ft × 3½ ft × 4 ft (depth) and a maximum speed of 2.5 mph. Alexander gave 30 ft × 4 ft × 5 ft (4 mph). Coker places her diving planes roughly amidships, so that she could change depth without taking on any angle, but the contemporary drawing and painting suggest that they were forward, as on *Pioneer*.

19. Perry, *Internal Machines*, reports that standard practice was to trim down *Hunley* until only her hatches and small conning tower were above the surface. Using her planes, (i.e., maintaining small positive buoyancy), she dove when her target was in sight. Leveling off, she steered toward her target's shadow. She left her towed torpedo against the target hull and, once past the target, headed for the surface. In the one test of this method, the resulting explosion rolled the submarine over. *Hunley* could use her spar torpedo awash, with the hatches open (for easier breathing and thus for better propulsion), relying on their high coamings to avoid swamping.

20. According to a Confederate deserter (reporting on 7 January 1864), *Hunley* had drowned another crew at Mobile before coming to Charleston. It appears that she sank on 15 October because she dived at too steep an angle and buried her bow in the bottom. Unfortunately, the ballast tanks had open tops, so as the boat went down bow first with full tanks, water from the after tank could spill out and run forward, pushing the bow further down. This was even worse than the free-surface instability later inventors suffered in diving with partly full (but closed) tanks. When she was found, the after tank (but not the forward one) had been pumped dry, and the drop keel bolts had been loosened but not released. Bolts had been loosened in both hatchways, but apparently water pressure made it impossible to open the hatches. Reportedly, however, *Hunley* made numerous successful dives, including one lasting 2 hr and 35 min (largely because seaweed had clogged a ballast pump). Apparently, there were numerous training runs, averaging four nights a week, out as far as 7 nm. Typically, the boat dived to 6 ft and surfaced frequently for air and observation (porpoising, in a later term).

21. Barber probably obtained his information from an account in *Harper's Weekly*, 30 January 1864, that quoted A. M. Olivier de Jalvin's account in *Le Monde Illustre*, which in turn gave news (presumably via blockade runner) from Mobile, Alabama. In this article, the inventor's name is spelled "Anstilt," but all later writers have used the spelling given here. According to this account, Alstilt's boat was iron, 23 yd long, with a hermetically sealed deck and a diving plane ("horizontal rudder") at the bow for vertical control. A pressure gauge measured depth. In this account, the significance of the 3 ft is that the boat is invisible if

she lies 3 ft or more below the surface. The boat was intended to release a remotely detonated buoyant mine as she passed under her target (the mine also could be percussion detonated to attack a moving ship passing over the submarine). There was no reported submarine activity during the Battle of Mobile Bay in August 1864 (there were, however, mines), and no contemporary account mentions the capture of Alstilt's submarine.

22. D. L. Canney, *The Old Steam Navy: The Ironclads* (Annapolis, Md.: Naval Institute Press, 1993) 20–21, 25, reports that Bushnell, a Connecticut entrepreneur and railroad investor, was already clearly interested in naval issues. He was partly responsible for two of the first three U.S. Navy ironclads, *Galena* and *Monitor*. On 3 August 1861, Congress appropriated $1.5 million for one or more ironclads, their designs (submitted by prospective builders) to be evaluated by an expert board. Bushnell had already submitted his *Galena* proposal on 28 June. He apparently acted as John Ericsson's agent for the *Monitor* design; Secretary of the Navy Gideon Welles later recalled that he met Bushnell in Hartford, was impressed by the idea, and sent Bushnell to Washington to meet the navy board there.

23. Holland published an account of Sweeney's test in *Cassirer's Magazine*, May 1897.

24. Barber "Submarine Boats," regards the whole saga as a fiasco: "A superior boat could probably be built for one-fourth her purchase money." The author is indebted to Donald L. Canney for certain details of the "Intelligent Whale."

Chapter 3

1. Holland claimed that the French boats incorporated elements of his *Fenian Ram* (see below), revealed when foreigners watched it being built. It seems more likely that several designers arrived at roughly the same conclusions independently, particularly since Holland himself drew on standard contemporary torpedo practice. Laubeuf won an 1896 French Ministry of Marine competition with a proposal that a standard torpedo boat hull be wrapped around a pressure hull. The price paid for good surface performance was very slow diving, but that was partly because the boat needed a steam plant to provide the necessary power. According to H. le Masson, *Les Sous-Marines Francais*, rev. ed. (Brest-Paris: Editions de la Cite, 1980), Laubeuf's *Narval* used the hull of a standard Normand torpedo boat (No. 130–144 class). Underwater endurance was 60 nm at 3.25 kt and 11 nm at 5 kt. Surface range was at least 500 nm at 6.5 kt and maximum sea speed was 10 kt. le Masson claimed that *Narval* could dive in 20 min; that was cut to 5 min in *Sirene* (1901) and to 4 min in the *Aigrette* class. According to Nicholas Lambert (private communication), however, *Narval* took 30 min to dive, and maximum underwater endurance was only 27 nm. Presumably, le Masson quoted trial, rather than operational, data. The French switched to diesels to cut diving time. The 1896 competition and its results were reported in Office of Naval Intelligence (ONI), *Information from Abroad*. These annual volumes, now in many libraries, were the main source of U.S. official knowledge of foreign technical developments. Many French naval officers preferred the all-battery *Gustave Zede*, which made a celebrated torpedo attack on the French battleship *Magenta*, in January 1898. (Minister of Marine Edward Lockroy was on board at the time.) The French Navy continued to build submarines (designed primarily for underwater performance) after it began building Laubeuf's submersibles. Laubeuf designs were used by France, Peru, and Greece. Italian double-hull designs by Cesare Laurenti were used by Italy, Sweden, Portugal, and Brazil, with a few in Denmark. Double-hull Krupp designs were used by Germany, Austria, and Norway, with a few in Russia and Italy.

2. This date has also been given as 1859. According to Frank T. Cable, *The Birth and Development of the American Submarine* (New York: Harper & Row, 1924), one of Holland's earliest sketches showed a boat powered by a gunpowder engine, one of the few available internal combustion types. Simon Lake, *Submarines in War and Peace* (Philadelphia: J. B. Lippincott, 1918), reports that Holland's son claimed that the ramming attacks of the Confederate ironclad *Merrimac* convinced Holland that a ram could defeat an ironclad. Reports of the "Intelligent Whale" convinced Holland that the enormous physical obstacles to a successful submarine could be overcome.

3. This account of Holland's work is based largely on R. K. Morris, *John P.Holland, 1841–1914, Inventor of the Modern Submarine* (Annapolis, Md.: U.S. Naval Institute, 1966). Morris worked from Holland's papers.

4. Cable, *Birth and Development of American Submarine*. This project is not described by Morris.

5. Cable, *Birth and Development of American Submarine*. Patented in 1874, Brayton's was among the few internal combustion engines then available. Holland used Brayton engines in his first four submarines. Cable implies that the Fenians supported Brayton because he was a supporter of their cause. At least in the 1878 boat, the internal combustion feature of the Brayton did not work; Holland had to run the engine on steam passed through a rubber hose from the boiler of a launch. Thus powered, Holland's boat performed underwater for an hour.

6. Holland's papers show a related submarine ($12\frac{1}{2}$ ft long, displacing 1.3 ton) equipped with a very simple periscope that he claimed he used for experiments in the Passaic River in May and June 1878. Morris suggests that this plan was an idealized afterthought because only his Zalinski boat and *Plunger* had periscopes. The dates suggest that Holland was thinking of some modification to *No. 1*, rather than of a separate boat.

7. Visitors to the yard where *Ram* was built reportedly included Italians, Germans, Russians, Swedes, and Turks. Although there was no official U.S. interest, according to Cable, *Birth and Development of American Submarine*, *Ram* greatly impressed several navy officers who later became Holland's supporters; they included Capt. (later Rear Adm.) George H. Converse (BuOrd). Cable *Birth and Development of American Submarine*, claims that two high-ranking Turks asked Holland to design a similar submarine for their government. A few years later, Turkey bought Nordenfeldt submarines. According to Cable, *Ram* took two years to build and cost $13,000.

8. These dimensions were chosen so that *Ram* could be carried in a standard railroad boxcar.

9. Pneumatic guns were attractive because contemporary gun propellants administered so sharp an acceleration that it was impossible to make usable high-explosive shells. U.S. Navy interest culminated in the "dynamite gun" cruiser *Vesuvius* built about a decade later. Holland claimed that his pneumatic gun could fire a projectile carrying 100 lb of explosive for 50–60 yd underwater or 300 yd over water.

10. According to Cable, *Birth and Development of American Submarine*, 80, Holland ran underwater by using the Brayton as an air engine; he could get 2 hr at full speed (a bit less than 7 mph) on a tank of 400-psi air. Observers were apparently impressed by the "dextrous swiftness" of her dives.

11. According to Cable, *Birth and Development of American Submarine*, the 16-ft model was still incomplete without the gasket to make her hatch watertight and without machinery (the operator would use his hands and feet for propulsion).

12. ONI, *Information from Abroad* (1889), 453–454. *Gymnote* was described as an enlarged manned version of the standard

Whitehead torpedo, 59 ft × 11 ft (29.5 tons), using stern planes for vertical control. Power was supplied by 564 alkaline storage cells (300 lb of battery per HP). Estimated speed was 10 kt for 6 hr (60-HP motor). Except for propulsion, the designers, Dupuy de Lome and Gustave Zede, seem to have come to much the same conclusions as Holland.

13. W. S. Murphy, *Father of the Submarine: The Life of the Reverend George Garrett Pasha* (London: William Kimber, 1987). Nordenfeldt's submarines were all designed by George Garrett (their relationship was similar to the one that later developed between Issac Rice and Holland). Unlike Garrett, Nordenfeldt envisaged the submarine as a torpedo boat that would operate mainly awash, submerging only to attack. Garrett completed a man-powered submarine in July 1878 and the steam-powered *Resurgam* on 21 November 1879. The latter relied entirely on her planes (balance rudders) to dive; she had no ballast tanks whatever, being designed to float awash. Garrett's Nordenfeldts added down-haul screws and ballast tanks, with their free-surface problems. Murphy considers Garrett's timing particularly unfortunate: just two years later there would be usable storage batteries, but in 1879 there was only steam and the steam storage boiler (Lamm fireless boiler, patented in 1872). Garrett apparently met Nordenfeldt while planning *Resurgam,* and Nordenfeldt might have helped to finance it. The boat sank under tow off Wales (her hatch did not seal from the outside). Because the loss did not reveal any design defect, Nordenfeldt took on Garrett in 1881 as a partner in building a much larger boat. Murphy credits her elongated "cigar" or torpedo shape to Nordenfeldt; Garrett preferred a cylindrical midbody with pointed ends. Nordenfeldt's company was taken over in 1888 by his competitor, Maxim (the comapny eventually became Vickers-Maxim). His failure to sell a boat to Russia or to the United States ended his interest in submarines.

14. ONI, *Information from Abroad* (1885), 134–135, describes Nordenfeldt's first boat (64 ft × 9 ft, 60 tons). At this time, she had remained underwater for as much as 1 hr, at a depth as great as 16 ft, and had maintained set depth within 1 ft. The greatest distance made on stored heat, closed up, had been 16 mi at 3 kt. She had made something over 8 kt surfaced and had survived rough weather during a 150-nm surface run. This boat was designed to dive to 50 ft (and would have collapsed by 100 ft). Although unarmed, she was designed to carry one torpedo tube (three Whitehead torpedoes) and one Nordenfeldt controllable towed torpedo.

ONI, *Information from Abroad* (1886), 258–259, describes a public trial of Nordenfeldt's boat at Landskrona, Sweden, in September 1885. The anonymous author noted that she was very slow underwater and took 12 hr to get up sufficient steam to operate. On the other hand, even at light draft she was barely visible at 1,000 yd. She took 20 min to trim down to the awash condition, from which she could quickly dive to just under the surface. Senior British naval observers at Landskrona were much impressed. Admiral Arthur, one-time British naval attaché at Washington, commented that all future torpedo boats should be submersible, albeit briefly. After the trials, the Greeks bought a Nordenfeldt (the first bought by any government), armed with one torpedo tube, that dived to 30 ft and once remained submerged for 6 hr. She easily made her contract speed, 8.5 kt, and ran 10 nm while closed up (though not submerged). The Turks then ordered an enlarged version (100 ft × 12 ft, 160 tons) with two tubes. Her haul-down screws were at her ends, rather than in sponsons amidships. Rated surface speed was 12 kt and range was 300 nm; she was intended to dive to 50 ft. ONI, *Information from Abroad* (1887) 342, reports that Nordenfeldt's final boat

(123 ft × 12 ft, 243 tons submerged) was launched at Barrow, England, in March 1887 for Russia but wrecked en route to Kronstadt for a demonstration. She was credited with a range of 1,000 nm at 8 kt (20 nm closed up, in which case she could make 6–8 kt). She made about 13–14 kt surfaced with fires lit. Armament was two torpedo tubes (four torpedoes) and two Nordenfeldt quick-firing guns. Unlike her predecessors, she was more tubular (the earlier ones had sharper ends). She had 1-in steel over her two conning towers and her turtleback.

ONI, *Information from Abroad* (1888), 416, indicates that the new shape was intended to reduce "the dangerous and eccentric movements of the earlier models, which occurred on any sudden variation of the speed."

15. Field, *Story of the Submarine;* according to ONI, *Information from Abroad* (1886), 259; however, Tuck's boat had only a single propeller and using planes, dived with positive buoyancy. This volume does not mention Tuck's *Peacemaker.*

16. ONI, *Information from Abroad* (1886), 259; and Sueter, *Evolution of Submarine Boat* (who does not mention Tuck's boat), describe the trials of Baker's submarine, in which she failed to maintain an even keel underwater but did reach a satisfactory speed. Two men in the boat remained underwater for 1 hr and 45 min. Sueter says, "If Mr. Baker had provided his boat with a propelling system quite distinct from the diving arrangements, no doubt the boat would have been fairly successful, as all the details were carefully worked out."

17. William W. Kimball, "Appendix," in Cable, *Birth and Development of American Submarine.*

18. Lt. W. C. Babcock, "Submarine Boats," in ONI, *Information from Abroad* (1888), 408–420.

19. This was not the *Plunger* that won the second competition. According to Babcok, "Submarine Boats," this single-screw steamboat relied entirely on diving planes for submersion. There is no mention of any electric power plant for submerged operation. Dimensions were 85 ft × 10.9 ft (diameter), displacement (light) 98 tons. Surface speed was 15 kt; submerged speed was 6–14 kt. Armament was one "pneumatic submarine tube," presumably an underwater dynamite gun, and one 8-in gun for surface use. The Nordenfeldt was the type that had been recently built for Russia.

20. The eight contestants included Tuck and Nordenfeldt. Lake later claimed that he had completed his first design (including hydroplane depth control, bottom wheels, and a diver compartment) at the age of 14 (i.e., in 1880). His father discouraged him, but he was inspired by the announcement of the 1892 competition. He claimed that four of the five members of the 1893 board favored his design, but that the constructor on the board rejected it for fear that it might fly off an underwater precipice while running over the bottom. He also thought that the navy rejected his ideas because of his total lack of backers and of a shipyard. In 1915, Lake published a sketch of his 1892 design, with hydroplanes fore and aft and a trim vane (leveling vane, pendulum operated) right aft. Beside the usual pair of propellers, he showed down-haul screws fore and aft and maneuvering screws (like those of some modern ships, pushing to the side) forward. The boat had a heavy drop-keel and a double hull, with three wheels. She would have been armed with pairs of torpedo tubes fore and aft, as well as a gun topside, and would have had a folding periscope. She would have been powered by a 400-IHP steam engine (70-HP electric motor submerged); dimensions were 80 ft × 10 ft (115 tons).

21. Morris, *John P. Holland.* Cable *Birth and Development of American Submarines,* however, claims that Congress revived the competition largely because of fear of war with Britain over Vene-

zuela. Secretary of the Navy Herbert feared a disaster like that of the Civil War *Hunley*: any floatable underwater vessel surely would be endangered by the explosion of its weapon. He was placated by a crude experiment. A watertight tank (an old Lay torpedo casing) carrying a cat, rooster, rabbit, and dove was placed on the bottom, and charges of guncotton were exploded at decreasing distances, down to 100 ft. The first casing leaked, but a later one protected its inhabitants. The cat and rooster survived apparently unharmed; the rabbit and dove died.

22. BuOrd was responsible because the submarine was conceived as an item of ordnance. Only after Holland's later submarine *Holland* was accepted in 1900 did C&R gain control over submarine construction and acquisition. Lambert (private communication) points out that A. K. Wilson, not Beresford, actually invented the twin tubes.

23. The navy convened a board to consider re-engining *Plunger*. After the Holland Co. decided to back out, there was some recrimination within the Board on Construction.

24. For example, Lt. Comdr. Kimball: "Give me six Holland submarine boats, the officers and crew to be selected by me, and I will pledge my life to stand off the entire British [Flying] Squadron ten miles off Sandy Hook without any aid from our fleet"; Rear Adm. James E. Jouett, former president of the Board of Inspection and Survey and a veteran of Mobile Bay (where mines had been so effective against the attacking fleet): "If I commanded a squadron that was blockading a port, and the enemy had half a dozen of these Holland submarine boats, I would be compelled to abandon the blockade and put to sea to avoid destruction of my ships from an invisible source, from which I could not defend myself"; Capt. (later Rear Adm.) Alfred T. Mahan: "In our present unprotected condition, the risk of losing the money by reason of the boat's being a failure is more than counterbalanced by the great protection the boat would be if a substantial success."

25. Kingston (flood) valves set into a boat's bottom admitted water up into her tanks. Generally they were remotely controlled by levers in the control space. Electric Boat submarines had Kingstons amidships venting into a watertight duct keel. On surfacing, pre-WW I U.S. submarines opened Kingstons, blew part of the ballast water out into the duct keel (and thence into the sea), and pumped out the rest using a high-volume bilge pump connected to the duct keel at its after end (amidships in the case of the final World War I S-boats, the S-42 series). Prior to the World War I S-boats, the duct keel ran under all a boat's ballast tanks. At least the production Electric Boat ("Holland") S-boats (S-18 and later units) had a duct keel running forward only to the bank of Kingstons under the control room. The forward ballast tanks (Nos. 1 and 3) had their own remotely-controlled Kingstons (Larner-Johnson valves) communicating directly with the sea. It seems likely that this change was an attempt to speed diving by allowing the forward tanks to fill more quickly, and thus to bring the boat's head down.

Since the duct keel was patented, Lake submarines had far more elaborate piping arrangements. C&R developed a compromise in its "government" S-boat design (S-3): tanks drained into a pipe running along the keel. However, that pipe was not watertight, so it could not support suction from the bilge (ballast) pump.

Kingstons opened and closed relatively slowly. During WW I, the Germans replaced them with large quick-opening flapper valves for faster diving. They were not watertight when closed, so residual water could not be pumped as a boat surfaced. Instead, the Germans used low-pressure (7 psi above atmospheric pressure) rotary blowers (so did the British). Once the tanks were

dry, air in them (held because the vents above the tanks were closed) kept water out (the boat "rode the vents"). U.S. S-boats built during WW I could not ride the vents because their ballast tanks were too leaky. The V-1 class introduced German-style rotary blowers and retained Kingstons but eliminated the duct keels of Electric Boat designs.

A British wartime observer, Stanley Goodall (later Director of Naval Construction Sir Stanley), commented that the U.S. preference for Kingstons over the use of the vents was disadvantageous in a large submarine such as S-3 (the "government" prototype), which he visited while it was under construction. The valves had to be large, and the lines of flow to the forward and after tanks were devious and comparatively long. Goodall also thought the Kingstons likely to leak despite measures to avoid that.

Comdr. Bowers, a postwar British visitor to C&R, saw little point in retaining Kingstons; omitting them would mean one less complication to worry about. He reported that the British had never had power-operated Kingstons (as the U.S. Navy had in the later S-class), and on service never closed these valves. (C&R correspondence, memorandum of 12 January 1922 in file 22-SS-15, NARS RG 19).

26. At this time and for many years afterwards, the assistant secretary was in charge of shipbuilding.

27. Holland trimmed by adjusting the load of pig iron ballast on board. Cable preferred leaving the forward ballast tank partly empty. Holland disliked the free surface involved, but it worked. When the boat was rebuilt, he provided two small trim tanks that could adjust for changes in the specific gravity of the water or in the load on board. The compensating tank for torpedo firing (WRT tank) was added about April 1899.

28. "History of Electric Boat (1899–1949)" (mimeographed paper clearly produced by Electric Boat Company), Rare Book Room, Navy Department Library. Rice decided to form Electric Boat after riding Holland's submarine through New York harbor on 4 July 1898. He was then president of the Electric Storage Battery Co. (later Exide) of Philadelphia, which made the batteries in the submarine. Holland assigned all his patents to Electric Boat in return for 5 years' employment. It used the Holland Co. name after Holland left in 1904. Shortly after being formed, Electric Boat took over the Electro Dynamic Co. (which made motors) and Elco (which built electric launches and yachts). Electro Dynamic built the A-boat motors. Elco is probably best known for WW I patrol boats and WW II PT boats.

29. Cable, *Birth and Development of American Submarine*, 169, attributes this very high cost to "interminable changes" made as Holland tried to perfect his design. Presumably, Rice feared similar continuous changes in the later boats for the Navy. Cable recalled (p. 104) that Holland received $25,000 toward his submarine from a wealthy New York woman, otherwise unidentified.

30. Morris, *John P. Holland*, lists those present. Lambert (private communication) suggests that only Dewey's aide, Lt. Harry H. Caldwell, might have been present because Dewey later said of the trial, "I am told that. . ."

31. Presumably, the price was cut partly because the navy had already spent $99,716 on the abortive *Plunger*. The minutes of the Board on Construction show considerable resistance to buying *Holland* for $165,000 or to accepting Holland's offer to sell one or two improved boats for $170,000. Rear Adm. Charles O'Neil (BuOrd) broke a deadlock: if the company settled the *Plunger* account, the department would be justified in buying one improved boat ("under proper guarantees and specifications," a phrase inserted by Rear Adm. Royal B. Bradford of the Bureau of Equipment) "for the purpose of further aiding in the develop-

ment of submarine boats." This decision was leaked to the press (presumably by Rice), and the congressional supporters were able to change it.

32. Electric Boat used the Holland Submarine Co. name through about 1910. Its designs are therefore often identified as Holland types. According to its testimony during 1908 congressional hearings, the company then had 250 to 400 employees and sublet part of the Fore River yard to manufacture patented equipment.

33. *Plunger* was completed with a long tube and two long torpedo skids; the other *Adders* were completed with short tubes but with two long torpedo skids. Each boat was therefore credited with three torpedoes. Initially even the short weapons had to be dismantled to be loaded, but framing was changed during modernization so that torpedoes could be loaded intact. The breech of *Plunger*'s long tube, extending over the forward part of the battery, blocked access. To load even a dismantled torpedo into the submarine, the ladder to the conning tower had to be unshipped. Torpedoes on the skids blocked access to the wheel controlling the stern planes and, on the other side, to the valves of the adjusting tank. To load the port torpedo, the handles of the Kingston valves of the midships and auxiliary tanks had to be removed. Too, the heavy weight of the long torpedo required that its compensating tank be quite large. Reloading was slow because it took so long to transfer water from the tube to the loading tank and from the loading tank to the equalizing tank. In August 1907, a board of officers at Newport requested that *Plunger* be refitted with 3.55-m, rather than 5-m, torpedoes. The board rejected the only advantage of the big torpedo, greater theoretical range, as unimportant. The Navy Department agreed (NARS RG 19 correspondence, file 16351E162, 28 August 1907).

The estimated cost of the change was $205. In November, it was proposed that the boats built with 3.55-m torpedoes be modified with shorter skids. Again, the Navy Department agreed, and the boats eventually carried five short weapons.

34. These engines used 50-psi air from six storage flasks.

35. The Hovgaard submarine exemplified fear of Holland patents. In February 1901, William Hovgaard, a highly respected Danish naval constructor (later an important C&R advisor) offered the U.S. Navy a submarine design for $750 (with details, another $2,000). There was no particular reason to suppose that it would be very valuable; one member of the Board on Construction called it a "grab bag proposition". Capt. Charles D. Sigsbee (ONI) however, argued that "Holland's people are on the qui vive; they might secure Hovgaard's design and then the Government would have to pay for it." Naval Constructor J. W. Woodward, later responsible for modifying the *Adders*, saw the plans as the basis for a better critique of Holland's and other projected plans. Admiral Bradford wanted them as a club to control Holland's organization.

36. According to Morris, *John P. Holland*, Holland claimed that a pair of new French engines at the ends of the boat (using snorkels) would drive his 96-ft boat at 26 kt submerged. A pair of high-energy batteries (1,200 BHP each) would drive her at 7.5 kt. The special naval board considered very high underwater speed unsafe. It appears that Holland tended to overestimate grossly the underwater speed of his boats. In December 1906, a skeptical Board on Construction asked Holland to explain in writing why his views were so different from those of British and French experts (minutes of the Board on Construction, NARS, RG 80).

37. The crankpit of the 4-cylinder gasoline engine was airtight. It drew intake air through piping in the engine room, which

created a draft through the open conning tower hatch. When boats were modernized, the crankpit was also piped to a ventilator in the after end of the boat. According to a description of the *Porpoise* modernization, this piping was of such length and diameter that air friction in it would prevent backfire gas (mainly carbon monoxide) from being diffused through the boat. It was apparently quite successful. In 1906, Lt. L. S. Shapley, commanding officer of *Shark* and *Porpoise*, reported that it practically prevented odors of backfires from getting into the body of the boat and kept the air in the engine room constantly circulating.

The engine could run on any two, rather than all four, cylinders (e.g. to provide half power). Its seawater coolant, circulated by a 40-gpm pump geared to the engine, was dumped overboard via a water jacket around the exhaust pipe. In a modernized *Adder*, each of four engine exhaust pipes was closed at the muffler by a soft rubber ball: pressure pushed the ball up to allow the cylinder to exhaust, and the ball protected the cylinder from spray on the other strokes or when it was not in use (the muffler could be sealed by a cast iron box). As completed, the boats had flapper valves on the muffler.

The 2000 psi engine-run air compressor charged air flasks on either side of the boat; it was also led to a reducing valve (cutting pressure to 50 psi, for the 50 psi air flask in the bow, on the port side of the torpedo tube) and then via another reducing valve to a 10 psi line used to blow ballast tanks.

When *Pike* and *Grampus* were being modernized at Mare Island, Naval Constructor H. A. Evans complained that their gasoline tanks leaked dangerous fumes. He reported that not only was a strong odor of gasoline always present, but that the crews, who had served on East Coast A-boats, found that normal; that there was always a decided smell of gasoline in these boats. Evans argued that the fuel tank and piping would have been unacceptable even had the fuel been heavy oil. Gasoline fumes could easily be exploded by sparks from exposed electrical switches and motors; moreover, the attitude of the crew showed that the crewmen did not realize the danger. Electric Boat's L. Y. Spear disagreed: surely the danger of gas fumes was nothing new. If Evans were right, it was difficult to understand why none of the more than 30 Electric Boat-built craft had suffered a gasoline explosion. He argued that Evans mistook conditions on board badly abused boats at the end of their pre-modernization lives for those on board operational submarines. By the time Evans saw the boats, they were incapable of operating, and because overhaul was imminent no attempt was being made to maintain their fittings or equipment. Gasoline odor was only one of many symptoms of their overall condition.

The 60 battery cells were in two lead-lined tanks (35 cells in the forward group and 25 in the after group) beneath portable hatches forming the main deck; 30 of the forward cells were connected in series to form the forward battery, and 5 of the forward and all of the after cells formed the after battery. By throwing a switch, the batteries could be connected to the motor either in series or in parallel (for half power).

Initially the cells were in individual lead receptacles. As a boat rolled in a seaway, acid could slop from the open-top cells to cause short circuits. In November 1903 the Bureau of Equipment (BuEq, responsible for electrical equipment) ordered the electrolyte placed in hard rubber cells inside tanks that would collect spilled acid. BuEq then demanded protection against the shock of collision or grounding. Electric Boat proposed a wooden framework in the battery tanks to take the weight of the cells, which would be separated by wooden spacing pieces. Sealing compound, poured between them nearly to their tops to form a fore-aft waterway between each row, would carry away acid slopped out of cells into 5 lead-lined tanks at the after end of each battery tank. Other features were hard rubber cap pieces with ribs to support the carrying bars and prevent plates from shifting, covers with acid-proof metal fastenings, a new battery deck, and a new ventilator. New bus bars and supporting bars were also needed. This new battery arrangement, which BeEq and C&R accepted, raised the cost of modernization by about 30 percent.

The motor was designed for a maximum speed of 800 RPM, far beyond normal engine speed, hence the need to change propeller pitch for maximum efficiency submerged. By 1905, this shift was no longer practiced, however, as submariners apparently accepted a considerable loss of efficiency when submerged. Data, including battery description, are from Lt. Charles P. Nelson, *General Instructions for the Care, Preservation, and Handling of Submarine Torpedo Boats* (a handbook for the *Adder* class), 1905 (NARS RG 19 correspondence, file 17693E2); Nelson commanded the submarines at Newport. Some details of the battery modification are from L.Y. Spear (Electric Boat), letter to Comdr. F. F. Fletcher, then Inspector of Ordnance (i.e., in charge of submarines) at Newport, 12 February 1904 (NARS RG 19 correspondence, file 16350E5).

When *Moccasin* was laid up awaiting a new battery, C&R saw an opportunity. The low underwater speed of submarines placed them unduly at the mercy of currents and tides. Greater unit capacity (e.g., for another 2–3 kt) would be well worthwhile, even at the cost of shorter battery life (particularly since batteries were used in spurts, rather than continuously). Marked improvements in car batteries suggested that submarine batteries, too, could soon become much more efficient. Manufacturers could be asked to develop sample cells that incorporated the mechanical improvements (described above) already planned for *Porpoise* or *Plunger* (From NARS RG 19 correspondence, file 16350E4/10).

The car battery idea ultimately resulted in the abortive Edison "ironclad." *Moccasin* modernization was delayed first by the search for a new battery and then to await experience with the *Porpoise* and *Shark*.

38. This was requested by the *Adder* trials board. Cable, *Birth and Development of American Submarine*, reports that steel had been substituted for cast iron because of experience with *Fulton*. He does not mention the report of the trials board, which is in RG 38, NARS.

39. Cable, *Birth and Development of American Submarine*, and L. Y. Spear, "Submarine Torpedo Boats—Past, Present, and Future," paper delivered at a meeting of the Society of Naval Architects and Marine Engineers (SNAME), 21 November 1902, provide these details about *Fulton*. The *Adders* were differently geared from the British boats, with a maximum propeller speed of about 230 RPM, rather than 320 RPM. In 1912, the British Director of Naval Construction credited the British boats with 7.5 kt at 160 BHP, probably in light condition. Vickers estimated full speed surface endurance as 236 nm (355 nm at half power). But, A. N. Harrison, *The Development of HM Submarines, From Holland No. 1 (1901) to Porpoise (1930)* (Bath, England: Ministry of Defence, Ship Department, 1979 [BR 3043]) considers these figures unrealistic. Submerged, the British submarines made 7 kt on an overload rating of 80 BHP (the engines were rated at 70 BHP); they had to make at least 5–6 kt to submerge and to maintain control submerged. BuEng considered the heavy-duty engines in the A class far more reliable than any later submarine gasoline engines.

40. Sueter, *Evolution of Submarine Boat*, states that *Adder* took 29 min to dive from light condition (*Pike* managed in 15, presumably taking advantage of earlier experience); however, she took 4 min to dive with main ballast tanks blown and other tanks full. Once trimmed to dive, actual submergence took only a few seconds.

41. Diving was slow partly because the appropriate diving angle (0–2.5 degrees) was reached by trimming down (by flooding the forward trim tank), rather than by relying on the boat angle imposed by the planes. Too, for safety, instructions required that 200–300 lbs of buoyancy be retained while diving. Buoyancy was reduced slowly, first by filling the small midships and adjusting tanks (with air kept ready to blow them instantly, as they were the boat's emergency tanks); only then was the main ballast tank filled, its air vented overboard to avoid raising pressure in the boat. In calm water, the auxiliary tank would be carefully flooded to that point. In rougher water, a boat's buoyancy would change rapidly as waves broke over her conning tower. Buoyancy could be judged by how much flooding or blowing of the adjusting tank (50 lb or 200 lb at a time) was needed to make the boat begin to rise once her hull was under water.

Under 1905 instructions, the auxiliary tank had to be shut off (or even blown) if the boat became too heavy. For example, as soon as the deck was under, it had to be switched from its Kingston to the more controllable flow via the adjusting tank. As a rule of thumb, if the axiliary tank was shut off just before water reached the bottom of the lower row of eye ports in the conning tower, the boat would continue to sink until the top of the tower went under but would then bounce up and settle to about the right buoyancy. Trimming down to dive was expected to take about 6–10 min and diving about 3 min more.

The single main ballast tank (frames 18–31, 378 cu ft) was by far the largest in the boat. The other major tanks were: auxiliary ballast (frames 19–23, 128 cu ft, with a $3\frac{1}{2}$-inch Kingston), forward trim (frames 37–39, 29 cu ft), after trim (frames 0–1, 11 cu ft), amidships tank (frames 20–22, 17 cu ft); and gasoline tank (frames 32–36, i.e., forward; 100 cu ft). By 1905 boats also had a special cylindrical measuring tank (602 lbs of salt water) on the starboard side above the battery deck amidships, connected to the sea, the auxiliary tank, and the forward and after trim tanks, as well as to a Taber reversible pump and to a 50 lb air line for blowing. According to Nelson, *General Instructions:* "As this is the most important tank in the boat, both for fine trim and for emergency purposes, every officer and man should be thoroughly familiar with its detailed operation." All tanks flooded and drained via a main water line extending fore and aft on the port side of the boat; it also could be used to transfer water from one tank to another. In later Electric Boat submarines, tanks flooded and drained via a duct keel, which greatly simplified piping arrangement (compared, for example, with Lake's submarines).

Tanks were designed to take up to 10 psi (to be blown by 10 psi air). In February 1907, when *Pike* and *Grampus* were being modernized at Mare Island, Naval Constructor H. A. Evans suggested that all tanks with outboard connections should have the full hull strength equivalent to 100 ft test depth (50 psi, including a 5 psi margin of safety), citing a 1905 remark by Capt. R. H. Bacon, who was in charge of British submarines. Evans feared that Kingstons were not strong enough to seal these tanks from outside, citing water tests in which they leaked badly (Electric Boat's L. Y. Spear replied that Evans had tested the tanks incorrectly by putting water inside; the pressure exerted by water *outside* the tanks sealed the Kingstons). Evans also argued that main ballast tanks should be blowable at any safe depth (i.e., at 50 psi), citing Bacon's statement that the British A 1 (effectively an enlarged *Adder*) had been lost due to a conning tower leak which her pumps had been unable to handle. If the tanks could be blown at 50 psi, moreover, piping could be simplified by eliminating the low-pressure (10 psi) line altogether (NARS RG 19 file 16348E40).

Electric Boat suggested that the *Adders* be fitted to blow their main ballast tanks automatically. At the 60- to 75-ft depth at which they would operate, outside water pressure would be about 30 psi, so 50 psi air would provide a 20 psi blowing margin. New submarines were being designed with 100-psi tanks; the company suspected that an *Adder* was inherently limited to about 60–75 psi. The company suggested that only the main and auxiliary ballast tanks (which were separated from the sea by quick-opening Kingstons) need be strengthened. If the Kingstons leaked, these tanks would indeed be subject to full sea pressure. It would be best to fit them with pressure gauges (as in *Plunger*, *Porpoise*, and *Shark*) and strengthen them. The smaller auxiliary and trimming tanks were never full when the submarine dove (leaving a margin in the event they leaked), and double valves (at least one of them a positive screw-down type) isolated them from the sea outside. Moreover, the company argued, changes in the behavior of the boat submerged would quickly tell anyone on board that they were flooding. The company agreed that all the tanks could be strengthened to take 50 psi, but considered that sort of improvement less important than tightening connections to the sea. Finally, Electric Boat wanted 10 psi air retained, for use in normal circumstances and for economy of air (it was needed anyway to load the torpedo tube).

A cylindrical loading tank held the weight of water displaced by the torpedo; the forward torpedo compensating tank held the weight of water surrounding the torpedo in the tube. Using these two tanks the tube could be completely emptied without changing the boat's trim. The center of gravity of the water in the loading tank had to be directly abreast that of the torpedo in the tube.

At the command to dive, the diving rudder (plane) was worked very slowly to zero angle: a level plane should keep it at the trimmed down angle for the propeller to drive it down. If the bubble (of the clinometer) went to zero and stayed there, the boat needed more plane angle; Nelson suggests that 1½ or 2 degrees would start the bubble aft: "When bubble gets to 3 degrees aft and [is] still moving aft, bring [plane] quickly to hard rise and hold there till bubble stops going aft, then bring [plane] quickly to about 3 degrees rise or zero. The bubble should now be about 6 degrees aft and slowly coming forward. By carefully working [plane] to 0 and 1 or 2 degrees to dive, the boat will slowly level up . . ." A boat coud be held at the desired depth by slowly working the plane between about 1½ degrees of dive and rise, depending on whether the bubble (indicating the angle of the boat) showed that she was pointed up or down. Nelson states: "Steer by bubble and not by depth gauge, as invariably the boat will continue to rise or dive after the inclination has been changed in opposite direction . . . The clinometer bears the same relation to the diving rudder [planes] as the compass does to the steering rudder. By watching [it] the man at the helm can always anticipate movement of boat."

In these and later Electric Boat craft (through the S-boats) the diving planes were balanced, so that dynamic forces would soon move the plane to zero angle if a control rod broke. Running at constant trim with the stern plane disabled, an *Adder* would porpoise at a dive/rise angle of 6–10 degrees and submerge about 20 ft between dives. The boat was so small that she could be trimmed by sending two men forward or aft. After the submerged boat steadied down, depth could be maintained by moving one man no more than 5–6 ft forward or aft of the center of buoyancy. If the planes were jammed at hard dive, the boat might take an angle of more than 12–14 degrees and go down very quickly. To stop her, the amidships tank could be blown and the motor stopped and backed (hard down forward was hard rise when the boat ran aft). All quotations are from Nelson, *General Instructions*, 2-5, 42-49, 67-68.

Other data on A-boat diving behavior was provided by a 7 January 1910 report by the Pacific Submarine Flotilla of operations off Sausalito, California during September-November 1909 (NARS RG 19 file 16348E110). Time to trim down to dive varied with the amount of gasoline on board, averaging 10 min (the best time was 7 min). Boats required, on average, 6 min from the time engine was shut down to dive 15 ft, including closing down, filling tanks, and going ahead under motor power. The boats made their deepest dives off the San Francisco lightship, reaching 62 ft in 9 min using the stern planes, and taking 4 min to surface, having blown the midships and adjusting tanks at 20 ft. The flotilla reported badly leaking main ballast tank Kingstons in *Pike* (her pressure gauge showed 30 lb, practically sea pressure) and a slight leak in *Grampus* (the gauge registered 10 lb at 62 ft). *Pike's* main depth gauge pointer would not go beyond 47 ft, so a mercury gauge had to be used for greater depths. Both boats suffered from leaky muffler valves (all their spark plugs grounded, so their motors would not start when they surfaced). The flotilla concluded that the existing valves were unsatisfactory below 30 ft.

42. Apparently the first serious U.S. submarine accident was *Porpoise's* deep August 1904 dive. An investigating board found that the submarine had lost buoyancy as the result of leaky valves (both main ballast tank Kingstons, the midship Kingston, the auxiliary ballast tank Kingstons, and many valves on the main water line), the weakness of the water line, and the inability of the rotary pump (which had a friction clutch) to work against heavy pressure. The investigating board wanted a large hand pump, capable of pumping against any pressure the hull could stand, installed on the port side under the engine room floor plates. Both hand and power pumps should be positive in action and, if possible, installed in duplicate. All water piping and ballast tanks should be strengthened against any pressure the hull could stand (Lt. L. S. Shapley [commanding the Newport submarines] letter, 22 August 1904, NARS RG 19 correspondence, file 16350E).

A 2-cylinder reciprocating bilge pump, usable against 200-lb pressure and positively geared (rather than clutched) to the propeller shaft, was installed on board all the *Adders*. *Porpoise* was judged unusable until she had been modified.

43. According to Nelson, *General Instructions*, 60, when light, the boats were sluggish on the surface (turning circle of about 200 yds). When diving or awash, with the stern deep in the water, the circle was reduced to about 75 yd; fully submerged, it was only 42 yd: "[the boat] is very sensitive to her helm and turns . . . quickly." The magnetic compass was too sluggish for such sensitive steering, as it had to be close to so much magnetic material. A boat could get well into a swing before the compass showed it at all, and the compass vibrated so badly while steadying down that the helmsman might well find it impossible to stop on the desired course. The boat could still be steered by periscope, as the helmsman could see any deviation from course. Going astern either surfaced or submerged, "she will continue to swing very rapidly in whichever direction she starts swinging, and apparently will turn equally fast either with or against the helm." Submerged, "she will back in a circle as on the surface, but if carefully handled her depth can be kept under control, as

she steers very well in the vertical plane." Boats tended to raise their sterns when backing underwater, so Nelson advised using the planes (or, in an extreme case, men placed aft) to pull the stern down and keep it level.

Nelson (p. 46) found the boats rather wet even in a moderate seaway. Because their buoyancy was concentrated amidships, they rose slowly to a short choppy sea and therefore tended to drive through it; they did better in a long swell. In a choppy sea, Nelson recommended applying full power, as the big bow wave would tend to break up the sea into spray.

44. Trials board reports for this class are in Board of Inspection and Survey (INSURV) reports, Vol. 1, RG 38, NARS. A drawing of *Plunger* suggests that, by about 1905, the diving plane wheels had been moved down to the conventional horizontal position, but no photographic evidence has been found.

45. As modernized, boats had three ventilating fans: a rotary reversible air pump in the engine room (at frame 14: original equipment) and two one-way exhaust blowers (each ⅛ HP), with each exhausting through its own ventilator, forward of the conning tower. Although the starboard fan was intended to ventilate the battery (the conduits for the port fan were of lighter material, not as well suited to resist the acid in battery exhaust gas), either fan could be switched between battery and boat ventilation. Putting both fans on the battery, however, risked vaporizing the electrolyte, which would ground the battery by condensing on the insulators of the battery plates and on the battery covers (Nelson, *General Instructions*, 59-61).

A 21 June 1906 report from USS *Shark* praising the new ventilation system, asked only that one of the two fans be made reversible, so that air could be drawn into the boat even if the conning tower hatch were closed.

46. In theory, the small propeller began to turn only after the torpedo was fired. The weapon armed after a set number of turns, in theory equivalent to a set distance from the firing ship. A special guard was designed for the B- and C-boats, but their very different torpedo tube configuration eliminated the problem.

47. Boats differed slightly. Despite reports to the contrary, it appears that none of the boats was completed with bilge keels. They were fitted only on modernization (and not in *Plunger*).

48. J. W. Woodward, report to C&R, 1 December 1904 (16351 E55 in RG 19 correspondence, NARS), in discussing changes to *Plunger* mentions a total of *three* torpedoes, so she may have been completed with Mk IIs. INSURV reports indicate that her sisters all had five short 18-in torpedoes.

Chapter 4

1. With their large fields of view and consequently reduced-size images, fixed periscopes could not be used to judge the distance to the objects they showed. Interest in rotating periscopes was inspired by a summer 1903 installation in *Fulton*. Her revolving walk-around hand-turned altiscope (periscope) passed through a stuffing box forward of the conning tower. The steering gear shaft was extended forward so that a man could steer by the periscope, but no compass was fitted there. The conning tower wheel had to be used to steer the boat by compass or when the periscope was scanning the horizon. By March 1904 the periscope (now with a fixed eyepiece and a motor drive) had been moved to the conning tower.

Electric Boat proposed that the CO use the periscope; the helmsman in the body of the boat would steer an ordered course by compass. Alternatively, the CO could take charge and steer by periscope. Electric Boat claimed its redesigned periscope showed objects at their proper distances with maximum light intensity:

"One can see almost as well by periscope as by eye at night and in thick weather." The only drawback was that the image revolved as the periscope turned; objects directly astern were seen upside down (Holland Torpedo Boat Co. [Electric Boat] letter replying to C&R request for a price quotation for installation of the *Fulton* periscope in an *Adder*, 29 March 1904, NARS RG 19 correspondence, file 16350E).

On 14 April 1904, Lt Charles P. Nelson, commanding the submarines at Newport, asked for Electric Boat's revolving motor-driven conning tower periscopes in *Plunger*, *Porpoise*, and *Shark* (his other two boats already had fixed periscopes) for efficient handling in day or night attacks. If the instrument had to be installed in the body of the boat, he wanted a special compass and wheel at the eyepiece. Because installation might take 2–2½ months, he wanted an early decision to make the boats ready for summer exercises (NARS RG 19 correspondence, file 16350E13).

By this time C&R already planned to install a *Fulton*-type fixed-eyepiece periscope in *Plunger* (while new battery cells were installed).

Unfortunately, the conning tower unit required new castings, which would take 90 days to make. To avoid installing new conning towers in *Porpoise* and *Shark* prior to the *Plunger* test, C&R ordered experimental installations in the bodies of these boats (which it expected could be completed in 30 days, in time for summer 1904 exercises). The order was urgent; the only two revolving periscopes Electric Boat had on hand were intended for foreign customers. By May, Electric Boat had completed installation plans for a manual periscope in *Shark* and a power-operated fixed-eyepiece periscope (with binnacle) in *Porpoise*. In each, the periscope would be installed at frames 16–17 abaft the conning tower (rather than forward of the conning tower, as C&R wanted) because, in that position, it would not interfere with torpedo loading, would provide a slightly higher objective (top) lens for the same total tube length, and would allow the commander at the eyepiece to see the depth gauge and diving plane gear; also, he could more readily pass to the conning tower.

The periscopes were installed at Newport (material was shipped in July 1904). C&R hoped that the COs of the two submarines would compare the two types of periscopes (Electric Boat preferred the powered unit in *Porpoise*), but each declared himself fully satisfied with his own version. The *Shark* type was simpler and lighter, but the steering gear (adjacent to the eyepiece) blocked about 30 degrees of its arc. The *Porpoise* type produced the confusing revolving image. The tall periscope tubes were held in place by guy wires. Within a few years, there were numerous complaints that the tubes vibrated badly when the boat ran submerged. In November 1909 Lt. Bingham commented that *Plunger*'s periscope was useless above 6 kt. He wanted the short after periscope (then installed) replaced by a much taller rigidly mounted walk-around type. The boat's home yard, Charleston, commented that, because the periscopes were 6 ft apart, they could not be stayed by stanchions as on later classes. Unless the guy wires had exactly the correct tension, each periscope would be thrown out of the vertical. In March 1910, the yard offered to install two fixed-eyepiece units, one in the conning tower and one 18 in forward of it, held together against vibration by shears. Estimated cost was $5390. By this time *Plunger* was very nearly worn out, and nothing was authorized (RG 19 correspondence, file 16350E).

The officer commanding the two West Coast boats continued to press for periscopes. C&R initially planned to buy two more instruments, but then *Porpoise* suffered her diving accident and had to go into New York Navy Yard for major repairs. C&R took this opportunity to modernize both *Porpoise* and *Shark*. Because they were expected to be out of commission for a considerable time, their periscopes were removed and shipped to the West Coast for installation (also abaft the conning tower) on board *Grampus* (manual unit) and *Pike* (power unit). C&R hoped (wrongly, it turned out) that a proper comparison could be made because both boats were commanded by a single officer. The two East Coast boats received improved instruments turned by both hand and power.

2. Similar tanks were called "regulators" in older submarines and "negative tanks" in fleet boats.

3. The false bow was included in the requisition that C&R sent to the Holland Torpedo Boat Co. (Electric Boat) in November 1903. In February 1904 Electric Boat pointed out that the desired battery work (to protect against shock) would add $3000 to the original estimated (and authorized) $9700. To save money, the false bow was abandoned. "From our experience with *Plunger*, which has a considerably higher bow, and from model experiments with still higher bows, we expect little practical effect at full speed." The new higher conning tower carried the hatch (through which the engine drew its air) high enough above water to ensure uninterrupted air supply to the engine (NARS RG 19 correspondence, file 16350E).

4. Dates are from *Dictionary of American Naval Fighting Ships*, 2d ed., Vol. 1, pt. A (Washington, D.C.: Naval Historical Center, 1991), 1. The work was done at the Lewis Nixon Yard. (The *Dictionary* says it was done at Electric Boat's New Suffolk base, but that had no facilities).

5. Initially, the fixed-eyepiece periscope on board *Plunger* seemed quite satisfactory. By January 1908, however, Lt. Guy W. S. Castle, commanding the First Flotilla (*Plunger*, *Porpoise*, *Shark*) wanted a replacement, preferably of the *Porpoise* or *Shark* type (NARS RG 19 correspondence, file 16351E176). A new torpedo compensating system was unsuccessful. The water motor that moved the torpedo into the tube measured the rate at which the torpedo compensating tank had to fill.

6. Woodward's changes seem to have been inspired by the first CO (responsible for both boats), Lt. F. L. Pinney, and his successor, Lt. C. P. Nelson, based on trials and seagoing experience. Their November 1903 letters, in NARS RG 19 correspondence file 14907E (E59 of 14 November 1903 summarizes them), request:

—a conning tower high enough to extend above moderate waves, giving a better view. Even in smooth water, the eye slits in the tower were so low that little could be seen through them, and in rough water waves washed completely over the low tower; only objects very close aboard could be seen. The higher the tower, the deeper the submarine's hull (and hence the propeller axis) could be while trimming down to dive. The shorter the conning tower, the nearer the propeller to the surface when the bow was trimmed down. There it could churn the water to produce a visible disturbance, which gave away the boat's position.

—an amidships ballast tank with capacity equal to the displacement of the conning tower: once the submarine was trimmed down, with only the tower above water, flooding this tank would bring her underwater.

—a separate air intake (induction) for the engine would allow it to run when the boat was in diving trim. It would be a pipe either the height of the conning tower, or passing through it, with suitable valves. The officers also wanted a permanent ventilator trunk for the battery fan.

—a better altiscope giving an all-round view, and making it possible to estimate distances to objects seen. This revolving (rather than fixed) device could be mounted in the conning tower.

—a separate helmsman; the CO normally should not steer the boat. Submerged, the boat was so lively that she quickly veered off course if the CO (acting as helmsman) was distracted by watching the depth gauge or giving directions. Pinney wanted the helmsman in an enlarged conning tower. Nelson wanted a second wheel for the CO at the periscope since "in running down a target or sighting, where very accurate steering is needed, the man at the periscope must have a helm." The helmsman could be in the body of the boat.

Nelson wanted some means of hovering, i.e., of maintaining depth without running through the water. Otherwise the boat would broach in the face of the enemy if its motor failed during combat. Hovering required some means of adjusting the boat's buoyancy. Nelson suggested doing that by regulating her displacement, using a cylinder, open to the sea, the volume of which could be varied by moving a piston. This idea had been tried in England (on a much larger scale, to regulate the whole buoyancy of the boat) in the previous century by George Garrett and then by J. F. Waddington.

The alternative, which was adopted, was a small cylindrical "adjusting" or "regulating" tank (capacity 602 lb of seawater) connected to the auxiliary, forward, and aft trim tanks, to the Tabor reversible pump, and to the sea. Using the tank, the boat could be made a bit heavier if she began to rise, a bit lighter if she began to sink. It could be blown by 50 psi air (outside sea pressure at 100 ft depth was 44.4 psi), and it was connected to a new mercury column depth gauge. Aside from its primary purpose, permitting hovering, the tank could be used for trimming in rough weather and to compensate for changes in water density. If the bilge pump failed, water from the main or auxiliary tank could be pumped into the adjusting tank and then blown or pumped overboard against a head down to the boat's operating depth.

Because the main ballast Kingstons were not in the lowest part of the main ballast tank, its lower part could be emptied only via the 2-inch water line. However, moving the Kingstons would have been too expensive. Woodward solved the problem by adding a spout.

As gasoline was burned, the water line fed water into its tank (it was removed by bilge pump). Gas fumes seeped back into the ballast tanks via the water line, and then into the boat via the vent pipes when those tanks were filled. Woodward supplied a separate source of compensating water.

Pinney proposed that one boat be selected for experimental work (*Plunger* was chosen).

Woodward details further changes to *Plunger* in a report to C&R, 1 December 1904 (NARS RG 19 correspondence, file 16351E55). The auxiliary ballast tank was modified to fill more quickly. The ballast tanks were fitted with new gauges and with more reliable suction pumps.

7. Lt. Nelson commanded all the boats; none had her own CO. Nelson wanted each boat had to have her own CO before she left her fixed base (he believed that the CO could be trained in 2–3 months). He was still exploring the boats' capabilities. They had attained a depth of 100 ft, both by submerging under way and by sinking dead in the water (i.e., by losing buoyancy; these experiments tested the strength of the pressure hull and the pump). Nelson also tested the effects on maneuvering qualities of currents, of shifting ballast, of changes of trim under way or stationary, and of loading and firing torpedoes submerged. Without periscopes, his boats could not work in rough weather; when they tried to do so, waves cut off the view from the small conning tower. Nelson stated: "Until suitable periscopes are fitted, nothing of value can be ascertained as to the sea-going qualities or capabilities for attacking in different kinds of weather or sea."

The Board of Inspection and Survey agreed: on 23 April it strongly endorsed Nelson's plea that *Shark* and *Porpoise* be equipped with periscopes Modification of *Plunger* had not yet begun (NARS RG 19 correspondence, file 17693E).

8. About February 1904 C&R suggested that the two modernization projects, the hull (sea-keeping) changes (C&R) and a new battery (BuEq), be combined on one boat. No money was available for *Porpoise*, which was favored because she was identical to five other *Adders*. Instead, *Plunger*, which was slightly different, was selected, because there was still a $25,000 balance under the old March 1893 Act that provided for building a submarine and experimenting with her. (*Plunger* had replaced the original abortive *Plunger* bought under the 1893 Act; for a time she, not *Holland*, was designated Submarine No. 1.)

On 29 November 1904, Lt. L. S. Shapley (CO of the Atlantic boats), who had just seen the last two trials of the modernized *Plunger*, asked that *Porpoise* be similarly modernized, with new batteries, conning tower, ventilating system, and so forth. Battery acid spilled when she rolled, she lacked a ventilating system (there was no effective way of ridding her of gas), and the short conning tower was ineffective for surface work in a heavy sea or at night without a periscope. Nor was there any way of definitely regulating her buoyancy; however, that could be done to a certain extent with hand pumps. *Porpoise* was then in New York Navy Yard for emergency repairs following her deep dive.

In December 1904, C&R suggested that two Atlantic boats be modernized for tactical trials, at an estimated cost of $31,500 per boat. Because money would come from the maintenance account, these refits had to be more austere than that approved for *Plunger*, although they would include sufficient repairs to make the boats safe.

On 27 December, a board of inspection listed essential safety repairs to *Porpoise*. Her old sea chests, which were part iron and part steel, had to be replaced; some did not fit properly, and the valves were of odd designs. The brass main water line should be replaced with iron. The board fully agreed with the report of Naval Constructor J. H. Linnard, who had analyzed the incident, that both hand and power pumps should be positive in action and installed in duplicate (that became possible with power pumps only after boats had grown to the point of having two propeller shafts, each driving its own pump). It turned out that not all tanks could be hard. The board therefore suggested a midships hard tank, into which all the other tanks could discharge, that would discharge overboard. This "adjusting tank" or "measuring tank" (first fitted to *Plunger* [see Chapter 4] then to the other A-boats) was expected to decrease the danger of overpressure. At night and in rough weather COs found it difficult to judge how deep the boat was in the water, so the board wanted a "buoyancy gauge," a small tube leading from an outboard well to a glass in the conning tower, to show (in effect) a waterline undisturbed by ripples. Ventilation was clearly vital, since gasoline was used for power, and the battery gave off explosive hydrogen. The board therefore wanted two No. 1 fans installed, as in *Plunger*, to do the work of the No. 0 fan used to carry off battery hydrogen. COs found their conning towers too low, so the board called for higher ones, as in *Plunger*. The board also suggested a combined gas and water gauge installed in the gas tank; and, to allow for quicker reactions, it wanted dials installed that would show the man at the periscope the amount of water in each tank. The board also wanted the torpedo loading hatch to be enlarged so that fully assembled torpedoes could be loaded.

Estimated total cost was $6115. C&R suggested that all alterations not essential for safety be deferred pending experience with the *Plunger* modifications. New York Navy Yard offered to complete parts of the refit while the boats were in drydock to obviate any need for Electric Boat to dock the boats while making its modifications. The yard's improvements were: bilge keels; spouts for the main ballast tank Kingstons so the tanks could be blown out completely; separate water flood and blow connections to the gasoline tank; sea valves for the adjusting tank; and alterations to the after superstructure to allow easier access to the muffler pipes. This program was approved (by telegram) on 23 January 1905 for *Porpoise* and *Shark*.

Work was delayed. *Porpoise* suffered a battery explosion in drydock (26 January 1905). The navy yard hoped that Electric Boat could complete its work at nearby Bayonne, New Jersey, but in April the company wrote that it was too late; it was moving its technical offices and workshops to rented space at the Fore River shipyard in Quincy, Massachusetts. Boats would have to be moved there. The Navy Department ordered all work done at the New York Navy Yard. The boats were not completed until 1906. By that time their modifications formed the pattern for those planned at Mare Island (for *Pike* and *Grampus*) and at Norfolk (for *Adder* and *Moccasin*). Note that the two Pacific boats received their bilge keels as part of modernization, not as originally built (as has sometimes been reported; the keels are included in a list of modernization items in NARS RG 19 correspondence, file 16348E).

9. A-2 (*Adder*) and A-4 (*Moccasin*) were run very hard at Newport. In December 1903 they were towed to Norfolk for refits, including battery replacement. Early that month *Moccasin* grounded north of Currituck Beach Light House. She took about a month to salvage, her battery being ruined in the process. Both boats were laid up in the Reserve Torpedo Flotilla at Norfolk to await modernization. Meanwhile A-6 (*Porpoise*) and A-7 (*Shark*) were modernized at New York Navy Yard (*Porpoise* September 1904–February 1906, *Shark* at about the same time). Similar modernization of the remaining boats (*Adder, Moccasin, Grampus, Pike,* and *Holland*) was authorized on 29 Oct 1906. *Holland* was still on this list as of June 1907, but she was soon deleted.

The two Pacific boats (*Pike* and *Grampus*) were laid up in November 1906 for modernization at Mare Island Navy Yard. Changes generally matched those to the earlier boats: the new conning tower with periscope abaft it, a new artificial ventilation system, the adjusting tank, piston rather than rotary pumps, new hand pumps, new battery arrangements, rubber ball valves for the muffler, a new midships ballast tank, and bilge keels. The main hatch was enlarged for torpedo loading, torpedo loading and compensating gear fitted, a new heavier torpedo tube breech fitted, and the air system remodeled.

In October 1907 work on *Adder* and *Moccasin* (at Norfolk) was suspended to speed work on ships about to leave for the Pacific (the Great White Fleet). On 18 February 1908 work was suspended because the estimated cost exceeded 20 percent of the cost of new boats, hence required congressional authorization. That was forthcoming, and work was ordered resumed on 1 July 1908 (i.e., on the first day of FY 09). Work was completed in 1909. There were some changes: the foremast, which had carried the torpedo davit, was cut down to reduce drag underwater (torpedoes then had to be handled by the boat's tender). Pressure gauges were installed in the tanks. A 2000 psi external air line was added so that the air flasks could be charged from outside the boat when she was closed up. Extension ventilators were fitted. Lifting shackles were fitted to the stern so that it could be lifted to allow examination of mufflers and rudders. A vent was installed at the fore end of the torpedo tube so that no air pocket would form as the boat dived.

Together with *Plunger*, the first two boats modernized formed the First Submarine Flotilla in March 1907. They were sent to the Philippines in 1908. There, presumably at the initiative of their COs (C&R central files apparently do not mention the change), Cavite Navy Yard added big conning tower fairwaters and false bows for better underwater streamlining. *Adder* and *Moccasin* followed in 1909, and on 23 February 1910 Olongapo Naval Station asked that they, too, be fitted with false bows. Evidently C&R had not been consulted, because it asked for details of the gain in speed achieved by adding the new bow. Replies (NARS RG 19 correspondence, file 14907E168 of 17 December 1910 and 14908E129 of 23 December 1910) showed:

	Adder		*Moccasin*	
	Bow off	Bow on	Bow off	Bow on
Surfaced	7.43	7.67	7.83	8.04
Submerged	5.41	5.44	5.32	5.44
		at 370 amps		

Ens. J. M. Murray, CO of *Adder*, reported that without either bow or fairwater, underwater speed was 5.23 kt, and drain on batteries 380 amp at full speed. The fairwater added 0.18 kt and saved about 10 amp. The CO of *Moccasin* considered the false bow valuable in a heavy swell or a rough sea; speed increased materially because less rise was needed on the planes to keep the bow up. During a run from Olongapo to Cavite (*Adder* with the bow versus *Moccasin* without it), *Adder* invariably gained in rough weather, *Moccasin* in smooth (she had been slightly faster before *Adder* had the bow added). In any sea, the bow broke up the water, making the deck much dryer and more comfortable for the crew. Given these data, C&R approved false bows and fairwaters for the remaining three boats (*Grampus*, *Pike*, and *Plunger*). Apparently the two Pacific Coast boats did not receive their new bows until they reached the Philippines in 1915.

About 1915, conning tower fairwaters were extended well aft to cover submarine bells (for underwater communication) and the marker buoys formerly abaft the conning tower were moved into the false bows. INSURV complained in 1915 that a boat running her engine on the surface made so much gear noise that her crew could not hear the bells' signals or warnings.

10. The flying bridge was proposed by Lt. Guy W. S. Castle, commander of the First Submarine Flotilla (Atlantic A-boats) on 19 January 1908. Castle noted that, in the recent run from New-port to New York "during perhaps the severest weather yet experienced by submarine boats in our service, when officers and men on deck were continually drenched, boots and oilskins were of little use." The boat could not really be navigated from inside a closed conning tower "as buoys, etc. can only be seen when close aboard and the officer at the wheel must also keep a sharp lookout for passing vessels." Castle proposed a pair of angle-iron skids onto which a flat grating, clear of spray, could be fitted. With a portable trunk added to the conning tower hatch, the hatch could be kept open (to run the engines) in rough weather; the trunk was made in pieces so that it could be carried back down the hatch. The skids would protect the conning tower hood in the event of an underwater collision. Rising above the conning tower, the unprotected hatch might easily be sprung in the event of a collision. Without any watertight door at the foot of the conning tower, water would pour into the body of the boat. Castle believed that French submarines had skids to protect their conning towers: "In the very recent collision of the two French submarines, while submerged, it is reported that a conning tower was damaged, so as to admit water into the boat." According to Castle, "the need of these bridges has been known for a long time, but has not been previously requested because not until now has a practicable scheme suggested itself."

The COs of *Porpoise*, *Plunger*, and *Shark* wanted the bridges

fitted before the boats went south in the spring for major maneuvers. Their home yard, New York, approved, as did C&R (24 January 1908). The Board on Construction ruled that the bridge was desirable but not necessary, so it should be tested on only three boats and compared with others of the flotilla. On 20 February the Navy Department authorized installation only on board *Plunger*. Her CO, Lt. P. P. Bassett, was enthusiastic; on a run from New York to Newport and back in April, he was able to keep the conning tower hatch open, even when seas broke over the bridge. The only question was whether the bridge would affect underwater handling. It turned out that the framework had no effect; the grating and hatch extension were removed before diving. In January 1910, the Pacific Submarine Flotilla reported that its two A-boats handled better submerged with the bridge shipped than without. New York Navy Yard fitted flying bridges to *Octopus* and the three *Vipers*, and by June 1908 the supervising constructor at Quincy had been ordered to arrange for them to be fitted to the C- and D-class submarines then under construction (NARS RG 19 correspondence, file 16351E151).

11. Although second periscopes were ordered in 1908 for later submarines, it was apparently initially considered impractical to add them to the A-boats. Probably that was because the two available positions, in or just forward of the conning tower, and well aft in the hull, were so far apart, with the likely CO position so far abaft the helmsman's. C&R said as much in a 1910 review of U.S. periscope practice.

In May 1909 the CO of *Moccasin*, which was about to be shipped to the Philippines with *Adder*, asked that the walk-around periscopes then being removed from *Cuttlefish* and *Viper* (for replacement by Goerz instruments) be fitted to *Adder* and *Moccasin* in place of their unsatisfactory fixed-eyepiece ones. C&R demurred briefly because installation of the Goerz units was not yet complete (it approved on 4 June, and the Navy Department approved on 7 June 1909). The new periscopes could either replace or supplement the existing periscopes, at the COs' discretion, and the periscopes were shipped to the Philippines with the boats. The bureau then approved the CO's proposed periscope location (for the helmsman, forward of the conning tower, *not* in a casting like that on *Plunger*) and forwarded a plan to Norfolk. This design was then implemented in *Porpoise* and *Shark*, which were already in the Philippines (no relevant correspondence has been found, but it is clear from the *Adder*/*Moccasin* file that no earlier two-periscope design existed, so *Moccasin* must have come first). In *Adder* and *Moccasin* the helmsman's instrument was a walk-around, but the CO had a fixed-eyepiece periscope; *Shark* and *Porpoise* each had two walk-around periscopes. *Pike* and *Grampus* were fitted with second (forward) periscopes after they arrived in the Philippines, some years later (NARS RG 19 correspondence, file 14907E).

None of these installations seems to have been related to that on board *Plunger*. She had a second (hull walk-around) periscope installed by mid-1909, possibly in reply to a request to move her conning tower periscope back into her hull (surviving correspondence files do not indicate when or why the periscope was installed). This after instrument, 6 ft abaft the conning tower, may have been installed to match the hull periscopes of the other boats, though it was much shorter than theirs (and than the conning tower instrument). On 6 November 1909 the boat's CO, Lt. Chester W. Nimitz, urgently requested a Goerz periscope in the conning tower and another just forward of it in place of the after walk-around. In response, the boat's home yard, Charleston Navy Yard, recommended replacing both periscopes with fixed-eyepiece erect-image types (Goerz type) and moving the after periscope forward so that the two could be braced together. No walk-around periscope could be installed forward because of interference with the steering gear and with the web frame of Frame 22. It is not clear how Norfolk Navy Yard managed to install walk-around periscopes forward for helmsmen in the other boats, and the Charleston correspondence does not refer to the Norfolk plan.

12. Electric Boat might have offered substantially smaller designs. An EB 8 drawing, surviving in Naval Sea Systems Command (NAVSEA), shows a much shorter submarine, about 50 ft long. An EB 12 proposal drawing at the Submarine Force Museum also shows something much shorter than an A-boat. The B class was EB 16; nothing is currently known of the designs corresponding to the missing numbers. Electric Boat counted *Holland* as EB 6, so EB 7 was the first post–*Holland* design.

13. J. D. Scott, *Vickers: A History* (London: Weidenfeld and Nicholson, 1962), 61–68, outlines details of Vickers' involvement with Electric Boat. Under the October 1900 agreement, Vickers had to pay 50 percent of the profit on every submarine it built to Electric Boat. That percentage was halved and the term reduced from 35 to 20 years in May 1902. Electric Boat agreed to pay Vickers 25 percent of the profit on any boat it built for the Royal Navy. The license allowed Vickers to sell boats abroad, but the Admiralty contract that gave Vickers a monopoly on British submarine construction also barred foreign sales. On 31 March 1911, the Admiralty gave the required 2-yr notice that the monopoly was to end (it wanted alternative souces of supply); after March 1913, Vickers could compete with Electric Boat on the world market. The only exceptions to the Admiralty agreement had been C-class submarines for an important British ally, Japan: two under the Japanese 1904 program and three under the 1910 program, all shipped to Japan in sections.

14. On 13 October 1900, the Admiralty informed the Holland Co. that it wanted to buy five submarines. Price per boat was £35,000 ($165,000). Stipulated surface speed was 8 kt in fine weather (7 kt in ordinary weather); radius of action, 250 nm at full speed; submerged speed, 7 kt (radius on batteries to exceed 25 nm and oxygen endurance with all hatches closed, 15 nm [3 hr]; it is not clear why the two endurance figures do not match, and the oxygen endurance seems much lower than it should have been). Depth had to be maintained within 4 ft (average 2 ft). Test depth was 100 ft, and time to go from full speed on the surface to submerged was 2–10 min. Vickers substantially modified the detail design during construction, blanking one main ballast tank. Harrison, *Development of HM Submarines*, believed that Vickers had to redraw many of the American drawings because the company was building ahead of the *Adders*. *Fulton*, the real prototype, however, came earlier. In February 1902, Cable redrew plans to fix diving angle controls (to preclude one-man control); this delayed British submerged trials until May 1902.

15. Cable, *Birth and Development of American Submarine*, claims active foreign interest in Holland submarines as early as 1899.

16. Capt. F. G. Babbitt, "A Submarine for the Tsar," *Proceedings of the U.S. Naval Institute*, April 1970, decribes Holland Co.'s offer to build six submarines in Russia in 1901 and again in 1903. In December 1903, the Nevskiy Works made a formal proposal to the Russian Naval Technical Committee. The Navy Ministry ordered the boats in April 1904 for completion by 1 September.

17. The Kaigun-Holland (Navy-Holland) No. 6 was 73 ft 10 in × 7 ft (63 tons submerged); No. 7 was 84 ft 3 in × 7 ft 11 in (95 tons submerged). Unlike earlier Holland boats, they were substantially faster on the surface (8.5 kt) than submerged (4 kt). Presumably, they had smaller motors (22 BHP) because their engines took up more space.

18. Correspondence relating to both Lake and Electric Boat for the period 1901–1905 was collected under Serial 18131 in NARS RG 80 (box 684) and also printed as a congressional document. It includes the 1903 trials board report on Lake's *Protector*, but not the 1904 Fulton trials board report leaked to the public.

19. If the planes are close enough to the longitudinal center of gravity, the submarine can rise and fall in the water without changing trim, like an elevator car. Apparently, this effect was quite pronounced in the *Skipjack* (SSN 585) class. The British Vickers B class had conning tower fins.

20. In a Holland boat, the space forward of the engines was occupied by the conning stand and torpedoes and tube. *Protector* had a clear centerline passage running its length, with four transom seats that could swing up to form berths for eight men, a collapsible mess table, and a pantry and electric stove just forward of the engines. In February 1905, Lt. Comdr. W. Irving Chambers reported that the crew had lived on board for weeks at a time (memorandum in General Board series 420-15, NARS). According to Chambers, Lake had reduced the length of the *Protector* by 17 ft 6 in at the suggestion of the Board on Construction. Lake claimed that, because his boat submerged on a level keel, she could be easily lengthened (e.g., for greater range and offensive power). As she submerged at an angle, the bow of a lengthened diving boat would be substantially below the rest of the boat and experience considerably more water pressure. Chambers was much impressed by how easily Lake's submarine was operated "without much regard to system or organization." A similar casual approach to operating a Holland boat would surely sink it. Controlled by an awkwardly placed overhead wheel, Holland's stern planes needed constant attention. "Every time I have witnessed the operation of that wheel I have been impressed with the idea that the exhausting work must sooner or later cause the operator to grow careless and allow the boat to take long deep dives, " Chambers wrote. *Protector* was also far more seaworthy than a Holland. She had often run the 98 nm between Bridgeport, Conn., and Newport, R. I., without assistance. Chambers continued: "I have seen her enter Newport, after rounding Point Judith, in a strong breeze and a nasty sea, with her supply sloop in tow, and this feat was performed with one screw only, the other having been disabled on picking up the tow."

21. L. Y. Spear, "The Development of Submarines," paper delivered at SNAME, November 1906. On trial at Newport, *Protector* made 7.44 kt surfaced and 3.8 kt submerged, and the latter speed required 100 BHP (2½-hr rate rather than 3-hr rate). Lake claimed that with his original propellers (changed in November, 1903) he had achieved 10.65 kt surfaced and 6 kt submerged. Spear rejected Lake's claim that the propellers were the problem: the Russians had obtained much the same ratio of speeds with their Lake and Holland boats.

22. Simon Lake, *The Submarine in War and Peace* (Philadelphia: J. B. Lippincott, 1918) (and other books and articles), claims to have influenced several prominent European builders. Lake moved to Berlin in 1904. He claims that Krupp wanted to build his submarines under license both in Germany and in Russia. The Russian plan was aborted by the 1905 revolution. Then, according to Lake, Krupp found that the U.S. patents did not apply to Germany, so it based its U-boats on pirated Lake data and ideas. Krupp claimed that its submarines were designed by a Spanish engineer, Raymondo Lorenzo d'Equevilley-Montjustin, formerly employed by Laubeuf, whom it hired in 1902. Eberhard Roessler, *The U-Boat* (London: Arms and Armour, 1981), gives details of d'Equevilley's contribution.

Lake also claims that he advised both Maxime Laubeuf and Cesare Laurenti (commercially far more successful than he), who had underestimated the importance of longitudinal stability, and that they had later accepted his ideas on a combination of such stability and hydroplanes (both for even-keel operation). Lake surely exaggerated. All three Europeans placed their ballast tanks in their full double hulls. Lake thought of the outer hull (superstructure) as a sea-keeping device. He carried ballast inside the pressure hull, as in an Electric Boat submarine.

23. The Board of Inspection and Survey considered that this mode of operation would merely cut the boat's underwater radius without making it nearly as fast as its surface target.

24. Apparently, the air duct was nearly as high as the periscope. In 1903, Lake asked for a special test run with only periscope and air duct (for the gasoline engine) above water, followed by a dive 30 sec after a signal was given. He wanted to show how close he could come to a target without being seen.

25. Chambers, memorandum, also indicates an enclosed toilet, apparently a new feature. Chambers considered it more important than in a surface ship.

26. Chambers, memorandum, notes that torpedoes could be loaded from within the submarine, but the 1903 trials board reported that they could be loaded only through the muzzles, a feature it considered undesirable. It is often not clear whether Lake's writings describe an existing or an envisaged feature.

27. As a veteran railroad lawyer, Rice certainly would have known how to influence Congress. He later claimed that members of the House Naval Committee welcomed his efforts because several of its members already favored submarines and that, without his lobbying, the navy never would have bought submarines at all. In January 1903, Congress investigated charges by Representative Montague Lessler that Electric Boat had bribed members of the House Naval Committee to vote for more submarines. Lessler initially claimed that the had been offered a check for $5,000; Rice's friends demanded a public investigation to clear the company's name. His enemies tried to keep the investigation secret, but one of them apparently could not resist a newspaper leak. In public, Lessler had to water down his charge to the point where the investigation collapsed. Rice described the situation in a 24 February 1903 letter to Vickers (EBC III-68 in a series of Electric Boat correspondence reproduced as reference material for Scott, *Vickers;* the author is grateful to Nicholas Lambert for a copy). He had decided to forgo further congressional lobbying in favor of a direct approach to the Navy Department. The Senate had voted unanimously to include submarines in the 1901 and 1902 programs, but the appropriation died in conference with the House. Returning from Europe early in 1903, Rice found the House Naval Committee willing to buy five boats. Two members had switched, for a 10–7 majority, but they turned back after Lessler's investigation.

Rice carried the fight to the floor of the House. He abandoned the original bill, which mentioned the Holland Co. by name; such partiality would arouse strong antitrust sentiment: "As long as the Holland type is the only type, we would have a monopoly of the business whether we are mentioned by name or not. If, on the other hand, Lake or anyone else should perfect a type superior to ours, we would lose the business, no matter under what name the legislation might be had." Rice recalled a 1902 proposal by Admirals Charles O'Neil and Francis T. Bowles that $500,000 be appropriated to buy any boat equal to or superior to the government boats. This bill had been reintroduced in a form more favorable to Electric Boat; Rice strongly advised that it should be taken up and rewritten as an amendment to the 1903 appropriation bill. The committee supported it unanimously, and the House then passed it overwhelmingly. At this time, Rice believed that Lake's boat would not be ready to compete before the 1 August deadline fixed by the new act ("even if it were, its method of construction has such inherent defect that we have nothing to fear from it").

28. This account is adapted from a statement by Bowles to the Board on Construction in 1904 on behalf of Electric Boat to support a claim that the 1903 and 1904 submarine funds should be combined. Bowles was then president of Fore River Ship and Engine Co. Lake took credit for setting up the 1903–04 competition. The third hopeful, Sub-Surface Torpedo Boat Co., offered a semisubmerged boat. It was represented by H. A. Herbert, former secretary of the navy who had bought the *Plunger.* The act was worded to cover both submarines and subsurface torpedo boats.

29. New screws (with new shafts) could be fitted only in drydock. Lake also planned to rearrange the vertical and horizontal rudders, to replace the small diving plane (hydroplane) hand wheel, and to improve the batteries.

30. Babbitt, *Submarine for the Tsar,* notes that the Russian Commission for Submarine Design considered *Protector* too slow underwater. Despite Lake's claims, the Russian Navy's Diving School considered her unsuitable. After outbreak of the Russo-Japanese War, the Russian purchasing agent in the United States, Capt. 2 Rank A. G. Butakov, played up the boat's claimed advantages and warned that the Japanese might buy first. On 12 April 1904, he bought the *Protector* and five more Lake submarines for $250,000 each. *Protector* arrived in Kronstadt on 15 June.

31. Dimensions of the five Russian boats were 73 ft × 11 ft 3 in (hull depth). *Lake X* was 85 ft 9 in × 11 ft 3 in. Because the United States was neutral, both Lake and Electric Boat had to ship their boats covertly aboard ships nominally carrying coal to Russia. *Protector* was loaded at sea, by wrecking crane, near Sandy Hook. *Fulton* was towed out and hoisted aboard a freighter in Gardiners Bay, off Long Island, after the ship had cleared customs. Both companies doubted U.S. government permission to export.

32. Fore River gained this status in 1904. According to Morris, *John P. Holland,* 130, after Holland's 1906 failure, Holland charged that Electric Boat used Fore River because the latter's president, former Chief Contructor F. T. Bowles, retained undue influence with the Navy Department.

Bowles had become head of Fore River in November 1903; the submarine orders followed early the next year. Bethlehem Steel bought the yard in 1913. It had already bought Union Iron Works, Electric Boat's West Coast subcontractor, in 1905. By 1914, then, Bethlehem Steel was Electric Boat's main submarine builder, the only exception being the second-source West Coast yard, Moran Bros. of Seattle.

33. Lt. Kenneth Whiting, "Tactical and Maneuver Data for Present U.S. Submarines" (June 1914), Naval War College Archives.

34. Ibid. Whiting credits the C class with a 2,000-yd torpedo range (1,000-yd for A and B classes, 4,000-yd for later submarines). He credits C and later classes with a 50 percent hit probability (presumably for war game calculations), compared with 33 percent for A and B classes.

35. In June 1908 Comdr C. C. Marsh, BuNav's submarine specialist, argued strongly that the boats should be fitted with submarine bells. "No vessel that goes to sea is unprovided with signalling equipment, but submarines lack it when submerged." This point had already been raised, in August 1907, by the *Octopus* (C-1) trials board, of which Marsh was a member. *Octopus* had air connections for the bell, but no bell had been installed. Marsh's comment was combined with the endorsement for the second periscope for SS 12-19, the repeat C and D classes. By this time Electric Boat held the patent on submarine signaling equipment. When it was required in the FY 09 boats, both Lake and Laurenti protested that Electric Boat would enjoy an unfair advantage; the navy agreed to provide Electric Boat signalling

equipment for them as GFE (government-furnished equipment). In December 1908 air-operated submarine bells and microphone receivers (two per submarine, one in each of two tanks) were approved for the repeat C and D classes (SS 13-19) (NARS RG19 correspondence, file 22700E106).

The bells seem to have had their first real test in a March 1911 exercise by the Third Submarine Division, during which *Narwhal* and *Grayling* communicated at a range of about a mile. Their COs were enthusiastic but wanted greater sound volume. Mare Island fitted *Grampus* and *Pike* with submarine signal bells and receivers about April 1910; other *Adders* apparently had theirs fitted in the Philippines.

36. Sea-keeping comments are from A. I. McKee, "Development of Submarines in the U.S. Navy," in *Historical Transactions of the Society of Naval Architects and Marine Engineers 1893–1943* (New York: Society of Naval Architects and Marine Engineers, 1945). McKee was then a senior U.S. Navy submarine designer.

37. Cable, *Birth and Development of American Submarine*, describes this performance as nearly impossible for a modern submarine of that time (1924).

38. The test period was extended because the test area in Narragansett Bay could be frozen in early March. The date for bids to be opened was extended from 18 February to 30 April 1907.

39. Lake apparently expected to use his third Russian boat (Newport News hull number 53) as his next demonstrator. She was the only one launched in the United States (17 October 1904) and the last delivered (23 February 1905; the first two [of five] were delivered on 17 October 1904 and the second pair on 2 January 1905). Lake complained, *Submarine in War and Peace*, that the Navy had refused to give him another 10 days for trials; presumably this was in 1904, and he then sold the boat to Russia. The larger Newport News hull number 56 became Lake's demonstration boat (*Lake XV*, later called *Defender*). Data and 1906 launch and completion dates are from a Newport News hull list provided by Jack Schnaedler of that yard.

Lake XV ran demonstration trials as late as 1908. During or after WW I, she was rebuilt (as *Defender*) with a shark bow. In this form she was tested briefly by the navy in 1929 as a platform for salvage divers. *Defender* had the following characteristics: 92 ft 7 in overall (spindle hull 75 ft 4 in long) × 11 ft 3 in; 185 tons light. Machinery: 2 × 120 BHP White & Middleton gasoline engines (four 10 × 12 in cylinders, 300 RPM) = 8.5 kts light, 7.5 kts awash; 2348 gal gasoline in welded tanks in the superstructure; range 500 nm at 8 kt, 850 nm at 6 kt light, 500 nm at 7 kt awash. With engines and motors, 9 kt surfaced. Battery: 60 cells (Gould improved type: 3475 amp-hr); endurance 5 hr at 5 kt submerged (maximum 6 kt submerged). She was tested to a depth of 137 ft. Complement: 1 officer and 7 men (accommodation for 10). Three 45 cm × 5 cm torpedo tubes (space for 2 reloads). She had a diver's chamber, two hydraulic guide wheels, and two drop keels, about 5 tons total.

40. Superiority of *Octopus* over *Lake XV* by categories:

Surfaced speed	45%
Submerged speed	100%
Structural strength and safety submerged	60%
Number of torpedoes	33%
Time to submerge	54%
Stability underwater	72%
Surface radius	100%
Submerged radius	350%

From L. Y. Spear, quoting the trials board in testimony at the 1908 House hearing on submarine contracts (House Resolution 288).

41. Bids were dated 30 April 1907. Electric Boat offered 13 kt surfaced and 8 kt submerged for its 133-footer (278/340 tons) and 10.5 kt sufaced and 8 kt submerged for its 105-footer (239/274 tons). Surfaced endurance at maximum speed was, respectively, 780 and 525 nm; submerged endurance (for both), 3 hr at 8 kt (55 nm at 6 kt). Each carried four torpedoes.

Lake offered the information provided in the table at the bottom of this page.

Speeds are surfaced/submerged. Endurances are (in nm) surfaced/submerged at full speed/submerged at 6 kt. The 85-footer showed about 17-nm endurance at 5.8 kt submerged. The number in parentheses after the number of torpedo tubes is the total number of torpedoes. All of these boats were intended to submerge to 200 ft (as in Electric Boat designs). The 85-footer was *Lake XV*; the 100-footer was the Austrian submarine. None of these designs was finally chosen for *Seal*.

42. L. Y. Spear (Electric Boat) letter to superintending constructor, Fore River (where the boats were being built), 15 October 1907, outlining his company's reactions to the board recommendations. In response to the *Octopus* trials board, the Navy Department was considering, but would soon again reject, the second periscope. Spear states: "submarines of equal or greater displacement than the *Octopus* [should have] two periscopes, one of which should be fitted into the body of the boat." Central torpedo firing apparatus, however, would be an unnecessary complication. The second pair of torpedo tubes required a larger hull (as in the D-class). Spear offered independent torpedo caps for the repeat C class, but not for the larger D class then on order. Then he had to design separate shutters for the D-boats, only to have the Board on Construction agree in January 1908 with C&R and BuOrd that their disadvantages outweighed any advantages.

The engine was noisy because it had to be compact and powerful yet reliable; when *Octopus* was designed, no suitable engine yet existed either in the United States or abroad (an engine offered by the Standard Motor Co. of Jersey City promised sufficient performance, but failed to provide it). It would be best to provide

Dimensions (ft)	Displacement, Submerged (tons)	Cost (in thousands)	Speed	Endurance	Torpedo Tubes
85 × 11-10.5	235	$225	8.75/6.75	390/15/25	3(3)
100 × 11-10.5	275	300	10.5/8	750/16.5/32	3(3)
100 × 11-10.5	250	235	11/8.5	600/18.5/40	3(3)
142 × 12-6	500	450	13.5/9	500/21/32	4(10)
142 × 12-6	425	365	14.5/9.5	400/20/36	3(3)

a bulkhead to keep engine noise out of the control room. Nor did Spear believe that the 250 HP engine could be made reversible, like a small 4-cycle gas engine, without a major redesign and lengthy trials. The board disliked the alternative, which was to reverse by switching to electric power. Spear pointed out that the shift was very quick, because the motors were on the same shafts, connected by friction clutch: if the motors were disabled, the boat would be powerless in any case.

The board wanted (and Spear provided, in the D-class) subdivision to isolate the storage battery, machinery space, and partial crews' compartments, partly to provide escape air locks and hatches. Although it did not call for a one-compartment standard, later correspondence implies that the bulkheads were so arranged (on 31 May 1908 Lt C. E. Courtney argued that it would be better to move a bulkhead to free space for a walk-around periscope than to keep it where it was, on the theory that the periscope was insurance against having a collision, whereas the bulkhead was insurance against sinking after the collision occurred).

The board did argue explicitly that any future design should guard against any leak above the battery, which would probably be fatal. Electric Boat's U-shaped tank (which the board called a double bottom) already extended well up the boat's side to a few inches above the horizontal axis. The board wanted it carried a bit further, to meet the superstructure above the pressure hull. This Spear could not provide. Nor could he provide the independent air supply for automatic blowing; he saw little point in it. Thus far, automatic blowing had failed only because of cracked stop valves, and the same valves would have to be used in any new independent system. The extra tank and reducing valve would take up space and add complication.

At this time, and at least through World War I, standard U.S. practice was to provide an air supply that would automatically blow ballast tanks when the submarine reached a set depth, as a peacetime safety feature. During the war, submariners would discover that occasional excessively deep dives were a means of evading depth-charging. For example, the British officer who took over H-11 in the United States remarked that he much preferred manual blowing controls to any sort of automatic blow.

43. On 15 December 1907, Lt. C. E. Courtney, commanding the Second Submarine Division (*Octopus* and *Viper*s), asked for a second periscope. The leading foreign navies all fitted two periscopes to each submarine. The commander, alone at the periscope in the one-man conning tower, was badly overloaded. He used his left hand to ring main motor bells (for going ahead, stopping, backing) and to push buttons to issue steering commands. He controlled the periscope motor with his right hand and looked through the periscope with his right eye. With his left eye, he kept track of the compass and the rudder indicator. He had a speaking tube to order torpedoes fired, tanks flooded and blown, planes moved up and down. In surface ships, which were so much simpler to operate, such duties were always divided among several men. Courtney thought that the commander should be moved down into the control room and provided with his own periscope, so that he could conn the boat and make other decisions rather than handle equipment. Moving the commander into the body of the boat would give him immediate access to all the crew (except the planesman). No man could both steer and simultaneously search the horizon.

Courtney stated: "During the trials last summer, the periscopes were kept pointed ahead, and the tenders gave notice of dangers in other directions." The fixed-eyepiece periscope in the conning tower (the only type that would fit in that limited space) should be used only for steering, with its operator keeping a

lookout over only a 26 degree field of view. A walk-around periscope let into the control room would be used to search the horizon, and also for submerged navigation, because it could be easily used to take bearings (and the boat's course plotted by cross-bearings). The second periscope could be easily fitted through the existing forward ventilator tube. The bridge fairwater could help support it. Later it would turn out that keeping the two periscopes close together made it easy to brace them and thus to avoid vibration (probably caused when vortices shed by the forward periscope hit the after one) (NARS RG 19 correspondence, file 17693E3).

Comdr. (later Adm.) Albert Gleaves, then Inspector of Ordnance at Newport, supported Courtney's idea. So did Rear Adm. W. H. Bronson, chief of BuNav. On 13 January C&R ordered New York Navy Yard to buy four periscopes for the Second Flotilla. *Octopus* was in Electric Boat hands, and that company installed her second periscope; the *Viper*s were refitted at New York Navy Yard. By 29 May BuNav was asking for improvements to the walk-around periscope already installed on board *Octopus*: it wanted a pelorus circle (so bearings could be taken) and vertical and horizontal scales in the focus of the eyepiece, to estimate range.

The steering wheel was already in the body of the boat. The natural next step, then, was to give the helmsman a walk-around instrument let into the body of the boat, rather than have him rely on push-button signals from a man at the fixed-eyepiece unit in the narrow conning tower. This idea was embodied in the E- and F-class designs submitted by Electric in the fall of 1908 for the FY 09 program (EB-19 and -20). In these craft the conning tower was virtually eliminated.

Correspondence concerning Lt. Courtney's proposal makes no mention of the earlier proposal by the *Octopus* trials board (NARS RG 19 correspondence, file 17693E3).

44. Electric Boat submitted a drawing of its proposed improved torpedo director on 30 January 1909 (NARS RG 19 correspondence, file 22700E122). To solve the torpedo deflection problem, how far ahead of a moving target the submarine should aim, the director modeled it in the form of three bars set under a walk-around periscope. One bar, fixed along the sight line of the periscope, was set at the estimated range to the target, in thousands of yards. It connected bars representing target course (length set for target speed) and submarine (hence torpedo) course (length set for torpedo speed). If the bars were properly set, swinging the submarine so that the sight line bore on the target would place the torpedo on the proper deflection course. Later much the same kind of triangle-solver would indicate proper torpedo gyro angle. The device also had a firing buzzer, by means of which the submarine's CO could order firing as soon as the submarine reached the proper firing angle. This type of director became impractical when American submarines adopted retracting periscopes during WW I, but the basic idea of mechanically solving the firing triangle problem persisted.

45. In a 31 May 1908 critique of the D-class design for BuNav's Capt. Marsh, Lt. Courtney protested that officers should have curtained bunks and enlisted men bunks with air mattresses. The head was not enclosed, but any permanent structure around it would limit access to the battery. In the next boats (E and F classes) a light portable structure was fitted. These boats also had more powerful blowers. Better engine room ventilators were needed. Ducts were on the bottom of the engine space to collect gasoline fumes, which are heavier than air. There they could not collect leaked exhaust, which is lighter than air. Because the engine ultimately took its air through the conning tower hatch, it would draw cold air through the crew quarters in winter; a

separate air induction was needed (NARS RG 19 correspondence, file 17693E).

46. About August 1908 the navy approved Electric Boat's proposed changes, including an additional (fixed-eyepiece) periscope. In December it asked the company to install instead a walk-around periscope with a torpedo director. Electric Boat objected. Plans of D-1 show a bulkhead (with the periscope within, rather than outside, the control room). The CO of *Grayling* (D-2), in a letter of 16 December 1909 describes the boat's second periscope as an old type like that on board *Octopus* (i.e., with a fixed eyepiece); he wanted the forward bulkhead cut away so that the instrument could be converted to a walk-around type suitable for installation of a torpedo director (NARS RG 19 correspondence, file 17693E).

47. The EB 18A design was practically identical to EB 18, except that the torpedo room was lengthened by 1½ ft to accommodate Mk V rather than Mk III torpedoes in tubes 8 in longer (total length 136 ft 4½ in) and it displaced 3 tons more. Additions included a periscope in the body of the boat, torpedo firing control at the boat commander's position, a portable bridge extension, a larger compass for underwater work, and a submarine signal bell and receiver. Like EB 18, EB 18A was fully subdivided, which precluded the internal arrangement in favor by late 1908.

48. Lt. D. A. Weaver, commanding *Salmon,* reported that her electrician's log showed the special run, at 1200 amp, rather than the usual limit of 1000 amp (letter of 26 October 1910, NARS RG 19 correspondence, file 25997E).

49. Few 5-m torpedoes were made. A Torpedo Board meeting on 27 June 1911 at the E. W. Bliss Co.'s Sag Harbor, New York test site suggested lengthening the tubes of the B, C, and D classes, where structurally permissible, to take the standard 5.2 m weapon. Apparently that was not possible for the B-class. The board had been convened by the Acting Secretary of the Navy (NARS RG 19 correspondence, 17693E268).

50. Lake went too far. Early in 1908, Representative George L. Lilley of Connecticut, where Lake's company was based, charged that Electric Boat had paid members of Congress to instigate the FY 09 change from four to eight submarines at the cost of a reduction in battleships from four to two. The bill was later amended to force the secretary of the navy to buy repeat *Octopus*-class submarines unless a better design had been offered and *demonstrated* by 1 October 1908. That effectively gave Electric Boat the contract. Lilley wanted Lake to be permitted to compete on the same basis as in 1907. After extensive (1,659 pages) hearings, a Select Committee decided that no corrupt activity had been proved. Testimony revealed the somewhat irregular way in which Lake had overturned the 1907 trials recommendation and showed that he had not been above hiring former government officials for their contacts. The charge and the hearings, however, presumably had served adequate notice that Lake, like Electric Boat, could exert pressure on Congress. The report of the 1908 hearings (House Resolution 288) includes the Lake and Holland correspondence of 1901–1905.

51. Neither Lake's Russian boats nor *Lake X* made their designed speeds. In 1907, *Lake X* made 7.59 kt surfaced and 5.65 kt submerged (only intermittently) against promised speeds of 9 kt and 6.75 kt.

52. As No. 19½, Lake's boat clearly had been slipped into the series. Electric Boat submarines bought after the 1907 trials were numbered 13 through 19.

53. Whiting, "Tactical and Maneuver Data."

54. Ibid.

55. In a memorandum submitted when G-1 was delivered (INSURV reports, vol. 61). Lake claimed that the trainable tubes would be particularly well suited to current night attack tactics, during which the submarine operated on the surface.

56. The Taft Board seems to have been prompted partly by the need to fortify new U.S. possessions, including the Philippines, Guantánamo Bay, Puerto Rico, and the Canal Zone, and partly by perceived changes in weaponry since 1886. The U.S. position in the Caribbean had been settled in 1903, with the decisions to acquire Guantánamo Bay and the Canal Zone. The Panama Canal ultimately justified the concentration of the fleet because it allowed the full fleet to pass quickly from the Atlantic to the Pacific.

57. Lt. Edward Kittle, "The Sphere and Scope of the Submarine in Coast Defense," in General Board 420-15 (1905). Kittle, a General Board planner, forwarded his report to the Taft Board in April. Controlled mine fields became less and less useful as naval gun range increased and ships could remain farther out to sea (hence much harder to localize and attack with specific mines). That left contact mines. According to the U.S. naval attaché in London, Russo-Japanese war experience (involving the first large-scale mining) had impressed the British with the danger of their own mines, onto which navigational errors might lead their ships. (The battleship of a Russian commander, Adm. Stepan O. Makarov, had been sunk by a Russian mine.) The indiscriminate character of contact mines might well result in international restriction on their use. Submarines and torpedo boats were better: they could operate farther offshore, with much better discrimination. No blockading squadron within submarine range could be considered safe. A fleet could anchor safely only if protected by deep nets or by a dense protective field of contact mines.

58. At this time, the perceived threat was more likely that a European power would use its Pacific squadron to attack the Philippines in the context of a larger war. The most immediate threat to U.S. control over the Philippines in 1898 was the local German colonial squadron.

59. EB 20A and EB 20B were offered for $429,000; EB 20D, for $418,000. The smaller EB 19A cost $380,000 (NARS RG 80 Entry 26506 [FY 09 submarine contracts]).

According to Electric Boat's description of its FY 09 alternatives, EB 18B abandoned the complete bulkheading of EB 18 (the original D-class) in favor of a better midships arrangement. In response to the *Octopus* trials board, the main and auxiliary ballast tanks extended above the line of maximum hull diameter (the hull axis). This version also had slightly more fuel (6400 versus 6150 gal, for 1400 nm at 10.5 kt versus 1350 nm at 10.5 kt) and more powerful motors (580 HP, for 11.25 kt at the 1 hr rate and 9 kt versus 8.5 kt at the 3 hr rate). EB 18C was powered by a lighter double-acting gasoline engine; the weight went into higher power (13.5 kt surfaced, 11.25 kt submerged) and fuel (7550 gal, for 1680 nm at 10.5 kt).

EB 19 was bulkheaded like EB 18B and EB 18C, and had better lines for surface speed (134 ft 10 in × 14 ft 5¼ in [maximum 14 ft 6⅞ in], 340 tons submerged). It had 4-cylinder 500 BHP diesel engines, with slow-speed 520 HP motors to match the slower engine speed (400-RPM). Speed was 13/11 kt. Diesels brought much better endurance: 1625 nm at 13 kt, 2475 nm at 11 kt; maximum (with oil fuel in ballast tanks) was 3465 nm at 11 kt. This design introduced bow planes into Electric Boat practice.

EB 20 was an enlarged EB 19 using the same hull form (142 ft 7 in × 15 ft 3 in [15 ft 4⅜ in max], 400 tons). EB 20A used a 6-cylinder diesel (800 BHP at 400 RPM) with the same 520 HP motors (14 kt surfaced, 10.5 kt submerged; surface radius 1120 nm at 14 kt, 2500 nm at 11 kt, maximum 3500nm at 11 kt; submerged 8 kt for 3 hr). EB 20B traded off a smaller 600 BHP engine (surface speed 13.5 kt) for more battery capacity (for 8.5 kt for 3 hr) and motor power (620 HP, 11.25 kt); fuel capacity was reduced from 6150 to 5800 gal (radius 1417 nm at 13.5 kt, 2350 nm at 11 kt, maximum 3300 nm at 11 kt). Unlike EB 20A, this version had its two batteries separated mechanically. The torpedo and engine room were separated off by permanent bulkheads.

EB 20C was a gasoline-engined (800 BHP at 500 RPM) version of EB 20B, with higher-speed motors to suit. Surface speed increased to 14 kt, but gasoline gave far less endurance: 770 nm at 14 kt, 1600 nm at 11 kt. Because gasoline could not be stowed in ballast tanks, there was no maximum figure. EB 20D used the double-acting 6-cylinder engine BuEng favored (800 BHP at 400 RPM). Although gasoline capacity was increased to 7100 gal, radius increased only to 980 nm at 14 kt or 1925 nm at 11 kt.

60. L. Y. Spear letter to Superintending Constructor at Quincy (Fore River), 12 November 1908, describing these designs. Spear points out that two walk-around periscopes (as in the E and F classes) had to be placed far enough apart (fore and aft) not to interfere with each other, and therefore precluded installation of shears that would support both against vibration. Complete separation would increase underwater resistance and, probably, the telltale wake of the periscopes. If the two observers were on different levels (as in the D class, as built), one periscope could be walk-around and the other fixed-eyepiece. Spear argues that this arrangement minimizes resistance and disturbance in the water, and makes for maximum rigidity (vibration was then a major problem). He points out that the periscopes could be designed to retract, so that only one need be exposed when close to the enemy. In that case, he would favor using a pair of walk-around instruments, each of which could be fitted with a torpedo director. This seems to have been the first U.S. proposal for retracting periscopes, which Spear almost certainly knew were already in use abroad.

61. The very small conning tower provided little access to the bridge; therefore Electric Boat provided a collapsible hatch trunk from the main deck. After March 1911 operations by the Third Submarine Division (*Stingray, Tarpon, Bonita,* and *Snapper*), intended largely to test their ability to operate away from a tender for three or four days at a time, their COs asked to turn in both their cruising bridges and their hatch extension trunks. They argued that the bridges made for slow diving. They feared that the existence of the trunk might tempt a CO to leave its hatch (on deck) open in a seaway; a high wave might damage the trunk and so begin to flood the boat. If trunks were fitted only in calm weather, access to the bridge generally would be via the narrow conning tower. The trunks were actually discarded but the bridges, which could be dismantled in 10–15 min, remained. Electric Boat argued that there was no real alternative to the external trunk, because the conning tower was too narrow to be used as the access trunk to the bridge. The company solved the problem in the next design (H class) by enclosing a permanent ladder in the conning tower fairwater. For the E and F classes, the company offered a non-collapsible trunk (for long surface cruises) that could be carried on board a submarine tender when not in use (Electric Boat, letter, 20 June 1911; Electric Boat letter, NARS RG 19 correspondence, file 17693E).

62. Very nearly echoing Simon Lake, Electric Boat explained that a boat with planes at both ends could dive on very nearly an even keel, as the planes could be used to provide a vertical thrust without a turning moment. Alternatively, they could induce a trim angle without a vertical thrust. Clearly, at some size, boats should be able to dive at very moderate angles, but there was no way to determine the critical displacement. If bow planes on the E- and F-boats proved unsuccessful, they could be removed, but they would be difficult to install after the boats were

completed. Bow planes also might be useful for higher-speed control underwater (all the designs except EB 18A were faster than earlier boats). Somewhat later submariners would argue that bow planes were important to prevent bows from rising as they fired torpedoes; some COs went so far as to risk sinking by making their boats bow-heavy before firing.

At this time, U.S. submarines apparently had no special torpedo firing compensating tanks (WRT tanks), although (see above) such tanks certainly were installed at least in the A-class. Stanley (later Sir Stanley) Goodall, the British constructor assigned to the U.S. Navy Department during World War I, remarked at the time that U.S. submariners relied on an enlarged forward trim tank for this purpose. Goodall's comments are in ADM 229/97, folio 14 (PRO, Kew, England). WRT tanks do appear in post-World War I U.S. submarines, perhaps as a consequence of Goodall's influence. They were introduced in the final S-boat series (Electric Boat S-42 through S-47, Lake S-48 through S-51).

63. "The Development of the Holland Submarine Boat," *Engineering,* 17 November 1911, 655–660, 670.

64. Whiting, "Tactical and Maneuver Data," lists six torpedoes (two reloads), but Office of Naval Intelligence, *Data on Submarines,* ONI Publication No. 17, November 1917, lists only four (no reloads) for the E and F classes (table of U.S. submarines, p.10). By 1917, reloads might have been landed to compensate for other added weight.

65. Lake initially offered 300 ton (submerged) and 310/400-ton boats. The 300-tonner met the requirements; the bigger boat was $\frac{1}{2}$ kt faster surfaced and submerged and added a pair of deck torpedo tubes. Later Lake offered two larger designs: 135 ft × 12$\frac{1}{2}$ ft (410 tons submerged, 4 torpedo tubes) and 161 ft × 13 ft (6 torpedo tubes, 2 forward and 4 trainable deck tubes in the superstructure). The smaller boat, probably related to the Russian *Kaiman,* was expected to make 15/9.5 kt, with surface endurance 1,000 nm at 14 kt and 3,000 nm at 8 kt; submerged endurance was 3 hr at 8 kt and 24 hr at 4 kt. This design included Lake's trademark guide wheels, drop keel, and diver's compartment, and had separate navigating and captain's "turrets" (each with its own periscope) covered by a combined conning tower and sighting hood with deadlights. The turrets could be used as escape chambers (a feature the submarine force later espoused). The larger boat was an improved version of the *Seal* (G-1) design Lake was then completing (it would be laid down in February 1909). Lake estimated that it would make 16 kt surfaced and 10 kt submerged, with 3-hr underwater endurance at 8 kt and 25 hr at 4 kt; surface endurance was 1,200 nm at 14 kt and 3,500 nm at 8 kt. A photograph of the towing tank model of the 161-footer, which accompanied Lake's proposal, shows that it was a more streamlined version of *Seal.*

66. Lake made his proposal in March 1909. Presumably, he badly wanted to avoid the extra cost of drawing and lofting a new hull. Perhaps he hoped to use Russian plans for the smaller submarine; but by 1909 that might not have been practicable. Lake offered a higher speed (14.5 kt versus 14 kt surfaced, 10.5 versus 9.5 kt submerged for 1 hr) and greater endurance (80 hr at 14.5 kt versus 70 hr at 14 kt). The only significant drawback was a small reduction in metacentric height. The board was perfectly happy to dispense with such features as wheels, a superimposed conning tower, after anchor weights, and a diver's air lock, which it had never asked for in the first place. The contract price was $410,000; Lake commented that, if built without the advantage of the G-1 hull work, the new boat would have cost $35,000 more (he had bid his 161-footer for $460,000 in 1908). G-1 was expected to cost $450,000 (NARS RG 19 corre-

spondence, file 24256E3). Lake's 17 November 1908 proposals are described in NARS RG 19 correspondence, files 26506E/23642E8.

67. In April 1916, Lake claimed that when the government took G-2 over in 1913 it refused her captain's request to run official trials. Presumably, Lake's point was that the time since had been devoted to crippling changes made by the government. He was trying to justify major new orders for his reorganized company. Comments on this and other G-boats are from an undated (probably 1916) research memorandum, "Submarines of the United States Navy," prepared by the C&R Preliminary Design section (National Archives RG 80 Entry 449, miscellaneous papers).

68. All three Lake submarines were limited mainly to training and experimental work during and just after WW I. Although commissioned in 1912, G-1 appears to have seen little operational service before her two near-sisters entered service in 1915–16. Although these boats made relatively long runs between New York and Charleston during the 1915 summer war games, their engine foundations needed extensive strengthening and they often broke their crankshafts. G-2 required an extensive overhaul (26 March 1916 through 28 June 1917) not long after entering service. In May 1916, the Submarine Flotilla excluded the G-boats (and the D and E classes) from its proposed operational submarine plan.

69. Laurenti's first submarines were the *Glauco* class, launched in 1905–09 at the Venice Navy Yard. His later boats were built by G. Asaldo–San Giorgio & Co. at La Spezia, with engines by FIAT. Laurenti began a campaign for a U.S. order with a 3 July 1907 request that the U.S. naval attaché in Rome visit one of his submarines.

70. G-4 was unusual in using controllable-pitch propellers, which Laurenti claimed could absorb power over a very wide range most efficiently. As offered to the navy, she would have had an unusual battery arrangement, 70 large and 12 small (half-capacity) cells, to suit her configuration, for an average output of 143 volts. As completed, she had a conventional 2 × 60 cell battery.

71. Lambert (private communication) reports that the Atlantic submarines began progressive endurance trials in the spring of 1910, the initial objective being a continuous 12-hr engine run of more than 100 nm. Engines were initially very unreliable: in August 1910, only one of six submarines returned after a day's cruise with both engines running. By November, most problems had been cured; the gasoline-powered submarines worked. Once engine problems had been solved, the flotilla began to exercise its wartime plan for protracted, independent operation from a tender, a 4-day cruise along a coast that it was expected to protect. Noise and gasoline fumes kept crew members from sleeping, so that they were not good for more than 3 or 4 days at a time. Submarines trying to operate longer had to anchor at night. Stores and fresh water proved inadequate, even for 4 days.

72. D-3 ran 135.8 nm submerged (including a run at 60 ft for 1 hr), D-2 ran 123 nm submerged, D-1 ran 118 nm, and the others less. No tenders were used.

73. A February 1913 cruise from Norfolk to Guantánamo Bay (1,814 nm) by the D-boats and the first diesel submarines (E-boats) was unsuccessful. The boats averaged 9 kt daily for 16 days, with four stops. The senior officer reported that E-boat engines were so unreliable that they might have to be repaired about every 24 hr; they could not be considered effective for coast defense.

74. C-class engines were shipped to Panama but not installed.

75. From one of a series of questionnaires, 27 May 1915, for D-1, D-2, G-2, E-1, E-2, K-2, K-5, and K-6. The fleet exercise was designed to test whether submarines were "capable of operating . . . from 300 to 400 miles from a base in all weathers encountered." Each CO was asked whether the submarine had successfully spent the 7 days of the exercise away from her base, and how many more days she could remain away efficiently. The exercise was conducted in fine weather. One striking feature of the questionnaires was the fraction of unqualified men, typically about a third to almost half.

76. For a remarkable fictional account of what life on this gasoline-powered boat must have been like, see J. Biggins, *A Sailor of Austria* (London: Mandarin, 1992; New York: St. Martin's Press, 1994). Biggins calls his boat U 8, but from his description she is clearly U 12 (the real Austrian U 8, built by Germania, was taken over by the German Navy in 1914).

77. Erwin Sieche, in *Conway's All The World's Fighting Ships 1906–1921*, R. Gardiner, ed. (London: Conway Maritime Press; Annapolis, Md.: Naval Institute Press, 1985), 342–343. According to Sieche, the Hay-Whitehead design was attractive mainly because it was available; Whitehead had already built three of the submarines for Denmark, and six more had been built in Danish yards. The Austrian Navy was well aware of deficiencies in the design, and the program suffered further because orders had to be split between Austrian and Hungarian firms. Sieche describes the class as "unreliable and unfortunate." Sieche based his work on Austrian naval archives.

78. Hay later designed submarines for Wm. Denny & Bros., a major British shipbuilding firm. Although Electric Boat did not list them as its own, the Hay-Denny boats were presumably derived from Electric Boat practice. They were the Dutch *0 7*, *K II*, and the *K V* class.

79. S. D. Klimovskiy, "*Kaiman*-Type Submarines," in *Sudostroyeniye* (Russian shipbuilding journal) No. 8 of 1990, pp 64–68. Neither Klimovskiy nor any Western writer mentions the trainable torpedo tubes which are so evident in Lake Co. photographs of *Kaiman*, and which are mentioned in contemporary Lake literature. Tests on the earlier *Protector* suggested to the Russians that it could be developed into a long-range cruiser. In September 1904 Lake's European office offered to build ten 400 ton cruisers for Russia, powered by two 300 BHP engines on each shaft (16 kt, range 4000 nm at 8 kt, 7 kt submerged), armed with four torpedo tubes and two 47-mm cannon. That November the Russian trials commission rated the *Protector* as suitable only for coastal work, but recommended building ten larger ones (radius at least 3000 nm) for the Pacific Coast (five each for Port Arthur and Vladivostok). The Russian submarine expert, I. G. Bubnov, doubted that the proposed 400-tonner could manage either the 4000 nm range or the projected 15 kt speed, but on 15 February 1905 the mine (i.e., torpedo) department of the Russian Navy approved specifications for four long-range submarines, which became the *Kaiman* class. A contract was signed on 1 April 1905 for completion the following year. Lake offered the 125-footer he had designed in 1901 and opened a design office in Berlin to support the project.

By this time the boat had grown to 40.2 × 3.85 m (132 × 12.6 ft). Two 300 BHP Wright & Middleton gasoline engines would drive each of two shafts (boats were completed with one 8-cylinder 400 BHP engine and one 4-cylinder 200 BHP engine per shaft); the 60-cell (6900 amp-hr) battery fed a pair of 100 HP motors driving adjustable-pitch propellers. Test depth was 45 m (147.6 ft). Ballast was carried in the ends of the watertight superstructure, with trim tanks at the ends of the pressure hull. Other tanks were amidships and wrapped around the conning tower. Hull tanks could fill through a large Kingston and four flood valves, but water had to be pumped (using two pumps) into the superstructure tanks. Armament was four 45 cm tubes in the superstructure (two bow, two revolving) with four reloads in storage tubes plus 47-mm guns in the conning tower pointing fore and aft.

Klimovskiy points out that Lake's continual changes in plans seriously delayed the project; so did strikes. A January 1906 design review by the Russian Naval Engineering Committee concluded, among other things, that Lake's trainable torpedo tubes might damage torpedoes as they ran out, that it was undesirable to locate the guns in the bridge structure, and that the paraffin-soaked wooden superstructure was a fire hazard. Lake chose to consider these comments as advice, not direction. Only after three boats had been launched (and one completed for trials) did he agree to replace the trainable bow tubes with a lightweight wood structure and two Dzhevetskiy (Drzwiecky) torpedo launching frames (which were then standard in Russian submarines). The bow hatch could then be kept open in a strong wind. The forward gun was moved onto the foredeck, the after one replaced by a superstructure housing a messenger buoy, a small motorboat, an enlarged muffler, and improved engine induction valve, and electric capstans for the underwater anchors.

As completed, *Kaiman* displaced 382 tons surfaced (425 tons awash) and 447 tons submerged. On trials (1909) she achieved only about 10.6 kt at 1200 BHP. Because her battery capacity was much greater than planned (7030 Amp-hr), it took 12 hr to charge. To cure her stern-heaviness, her underwater anchor and wheels were removed. Work on fitting out the other boats dragged on; on 9 October 1909 the Lake Co. was dismissed from fitting-out work. Further trials revealed more overweight; lead ballast keel and powered wheels (about 20 tons) were removed. To add buoyancy three hollow cylinders ("displacers") were added on each side of the stern and timbers were added to the superstructure. In December 1910 the mine department ordered the forward four cylinders removed from each eight-cylinder engine, reducing surface speed to 8–9 kt. According to Klimovskiy, nothing could cure the boats' problems. For example, wood superstructure beams swelled when wet, warped, and cracked in the sun; water entered deck tanks; soaked wood deck planking reduced buoyancy when the boat submerged. As completed, the boats hardly resembled the design Lake had sold in 1905.

Problems with this class presumably made it impossible for Lake to sell any later boats to the Russians.

The Austrian U 1 and U 2, launched in February and April 1909, were intermediate between *Lake X* and *Kaiman*.

80. The Nevskiy Works, which had an Electric Boat license, sold both EB 31A (*Narval* class) and EB 27B to the Russian Navy.

According to E. P. Ignatyev, "*Narval* Class Submarines," in *Sudostroyeniye* No 2 of 1991, pp 74–76, these submarines were the three Black Sea Fleet submarines bought as part of the "small shipbuilding program" approved by Czar Nicholas II on 12 July 1907. In the summer of 1909 the Main Naval Staff produced specifications: 12 kt surfaced, 10 kt submerged, range 1000 nm surfaced and 100 nm submerged. On 3 June these characteristics were circulated among interested Russian firms, 16 of which responded. A committee of the Russian Naval Technical Commission (MTK) under Capt. 1st Rank Beklemishev rejected all projects powered by only a single engine or designed by yards which had not yet produced a submarine. That left only the Nevskiy works (490 tons) and Baltic works (450 tons) designs.

Then, in September, Capt. 1st Rank Stal', deputy to the chief of the main naval staff, asked that the submarine be capable of 16 kt surfaced and 12 kt submerged. It is not clear where these figures, which were quite ambitious, originated. The Russian chief constructor warned the MTK that these characteristics

would require a displacement of 1000 tons. Any builder would need three months of model testing to ensure success. Late in November the construction department estimated that the submarines would probably displace 750/950 tons.

As required, the Nevskiy Works reported only a price and displacement. The Baltic Works offered a complete set of drawings of a 600 ton submarine. Each had its supporters. Finally, in December Navy Minister Vice Adm. Vogevodskiy decided to order three submarines from each yard, given the urgency of building up the Black Sea Fleet. The Nevskiy boats were the *Narvals* (the Baltic Works craft were the *Morzh* class). Their design offered a surface speed of 17 kt and a submerged speed of 12 kt. Although the MTK hoped that all construction would be done in Russia, on 23 November 1910 the Nevskiy Works had reported that the engines would be 850 BHP 2-cycle MANs built in Germany (ultimately they could be license-built in Russia). To cut weight, the designers had to cut battery capacity. To achieve the required underwater speed with that reduced capacity, they had to accept a higher battery discharge rate, which in turn cut battery life to about one-eighth that of a U.S. K-boat. After a June 1911 design review, designed surface speed was reduced to 16 kt and submerged speed to 11 kt in the interest of increasing underwater endurance. This reduction was *not* noted in the influential November 1911 *Engineering* article.

The boats were formally ordered on 9 July 1911 for completion within two years. The 27 July 1911 engine contract with MAN called for delivery of the first engine in 11 months, and of the 5th and 6th after 15 months. Electric Boat supplied compressors, air flasks, and pumps. As laid down, the submarines were expected to displace 621/944 tons. In fact construction was slow (boats were not launched until 1915) and the MAN diesels were never delivered. Instead, each had four 160 BHP units; maximum surface speed was only 9.6 kt (10.5 kt in *Narval*). Nor were they completed with the planned revolving deck torpedo tubes; they got drop-collars instead. Unlike contemporary Russian-designed submarines, these boats had negative tanks and ballast tanks filled by gravity (rather than by pumps). Reported diving time was 1 minute.

The *Ersh* class minelayers (*Ersh* and *Forelle*), a modified version built under the 1912 Program, had revised ballast tankage (displacement 655/750 tons).

Once WW I began, the Russians ordered more Electric Boat submarines, beginning with U.S.-built H-boats (AG-class) under a 1915 Emergency Program. The Russian 1916 Program included a double-hull B-class reportedly influenced by Electric Boat practice (i.e., by the *Narval* class) and a parallel Electric Boat-designed double-hull G-class (28 boats, 265 × 23 × 13 ft, 952/1289 tons, 16/9 kt, 2 × 75-mm guns, 2 machine guns, 10 torpedo tubes [probably 4 athwartships], 6 drop-collars, 10 mines). The first 14 were laid down in 1916–17 but abandoned after the Revolution. Unfortunately, no Electric Boat design number is known. Data on the B- and G-classes are from R. Gardiner ed., *Conway's All the World's Fighting Ships 1906–1921.*

According to V. G. Andriyenko, "Small Submarines of Holland Type 27B" in *Sudostroyenie* No. 1 of 1991, pp 74–77, these boats were intended as mobile torpedo stations to defend passages through the minefields around the modernized Kronstadt fortress; work on these boats began in 1908. Six small submarines and their tenders were included in the 1910 phase of the work (finances limited the project to three boats). They were an Army Ministry project; the Navy Ministry was far more interested in long-range seagoing submarines. Specifications were developed at a 9 March 1910 conference held by the naval general staff. Naval officers at the conference rejected the idea; the Navy Ministry decided to limit its role to advice, including providing specialists during construction.

During the latter half of 1910 the ministry chose a Nevskiy (Electric Boat) design over one by the Baltic Works. The specifications envisaged 25–30 ton boats; the Baltic Works offered 40 tons, the Nevskiy works 32 tons. The Baltic Works offered the required 100 nm surface range (18 nm at 3 kt submerged), but Nevskiy offered 150 nm surfaced. Both yards offered the required speeds, 8 kt surfaced and 6 kt submerged. Both yards claimed to meet the requirement to dive in 4 min. but the Nevskiy boat could dive twice as deep (down to 30 m), carried more compressed air (with a more powerful compressor), and carried its torpedoes in tubes rather than in dropping collars. All its controls were centrally located. New features included a diesel engine (the Baltic Works offered a "kerosene" engine) and Edison nickel batteries (which Andriyenko describes as both more compact and safer than lead-acid units). The naval technical commission (MTK) disliked the new batteries, and demanded a two-year guarantee (Given U.S. experience, they were clearly correct). Other characteristics of the Nevskiy design were: dimensions 20.35 × 2.15 × 1.83 m, displacement 33.1/43.6 tons. Power: 50 BHP surfaced, 35 HP submerged. No reloads were carried for the two torpedo tubes.

Some Russian documents mention a Type 13, perhaps an Electric Boat design designation (EB 13).

81. The story of the C class and the replacement is told in detail in F. Abelsen, "Ubatene som vi aldri fikk: C-klassen," *Norsk Tidskrift for Sjoewesen*, March 1991, 17–24. Abelsen includes scale plans of various versions of the C class. C-class characteristics are given as: 220.6 tons, 34.35 m × 3.61 m, one 4-cylinder Sulzer diesel (type 4Q.28) of 300 EHP (425 RPM) for 10.75 kt (9.75 kt submerged); range 1,100 nm/9.5 kt; diving depth, 50 m; complement, two officers and eight enlisted men; and armament of two 45-cm (18-in) torpedo tubes and four torpedoes (45 cm × 5.7 m, which is an unusually great length for this caliber).

82. Vickers supplied engines for the Spanish C class and reviewed its design; its papers refer to it as 309V (Electric Boat called it 3090). EB 707D also might have been offered to Spain. Vicker's papers suggest that Electric Boat competed for the Spanish contract for a fast (20-kt) submarine, the D class, but Vickers won.

83. Electric Boat tried to sell submarines to Argentina, Brazil, and Chile after World War I. Fragmentary company records at the Submarine Force Museum indicate that Vickers offered Design 309V to Argentina, for completion in 24 months, and that 707KB was offered to Brazil. The Argentine offer was apparently made against Armstrong, and was part of a larger package including surface ships. Argentina ordered French submarines, then switched to Italian. Brazil bought Italian submarines. Chile had bought twice from Electric Boat (first the abortive pre-1914 EB 19s, then the wartime H-boats transferred by Britain), but in the late 1920s she bought Vickers designs.

Other export designs of this period include 309T (93T), 309VB (93VB), 506A (65A), 509C (95C), 707DE, 707J, and 803N (38N). No characteristics are available. It is tempting to associate 707DE with Denmark, which bought three new submarines in the 1920s (clearly smaller than this design). At some point Electric Boat began to designate export designs in a new 1000-series. References in available company records show Designs 1006A, 1009, 1014C, 1019A, 1020A, 1025 (fleet submarine, November 1926), 1026 (fleet submarine, November 1926), 1027 (fleet submarine, November 1926), 1028 (fleet submarine, November 1926), and 1064 (October 1931, probably for Norway; note that the Norwegian B-class was 406B/64B). Again, details are lacking.

84. Although contemporary U.S. papers do not mention the foreign disasters, it seems noteworthy that escape and salvage concepts cropped up suddenly in 1909–11. These themes did not receive much attention again until the S-4 disaster of 1927. On 15 April 1909, Ens. Kenneth Whiting (CO of *Porpoise*) made a publicized escape from his boat's torpedo tube (in 1910 there would be entries *into* a bottomed submarine via her tubes). Apparently, Whiting was severely reprimanded; intense interest in submarine escape only came somewhat later. Experiments with a marker/messenger buoy that would carry a telephone to the surface were authorized in September 1910. Tests on board a C-class submarine were authorized in June 1911. Meanwhile, interest revived in other forms of escape; a man successfully left the conning tower of *Viper* (B class) in a flooded dry dock at Charleston on 1 July 1911. The marker buoy developed at this time was not adopted; U.S. submarines did not carry messenger buoys until the 1930s.

Chapter 5

1. Lt. Comdr. W. V. Pratt, in an extraordinary 1914 paper for the Naval War College, proposed making transports the primary targets in defense of the Caribbean against a German assault. The college had posed the problem of defense by torpedo craft, with the main fleet being occupied in the Pacific. Pratt argued that any landing had to be stopped wtihin 48 hr, partly because anti-American sentiment in the Caribbean might make the Germans almost impossible to dislodge once they had consolidated their position. Pratt's was the only solution considered viable. (Pratt's paper is in the Naval War College archives.)

2. Firing doctrine was embodied in tactical tables showing the proper bearings on which to fire torpedoes for every possible formation. Group tactics are from Lt. Comdr. (later Admiral) Chester Nimitz, description of submarine tactics, 17 May 1912 (General Board 420-15 file, NARS). Prompted by Rear Adm. Robert Griffen (BuEng), the General Board requested the paper. It projected existing practice to the fleet submarines, which were then controversial. Nimitz was the new Senior Group Commander, Atlantic Submarine Flotilla. He had joined the submarine force as CO of *Plunger* in 1909. After commanding the Atlantic submarines, he went to BuEng, where he was responsible for submarine and surface ship diesel development (he had a finger crushed in the process). His Atlantic submarine post was left unfilled until the summer of 1914. During WW I, Nimitz was Atlantic submarine force engineering aide and then chief of staff under Capt. S. S. Robison.

3. This proposal was made as part of a May 1909 tactical paper (General Board 420-15 file).

4. Earlier foreign attempts at a snorkel were apparently defeated by back pressure. Lake patented, but did not try, a snorkel (U.S. Patent 726947). From the C class on, engines had to be operable in the awash condition (i.e., with main ballast tanks flooded and the conning tower clear). E-1 tested her air intake valve in August 1912 but only when fully surfaced; the flotilla commander refused to try it awash. G-1 had an air intake valve for use when only the conning tower was above water, but on trial the contractor refused to operate in this condition. G-2 and G-3 had the special air induction valves, but they were not installed on G-4 because the Submarine Flotilla said that it would never run a submarine's engines with the boat partly submerged. The K class had an oval ventilator (6.5 in × 10 in) between the periscopes. K-2 ran her engines with the after and main ballast tanks full, and, on trials, K-5 ran both her engines with hatches closed and only the ventilator open.

5. R. S. Edwards, RG 80 (SecNav Correspondence). Edwards

commanded Submarine Division (SubDiv) 1 (Atlantic Fleet). There is one postscript. During WW I, the Italian Navy received U.S. H-class submarines, which presumably incorporated the special ventilators between their periscopes. Capt. E. Ferretti, who headed the Italian Navy's Submarine Division at Taranto in 1917–21, proposed that the ventilator be extended so that a submarine caught on the surface could dive without turning off her engines. As head of naval engineering at Naples in 1924, he ordered a test installation on board an H-class submarine (H-3 ran successful trials in November 1925). Similar gear, designed in 1933–34 for the new *Sirena* class, was tested successfully, but the project was abandoned in 1937. During WW II, the Germans searched unsuccessfully for Captain Ferretti. Their snorkel work (which ultimately led to the U.S. snorkel), however, was based on Dutch work apparently unrelated to Ferretti's. See *Maritime Defence*, April 1991, 111–112.

R. Compton-Hall, *Submarines and the War at Sea, 1914–1918* (London: Macmillan, 1991), 45, recounts two wartime instances of British submarine COs extemporizing snorkels: C-3 used an extended ventilator, and E-35 used a 6-ft–long pipe through a 6-in collar in a wooden plug in the conning tower hatchway. Neither was officially sanctioned, and no letter in the U.S. file on the British wartime submarine service mentions these or similar devices. While on anti–U-boat patrol, E-35 ran her main engines and charged her batteries at periscope depth, even in heavy weather, and used a tarpaulin below the hatchway to direct any water entering into the beam torpedo tube well (from which it could be removed by bilge pump). Compton-Hall probably took these data from contemporary letters on file at his Royal Navy Submarine Museum. The experiments had no sequel, perhaps partly because the British submarine service was so decentralized that few in it heard of them at the time.

6. Cage was general manager of the new Los Angeles Submarine Boat Co. of Long Beach, California, which bid on SS 40–47 in August 1912. The bid was rejected because of the company's inexperience, but the navy was interested enough in the engine to appoint several boards to examine the company's claims. In June 1913, Cage claimed that he had remained underwater for 36 hr (breaking a record set by USS *Octopus*, C-1), while running a gas engine without fumes in the boat. In November, a trials board objected that a full-size submarine could not accommodate enough air. Even so, the navy offered a West Coast H-boat or K-boat for trials. The system was to be installed at a navy yard at company expense, but the fleet commander was unwilling to divert an operational submarine in increasingly dangerous times. A. R. Neff (who had been Lake's Washington agent) acquired the Cage patents between January and July 1915. CNO Benson forwarded plans and specifications for a Neff conversion of G-1 in December 1915. Letters were prepared for the secretary of the navy to request money from Congress, hence its inclusion in the big 1916 program.

7. After firing an initial salvo, the submarines would go deep to reload, then reattack individually.

8. Spear referred to a "special engine" (a Vickers diesel) being installed on board the F class, with a specific consumption 30 percent less than the best gasoline engine. Its greater weight would reduce surface speed about 4 percent. Normal radius of action at full speed, however, would increase about 80 percent (maximum radius about 110 percent), and fuel cost per mile would be halved. Spear might have avoided specifically mentioning diesels for patent reasons (see Appendix A).

9. Typical battery capacity at half-speed (about one-eighth power) was about 15 hr. Spear was not concerned with very low speeds. Later, a submarine's endurance at minimum controllable

speed, perhaps 1–2 kt, often determined her chance of evading pursuers by exhausting them.

10. Spear argued that more tonnage could buy deck tubes and external torpedo racks, but neither could be fired really accurately. Too, torpedoes were so delicate that they had to be accessible from within the submarine.

11. In August 1910, the Atlantic Torpedo Fleet proposed that the FY 11 boats (K class) have conning towers above their hulls that were large enough for three men. They would contain all navigating facilities (e.g., compass, hand and power steering gear), and be fitted as escape chambers (air locks). The flying bridge would be atop the conning tower. Boats were to have two periscopes, as close together as possible, the after (higher) one having its eyepiece in the operating compartment, the forward (upper) one in the conning tower. The General Board accordingly modified the circular for the FY 10 boats (H class) in October 1910, but the proposed FY 11 circular allowed for an alternative placement of the forward periscope in the hull. In April 1911, the Submarine Detachment of the Atlantic Torpedo Fleet rejected the alternative; the periscope positions had been chosen on the basis of careful experiments, including dummy attacks on the battleship Vermont in Cape Cod Bay in 1909.

Lt. D. A. Weaver, CO of *Salmon*, wrote 26 October 1910 to support the larger conning tower (NARS RG 19 correspondence, file 25997E). Not only was his conning tower too small, but the new E and F class boats would have even smaller ones. In rough weather Weaver navigated from the conning tower and even kept the lookout there. In night (surface) attacks, the boat had to be handled from inside the conning tower, as the periscope was practically worthless. Despite its cost in underwater speed, Weaver badly wanted a two-man conning tower.

12. Even in this case, Electric Boat used its special export design numbers. It designated the U.S. H class as EB 26A; the boats ordered for Russia but taken over by the U.S. Navy became EB 26R. Export designations were 602E for England; 602F, 602GF, and 602L for Russia; 602G, 602GX, and 602K for Italy, a total of 39 in addition to the original U.S. boats. The British Admiralty ordered 34 modified H-boats, of which 10 were canceled in November 1917. See E. C. Fisher, Jr., "The Subterfuge Submarines," *Warship International*, vol. 3, 1977, 200–226.

13. Gardiner, *Conway's Fighting Ships*, 397, notes that China tried to obtain the six Russian boats in 1918. It had tried to buy other H-boats in 1915. Chinese sailors had arrived in the United States for H-boat instruction, but no boats were ordered because of lack of money.

14. There might have been fear that the new Taft administration, less navy-oriented, would see submarines as an inexpensive alternative to battleships.

15. Electric Boat, Lake, Laurenti, Flint & Co. (New York), Nordenfeld (Boston), and the Risdon Iron & Locomotive Works (San Francisco) all received FY 11 bidders' packages. Flint was Laubeuf's agent (boats would have been built by Newport News). Nordenfeld seems also to have been an agent, possibly for Denny, a British shipbuilder. Risdon would have been Lake's West Coast yard. Flint had to drop out when Laubeuf was delayed in France by family illness; the company could not provide a proposal soon enough. Nordenfeld dropped out because of what it called prohibitive government requirements involving diesel engines. Bids from Electric Boat, Lake, and Laurenti were opened on 14 March 1911.

Electric Boat offered two basic designs, the 470-ton EB 29 and the 521-ton EB 30, each with variations (A, B, C, D) at successively lower prices. The main reductions were the gyro compass and about $15,000 of machinery spare parts. The appropriation would pay for four East Coast EB 29As, EB 29Bs, or EB 30Bs. The conning towers of these designs all lacked the required hand steering station and were not fitted as escape chambers. These omissions were made to minimize conning tower size (e.g., the escape chamber required levers and valves to admit water as needed). The two materiel bureaus (C&R and BuEng) favored EB 30B for its greater endurance and recommended building two on each coast. The omission of the gyro compass was accepted and then applied to the FY 12 circular. The Electric Boat designs were submitted on 14 March 1911.

Lake offered the 485 ton design A-4, the 495 ton A-5, and the 600 ton A-6. A-5 added 2 torpedo tubes and guide wheels in the forward end of the hull to A-4, at a cost of about 10 tons. The bureaus observed that there was little in their experience to suggest that Lake would deliver on time and that none of his boats had yet been tested. It would be best to avoid buying any more until G-1 and G-2 had been tried.

Laurenti offered a 364 ton (370 metric ton) C-535 and a 423 ton (430 metric ton) C-522. C-535 was essentially G-4 with all torpedo tubes moved to the bow and with heavy oil (probably diesel) engines. The bureaus rejected both designs: although they were smaller than either the Lake or the Electric Boat craft, with less full-speed endurance and slightly less service test speed, they were much more expensive.

Bid data and conclusions are from NARS RG 19 correspondence, file 26000E. The Submarine Force Museum has a drawing of a Nordenfeld 300 ton submarine described as the company's Model 105.

16. A variety of more detailed guarantees were later added: diving time (to pass from 14 kt light to 8 kt submerged), 6 min; variation in depth for 10 min at 9.5 kt, 1 ft (2 ft at 10.5 kt); depth variation while firing four torpedoes (full salvo) from the bow tubes at intervals not exceeding 10 set at 9.5 kt, 2 ft; depth variation while loading four torpedoes within 9 min at 9.5 kt submerged, 3 ft; ability to rise to periscope depth from 60 ft and return without porpoising; time to reverse engines at 14 kt in light condition, 5 sec. Engine reliability would be guaranteed by a 24-hr endurance run at 13.5 kt or more.

17. ONI, *Data on Submarines*, 10–11, footnote to a table of U.S. submarine data. Endurance figures for lubricating oil and battery water had yet to be calculated. Presumably, real endurance was limited by engine (un)reliability.

18. Electric Boat was installing stern tubes in two modified E-boats for Chile (taken over by Canada in 1914). The company later said that it had tried to dissuade the Chileans, partly for fear that torpedoes fired astern would be sucked back by the propellers. Now that submarines carried eight torpedoes, about all that the gunner's mates could handle, there was little point in having more tubes. U.S. submariners suspected that interest in stern tubes was a relic of earlier tactics used by submarines armed with only a single bow tube. With a stern tube, they could reattack either by turning or by passing under the target. All Atlantic submarine commanders rejected stern tubes. Pacific commanders feared that the caps would foul propellers and rudders. SubDiv 3 argued that the tube would cramp the after end of the submarine; it was better to leave space for more reliable machinery. Lake had introduced a stern tube only because his submarine's superstructure already provided the necessary space.

19. Laurenti's fast submarine design inspired British interst in fleet submarines; however, no such submarine was apparently ever built by Laurenti's yard, FIAT-San Giorgio. Pre–WW I Laurenti submarines built for Italy, Brazil, Denmark, Greece, Portugal, and Spain generally displaced no more than about

250–300 tons surfaced. Somewhat larger boats, built under license in Japan (as the F-1 and F-2 classes) just after WW I, were powered by FIAT diesels. Laurenti did design a 730-tonner for Germany, which was laid down in 1913 and taken over by Italy during WW I. In common with contemporary U-boats, it was not particularly fast (the Germans bought it to gain information on FIAT diesels). Among Laurenti designs, the WW I *Adrea Provana* class (760 tons, 16 kt) came closest to a fleet boat.

20. Electric Boat described EB 32 as a repeat K-1 with the stern tube omitted. Lake offered three series: A-7 a repeat *Turbot* but with one tube aft, rearranged machinery, and the diving compartment and bow rudders omitted); E (hull axis horizontal aft, rising forward); and F (hull axis rising fore and aft). E-2 had two conning towers, one extendable. E had four bow tubes; E-1 had six. The F series had single stern tubes plus four or six bow tubes. The earlier Lake boats were 161 ft long, but E and F were larger (E, 165 ft × 14 ft 9⅛ ft; F, 163 ft 6 in × 14 ft 9⅛ in). Lake underbid Electric boat ($430,500–$463,000 against $483,000–$524,000) but could not offer construction on the West Coast. The C&R/BuEng evaluation (dated 21 September 1911) of the FY 11 bids (opened 1 September 1911) is given in NARS RG 19 correspondence, file 26825321. Although Lake had already received three contracts, his first boat (G-1) was over a year overdue (contract trial date was 3 May 1910). They therefore wanted to limit the FY 11 program to four Electric Boat submarines. Given Lake's later problems, the navy was lucky not to have accepted his 1911 bids. Data are from a C&R blueprint tabulation of bids.

21. The submariners argued that detection, even during the pre-firing run-in (about 10 min, 3,000 yd), might spoil a shot. They wanted longer periscope range (6,000 yd) and better depth control and steering (which amounted to pointing because the torpedo track could not yet be angled) at periscope depth.

22. The 3 in/23 turned out to have the unnerving habit of retracting suddenly and unexpectedly. This was often due to the shock of firing, but it sometimes occurred randomly.

23. The results were probably two undated C&R lines plans (ca 1912: C&R 22591) marked "Submarine Torpedo Boat—Flotilla Board Characteristics." They represented both Electric Boat's single- and double-hull (as in EB31A) configurations. It is not clear to what extent Electric Boat influenced (or executed) those designs.

24. Electric Boat, Lake, and the Los Angeles Submarine Boat Co. all submitted bids, which were opened in December 1912. Electric Boat offered EB 37F and F(a), EB 37G and G(a), EB 39D, and EB 39E. EB 37F and 39E used crosshead engines and slow-running 240-RPM motors; 37G and 37D had standard 2-cycle trunk type engines and faster-running (320-RPM and 295-RPM, respectively) motors. All motors developed 170 HP per shaft underwater. The suffix (a) indicated a longer-life battery. EB 39 was a big double-hull submarine. Its normal radius of action would be too short, but Electric Boat offered to use two ballast tanks for reserve fuel, in order to reach the required 5,500 nm. The bureaus found this configuration so desirable that they asked for one (choosing the EB 39E version, to test the crosshead engine) even though its diving depth was only 150 ft. They also wanted four EB 37G(a)s. EB 39E became the experimental submarine M-1; the others were the first four L-boats.

Lake offered A-8 and F-7 and F-8. F-7 had the required 4 bow torpedo tubes and 1000 BHP engines; F-8 added 2 bow tubes and a stern tube, and had 1200 BHP engines. The bureaus considered its higher cost unwarranted. A-8 could not reach the desired radius of action; it was small and hence unlikely to be a good sea-keeper. The bureaus suggested that one F-7 be built at Bridgeport and two more on the West Coast by Craig Shipbuilding. As of 30 January 1913 the projected dimensions of the F-7(a) design were 165 ft (overall) × 14 ft 9 in (moulded) × 13 ft (maximum 14 ft 2 $\frac{1}{2}$ in), 504 surfaced/578 submerged tons; surface power was 1000 BHP = 14 kt; submerged power was 400 HP = 10.5 kt (8 kt for 3 hr). Fuel capacity was 11,800 gal (21,800 gal maximum), plus 860 gal of lubricating oil, for a designed endurance of 3150 nm (5000 nm on maximum fuel) at 11 kt (or 120 hr at 14 kt). The design showed 4 tubes (plus 4 reloads) forward and a 3 in gun with 30 rounds of ammunition. The boat would have one horizontal rudder (diving plane) aft, 4 hydroplanes amidships, and 2 planes forward, all with hand and power control. The oval conning tower would be about 8 ft × 4 ft, and there would be two hand-rotated periscopes with a 45 degree field of view (and with a magnifying eyepiece offering a 20 degree field of view). By this time, Lake was also offering a Type G, 175 ft long (830 tons), presumably to compete with EB 39. No further details are available. After Lake went bankrupt, his L-boats were built to a new design.

The Los Angeles Submarine Boat Company offered Cage's submarine, which was powered underwater by compressed air; the bureaus were interested, but they could not buy a full-size submarine on the basis of the company's nearly complete 75 ft scale-model. The company's drawing shows an unusual boat, with two propellers on sponsons roughly abeam the conning tower, which is set well forward of amidships. Air flasks for power are clustered around the four bow torpedo tubes, in a double bottom extending aft to about amidships, and in the stern. The two reciprocating air engines are amidships, abaft the conning tower. A gun is mounted in the bow under the boat's weather deck. Dimensions: 178 ft (pp) × 12 ft (mld) × 11 ft 9 in (mld); height 15 ft (mld). These data are taken from C&R blueprints 23992 A through 23992 F.

Late in 1912 estimates were requested of the cost to build a submarine at Norfolk Navy Yard. Presumably, this inquiry was part of the process that led to the 1913 order for L-8 from Portsmouth.

25. EB 39J and 39K were each 196 ft 3 in × 19 ft $\frac{1}{2}$ in, 488/676 tons, powered by 420-BHP diesels, and armed with four bow tubes. Like M-1, they had a test depth of 150 ft, rather than the usual 200 ft. The two versions differed in power plant: 840 BHP versus 1,200 BHP for 14 kt; endurance was 2,400 nm (normal)/5,500 nm (maximum) at 11 kt. Submerged speed was 10.5 kt. The small EB 38H was expected to make 11 kt surfaced (9.5 kt submerged); normal endurance was only 950 nm. Lake offered a 451/527-tonner (165 ft × 14 ft 9 in), but by the time bids were opened his company had gone bankrupt. Data are from a C&R blueprint tabulation of bids.

26. EB 37L: 168 ft 8 in × 17 ft 5 in × 13 ft 7 in, 453/611 tons; EB 37 M: 168 ft 4 in × 17 ft 5 in × 13 ft 10$\frac{1}{2}$ in, 458.8/547.1 tons; EB 39M: 197 ft × 19 ft $\frac{1}{2}$ in × 11 ft, 489/730 tons (the difference in submerged displacement reflects the double hull); EB 68A: 172 ft 4 in × 18 ft $\frac{1}{4}$ in × 14 ft 5 in, 520.6/684 tons. Expected surface speed was 13.5 kt for EB 37, 14.75 kt for EB 39, and 14 kt for EB 68A (10.5 kt submerged, except 10.25 kt for EB 37L). Endurance (nautical miles), respectively: 3,300/6,000, 2,800/5,500, 2,700/6,500, and 3,000/6,000, all at 11 kt and all normal/maximum (fuel in ballast tanks). Note the increased capacity associated with the double-hull EB 39. The bigger EB designs were expected to cost $550,000, the smaller ones $523,000–$531,000. Union Iron Works offered EB 37L, 37M, and 61C, a modified N-boat.

27. Lake's design numbers were 24-H, H-1, K, K-1, M, M-1, and P. Presumably, the use of numbers instead of letters was due to the reorganization of his company. All were 175 ft ×

16 ft 3$\frac{3}{8}$ in × 13 ft 10$\frac{1}{4}$ in, 485/637 tons, powered by two 2- or 4-cycle, 6-cylinder Busch-Sulzer engines (14/10.5 kt or 11 kt). Each boat was armed with four bow tubes and one gun (30 rounds). Guaranteed diving time was 8 min. Lake boats had six compartments versus five in EB boats. Cost was $534,000–$545,000.

28. New York Shipbuilding Corp. (NYSB) and Newport News Shipbuilding & Dry Dock Co. each offered the same design. Hower Co. offered a Laurenti submarine. Sloan Danen offered a midget submarine (the $15,000 Davidette). C&R's price list also included three navy yards: Norfolk, Portsmouth, and Puget Sound; the latter was awarded O-2, although Portsmouth's estimate was considerably lower, $423,000 versus $484,000. The NYSB/Newport News design was 165 ft 6 in × 17 ft 2$\frac{1}{2}$ in × 12 ft 8 in, 490/700 tons, powered by two Dutch-type Werkspoor 4-cycle, 500-BHP diesels (14/11 kt); it was expected to cost $550,000. Armament was four bow tubes (eight torpedoes) and one gun with 30 rounds. The Laurenti boat was 177 ft × 16 ft 3 in × 11 ft 4 in, 417/630 tons, powered by two 2-cycle diesels (15/10 kt), and armed with four bow or three bow and one stern or four bow and one stern tubes, with two torpedoes per tube. Endurance was 1,100 nm, and cost was $330,000 for each of four boats. The Davidette was 48 ft × 5 ft 7 in, powered by two Sterling gasoline engines (360 BHP, 20 kt for 9.81 hr; 10 kt submerged, 5 kt for 4 hr). Neff bid a K-boat powered by two 500-BHP diesels and carrying 160,000 cu ft of air at 2,500 psi, but no figures were given on estimated submerged endurance.

29. General Board hearing, 11 April 1918.

30. H-boats served in Britain and Italy during WW II. As before WW I, boats entirely adequate for short-range European operations offered little to a U.S. Navy whose home bases were so far from potential enemies.

31. John Alden (private communication) recalls hearing at Submarine School in 1944 that plans were prepared to put radar on the O-boats and use them in combat if necessary; this was not done.

Chapter 6

1. This was the *Narval* class (design EB 31) of the Black Sea Fleet, designed for two 850-BHP diesels (16 kt). As built, submerged displacement was 994 tons (1,045 tons in *Narval*). Ironically, like the T-boats, these submarines ended up with tandem diesels, in their case, 160-BHP NELSECOS. The T-boat seems to have been a stretched *Narval*. Surface displacement was 621 tons.

2. BuEng expected a French attempt to reach 1,200 BHP to fail. It might have misinterpreted a French attempt to build a 2,400-BHP engine as an attempt to reach a *total* of 2,400 BHP in a two-engine boat (presumably it could not imagine how ambitious the French were). According to Confidential Navy Department Bureau of C&R Bulletin No. 36, 1 August 1911 ("Notes on British, French, and German War Material," a report of a visit to those countries by Naval Constructor R. H. Robinson), 18: "I saw a contract with the French navy department for two [diesel] motors, 2,400 horsepower each, 8 cylinder, 350 RPM, 2 cycle, trials to be in 11 months from June 1. . . These motors will give a surface speed of 21 knots to a boat 800 tons and which is to have 11 knots submerged speed." Cylinders were to be arranged in two groups of four at the ends of each engine, with air cylinders (for compressors) in between.

According to Lambert (private communication), the French Navy decided in July 1910 to order French-designed 2-cycle diesels instead of MAN's 4-cycle engines (which had been used until then) specifically to obtain enough power to drive a submarine at fleet speed. These diesels were ordered (as 2,000-BHP units) in September 1910, when the French had yet to perfect a 420-BHP diesel for their 1906 submarines, and when 30 submarines still awaited diesel engines. The main European diesel firm, the German MAN company, had already rejected the order as too ambitious. Dr. Rudolph Diesel reportedly predicted trouble, as the French envisaged a combination of high piston speeds and light-weight construction. In the spring of 1911, the French submarine designers asked for 20 percent more power to reach the 21-kt goal. The diesels' builder, the Soc. de la Loire, abandoned the contract in December 1911, and a Belgian firm, Carels, had to take it over. It derated the units to 1,800 BHP and then to 1,200 BHP. By July 1912, the French accepted that 900 BHP was a practical limit. One of the two boats, *Gustave Zede,* used steam engines instead. About this time, the French had to derate MAN 650-BHP, 2-cycle diesels to 400 BHP in smaller submarines (*Clorinde* and *Amphitrite* classes).

3. Nimitz, description of submarine tactics (see chapter 5), includes fleet submarines. He imagines a flotilla approaching, destroyerlike in formation, then diving together to fire a salvo together from long range (about 3,000–4,000 yd) at a column of battleships and disrupting it so as to provide U.S. battleships with a considerable gunnery advantage. Nimitz lectured at the Naval War College in June 1912; according to Lambert (private communication). That encouraged the college president, Rear Adm. William Rogers, to form a committee of three officers to examine the tactical possibilities of submarines engaging a battle squadron at sea. It inspired the October war games, as described in this text. The War College submitted its report to the General Board in December 1912. Rogers concluded that it would be well worthwhile to reduce submerged speed in order to buy the increased surface speed needed by a fleet submarine. Nimitz became interested in long-range shots to disrupt formations, rather than necessarily to sink specific ships. In September 1912, he had the rules of the annual torpedo firing changed to penalize submarines firing at *less than* 2000 yd. After July 1913, E-boats had to fire at 3,600 yd.

4. According to Harrison, *Development of HM Submarines,* the British Submarine Committee, in February 1912, called for a 20-kt, 1,000-ton "overseas" submarine specifically to work with the British battle fleet. It was to have had two bow, two beam, and two stern torpedo tubes; the British adopted beam tubes because they feared that large submarines (from their E class onward) were not maneuverable enough to make end-on attacks. According to Harrison, the committee was inspired to propose these characteristics after British officers were favorably impressed by a fast Laurenti submarine they saw during an August 1911 visit to the FIAT-San Giorgio shipyard at La Spezia, Italy. According to Nicholas Lambert (unpublished thesis), British official interest in fleet submarines dates much further back. Laurenti designs were important because, under the Vickers contract, the Admiralty could not pay for design development by any other company until March 1913; however, it could buy designs off the shelf. Fleet submarines built in British yards then encountered the usual serious problems with the required high-speed diesels. When the British asked FIAT to offer an 1,850-BHP diesel, Laurenti proposed using a 4,000-SHP geared steam turbine plant instead. It was installed in HMS *Swordfish,* the first British steam submarine. The Admiralty developed a sketch design for its own 10,000-SHP, 24-kt steam submarine in the spring of 1913. It was rejected at the time because it represented so great an increase in displacement, and because the Admiralty wanted to wait for experience with *Swordfish* before building a much more powerful steam submarine. As it turned out, *Swordfish* could not make the required speed nor could the three-shaft diesel J class of 1914, hence the development of the

British K-boats, which so impressed U.S. officers during WW I. It is unlikely that the pre–WW I U.S. Navy was aware of the conclusions of the 1912 committee, but it is intriguing that they so paralleled U.S. thinking.

According to Harrison, the K-boats themselves were inspired by incorrect reports, received in the fall of 1914, that the Germans were building 22-kt U-boats. In his very full account of U-boat design, Roessler, *The U-Boat,* betrays no such official design but does include a 4,000-SHP, 20-kt steam submarine conceived in 1912 by d'Equevilley, Krupp's senior designer (p. 32). Unlike the British K-boats or the French steam submarines, d'Equevilley's was intended to use stored steam for underwater propulsion. According to Roessler, the Germans did discuss such power plants publicly before WW I.

According to Lambert (private communication), the French became interested in fleet submarines as early as the fall of 1907. It is not clear when this interest became public.

The Russian move toward a fleet submarine was epitomized by Electric Boat's *Narval* (Russian 1911 Program) and the 18-kt *Bars* class ordered under the Russian 1912 Program. Because of a severe diesel shortage, only two of these boats even remotely approached their designed high speeds.

5. Engine redesign is described in undated C&R Preliminary Design memorandum, "Submarines of the United States Navy." (See chapter 4, note 49.)

6. This engine was to be used primarily to carry the "hotel" load and to provide a finishing rate on battery charging. It could have provided emergency propulsion via the battery to the main motors.

7. It is very striking that this *submarine* was assigned a *destroyer* name (i.e., the name of a deceased naval officer). Presumably, the naming reflected the hopes of the fleet submarine advocates that their craft might ultimately replace destroyers as fleet torpedo craft. The author is indebted to John Alden (personal communication) for this suggestion.

8. According to Lt. S. E. Halliday, *Notes for the Main Engine and Submarine Propulsion Course,* New London, about 1917 (OpNav Submarine Division papers, Operational Archives), the 175°F temperature of the big plant would have radiated through the submarine's skin; within, it would have been confined by a coffer-dam. In 1915, the industrial manager of the New York Navy Yard, who knew about foreign (probably French) steam submarines and also about the fleet submarine, suggested that the unreliable diesels of E-1 and E-2 be replaced by steam turbines. He invited the Talbot Boiler Co., which produced the lightest and most compact available boiler, to submit a bid. BuEng included this idea in a pamphlet, "Undeveloped Methods Proposed for Motive Power of Submarines."

9. Secretary of the Navy Edwin Denby, order on the disposition of existing submarines, 30 July 1921 (OpNav Submarines Division files, NARS) includes removal of the second pair of engines from each T-boat (which would be reclassified as 15-kt boat), but that was never done. C&R suggested that the bow and stern main ballast tanks be converted to fuel tanks to increase cruising radius to 9,170 nm at 14 kt. That would still leave a sufficient 23 percent reserve buoyancy. To speed diving, the Kingstons could be replaced with flapper valves (as in S-3 through S-9). Adding remote control for the main ballast vents as well as reliable controls for the planes, would help the boat stay within her narrow depth envelope. Two 18-in tubes could be added aft and 2 spare torpedoes stowed in the motor room, for a total of 16 torpedoes (Electric Boat had already drawn up plans for this change). The 4-in guns could be provided with useful platforms. Effective hydrophones (MV and SC) could be

installed. The T-boats just were not worth all this effort. C&R suggestions are from Bureau of Construction and Repair to Chief Constructor, 2 February 1922 (RG 19 Entry 105 Box 80 [File O-SF-1], National Archives), a critique to help decide the fate of the T-boats.

10. In theory, lubricating oil capacity sufficed for 3,065 nm at 14 kt. Actual oil consumption was excessive. T-2's oil sufficed for only 1,883.3 nm at 19 kt; this was due partly to increased piston clearances, partly to leaky lines and joints (likely resulting from engine vibration), and partly to excessive amounts of lubricating oil supplied by hand (6 gal/hr).

11. A submarine facing depth charges would try to dive under a barrage; a T-boat could not dive quickly for fear of getting part of her 270-ft length well under her 200-ft collapse depth. In a fleet action, light cruisers and destroyers would be too busy to circle and drop depth charges. A submarine working alone might well encounter destroyers free to concentrate on depth charging.

12. All were 5⅛-in Kollmorgen instruments raised by motor winch: a short (16 ft 1½-in) bifocal periscope in the conning tower and a low-power periscope (26 ft) and alti-periscope (26 ft 8 in) in the operating compartment. There were no wells; the first two periscopes traveled 5 ft 6 in and the third, 6 ft 6 in.

13. T-2 was kept in commission at New London until she broke down. By 1924, the T-boats were described officially as of "practically no military value. . .it is considered highly undesirable to spend further money on them to attempt to modernize them or improve their present condition." (Material collected in reply to questions by Sen. William H. King, 29 April 1924, in OpNav Submarine Division papers.)

14. BuEng developed a theory of balanced submarine machinery design in 1916, as part of the navy's move to develop an internal capability for submarine design. It began with the fact that the same motors that drove the submarine underwater also were the generators that charged the battery. The bureau also believed that diesels could operate efficiently only at one rating. That implied that the diesel should put out the same power whether it was charging the battery or propelling the submarine, so generator power (hence, roughly, motor power) ought to match diesel rating. Submarine designers did not share BuEng's idea of efficiency. Motor/generators were rated well below maximum diesel power, partly because they had to match battery characteristics. Batteries discharged rapidly but recharged much more slowly; there was a definite limit on how quickly energy could be poured into them, hence how powerful the charging generators could be.

15. A 31 December 1917 Atlantic Fleet report of a visit to a K-boat was circulated within the General Board, whose chairman, Adm. Charles J. Badger, commented that the 1919 characteristics were very similar to the K-boat, apart from providing a heavier armament. Conceived in 1912 and designed in 1913, the K-boat was nearly contemporary in concept with the U.S. fleet submarine.

16. Lt. Comdr. H. M. Bemis, USN, describes British K-boat diving practice in a 1918 report (OpNav Undersea Warfare Division papers, Operational Archives). In theory, a K-boat could dive in about 4 min; the record was 3 min 42 sec, but that nearly boiled the crew. In practice, after tanks were flooded, there was an anxious 2-min wait for word that all had been secured aft. If this word did not reach the control room, flooding was stopped. Bemis had heard that K-13 was lost when she submerged without securing a boiler room. The big K-boat had enormous momentum; at a steep diving angle, her flat deck could act as a plane and overwhelm the effect of the bow planes. For example, a boat diving with negative buoyancy at more than a 3-degree down

angle would almost certainly hit bottom. Only a short time before Bemis's visit, a K-boat diving at an excessive bow angle touched bottom at 185 ft while the stern was within a few feet of the surface. Tested to 100 ft, the K-boat hull was considered safe to 125 ft. Bemis reported that K-8 took 11 min to submerge. Upon the signal to dive, the boilers and turbines were secured in a little less than 2 min; this included shutting down the blowers, shutting off the burners, lowering the smoke pipes, closing the ventilators, securing the turbines, and throwing out the clutches. A few minutes after diving, the temperature was 160°F in the boiler room and 90°F in the engine room. No one remained in the boiler room, which was opened up for inspection every 30 min. Men assigned to the engine room usually went forward into the beam tube compartment but returned frequently to check conditions in the engine room. COs considered it very important to know for sure that both engine and boiler rooms had been secured; they used some repeat-backs. Quick dives were difficult. Bemis reported that the big K-8 handled well underwater except for a large turning circle and slow turning. It took about 10 min to surface and get to full-ahead power on both turbines. These considerations of length, planing effect, and momentum all affected later U.S. fleet submarines.

17. The British tried to solve the problem by escorting the K-boats with light cruisers; eventually the K-boat flotilla was led by a light cruiser. That they never solved the identification friend or foe (IFF) problem was demonstrated in the disastrous 31 January 1918 "Battle of May Island," in which K-4 and K-17 were sunk by collision.

18. According to an unsigned compendium of WW I U-boat data in the OpNav Submarine Division file: "In a danger zone it was customary to proceed with one main engine serving for both propulsion and for charging the battery, the opposite motor running for [surface] propulsion; the submarine was thus ready for instant diving, needing only to stop one engine." According to a U.S. officer visiting them, British E-boats, at least as of August 1917, could not have operated that way because they were unable to run one motor at a time, although planned switchboard changes would make that possible.

19. A note in the C&R file asks why Emory S. Land, C&R's submarine expert, limited length to 300 ft. He seems to have wanted the fleet submarine to fit both Lake and Electric Boat facilities, the former being much more difficult to extend. Land also chose the initial displacement target of 1,600 tons.

20. G. F. Weir, *Building U.S. Submarines, 1914–1940*, No. 3 in series, Contributions to Naval History (Washington D.C., Government Printing Office, 1991), notes that this was Busch-Sulzer's last foray into the U.S. submarine market. He suggests that the company gave up because it doubted that the market was worth pursuing; however, the parent Sulzer company produced submarine engines through the 1930s, e.g. for the Imperial Japanese Navy.

21. Characteristics: 325 (LWL) × 24 ft 8 in (molded)/24 ft 9 in (extreme) × 14 ft 9.5 in; 1,900 tons surfaced, 2,372 tons submerged; 6,000 nm normal/11,750 nm maximum (with oil stowed in ballast tanks) at 11 kt (fuel oil capacity, 160 tons normal); two 2,000-BHP and two 900-BHP Busch-Sulzer diesels; two 1,100-HP motors; 120 battery cells (S-1 type). Armament: one 5 in/51 gun, two machine guns, four bow and two stern torpedo tubes. The design showed three periscopes, each of 30-ft optical length, and one 60-ft telescopic mast to support the radio antenna (the radio experts required three masts, to keep antennas completely free of spray thrown up by the bow or aft by the following sea). Complement: five officers and 50 enlisted men. Longitudinal coefficient: 0.597. Habitability: 457 cu ft per man, compared

with 283 cu ft in U-141 and 237–293 cu ft in S-3. The forward periscope was located off the centerline to offset the radio antenna tube.

22. The two-foundation arrangement was adopted in December 1919.

23. Lake Co. was used for a variety of calculations at this time.

24. An alternative soda boiler plant capable of underwater operation could not produce the sort of power required. BuEng seriously considered reviving the Nordenfeldt steam-storage scheme of the 1880s; it argued that Nordenfeldt's submarines had failed more because of their poor depth control than because of any power plant problem. Unfortunately, stored steam also made the interior of the submarine uncomfortably hot. The idea of storing heat for underwater propulsion was revived in the 1970s in the form of a graphite heat sink proposed as part of a DARPA (Defense Advanced Research Projects Agency, now ARPA) program to study advanced non-nuclear submarines.

Chapter 7

1. This range rather exceeded what had been achieved. The best average radio range was only 30 nm, although West Coast submarines had achieved 100 nm under very favorable conditions with a masthead height of 40 ft. It appeared that a 60-ft mast would be required for reliable radio communications at 100 nm. Radio range also depended on the length and spread of the aerial. The fleet submarine Schley was being designed for an aerial length of 200 ft, a spread of 8–13 ft, and a masthead height of 60 ft; all of these dimensions would greatly complicate any attempt at rapid rigging and unrigging (for surfacing and diving). The submarine's oscillator and receiver were to allow submerged communication to 10 nm at not less than 20 words/min. Recent (1916) tests of the Fessenden underwater oscillator had shown that boats on diverging courses could communicate reliably at 6 nm and less reliably at 8–11 nm (parts of words in Morse Code were received). Approaching boats could not establish reliable communications, however, until they were within 2 nm of each other.

2. The submariners' views were summarized by Adm. A. W. Grant, Submarine Commander Atlantic, 4 February 1916.

3. As an example of Electric Boat's power over U.S. submarine design, Steam Engineering had no access to curves of effective horsepower for contemporary U.S. submarine hulls, even though the data had been taken at the navy's test tank. This information was the property of Electric Boat.

4. In contrast to earlier estimates, the Submarine Force assumed that a surfaced submarine could be seen at 12 nm. Submerging at that range, she would run in at about 8.5 kt. She would use her periscope almost continuously when within 3 nm of the enemy. The enemy would try to escape upon sighting the periscope at about 2 nm; the submarine would accelerate, fire (at a range of about 2,000 yd), and either escape or turn to another target. In either case, she would have to run back out to the 12-nm circle before surfacing. A coastal submarine could run for 3 hr at 8.5 kt, so the initial 10-nm run-in would use up more than a third of her battery and leave very little time for full speed. Higher underwater speed would make it easier to catch a fast enemy, but analysis showed that there was little point in raising it above 12–13 kt. Remarkably, there seems to have been no fear that, upon sighting a periscope, a prospective target would turn to ram the submarine.

5. Electric Boat offered a repeat O-boat (EB 68C), as well as an enlarged coastal boat (EB 77A) and an 800-tonner (EB 73A). Lake offered his O-boat (24-M-1) and two new designs coastal

design 31 and 800-ton design 30 (in versions powered by either 2- or 4-cycle Busch-Sulzer diesels). His design 31 was shorter (175 ft versus 186 ft 1½ in) and smaller (495/598 tons versus 569/755 tons) than Electric Boat's 77A. EB 77A and EB 73A and both of Lake's new designs were chosen. Schneider offered A (208 ft 4 in × 19 ft 8¼ in, 629/905 tons, four bow and one stern tubes), B (196 ft 10¼ in × 19 ft ⅜ in, 526.5/762.0 tons, two bow and two stern tubes), and C (213 ft 3 in × 19 ft 8¼ in, 605/875 tons, two bow and two stern tubes). All were to have been powered by 6-cylinder, 2-cycle diesels. The new Lake and Electric Boat designs (and the Schneider boats) each had 21-in tubes, with one reload per tube (EB 73A offered a second reload in wartime only). The Electric Boat and Lake designs offered a deck gun with 98 rounds, rather than the 30 rounds of the L-boats. Data are from an undated C&R list of bids, probably April 1917. By that time, Lake was offering four to eight boats.

6. Emory S. Land, General Board hearing, 11 April 1918. The question was whether the navy should buy H-boats that Electric Boat offered to mass-produce.

7. As of the summer of 1923, the "Rules for Engineering Competition" would allow the navy boats (S-3–S-9 and S-14–S-17) 125 sec from going ahead on the engines to completely submerged. Unfortunately, the usual expedients for quick dives could not be used. Ballast tanks leaked so badly that boats could not run on the surface partly ballasted down. Similarly, they could not "ride the vents" (with Kingstons open and vents closed). Asiatic Fleet submarines tried "banking the tanks" (the tanks were partly filled, then sealed by closing both Kingstons and vents). Because the tanks leaked differently from starboard to port, the submarine tended to list as time passed; tanks could not be banked for more than 5–10 min.

8. In April 1919 Lt. Comdr Lewis Hancock, Jr. of the OpNav submarine section (and prospective CO of S-2) commented that the boat's problems could be traced largely to its flat-topped main ballast tanks, which Lake had adopted because Electric Boat had patented U-topped tanks (the patent expired in 1918). The flat top was difficult to stiffen (hence required additional structural weight) and to vent (a film of air could form along its top). The top of the U-topped tank could surround other elements of the boat (e.g., the battery), whereas they had to be placed atop the flat tank. Space outboard of such elements was a total loss in a Lake boat; therefore, too much had to be squeezed into the control room: all water ballast pumps and main and auxiliary switchboards. The flat tank-top was both the deck of the control room and the bilge collecting water from the pump glands and the conning tower. Because it would be almost impossible to flush dry, coamings had to be installed around the bottoms of the switchboards to keep water from splashing onto the switches. Surely, it would be difficult to work in a space whose deck was always wet. U-shaped tanks accommodated pumps between their tops and the floor plates or against one side of the boat, and water could drain into a properly built bilge. Torpedo impulse and 100-lb air tanks had to be installed in S-2's superstructure because the flat tanks left so little overhead space inside the pressure hull. Nor was there space for windlasses to move periscopes up and down (but Lake had a successful pneumatic system, and C&R was considering a hydraulic [telemotor] one). Some high-pressure air flasks had to be placed inside the main ballast tanks, into which they could leak air.

Without an Electric Boat style duct or drain (the patent for which would expire in 1925), Lake had to use separate suction pipes from each tank, whose contorted shape wasted pump power in overcoming friction. The forward and after trim tanks were so large that, as in Lake O-boats, they could form free surfaces (C&R was installing swash plates to solve this problem in the O-boats). Without Electric Boat's patented trim line, the regulator tank amidships could not be connected directly to the forward and after trim tanks. Hancock expected the main ballast tanks to flood too slowly, partly because flooding area (only one 17-in Kingston in the forward tank, two 15-in Kingstons in the middle and after ones) was too small, and partly because vents were insufficient and poorly located.

According to Hancock, experience showed that the watertight superstructure "cannot be depended upon when most needed—in rough weather. Sooner or later, the structure is strained sufficiently to open the flood or vent valves, thus destroying the watertight feature. This is especially serious on the S-2, as the battery and hull ventilation, and engine induction systems, are directly dependent on the water tightness of the superstructure."

C&R accepted the known weakness of Lake designs to avoid more patent-infringement suits by Electric Boat. In the spring of 1919 Lake's *Seal* (G-1) was still being litigated in New York. C&R had suggested that Lake avoid the duct keel patent by placing a drainage pipe inside the keel and making the latter non-watertight, but Lake did not do so. The bureau considered S-2 more seaworthy than Electric Boat's S-1 (less so than its S-3), but only if the superstructure remained watertight. Lake wanted to fit a bow buoyancy tank (which would be done about 1921) but C&R wanted installation delayed so that the three S-boat prototypes could be compared as designed. Certainly S-2 showed much less watertight superstructure than earlier Lake designs. C&R pointed out that S-2 was then the fastest submarine in the U.S. Navy apart from AA-1 (T-1) (NARS RG 19 correspondence, file 22-S-5 Serial 55352).

S-2 had provision for Lake's trademark midships planes, but they were not installed, pending experience with earlier types. She also had space and weight provision for a gyro-stabilizer (which was never fitted). It had been tried on G-4 and on some L-boats. By early 1918 such stabilizers were disliked for the large forces they exerted on boats' hulls (which had only a moderate effect on boats' rolling). Comments by S. Goodall, ADM 229/97, letter 14.

9. On 1 August 1918 the navy ordered a total of 24 new S-boats, 16 from Electric Boat (2 under the 1 July 1918 Appropriation Act, 14 out of the Emergency Fund) and 8 from Lake (all under the 1918 Act). Only six were built: S-42 through S-47. The others were tentatively designated S-48 through S-57; the Lake boats would have been S-58 through S-65. Contemporary correspondence concerning redesign refers to S-68 through S-71, to be built at Portsmouth Navy Yard. Presumably S-66 and S-67 were planned for Mare Island. A reference to a total of 34 second-series S-boats may refer to the four (S-10 through S-13) then still under construction at Portsmouth, which were completed with stern tubes but without other modifications that applied to the S-48 series. No boats with names (numbers) above S-65 were ordered, and no hull numbers (SS numbers) were assigned to them. Presumably there was no need to order submarines formally from the two navy yards. When 10 Electric Boat and 4 Lake submarines were canceled on 4 December 1918, the names S-48 through S-51 were assigned to the four surviving Lake boats, to avoid gaps in the S-series.

Revised specifications for all these boats were circulated on 20 November. They called for a 4 in/50 gun (as had already been adopted for S-1 through -41), a mine defense bulkhead just abaft the torpedo tubes, longer housing periscopes (requiring rearranged tankage in Electric Boat craft), six 18 in bow torpedo tubes (instead of four 21 in) and a single stern tube, and such new standard features as a chariot bridge and revised radio mast-

ing and enlarged radio room. Kingstons and vents were to be powered. Electric Boat submarines would have their tankage revised so that they could stow emergency oil fuel in main ballast tanks. About this time the specification was also changed to include WRT tanks for the torpedo tubes.

These were enormous changes. C&R knew it could either (i) settle for the existing designs, modifying it as might be possible; (ii) revising the existing designs (the bow of the Electric Boat type might be modified to take six tubes for 5.2 m long-warhead 18 in torpedoes); or (iii) suspending the program while entirely new designs were prepared.

Early in 1919 C&R formally decided to abandon the 18 in bow tubes in all the new S-boats, and to give up the mine defense bulkhead in Electric Boat craft on the ground that it would be ineffective (similar arguments would probably apply to C&R craft). A letter to this effect is in NARS RG 19 file 22-S163 etc. However, a WRT tank was installed forward and the main ballast pump moved from aft to a new position directly under the control room; a prominent access hatch was also provided under the breech of the 4 in gun. These changes are apparent in inboard profiles of the S-boats preserved in the U.S. National Archives, but they do not appear in the early 1919 letter. These boats were somewhat longer (225 ft 4½ in versus 219 ft 4½ in overall) and slightly beamier (20 ft 11 in versus 20 ft 6¼ in) than the earlier series. They displaced slightly more (963/1135 tons versus 930/1094 tons). This growth cost about half a knot in surface speed, but the later boats were half a knot faster underwater. Although normal fuel capacity was about the same (16,529 versus 15,100 gal), the later boats had considerable emergency fuel tankage (total 40,541 gal), which increased cruising radius from 6153 nm to 9500 nm (as listed in 1939; a 1934 table showed 10,000 nm at 8.1 kt versus 8950 nm at 9.5 kt). The larger hull cost mileage: normal endurance fell from 3420 nm to 2510 nm. Rated stores endurance for both types was 75 days, but for the first time, reserve fresh water (2,953 gal) was provided (normal capacity was 1062–1075 gal versus 1017 gal). Rated tactical diameter (surfaced) was cut drastically, from 650 yd to 330 yd (submerged tactical diameter, 800 yd, did not change); the late Electric Boat S-boats were apparently by far the handiest of the series. The Government S-boats were the worst, with surface tactical diameters of 800 yd (900 yd in the S-10 group). Rated diving time for all Electric Boat S-boats was 75 sec, compared with 120 sec for S-14 (75 for S-10), 120 sec for a V-boat, and only 50 sec for an R-boat (tactical diameter: 300 yd surfaced, 425 yd submerged). All boats in both series had 8-cylinder 600 BHP NELSECO diesels. All had electric motors rated at 550 HP but capable of 750 HP (Ridgeway motors in the S-18 through S-29 sub-series could make 1175 HP at 340 RPM). Tactical diameter and diving time data are from a SubDiv 12 report on the effect of new construction on the submarine force, 25 April 1934, NARS RG 19, file SS/L9-3.

The S-42 group could be recognized by a prominent gun access hatch trunk forward of the conning tower fairwater. S-1 had been designed with a similar hatch, but the S-18 group cut that to an ammunition-passing trunk, probably to accommodate the big 4-in/50 gun added during construction. The S-42 group was redesigned after the decision to add the big gun, so it restored the hatch. Of this group, S-43 emerged from a 1925 refit with her skeg cut down sharply. This modification was altogether unrelated to the later safety program; it may have been designed to speed diving. No other submarine appears to have been similarly modified.

On 12 November 1918 C&R ordered the industrial manager at Portsmouth to develop corresponding modifications to its own design, initially as the S-68 to S-71 class. Additions specific to the "government" design were a new safety tank with about the same volume as the conning tower (including periscopes and fairwater), a small tank for balancing (hovering) with a volume of about 500 lbs, and an enlarged low-pressure (ballast) pump with a higher-capacity drainage system for the main ballast tanks (presumably for quicker diving). The C&R request made no mention of a WRT tank, but one was included in the modified design. The stern planes were to be relocated and the propeller shafts rearranged to take larger propellers driven by more powerful engines (on 30 November the shipbuilding supervisor at the Lake yard in Bridgeport was told that boats to be built there would have more powerful engines, and in December Lake was told to design for 900 BHP Busch-Sulzers, which were expected to drive these boats at 15.5–16 kts). Boats would be lengthened to incorporate these changes. See NARS RG 19 C&R correspondence, series 22-S-153 etc. Drawings of S-48, the lead ship of the new series, do not show any marked change, although the rebuilt S-14 group later showed something like an Electric Boat-style duct keel, with the ballast pump aft and Kingstons amidships.

10. The General Board recommended rearming the O-boats in August 1918. The guns were ordered, and at least some were manufactured. Late in October 1919, however, OpNav decided to save $208,000 by not fitting them. When the O-boats were recommissioned in 1940, the prospective commanding officer of O-2 recommended that the 3-in/23 be landed, particularly given its poor performance in battle practices during the 1920s. Two of his colleagues agreed; they wanted 0.50-caliber machine guns instead. A 3-in/50 was considered but rejected, partly because the gun deck would be very wet except in the calmest weather. Removal greatly improved stability and added berthing space. The General Board and then the secretary of the navy approved the proposal in April 1941; the 0.50 was mounted atop the conning tower.

11. The General Board in a 1919 comparison of the two builders in connection with the new fleet submarine project, cites an unfortunate experience with Electric Boat and suggests that, if pressed, the department should "hinge [refusal to deal with Electric Boat] on the quality of their diesels, practically all that Electric Boat actually builds (mainly failures)." Lake was "loyal to government and [has] good morale, but inadequate plant, cannot launch a 340-foot fleet submarine."

12. In July 1923, OpNav reported a 6-mo trial by Submarine Division 3, during which all officers and men lived and messed on board continuously. The boats ran from the tropics (temperature well above 100°F) to northern waters in winter.

13. McKee, "Development of Submarines." Until 1920, ventilation was provided only by the draft resulting from the engine intakes. Thus, the only adequately ventilated space lay between the conning tower hatch and the engines. In the new system, every compartment was provided with a positive source of air and an exhaust. This change might have been inspired by the captured U-boats.

14. From an undated (probably 1923) paper by Lt. Comdr. R. F. Jones and Lt. G. H. Marlin, both U.S. Navy Medical Corps, in the OpNav Submarine Division file. It was probably written in connection with a 30 July 1923 OpNav request for a comprehensive plan to modify Electric Boat S-boat ventilation, following a 3-mo test by SubDiv 3. Jones and Marlin wanted better toilet and berthing facilities, particularly berths for all assigned personnel. In new submarines, ventilation for living spaces had to be separated from that for engine and motor rooms, and ventilation piping had to be kept as straight as possible to reduce resistance.

15. Presumably, hot humid weather exacerbated an existing problem. Diesel fuel collected carbon and deposited it in tiny cracks in motor insulation, thus shorting out the motor. Better types of insulation (plastics) eventually reduced the number of cracks, although they were also brittle. Insulating rubber was made more wear-resistant and plastics became more useful, just as the change to nuclear power drastically reduced dependence on DC motors with their carbon brushes (and did away with diesel fuel).

16. Other projected characteristics: dimensions, 275 ft × 30 ft × 17 ft 6 in; displacement, 2,920 tons; test depth, 250 ft; speed, 12 kt surfaced, 6 kt submerged; radius of action, 18,000 nm at 9 kt, submerged radius, 40 nm. The tanker would carry 840 tons of cargo fuel (140 tons per S-boat per fueling) plus 450 tons for herself. Defensive armament would be two torpedo tubes (eight torpedoes) and one 4-in gun.

17. There was no inkling that the need to make fueling arrangements by radio would expose the tankers to detection and thus to destruction, as was the case with the German "milch cows" of WW II.

18. Two S-boats were lost by ramming: S 51 by merchant ship *City of Rome*, 25 September 1925; and S 4 by the Coast Guard destroyer *Paulding*, 17 December 1927. S 5 previously had been lost on trials when she flooded through her main induction, 1 September 1920.

19. An expert board was appointed by the Navy Department on Presidential authority. On the board's recommendation, the bureaus drew up an extensive safety program. Money for a 2-year program was approved for FY 31 and beyond; the most expensive changes were stronger bulkheads for 60 Electric Boat submarines (O-, R-, and S-boats). In April 1930 the Chief Constructor, Rear Adm. George Rock, proposed that alterations be limited to submarines to be retained under the new London Treaty limit of 52,700 tons. That eliminated the O-boats and most R-boats. The Secretary of the Navy ordered all Battle Fleet S-boats modified by the end of June 1932, with the required three structural bulkheads (adding one to some boats, such as S-29) with new doors (all proof against 88 psi pressure) and a new permanent buoyancy tank to be used for fuel. Mare Island was expected to complete each boat in about 3–4 mo.

A list of desired modifications for the Electric Boat craft was drawn up in October 1929. Both end compartments (torpedo room and motor room) would be strengthened by installing the new bulkheads, to withstand water pressure if the pressure hull was breached. Each end compartment would be fitted for survival (with stowage for rations) and for escape (stowage for Momsen lung escape devices, with oxygen lines to charge them, and by fitting an escape hatch with a skirt, to hold the air bubble with which a man would rise). A new escape hatch had to be cut into the motor room aft and the skeg atop the pressure hull cut away. This modification was the only really visible effect of the safety program. The torpedo loading hatch was modified so that it could be opened from inside. Other changes were: (1) 2 air supply valves installed in each main compartment; (2) the bulkhead ventilation valve in the bulkhead between the after battery and engine room was replaced with a valve of the type used in the V-class; (3) a separate strongback was installed on the torpedo loading hatch; (4) separate air salvage lines were installed for each main ballast tank; and (5) an outlet with removable cover placed in the ventilating duct in the battery room(s) and control room.

Special modifications were planned for S-22: (1) marker buoys at each end, releasable from the end compartments; (2) strengthened structural bulkheads (Nos. 30 and 101); (3) an escape lock with side door over the torpedo room; (4) padeyes to attach three pairs of 80-ton pontoons for salvage; and (5) a buoyancy compartment in No. 3 main ballast tank (and a bow buoyancy tank built up over the bow) to compensate for the added weight. These modifications were carried out, but the external bow buoyancy tank was removed before 1941. S-22 had escape hatches raised above her deck.

It appears that all boats had their bulkheads reinforced and new doors installed, but the hatch and skirt in the motor room may not have been installed on all of them. Unfortunately it is difficult to be sure which boats were modified before 1941. Photographic evidence is somewhat ambiguous, and booklets of plans with the appropriate dates have not survived for all the Electric Boat S-boats. It does not seem certain that the following boats were modified: S-20, S-22, S-23, S-26, S-29, S-30, S-34, S-36, S-39, S-40, and probably S-42 through S-47 (S-45 may not have been modified). At least the earlier S-boats modified had no marker buoys. The buoys were, however, installed fore and aft on R-boats serving for training at New London, which were also modified: certainly R-2, R-4, R-10, R-12, R-13, and R-14, and probably also R-4 and R-11.

Although marker/messenger buoys had been developed before 1914, few contemporary plans of U.S. submarines show them. They were included in tentative October 1917 characteristics for new fleet and ASW submarines. A British attaché, Stanley (later Sir Stanley) Goodall, who eventually became British Director of Naval Construction, commented in 1918 that although some U.S. submarines had buoys, many COs feared that the buoy would not detach properly in the event of a sinking. Others feared that they would detach too easily in the event of depth charging. Goodall's comments are in his letter 14 to the Admiralty (ADM 229/97 in the PRO, Kew, England). Apparently it was not until about 1930 that a satisfactory buoy was developed.

Relatively minor improvements were planned for the C&R-designed boats. For example, plans for S-3 called for (1) removing ventilating valves in the engine room bulkhead and blanking off those openings; (2) installing power operated side Kingstons; (3) installing stowage for pyrotechnics and identification signals.

The S-4 disaster also led to the development of the McCann rescue chamber; the two prototypes for this were made from the halves of the aircraft hangar installed on board S-1.

S-4 herself was never completely reconditioned after her sinking. Her engine and motor rooms were used to test new submarine rescue devices, such as pontoons and the new rescue chambers. Ready for initial tests on 10 December 1928, S-4 was towed to New London. After tests there, she was towed to Key West, and then to Portsmouth. In 1931 the Submarine Force commander recommended that she be decommissioned, but instead she became part of a new Submarine Safety Test Unit (ordered formed 20 October 1931). In this form she was used for training and salvage drills at New London, Coco Solo (Panama), San Diego, and Pearl Harbor. For example, she arrived at Coco Solo 19 January 1932 and was twice bottomed in the harbor of Porto Bello, Panama, then raised by the stern by the rescue ship *Mallard*, using the pontooning method developed in the S-4 and S-51 salvage operations. About 85 percent of the submariners of SubDiv 3 took the opportunity to practice Momsen Lung escapes from her motor room. She also demonstrated and instructed in the Rescue Bell, at this time the only pure rescue device available to save the crew of a bottomed submarine. In August 1932, S-4 left under tow for Pearl Harbor, to train SubDiv 4. The Submarine Safety Test Unit was abolished and S-4 decommissioned on 7 April 1933 at Pearl Harbor.

One lesson of the S-4 experiments was that pontoons were of no value in crew rescue. In his FY 33 report, the Submarine Force commander commented that had this point not been demonstrated, considerable effort might have been dissipated in an emergency in getting pontoons to the scene of a sinking.

By this time all Battle Force submarines had seatings for rescue chambers *except* S-23, S-24, S-31, S-32, S-33, S-34, and S-46, all of which were due for refits in 1933–34.

20. Decommissionings would begin in July 1936. The planned July 1937 group consisted of the S-10 class and the V-1 class. The latter boats were included because (1) their great displacement blocked so much further construction, (2) they were so expensive to operate and maintain, and (3) they were unsuitable for reassignment to shore bases when replaced by new submarines. The six R-boats would be retained as long as possible (in this table, until July 1939) for training at New London, because they were so inexpensive and their small displacements had so little effect on the overall U.S. tonnage allowance. If the treaty were abrogated (as it was), the CNO wanted to retain the older single-hull S-boats in commission, because their structure was readily accessible for examination and repair under a relatively inexpensive refit program. The double hull boats were considered harder to maintain, hence not worth keeping much beyond the statutory 13-year age. At this time CinC Asiatic Fleet also wrote that he was much concerned about newly discovered severe corrosion in the double-hull S-boats. Earlier corrosion problems led to the placement of fuel (rather than ballast) tanks in the ends of the submarine *Dolphin*. The August 1934 evaluation is by the Submarine Force (signed C. W. Cole), FF4/L9-3/A4-1 in NARS RG 19 correspondence, file SS/L9-3 and other data are from NARS RG 19 formerly classified correspondence, file SS/L9-3.

21. The U.S. plan for a European war then envisaged operating S-boats from Gibraltar and Britain against Axis shipping. The OpNav War Plans Division proposed that 10 Holland S-boats be retained to train for overseas operations; it suggested that the British receive 6 Holland S-boats (SubDiv 51 less S-1, i.e. S-21 through S-26 and S-29) and 12 R-boats (SubRon 3). Three more S-boats (S-1, S-20, and S-48, plus *Mackerel* and *Marlin*) would continue experimental operations, and 10 Holland S-boats (SubRon 5, less SubDiv 51: SubDivs 52 and 53) would form a mobile unit based on Bermuda and available for overseas duty. The 7 Government S-boats would operate out of Coco Solo to defend the Canal Zone. The British did receive 6 Holland S-boats but only 3 R-boats.

Chapter 8

1. Lt. J. H. Austin, 27 June 1918 (Undersea Warfare Division papers, Operational Archives), report of his visit to the British Hydrophone Experimental Station, Hawkscraig.

2. Lt. (jg) Eric L. Barr, 26 March 1918, report by CO of K-1. The required enlisted men for each watch were three deck force (gunner's mates or other rated), two electricians (one general, one radio), and four engineers (one machinist's mate, two engine men, one lower rating), in addition to a chief machinist's mate (constantly needed to overcome breakdowns, hence not a watch-stander), cook, and messman, for a total of 30 enlisted men, plus three officers. In a crash dive, the gunner's mate secured aft (main vent) and controlled the main diving planes; the other two deck force petty officers secured the conning tower and main induction and steered the boat. The electrician controlled the main motors; the radio electrician (the listener on patrol) secured the forward ventilator and opened the main ballast vent. The machinist's mate and the engine men secured engines and the engine room. The lower-rated engineer opened the auxiliary main ballast vents and passed the word from the engine room. A properly crash-dived boat "must be under in less time than it

takes the average man to be fully waked up from sleep. Therefore the necessary men must be up, awake, and on the alert."

3. Lambert (private communication).

4. The British-built improved H-boats were lengthened, mainly in the central compartment, to approximate the U.S. L class. U.S. officers believed that the British still found them too small for anything but harbor or coastal work. In fact, the British liked them for their larger bow salvo (four rather than two torpedoes in a British E-boat) and used them in the Mediterranean and Adriatic, rather than in the North Sea. Emory S. Land heard that they had stability problems. He claimed that Electric Boat had bribed its main proponent, Lt. Comdr., of (later X-craft fame) C. H. Varley, RN. Land testified: "It seems [Electric Boat] accomplish their ends by any means they see fit. I therefore discount any statement Lt. Varley makes of the popularity of the H-boat in Great Britain. This can be confirmed by other submarine naval officers in the Dept." (General Board hearing, 15 April 1918). In April 1918, the Board of Inspection and Survey found that the N-boat (in effect an updated H-boat) could not "remain at sea and compete with O-class, which are themselves none too large or seaworthy. . . the small boat possesses no advantage over the larger one in facility of handling or quick submergence."

5. When Land repeated his preference for the 800-tonner in a July 1920 paper before the British Institution of Naval Architects, A. W. Johns, chief constructor for the Royal Navy, argued that submarine tonnage was determined by available engines, typically 1,000–1,200 BHP for 850 tons. As soon as the Germans got more powerful engines (1,750 BHP), they built larger U-boats (1,150 tons in U-135). The 3,000-BHP engines intended for the U-148 class allowed for 2,150 tons (surfaced).

6. Submarine Board, Report 6, 1918; RG 80, NARS.

7. Some wartime diesels might have vibrated badly because they had steel, rather than composition, bearings.

8. In May 1918, the British Grand Fleet sortied within an hour of a contact report but missed contact by 25 mi, reportedly because a submarine CO, sighting several capital ships, thought they were British and therefore waited 4 hr to report. Submarines were then ordered to report all surface craft unless their nationality was confirmed by exchange of signals or some other distinctive mark. They were not to attack other submarines at night unless absolutely sure they were U-boats (during the spring of 1918, a British J-boat from Blythe unsuccessfully attacked a boat from Harwich or Yarmouth). The choice of patrolling on the surface or submerged was left to the individual CO. The British assumed that the Germans would detect and locate their boats when they radioed but considered the risk well worthwhile. In addition to lookout duty, each North Sea submarine depot was assigned a certain number of Grand Fleet stations to be occupied immediately in case of a fleet action.

9. The pre-Jutland U-boat concentrations failed partly because boats had to be sent out so far in advance that some had broken down by the time the German fleet sortied. There was also bad judgment: a U-boat missed the damaged British battleship *Marlborough* because she fired from 3,000 yd. By way of contrast, U-boats sent out in August 1916 sank two British light cruisers.

10. The immediate cause of U.S. entry into the war was that Germany (in the "Zimmermann telegram") explicitly promised Mexico the return of territory lost in 1848 should she enter the war on the German side. It was widely believed, however, that American revulsion at unrestricted submarine warfare made the declaration of war possible. The Germans abandoned unrestricted submarine warfare several times in the face of strong U.S. protests, which generally resulted from the indiscriminate killing of American citizens. The Germans prosecuted un-

restricted warfare in the Mediterranean in 1916–17, where it did not risk U.S. casualties.

11. In 1919, the U.S. naval planning staff in London was asked to study the abolition of submarines. Its covering memorandum compared Japan with Britain. Little dependent on overseas commerce, the United States did not face reprisal if she attacked Japanese shipping: "Our submarines based in Philippines and on Guam would be within striking distance of her coasts and would be a grave threat to the commerce on which her existence depends . . . there is no quicker or more efficient method of defeating Japan than the cutting of her sea communications." The two main submarine roles in a war against Japan would be defense of the Philippines and commerce warfare. Submarines also would be useful scouts. High officials of an unnamed wartime ally (almost certainly France) said that, had their country been in Germany's position, unrestricted submarine warfare would have been entirely justified (France resisted limitation of total submarine tonnage at the 1921 Washington Conference). The memorandum included an apparently pro forma argument that the United States should support abolition because the national conscience would not support a U.S. antishipping submarine campaign like the German campaign. It was probably known that the British would reject abolition: any power could easily begin submarine construction covertly, as the Germans did in 1933–35. The memorandum and the planning section report (No. 68, 18 January 1919) are in GB 420-15, folder for 1919. Arguments justifying the German offensive are in GB 420-15 and in lectures delivered by Capt. T. C. Hart to the Naval War College and to the Army War College in 1919 and 1920 (Naval War College archives). Hart argued that the German offensive was actually humane. Although the Germans had sunk over 12 million tons of merchant ships and killed 10,000 to 12,000 Allied seamen, about this number of men had died in a single day of intense battle on the Western Front.

12. According to Lambert (private communication), British submarine patrols in the Irish Sea were proposed by Capt. Martin E. Nasmith, who had learned in the Sea of Marmora how the threat of enemy submarines could affect a submariner. Nasmith was named CinC of British submarines in Ireland specifically to implement his ideas.

13. British submarines were being run very hard. According to a 6 September 1918 report by Lt. Comdr. H. M. Bemis, who was assigned to HMS *E-29* (OpNav Submarine Division papers, Operational Archives), a patrol by British E-class submarines lasted 10 days. Upon return, half the crew was given 3 days' leave while the base made major repairs. The boat was then placed on 2-hr notice. Two or three weeks generally elapsed between patrols, but the 2-hr notice precluded major repairs; boats were run until they broke down and were decommissioned for a dockyard refit. Each day, two boats were detailed as duty boats, their crews either on board or on the tender. Since 1915, there had been no overnight leave at all except for the 3 days following each patrol. *E-29* had not been refitted or drydocked for 18 months. Bemis was on board when *E-29*'s CO and 17 of her 29-man crew collapsed with influenza. Temporarily in command, Bemis managed to operate the boat with just enough men to handle the planes (2); to steer (1); this man also controlled the periscope and worked the voice pipes to the motor room and to the LP blower); to work the switchboard (1), the Kingstons and blow valves (2), the radio (1), and the engine room (1); and to act as lookout (1). Bemis commented drily that it was simple, except that different stations were sometimes manned by other than their regular personnel.

14. According to papers collected for a postwar official history,

the Azores decision was prompted as much by the Navy Department (presumably OpNav) and by Adm. H.T. Mayo, CinC Atlantic Fleet, as by anyone else (papers of OpNav Submarine Warfare Division, Operational Archives).

15. SubDiv 5 operations are summarized in its war diary (Submarine Warfare Division papers, Operational Archives).

SubDiv 5, 1 December 1917 to 1 November 1918:

	AL-1	AL-2	AL-3
Days at sea	115.9	125.4	134.0
Days on patrol	76.5	83.0	89.0
Miles on surface	12,072.3	17,562.3	12,093.8
Miles submerged	2,353.0	1,879.0	3,120.0
Hours submerged	1,245.4	1,163.1	1,669.2
Enemy sighted	3	5	2
Enemy attacked	1	0	0
Torpedoes expended	4	0	0

	AL-4	AL-9	AL-10	AL-11
Days at sea	90.2	108.0	136.6	106.2
Days on patrol	60.0	62.0	95.0	78.0
Miles on surface	10,871.6	12,251.8	15,617.3	13,066.3
Miles submerged	3,126.0	2,058.6	2,891.8	1,906.8
Hours submerged	1,285.1	954.8	1,794.5	1,597.0
Enemy sighted	5	1	2	3
Enemy attachéd	2	0	0	1
Torpedoes expended	5	0	0	2

16. The detachment commander proposed his three billets 3 days before sending out the submarines, based on a combination of intelligence and projection of German intentions. They had to be approved by CinC Coast of Ireland Adm. Lewis Bayly, RN.

17. AL-10 spotted two U.S. destroyers. She crash-dived to 60 ft and turned to evade their depth charges. She surfaced after the lights had been knocked out and the motor switches thrown open. Before the destroyers began to fire, the CO and executive officer (XO) had fired all of their signals. It turned out that the CO of the leading destroyer had been the roommate of the submarine CO at Annapolis. The British devised the most exotic recognition signal, the "whale spout," a pipe through which water could be pumped to form the dots and dashes of Morse letters. It impressed U.S. officers on duty in European waters, but it was not adopted.

18. In October 1918, it was estimated that 4,000 new trained enlisted men would be needed for the big submarine program. In the past, a man had not been considered qualified before he had served 6 mo on board a submarine. By that time, only 25 boats were available for training in home waters. The navy therefore started special submarine schools for enlisted men at New Lon-

don, Coco Solo (Panama), and San Pedro (California). Only the New London school long survived the war.

19. This was exactly the point raised by Chief Constructor Rear Adm. E. L. Cochrane during WW II in connection with the thick-skinned *Balao* class: the maximum pressure against which the pump could work, not merely the strength of the pressure hull, determined how deep the submarine could safely operate.

20. The idea seems to have come from the Submarine Force. The schooners were actually unarmed submarine tenders, rather than Q-ships, because their crews were in uniform. The U.S. Navy was apparently unaware of British operations with small submarines towed by trawlers (1915). For the U.S. operations, see E. F. Beyer and K. M. Beyer (J. W. Klar and C. C. Wright, eds.),"U.S. Navy Mystery Ships," *Warship International* 4 (1991), 322–372.

21. By division, the following were submarine activities during 1918: SubDiv 1 (C-boats at Coco Solo); all but C-2 and C-3 made submerged patrols; on 22 May, C-2, and C-3, and *Tallahassee* (tender) were sent to Virgin Islands for patrol, then moved on 21 June to Key West, Florida, to operate with K-3 and K-4 until 1 September, when they returned to Coco Solo.

SubDiv 2 (D-boats and G-boats at New London for training and experiments; all but G-3 and, later, D-1 had gasoline engines): At the end of the war, 19 submarines were based at New London, 2 of which were scheduled to sail for Bermuda for winter ASW patrol.

SubDiv 3 (K-3, -4, -7, -8, plus H-1 and H-2, which arrived at Key West 8 January 1918 from Honolulu, Hawaii, and went to Philadelphia for repairs): K-3 and K-4 patrolled off Key West and K-7 and K-8 off Galveston.

SubDiv 4: Azores (E-1 and K-8 returned to New London). By October 1918, they were scheduled for replacement by SubDiv 6.

SubDiv 5: AL-boats at Bantry Bay.

SubDiv 6 (Lake L-boats, M-1, E-2): East Coast ASW patrol; L-5 and E-2 from Hampton Roads, L-6 and L-7 from Charleston, L-8 and M-1 from Cape May, New Jersey, and New London. The Lake boats (tender *Alert*) sailed 12 October to Ponta Delgada in the Azores.

SubDiv 7 (N-boats): N-1–N-3 arrived at New London from the Pacific Coast on 7 February, after completing the entire trip from Puget Sound practically without casualty. This was the longest cruise performed to date by any U.S. submarine without breakdown. N-1 and N-2 patrolled off Provincetown and N-3 off New London. In October, the four later N-boats, which had just completed shakedown, began continuous submerged patrols.

SubDiv 8 (O-3–O-10): Special operations from Delaware Breakwater (tender *Savannah*). Near the end of the war, they were assigned to Bantry Bay for operations off the French coast. They got to Ponta Delgada in the Azores before the war ended.

SubDiv 10 (O-11–O-16): Assembled at Coco Solo for service in the Virgin Islands.

SubDiv 14 (R-15–R-20): At the end of the war, these new boats were assembling in Long Island Sound for service on the Atlantic Coast or in European waters.

These statistics are from 1 January–21 October 1918 Summary (Submarine Warfare Division papers, Operational Archives).

22. As a lieutenant in charge of the British submarine attack school, Martin E. Nasmith (famous for his later exploits against Turkish shipping in the Sea of Marmora) invented the Attack Teacher in 1912. He soon discovered the difference between track and bow angle. The British distinguished approach from attack: maneuvering into attack position versus maneuvering after reaching firing range but before firing.

23. The Nasmith Director was a simple angle-solver using own course, target bearing, and angle on the target's bow. Its accuracy depended on the CO's ability to judge the angle on the bow. Nasmith also invented the Is-Was, a means of checking estimates of target course and speed.

24. Pre–Attack Teacher techniques were based on bow angle, the bearing of the submarine as measured from the target's bow.

25. The gyros of all U.S. Bliss-Leavitt (not Whitehead) torpedoes could be angled, but submarine torpedo tubes were not arranged to set angles until 1917–18. The capability to adjust torpedo angle probably explains why the U.S. Navy placed destroyer torpedo tubes along the sides, rather than the centerline. A destroyer could fire all 12 tubes, not just the 6 on one side, at a target ahead of her. Many wartime British E-boat commanders tried to double their salvos by throwing off the gyros of their broadside tubes, so that the torpedoes eventually took up a course about 90 degrees from the tube, in line with the two bow tubes. They could not be sure of how far the torpedo would advance before turning, and this expedient rarely worked. The British could not angle their WW II torpedoes.

It is not altogether clear just when tubes were modified for angled fire. However, it is suggestive that draft characteristics for fleet and ASW submarines circulated October 1917 seem to have been the first to mention this facility. It must have been novel, since Electric Boat asked for an explanation (did C&R mean different running depths?). In March 1918 C&R informed the two builders that all future torpedo tubes would be fitted for angled fire. Oddly, given the British rationale for broadside tubes, tentative 12 October 1917 characteristics for a new fleet submarine called for one 21 in tube on each beam plus four bow tubes, all to be capable of angled fire. The characteristics are in NARS RG 19 correspondence, file 22-S (1915–1926 series).

26. According to Lambert (private communication), many British submarine COs set their torpedo speeds before going on patrol by moving the reducer valve. Settings could be chosen by the CO; for example, Lt. Robert Ross Turner (E-38) used 18 kt instead of the ususal 25 kt. British submariners could not close many U-boats, which were often spotted at 3,000 yd, an extreme torpedo range, hence the "submarine monitor" (M class) armed with a single 12-in gun, salvaged from a pre-dreadnought battleship, to attack surfaced U-boats. The gun was expected to pop up for a single shot (aimed from periscope depth), which would arrive before the U-boat could dive. It was not too different in concept from a modern submarine-launched anti-ship missile, such as Sub-Harpoon. By 1918, the U.S. Submarine Force was aware of the M class and of its logic, but it produced no parallel proposal. The 1922 Washington Treaty set maximum gun caliber at 8 in.

27. In March 1920, one trainable SC or MB, one deck, and one keel Y-tubes were authorized for each submarine (no keel tube would be installed in any submarine on which work had not yet been done.) In November, BuEng suggested that the superior MV replace the Y-tube on board later (ultimately all) S-boats. T-boat MVs were canceled when they were laid up. SC installations were stopped early in 1921 in hopes that a better trainable device soon would be available (submarines without SC had the inferior Y-tube) but were resumed in February 1922 because there was no money for a new set. By that time, BuEng was working on "supersonics" (sonar). In January 1925, CinC U.S. Fleet drew up a standard sound outfit:

• supersonic outfit, including projector (19 in diameter), total 5,470 lb, for accurate short-range echo detection and ranging

• electric (MV) receiver, including compensator and blisters (2 ft × 14 ft), total 6,560 lb, possibly to be eliminated altogether
• rotatable receiver (MB or SC tube) for long-range detection, to replace MV if sufficiently developed
• oscillators for only V-4–V-6.

By June 1927, all U.S. submarines had 540-Hz oscillators and SC tubes. S-boats (except S-2, S-14–S-17) and V-1–V-4 all had MV. Older submarines and S-14–S-17 had Y-5 tubes (exceptions were O-1, O-2, R-10, R-13, R-17, and R-22, which had MV). Orders for replacement of Y-5 by MV had been issued to yards for S-14–S-17 and the remaining R-boats. Replacements in O-3, O-4, O-6–O-10, and S-2 had been authorized, but orders had not yet been issued. All decommissioned K-, L-, O-, and R-boats had Y-5. The new V-5 and V-6 were scheduled for supersonic and sonic equipment.

28. Comdr. W. L. Friedell, "Characteristics and Limitation of S Class Submarines," lecture at Asiatic Fleet War College, Chefoo, China, 22 July 1923 (Naval War College archives).

29. It turned out that the Germans had come nowhere near matching British construction rates, partly because they had never simplified U-boat designs for quick production.

30. The remarks quoted here are by U.S. submariners who served on board captured U-boats, and who much affected U.S. submarine policy in the decade that followed. The bureaus' views had far less impact on overall policy, but they certainly affected the details of U.S. post–WW I submarines. On 1 April 1920, C&R published a lengthy Confidential report, Bulletin 103, "Report on German Submarines," 2613–2671, one in a series of C&R Confidential bulletins that describes C&R-related features of the U-boats in some detail. (The author has been unable to find corresponding BuOrd or BuEng reports.) As might be imagined, the C&R report is not entirely favorable. It criticizes U-boats for their excessively elaborate, complicated, and intricate fittings. U.S. submariners who had served on the U-boats suggest that the elaborate mechanism, in fact, was vital; however, after WW II, U.S. designers pointed out that the new U-boats were likely to be unreliable because they were unduly complicated. Numerous cables and pipes passed through otherwise watertight bulkheads (in one case, 35 electric cables). There were also unduly elaborate "shore connections" through the pressure hull, even including an oxygen connection to charge flasks for air purification. "There is ample evidence that public opinion forced [adoption of] some of the [excessively elaborate emergency fittings]; that the submarine service could get anything that was suggested; also that every effort was made to attract men to the submarine service by all sorts of safeguards, both essential and nonessential . . . submarines had special food supplied. Many of the older boats were modernized or made more comfortable by the addition of officers' quarters, insulation, wash rooms, small showers, transoms, lockers, etc. It appears that much more was done for the officers' comfort than for the men. Boats long in service or in from long cruises were very dirty and ill smelling" (p. 2615). Ventilation is described as "very elaborate compared with other services (British, French, Italian, and United States) and has many intricate leads, cross connections, and fittings. Bulkheads and strength [pressure] hull are pierced indiscriminately. As a ventilation system . . . it should be very efficient, as no compartment is overlooked and any number of leads are taken off the main line—in some cases, without any apparent rhyme or reason" (p. 2632).

Ballast tanks were controlled by three wheels in the control room, via long lines of shafting running through the bulkheads.

C&R finds this technique objectionable, preferring the British telemotors.

The C&R report includes some notes by a lieutenant Commander Bowers RN, who was escorted around U-boats at Kiel and Bremen by Kpt-Lt. Steinbrinck, a wartime "ace" (responsible for sinking more than 200,000 tons of merchant ships) who had commanded a UB, a UC, and one other boat in wartime (pp. 2640 ff). Steinbrinck reported that the later U-boats had very limited stability; the U-140 class was credited with a GM of only 3 in. As a consequence, U-144 once listed 40 degrees when a tank on one side flooded but the opposite tank did not. He described the class as good divers, better submerged than on the surface. Steinbrinck claimed that some British submarine torpedoes hit U-boats but failed to explode. He implied that the Germans knew nothing of torpedo gyro angling; however, according to C&R's description of German periscopes, "above the main pelorus ring is a revolution ring with catches every 15 deg to correspond with the settings of the torpedo gyro angling device" (p. 2665).

The engineer at the Weser Werft in Bremen pointed out that German U-boat construction had been seriously delayed because of the sheer number of distinct types built (he thought that, had Germany built only a single type, she would have built enough to win the war). He considered the "mittel" U-boats (800–850 tons) best. High submerged speed was of no importance; the usual 9 kt was enough.

According to an unsigned compendium of U-boat data in the OpNav Submarine Division files, late U-boats dispensed with retractable bow planes. The planes were mounted as low as possible in the bow so that they would be effective as soon as they were depressed into the diving position. At high speed, unfortunately, the planes might be damaged. This practice was therefore unattractive to a postwar U.S. Navy interested in high surface speed. The compendium also mentions the Germans' attempts to make their diesel exhaust invisible; they claimed that British exhaust could be seen at 8 nm.

32. To Daubin, U-111 in drydock looked like a yacht, whereas the single hulls of U.S. submarines "bellied out." Letter, 1 July 1927 (OpNav Submarine Division files), in connection with designs for a new U.S. submarine.

33. Because U.S. submarine vents leaked, the S-boats could not ride their vents to crash-dive.

34. C&R tried to defend its design: in 1919, it said that a comparison between S-3 and U-111 clearly favored the former. It claimed that U-111 was slower, both submerged (7.8 kt versus 12.4 kt) and surfaced (13.8 kt versus 14.7 kt). Trials showed that, when tuned, U-111 could exceed 17 kt surfaced, and she was a much faster diver. Officers who remembered the 1919 claims would distrust C&R's 1927 arguments against using U-135 as the prototype of future U.S. submarines.

35. Several modern designers have suggested to the author that methods of computation in use in 1914–18 were probably far too crude to support such a judgment; probably the Germans made their choice when they began building U-boats and never reviewed it. This issue did not arise in C&R's 1920 study of U-boats mentioned earlier.

36. Lt. H. W. Koehler, 12–13 February 1919, letter from Berlin (Submarine Warfare Division files, Operational Archives), describes contemporary events and views in Berlin, and predicts that the Germans would try again (as they did).

37. The former U-boat CO did not fear using his radio freely because British direction finders could not direct a destroyer to his position until hours after he had left. Only at the very end of the war did it occur to him that radio direction finding made evasive convoy routing possible.

Chapter 9

1. Typical distances were Honolulu to Nagasaki, 3,976 nm, and to Yokohama, 3,400 nm; Seattle to Manila, 7,247 nm.

2. Plans dated 8 June 1920, in Secretary of the Navy/CNO classified papers (RG 80, National Archives, reproduced in the NARS microfilm of these papers for the period 1919–1927). The war planners enclosed a copy of the Submarine Section of a 28 April 1920 Plans Division paper on the use of submarines against enemy trade in a Far East war.

3. Planning figures were based on a 1-year war (i.e., no major refits), 20 percent safety factor, and allowance of 200 nm per day equivalent on station for cruising and battery changing.

4. On 22 September 1919, the General Board had proposed a 12-submarine program.

5. During the summer of 1936, with the 1930 London Treaty about to expire, Britain invoked the clause to avoid scrapping 40,000 tons of overage destroyers to counter what it considered abnormal building by France and Italy. The United States matched the British step. Japan lacked sufficient overage destroyer tonnage to fill out her enlarged allowed tonnage, so she retaliated by retaining overage submarines. The extra U.S. submarine tonnage matched the Japanese tonnage.

6. Mk XI was the first torpedo BuOrd designed; earlier ones had been developed by E. W. Bliss Co. Production began in 1927, but Mk XI was superseded in 1928 by the very similar Mk XII. About 200 Mk XII torpedoes were made (no figure for Mk XI is available).

7. BuOrd standarized this generation of torpedoes by making the Mk XV destroyer torpedo a Mk XIV with a longer air flask for greater range. Mks XI and XII were limited in performance because they were limited in length (to 271.06 in) to fit a standard submarine torpedo tube. In Mk XV, another 5.5 in bought an additional 100 lb in warhead.

8. E. W. Jolie, *A Brief History of U.S. Navy Torpedo Development* (Newport: Naval Underwater Systems Center Technical Document 5436, 15 September 1978). During WW II, 13,000 Mk 14 and 9,700 Mk 23 torpedoes were made. Ironically, Mk 23 was unpopular because submarine commanders came to appreciate the long-range option when attacking in the face of aggressive ASW forces.

9. The $25 million (hull and machinery) C&R design employed two tiers of tubular pressure hulls: three 20 ft above two 22-ft × 226-ft tubes each containing two boiler rooms, with two boilers each. Tubes were held in place by deep framing. The surface power plant would be 52,500-SHP steam turbines (25 kt) plus two 2,000-BHP battery-charging diesels (2,000-HP motors for submerged power). A 21 July 1920 sketch showed a 20,000-ton ship (625 ft LWL × 72 ft 10 in × 30 ft) armed with four 12-in/50, plus 10 bow and four stern tubes. A 2-in deck (4.5 in at the deck edge) would meet a 6-in belt extending to 3 ft below the waterline. Craven wanted a surface radius of 20,000 nm and a submerged endurance of 50 hr at 3 kt. For so long a submarine, test depth was set at 400 ft. C&R and BuEng preferred 8-in or 9-in guns.

10. The S-1 test was formally proposed about September 1921. By December 1921, BuAer was working on an airplane for destroyers and submarines; preliminary design had progressed to the point where the bureau knew that it could be stowed in a cylinder with dimensions of 5 ft 9 in × 22 ft 9 in. BuAer wanted the airplane incorporated into the cruiser submarine design. In February 1922, C&R offered preliminary data, including a sketch of an installation on board S-18. Flooding the hangar would cause problems but would not be catastrophic (it would be disastrous on S-42–S-47). S-1 was chosen for the test because she was due

for overhaul. In January 1924, BuAer asked for similar arrangements on all S-, T-, and V-boats. It appeared that the widened deck aft would actually increase underwater maneuverability without much added drag (the bridge structure, guns, and rails already imposed enormous resistance). BuAer wanted a larger tank (diameter of at least 6 ft 9 in, the minimum for a small flying boat, and 10-ft diameter in new submarines) to allow quicker assembly of the airplane. Three small airplanes (Loening Kittens) had been ordered in 1918. In 1921, three small KF-1 seaplanes were ordered from the Martin Co. (*not* Glenn Martin). In 1922, the navy bought two small German Heinkel-Caspar aircraft. None of these aircraft actually flew from a submarine, though apparently all were considered. In 1923, the navy received six Cox-Klemin XS-1s and six Martin MS-1s; one of the latter was tested in October and November 1923 on board S-1. A modified XS-1 (XS-2) and the MS-1 were test-flown from S-1 in the fall of 1926. Neither airplane was altogether suitable, but the project was revived in 1929 with the Loening XSL-1, which could be folded and unfolded quickly enough to be worthwhile. Authority to design the required hangar was apparently withdrawn after the British M 2 sank when her large hangar flooded. BuAer notes are from C&R files (NARS RG 19) and notes on aircraft from T. C. Treadwell, *Submarines with Wings* (London: Conway Maritime Press, 1985), 33–45.

11. From a V-4 design history held by the current submarine design division in NAVSEA. The V-1s were not yet at sea. According to other accounts, the model basin disliked the dory bow, but its tests had all been run in smooth water. Rear Adm. M. M. Taylor, who commanded the Control Force (the submarines operating in the Atlantic), asked for comparative tests with a German U-boat hull form in simulated waves, rather than in smooth water. This time, the bulbous bow came in second best. Commander Submarines Battle Force (Rear Adm. Ridley McLean) later commented that V-4 performed remarkably well in a heavy sea.

12. The Control Force was one element of a U.S. Fleet organization ordered on 6 December 1922 (effective 1 January 1923). It was comprised of the former Submarine Force Atlantic plus a mine division (the large minelayer *Shawmut* and a pair of destroyer minelayers). Submarine Force Pacific became the submarines of the newly established Battle Fleet. The other main elements of the U.S. Fleet were the Scouting Fleet (in the Atlantic, built around the six oldest battleships) and the Fleet Base Force (the Pacific fleet train). The Asiatic Fleet was separate. In theory, the Control Force would have two distinct wartime roles: (1) its submarines and destroyer minelayers would blockade Japan and (2) a force built around the minelayer would seize and hold an advanced base for the main fleet. Clearly, peacetime forces were inadequate; in theory, the Control Force was a nucleus around which a force could be extemporized in an emergency. Of the elements of the U.S. Fleet, the Control Force came to be considered the worst suited for its wartime mission. From 1927 on, successive fleet commanders called for reorganization along type lines; submarines would once more form a Submarine Force. This type of organization was ordered into existence on 10 December 1930 (effective 1 April 1931); the new Submarine Force was responsible for all submarines of the U.S. Fleet, based at New London, Coco Solo, and Pearl Harbor (the Asiatic Fleet submarines were separate).

13. The spherical Mk 11 would resist tidal action. The elongated Mk 10 would not do nearly as well, and it would be visible from the air. The Mk 11 antenna mine would fire when a ship approached too slowly to break the chemical horns of a Mk 10. The General Board found that it liked Mk 11 so much that further specialist minelaying submarines should be built, but that was

never done. The secretary of the navy approved the General Board decision not to convert the ship on 2 January 1940.

14. Although *Argonaut* was sent to Australia to carry landing parties to Japanese-supplied islands, she was lost while attacking a Japanese convoy.

15. In mid-1924, C&R sketched three 2,880-ton submarines: a 17-kt cruiser carrying 30 (rather than 24) torpedoes, a 15-kt minelayer carrying 80 (rather than 60) mines, and the 17-kt hybrid. Each carried two 6-in guns and had a radius of action of 18,000 nm, as in V-4. Each had a 180-cell battery. The cruiser or hybrid would have cost $5.9 million and the minelayer, $6.35 million (these figures probably include one outfit of ammunition).

16. April 1925 sketch design shows the following characteristics: 345 ft × 34 ft 4 in × 15 ft 8 in = 2,896 tons surfaced; ballast, 1,167 tons. Two 2,350-BHP main engines, one 450-BHP charging engine, two 1,200-HP motors, two 120-cell batteries; 17/8 kt. Endurance at 10 kt: 6,000 nm normal, 18,000 nm maximum. Underwater: 36 hr at 1.5–2.5 kt. Stores for 90 days. Four bow and two stern tubes (24 torpedoes), two 6-in/53 guns (200 rounds per gun), one airplane. Seven officers and 66 enlisted. Test depth: 300 ft. Protection: 30-lb STS on conning tower, 50-lb STS over upper strake of pressure hull.

17. BuEng wanted to increase the spacing between engine and motor by 10 ft and to place a small flywheel at the after engine flange to move the critical frequencies from 200, 246, and 387 RPM to 109, 151, and 415 RPM. On the basis of towing tests of the V-4 model, 151 RPM would correspond to about 6.7 kt, and 415 RPM would be above the normal speed range; 246 RPM corresponded to 10.09 kt, very much within the important speed range.

18. General Board files suggest that the earliest such suggestion came from Lt. Comdr. Sherwood Picking, CO of V-1, in a March 1926 letter to the secretary of the navy. He wanted to base the mobilization submarine on U-111, which he had commanded for the U.S. Navy postwar, with some minor sacrifices to gain half a knot. His call for prototypes was strongly supported by the Control Force, C&R, and BuEng. The timing (the full correspondence was forwarded to the General Board in October 1926) suggests that the Picking letter was an important factor in the creation of the Submarine Officers Conference. U-135 was a modified U-111.

19. In theory, a longer boat had to be safe to a greater depth because, at a given angle (inclination), she would extend deeper into the water. At this time, there seems to have been very little interest in the tactical advantage of greater diving depth.

20. Direct-drive ratings were maximum; generator ratings were those formerly used for sustained operation. The 1,750-BHP BuEng diesel could sustain 1,400 BHP; the 1,200-BHP engine was normally rated at 1,000 BHP. Presumably, C&R could achieve acceptable speeds only by uprating the BuEng diesels, a risky practice.

Chapter 10

1. In a 1923 Naval War College game, three V-boats armed with long-range torpedoes ran parallel to their capital ship targets and fired beam shots (90-degree angle) to concentrate all their torpedoes against these fast ships. Rules made for numerous misses (it was assumed that half the torpedoes would not run true), so players had to use the densest possible salvoes, combining bow and stern tubes in beam shots. In February 1923, Capt. T. C. Hart wrote that this game had been more illuminating than four years of sea experience. It convinced Hart that submarines with maximum speeds approaching fleet speed were useful and that all torpedoes should be instantly adjustable for either very high speed or very long range.

2. Mk 1 incorporated Arma's new 14-inch plotter. Originally it did not allow for a dive *under* the target; the TDC had to be fitted with a slew switch. Ford built 12 Mk 2s, which were ultimately replaced by Mk 3s. It proved ineffective because Ford had to make some massive assumptions about the fire control problem to shrink its size. Arma was apparently unaware of the Mk 2 program. Arma originally made searchlights. During World War I the U.S. Navy asked Arma to develop the German Anschutz gyroscope as an alternative to the U.S.-developed Sperry gyrocompass. During World War II, the U.S. government merged Arma with the German-owned (and U.S.-nationalized) Bosch Corporation, to form Bosch-Arma. Bosch-Arma was an important developer of ballistic missile guidance systems. It survives as part of the United Technology Corp., making fuel-injectors for tanks. I am grateful to Terry Linnard, who is writing a history of U.S. torpedo fire control, for these details.

3. The TDC was generally supplemented by a variety of simpler devices that had been developed to expedite calculations and minimize errors (e.g., to check an evolving TDC solution). They also ensured against the failure of the TDC itself. Some dated back to WW I. Typically, they were the submarine attack course finder, the Mk 1 angle solver (for straight shots), the Mk 6 and Mk 8 angle solvers (for angled shots), a separate range keeper, and a distance-to-track table or slide rule. For example, the track angle could be determined either by the attack course finder or by the TDC. The difference was that the instruments could find the parameters for a particular shot, whereas the TDC continuously solved the attack problem.

4. Destroyers performed far better than submarines after their sonar controls were moved to the bridge where the CO could see them. The Experimental Division (late Naval Undersea Systems Center) at New London had already proposed installing a JK passive sonar directly above the conning tower to provide such a direct input. The Submarine Officers Conference took up the TDC location in March 1938. Initially, it seemed that the conning tower would have to be much larger (8 ft longer, 6 in wider), but that April Portsmouth offered a layout requiring only 1 ft of additional length. In August, contract plans of the *Tambor* class showed the conning tower as 8 ft × 15 ft 10 in (adding 8 tons of displacement). The conference voted 13–2 to move the TDC and 14–1 to move the sound controls.

5. About 1937, it was discovered that sonar could detect the sounds of nearby aircraft put into the water. SubDiv 13 tested an "acoustical aircraft detector" for several years prior to 1940, but without much success.

6. From a BuShips Submarine Maintenance Division report (RG 19 wartime correspondence, NARS); the latest submarine listed was *Seawolf* (JK-4, JL-5, NM-10, and QCH).

7. The account of the Portsmouth caisson is based on notes from Comdr. John Alden's interview with Rear Adm. Andrew I. McKee, 9 January 1974, provided by Alden. McKee was at Philadelphia Navy Yard in 1931–34 and at Mare Island in 1935–39, so his comments on a test (about 1934) are not first hand; he was in charge of the submarine type desk in C&R in 1926–30 and was planning officer at Portsmouth in 1940–45. The account of the two-caisson test is from Alden's interview with Rear Adm. Armand M. Morgan, 2 May 1974, transcript provided by Alden. Morgan was at the Production Department of Portsmouth Navy Yard in 1934–38 and was head of submarine design within BuShips between April 1938 and February 1945. Morgan recalled that when welding was introduced, two test caissons, each 30 ft long, representing full-scale pressure-hull sections, were built specially to compare welding with the earlier riveted construction. The caissons were lowered to 120 ft and depth

charges exploded. The first shot sank the riveted caisson, as its joints popped. The welded one merely bent. The next test used a double-hull section, but caissons were used after that to test equipment, such as battery cells. In fact, the use of these caissons focused interest on such internal features, rather than on overall hull construction. Morgan credits the idea of testing a battery cell to a Lieutenant Dana on the BuEng diesel desk. The first test used only a battery jar filled with water. It burst, so the next time a real cell was used. It also broke. The first proposed solution was to put a layer of thin steel between two layers of rubber, but that cost too much weight. Then Lt. (later Rear Adm.) E. E. Yeomans suggested using a thin layer of flexible rubber. Morgan considered the shockproof battery jar one of the most important wartime features because a large percentage of lost German U-boats had sunk as a result of battery failure; he believed that the U.S. Navy suffered no such problems.

8. Pacific Fleet Submarine Force, "Enemy Anti-Submarine Measures," undated, prepared at Pearl Harbor. The copy in the OpNav Submarine Division files (now in the U.S. Navy Operational Archives) was sent by Capt. K. G. Hensel on 17 June 1946, so this report must have been prepared soon after the end of WW II. The report describes an attack on *Puffer* (Lt. Comdr. M. J. Jensen) on 9 October 1943. Morale held up until the air conditioner was turned off to reduce the drain on the battery. Many of the crew were convinced that the boat was finished. In fact, she survived, but the air conditioner would not have been a very great electrical drain. The badly shaken crew had to be dispersed once the submarine returned to base. J. D. Alden, *The Fleet Submarine in the U.S. Navy* (Annapolis Md.: Naval Institute Press, 1979), points out that although air conditioning could not renew the air in a submerged boat, it could leach out such annoyances as grease and smoke.

9. Lt. Comdr. R. W. Christie argued that the new magnetic exploder made larger salvos unnecessary (see Chapter 12).

10. Deck stowage of torpedoes (in pressure-proof containers) was first tried in 1933 on board V-4, V-5, and V-6. In March 1933, the General Board approved a January 1933 proposal to stow three torpedoes on deck in the new *Dolphin*.

11. In February 1923, BuOrd reported initial experiments toward development of an anchored mine interchangeable with a 21-in torpedo (on a one-for-one basis). In April 1933, BuOrd described its new Mk X mine: 13 ft 3½ in long, 2,080 lb (a 20-ft Mk XIV torpedo weighed 2,879 lb). Because each mine displaced one torpedo, minelaying was uneconomical. When skids were lengthened to accept longer torpedoes, the mine was shortened so that two could fit each skid and each tube.

12. The poppet valve, devised by Lt. M. M. Dana at Portsmouth Navy Yard, eliminated the bubble by venting air and water from the tube into the bilges. It was ordered installed in February 1941. The submarine officers wanted BuOrd to use a piston to launch torpedoes, as the Germans and French later did. To accommodate it, the tube had to be 2 ft longer (also wider). Its piston could launch a short torpedo, or it could fire a long one by air. Unfortunately, the spindles used to set torpedo gyro, depth, and speed were all located at set distances from the torpedo tail. They would have to be in different places along the length of the tube, depending on whether it was firing with or without a piston. It would have taken an even longer tube to fire either long or short torpedoes by piston.

13. On trial, *Shark* (Electric Boat FY 34 type) developed 4,500 SHP (from 5,200 BHP), rather than 4,300 SHP, and made 20.4 kt.

14. C&R's study was delayed by the press of other work on the FY 38 program. By November 1936, C&R and Electric Boat

had both worked up alternative schemes. C&R suggested widening the existing dory bow (there was little point in adding length) at a likely cost of about 40 tons and 0.2 kt. Electric Boat dropped the forefoot to add the tubes below the four-tube nest. The boat would be about 36 tons heavier, she would pitch a bit more, and added length would make her a bit faster on the surface.

15. Those who disagreed felt that 10 or so tons of additional negative buoyancy could not make much difference; it was better to dive more steeply and to correct slightly negative. The tank was blown before the submarine reached her ordered depth, to avoid overshooting. It was vented inboard to avoid leaving a telltale bubble.

16. Previous classes had been designed to operate at 80 percent of test depth. *Gatos* were designed to operate at full test depth, which was increased to 300 ft.

17. Adm. Armand F. Morgan (Alden interview) considered that these tests provided more useful information on the effects of such explosions than all the wartime experience—and, moreover, in time to save many wartime U.S. submarines. He attributed the tests to Comdr. F. S. Low, then on the OpNav staff. Low later coordinated U.S. Atlantic ASW efforts as commander of the Tenth Fleet and, in 1950, directed an important analysis of ASW issues.

18. Program data from S. S. Roberts, "U.S. Navy Building Programs During World War II," *Warship International* 3 (1981), 218–261. Dr. Roberts makes it clear that hull numbers were not assigned in sequence.

19. According to the official submarine history, *Submarine Commands*, vol. 2 (undated), 473, Cramp was assigned naval orders at the personal direction of President Roosevelt, who as assistant secretary of the navy had been responsible for warship production during WW I.

20. University of Pittsburg Historical Staff at Office of Naval Research, "The History of United States Naval R&D in World War II," undated manuscript held by U.S. Navy Operational Archives (probably written about 1948), cites reports by U.S. observers in Britain early in 1941: both sides were using heavier depth charges. According to Admiral Morgan (Alden interview); deeper diving was largely a matter of hull steel thickness, rather than of steel strength. Hulls usually failed not by tearing (yield) but by buckling (instability), and the solution to buckling is a larger radius of gyration (i.e., a thicker plate). Stronger steel is not enough; there must be stronger framing to hold it in place. Admirals Morgan and McKee made their calculations a few days after the Pearl Harbor attack, while Rear Adm. E. L. Cochrane, chief of BuShips, was at Pearl Harbor inspecting the damage. They guessed the hull would fail at 925 ft (if it was built of HTS), but settled on 650 ft because McKee feared that HTS might not be available (boats would have to be built of mild steel). That equated to a test depth of 450 ft. Returning, Cochrane rejected the new depth as excessive. Morgan said that he actually had wanted 600 ft, and he had cut it to 450 ft, "knowing you'd overrule me." Despite the nominal 400-ft test depth, Morgan wrote all of the specifications for the new type for 450 ft (with the usual 50 percent safety factor).

21. The yield point (which determines crush depth) of wartime HTS was reduced from 50,000 to 45,000 lb/sq in because chrome-vanadium alloy had to be replaced by titanium-manganese. The earlier mild steel (MS) had a yield point of 33,000 lb/sq in, but a slightly greater elongation (23 percent versus 20 percent). The change from MS to HTS alone should have increased diving depth by a factor of about 1.5. Alden, *Fleet Submarine in U.S. Navy*, ascribes the idea for converting the increased margin to pressure hull steel to McKee. He quotes McKee as fearing that

wartime submarine commanders might be overconfident of their ability to dive well below test depth. In October 1944, for example, *Salmon* reported that she had gone to 600 ft during a severe depth charging. The prospective commanding officer of *Bowfin* said that he would not hesitate to go to 1,000 ft. McKee knew that models showed a *Gato* failing at 550 ft (*Salmon* was not as strong) and that the small-scale model of the heavy hull version had failed at 909 ft. He suspected that *Salmon* had overestimated her depth, and he arranged to lecture all prospective submarine commanding officers at Portsmouth on hull strength. McKee considered the heavy-hull submarine safe to 600 ft but not too much below that.

22. Earlier submarines, which lacked variable tanks, also had their No. 4 main ballast tanks converted to fuel ballast tanks, for a total capacity of 116,000 gal. According to Admiral Morgan (Alden interview), the added fuel tanks were his own initiative, based on his reading of wartime patrol reports. Morgan visited Pearl Harbor in 1943 and asked Adm. C. A. Lockwood whether he wanted more fuel. He proposed converting some ballast tanks to fuel ballast tanks. Lockwood's squadron and division commanders asked for about 50 tons; Morgan gave them 64. He thought that a few dives would flush out any oil residue left after the fuel was burned. It is not clear why wartime submarines did not suffer from the oil slick problem so prominent before the war.

23. Prewar motors developed 1,375 HP at 1,300 RPM, driving through herringbone reduction gears with a 4.5:1 ratio. The direct-drive motor developed 2,700 HP surfaced (1.330 HP submerged, using one armature rather than two). As of August 1945, 26 of the planned 39 conversions had been completed.

24. Rear Adm. Armand M. Morgan to Comdr. John Alden, undated letter, 1974. Morgan suggests that this was a prewar initiative by then Capt. C. A. Lockwood (in OpNav); the author has not seen any supporting documentation. He thinks the test was in *Seadragon* or in that class. Several navies tried superstructure tubes during WW II, with similar unhappy results. However, tubes were installed when the big V-boats were modernized in wartime (see chapter 9).

25. Alden, *Fleet Submarine in U.S. Navy*, reports that removal of the bridge steering station was authorized on 15 January 1942, followed on 9 March by reduction in bridge and conning tower fairwater. Removal of the conning tower deadlights had been proposed prewar, but was approved only after *Plunger* (SS 179) was depth charged on her first war patrol. On 26 September 1942, the sheathing around the periscope shears was ordered removed, which resulted in the characteristic wartime openwork structure.

26. In January 1946, CNO directed BuOrd to buy enough 5-in/25 deck guns to provide each active submarine with two and each inactive submarine with one (i.e., to standardize on this weapon). There was considerable opposition to this expenditure.

Chapter 11

1. These characteristics were: 715 tons normal surfaced; trial speed 14/9.5–10 kt; 200-ft test depth; fuel oil 50/100 tons, 2,500/5,000 nm at 10 kt (factor of $\frac{2}{3}$ applied to estimated surface radii). Six 21-in bow tubes (written in: "if practicable, certainly four"), 10 torpedoes, one 3-in gun, complement 35, stores for 25 days, habitability slightly superior to R-boat.

2. Hart's proposed characteristics (clearly based on a sketch design study) were: 1,250 to 1,280 standard, LOA 280 ft, machinery space 52 ft, otherwise as *Perch*; complement five officers and 42 men; six bow and two stern tubes (18 torpedoes); no change in guns; two reversible main engines driving through hydraulic

clutches and reduction gears, each about 2,000 BHP; two auxiliary engines, about 300 BHP each, driving generators. Maximum speed with normal fuel and foul bottom 18.5–19 kt. Battery about as in *Perch* with main motor power for 8.5 kt submerged. Maximum fuel 80,000 gal, not over 40 percent of it in fuel ballast tanks. Reserve buoyancy with normal fuel 28–30 percent, 60 days' provisions.

3. Electric Boat's 13.5-in × 15.5-in engine required a pressure hull diameter of 14 ft 3 in; C&R was planning on 13 ft 8 in or 13 ft 9 in.

4. The Germans credited U-25 and U-26 (Type IA) with a standard displacement of 712 tons; surfaced, 862 tons; and submerged, 983 tons. A pair of 1,540-BHP MAN engines drove them at 17.8 kt; endurance was 6,700 nm at 12 kt. They had four bow and two stern tubes (14 torpedoes). The small U.S. submarines were later compared with the smaller Type VIIC, the standard German production boat for much of WW II (769 tons surfaced, 871 tons submerged). Two MAN 1,400-BHP diesels drove her at 17 kt surfaced (7.5 kt submerged). She had four bow tubes and one stern tube (14 torpedoes, including 2 externally-stowed reloads).

5. For these points, the author is indebted to D. K. Brown, who studied different navies' approaches to submarine pressure hull structure. He believes that the Germans were lucky to hit upon approaches that U.S. and British designers discovered analytically postwar.

Chapter 12

1. According to USF 25, *Current Submarine Doctrine* (1939): "Under the limitations imposed by the laws of war and as interpreted in the Treaty of London, submarines cannot be used effectively against merchant ships without running undue risk of destruction" (p. 2). However, "submarine operations against enemy commerce are limited to attacks on convoys, or attacks on positively identified armed enemy shipping, *unless unrestricted commerce destruction is directed as a last resort*" (italics supplied) (p. 11). Some recent U.S. writers have suggested that, at least from the late 1930s, U.S. submariners did expect to execute unrestricted submarine warfare.

2. After the war, the Joint Army-Navy Assessment Committee (JANAC) credited U.S. submarines with sinking a total of 5.3 million tons (1,314 ships) of Japanese shipping, 55 percent of the total lost, plus probably another 78 ships (263,306 tons). That included 1 battleship, 8 carriers, 11 cruisers, and lesser combatants. The JANAC figures were generally considered conservative. At the end of the war, the Japanese government estimated that it had lost 1,750 steel merchant ships (4.871 million tons) to submarines (including Allies), compared with 876 ships (2.727 million tons) to air attacks, 239 ships (513,700 tons) to mines, and 264 ships (718,000 tons) to all other causes. German U-boats sank about 11 million tons of Allied merchant shipping in WW I and about 14.4 million tons in WW II; these figures reflect not only the success of the U-boats but also the much greater size of the Allied merchant fleet.

3. Japanese ship and convoy movements were often predicted on the basis of code-breaking. See W. J. Holmes, *Double-Edged Secrets* (Annapolis, Md.: Naval Institute Press, 1977). According to Clay Blair, Jr., *Silent Victory* (Philadelphia: Lippincott, 1975), attacks were sometimes frustrated because Japanese warships unintentionally deviated from their ordered routes; the submarines were not fast enough to make up the difference.

4. Notes on U.S. tactics are mainly from *Submarine Warfare Instructions*, (1946, rev. 1952), USF 9, postwar standard manual.

5. Data on wartime attacks are from *Submarine Warfare Instruc-*

tions, and from Pacific Fleet, *Confidential Submarine Bulletin* (1945 issues). Prewar and wartime doctrines are from USF 25, *Current Submarine Doctrine* (1939, 1944); this handbook preceded USF 9. These publications probably do not fully reflect wartime practices. Comdr. John Alden (communication to the author) recalls that, at Submarine School in 1944, "Skippers fresh in from the Pacific told us flatly to ignore doctrine and rely on experience and common sense."

6. Prewar submariners expected to dive 30–40 nm ahead of a target to avoid aircraft. The Japanese lacked radar-equipped aircraft, which the Allies found so effective in the Atlantic. Although their 901st Air Fleet was formed (solely to escort convoys) in December 1943, large-scale use of radar-equipped ASW aircraft was not reported until the following fall. Japanese aircraft radars were then credited with the ability to detect a submarine at 12 nm; toward the end of the war, U.S. submarines reported numerous night air contacts. Japanese doctrine limited radar to night and low-visibility weather on the ground that visual search was more reliable. There was considerable emphasis on magnetic anomaly detection (MAD).

7. The anonymous official author of the Pacific Fleet analysis of Japanese ASW (in the Submarine Warfare Division files of the Operational Archives at the Washington Navy Yard) gives a striking example of the virtues of a surface attack: "Another great aid to evasion was to get some good hits in a convoy before the depth charges started. The submarine that got its licks in first was apt to escape much more lightly than was the one whose attack failed. After the torpedoes started going off, the confusion was so great that anything could happen. Cdr. H. G. Munson recounts that on the night of 18 August 1944, when *Rasher* got 16 torpedo hits in a convoy in 2½ hours, she underwent one of the most intensive depth-charge attacks of the war. *Rasher* lost count of the number of depth charges when it passed 250. During the whole time *Rasher* was on the surface enjoying the show."

8. According to University of Pittsburgh Historical Staff, "History of United States Naval R&D," SD was conceived in 1940 by Rear Adm. H. G. Bowen, former chief of BuEng (thus well aware of early radar work because his old bureau was responsible for electronics). The omnidirectional antenna was accepted to avoid underwater resistance (in 1941 OpNav hoped that a directional antenna could be developed, but that would have been far too large at SD's 2.63-m wavelength). NRL began work in March 1940, and the production contract went to RCA.

According to the BuShips "Radar Installation Plan" of 11 July 1941 (U.S. Navy Operational Archives, document C-S67/36(485)), the first SD would be available for installation in October 1941, production of 60–135 following at 7 per week. The first SJ was expected in January 1942. At this time all submarines were to be fitted with SD, but only modern ones with SJ. A revised plan dated 30 August 1941 showed 60 SD and 100 SJ. A detailed plan dated 1 February 1942 showed SD in every submarine, supplemented by SJ in *Barracuda* (V-1) and all later submarines. In fact rebuilt "Holland" S-boats were fitted with SJ, sometimes without SD. At this time only *Cuttlefish, Plunger, Pollack, Pompano, Tuna, Gar, Grampus, Grayback*, and *Drum* had operational SD radars. No SJs had been installed.

A BuShips document, "Shipboard Search Radar Program" of April 1945 (in U.S. Navy Operational Archives, Command Files) divides the wartime radar program into three phases: introductory (1940–42), improvement (1943–44), and replacement (1945–47). SD, SD-a, SD-1, SD-2, SD-3, and SJ were produced during the first phase. Improved (second phase) versions were SD-4 and SD-5, SJ-a and SJ-1, and ST. Replacement radars were ST-a and ST-1; SV, SV-a, and SV-1; and SS and SS-1.

According to this report, the first range-only SD was installed late in 1941. It incorporated a diplexer, so that it and the submarine's TBL radio could be used simultaneously. Performance against low-flying aircraft was disappointing due to the radar's low frequency (which brought its lowest lobe well up from the sea surface). The only indicator was an A-scope with one range scale (30 nm). Peak power was 100 kW (8 microsec pulses, repetition rate 60 Hz). Typical ranges were 20 nm for a bomber and 14 nm for a fighter at 10,000 ft, and 5 nm for a destroyer.

Sixty were made; they were field-modified to SD-a by the summer of 1942. This version had a new horizontally- rather than vertically-polarized antenna. SD-1 (20 made) was a version for submarines with fixed rather than retractable antenna masts. Not enough SD's had been made, so a contract for 60 SD-2s (virtually identical to SD-a except for added provision for IFF) was let. The first was installed in the fall of 1942. SD-3 was a small-boat version with a directional antenna (but with the same below-decks electronics). Some of the 125 made were converted back into submarine sets, since better patrol boat radars soon appeared. SD-4 (104 delivered July 1943–July 1944) was similar to SD-2, but with 15 and 60 nm range scales. SD-5 was the final version, with a new indicator (20 and 80 nm scales) and receiver, and with power increased to 130 kW (the last of 86 was completed December 1944). SV was the 750 kW S-band replacement, using SJ-1 indicator components. SVa and SV-1 used SS indicator components.

The first microwave SJ (total of 160 made) was installed in June 1942. The first version was manually-trained, with only an A-scope with main and precision sweeps (10 and 30 nm range scales); a PPI (with automatic scanning) was later added. SJ-1 had a higher-powered transmitter (50 rather than 30 kW): 300 were produced between August 1943 and February 1945. SJa was the equivalent field change to an existing SJ; 170 kits had been produced by April 1944. SS was the X-band replacement. SS-1 incorporated aided-tracking.

ST used a radar transmitter related to that of the contemporary Mk 13 on board battleships. Although in theory it was a range-only radar, in fact its 30 deg beam could measure a bearing to within an accuracy of 3 deg. Production of 254 sets began in July 1944; by 1 March 1945, 139 had been delivered and 95 had been installed. ST initially used the SJ A-scope. ST-1 and ST-a (the equivalent field change) used the radar components of the new SS surface-search radar, a waveguide switch connecting them to either the SS or the ST antenna. These versions could also transmit (and receive) voice signals at radar frequencies, for boat-to-boat semi-secure communication.

9. After the war, the U.S. Navy learned that the Japanese had developed a shipboard radar detector as early as 1942. Most escorts had it by 1944, and at least the surface ship version was directional. Installations on board aircraft did not begin until December 1944. Carrier task forces had first priority, with few going to ASW aircraft. According to the early postwar Pacific Fleet account of Japanese ASW, Japanese aircraft definitely did not home on U.S. submarine radar emissions. However, military historian Dale Ridder found accounts of just such homing in the files of the postwar U.S. Strategic Bombing Survey, now in the NARS military branch (private communication).

10. In May 1945, submariners at Pearl Harbor asked the NRL team there to provide ST with a PPI display so that it could be used as a search radar (its beam was narrower than that of SJ). *Thornback* was so equipped (in Rube Goldberg fashion): the TDC transmitter on the Type 4 periscope powered a selsyn that drove the PPI normally used by the SJ surface-search radar.

11. APR-1 (also designated SPR-1) covered a range of 80–1,000 MHz; it could be supplemented by APR-5AX/SPR-2 (1,000–3,500 MHz, i.e., S-band). The initial antenna was a short stub (APR stub) extending horizontally from the forward periscope shear. It was not particularly directional, and it was intended mainly for early warning while the submarine operated at radar depth. When fully surfaced, it could be used as a search antenna to gather electronic intelligence. By 1945, the stub had been supplemented by more directional dipoles on either side of the submarine. The APR-1 side antenna (DBU, also known as XCV and 66AJO) consisted of four sets of dipoles, two of which (for high [300–1,000 MHz] and low [80–300 MHz] bands) were mounted on a reflector on each side. They were supplemented by a short stub extending horizontally from the forward periscope shear. The APR-5 antennas (DBV) were a pair of dipoles, one on either side of the periscope shear, near the APR-1 stub. Until they became available, submarines received cone antennas in small fairings (AS-44) intended to perform the same early warning function as the APR-1 stub, at a higher frequency. Each APR-1 dipole was connected to an antenna switch, which could connect either both high- or low-frequency antennas, or any one antenna to the APR-1 receiver. Switching back and forth (lobing) gave an approximate idea of target bearing (for greater accuracy, the submarine had to swing). Much the same applied to APR-2. The antennas all fed an SPA-1 pulse analyzer that showed pulse repetition rate and pulse width. An earlier search receiver, ARC-1, was carried by the submarine *Drum* during a patrol off Japan in October 1942.

12. Boats typically had two retractable sound heads in their bottoms, port and starboard, one QB, the other QC back to back with JK in a spherical head. All units fed into the WCA sound stack.

13. TDM was a faster sweep for the QB sound head (Field Change 31 to WCA/WDA). NRL's OL was a short-ping modification (Field Change 6 to WCA-2): the QC stack put a 10-msec pulse through the QB sound head. These QBs were fitted with chemical recorders, and the range was periodically marked as the paper moved down. Such recorders had been invented by the Royal Navy as a surface attack aid (the trend in range showed when depth charges should be dropped). Chemical recorders were the first U.S. visual sonar displays. In OL, a mine appeared as a short dash on the chemical range recorder paper. The sonar pulse had to be short for sufficient range discrimination. OL was first tested on board *Thornback*; in May 1945, it was installed at Pearl Harbor on *Devilfish* and *Kingfish*. The University of California developed the improved SOD (small object detector), inspired by the British harbor defense (Type 135) and small craft (Type 150) Asdics. Formally authorized in June 1944, SOD used a higher-powered 0.5-msec ping. It was tested on board USS *Flying Fish*. Columbia University used much the same principle in its MATD (Field Change 9 to WCA-2, used with TDM and OL). It used a 5-msec ping and a PPI display. The QB head (with a QC driver) slowly sector-scanned through 60 degrees on either side of the bow. In the passive torpedo detector mode, the QB rotated at 12 RPM. A noise (torpedo screws) showed as a dip in a ring on the CRT (cathode-ray tube), the size of the dip being proportional to loudness. In tests on board USS *Redfin*, the torpedo detection feature proved useful in evading escorts.

14. USF 25, *Current Submarine Doctrine* (1944).

15. The first postwar Submarine Officers Conference enthusiastically endorsed triangulation ranging because it avoided any telltale sonar or radar emission. The wartime TLR became XJAA, its two JTs held on target by automatic target followers. Bell Laboratories' XJAB used two rotating-sphere hydrophones, their relative phases displayed on a two-pen recorder. Nulls in the trace indicated the angle between them, XJAC (NRL) worked with the new Mk 31 fire-control computer, which could accept sonar, radar, and optical data. Hydrophone outputs were dis-

played on a sector-scan indicator (CRT). Data were transmitted to the Mk 31 (rather than to the angle solver used by XJAA and XJAB). Mk 31 could also triangulate vertically to compare target elevation angles at different submarine depths (the difference in depth was the baseline; it could allow for refraction effects on the sound path). This technique, not altogether practical in 1945–46, is now common. In September 1945, XJAA was due for tests on board *Quillback* in November 1945. XJAC and Mk 31 were due in March 1946. The Underwater Sound Laboratory installed a tiltable, trainable set of crossed-line hydrophones (of the sort needed for XJAC) on board *Permit*. Preliminary tests showed good performance at short ranges, and suggested that the hydrophones might help a submarine escape surface attack. *Seacat* (SS 399) was fitted with a more elaborate vertical triangulation sonar, XDG, during a 1950 refit at Philadelphia, and redesignated AGSS because the equipment filled her forward torpedo room. Then, the hydrophones collapsed during the trip down to Key West for tests; XDG failed.

16. An FM (frequency modulated) sonar, QLA emitted continuously, varying its frequency from 36 kHz to 48 kHz at a rate set to match the selected range (300 ft or 300–3,000 yd). Both transmitting (broad beam) and receiving heads rotated continuously at an average speed of 4 RPM. The radarlike PPI display could be used to avoid mines and other obstacles. The University of California Division of War Research conceived this "Echoscope" for surface ASW in June 1941; it was tested successfully aboard the ex-destroyer *Semmes* in the fall of 1942. By March 1943, it had a radarlike PPI display, which interested the submarine force. In December 1943, Commander, Submarines, Pacific (ComSubPac) saw the Echoscope system; 1 set was installed on S 34 in March 1944, then transferred to the new *Spadefish* (SS 411) before her completion. Unfortunately, the topside sound head was damaged on patrol. NDRC authorized 5 more sets in May 1944. Tests at San Diego on board *Tinosa* (SS 283, September 1944) were disappointing as a result of local sound conditions. Then *Bowfin* (SS 287) very successfully penetrated a dummy mine field on Penguin Bank, Hawaii. A total of 29 sets were bought. QLA was installed on board *Tunny* (282), *Skate* (305), *Bonefish* (223), *Seahorse* (304), *Crevalle* (291), and *Flying Fish* (229) in rapid succession. In October 1944, 12 more QLAs were ordered. About May 1945, *Runner* (476), *Pogy* (266), *Sennet* (408), *Jallao* (368), *Torsk* (423), and *Piper* (409) were urgently modified at Pearl Harbor specifically for the "special mission" into Japanese waters. Four more submarines were modified on the West Coast: *Stickleback* (415), *Pargo* (264), *Hoe* (258), and *Flasher* (249). Also in May, 25 improved QLA-1s were ordered. After the first mine field penetration data had been analyzed in July 1945, more QLA-1s were ordered, but they were canceled at the end of the war. Most of the 25 earlier sets had been delivered for tests by that time. Production ended because planned postwar sonars were more promising, although SubPac protested that many wartime promises of better equipment had not been kept. Postwar mine-evasion sonars, such as BQS-14 and -15, were based on QLA. Like QHB, Harvard's alternative QKA sent out a short (3–5-msec) omnidirectional ping. Instead of a commutator, QKA used preformed receiving beams; it proved useful as a depth charge locator, with a single ping indicating both range and bearing. The prototype was installed on board *Spadefish* in May 1943 and the first production model on board *Tinosa* in October 1944, but QKA did not enter large-scale service.

17. Mk 3 was converted into Mk 4 by a field change, in which a new receiver section (10 inches wide) was inserted between the two position keepers.

18. Like SS, the stabilized K-band radar (1-degree beam) would be precise enough for gun fire control. There would be an associated periscope radar.

19. BuOrd began the magnetic exploder project, G-53, in 1922 and blew up the obsolete submarine L 8 on 8 May 1926. It has been generally assumed that submarine commanders were unaware of the nature of the highly secret magnetic pistol. That now seems less likely. In connection with optimal salvo size, Lt. Comdr. R. W. Christie (then CO of USS *Narwhal*) wrote on 24 October 1933 that the new BuOrd magnetic pistol (cover-named "Index Mechanism") would negate all side protective systems. It was to be issued with the new Mk XIV torpedoes for *Cachalot* and *Cuttlefish* and could be applied to earlier long torpedoes. A torpedo so equipped could carry more explosive because not all of the charge had to be in its nose. The letter (coded A16-3/SS167, in General Board 420-15 file) is an endorsement of a SubDiv 12 letter on fleet submarine improvements. BuOrd was less unique than it thought. Britain and Germany, at the least, also developed such pistols, also considered them terribly secret, and suffered serious failures. For example, failures of British magnetic pistols apparently saved some Italian ships at Taranto in 1940. U.S. observers reported the failure of British magnetic exploders early in WW II, but BuOrd conducted no tests of its own. The Germans deactivated all their magnetic pistols in 1941 and developed an entirely new active-magnetic device, the ancestor of modern magnetic torpedo pistols. The active exploder creates a magnetic field that is disturbed by the target, whereas the passive exploder relies on the ship's magnetic field and is apparently bedeviled by local changes in the earth's field.

20. In 1945, U.S. submariners claimed far more Japanese tonnage than later analysis showed had been sunk. For many years, the difference was a matter of great contention: CO after CO actually saw explosions, yet ships were not credited to them. J. D. Alden, "ULTRA Revisited," *Submarine Review* 2 (1992), believes the reason is probably a previously unsuspected series of premature explosions. Commander Alden carefully compared submarine patrol reports, which showed the claimed explosions, to Japanese after-action reports intercepted and decoded during WW II by the U.S. Navy. These "ultras" (so named after their classification status) were often the basis for postwar sinking credits.

21. Work began in 1915 with a contract to Sperry Gyroscope Co. for a 7¼-in × 72-in (90-lb without warhead) weapon stabilized by the gyro effect of its motor (3,800 yd at 25 kt). By 1918, no torpedo had been built. The project was taken over by the Navy Experiment Station (and then by the Naval Torpedo Station) at Newport, which designated it Electric Torpedo Mk 1 and Mk 2. By 1941, nothing had come of either project.

22. More than 1,700 Mk 16s were made. The last Mod 6 was withdrawn from service in 1975. Mk 42 was Mk 16 redesigned for pattern running, with a new depth mechanism suited to 60 kt. Expected to reach at least 20,000 yd at 40 kt, it was abandoned in 1952 in favor of further Mk 16 development.

23. Of 106 Mk 27s Mod 0 fired in combat, 33 hit (24 ships sunk and 9 damaged); wartime production was 1,100. Mk 27 swam out because an evading submarine might not fire until after she had passed below maximum pneumatic firing depth. The torpedo had to be narrower than the tube so that water could run around the torpedo to reach its propellers, hence the 19-in diameter of Mk 27 and the postwar Mk 37.

24. Of 16 Mk 28s fired in combat, 5 hit; wartime production was 1,750. Mk 29 was an abortive improved version using a seawater-activated primary battery (12,000 yd at 21 kt or 4,000 yd at 28 kt). It could be set for either straight runs or homing. It was canceled in April 1945. At full speed, its self-

noise was about equal to that of Mk 28 at its full speed of 21 kt; at low speed, it was much quieter than Mk 28. A planned postwar follow-on, Mk 38 (10,000 yd at 35 kt using a primary battery) was postponed, pending development and evaluation of Mk 37, and then canceled in the early 1950s. Mk 33 was a short (156-in, 1,795-lb) passive electric torpedo using a new type of electrohydraulic control system. It was canceled in 1946 after 30 had been made, but some features were fed into the later Mk 35 program.

25. Capt. K. G. Hensel, memorandum to Capt. George M. O'Rear, 12 February 1946 (Submarine Warfare Division files, Operational Archives). In July, Hensel proposed to "try to stir things up, for the next war, on the idea of a jet type or Walter Cycle (Turbine 300-ton U-boat) Torpedo making 100 kts or so." SORG studied the effect of very high torpedo speed (100 kt) on hit probability.

26. Pacific Fleet Submarine Force, "Enemy Anti-Submarine Measures." The author has relied heavily on this report because it is the only available summary of U.S. experience against Japanese ASW.

27. *SubPac Submarine Bulletin* (June 1945): 65, report of recent Tenth Fleet ASW Operations Research Group (ASWORG) report. Noise was measured at 200 ft. The reduction was so drastic that silence could be ruined by something quite trivial, such as careless stowing of gear (e.g., a can of tomatoes) between the hull and a vibration-isolated auxiliary.

28. Data from *Submarine Commands*, vol. 2, and from National Defense Research Committee, volume on *Sonar Countermeasures* (Underwater Sound Equipment VI, Washington, D.C., 1946, declassified 1972). The table at the bottom of this page is from *Pacific Fleet Submarine Bulletin* (June 1945): 60.

NAC frequency band and time delay had to be set before launching; some early duds were ascribed to failure to return the time delay lever to the "operate" position. NAE was designed to protect a diving submarine from a homing torpedo, such as the U.S. Mk 24 (no such Japanese weapon ever appeared). It could also jam sonars and even passive sonic (LF) equipment. FTS was first used in the summer of 1944 (by *Seahorse*). *SubPac Submarine Bulletin*, (March 1945): 65, describes it as ineffective against poor or badly used equipment, but "its deception value increases as the enemy's skill and equipment improve." At this time, the Mk II grenade was still under development.

29. It is widely believed that U.S. submarines were lost because their true test depth was inadvertently given away (in the form of a boast, in the press, that they often survived because depth charges were set too shallow). Pacific Fleet Submarine Force, "Enemy Anti-Submarine Measures," 11–12, states that test depth was the one technical secret the Japanese failed to obtain. The author commented rather bitterly that many prisoners of war believed that all technical information was worth keeping secret and hence endured much unnecessary torture. The author considered that keeping extra effective operating depth

unknown to the Japanese was a great advantage because it was space they did not normally try to search. That was quite aside from the advantage gained from the additional time required for a depth charge to reach a deeper submarine, which therefore had a better chance of evasion. Apparently, U.S. submariners accidentally discovered quite early in the war that they could dive their nominally 300-ft submarines to 400–500 ft when they were driven down by attacks and loss of control. Apparently, the Japanese failed to make much use of the material available to them. For example, they raised USS *Sealion* "but it is doubtful that they learned much from her. . . . They got nothing from submarines sunk in shallow water." The U.S. Navy first discovered the Japanese ASW intelligence failure when it obtained the April 1944 Japanese summary of ASW action between June 1943 and March 1944, put out by their Battle Lessons Investigation Committee. Discussions of U.S. tactics showed obvious errors. For example, in a 9 November 1943 attack on *Akatsuki Maru*, the Japanese believed that they encountered eight torpedoes, four of which hit (they were duds). In fact, USS *Seawolf* fired only four. The Japanese credited U.S. submarines with surface speeds of 24–25 kt (20 kt submerged), estimated that radar was used to fire torpedoes, and stated that curved (gyro-angled) fire was rarely used. On the other hand, except for the Japanese failure to discover U.S. diving depths, the report considered Japan's technical intelligence quite good.

30. It was estimated that the probability of a successful attack was roughly proportional to the turning circle of the submarine, which in turn might be proportional to the length of the submarine (for similarly proportioned hulls and rudders).

31. This could not be derived from actual experience. Instead, numerous runs were made with an attack teacher, in effect, a simulator of an ASW attack.

32. BuShips also produced a graph of the declining value of depth charge barrages with depth because of the increased dead time between the moment of dropping the depth charge into the water and its arrival at the submarine's position, as estimated at the time of dropping. The submarine, of course, would begin to evade as soon as the charge was heard hitting the water. The curve seemed to show a knee at 500 ft. Much depended, however, on the rate at which the charge sank. A typical barrage of slow-sinking (8–9 ft/sec) charges (six Mk 6 and three Mk 7) was credited with a 5.7 percent chance of sinking a submarine at 150 ft, but that figure fell to 1.1 percent at 400 ft and 0.3 percent at 600 ft. The new Mk 9 teardrop (22.7 ft/sec) had a proximity fuze in some versions to make up for errors in estimating submarine depth. On the other hand, it carried much less explosive, so these figures did not imply that its performance against a submarine 1,000 ft down was equivalent to that of a Mk 7 at 400 ft.

33. Schemes are described on calculation sheets retained by the new submarine design section of NAVSEA. The first postwar projects were a continuation of this series. Data on missing

	NAC	NAE	Mk II Grenade	FTS
Frequencies (kHz)	15–19 17.5–22.5 21.5–27.5	4–40	2 and below	——
Maximum ejection depth (ft)	400	150	1,000	350
Delay to start	0,3,5,7,10 min	None	30 sec	27 sec
Duration (min)	10–15	5–8	6	At least 4
Operating depth (ft)	50	40	Descends 1 ft/min	Launch point
Counters	Sonar	Acoustic weapon	LF passive	Sonar

scheme numbers are either very limited (e.g., length and pressure hull diameter only) or missing. Data presented later are from General Board files on the 1945 submarine and represent specific schemes.

34. U.S. forces captured a U-boat snorkel at Toulon in southern France in the fall of 1944, and Portsmouth was assigned development of a U.S. snorkel incorporating its upper part (carrying the crucial valve that closed the tube when a wave broke over it). Drawings existed by January 1945. In March 1945, the old submarine R-6 was assigned to Portsmouth to test the snorkel. The yard planned to begin with dockside tests to determine the effect of negative pressure on the ship. The diesel would exhaust through a pipe led 4 ft below the waterline to simulate a standard snorkel installation. The first reference in the boat's deck log to running underway on the snorkel is for 7 June 1945 (runs between 0832 and 0849 and between 0857 and 0913). This may have been her first day at sea after the refit. The log also shows runs on 19, 21, and 25 June, and on 5 and 6 July. R-6 was sent to Port Everglades in August 1945; her log shows her snorkeling on 11 September. On 7 August, OpNav approved a similar simulated snorkel to be installed on the fleet submarine *Sirago* upon completion and before she went to sea. That seems not to have been done (*Sirago* was completed just as Japan surrendered); Portsmouth did most of its snorkel work on a unit mounted on a water tower. The crucial difference between R 6 and *Sirago* was that the former, like German U-boats, had a 4-cycle engine that drew less air than the 2-cycle diesels of the fleet boats. The Germans thought it impossible to develop a snorkel for a 2-cycle diesel.

35. A contemporary BuOrd study showed three alternatives for 24-in torpedoes:

Weight (lb)	10,000	7,000	5,000
Length (ft-in)	37-2	30-0	standard length (21 in)
Range (yd) at speed (kt)	24,000/45 15,000/60	20,000/45 10,000/60	6,000/45
Warhead (lb)	3,000	2,500	2,000

BuOrd argued that existing 21-inch torpedoes were sufficiently lethal; it was better to have greater numbers of torpedoes. Greater range and higher speed did not require larger caliber.

36. The Canadian report is in the Submarine Warfare Division files in the Operational Archives. The author used it because it was so much more detailed than the U-858 report.

37. During the fall of 1944 (e.g., October 1944 in the case of U-1228), snorkel U-boats were coated with material effective at X-band and not bad at S-band. U-boat crews believed that coated snorkels could not be detected; they stopped using their intercept receivers to detect approaching bombers with S- and X-band radar. From a 12 June 1945 report by members of the MIT Radiation Laboratory and the Harvard Radio Laboratory, describing a visit to the four U-boats (including U-805 and U-1228) then at Portsmouth. The 95 percent reduction in reflectivity should have reduced target range by something over half (range is proportional to the fourth root of target strength). Canadian tests of U-889 showed shipboard radar range reduced by about one-third. Air radars at low altitude sometimes actually did better against the coated snorkel. An ASV Mk VA S-band radar detected the coated snorkel at 7.5 nm, the uncoated one at 2.5 nm.

38. The Canadians concluded that German claims of U-boats snorkeling in all weather were less than credible. They found it surprising that transiting U-boats did not use their snorkels more instead of running on their batteries. British-trained crews liked snorkeling because they instinctively associated the sound of

engines (rather than motors) with running on the surface. They could also smoke while snorkeling. On the other hand, the planesmen had to maintain depth much more precisely, and the engine room had to be able to shut down promptly in case of an inadvertent dip.

39. These notes are based on the submarine report of the U.S. Naval Technical Mission to Japan (report S-01-1, January 1946) and on the massive compilation of material on Japanese naval development written by Dr. E. Lacroix in *The Belgian Shiplover* (particularly Number 1/72 pp 16, 21–22, 24–28; 2/72 pp 133–134, 142; 3/72 pp 227–229; 1/73 pp 29–30; 3/73, pp 115–116, 244, 247; 4/73 pp 333–334; 1/74 pp 28–29, 32, 33; 3/74 pp 212–214, 220; 2/75 pp 26–27, 32, 38/9). The Naval Technical Mission described the hydrodynamic work on the I-201 class; the comparison is to German work described in the corresponding reports of the U.S. Naval Technical Mission to Europe (the Japanese seemed far more aware of problems of underwater instability). Note that because they had built some very fast midget submarines prewar, the Japanese were probably uniquely aware of the problems entailed in high-speed underwater runs. Their submarines were never placed into service by the U.S. Navy because it was impossible to replace their awkwardly-placed car-type batteries.

Appendix A

1. Max Rotter, chief engineer of Busch-Sulzer, "The Diesel Engine in America" (paper delivered at 1915 San Francisco International Engineering Congress); reprint, *ASNE Journal*, (1915): 1010–1019. Carnot seems to have been the first to represent a heat engine by a cycle corresponding to a closed curve on a pressure-volume diagram. The area of the curve gives the work the engine extracts from the heat fed into it. In Carnot's ideal cycle, heat is added and extracted only at constant temperature; otherwise the working fluid expands or contracts without losing or gaining heat. Diesel learned of Carnot's theory at an 1878 lecture given by Carl von Linde; Diesel soon began selling von Linde's ammonia ice-making machines (in effect, reversed heat engines). They were made by Sulzer Brothers of Winterthur, Switzerland, later an important diesel engine builder. At first, Diesel took Carnot too literally. He sought a long slow burn (to maintain constant temperature for the first 10 percent of the stroke). To avoid losing heat during the rest of the power stroke, he did not cool his cylinder. The piston stuck, destroying the prototype engine after only a few revolutions. Diesel's backers were so impressed by his clear understanding of the physics of high efficiency that they kept financing him. Workable diesels burn their fuel (i.e., heat the working fluid) at constant pressure rather than constant temperature. Dr. Diesel calculated that for maximum output per cylinder, an engine using air as its working fluid had to operate at 30–40 atmospheres (up to 590 psi) and 500–600°C, which implied a combustion temperature of 1,600–1,800°C, far beyond the ignition temperature of any likely fuel. To avoid premature ignition, fuel could not be introduced until compression was complete. Thus compression-ignition, which is usually considered the basis of Diesel operation, was only a byproduct of Diesel's idea.

2. D. Clerk, *The Gas, Petrol, and Oil Engine* (London and New York: Longmans, Green, 1910). The modern idea of compression followed by constant-volume ignition (i.e., all the air is introduced, mixed with fuel, and then the mixture is ignited together) was first suggested by Barrett in 1838. A practical cycle of this type was described in 1862 by Beau de Rochas and implemented by Dr. N. A. Otto (who had been working on this concept since 1855) in 1876. Otto displayed his first "Silent Engine" at the 1878 Paris Exposition. This heavy engine used an open flame to ignite

its fuel-air mixture. Carl Daimler produced the first lightweight high-speed gasoline engine (using a surface carburetor and open-tube ignition) in 1883. The Otto cycle was also adapted to heavy oil fuel, using a spray vaporizer and a spark plug (probably first by Priestman in England about 1885). None of the prototype engines was particularly powerful, so steam remained the only possible submarine surface power plant until the very end of the 19th century. The Brayton engine that Holland originally used was a relatively successful example of an earlier class of engine in which compressed air ignited at constant pressure.

3. E. C. Magdeburger, "Diesel Engines in Submarines," *ASNE Journal*, 1925; 572, a U.S. Navy diesel expert, claims that the U.S. Navy had been unique in building successful gasoline-engined submarines (presumably the C and D classes), "despite the dangers from explosions and the so-called gasoline-jags."

4. Although Electric Boat files include an Otto Co. design for a 250 BHP (350-RPM) engine (dated August 1901), Electric Boat clearly developed and built (at Fore River) the 250 BHP B- and C-class engine. Board on Construction files describe an April 1906 demonstration of an Electric Boat engine similar to those being built at Fore River for *Octopus* (C-1) and the B-boats. When the *Octopus* trials board criticized it in 1907, L. Y. Spear stated that the engine had been developed by Electric Boat because no compact yet reliable 250 BHP gasoline engine yet existed, either in the United States or abroad. The company's trials of an engine made by the Standard Motor Co. of Jersey City had been unsuccessful. This type of engine was also used in Electric Boat's Austrian submarines.

Spear suspected that critics familiar with the existing, relatively quiet, 140 HP engines did not understand how great the step to 250 HP had been. To gain reliability, Electric Boat concentrated on dissipating the engine's heat, using double inlet and double exhaust valves in each cylinder head, plus a third exhaust valve at the bottom of the stroke. Multiple valves, especially with their mechanism exposed for easy access, were noisy, but they were much more likely to remain tight than quieter single large valves. On the basis of numerous trials in the United States and abroad, Spear doubted that a reliable yet quiet engine of the required power could be produced.

Craig became well known as the designer of a gasoline engine that won the Bermuda race in 1908. The extra exhaust valve at the bottom of the stroke was his trademark. Presumably he designed the 250 BHP engine while working for Electric Boat.

The three series of NELSECO 250 BHP gasoline engines were not quite identical. The B-class engine had 11 in diameter cylinders (12 in stroke) and ran at 450 RPM. Each cylinder had 4 valves (2 inlet, 2 exhaust) in its head, plus the auxiliary exhaust valve, the port to which was controlled by the piston (the valve was operate by a lever and cam on the main shaft). The C-class engine had similar cylinders, but ran at 500 RPM. It had a lower exhaust header for each 3 (of 6) cylinders, a single upper header for all six. D-class cylinders were bored out to 12 in diameter and had single inlet and double exhaust valves in their heads. None of these engines was reversible. Data from individual submarine operating manuals in Box 210, C&R Confidential files, NARS RG 19.

BuEng considered the Electric Boat engine no noisier than others of similar power, but it disliked its inability to reverse and its clutch coupling. When the *Octopus* trials board asked that the engines be made reversible, Spear argued that expensive and time-consuming redesign and new trials would be needed; better to use the motors to reverse.

By 1908, the Board on Construction was examining numerous complaints about these engines; Lt. C. E. Courtney, the flotilla commander, went so far as to declare the engines unsuitable for naval use, hence, in effect, unusable in the new FY 08 submarines (SS 13–19: repeat C-boats and D-boats). *Tarantula* had given the least trouble, *Cuttlefish* the most. However, *Tarantula* had a cracked cylinder after a run from New York to Annapolis and therefore did not try an endurance run. Arriving at Annapolis on 5 March 1908, *Viper* broke down after 16 hr of a 24-hr endurance run because of a hot wrist pin in No. 6 cylinder. *Cuttlefish* had to stop after about 6 hr as a result of considerable damage. Water got in through the exhaust (Electric Boat fitted an extra valve) and circulating (cooling) water passed into the cylinder via a gasket under the cylinder head. Courtney wanted to water-cool the pistons, but Electric Boat objected that the pistons of the new engines were smaller than those of the *Adder*s, which successfully ran full-power trials after 3 years. Heating did limit the diameter of any non–water cooled piston to about 12 in. Courtney also found the valves noisy and poorly arranged (just over the combustion chamber, they felt the full force of each firing; any valve that broke fell right into the cylinder and wrecked it). Electric Boat argued that it had done its best under very difficult and especially cramped conditions. Exhaust pipes had carried away; Electric Boat pointed out that they were not water-jacketed (which would have solved the problem) because originally it had been planned to use them to heat the boats. Overall, the board tended to support Electric Boat. Officers often did not realize that they had been overloading their engines. For example, the day after *Cuttlefish* broke down, she ran easily at 9 kt (which the officers considered low speed); but her contract speed was 8.75 kt. Trials of the Austrian engine were "rather favorable" to Electric Boat. They were much improved in details, such as special lubrication for the wrist-pins and cooling water that was kept farther from the cylinder bore. The board thought they would give good results at 250 BHP (500 RPM; the *Viper* engine was designed for 450 RPM). The *Adder*s had adjustable-pitch propellers so that they could run at higher RPM and the board doubted that higher RPM would cure *Cuttlefish*. It thought valves were the main issue. As an alternative, it wanted the single-acting Standard engine of the Portsmouth Ferry tested for endurance and maneuvering. This engine, however, was not adopted.

5. Figures given by A. P. Chalkley, "Submarine Engines," in *ASNE Journal*, 1915, 471–477, reproduced from *Cassier's Engineering Monthly*. Presumably, the much heavier weights commonly quoted for U.S. engines include auxiliaries.

6. This litany of problems is taken from E. C. Magdeburger, "Diesel Engines in the United States Navy," *ASNE Journal*, April 1949, 45–93.

7. There is no evidence of U.S. understanding of torsional vibration before 1914.

8. J. F. Kirkland, *Dawn of the Diesel Age: The History of the Diesel Locomotive in America* (Glendale: Interurban Publications, 1983), gives details of Diesel's early work.

9. The French encountered problems with diesels, so several of their submarines, including their numerous *Pluviose*-class submarines (launched 1907–10) reverted to triple-expansion steam.

10. In 1903, the British decided to install Hornsby-Ackroyd engines in *A 13*. These engines, patented in 1888, were not quite diesels. Rather, they were heavy-oil versions of the Otto (gasoline) engine, using a hot bulb or rod to gasify oil and then to ignite the gas-air mixture. The rod or bulb was heated by blow lamp before the engine started; once running, the engine kept it hot enough. Because the gas-air mixture was present throughout much or all of the compression stroke, these engines had to be designed to avoid pre-ignition by excessive compression (hence

heating) of the gas-air mixture. As a consequence, they had to run at low compression ratios, which reduced power production per cylinder by about 20–30 percent, compared to a gasoline engine. Even then they suffered because they could not maintain the sort of precise temperature control which, in theory, they required. By way of contrast, a diesel injects its fuel only *after* the air has been heated in the cylinder, hence it needs not limit compression to avoid pre-ignition.

The Germans used the somewhat similar 2-cycle Korting engine for their first U-boats. To start, it was turned over for about 10 min by the main motor, its intake air being heated electrically. Neither engine had any U.S. naval equivalent.

The British soon adopted Vickers diesels, which proved successful. Wartime U.S. observers thought these engines quite similar to (though larger than) the contemporary NELSECOs. Some thought that Vickers' success showed that NELSECO's problems were very curable. The standard Vickers used a 4-cycle, 14.5-in × 15-in cylinder and developed about 100 BHP per cylinder at 380 RPM. According to Lambert (private communication), British documents show that its heavy (and expensive) construction was a deliberate, and reasonably successful, counter to torsional vibration (which was not well understood at the time). A British World War I observer, Stanley Goodall (later Director of Naval Construction), found AA-1's engine foundations noticeably lighter than those in British submarines. After inspecting the submarine's tandem engines, he wrote that he much preferred the steam turbines of British K-boats.

At the outbreak of war, Vickers engines were much disliked because of compressor failures. Vickers therefore developed a solid injector, which required very light oil. To U.S. observers, the engine's smoky exhaust demonstrated its inefficiency. These engines used their oil fuel for lubrication: 10 percent of fuel as of February 1912; probably 5 percent later. By 1918, the British used a maximum cylinder pressure (over 600 lb) about 100 lb more than in the U.S. Navy. U.S. officers attachéd to the British submarine force reported that engines required considerable maintenance (e.g., overhauls after the usual 50 hr of diesel operation during a 7-day patrol consumed much of the 5 days in port between patrols; a gang of seven men on the depot ship continually overhauled valves to keep them tight under the high pressure used to inject the fuel. Had MAN engines not become available, the postwar U.S. Navy probably would have tried to copy some features of the Vickers engines.

11. E. Roessler, *The U-Boat* (London: Arms and Armour Press, 1981), provides details of German diesel development. MAN was apparently permitted only to export diesels (and designs) derived from its unsuccessful 2-cycle series; at least through 1915, the German Navy apparently kept MAN's 4-cycle diesels secret. The U.S. engines were recognizably MAN's, rather than Krupp's. Krupp used more valves in the cylinder head (three) and drove its scavenging pumps from the ends of the crankshaft; MAN used each piston to drive its own scavenging pump (part of the same casting).

12. The upper of two sets of ports, controlled by a valve, supplied extra air for the next cycle after scavenging air from the lower port had blown out most of the burnt gas. Objections were that exhaust temperatures were too high for the cylinder wall and that scavenging would be inefficient because the scavenging ports opened after the exhaust ports, then reclosed after the exhaust ports closed.

13. A typical 1915 Polar submarine engine produced 350 BHP at 500 RPM, using six 290-mm × 300-mm cylinders. Unlike most of its contemporaries, it was directly reversible, the exhaust and inlet valves being interchanged (the camshaft was moved lengthwise).

14. Magdeburger "Diesel Engines in the United States Navy," 54. Magdeburger began at MAN's Russian licensee (probably Nobel Diesel in St. Petersburg), emigrated to the United States in 1910, and joined Busch-Sulzer in 1912; when he went to BuEng in 1922, he became its senior diesel expert. His 1949 article commemorated the landing of the first Diesel engine in the United States (1898). In December 1908, Electric Boat said that its engine was definitely beyond the experimental stage. It had been operating a 500-BHP, 380-RPM (13-in × 14.5-in, 118 lb average mean pressure) engine for about a year, including 7 mo of tests. It later built two 600-BHP engines lighter than the prototype (as a result of different framing). Each of these engines was far more powerful than the unit that Electric Boat proposed to install in U.S. submarines.

15. Details from an undated and unsigned mimeographed *History of the Electric Boat Co., 1899–1949*, probably written for Electric Boat, in the Navy Department Library. Engine designations are from NELSECO, *Reference List of Engines Built and Building*, corrected to 1934 and to 1940, provided by the Submarine Base Museum and Library. The list omits the 50-BHP engines of Electric Boat's three Russian midget submarines; presumably, it did not make these units.

16. Magdeburger, "Diesel Engines in Submarines," 581–582. Air compressor valves broke and dropped into the compressor cylinders; water-cooled exhaust valves often cracked; water-cooled main bearings (abandoned in later engines) leaked and salted up the lubricating oil; cylinder studs between the separate cylinders snapped (nuts from some cylinders rested on the next in line). Compactness and light construction were the real culprits.

17. McIntosh & Seymour was a U.S. company specializing in pipeline-pumping, stationary, and marine engines. It supplied engines to ALCO (the locomotive maker) after that company split with General Electric.

18. Magdeburger, "Diesel Engines in Submarines," 605. Built by James Craig E&M Works of Jersey City, this 4-cycle engine had a valve-controlled auxiliary exhaust port at the bottom of its cylinder. That was also a feature of Craig's early U.S. submarine gasoline engines. This type was not developed further.

19. Electric Boat probably bought the German rights to avoid patent trouble. In 1909 (see chapter 5), Spear spoke of "heavy oil" engines rather than Diesels (to avoid mentioning what amounted to a trade mark, such as Xerox, which would have entailed separate payments). Presumably, the Vickers design was too heavy; attempts to save weight might explain the problems with the E- and F-boats. In 1897, Busch bought sole rights to all of Diesel's existing and future U.S. patents. They would not have expired by 1908.

20. Although they had the same designation as the earlier engines, diesels in the L class differed in detail, such as having two scavenging valves (rather than one) in the cylinder head. After diving, their exhaust valves let salt water into the cylinders, past the piston rings, and into the crankcase, which occasionally resulted in breaking a cylinder casting.

21. The outbreak of war in 1914 cut NELSECO off from MAN. This engine was NELSECO's attempted redesign. Magdeburger, "Diesel Engines in Submarines," 590, describes it as extremely heavy. Service problems included cracks in the outside of the water jackets and excessive oil leaks into the bilges. Both seem attributable to vibration. M-1 was presumably tighter internally than earlier single-hull boats. According to Magdeburger, the engines were successful in wartime, but the postwar crew of M-1 could not make them work properly and they were soon scrapped.

22. Magdeburger, "Diesel Engines in the United States Navy," 61, claims that this engine was doubled up from the existing

NELSECO 4-cylinder, 120-BHP (9-in × 12.5-in) commercial engine to meet a dire need for a reliable submarine engine.

23. Lambert (private communication).

24. Magdeburger, "Diesel Engines in the United States Navy," 65, reports that BuEng preferred 4-cycle engines because these units had succeeded, and because the Germans had used only 4-cycle engines in wartime.

25. A design for Spain might have been the prototype. The first engines for the Spanish B class had lower serial numbers than 8-EB-15s for the U.S. S class, but they were delivered later. The Electric Boat list does not show the engines originally built for S-1, the prototype. Engines delivered for S-1 in 1921 (600 BHP, 340 RPM) are numbers 525 and 526, much later than any in the S-class series except S-47 (1925, numbers 562 and 563).

26. Magdeburger, "Diesel Engines in the United States Navy," 68; and "Diesel Engines in Submarines," 601–602. The two alternative solutions were NELSECO's 8-in crankshaft replacing the original 7-in shaft (which displaced the critical speed from the full power speed at which it was originally located, leaving only 5½ and 6½-order minors in the upper range of speeds) and New York Navy Yard's friction damper. Although the latter worked well in shop tests, it did not stand up in service. The problem was first encountered in the NELSECO-designed (but Navy Yard built) engines of the S-3; the S-1 engines broke up during final trials. Fortunately there was sufficient room in the "Holland" S-boats to install the new crankshafts. Eventually it was possible to reduce even the minor criticals by changing the camshaft to get a better firing order of the cylinders. S-3 was a more difficult proposition, since in her case there was insufficient space for the heavier crankshaft. These engines therefore had to be operated at reduced RPM. That was one reason why S-3 through S-9 were among the first S-boats to be discarded. It also explains the decision to complete S-10 through S-13 with Navy-built MAN engines. Later S-14 through S-17 were rebuilt with similar engines, although apparently their original 4-cycle Busch-Sulzers were quite satisfactory. The 2-cycle Busch-Sulzers on S-48 through S-51 initially gave excellent service, but after a time torsional vibration broke three crank shafts in close succession; the critical speed turned out to be 310 RPM, a favorite battery-charging speed. Both elastic couplings and heavier crankshafts were tried. In the summer of 1923 S-50 was fitted with an experimental elastic damping engine coupling intended to lower the critical frequency below the usual operating range. Friction vibration dampers at the free end of the crankshaft did not stand up to the severe fourth-order critical at the engine's rated RPM. The heavier crankshaft seems to have been accepted in the fall of 1923. It was first applied to S-51, then to S-48 through -50. Fortunately there was sufficient space.

27. According to Magdeburger, "Diesel Engines in Submarines," 593, these Swiss-built engines proved too large for the hull; they were relatively inaccessible. Water and oil pump drives were too light, it was difficult to lubricate the air compressor drives, and the fuel pumps were poorly located at the operators' feet. The smaller American-built Busch-Sulzers were considerably modified, both on the basis of experience with G-3 and with stationary diesels in the United States. The later 600-BHP version encountered trouble, mainly because of a weak pump drive and inefficient oil coolers.

28. Kirkland, *Dawn of the Diesel Age*, reports that Busch decided to make diesels because the Prussian State Railways contracted with Sulzer for a diesel locomotive in 1906. Locomotive engines powered later U.S. diesel submarines. Busch-Sulzer's only locomotive engine was a 10-cylinder, 2-cycle unit for a GE engine on the Illinois Central (1935: 14 in × 16 in, hence presumably far too heavy for U.S. submarines).

29. Magdeburger, "Diesel Engines in the United States Navy," 69–70, reports that the intricate thin-walled castings in the MAN engines were difficult to copy; they were made mainly by the Naval Gun Factory (Washington Navy Yard). Engines were assembled at the New York Navy Yard. Overall design was simple, with cast steel bedplates and cylinder housings. These engines reversed reliably on air. France also copied the wartime MAN engines. Japan not only bought them but also hired German experts (in what the U.S. Navy considered a violation of the Versailles Treaty). C&R rejected Krupp's 1921 offer to sell complete U-boat plans, on the ground that it did not want numerous German submarine experts in its own design offices.

30. Ibid., 70.

31. Ibid., 68. Magdeburger cites F. M. Lewis, "Torsional Vibration of Irregular Shafts," *ASNE Journal*, 1919, as the first U.S. Navy attempt to calculate critical speeds. More elaborate analyses of the torsional problem were published in the mid-1920s: F. M. Lewis, "Torsional Vibrations in the Diesel Engine," *Transactions of the Society of Naval Architects and Marine Engineers*, 1925; and Porter, "The Range and Severity of Torsional Vibrations in Diesel Engines," *Transactions of the American Society of Mechanical Engineers*, ASME-APM 50-8, 1928. The references are quoted by J. S. Leonard in a comment on the Weir paper (see note 33), *Naval Engineers Journal*, July 1989, 145. Apparently, BuEng was extremely fortunate that its arbitrary demand for a larger-diameter crankshaft in the S class solved the vibration problem sufficiently well for the S-boats to operate successfully. As late as 1943, the navy asked the Society of Automotive Engineers to form a committee on torsional vibration.

32. Alternatives to electric drive considered at this time were pneumatic drive, hydraulic drive, fluid drive (a hydraulic clutch, as in an automobile), and combined fluid and electric drive. The first two were considered too complicated and too inefficient. Fluid coupling completely isolated the propeller shaft from the pulsing torque of the engine, smoothing it out, but it did not solve the critical speed problem. With reduction gearing, propeller shaft RPM had to be in some definite ratio to engine RPM: to cover a wide speed range, the engine also had to operate over a wide range of speeds. A fast-running, lightweight engine had to be geared down to turn a low-RPM propeller.

33. G. F. Weir, "The Navy, Industry, and Diesel Propulsion for American Submarines 1914–1940," *Naval Engineers Journal*, May 1989, 207–219. The four S-boats, newly re-engined with MAN diesels, were used. February 1928 trials with S-14 showed that such operation strained the motor. All four boats were then sent to Coco Solo for hot-weather trials. They also overheated, but the Board of Inspection and Survey solved the problem by closing off the engine room and drawing ventilation air through the motor room.

34. In 1933, Electric Boat produced an experimental diesel generator engine, 16VM1, for S-20. The special engine was removed in December 1939. Data on BuEng 1929 alternatives are from memoranda presented by the bureau to the General Board, in connection with the V-7 design, in the 1929 General Board *Hearings*.

35. The board thought that contemporary Italian (*Balilla* class) and Brazilian (*Humaita* class) submarines were much faster than the U.S. V-7, then being designed to about the same displacement. C&R stated in September that the two engines of the Italian submarines, originally rated at 3,000 BHP for 19 kt, had been derated to 2,200–2,300 BHP because of torsional vibration. The Brazilian submarine, somewhat smaller than her U.S. contemporary (about 1,400 tons standard) had two 2,300–2,400-BHP engines; her engines would drive a V-7 hull of her displacement at 18 kt (reportedly *Humaita* made 18.07 kt on reduced power).

U.S. submarines could have been made faster by lengthening the nonwatertight ends at a cost in maneuverability; C&R wanted submarines as short as possible. Gardiner, *Conway's All the World's Fighting Ships,* credits *Balilla* with 4,900-BHP diesels (17.5 kt). *Humaita* apparently reached 18.5 kt on trials.

36. As of September 1930, the three series were:

Cylinders	Bureau (BHP/RPM)	MVu (BHP/RPM)	WV (BHP/RPM)
6	1,200/450	1,050/480	——
8	1,750/380	1,400/480	600/700
10	2,000/380	1,750/480	1,000/700

The license-built M9Vu 40/46 powered the *Cachalot*s.

37. The license agreement was signed on 25 February 1931. Electric Boat had to sign a separate agreement for the diesels it built for *Cuttlefish.* $500,000 in production funds was included in the FY 32 budget allocation of $3.5 million for submarine diesels. Budget figures are from Weir, "Navy, Industry, and Diesel Propulsion."

38. Robinson's goals are listed by Alden, *Fleet Submarine in the U.S. Navy,* 43. According to Magdeburger, "Diesel Engines in the United States Navy," Robinson thought that the navy could exploit engineering talent idled by the depression to produce a new standard range of lightweight, high-speed diesels, to be made at low cost on production lines. See also J. D. Alden, "High-Speed Diesel Engine Development in the U.S. Navy," *Naval Engineers Journal,* August 1979, 43–49. The decision not to depend on MAN proved fortunate. The FY 35 report of the C-in-C U.S. Fleet describes *Cuttlefish* and *Cachalot* as unsatisfactory due both to their overall engine installation and to their wide bands of critical speeds. Two years later (FY 37), these boats were still described as very unsatisfactory, and the big *Narwhal* and *Nautilus* were encountering vibration problems. Their batteries were also aging badly.

39. H. G. Bowen, *Men, Machinery, and Mossbacks* (Princeton, N.J.: Princeton University Press, 1954). This looks like hindsight. BeEng had been happy to buy the MAN engine for the *Cachalot*s, and the HOR diesel was a MAN design. Admiral Bowen, Robinson's successor (1935), emphasizes the need to escape foreign dominance in machinery, particularly in his dealings with turbine makers.

40. Comdr. Holbrook Gibson, "U.S. Navy Diesel-Engine Requirements," *Mechanical Engineering* 53, no. 12 (1931): 875, states: "The requirements of [diesel locomotives] approach very closely those of a diesel engine for the submarine service. It is well known that this application . . . is progressing steadily and surely, and that great strides are being made in the development of the locomotive type of engine." Note the contrast with Admiral Yarnell's 1929 pessimism. With the exception of 1927–29, Gibson had been responsible for BuEng submarine machinery design since 1924. He had been Sims's submarine chief of staff at the end of WW I and had then commanded a captured U-boat. Kirkland, *Dawn of the Diesel Age,* reports that considerable work already had been done by ALCO in combination with Ingersoll-Rand (IR), Baldwin, General Electric, and Westinghouse. ALCO-IR dominated the pre-depression market; it sold 96 engines in 1925–29, but only 7 were shipped in 1931 and none in 1932. By 1936, the railroads were ready to invest in new engines, but Baldwin, GE, and Westinghouse had all withdrawn (Baldwin produced steam engines, so it could afford to wait for the diesel market to develop). GM (Electro-Motive Corp, EMC) dominated the market because, unlike Baldwin, it concentrated on diesels.

ALCO remained in the market, but its engines were much heavier than GM's. Companies other than GM sold a total of 190 diesel-electric locomotives in 1925–36.

41. The time was ripe because railroads were desperate to stimulate passenger travel. According to Kirkland, *Dawn of the Diesel Age,* both Burlington and the Union Pacific conceived high-speed articulated diesel trains powered by the new 20-lb/BHP engine and ordered them from, respectively, Budd Car and Pullman. The Pullman train was completed first, but Winton could not supply its new engine in time, so it was powered by a light-oil 191A (vee-12, 600 BHP at 1,200 RPM, 7.5 in × 8.5 in). Burlington's Pioneer Zephyr got the first 201A (8-cylinder in-line, 600 BHP at 750 RPM). Also, according to Kirkland, Kettering later claimed that he began working on a 2-cycle engine in 1928; by 1930, he was sure that it could work. GM apparently realized in 1929 that potential sales of diesel locomotives could support a production line. Kettering had General Motors buy two Cleveland companies: Winton (20 June 1930) and the Electro-Motive Co., which actually built the locomotives (31 December 1930). He had bought a Winton diesel for his yacht a few years earlier. The Century of Progress engine powered a Chevrolet production line. Kettering's biographer, S. W. Leslie, dates his key confidential meeting with Capt. H. G. Bowen, then assistant head of BuEng, to March 1933, but March *1932* is likelier. Bowen requested the meeting and promised Kettering a $500,000 study contract, according to Leslie, *Boss Kettering* (New York: Columbia University Press, 1983), 265. Kirkland, *Dawn of the Diesel Age,* does not mention the GM naval connection at all in his history of early U.S. railroad diesels, although he does mention some naval applications of other engines.

42. A scaled-up version was designed and a prototype built, tested, and type-approved but not manufactured: 1,700 BHP (supercharged) at 850 RPM; cylinders, 9 in × 12 in, 17.8 lb/BHP (compared with 11.2 lb/BHP in the prototype). Data are from J. S. Leonard, comment on Weir, "Navy, Industry, and Diesel Propulsion for American Submarines" (see note 33), *Naval Engineers Journal,* July 1989, 145. Leonard was formerly chief marine engineer at Electric Boat. The charge of low priority (because other business was more profitable) is in E. C. Magdeburger, "U.S. Navy Participation in Diesel-Engine Development," a paper presented at the Tenth National Oil and Gas Power Meeting of the American Society of Mechanical Engineers, 18–21 August 1937; reprinted in *Mechanical Engineering,* September 1937, 1.

43. Laskar Wechsler, who began work in the engine branch of BuEng in 1940, recalled in a comment on Weir, "Navy, Industry, and Diesel Propulsion for American Submarines" (see note 33), *Naval Engineers Journal,* July 1989, 146, that HOR engines in early fleet boats (SS 172–181 group) were so unreliable that they often left Pearl Harbor on four engines but arrived at Cavite on only one, having cannibalized the others for parts. Despite much unhappiness with these engines, a second (9-cylinder, rather than 8-cylinder) and then a final generation of HORs were ordered for 12 *Gato*-class submarines. The first, *Gunnel,* broke down completely in the Atlantic on her first patrol; her blower drive gear cracked, and it could not be repaired at sea (Alden, "High-Speed Diesel Engine Development," comments that the problem was due to improperly treated steel, and that other HOR boats did not experience unusually high rates of failure). All the HOR engines were replaced, in *Pompano* by GM 16-278As and in the others by FM engines. Some older boats were not re-engined until 1944. Historical Section, Submarine Commands, "Submarine Commands," draft historical narrative (classified Secret), submitted to Director of Naval History, 14 February 1946 (now declassified), notes that the HOR engines first suffered from

broken connecting rods, then blow-by in the stuffing glands that closed the combustion chamber below the piston, but that their worst problem was timing gear breakage resulting from lack of proper support (in turn caused by limited engine room space). According to Alden, "High-Speed Diesel Development," Magdeburger personally supported the HOR, and Admiral Robinson might have intervened personally in its favor when he returned to head BuEng (and then BuShips) in 1939. Alden suspects that crews disliked some of the engine's unfamiliar German features and its metric (rather than Imperial, e.g., inch) dimensions; it was also reportedly difficult to maintain.

44. For much of the material on battery construction and operation, the author is indebted to Jim Christley, who was a submarine electrician on Guppies and fleet snorkel submarines, and who taught the submarine storage battery course at Naval Submarine School for 3 years.

45. M. F. Hay, *Secrets of the Submarine* (New York: Dodd, Mead, & Co., 1917), 45–53. WW I batteries did far worse. According to Hay, who designed the Hay-Whitehead and Denny-Hay submarines for Denmark and the Netherlands, a typical specific gravity was 1.215, and a typical output per cell was 2 volts. An exhausted battery would produce 1.7 volts. Although Hay's book was clearly intended for a popular audience, his design experience lends it great credibility. Its preface was signed by Adm. H. T. Mayo, CinC, U.S. Fleet.

46. Ibid., 129. Hay gives an example, presumably typical of WW I U.S. practice. He estimates capacity at the 1-hr rate as 69 percent of capacity at the 3-hr rate; at the 5-hr rate, it rises to 111 percent, at the 10-hr rate to 127 percent, and at the 20-hr rate to 139 percent.

47. Ibid., 47. Hay estimates the life of a pasted-cell battery at 300 complete cycles, compared with 500–600 for a Planté. The modern battery described below would be good for about 500 cycles. Contemporary U.S. BuEng reports suggest that Hay considerably overestimated typical battery lifetime.

48. Alden, *Fleet Submarine in U.S. Navy*, credits this innovation with the survival of many fleet boats under depth charge attack; the loss of many WW I U-boats was attributed to gas generated when battery acid poured out and mixed with seawater. The soft rubber inserts were standard after late 1942.

49. The bureau's requisition, issued 15 August 1905, called for a capacity of 2750 amp-hr at the 5-hr rate, 3040 at the 8-hr rate, and 3300 at the 12-hr rate. The existing A-class battery was rated at 1840 amp-hr at the 4-hr rate. Plans of the battery tanks of both *Moccasin* and *Adder* were drawn up for prospective bidders. NARS RG 19 correspondence file 14907E.

50. According to Hay, *Secrets of the Submarine*, 48–51, the Edison battery was more robustly built than lead-acid batteries, had a longer life, and would stand much more careless handling, but those advantages were more than offset by its gassing and its high price, more than twice that of a standard lead-acid unit. It also heated as it was charged, and this heating generally stopped the charging for a time. Although the Edison was much lighter than the lead-acid battery, that mattered very little for units normally installed well below a submarine's center of gravity. Finally, the Edison had a much lower efficiency (a typical lead-acid battery would absorb 85 percent of the electrical energy passed through it, but the Edison would absorb only about 70 percent).

Appendix B

1. Unfortunately, C&R correspondence prior to 1915 is quite sparse (the post-1915 material is voluminous). Evidence for the 1912 policy shift includes proposed periscope specifications writ-

ten by K&E as well as a 1915 document celebrating the quality of new C&R-ordered documents. Too, in 1910 in connection with complaints by Lt. Chester W. Nimitz, CO of *Plunger*, the chief constructor, Rear Adm. Richard M. Watt, reviewed the periscope situation and noted his intention to buy six periscopes from Galileo and Goerz. Periscope descriptions appear in documents concerning individual boats, such as the operating manuals preserved in Boxes 209 and 210 of the C&R Confidential Files (NARS RG 19). Until late 1919, there were no standard periscope designations. Each instrument received a sequential registry number; in some cases, there was an awkward description (e.g., "replacement periscopes for K-4, -5, -6, -7,") that often had little relevance. To a limited extent, mention of various units after 1915 makes it possible to reconstruct parts of the earlier registry; at the least, the registry numbers indicate totals bought by the navy. Unfortunately, the registry itself is not available (the current periscope office retains only the post-1950 registry; it is not clear where, or whether, earlier records were stored). Thus, much of the early part of this appendix is necessarily based on very fragmentary data.

2. This was a matter of considerable controversy. Tests using the $1.2 \times /3.0 \times$ bifocal periscope on board L-1 were taken to show that a nominal magnification of $1.2 \times$ gave an observer the impression that objects were only 75 percent of their normal size. However, the unifocal ($1.2 \times$) instrument, however, seemed to give a full-size image. Late in 1917, the COs of SubDiv 5 (L-boats) argued that it would take a magnification of $2.6 \times$ to reproduce normal vision. C&R found this unlikely; if $1.2 \times$ looked like $0.75 \times$, then normal vision would require $1.65 \times$. The Germans did well enough with $1.5 \times$ (which the U.S. Navy adopted after WW I).

3. On 29 May 1908 BuNav asked C&R to provide range markings (graduated vertical and horizontal scales) in the focus of the periscope eyepiece, the graduations to correspond to a height of 10 ft at 1000 yds and to a length of 100 ft at 1000 yds. C&R bought Electric Boat's inexpensive eyepiece parts incorporating the required markings. WW I correspondence files refer to a new generation of such scales, presumably adapted to bifocal periscopes. To be in focus at both magnifications, the scale had to be inside the periscope tube, in a focal plane. Adding such a telemeter scale was expensive. An experimental telemeter was installed in A-5 about the beginning of 1917. The first orders for installation appear to date from May 1917. As of December 1917, however, tests in the Atlantic and Pacific showed that the telemeter was of little value beyond 1,500 yd and of no value in a seaway. C&R decided not to buy any more of these expensive instruments before more tests. A-5 then ran trials in the Philippines during April 1918; at 2,900 yd and at 650 yd, the telemeter scale range was accurate within 50 yd (at 1,575 yd, however, it was 225 yd off). An observer used a set of curves to connect telemeter readings to ranges. The 1918 trials seem to have been conclusive; the telemeter became a standard element of U.S. submarine periscopes.

4. Conventional coincidence range finders focus on the same point on a target from two ends of a base on board ship. The operator sees two target images (one from each end, typically an upper and lower part of the target) and brings them together (into coincidence). Effective range is limited by the length of that base. A stadimeter reverses the process by using, in effect, the length of the target (or a known length on the target) as its base and measuring the angle that length subtends. The operator sees separate images of two parts of the target and measures the angle by bringing them together. Accuracy is limited because the apparently known length may be in error (e.g., if a mast has

been cut down slightly or if a ship is at an angle to the line of sight). In 1912, B&L produced an unsuccessful experimental vertical-base coincidence range finder. In 1918, the U.S. Navy tested a British Barr & Stroud periscope incorporating a vertical range finder. Again, it was unsuccessful, partly because its images were too dim. BuOrd provided its first submarine periscope stadimeters just after WW I; by 1924, it had reached Mks V and VI (designs 30GRF and 30GFRD).

5. About the beginning of 1912, C&R asked the navy's rangefinder maker, Bausch & Lomb, to adapt a standard coincidence rangefinder to a submarine periscope. The company argued that it would have to be a separate unit, since a rangefinder required high magnification at the price of accepting a small field of view, the opposite of what a normal periscope should be. It proposed mounting the unit to a standard periscope. Through 1912 drawings were exchanged, and finally a unit with a 5-ft vertical base was built for installation aboard the submarine C-1, attachéd to the boat's forward (auxiliary) periscope (NARS RG 19 correspondence, file 13534A15).

6. This first Goerz order may date from 1908; no correspondence concerning it has been located. Installation was complete by early June 1909.

7. Because K&E was the main producer of BuOrd's periscopes for surface ships, such as battleships, it was naturally asked to make submarine periscopes. C&R correspondence files include a 1908 K&E request to bid on a U.S. submarine periscope. Presumably that year's purchase of Goerz periscopes was intended as the beginning of the sort of competitive procurement which only began in 1912. It is not clear why the 1908 project was aborted. Registry number 41 (see below) may have been the first K&E periscope bought by C&R. An early K&E brochure claims that the company had made over 95 percent of U.S. Navy *submarine* periscopes by 1913, but that figure cannot be correct unless it consists mainly of surface ship instruments.

8. In 1912, B&L was the main supplier of U.S. Navy range finders. It was asked to provide a range-finding periscope (using a vertical range finder; probably Registry number 44), which proved unsuccessful. The next B&L periscopes were probably a pair of L-boat replacements, Registry numbers 120 and 121, delivered in 1916. In May 1915, the company received a contract for numbers 134 and 135 (forward [auxiliary] walk-around periscopes for D-2 and D-3); it also made a new after periscope (133) for K-6. All three were delivered in May 1916. Even then, B&L was not very interested in periscope manufacture; apparently, in February 1918, Bausch himself took personal charge of this work and greatly accelerated it. B&L acquired a range-finder maker, Zeigmoller, in 1907 and, both before and after WW I, it was associated with Germany's Carl Zeiss.

9. Kollmorgen Corp. brochures reproduce its patent drawings for a periscope (U.S. Patent 1,006, 930: filed 20 October 1909 and patented 17 October 1911). These dates suggest that Kollmorgen designed the first K&E submarine periscopes. The only other domestic supplier was the Queen-Gray Co. of Philadelphia, which supplied the two periscopes originally intended for G-4 (Registry numbers 59–60). They were apparently unsuccessful. According to a 1920 note in the C&R correspondence file, they were never any good and were never installed (K&E instruments were substituted).

10. On 15 January 1903 C&R requested the new rotatable periscopes through the Superintending Constructor, Asst Naval Constructor Stuart Farrar Smith, at the Crescent Shipyard, where the A-boats were being built. Electric Boat's Vice President, L. Y. Spear, argued in a 28 January letter that only the wider field of view and the marked fore-and-aft line were practicable.

Any rotatable periscope would have to be let into the body of the boat rather than into her conning tower. It would no longer be within sight of the wheel in the conning tower. The steering gear shaft would have to be extended forward (to the periscope eyepiece) and an additional hand wheel fitted there for the helmsman. That in turn raised a question which would bedevil all single-periscope boats: who would use the periscope? The helmsman could hardly search the horizon while using his instrument to steer. On the other hand, the CO would want to be in complete control of the boat while running down a target. Spear argued that a helmsman could not look more than 30 deg either side of dead ahead without losing control. Much of the time, moreover, the helmsman would not be steering by means of the periscope; instead he would rely on a compass, which would have to be in full view at all times. It would be extremely undesirable to add another crew member as periscope lookout. The watertight connection through the hull presented special problems. To keep the helmsman's hands free to control the boat, any rotating periscope would have to be power-operated. All of these considerations would make the device more complex and costly. Spear proposed instead to replace the centerline deadlight of the conning tower with the periscope eyepiece, mounted in a watertight box. The periscope barrel could be emplaced in the box if needed; otherwise deadlights in the box would be usable by the occupant of the conning tower. He hoped for a 50-deg field of view (as built, the Electric Boat altiscopes had about a 60-deg field). This letter is in NARS RG 19, file 14908E8. On 6 February 1903 Smith reported to C&R that he agreed with Electric Boat that rotation was an impractical complication. The bureau agreed, and by summer both boats had fixed altiscopes. In November, their CO, Lt F. L. Pinney, and his prospective replacement, Lt. C. P. Nelson, both asked for rotating periscopes, which could have narrower fields of view and which therefore could produce larger images which might allow an observer to estimate relative distances. Too, during long submerged runs, they keenly felt their inability to see astern or to either side (their letters are in NARS RG 19, file 14907E59-61). Nelson pointed out that it was essential to have the helmsman steer while the CO at the periscope conned the boat; if the helmsman was distracted, the lively boat would soon turn off her course. On the other hand, in running down a target or a sighting, where very accurate steering was needed, the man at the periscope had to have direct access to the helm. Nelson wanted a second wheel (connected to the main wheel) for just that purpose, where the CO had access to it. Many of these arguments eventually led to demands for two separate periscopes, one for the helmsman and another for the CO. Meanwhile, C&R sought a better periscope. The Rev. E. L. Hubbard of Washington, D.C. suggested a multi-lens (probably bifocal) fixed periscope. C&R had one (plus an improved version) made at the Naval Gun Factory, the navy's precision manufacturing plant. Hubbard's elongated periscope was rejected because it could not be made to turn. Early in 1904 plans to provide the two Pacific Coast boats with altiscopes (in answer to their CO's complaints) were canceled in view of the unhappy experience of the two Atlantic test boats, and in hopes that the new rotating instruments would be satisfactory. Smith's letter is NARS RG 19, file 14907E139. Spear's concept of a periscope let into the forward deadlight of the conning tower led directly to the rotating-barrel/fixed-eyepiece type installed in *Plunger*(A-1).

11. The entire barrel turned. Initially the joint between barrel and fixed eyepiece was sealed by a cup of mercury. Electric Boat did not patent a conning tower periscope with a turning barrel (but fixed eyepiece) until 1906.

12. In a 20 May 1904 letter Spear described the rotating peri-

scope as similar to the earlier altiscope except with the field of view reduced to 25 deg. Its barrel would be steadied by guy wires led from a collar within which the barrel rotated. The tube would be rotated by a 1/4 HP motor. The point at which the periscope tube entered the conning tower was fitted with a coned surface, forming a ground joint, with washers and a lock-nut. The CO of *Plunger* (A-1) reported in 1907 that at a depth of only 20 ft the lock-nut had to be so tightened (to keep the joint watertight) that the periscope could not rotate at all. Later periscopes were fitted with a stuffing-box and roller bearings, which permitted rotation at depth.

13. The motor proved unreliable and for a time the conning tower periscope had to be turned by hand. That was particularly difficult for an officer who had to observe while steering. By 1907 this instrument was again motor-driven. All the other fixed-eyepiece periscopes were motor-driven.

14. An Electric Boat handbook for EB 7P (*Adder*-class) submarines (Submarine Museum Library) describes a 16-ft fixed-eyepiece periscope revolved by motor, with a special reversing switch, giving a 20–25-degree field of view. It could be centered exactly forward, and a pointer on a scale gave the bearing on which it was set. It is not clear whether this was the standard A-boat hull periscope. Certainly, the *replacement* periscopes for the A-boats were walk-arounds.

As of November 1907, the two Pacific boats, A-3 and A-5, both had 3.5-in periscopes dried by a calcium chloride pot above which air circulated naturally. The modernized A-6 and A-7 (*Porpoise* and *Shark*) had 3.25-in periscopes. A small pressure blower circulated dry air through them, piping it outside. *Plunger* (A-1) had a 3.25-in fixed-eyepiece periscope in her conning tower. The 4-in fixed-eyepiece periscopes of the B- and C-classes used the A-3 system. As of December 1907 New York Navy Yard reported that the *Porpoise* type was best because of its superior drying mechanism and its walk-around eyepiece.

15. Opinions of the fixed-eyepiece conning tower periscopes seem to have varied. On 27 August 1907 the CO of *Plunger* asked to have his conning tower periscope replaced by a walk-around hull instrument like that installed in *Porpoise* and *Shark*. A CO using the conning tower instrument could not supervise the work of the crew while the boat was submerged, and opening or closing the conning tower door changed the focus of the periscope (his particular instrument had an inefficient drying device, and its middle lenses could not be taken out without dismounting the entire periscope, an operation lasting an entire day; necessary frequent overhauls had left its lenses and prisms badly scratched). In a December 1907 letter reiterating these objections, the CO pointed out that foreign submarines generally had two periscopes: "while I do not consider this practicable in the *Plunger* class, I consider it absolutely necessary to battle efficiency that the one periscope should be efficient, and should be mounted abaft the conning tower [i.e., as in the modernized *Porpoise* and *Shark*] in order that the CO may have ready access to his charts and supervise the work of the crew" (NARS RG 19 correspondence, file 16351E).

In answer to further complaints about *Plunger*'s periscope, in December 1910 Chief Constructor R. M. Watt surveyed the current periscope situation (NARS RG 19, file 16351E216). Although the CO of *Plunger* disliked the rotating image in his fixed-eyepiece instrument, other COs, used to it, liked being able to judge the bearing of the object they were observing (Watt agreed that rotation confused anyone not used to the fixed-eyepiece periscope and was objectionable on that account). The alternative Goerz periscope lost some (but not much) light in its erecting prism. A special indicator in the focus of its eyepiece showed

the direction of the periscope head relative to that of the boat. Both types were attractive because they took up so little space. Watt considered a fixed-eyepiece periscope particularly well adapted for use by the helmsman, who would tend to look nearly straight ahead.

The alternative walk-around periscope did offer an observer a sense of direction (since the eyepiece was always pointed towards the object seen), but it also required far more clear space. Watt described the walk-around type as "particularly satisfactory" for firing torpedoes (one of the CO's roles), presumably because it was far easier than a fixed-eyepiece instrument to adapt to BuOrd's new torpedo director. He would therefore fit fixed-eyepiece units as CO periscopes only where there was too little space for a walk-around, as in the first two D-boats.

Watt wanted all periscopes motor-driven, with five speeds (from one revolution in 10 sec down to one in 65 sec).

16. C-1 had a nonerecting, fixed-eyepiece periscope, according to Simon Lake's comparison between G-1 and C-1 included in the former's trial report (INSURV records, Vol. 61 of trials books). A reference (in General Board files, 1912) to trials of a new type of fixed-eyepiece periscope, in hopes that it might be revived, seems to apply to the E-1 trial. According to notes on C-1 held by the Submarine Force Museum, the conning tower periscope had a 28-degree field of view, and its motor could make one revolution in 23 sec to 1 min 15 sec.

17. By January 1916, A-4 was reporting that her forward periscope could not be trained at all ("but gives good service in allowing a second person to check estimated range"). Two new conning tower periscopes bought for the C class were not so much better than their predecessors to be worth fitting the whole class. New units for the D class proved better; by mid-1916, C&R planned to buy five new conning tower periscopes for the C-boats. The issue was urgent; the Submarine Force commander complained that new trainable conning tower periscopes were needed (for his 8 C-boats and D-boats) because otherwise the helmsman could not steer directly for the target. The D-class conning tower replacements, which were rotated by hand, rather than by power, were bought in 1916; they were being made as of that August (Registry numbers 173–175; 176–180 were probably for the C-boats). The reconstructed Registry list suggests that no new fixed-eyepiece periscopes were bought for the A-boats and B-boats. B&L provided the walk-around replacement hull periscopes for D-2 and D-3.

18. In his 15 October 1907 letter to the Superintendent of Shipbuilding at Quincy concerning improvements to submarines (see note to chapter 4), L. Y. Spear wrote that "we are now engaged in developing an entirely new form of periscope which gives an instantaneous view of the whole horizon. The image, however, will be of such a character that this instrument can probably not be used effectively in torpedo firing where exact direction and reasonably accurate estimation of distance is required. Its probable use would be as a finder in a large sense, so that the CO of a vessel may, with exceedingly short exposure, keep himself advised of the location and movements of surrounding vessels and may in a general way correct his own course accordingly when completely submerged. For final observation and for torpedo firing, however, an instrument of the character now used will be required in addition. As soon as our development work on the new instrument is completed, we propose to submit a proposal to the Bureau [of C&R] as a change, looking towards the installation of two instruments. When the additional instrument is carried there will, of course, be some reduction in submerged speed."

19. From specifications for building SS 20 class, 1909, in Sub-

marine Base Museum Library. The FY 09 contract circular in Board on Construction correspondence (RG 80, NARS) called for two periscopes, preferably of walk-around type to show erect images in all positions; the contractor could provide fixed-eyepiece instruments only if they were demonstrated satisfactory for navigation and torpedo fire. One periscope was to have alternative magnifying and low-power eyepieces. As an indication of expected performance, each periscope's horizontal scale markings corresponded to 100 ft at 1,000 yd (vertical, to 10 ft at 1,000 yd). The Submarine Base Museum Library also has detailed specifications, marked "D-class" but probably for the H class (because the specification for the latter shows a larger periscope diameter). Both periscopes are to be of walk-around type, rotated by hand, "each mounted on a piston in a cylinder by means of which the entire instrument may be raised or lowered through a distance of about 5 ft. The operating medium is oil under air pressure. . . ." Specified diameter is $4\frac{5}{8}$ in, with a 5-in lower section, the two being screwed and soldered together, and the total length is about $19\frac{1}{2}$ ft for the forward instrument and about $20\frac{1}{2}$ ft for the after one (so that it could see over the top of the forward periscope). Field of view (at slightly over $1\times$ magnification) was 34 degrees; the forward periscope would be fitted with a high-power eyepiece of about $2\times$ power. Within each low-power eyepiece was a glass telemeter scale, each of whose horizontal and vertical gradations represented 100 ft at 1,000 yd. The forward instrument was provided with a torpedo director. Each periscope had a pelorus (a collar on the lower part of the vertical tube).

20. In 1917, in connection with proposals for the S-boats, Submarine Force Commander recalled that the E-boat periscopes housed too slowly, over too short a distance to be worthwhile, and suffered from mechanical problems. They were removed on the recommendation of the COs and the Atlantic Flotilla commander (RG correspondence 1915–1925, File 125 series, NARS). Defending the short housing distances then contemplated, C&R retorted that the problem was vibration.

21. G-1 Ship Information Book (copy in Submarine Force Museum). Lake probably measured fields of view from the center to one side (e.g., he credited the prototype *Adder* periscope with a 15-degree field, whereas an official navy description said 30 degrees). The standard measurement is the entire field, so his 3-in periscopes probably had 34-degree fields.

22. It later became obvious that the specification was too vague. It seems to have called for a walk-around periscope with a low power of $1.2\times$ to $1.5\times$ and a high power of $3\times$ to $5\times$ (C&R hoped for $5\times$, but was willing to settle for $3\times$; it later turned out that $3\times$, which is what the manufacturers offered, was grossly inadequate). Field of view at low power had to be at least 40 degrees. Some of these data are taken from the version of the specification sent to Electric Boat in 1916 for a pair of L-boat periscopes (forward 20 ft $11\frac{3}{4}$ in, aft 22 ft $7\frac{3}{4}$ in). In November 1918, recent U.S. periscopes were credited with a field of view of 32 degrees (effectively 27 degrees) at low power and 7–8 degrees at high power.

23. The run of consecutive Registry numbers (36–41) suggests a concerted experimental program, but, unfortunately, no documentation has emerged. Another Goerz periscope (bifocal, $1.5\times$/ $6\times$, Registry number 45) was installed, as the No. 2 periscope of Lake's first U.S. Navy submarine, G-1.

24. C&R note to BuOrd, 14 September 1915, in RG 19 correspondence series for 1915–1926, symbol 125 (periscopes), box 2109. This was in response to BuOrd complaints of poor periscope performance in 1914–15 Battle Practice and Elementary Practice. At about this time, the New York Navy Yard was referring to K&E periscopes in the A, L, and G classes.

25. Kollmorgen Corp., *The Submarine Periscope 1916–1991* (Northampton, Mass., 1991), and RG 19 correspondence 1915–1925, file 125 series, NARS records. The 5-in brass K-1 periscopes were unifocal ($1.2\times$), 12 ft 4 in (conning tower) and 22 ft 4 in (control room) long.

26. According to a request for financing for Kollmorgen by the navy's Bureau of Supplies and Accounts, 15 May 1918, incomplete Kollmorgen navy contracts amounted to (dates in parentheses): 1 K-class periscope, 15 percent complete (19 December 1916); 6 O-class sets (4 delivered to date: 31 March 1917); 3,240 Mk XXVI gunsights (25 delivered to date: 4 June 1917); 11 periscopes for S-3–S-13 (16 November 1917); 100 special telescopes (20 July 1917); modification of O-3–O-10 periscopes to alti-periscopes (9 February 1918); and modification of periscopes for C class (4 delivered: 7 May 1918). Electric Boat contracts were: changing 16 periscopes for O-boats (EB 68A type, 4 delivered, 19 May 1916); changing 6 periscopes for T-boats (EB 63C type, 12 September 1916); 1 alti-periscope for *Schley* (12 September 1916); 2 periscopes for *Schley* (19 April 1916); 40 R-class periscopes (EB 77A: 12 delivered, 5 April 1917); 3 periscopes for S-3 (EB 73A: 26 September 1917); and 72 periscopes for S-18–S-41 (5 April 1918). Kollmorgen also made the periscopes of the six H-boats ordered for Russia but ultimately delivered to the U.S. Navy. Kollmorgen reported in June 1918 that it had a satisfactory bifocal design and in August 1918 that it had a satisfactory general design for an alti-periscope. The stated 1916 order for an alti-periscope for *Schley* might represent a later revision; there is no other evidence of such early U.S. interest in that type of instrument.

27. In December 1917, U.S. manufacturers offered replacement single-power periscopes for the D-boats in about 8 mo; the British Admiralty was then obtaining periscopes a little more quickly (in 6–8 mo). Moreover, unlike C&R, the Admiralty used no specification but relied on its suppliers. C&R authorized purchase of two British periscopes as C-class spares. When they arrived in New York in May 1918, tests showed that they were about equivalent to U.S. designs (because the designs were privately owned, however, C&R could not obtain the relevant optical constants). By this time, typical British periscopes used $1.3x$ and $5\times–6\times$ magnification.

28. The specification written for the K&E periscope called for an optical length of 20 ft (plus or minus 2 ft) and an outer diameter of 5 in (upper end about $3\frac{1}{4}$ in, with a $3\frac{1}{2}$-ft taper for the forward periscope and a $4\frac{1}{2}$-ft taper for the after one). This might have been one of the first demands for a small-head, tapered periscope in U.S. service. These were to be walk-around units using a rigid outer tube within which the inner tube, containing the optics, rotated by means of a pair of handles at the eye end. The periscope had to be raised and lowered electrically through 4 ft in 15–30 sec. Unlike the existing L-boat periscope, this one would have only a low-power setting ($1.2x$).

29. Report from USS *Kearsage*, 4 April 1917. The ship was then in the Atlantic Reserve Fleet, so presumably this was a cover for an attaché or intelligence report. Specifications for building Electric Boat and Lake O-boats (dated 1916, Submarine Base Museum Library) include alti-periscopes, but it seems likely that these documents had been revised without being redated. The C&R file in NARS shows no reference to the alti-periscope before 1917.

30. Housing was the windlass type. Both $1.2x$ periscopes were 5-in diameter. Optical lengths were 19 ft $9\frac{15}{16}$ in and 22 ft $\frac{7}{8}$ in, with housing distances of 5 ft and 7 ft, so that both came down to the same housed length.

31. All on board T-1 were old-type, 5-in periscopes: a 16-ft $1\frac{1}{2}$-in bifocal periscope ($1.2/3.0\times$, 43/17-degree fields of view), a 26-ft unifocal periscope ($1.26\times$, 39-degree field of view), and an

altiscope (1.2/0.5×). C&R wanted more magnification (1.5×, 1.5/6×); in November 1918, it agreed to pay Kollmorgen for new optics for T-2 and T-3 (Nos. 1 and 2 became bifocal at 1.5/6× magnification, and the altiscope was converted into a tilting-prism instrument; designations were 10KA-0015 [No. 1], 20KA-0026 [No. 2], and 10KS-0026 [No. 3]).

32. Electric Boat units were 20 ft 3 in and 21 ft long, housing distances 4 ft and 4 ft 10 in, respectively. Lake's 5-in diameter periscopes were 16 ft 3 in and 17 ft 9 in, housing more than 4 ft 6 in and 6 ft, respectively.

33. The change from fixed periscopes to pneumatic housing units (as in the N class) was ordered in July 1917. The 20-ft 1-in alti-periscope housed more than 5 ft 1 in. The other two, 21 ft long, housed more than 6 ft and 10 ft. All were Kollmorgen instruments. Kollmorgen initially had trouble with the O-class bifocal periscopes; in October 1918, it proposed 2.4/9.6× to fit within the O-class periscope head. C&R considered that magnification entirely too high, although some of the submariners rather liked the idea. By this time, C&R planned longer periscopes: 24 ft (1.5×, housing 9 ft 4⅝ in), 28.5 ft (1.5/6×, housing over the same distance), and 23 ft (1.75×, housing over 14 ft 10⅛ in). At least in the case of O-10, the bifocal periscope was replaced by a new windlass unit in 1923. The single-power instrument was later removed, probably about 1926. The bifocal periscope was replaced by a longer instrument when boats were restored to service in 1941. By that time, the alti-periscope was gone.

34. They were 17 ft 9 in and 19 ft 3 in long, housing more than 4 ft 6 in and 6 ft, respectively.

35. K&E already had so much work that, about March 1918, it withdrew its bid. Too, K&E offered a larger periscope head than Kollmorgen, and its two-power and alti-periscopes needed a ground joint at the end of the operating lever, which was inferior to Kollmorgen's arrangement. It proposed a 1.25×–1.5× unifocal periscope (48-degree field of view) and a 1.25×–1.5×/3.5×–4× bifocal periscope (48/20.5-degree fields of view). The problem of S-boat periscopes led Spear to write to Land on 23 January 1918 that "the Chief [of C&R] will have nothing on me when I die, as the word 'periscopes' will be stamped not only on my heart but on all my other internal parts. . . ." Land penciled that "I take this with some saline solution." Problems included the supply of optical glass, labor difficulties in optical plants, enemy aliens in those plants, and difficulties in obtaining tubes that would be watertight and airtight not only in the factory but also in service.

36. C&R records contain Album XIV by Carl Zeiss, "Nedinsco" factory, dated October 1927. All periscopes on offer had an optical length of 7 m (about 23 ft), well short of U.S. requirements. Main tube diameter was 150 mm (5.9 in). Standard magnifications were 1.5× and 6× (fields of view, 40 and 10 degrees). The XIII.42 search (observation or navigation) periscope had a 55-mm (2.2-in) head. Elevation limits were +20 and −10 degrees. The XIII.62 antiaircraft periscope had a 60-mm upper section and could elevate from the horizon to the zenith. The attack periscope (XIII.52) had a 31-mm (1.22-in) head; elevation limits were +20 and −10 degrees. There was also a short (4–5 m, about 5–8 ft) night periscope (head 80 mm), whose head could elevate to the horizon. Nedinsco rated these periscopes in brightness, rather than in percentage of light transmission. At high power, search or antiaircraft periscope brightness was 16, compared with 11.8 in the attack periscope, and 49 in the night periscope.

37. The company offered four alternatives: 7278 (simple attack periscope), 7279 (full-option periscope), 7533 (cruising periscope with sky-search prism), and 8002 (large-diameter periscope). 7278 and 7279 were 150-mm × 30-ft bifocals (1.5/6×, 30- and 7.5-degree fields of view) with roll-top (+20/−10–degree) prisms and 38-mm (1.5-in) heads. The company claimed that using the right periscope grip for prism control was its own special feature (but C&R used much the same system). 7279 added range-finding and director features. The stadimeter (range estimator), using two prisms rotating relative to each other, measured angle (in minutes of arc) on a scale. The prisms were rotated out of the optical path when not in use. The illuminated fixed line of sight used an electrically driven gyro within the case. The integral torpedo director used the enemy course and speed to give director angle (the angle the periscope should make with the bow of the submarine when firing). The director scales were visible through the left eyepiece of the periscope (data were set using a knurled knob). The display included a true course repeater. The director could be used to set gyro angle. 8002 was 7.5 in × 36 ft, with a prism elevating to 70 degrees and depressing to −15 degrees, for sky-search. Barr and Stroud estimated 25 percent light transmission at 1.5×, 31 percent at 6×.

38. The prototype periscope (Registry number 705) was shifted to S-47 on 19 November 1932. Similar periscopes were tested on board S-18, S-22, and S-23 in the fall of 1933 (this group reported in November 1933). It turned out that the bow and stern made poor stadimeter marks; in September 1933, S-22 did better and quicker by measuring the distance between target masts. Experiments showed that, as a result of refraction in the atmosphere, effective maximum range was 7,500 yd (C&R soon wanted 16,000 yd, and Kollmorgen varied between citing the effective limit and pointing out that, because the instrument was measuring angle, it had no effective outer range limit).

39. Patent 1986731 dated 1 January 1935. In connection with Electric Boat's December 1937 query about exporting Kollmorgen periscopes with this feature, C&R stated that Zeiss developed an almost identical range/course angle finder, plans of which were obtained by B&L soon after they had been issued. Even so, C&R considered Kollmorgen's range finder/course finder confidential and did not want the combination of this feature and the stabilized line sold to a foreign power. The most likely buyer was the Soviet Union, which was then shopping for warship plans and equipment (at this time, it bought battleship and destroyer plans from Gibbs & Cox).

40. The outer ring showed the length of the target in feet (100 ft to 1,000 ft). The intermediate ring showed range in hundreds of yards, between 220 yd and 11,000 yd. The inner ring showed target height in ft (15 ft to 130 ft) and also course angle (0 to 85 degrees). In connection with an order for 20 new periscopes for new submarines, in 1935 Kollmorgen suggested that the outer ring be marked outside in feet, inside in course angle (30 minutes to 85 degrees). The intermediate ring would be range and the inner ring, height. That would speed operation by allowing the operator to set target length (for course angle) before taking range. C&R agreed. The stadimeter was operated by rotating a knob under the focusing knob. Turning it first produced the doubled image used for range finding. After the range was read off, further turning produced the horizontal double image used for course-angle finding. Reversing brought the two parts together. Further reverse turns brought back a single image, and finally the image was turned back into its normal horizontal position. Tests showed that the full cycle took 70–90 sec, so Kollmorgen added a small crank handle (in Registry number 730) to cut the time to 30–40 sec. In its 86KA-34 design, it cut time further.

Although the stadimeter proved quite valuable for rangefinding, apparently the course-finding feature was little used during WW II. COs were far too unwilling to expose their periscopes for more than a minimum time.

41. The *Perch* class is credited with a mix of 7.5-in and 6-in periscopes in a table of periscope assignments dated December 1937, after these boats had been completed. A 28 May 1938 list of submarine periscopes, however, shows pairs of 86KA-34s in each of the *Perch* class.

42. Penciled remarks on the cover sheet of the letter from B&L indicate that C&R did not want a foreign power to know that the U.S. Navy planned 40-ft periscopes. Another penciled note, however, indicates that B&L (hence C&R) would likely learn far more from Zeiss than Zeiss would learn from it. No papers in the C&R correspondence file describe a purchased Zeiss periscope, and there is no gap in the Registry list to allow for such an instrument.

43. On her shakedown cruise, however, *Saury* experienced considerable vibration at 4–5 kt, which built up and then damped down, particularly at bearings near the bow and beams. C&R concluded that the periscope shaft was shedding vortices, a phenomenon then just beginning to attract attention. (As an example of how new this understanding was, unexpected vibration caused by vortex shedding destroyed the new Tacoma Narrows bridge in Washington State in 1940.)

44. Details of Types 1, 2, 3, and 4 are from a June 1946 periscope manual (NavPers 16165). Designations and dates are from a Kollmorgen design list and log.

45. Production versions were 91KA-40T/1.414HA and 92KA-40T/1.414HA. Postwar, 106KA-40/HA and 109KA-40/HA were Type 2A (improved optics); Type 2B was 107KA-40/1.500HA; Type 2D, a major redesign, also strengthened for deeper diving, was 123KA-43.3/HA and 123KA-43.3T/HA; Type 2E was 124KA-36/HA; and Type 2F was 129KA-40T/HA. The T suffix stood for treated optics.

46. Kollmorgen remains dominant. The company's list of periscopes for the U.S. Navy shipped between 1939 and 1968 (Registry numbers 768–2418) shows only the following non–Kollmorgen instruments: the canceled wartime series (1282–1291), 3 Bausch & Lomb periscopes delivered in 1951 (1700–1702), and a few built by Sperry in the 1950s to establish an alternative source of supply (1790–1793 delivered 1958, 1840–1849 in 1959, 2019–2054, 2067–2079, probably 2142–2152, 2170–2186, 2202–2204, probably 2220–2245). Most of the Sperry units were Type 2s. Kollmorgen was responsible for all new designs. Apart from Types 2, 3, and 4, the only other wartime Kollmorgen production was 10 85KA-34Ts (numbers 1102–1111) to replace some old periscopes; they were shipped between 11 September 1943 and 19 February 1944.

INDEX

NOTE: Entries for ships' class names are identical to entries for the name ship of the class.

0.30-caliber machine guns, 127, 165

0.50-caliber machine gun; as submarine air defense, 165; *Triton's* inability to use in surprise attacks, 205

3-in guns; insufficient fire power of disappearing, 124–126; L-boat provision for, 81

3-in Mk IX gun, 85

3-in/23 gun; L-1 boat, 150; L-11 boat, 85; O-6 boat's disappearing, 168; proposed for cruiser submarines, 169; S-1 boat's disappearing, 124

3-in/50 gun; *Gato*, 206; *Marlin*, 226; *Pompano*, 196; R-1 submarine, 121; R-boats, 127; replacing 4-inchers on S-boats, 145; replacing 5-in/51 on V-1 boats, 113; *Tambor* class, 204

4-in/50 gun; added to S-boats, 126–127; added to T-2 boat during WWI, 103, 104; added to T-3 boat during WWI, 104; *Gato*, 215; *Snapper*, 213

5-in high-powered wet gun, 107

5-in/25 gun; *Archerfish*, 251; *Gato's* wet mount, 206; *Grouper*, 217; proposed for cruiser submarines, 168; proposed for post-WWII submarines, 249; submarine COs' option to install two, 215

5-in/51 gun; adoption as standard U.S. submarine gun, 218; Fleet Submarine 1919, 111; replaced with 3-in/50 on V-1 boats, 113; *Tambor*, 204–205, 214

6-in/53 cruiser gun, 168, 169

8-in/50 gun, 169

20-mm gun; described, 219; *Gato*, 215; *Grouper*, 217; *Mackerel* (SS 204), 225, 230; *Marlin*, 220–221, 226; *Pompano*, 196; *Porpoise*, 211; R-boats, 144; S-28 boat, 146; S-boats fitted with, 147; *Sunfish*, 167

40-mm gun; *Gato*, 215; *Grouper*, 217; S-18 boat's, 131; success of, 219; *Sunfish*, 167

76-mm antiaircraft gun, 90

800-tonner submarines; *see also* small submarines; Admiral Hart's studies, 221; demands for, 118; German U-boats inspiring desire for, 117, 151; prototypes included in FY 17-19, 119, 121

1,500-ton Cruiser Submarine 1929, 185

A-1 boat, 3

A-boats; *see also Adder* class submarines; gasoline engines, 255; standard features, 35; stricken, 87

AA-1 submarine, 101

Abbot, Lt. Comdr. H. L., 169–170

Active sonars; evolution of, 198; QB, 144, 198; range of Japanese, 247

Adder; history of, 286; modifications to, 33–35; open sea endurance trial, 33; trials for first U.S. Navy periscope, 270

Adder class submarines; *see also* A-boats; as advance over *Holland*, 27; consequences for Electric Boat, 28–29; described, 29–31; long periscopes, 271; ordered to Philippines, 56; purchased by Japan and Russia, 36

Air conditioning; *see also* ventilation systems; ventilators; *Argonaut* modernization, 176; first adoption as standard equipment, 200; *Nautilus*, 180; S-20 boat, 138; S-28 boat, 146; S-35 boat's, 131; S-44 boat, 145; S-48 boat, 141; S-boats rebuilt with, 147

Air locks, Lake's patented, 85

Air purifiers; *Alligator*, 12–13; use in WWI, 152; *Whale*, 16

Aircraft; alti-periscopes for spotting, 274–275; difficulties designing submarines to accommodate, 176; interest in placing aboard scout submarines, 163; Taylor's studies of long-range armored submarines carrying, 170–172; vulnerability to being spotted by patrolling, 165

Aircraft canisters, 124

AL-designations; assignment to SubDiv 5 L-boats, 152, 153; purpose of, 84

AL-series boats; *see entries for L-boats with same number designations*

Albacore (SS 218), 294

Alligator, 12–13, 53

Alstilt (*American Ram* builder), 16

Alti-periscopes, 268, 270, 274–275

Amberjack (SS 219), 294

Amberjack (SS 522), 304

American Laurenti Co.; FY 09 contract award, 56; FY 11 proposal for 20-kt submarine, 79; *Thrasher* (G-4), 64–68

American Ram, 16

American Revolution, submarine warfare in, 11–12

Angler (SS 240), 295

Antennas, *see* radio antenna masts; radio antennas

Antisubmarine warfare, *see* ASW

Apogon (SS 308), 298

APS-1 boat, 176

Arabia (SP-3434), 154

Archerfish, 251

Archerfish (SS 311), 298

Argonaut Junior, 31

Argonaut (SS 475), 303

Argonaut (V-4); batteries, 265; conversion to transport (APS-1), 176; described, 178; history of, 292; sonars, 198; V-4 boat renamed as, 176

Arma Corp., 240–241

Armored submarines, 170–172

Aspro (SS 309); 40-mm and 20-mm guns and radio antennas, 215; history of, 298

ASW (antisubmarine warfare); conducted against U-cruisers off U.S. coast, 154–155; first U.S. proposal for, 152; German opinion of Allied, 152; lack of Japanese airborne, 234; submariners favoring vs. surface ship convoying, 157

ASW submarine; prioritized by General Board, 158; proposed, 157

Atlantic Submarine Flotilla; demands for fast 800-tonner, 118; wanting transatlantic-capable submarines, 117

Attack tactics; against convoys, 233; British teaching U.S. Navy, 155–156; post-WWI, 165; taught to U.S. Navy by British Navy, 155–156; torpedo gyro-setting feature for, 137, 195–196

Attack Teacher, 155, 246, 267

Atule (SS 403), 302

Austria-Hungary Navy, 69

Auxiliary diesel generators; *see also* diesel generators; battery life prolonged by, 200; first inclusion in submarine design, 101; *Sargo*, 204; *Tambor* class, 204

Auxiliary engines; charging batteries using, 107; moved back to main shafts, 86; removal from main motor shafts, 81–83; Submarine 1919, 104–105

Auxiliary power plant ratings (kw), 306–311

B-1 boat (SS 10), 306

B-boats; *see also Viper* (EB 16); double-hull design, 90; false bows, 34, 43; flagstaffs and running lights, 42; gasoline engines, 255; proposals leading to, 35; rotating, fixed-eyepiece periscope, 271; sing-screw and superstructure design, 44; stricken, 87

Baker, George C., 21–22

Balao (SS 285), 297; data, 311; thick HTS skin, 209

Balkon/GHG passive sonar array, 252

Ballast, *Turtle's* lead, 11

Ballast tanks; *Adder* modifications, 34; conversion to variable fuel, 209; discontinuance and resumption of storing fuel in, 165; diving speed and, 130; duct keels and, 57, 60; early attempts to control buoyancy using, 6–9; experimental M-1 submarine, 83; on *Fenian Ram*, 21; fuel oil carried in, 137, 142; on G-1 submarine, 52; German UB-88 boat's saddle, 160; on Holland's underwater "airplane," 19; impediments to quick diving, 149; no longer storing fuel in, 202; removal of Kingstons from, 210; returned to fuel stowage, 204; S-3's separately flooded, 121–122; S-17 boat's, 129; U-shaped, 60

Bang (SS 385), 301

Barb (SS 220), 219, 294

Barbel (SS 316), 298

Barbero (SS 317), 298

Barr & Stroud periscopes, 280

Barracuda (F-2), 286

Barracuda (V-1); history of, 292; insufficient battery size, 265

Barrow, Robert F., 13

Bashaw (SS 241), 295; wartime modifications, 238

Bass (V-2); as built and as stripped for sinking, 114; bulbous bow, 112; as cargo submarine, 114; class data, 309; history of, 292; radio antenna masts, 110

Batfish (SS 310), 298

Bathythermograph (BT), 234, 247

Batteries; Alstitt's Confederate submarine, 15; *American Ram*, 16; auxiliary diesel generators prolonging life of, 200; charged by auxiliary diesels, 107; described, 263–265; doubled number of cells aboard *Octopus*, 46; G-1 submarine, 52; half-switching for longer endurance, 150; improvements to *Adder*s, 34; numbers of cells and types of, 306–311; proposed cruiser submarine, 168; proposed post-WWII submarine, 249; R-1 submarine, 121; rapid deterioration of K-2 and K-5, 78; replacement of Gould with thin-plate Exides, 88; *Salmon* class increased capacity, 202; *Sargo*, 204; Scheme O fleet submarine design, 107; slower evaporation of U-boat, 160; V-4 boat, 176

Battery tanks, 85

Battlecruisers; fleet submarines reducing mobility of, 100; as potential surface scouts, 163

Bauer, Wilhelm, 12

Bausch & Lomb periscopes, 269

Baya (SS 318), 298

Beam, submarine, 306–311

Beatty, Adm. Sir David, 105–106

Becuna (SS 319), 298

Bell Laboratories, SV radar, 236

Bells, signal; A-3 and A-5 submarines, 44; B-1 and A-7 submarines, 43; D class submarines, 57; H-2 submarine, 58; L-8 submarine, 85; underwater communications among harbor defense boats using, 76; *Vipers*, 46

Bergall (SS 320), 298

Besugo (SS 321), 298

Bifocal periscopes; advantages, 280; problems with, 267; proposed submarine cruiser, 169

Bilge pumps, K class, 81

Billfish (SS 286), 297

Blackfin (SS 322), 298

Blackfish (SS 221), 294

Blenny (SS 324), 299

Bliss-Leavitt Mk IV, IV-1, VII, X torpedoes, 50

Blisters; added to *Turbot* for stability, 65; S-20 boats' external fuel, 132, 137, 138; S-49 boat's passive MV system, 136

Blower (SS 325), 299

Blueback (SS 326), 299

Bluefish (SS 222), 294

Bluegill (SS 242), 295

Board on Construction; annual building program recommendations, 2; formation of, 1

Boarfish (SS 327), 299

Boilers; caustic soda, 21; for proposed steam-powered fleet submarine, 103

Bonefish (SS 223), 294

Bonita (C-4), history of, 286

Bonita (V-3), 200, 292

Bow; drawbacks of bulbous, 110; improved sea-keeping using false, 34; L-8 boat's limber holes, 86; learning to estimate angle on, 156; reducing wave making resistance with bulbous, 110, 112; S-20 boat's modified, 137, 138; V-1 boat's clipper, 111; V-2 boat's bulbous, 112

Bow caps; K-8 boat's rotating, 80; O-1 submarine, 93; request for independent, 80

Bow planes; introduced on E- and F-class submarines, 61, 62; vs. Lake's hydroplanes, 151

Bowfin (SS 287), 297

BQR-2 sonar, 156

BQR-3, 239

BQR-4 sonar, 156

Brayton engines, 20

Bream (SS 243), 295

Breathing tubes, 16

Bridge directors, 235

Brill (SS 330), 299

British Royal Navy; 1927 increased submarine building rate, 164; *Adder*s built for, 35; adoption of diesel-electric engine, 260; alti-periscope innovations, 275; in American Revolution, 11–12; Electric Boat's B-boats, 90; fleet submarines, 104; K-boat deployment, 105–106; purchase of H-boats, 78; Q-ships countering U-boats, 151; rating of R- and S-boats, 142; submarines' ability to keep blockading ships out to sea, 55; teaching U.S. Navy attack tactics, 155–156

British submarines; E-boat battery wiring, 150; periscopes, 269; R class, 158; WWI U-boat sinkings by, 151–152

"Browning" shots, 165

BT (bathythermograph), 234, 247

BuEng (Bureau of Engineering); 6-cylinder gasoline engine, 255–256; attempt to balance submerged and surface speed performances, 119; "balanced" 1,600 tonner submarine, 104; copying U-boat MAN diesels, 161; predicting critical diesel engine speeds, 258; proposal of composite power plant in *Salmon*s, 203; search for diesel-electric engine, 259–263; sonar development, 197–198; submarine design responsibilities, 1, 2;

suggesting FY 14 boat be ordered abroad, 68

Bugara (SS 331), 299

Building programs; Congressional desire for competing 800-tonners, 119; FY 09 East and West Coast contracts, 56; FY 10, 76, 77; FY 12, 79, 81; FY 14 General Board suggestion for advanced submarine, 83; FY 15's fleet submarine prototype, 101; FY 15's repeat K-boats, 85; FY 16 program characteristics, 86; FY 17-19 authorization for V-boats, 104; FY 17-19 inclusion of 800-ton prototypes, 119, 121; FY 18, 124; FY 19 V-1 through V-3 submarines, 113; FY 21 General Board requests, 163; FY 25 minelayer and cruiser characteristics, 174; FY 26 purchase of V-5 and V-6 cruisers, 164, 176–179; FY 35 characteristics approved, 200; FY 37 *Sargo* class, 204–205; FY 40 *Gar* class, 205; FY 41 *Gato* class, 206; FY 44 (1945 Combatant Building Program), 208; General Board's 1907 study affecting FY 09 policy, 55; introduction of annual, 2; Lake's offers for FY 09, 61; proposed 20-year (FY 28-47), 164; request for fleet boats for FY 19, 124; restoration of annual 6-boat program in FY 39, 164–165; suggestion to order FY 14 boat abroad, 68; WWI wartime experience affecting, 157–159

Bulkheads; on D-3 vs. D-1 and D-2 boats, 50; first use of subdividing, in submarines, 49; L-boat strong internal, 81; Laurenti's use of watertight, 66; mine defense, 127; R-2 boat's reinforced, 120; repeat K-boat's strong internal, 85; S-boat heavy, 128

Bullhead (SS 332), 299

Bumper (SS 333), 299

BuNav (Bureau of Navigation); submarine design responsibilities, 1; torpedo flotilla development, 6

BuOrd (Bureau of Ordance); attempt to control all periscope manufacture, 267; chemical fuel torpedoes, 245; deck guns for WWI, 127; designing turbine torpedoes for more than one setting, 156; fire-control system development, 218–219; Mk XIV torpedo development, 165; Mk XIV torpedo with Mk VI magnetic pistol, 242–243; submarine design responsibilities, 1; torpedo data computer (TDC) development, 196–197

Buoyancy; *see also* ballast tanks; 1887 Circular of Requirements requirement for positive, 22; early attempts to control, 6–7; *Octopus*'s limited reserve, 47; superstructures increasing reserve, 31; *Turbot*'s lack of reserve, 64

Buoys; elimination of aft marker, 146; released to indicate submarine position, 72; telephone-carrying messenger, 73, 142

Bureau of Navigation, *see* BuNav (Bureau of Navigation)

Bureau of Ordnance, *see* BuOrd (Bureau of Ordance)

Bureau of Ships, *see* BuShips (Bureau of Ships)

Bureaus, U.S. Navy; attempts to coordinate, 1; technological conservatism of, 2

Burrfish (SS 312), 298

Busch-Sulzer engines; as alternative to NELSECO engines, 258; as generators for fleet submarines, 107; installation in L-boats, 97

BuShips (Bureau of Ships); direct-drive motor development, 209–210; formation of, 1, 206; proposed post-WWII submarine designs, 248, 250; small submarine design, 229–230

Bushnell; Congressional authorization for, 81; SubDiv 5 Azores deployment, 152

Bushnell, Cornelius S., 16

Bushnell, David, 11–12

C&R (Construction and Repair); adopting welding in submarine construction, 200; alti-azimuth periscopes, 276; ASW submarine design, 158; comparisons of foreign and U.S.-made periscopes, 273; disagreement with fleet about periscopes, 280; foreign periscopes bought by, 271; post-V class submarine designs, 198; proposal for improvements to K class characteristics, 81; responsibility for U.S. submarine periscopes, 267; sketch designs for Long-Radius Submarine, 170; submarine design responsibilities, 1; suggesting FY 14 boat be ordered abroad, 68; trade-off study, 119; U-135's unsuitability for tropical patrols, 181–185; U-boat design and, 161; weaknesses in submarine design process, 2

C-boats; *see also Octopus* (C-1); changes to increase surface and submerged radius, 68–69; gasoline engines, 255; maximum time at sea, 68; proposals leading to, 35; rotating, fixed-eyepiece periscope, 271; stricken, 87

C-tubes, 156

Cabezon (SS 334), 299

Cable, Frank T., 25

Cabrilla (SS 288), 297

Cachalot (V-8); 1930 design schemes, 192; C&R 1928 design schemes, 186; data, 310; design evolution, 189–193; design schemes, 190; history of, 292; problems after entering service, 193

Cage (later Neff) system, 76

Caiman (SS 323), 299

CALSHIP (California Shipbuilding Corp.), FY 16 ships, 86

Canada; purchase of EB-19B submarine, 61; taking over EB 19B and 19E boats, 72

Capelin (SS 289), 297

Capitaine (SS 336), 299

Carbonero (SS 337), 299

Cargo submarines, conversion of *Bass* to, 114

Carl Zeiss periscopes, 270

Carnot, Sadi, 255

Carp (F-1), 286

Carp (SS 338), 299

Casings, *see* superstructures

Catfish (SS 339), 299

Causey, Lt. L. D., 152

Cavalla (SS 244), 295

Centrimetric radar, 235

Cero (SS 225), 294

"Chariot" bridge; G-3 and D-1 submarines, 65; H-2 submarine, 59; K-5 submarine, 81; L-8 submarine, 85; L-boats' permanent open, 153

Characteristics; for 800-tonner, 118–119; for FY 19 inspired by British fleet submarine, 104; K class submarine, 79–80; S-boat vs. coastal submarine, 119; in submarine design process, 2

Charles Whittemore (SP-3232), 154

Charr (SS 328), 299

Chile; H-boats transferred in compensation to, 78; ordering modified E-boats, 72

Chivo (SS 341); history of, 299; Mk 51 launcher, 219

Chlorine gas, 264

Chopper (SS 342); history of, 299; Mk 51 launcher, 219

Christie, Comdr. R. W., 221

Chub (SS 329), 299

CICs (combat information centers), 241, 249

Cisco (SS 290), 297

Civil War, submarine warfare in, 12–17

Clamagore (SS 343), 299

Clutches; friction, 46, 58; positive-engagement (claw), 58

CNO (chief of naval operations), 3–5

Coastal defense submarines; *see also* O-boats; R-boats; small submarines; acceptance for coast defense, 55; ASW patrols off U.S. coast, 154–155; designation as R class, 119; development of, 75–97; Emory S. Land's opposition to, 3; post-1919 change in mission of, 87, 97; recommended for FY 40, 222; submariners' dislikes of, 117

Cobbler (SS 344), 299

Cochino (SS 345), 299

Cod (SS 224); history of, 294; types 2 and 3 periscopes, 267

Collapse depths, 306–311; *Gar* class increase in, 205; increase to 900 ft, 209; proposed 800-ft, 249

Columbia University Division of War Research, 234

Combat information center (CIC), 241, 249

Comber (SS 527), 304

Compartmentalization; D class submarines, 49, 57; Lake boats vs. Electric Boat's boats, 85; loss of boats to collision because of less, 50

Composite drives, 202–204

Confederate submarines, 13–16

Conger (SS 477); fitted with JT triangulation listening ranging set, 239; history of, 303

Conning towers; B and C class designs, 45; CIC (combat information center) in, 241; defined, 9; elimination of periscopes in, 279; F class submarines, 62; first U.S. horizontal cylindrical, 178; guns moved forward of, 214; H-2 submarine, 59; *Haddo*, 244; improvements to *Adder*, 33–34; installation of walk-around periscopes in, 77–78; *Marlin*, 226; *Narwhals'*, 48; NDRC proposal for rearranging, 245; New London attack teacher, 246; proposed for E-2 submarine, 58; proposed small cruiser's small, 187; for proposed small submarines, 223, 224; *Protector's* double, 38; redesigned for O- and R-boats, 118; *Salmon*, 203; *Sea Lion*, 244; size reduction in D class, 60; submariners' dislike of L-boats' small, 118; submariners' proposals for large,

80, 118; TDC moved to, 197; *Thrasher's*, 67; V-1 through V-3 boats, 113; V-4 boat, 176

Construction and Repair, *see* C&R

Continental Motors Corp., 261

Control rooms; Laurenti's spacious, 66; need for torpedo-firing gear in, 49

Convoy escorts; countering U-cruisers off U.S. coast, 154; WWI U-cruisers forcing Allied use of, 151

Convoys, submarine attacks against, 233, 234

Coolidge tubes, *see* C-tubes

Corporal (SS 346), 299

Corsair (SS 435); conning tower CIC, 241; history of, 303

Corvina (SS 226), 294

Counterattacks, track angle and chance of, 155

Course finders, British Nasmith Director, 155

Covia (SS 245), 295

Crash-diving; design changes required for, 149; German U-boat provisions for, 159–160

Craven, Lt. Comdr. F. S., cruiser submarine proposal, 170

"Creep" dives, 161

Crevalle (SS 291); history of, 297; ST periscope and air-search radar mast, 236

Crew accommodations; *see also* habitability; *Bass* (V-2), 114; *Gato*, 206; German U-boat, 159; *Mackerel*, 225; *Marlin*, 226; *Thrasher's*, 67; V-1 boat's, 111

Croaker (SS 246), 295

Cruiser submarines; attempts to reduce size of, 180–186; C&R design changes to, 179, 185; characteristics proposed, 167–174; designs, 181; end of plans for big, 180; first formal proposal for, 166–167; originating in WWI proposal to build 54 scout submarines, 157; SC designation, 179

Cubera (SS 347), 299

Current Submarine Doctrine, USF 25, 234

Currupa (SS 359), 300

Cusk (SS 348), 300

Cutlass (SS 478), 303

Cuttlefish (B-2), 286

Cuttlefish (V-9); 32–33; 1930 design schemes, 192; as Americanized U-135, 189; design evolution, 189–193; dual periscopes and false bow, 43; flagstaffs and running lights, 43; history of, 292; as one of the last V-boats, 162–163; problems after entering service, 193

D-1 boat (SS 17); data, 306; May 1915 exercise results, 69

D-2 boat, 69

D-3 boats; hull periscope, 272; introduction of features planned for E and F classes, 50

D-boats; change of *Narwhal* designation to, 33; changes to increase surface and submerged radius, 68–69; design of, 48–49; engine runs and effective range, 68; gasoline engines, 255; re-engining with diesels, 49–50, 69; rotating, fixed-eyepiece periscope, 271; torpedo tube problems, 50

Dace (SS 247), 295

Darter (SS 227), 294

Daubin, Lt. Comdr. F. A., opinion of U-111 boat, 159
"Davids," 13
Davis guns, 127
DCDI (depth charge direction indicator), 248
DCRE (depth charge range estimator), 248
De Villeroi, Brutus, 12–13
Decoys, submarine, 247
Defender; described, 47–48; trials against Electric Boat, 48
DeFrees, Adm. J. R., 221–222
Denny-Hay submarines, 69
Dentuda (SS 335), 299
Depth charge direction indicator (DCDI), 248
Depth charge range estimator (DCRE), 248
Depth charges; evasive tactics, 248; post-WWI studies of, 161; risk from small surface crafts carrying, 150; *Tambor* tests leading to heavier, 205–206; test and collapse depths increased to evade, 205
Depths, *see* collapse depths; test depths
Devilfish (SS 292), 297
Dewey, Adm. George; and General Board, 2; *Holland VI* and, 26–27; request for submarines to defend Subic, 56
Diablo (SS 479), 303
Diesel engines; *see also* diesel generators; diesel-electric drives; direct-drive diesel engines; MAN diesel engines; adoption of, for FY 09 program, 56–60; *Argonaut*'s, 176; BuEng and MAN compared, 259; BuEng's procurement of, 259–263; experiments with running on compressed air, 76; first satisfactory, 87; fleet boat prototype's tandem, 101; functional description, 256; FY 16 reversion to 4-cycle design, 86; German alternative configuration, 107; installation aboard D class, 50, 69; Japanese and U.S. compared, 253; lightweight versions compared, 265; *Narwhal* modernization, 180; non-reversing, powering E- and F-boats, 58, 62; *Porpoise*, 200; proposed post-WWII submarine, 249; supercharging, 262; *Turbot*, 64; unreliability of, 60; V-1 through V-3 boats, 113
Diesel generators; *see also* auxiliary diesel generators; British Royal Navy's fleet submarine, 104; Busch-Sulzer engines as, 107; V-1 through V-3 boats, 113
Diesel, Rudolf, 255, 256
Diesel-electric drives; as solution to torsional vibration, 259; *Swordfish*, 204
Diodon (SS 349), 300
Direct-drive diesel engines; eliminating gear noise, 209–210; *Mackerel*, 225; *Marlin*, 226
Displacement; *see also* London Naval Treaty (1930); increase in planned cruiser, 179; Japanese increase, 253; *Salmon* increase in, 202; Submarine 1919, 105; submarine performance vs., 77, 118
Diver's compartments; G-1 boats, 51, 52; "Intelligent Whale," 16; U-1 and U-2 boats, 70
Diving; *see also* crash-diving; *Adder*'s lengthy process of, 30; additional holes drilled into superstructures for faster, 167; ballast tanks and, 130; "down

express" tank for quicker, 205; to escape depth charges, 161; G-1's lengthy process of, 51; Holland's underwater "airplane" vs. rivals' underwater "helicopters," 19; K-boat's slow, 106; limber holes for fast, 86; made quicker by sealing off engine room, 66–68; *Narwhals*' slow, 180; O-boats' (Lake) slow, 151; with partly filled ballast tanks, 6, 19; *Protector*'s even-keel, 38; Q tank and, 34; R-boat's (Lake) slow, 119, 151; reduction in angle of, 61; required expertise for, on *Adders*, 30; S-2 boat's slow, 121; speeds of U.S. boats vs. German U-boats, 229; T-boat's slow, 104; U-858 and U-889 boats' slow, 252; under thermal layers as evasion, 248; using independent planesmen, 155; WWII changes in procedure, 210
Diving planes; *see also* bow planes; change from riveted to welded skegs, 47; enabling unattended depth keeping on U-1 and U-2 boats, 70; on Holland's *No. 1*, 20; Holland's underwater "airplane," 19; Laurenti's linked fore and aft, 68
Docking keels, 175
Dogfish (SS 350), 300
Dolphin (V-7); *see also* V-7 boat; as attempt to reduce submarine size, 187; data, 309; designs leading to, 182; history of, 292; proposals leading to, 139; reduced number of annual battery cycles in, 200; use for training, 188
Dorado (SS 248), 295
Dorado (SS 526), 304
"Dory" bow, 159, 176
Double armature motors, 265
Double-hull submarines; ballast tanks in, 6, 8; Electric Boat's first U.S., 88, 89; FY 14 program, 83; lengthening of S-boat, 139; *Silversides*, 5; submariners' arguments for, 80; *Thrasher*, 66; uniqueness of Lake submarine design, 7–9
"Down express" tanks; kept flooded in wartime, 210; *Triton*, 205
Dragonet (SS 293), 297
Drum (SS 228), 294
DuBose, Adm. W. G., 224
Duct keels; D-boats, 57; E-2 submarine, 60; Electric Boat's B class, 90; Electric Boat's S-boat, 132, 135
Dugong (SS 353), 300
Dutch Navy, first submarine built for, 36
Dutch Nedinsco periscope, 279–280

E-1 boat, *see Skipjack* (E-1)
E-1 boat (SS 24), 306
E-2 boat; battery explosion, 265; design of, 58; May 1915, exercise results, 69; periscopes, 268; range of installed radio, 76; U-shaped ballast tanks, 60
E-boats; bifocal periscopes, 268; bow diving planes, 61, 62; diesel engines, 62; friction clutches, 58; housing periscopes, 272; introduction of, 56–60; torpedoes, 61
EB 16 boats, *see* B-boats; *Viper* (EB 16)
EB 17 boats, *see* C-boats; *Octopus* (C-1)
EB 27B boats, 44
EB 31 boats, *see Narval* (EB 31) class
EB-19B boat, 61
Eberle, CNO Adm. E. W., 280

Echo fathometers, S-boat, 131
Edison, Thomas, 265
Edwards, Lt. (jg) R. S., 75
Eel (SS 354), 300
Electric Boat Company; *see also Fulton* (submarine); 75-foot submarine design, 44; alti-azimuth periscopes, 276; attempts to sell submarines abroad, 69; bid to build diesel engines, 261; bottlenecks in building submarines, 157; consequences of *Adder* delays, 28–29; as contract design agent, 3; dominance in early submarine evolution, 2; double-hull B class design, 90; EB 16 and 17 submarines, 45–48; evolution of standard design, 57; first U.S. double-hull submarine, 88, 89; fixed-eyepiece periscope with all-round vision, 272; fleet submarine designs offered for FY 14, 100–101; FY 10 contract, 77; FY 14 program designs, 83–85; gasoline engines, 255; "general purpose" submarine proposal, 185; John Holland employment at, 26; large conning towers with periscopes, 118; loss of monopoly in FY 09 program, 56; manufacturing periscopes, 269; modifications to *Adders*, 33–35; O class submarines, 87; opposition to foreign boat purchases, 68; pasted plate batteries, 264; *Perch* class submarines, 200; permission to use steel tubes in periscopes, 267; post-WWI collapse of exports, 72; proposal for additional periscope in C and D classes, 48; R-1 through R-20 submarines, 119; rebuilding S-boats, 133; receiving largest S-boat contract, 124; rotating fixed-eyepiece telescopes, 270, 271; sale of H-boats to British, 78; sales to European navies, 72; single-hull S-boat design, 119, 134, 135; small submarines for foreign customers, 92; small submarines for U.S. Navy, 223, 224; submarines built for export, 35–38; switch to thicker hulls, 209; two-window bifocal periscope, 268; Vickers' 4-cycle diesel engines, 257; Vickers' financial support for, 36; WWII expansion of capacity, 206
Electric motors; direct drive, 209–210, 225; testing of high-speed geared, 200
Electric torpedoes, *see* wakeless torpedoes
Electronic intelligence (ELINT), 236–238
ELINT (electronic intelligence), 236–238
Emergency blowing, U-boat decentralization of, 160
Endurance; British Royal Navy's fleet submarine, 104; coast defense submarines' limited, 154; equated with engine reliability, 77; of Pacific submarines, 189; of planned steam submarine vs. diesel, 103; proposed cruiser submarine, 166, 168, 170; S-18 class, 137; Spear's opinions for best increasing, 76; submariner demands for greater, 117–118; *Tench*, 209; U-boat low-speed, 107; WWI need for increased low speed, 150
Engineering magazine, publishing accounts of Electric Boat submarines, 36
Engines; *see also* Brayton engines; diesel engines; gasoline engines; internal combustion engines; capable of

operating with submarine awash, 38; cruiser charging, 179–180; directly driving motor and propeller shaft on *Vipers*, 46; effect of closed ventilators on, 75–76; fleet submarine prototype, 101; H class reversible, 77; increasing power by placing on each propeller shaft, 66; proposal of three for new cruiser, 186; for proposed small submarines, 221–222; Scheme L-3 fleet submarine, 110; surface power (BHP), 306–311; too few for proposed small submarines, 230; U-1 and U-2 boats, 70; V-1 boat Fleet Submarine 1919 design, 111

Entemedor (SS 340), 299

Escape hatches; added to after motor room, 139; O-8 boat, 96; S-8 boat, 128; S-22 boat, 143

Escolar (SS 294), 297

Espada (SS 355), 300

Evaporators, O class introduction of, 87

Even-keel diving; *Protector*, 38; wartime inadequacy of, 151

Exide batteries, 264–265

F-1 boat (SS 20), 306

F-boats; bow diving planes, 61, 62; conning tower, 62; diesel engines, 62; diesel engines powering, 58; friction clutches, 58; housing periscopes, 272; non-reversing diesels powering, 58; relocation of periscopes on, 60; torpedoes, 61

Fairbanks Morse, 261, 262

Fairwaters, 9

False target cans (FTCs), 247, 248

False target shells (FTSs), 247, 248

Fathometers, S-boat echo, 131

Fenian Ram, 20–21

Fessenden oscillators; Electric Boat's single-hull S-boats, 134; replacing signal bells, 85; underwater communications among harbor defense boats using, 76

Fife, Capt. James, 227

Figure-eight hulls, 180

Finback (SS 230), 294

Fire-control systems; *see also* guns; described, 218–219; elements of, 215

Fiscal year (FY) programs, *see* building programs

Flasher (SS 249), 295

Fleet Submarine 1917; Scheme F, 122; Scheme I, 123

Fleet Submarine 1918, 105

Fleet Submarine 1919, 104–105, 107, 111; *see also* V-1 boats

Fleet submarines; *see also* scout submarines; Congressional authorization for, 86; Congressional authorization for FY 16, 101; designs for FY 17-19 program, 104–107; FY 15 prototype, 101; *Porpoise* as precursor to WWII, 198–200; possibilities developed in 1912 war games, 99–100; post-WWI forward-operations, 151; requested as potential submarine cruisers in WWI, 157; SF designation, 179; size requirement for speed and endurance, 110; WWI delays in building V class, 104

Fleets, submarine, General Board's 1907 study for deployment of, 55–56

Flier (SS 250), 295

Flounder (SS 251), 295

"Flying" bridges, 35

Flying Fish (SS 229), 294

Forfait, P. A. L., 12

Forrestal, James V., 250

French submarines; *Gustave Zede*, 100; *Gymnote*, 21

Friction clutches; E- and F-boats, 58; *Octopus*'s problems with, 46; relocation of periscopes, 60

FTCs (false target cans), 247, 248

FTSs (false target shells), 247, 248

Fuel; end of ballast tank storage, 202; increasing endurance by using denser, 76–77; return to ballast tank stowage, 204; S-20 boat's external blisters for carrying, 137; stored in ballast tanks, 137, 142

Fulton, Robert; attempts to control buoyancy, 6; submarine experiments and mine warfare ideas, 12

Fulton (submarine); construction and trials, 27–28; demonstration to foreign representatives, 36; described, 30; offered for sale to Navy, 35; sale to Russia, 42; trials, 40–42

Fulton (tender), 79

FY (fiscal year) programs, *see* building programs

G-1 boat (SS 19-1/2); change in designation from *Seal*, 33; data, 306; deficiencies of, 51–55; depth charge tests on, 161; distinctive stern, 87; U-shaped ballast tanks, 60

G-2 boat (SS 27), 306; *see also Tuna* (G-2)

G-3 (SS 31) boat, *see Turbot* (G-3)

G-3 (SS 31) class data, 307

G-4 boat (SS 26), *see Thrasher* (G-4)

G-4 (SS 26) class data, 307

Gabilan (SS 252), 295

Galileo periscopes, 270, 273

Gar class (SS 206–211), increased collapse depth, 205

Gar (SS 206); 5-in/51 gun, 214; history of, 293

Garfish (H-3), 287

Garlopa (SS 358), 300

Gas Engine and Power Company, 25

Gas turbine engine proposal, 248

Gasoline engines; 250-BHP aboard *Octopus* (EB 17C), 48; abandonment of by European navies, 56; disadvantages of, 255; G-4 as last U.S. submarine using, 64; problems with G-1's four, 51; proposed post-WWII gas turbine, 248; replacement with diesels in D class, 69

Gato class (SS 212–214, 228–230); data, 311; development of, 206

Gato (SS 212); described, 206; history of, 294; wartime modifications, 216

Gear noise; direct-drive motors developed to eliminate, 209–210; in *Holland* and A-boats, 30

General Board; 5-year plan for potential German-Japanese alliance, 157; and ascendancy of OpNav, 3–6; characteristics for 800-tonner, 118–119, 224; comparison of U.S. fleet vs. British and Japanese, 164; countering attempts to abolish submarines, 158–159; failure to realize lack of seaworthiness of small submarines, 77; Fleet Submarine 1919 characteristics, 107; FY 10 program

characteristics, 76; FY 11 request for tenders, 78; FY 16 request for fleet submarines, 101; FY 18 objections to proposed program, 124; FY 25 characteristics for cruisers and minelayers, 174; FY 40 characteristics for small-medium submarines, 224; proposed post-WWII submarine characteristics, 249; reliability of submarines for coastal defense, 55; revised small submarine characteristics, 229; submarine design responsibilities, 2

General Motors, 260–261, 262

"General purpose" submarines; in cruiser and fleet support roles, 189; Electric Boat Company proposal, 185; SS designation for, 179

German Navy; attacks on Allied trade, 151; projections of number of submarines in post-WWI, 157; purchase of first diesel U-boat engines, 256–257

German submarines, *see* U-boats (German)

Gibson, Comdr. Holbrook, recommending additional stern tubes, 187

Goerz periscopes, 270, 271

Goldring (SS 360), 300

Golet (SS 361), 300

Gould centrifugal trim pump, 209

Gould Plante batteries, 264–265

Grampus (A-3), 29, 32–33; history of, 286; modernized, 44

Grampus (SS 207), 293

Grampus (SS 523), 304

Grant, Adm. A.W., 6

Grayback (SS 208), 293

Grayling (D-2), 286

Grayling (SS 209), 293

Grayling (SS 492), 303

Greenfish (SS 351), 300

Greenling (SS 213), 294

Grenadier (SS 210), 293

Grenadier (SS 525), 304

Grouper (SS 214); described, 217; history of, 294

Growler (SS 214), 294

Grunion (SS 216), 294

Guardfish (SS 217), 294

Guavina (SS 362), 300

Gudgeon (SS 211), 294

Guitarro (SS 363), 300

Gun batteries; standard late WWII, 218, 219; underwater drag and, 126–127

"Gunboats," submarines converted to, 215, 219

Gunnel (SS 253), 296

Guns, 306–311; *see also entries for specific guns*; fire-control systems; C&R provision for in L class bidders' package, 81; delays in firing antiaircraft, 165; Electric Boat's B class 76-mm antiaircraft, 90; *Fenian Ram*'s 9-in pneumatic dynamite, 21; Fleet Submarine's 5-in/51, 111; *Gato*'s 20-mm, 40-mm, and 4-in/50, 215; *Gato*'s, 206; *Holland VI* pneumatic dynamite, 24; insufficient fire power of disappearing 3-in, 124–126; L-1 boat's 3-in/23, 150; L-11 boat's 3-in/23, 85; L-boat provision for 3-in, 81; *Marlin*, 226; O-6 boat's disappearing 3-in/23, 168; *Pompano*'s 20-mm and 3-in/50, 196; *Porpoise*'s 20-mm,

Guns (*continued*)
211; proposed for fighting enemy submarines on surface, 77; R-1 submarine's 3-in/50 deck, 121; replacement of 4-inchers with 3-in/50 on S-boats, 145; replacement of 5-in/51 with 3-in/50 on V-1 boats, 113; requested for U.S. submarines in European waters, 152; S-1 boat's disappearing 3-in/23, 124; S-18 boat's 40-mm, 131; S-boat deck, 127; S-boats fitted with 20-mm, 147; *Snapper's* 4-in/50, 213; *Sunfish's* 20- and 40-mm, 167; T-2 boat's 4-in/50, 103; T-3 boat's 4-in/50, 104; *Tambor* class, 204, 214; U-boat's two, 160; WWI usefulness against small surface craft, 150; WWII, 214–219

Gurnard (SS 254); gun access trunks, 218; history of, 296
Gustave Zede, 100
Gymnote, 21
Gyrocompasses, unreliability of WWI U.S., 152–153
Gyros, torpedo; ability to angle Bliss-Leavitt, 50; difficulties of gyro shots, 195–196; post-1918 attack tactics and, 137

H. L. Hunley, 15, 16
H-1 boat (SS 28), 287
H-1 (SS 28) class data, 307
H-2 submarine, design of, 59
H-4 through H-9 boats, 291
H-boats; diesel engines, 258; earmarked for training, 97; modifications from F class, 77–78; obsolescence of, 87; purchase by U.S. Navy after Russian Revolution, 72; WWI proving insufficient size of, 150–151
Habitability; *see also* crew accommodations; attempts to reduce cruiser size and, 186; German U-570 boat, 229; increasing submarine size, 166; M-1 submarine, 88; O class improvements, 87; U-boat, 160
Hackleback (SS 295), 297
Haddo (SS 255); conning tower, 244; history of, 296
Haddock (SS 231), 294; first SJ attack, 236; gun battery for wolfpack work, 218; history of, 287
Hajen, 36–37
Hake (SS 256); described, 242; history of, 296
Half-switches, 150
Halfbeak (SS 352), 300
Halibut (SS 232), 294
Halstead, O. S., 16–17
Hammerhead (SS 364), 300
Harbor defense submarines; described, 33–73; Holland's design for, 20
Harder (SS 257), 296
Hardhead (SS 365), 300
Hart, Adm. Thomas C.; austere design scheme data, 310–311; construction of 300-ft boat urged (as Capt.), 110; cruiser submarine proposals (as Capt.), 167–168; fleet submarine design recommendations (as Capt.), 106, 107; on German U-boat pressure hulls (as Capt.), 160; long-range submarines, support for (as Capt.), 151; repeating class of FY 38 boats, 204; as senior U.S. submariner (as Capt.), 6; shift from four 21-in to six 18-in torpedo tubes urged

(as Capt.), 127; small submarines and, 221–223, 224, 227
Harvard University Underwater Sound Laboratory, 234
Hawkbill (SS 366), 300
Hay, Marley, 69
Hay-Whitehead submarines, 69
Helvetia (SP-3096), 154
Herring (SS 233), 294
High-tensile steel (HTS) skin, 208, 209
HMS *Eagle*, 12
Hoe, sonars, 243
Hoe (SS 258), 296
Holland, 27; *see also Holland VI*
Holland, John; *see also* "Intelligent Whale"; building *Holland VI*, 24–27; forming Nautilus Submarine Boat Company with Zalinsky, 21; joining Rice in Electric Boat Company, 26; *Plunger* design, 22–25; as precursor to modern submarine designers, 11; self-propelled torpedo influencing, 17; selling boats to Japan, 37; underwater "airplane," 19–20; *Viper* (B) class, 29
Holland (SS 1), 306
Holland VI, 24–27, 286
Hooven, Owens, Rentschler, 262
Hoover, Comdr. J. H., 181
Housatonic, 16
Howard Grubb periscopes, 270
HTS (high-tensile steel) skin, 208, 209
Hulls; *see also* double-hull submarines; pressure hulls; single-hull submarines; adoption of HTS (high-tensile steel) for, 208, 209; difficulties in optimizing for surface speed, 110; EB 31 class, 72; figure-eight, 180; modifications to S-boat, 130; Scheme E fleet submarine design, 107; V-1 boat's bulbous, 111; *Walrus* single and double, 4
Hunley, H. L., 13–16
Hydrogen peroxide-fueled torpedoes, 245
Hydrophones; German "creep" diving to evade Allied, 161; L-10 boat's fixed-spot, 153; range of Japanese, 247; for submarines unable to listen while surfaced, 235

Icefish (SS 367), 300
Instability; *see also* stability; of Holland's rivals' submarines, 19; Holland's solutions for, 20, 21
Internal combustion engines; *Holland VI*, 25; pre-diesel vs. modern, 255
"Intelligent Whale," 16–17
Irex (SS 482), 303
Ironclads, 12–17

Jack (SS 259), 296
Jallao (SS 368), 300
Japan; merchant fleet sunk by U.S. submarines, 233; as most likely post-WWI enemy, 151; post-WWI plans for possible war with, 163–164; purchasing *Adders* for war with Russia, 36; rising tensions with U.S. after Russo-Japanese War, 55; violation of 1930 Treaty limiting submarines built, 164
Japanese submarines; engines, 253; projections of number of post-WWI, 157; use of sonar, 247
Jawfish, ex-*Fanegal* (SS 356), 300
Jefferson, Pres. Thomas, 12
Jellicoe, Adm. Sir John, 100

JK high-frequency passive sonar; described, 144, 198; installation on O, R, and S class boats, 142, 143, 145; *Mackerel*, 225
JP passive sonar; added to deck gear, 239; tested vs. JK, 144
JT line array sonar; *Crevalle*, 236; described, 239; *Hoe*, 243

K-1 boat (SS 32); history of, 287; SubDiv Irish Sea deployment, 152
K-1 (SS 32) class data, 307
K-2 boat; history of, 287; SubDiv Irish Sea deployment, 152
K-5 boat; faired periscope shears and Fessenden oscillator, 79; history of, 287; in May 1915 exercise, 78; standard WWI modifications, 81; SubDiv Irish Sea deployment, 152
K-6 boat; history of, 287; SubDiv Irish Sea deployment, 152
K-7 boat, 287
K-8 boat; history of, 287; rotating bow cap, 80
K-boats; assigned to Europe in 1917, 152; British Navy's deployment of, 105–106; comments on characteristics for, 79–80; diesel engines, 258; earmarked for training, 97; Gould paste batteries, 264; May 1915 exercise results, 78; repeat, 81, 85
K-tube fixed sonar array, 156
Kaiman class (Russian) submarines; *see also* G-1 boat (SS 19-1/2); *Alligator*, 53; described, 71, 72; features introduced by, 51
Keel sonars, 198, 226
Keels; D class duct, 57; E-2 duct, 60; Electric Boat's S-boat duct, 132, 135; heavy lead, 68; Model 2519's docking, 175; *Protector's* even-keel, 38; S-17 boat's box, 129; S-boat deck, 128
Kete (SS 369), 300
Kettering, Charles, 260–261
Keuffel & Esser periscopes, 268, 269, 273
Kimball, Lt. William W., 21, 22
King, Adm. Ernest J.; as CNO, 6; control of submarine production and outfitting, 6; postwar submarine construction, 208; proposed post-WWII submarine designs, 248, 250; small submarines and, 228
Kingfish (SS 234), 295
Kingston valves; *see also* ballast tanks; removed from ballast tanks, 210; size required for quick diving, 149
Kollmorgen periscopes, 269, 270, 273, 276, 280
Kraken (SS 370), 300
Krupp; sales to Norway, 72; U-boats in Austrian trials, 69
Krupp diesel engines, 256–257

L-1 boat; 3-in/23 disappearing-mount gun, 150; history of, 287; SubDiv 5 Azores deployment, 152; wartime modifications to, 84
L-1 (SS 40) class data, 307
L-2 boat; history of, 287; SubDiv 5 Azores deployment, 152, 153
L-3 boat; history of, 287; SubDiv 5 Azores deployment, 152
L-4 boat; history of, 287; near loss of, 153–154; problems firing torpedoes,

153; SubDiv 5 Azores deployment, 152, 153–154
L-5 boat (SS 44), 287
L-5 (SS 44) class data, 307
L-6 boat, 287
L-7 boat, 287
L-8 boat; described, 85; Exide's "ironclad" battery, 264; history of, 287; limber holes, 86
L-9 boat; history of, 287; SubDiv 5 Azores deployment, 152; war modifications to, 84
L-10 boat; fixed-spot hydrophones, 153; guns and periscope, 83; history of, 288; SubDiv 5 Azores deployment, 152
L-11 boat; Fessenden oscillator and 3-in gun, 85; history of, 288; problems firing torpedoes, 153; SubDiv 5 Azores deployment, 152
L-boats; AL-designations for SubDiv 5 boats, 84, 152; assigned to Europe in 1917, 152; at Berehaven, Ireland, 158; described, 81–83; earmarked for training, 97; insufficient size of, 151; reliance on SC-tubes, 156; submariners' dislike of small conning towers, 118; surviving German depth charges, 161; war modifications, 153
Lake, Simon; see also CALSHIP (California Shipbuilding Corp.); Kaiman class (Russian) submarines; Lake submarines; Argonaut Junior, 31; attempts to sell submarines abroad, 69; Defender, 47; destroyer yard, 157; G-1 (Seal) boats, 51–55; L-boats, 83; Lake X, 42–45; manufacturing periscopes, 269; "omniscope" periscope, 267, 272–273; out of business, 133; Protector submarine, 38–45; Tuna, 61–62; Turbot, 62–64; U-1 and U-2 submarines, 70
Lake submarines; Busch-Sulzer engines in S-boats, 124; change in designation from Seal to G-1, 33; designed for under-ice operations, 94; distinctive sterns, 87; double-hulled S-boat prototype, 119–121; engine changes to V-boats, 113; Gould Plante batteries, 264; L-8 boat with ship-type stern, 85; last designed for U.S. Navy, 126; N-5, 91; O-12, 93; R-21 through R-27 submarines, 119; redesigned R-boats for additional periscopes, 118; unusual superstructures and hulls of, 7–9; WWI deficiencies of, 151
Lake X, 42–45
Lake XV; see Defender
Lamprey (SS 372), 300
Lancetfish (SS 296), 297
Land, Emory S.; arguing need for larger submarines, 117, 151; comparing coastal submarine classes, 119; opinion of Electric Boat's O class, 87; opposition to small coastal submarines, 2–3
Lapon (SS 260), 296
Large submarines; see also cruiser submarines; fleet submarines; S-boats; scout submarines; C&R plans for FY 14, 83; Spear's skepticism of supposed advantages of, 76; submariners' 1910 request for compartmented, 79
Laubeuf, Maxime, 19
Laurenti, Cesare, 64; see also American Laurenti Co.
Lee, Sgt. Ezra, 11–12

Legarto (SS 371); gun battery for wolfpack work, 218; history of, 300
Lengths, submarine, 306–311
Leovy, H. J., 13
Limber holes; additional holes drilled into Sunfish's superstructure, 167; crash-diving requirement for more, 149; Gato's additional, 216; L-8 boat, 86; Tambor's additional, 214
Ling (SS 297), 297
Lionfish (SS 298), 297
Listening attacks, 156–157
Listening gear, WWI Allied innovation in, 156–157
Little, Capt. C. J., 106
Lizardfish (SS 373), 300
Lockwood, Capt. C. A.; gas turbines in post-WWII submarines, 248; Great Lakes tour in UC-97 boat (as Lt. Comdr.), 160; providing foundations strong enough for 5-in guns, 214–218; special weapons in post-WWII submarines, 249; tentative characteristics for patrol submarine, 222
Loggerhead (SS 374), 300
London Naval Treaty (1930); see also displacement; size, submarine; "escalator" clause, 164; forcing navy to discard S-boats, 139; Japanese response to, 253
Long Radius Submarine 1919, 169, 170; see also cruiser submarines

M-1 boat (SS 47); cross-section of double hull, 89; described, 88; experimental version, 83; history of, 287
M-1 (SS 47) class data, 307
Macabi (SS 375), 300
McArthur, Lt. Arthur, 33
McClintock, James R., 13
McIntosh and Seymour diesel engines, 259
McKee, Andrew, 208–209
Mackerel (SS 204), 293; built, 227; data, 311; described, 225, 228; war modifications, 230
McLean, Rear Adm. Ridley; proposal for aide to oversee characteristics and operations (as Lt. Comdr.), 6; on submarine reliability, 186
Magnetic pistol, 242
Magnification, periscope, 269
MAN diesel engines; BuEng copying U-boat, 161, 258; BuEng's purchase of license for, 260; feasibility of lightweight, in small cruisers, 189; problems switching from Vickers to, 77; S-20 boat, 137; S-48 boat, 139; S-boats re-engined with, 133; sales to navies, 256–257
Maneuverability; auxiliary rudder added to reduce turning circle, 210–211; proposed rudders for post-WWII submarines, 248, 252
Manitowoc Shipbuilding, 206
Manta (SS 299), 298
Mapiro (SS 376), 300
Mare Island; limited wartime (WWII) building capacity, 206; postwar submarine building, 208
Marker buoys; elimination of aft, 146; S-22 boat, 143; tests, 72
Marlin (SS 205); Adm. Hart's role in decision to build, 6; built, 227; data, 311;

described, 226; history of, 293; periscope, 281; proposed redesign of, 227, 228; war modifications, 220–221, 230
Marsh, Capt. Charles C. (as Comdr.), 6
Massachusetts Institute of Technology (MIT), 234, 247
MB passive sonar, 156
Medregal (SS 480), 303
Menhaden (SS 377), 301
Merchant ships, submarine attacks against, 233, 234
Meriam, Scovel S., 16
Mero (SS 377); history of, 301; SV air-search radar and bridge, 209
Merrimack (CSS Virginia), 12
Messenger buoys; development of telephone-carrying, 73; installed on O, R, and S class boats, 142
Michelsen, Adm. Andreas, 152
Midget submarines, 92
"Milch cows," 137
Mine defense bulkheads, 127
Mine Mk 27 torpedo, 245
Mine warfare; conducted by Turtle, 12; considered as strategic scout role, 163; hazards of submarine minelaying, 245; Robert Fulton's contributions to, 12; in Taft Board's recommendations for coastal defense, 55
Minelayers, submarine; FY 25 characteristics for, 174, 176; mine stowage proposals, 174; proposal for prototype, 157–158
Mines; degaussing required by threat of magnetic, 234–235; lack of German respect for in WWI, 161; sonar detection of, 240; stowage location aboard Argonaut, 178; Tambor class capability, 204
Mingo (SS 261), 296
Minnesota, 14
MIT (Massachusetts Institute of Technology), 234, 247
Mk 1-3 TDCs (torpedo data computers), 196; see also TDCs
Mk 6 computer, 218–219
Mk 6 stable element, 219
Mk 10/11 mines, 176
Mk 14 pepper signal, 247–248
Mk 14 torpedo directors, 145
Mk 16 torpedo; Mk 31 control of, 242; proposed post-WWII submarine, 249
Mk 18 torpedo, 243–245
Mk 19 torpedo, 245
Mk 20 pepper signal, 247–248
Mk 22 torpedo, 246
Mk 24 (Fido) torpedo, 245
Mk 27 (Cutie) torpedo, 245
Mk 28 torpedo, 245
Mk 30 torpedo, 246
Mk 31 computer, TDC and, 241–242
Mk 35 torpedo, 246, 247
Mk 51 rocket launcher, 219
Mk 101 computer, 242
Mk IX gun, 85
Mk VI magnetic pistol, 242–243
Mk XIV torpedo, 242–243
Moccasin (A-4), 30; battery ruined when grounded, 264; history of, 286
Model 2519 (cruiser), 175
Modernization, submarine; Argonaut (V-4), 176; of "Holland" S-boats, 145, 146; Nautilus and Narwhal, 180; post-WWI, 163–164

Monitor, 12

Moray (SS 300), 298

Morgan, Armand F., 208–209

Morrisey, Comdr. E. R., 279–280

Morton, Lt. Comdr. Dudley W. ("Mush"), 232–233

Motors; *see also* electric motors; capable of discharging battery in one hour, 49, 77; connected by friction clutches on E- and F-class boats, 58; double armature, 265; friction clutch problems aboard *Octopus*, 46; German-type creep, 252; HP of submerged, 306–311; main auxiliaries driven by separate electric, 83; *Porpoise*'s eight main propulsion, 200; problems ventilating S-boat, 137; U-1 and U-2 submarines, 70

Mufflers; introduction of wet, 210; *Snapper* and *Spearfish*, 213; *Sturgeon*, 212

Muskellunge (SS 262), 296

MV passive sonar system; described, 156; S-20 boat, 138; S-49 boat, 136; U-3 *Eel* towed line array use with, 149

N-1 boat; described, 92; history of, 288

N-1 (SS 53) class data, 307

N-2 boat; history of, 288; use for training, 91

N-3 boat, 288

N-4 boat, 288

N-4 (SS 56) class data, 307

N-5 boat, 288; standard sound gear, 91

N-6 boat, 288

N-7 boat, 288

N-boats; development of, 85–86; earmarked for training, 97; patrols off U.S. coast, 154

NAC decoys, 247, 248

NAD decoys, 247, 248

NAE decoys, 247, 248

NAG decoys, 247

Narval (EB 31) class; inspiring fleet submarine program, 100; Russian purchase of, 72

Narwhal (D-1); described, 180; history of, 286; initial SC designation, 179; inspired by German WWI U-cruisers, 179; sonars, 198; WWII modifications, 183, 184, 185

Narwhal (V-5), 292

Nasmith Director, 155

National Defense Research Committee (NDRC); coordinating civilian research, 234; JT sonar tests, 239; proposed rearranged conning tower, 245

National Industrial Recovery Act, 198

Nautilus (H-2), 12; conversion for operation in iced waters, 94; described, 180; exercise testing tactical value of surface speed, 200; FY 26 program authorization for, 179; history of, 287; vulnerability of external torpedo tubes, 180, 186

Nautilus Submarine Boat Company, 21

Nautilus (V-5), 292

Nautilus (V-6) data, 309

Naval Torpedo Station (Newport; as BuOrd's main experimental base, 1; Rhode Island), founding of, 11

Naval War College; 1909 proposal for submarine force, 76; defending logic of Pacific warfare, 189; fleet submarine requirements, 99–100; as navy's "think tank," 2; optimum "treaty" submarine, 191

Navigation; Holland's proposal to use compass for, 20; U.S. and British WWI submarines compared, 152–153

Naval Mk 10 torpedo, 245

NDRC (National Defense Research Committee); coordinating civilian research, 234; JT sonar tests, 239; proposed rearranged conning tower, 245

Nedinsco periscopes, 280

Needlefish (SS 379), 301

Neff, A. R., 76

Negative tank; *see* "down express" tanks

NELSECO (New London Ship and Engine Company), 257, 258

Nerka (SS 380), 301

Neutral buoyancy; as requirement in early submarines, 6; simulating while using listening gear, 156

New Ironsides, 16

New London Ship and Engine Company (NELSECO), 257, 258

Nielsen, Lt. Comdr. J. L., 160

Nimitz, Adm. Chester, fleet submarine design recommendations (as Lt. Comdr.), 107

NLMs (noise level monitors), 247

No. 1, John Holland's, 20–21

Noise level monitors (NLMs), 247

Nordberg diesel engines, 259

Nordenfeldt (Swedish arms manufacturer), 21

Norwegian purchases from Krupp and Electric Boat, 72

NRL (Naval Research Laboratory); integrating electronics systems, 241; interwar U.S. sonars, 197

O-1 (SS 62) boat; bow cap, 93; history of, 288; stern and skeg, 95

O-1 (SS 62) class data, 307

O-2 boat, 288

O-3 boat, 288

O-4 boat; assignment to convoy duty, 154; forward radio loop antenna fitting, 95; history of, 288

O-5 boat, 288

O-6 boat; fired upon by U.S. ships, 154; history of, 288; post-WWI radio-receiving antennas, 168

O-7 boat, 288

O-8 boat; history of, 288; modifications for greater safety, 96

O-9 boat, 288

O-10 boat; forward radio loop antenna fitting, 95; history of, 288

O-11 boat (SS 72); Exide's "ironclad" battery, 264; history of, 288

O-11 (SS 72) class data, 307

O-12 boat; described, 93; history of, 288; rebuilt for Wilkins Arctic expedition, 94, 97

O-13 boat, 288

O-14 boat, 288

O-15 boat, 288

O-16 boat; Exide's "ironclad" battery, 264; history of, 288

O-boats; Congressional authorization for, 86; diesel engines, 258; dimensions, 93; first satisfactory diesels, 87; laid up and stricken (Lake-built), 97; ordered scrapped, 208; retention for WWII use, 96, 97; safety modifications, 142

Octopus (C-1); *see also* C-boats; change in designation to C class, 33; data, 306;

design of, 45–47; history of, 286; Lawrence Y. Spear designing, 29; trials, 47–48

Odax (SS 484), 303

Oil slicks; fuel oil stowage in ballast tanks causing, 137; left by S-boats, 137; measures taken to prevent, 165

1,500-ton Cruiser Submarine 1929, 185

Ono, ex-*Friar* (SS 357), 300

OpNav (Office of the Chief of Naval Operations); *see also* Hart, Adm. Thomas C.; War Plans Division, OpNav; ordering WWII submarine expansion programs, 206; pre-World War II history of, 3–6; retaining old boats for training, 97; Submarine Section proposals for cruiser submarines, 170

Orca (K-3), 287

Osetr, see *Protector*

Otto engine, 34

Otto Gas Engine Works, 255

Paddle (SS 263), 296

Pampanito (SS 383); described, 208; history of, 301

Parche (SS 384), 301

Pargo (SS 264); 40–mm and 20-mm guns, 215; history of, 296

Passive sonars; *see also entries for specific sonars;* triangulation, 141; WWI Allied innovation in, 156–157; WWI development of, 149

Passive sound gear, K-5 submarine, 81

Passive underwater fire control feasibility (PUFFS), 239

Peacemaker, 21

Pendulums for maintaining trim, 21, 25

Perch class (SS 176–181), 200

Perch (SS 176), 292, 310

Perch (SS 313), 298

Periscope stadimeters; calibrating, 238; described, 269; as eyepiece attachments, 279

Periscopes; 1919 C&R standardization conference, 277; 1920 specification, 279; alti-periscope, 128; *Argonaut*'s, 176; attack tactics and, 155; attempts to standardize, 277–279; B and C class motorized, 45; conning tower installation of walk-around, 77–78; constant height eyepieces, 279; design problems, 267; difficulties manufacturing, 273; difficulties modifying submarines for housing, 274; E-2 submarine, 58; E- and F-class relocations of, 60; EB-19B's, 61; Electric Boat's fixed-eyepiece design, 49; Electric Boat's single-hull S-boats, 134; elimination of conning tower, 279; elimination of R-boat and S-boat conning tower, 118; evolution of, 267–283; first U.S. Navy, 270; fixed, 75; G-1 housing, 53; independent telescopes in, 269; installation aboard *Adder*s, 33, 35; installation of second, aboard B, C, and D classes, 48; L-8 boat's retracting (housing), 85; L-boats' housing, 153; lengths of U.S. and German compared, 229; long (hull-penetrating), 270–271; narrow head, 282; *Octopus* class vibration problems, 50; *Plunger*'s power, 34; pneumatic, 276; *Porpoise*, 211; pre-1919, 270; problems with rotating fixed-eyepiece, 271;

proposed cruiser submarine's bifocal and twilight, 169; prototype 7.5-in bifocal, 281–282; R-1's housing, 121; replacement of early nonretractable, 272–273; submariners' demands for housing, 118; submariners' proposal for walk-around, 80; T-boats' three retractable, 104; WWI design change, 274; WWI experience demonstrating need for retractable, 274, 275–276

Permit (SS 178), 292

Peruvian purchase of EB707D submarines, 72

Peto (SS 265), 296

Pickerel (F-3), 286

Pickerel (SS 177), 292

Pickerel (SS 524), 304

Picuda (SS 382), 301

Pike (A-5); history of, 286; modernized, 44

Pike (SS 173), 292

Pilotfish (SS 386), 301

Pintado (SS 387), 301

Pioneer, 13, 14

Pipefish (SS 388), 301

Piper (SS 409), 302

Piranha (SS 389), piston steam engines, 255

Piston steam engines, 255

Plaice (SS 390), 301

Plunger (A-1); data, 306; history of, 286; Holland's failure to deliver, 22–25; marker (reel) buoy tests, 72; periscope tests, 270; as prototype for *Adder* modifications, 34; unique fairing design of, 31

Plunger (SS 179), 292

Pogy (SS 266), 296

Pollack (SS 179), 292

Pomfret (SS 391), 301

Pomodon (SS 486), 303

Pompano (SS 181); early war modifications, 196; history of, 292

Pompano (SS 491), 303

Pompon (SS 267), 296

Porpoise; in 1942, 201; modernized, 44; periscope trials, 271; surviving diving beyond test depth, 30; war modifications, 211

Porpoise (A-6), 286

Porpoise class (SS 172–175); data, 310; as precursor of WWII fleet submarines, 198–200

Porpoising; abandonment of, 61; argued as unrealistic for hiding periscopes, 80; Holland's underwater "airplane," 19; to raise fixed periscopes, 75

Portsmouth Navy Yard; designation as specialist builder, 2; as design agent, 3; design changes for adding stern torpedo tubes, 127–130; double-hulled S-boat prototype, 119–121; modified *Marlin*, 227, 228; program to save weight, 204; S-3 boat design, 121–124; small submarine design, 227; switch to thicker hulls, 209; WWII building record, 206

Power plants; *American Ram*, 16; proposal for first dual, 15

Power trains; Electric Boat's characteristic, 57; *Protector's* two separate, 39, 40

Pressure hulls; in double-hull construction, 5; flat-floored, 90; G-1 curved, 51, 52; Laurenti's elliptically shaped, 66, 68; *Octopus's* body-of-revolution, 47; proposed cruiser submarine's multiple, 170, 172; S-49

boat's kinked, 136; thicknesses, 306–311; U.S. and British vs. German U-boat, 160; weakness of T-boat, 104

Price, Augustus, 16

Propellers; 19th century submarines, 19; adjustable-pitch on *Vipers*, 46; on George C. Baker's submarine, 21; *Protector's* twin, 39, 40; replacement of three-bladed with four-bladed, 210

Protector; see also U-1 boat; U-2 boat; described, 38–39; failure to participate in competitive tests, 40–41; sale to Russia, 41

Puffer (SS 268), 296

PUFFS (passive underwater fire control feasibility), 239

Q (quick dive) tanks, 33–34

Q-ships, 154

Q-ships (British), 151

QB series active sonars, 144, 198

QC series active sonars, 198

QH series scanning sonars; commutator, 240; Harvard University and, 234

QHB sonars, 240

QLA sonar, 240

Queenfish (SS 393), 301

Quick (Q) dive tanks, 33–34

Quillback (SS 424), 302

R-1 boat (SS 78); as completed, 121; history of, 289

R-1 (SS 78) class data, 308

R-2 boat; history of, 289; modified for safety, 120

R-3 boat, 289

R-4 boat, 289

R-5 boat, 289

R-6 boat; history of, 289; testing first U.S. experimental snorkel, 119

R-7 through R-11 boats, 289

R-12 boat; described, 144; history of, 289

R-13 through R-18 boats, 289

R-19 boat; history of, 289; telescoping radio mast, 122

R-20 through R-27 boats, 289

R-21 (SS 98) class data, 308

R-boats; 3-in/50 guns added to, 127; 21-in torpedoes, 118; coast defense boats designated as, 119; diesel engines, 258; elimination of conning tower periscopes, 118; experimental JP sonar tests, 144; improvements over H and O classes, 119; laid up and discarded, 119; modified according to WWI experience, 124; ordered scrapped, 208; redesigned conning tower for periscopes, 118; safety modifications, 142

Radar; British provision of U.S. with magnetrons for centimetric, 235; enabling submarines to surface, 1; increasing attractiveness of night attacks, 234; MIT's development of microwave, 234; S-boat refits installing, 131; SS X-band radar, 234

Radar countermeasures (RCM), 240, 241

Radar detectors, *Hake's*, 242

Radio antenna masts; *Bass's* telescopic, 110; counterbalanced U-boat, 160; L-8 boat's retractable, 85; R-19's telescoping, 122

Radio antennas; allowing underwater reception on S-44 boat, 145; *Bashaw's* HF whip, 238; *Cachalot's* limiting machine gun arcs of fire, 191; D class

boats, 57; DF loop for underwater HF, 217; enabling transmitting from periscope depth, 165–166; low-frequency reception by loop, 234; *Mackerel's* paired, 230; *Marlin's* loop, 220–221; O-4 and O-10 boats' radio loop, 95; O-6 boat's post WWI, 168; *Octopus*, 46; *Pompano's* HF, 196; *Porpoise*, 211; preventing diving while rigged, 76; S-45 boat's flat-top, 146; *Sunfish*, 167

Radios; first U.S. submarines with permanent, 61; long-range for proposed scout submarines, 165; low frequency signal reception, 166; proposal for HF, on fleet submarines, 107; proposed cruiser submarine, 167; ranges of first installed, 76; strategic scout requirement for long-range, 165; submariners' desire for reliable, 81

Range finders, submariners' rejection of vertical-base, 80

Rasher (SS 269), 296

Raton (SS 270), 296

Ray (SS 271), 296

Raytheon Corp., *see* Submarine Signal Co.

Razorback (SS 394), 301

RCM (radar countermeasures), 240, 241

Redfin (SS 272), 296

Redfish (SS 395), 301

Refrigerators, 145

Remora (SS 487), 303

Requin (SS 481); history of, 303; Mk 51 launcher, 219

Rice, Isaac; founding Electric Boat Company, 26; as Holland's partner, 25

Richson, Carl, 36–37

Rickover, Adm. H. G. (as Capt.), 209

Robalo (SS 273), 296

Robert H. McCurdy (SP-3157), 154

Robinson, Adm. S.S., 6

Robinson, Rear Adm. Samuel M., 260

Rochelle salt-active sonars, 198

Rock (SS 274), 296

Rocket launchers, 219

Roncador (SS 301), 298

Ronquil (SS 396), 301

Roosevelt, President Franklin D., 206

Rudders; auxiliary added to reduce turning circle, 210–211; proposed topside, 248

Runner (SS 275), 296

Runner (SS 476), 303

Russia; *see also Kaiman* class (Russian) submarines; Electric Boat's cruiser submarine, 100; purchase of *Adders* for war with Japan, 36; purchase of *Fulton* (submarine), 42; purchase of *Protector*, 41

Russian submarines, *Kaiman* class, 51

S-1 (SS 106) boats; described, 124; gun access hatch, 125; history of, 290; test of carrying airplanes, 177

S-1 (SS 106) class data, 308

S-2 boat; flawed design of, 124; history of, 290; as last Lake design for U.S. Navy, 126; slow diving, 121; stricken, 139

S-3 boat; described, 122–124; history of, 290; separate ballast tanks, 121–122

S-3 boat (SS 107), 308

S-4 boat; history of, 290; rammed, 139

S-5 boat, 290

S-6 boat; as C&R-designed boat, 127; history of, 290

S-7 boat, 290

S-8 boat; described, 128; history of, 290
S-9 boat, 290
S-10 boat, 290
S-10 (SS 115) class data, 308
S-11 boat; history of, 290; stern torpedo tube, 134
S-12 through S-16 boats, 290
S-17 boat; after refitting, 129; history of, 290; stricken, 139
S-18 boat, 290
S-18 (SS 123) class data, 308
S-19 boat, 290
S-20 boat (SS 125); engine room, 260; as engineering experimental ship, 137; history of, 290; wartime modifications, 138
S-20 (SS 125) class data, 308
S-21 boat, 290
S-22 boat; after refit, 143; history of, 290
S-23 through S-27 boats, 290
S-28 boat; history of, 290; refit, 146
S-29 through S-34 boats, 291
S-35 boat; described, 131; history of, 291
S-36 though S-43 boats, 291
S-42 (SS 153) class data, 309
S-44 boat; history of, 291; modernization of, 145
S-45 boat, 144; history of, 291; refit, 146
S-46 boat; history of, 291; underway, 147
S-47 boat, 291
S-48 boat; described, 140; history of, 291; as prototype for abortive S-boat reconstruction, 142; repairs and modifications to, 139, 414; stricken, 139
S-48 (SS 159) class data, 309
S-49 boat; described, 136; history of, 291; sonar tests, 197; stricken, 139
S-50 boat; history of, 292; sonar tests, 197
S-51 boat, 292
S-boats; 21-in torpedoes, 118; 800-tonners designated as, 119; battery capacity for endurance, 150; C&R vs. Electric Boat designs, 132; deficiencies of, 139–142; diesel engines, 258; diesel-electric drives as cure for unreliability of, 259; double armature motors, 265; elimination of conning tower periscope, 118; engine upgrades for Pacific battlefleet service, 133; guns approved for, 126–127; incorporating German features, 133; London Naval Treaty forcing discarding of, 139; modifications for stern torpedo tubes, 127–130; modified according to WWI experience, 124; ordered scrapped, 208; origins in plans for 800-tonners, 117–119; planned to replace A through R classes, 157; possible roles in war with Japan, 163; proposed replacement by 1,200-tonners, 165; safety modifications, 142; Scheme B design, 130–133; sonar tests, 197–198; wanted by submariners for FY 19, 124; WWI experience justifying move to, 151; WWII deployments of government-built, 147; WWII modernization of Holland-type, 145, 146; WWII modernization of Holland-type, 131, 145, 146
Sabalo (SS 302), 298
Sablefish (SS 303), 298
Saddle-tank submarines, 7
Safety modifications; O-8 boat, 96; R-2 boat, 120; S-4 boat's ramming disaster inspiring, 139

Salmon class (SS 182–187); data, 310; development of, 200–204
Salmon (D-3); described, 78; history of, 286; improved motors, 49
Salmon (SS 182), 292
Sand Lance (SS 381), 301
Sarda (SS 488), 303
Sargo cells, 264
Sargo class (SS 188–193); data, 310; development of, 204–205
Sargo (SS 188), 293
Saury (SS 189), 293
Sawfish (SS 276), 296
SC designation, 179
SC-tubes; development of, 149, 156; replaced by JK sonar, 198; use with Y-5 tubes, 156–157
Scabbardfish (SS 397), 301
Scamp (SS 277), 297
Scheme B-1 fleet submarine design, 106
Scheme C-1 fleet submarine design, 106
Scheme D fleet submarine design, 108
Scheme E fleet submarine design, 107
Scheme K fleet submarine design, 107–110
Scheme L fleet submarine designs, 110
Scheme L-3 fleet submarine, 110–111
Scheme O fleet submarine design, 107
Schemes 2 through 17 design data, 311
Schemes I, II, III (Adm. Hart's designs), 310
Schley (AA-1); see also AA-1 submarine; T-1 boat; fleet submarines ordered as near-repeat, 103; naming of, 101
Schley (SS 52) class data, 309
Schooners, countering U-cruisers off U.S. coast, 154
Scorpion (SS 278), 297
Scott, John K., 13
Scout submarines; see also cruiser submarines; fleet submarines; C&R's 1920 designs for, 172; interest in placing airplanes onboard, 163; OpNav estimates for, 164; proposed by submariners to General Board, 107; SC designation, 179
Sculpin (SS 191); history of, 293; overweight, 204
Sculpin (SS 494), 303
SD air-search radar; Argonaut, 176; described, 235; Gato, 206, 216; Mackerel, 225; Marlin, 220–221, 230; Narwhal, 185; Nautilus, 180; Pompano, 196; Porpoise, 211; S-17 boat, 129; S-44 boat, 145; S-boats rebuilt with, 147; Salmon, 203; Sturgeon, 212
SE (Steam Engineering); see also BuEng (Bureau of Engineering); submarine design responsibilities, 1
Sea Cat (SS 399); converted to "gunboat," 215, 218; history of, 301
Sea Devil (SS 400), 301
Sea Dog (SS 401), 301
Sea Fox (SS 402), 301
Sea Leopard (SS 483), 303
Sea Lion, 244
Sea Owl (SS 405), 302
Sea Panther (SS 528), 304
Sea Poacher (SS 406), 302
Sea pressure gauges, 150
Sea Robin (SS 407), 302
Sea-keeping; B class false bows for improved, 34, 43; bow buoyancy tanks for better, 130; emphasis on high

underwater speed vs. surface, 75; "flying" bridges for improved, 35; free-flooding superstructures for improved, 31, 38; German U-boat, 159; S-20 boat's bow modification for better, 137
Seadragon (SS 194), 293, 310
Seahorse (SS 304), 298
Seal (G-1), 286
Seal (SS 183), 292
Sealion (SS 195), 293; stern form accommodating four tubes, 202
Sealion (SS 315), 298
Seawolf (H-1), 287
Segundo (SS 398), 301
Semisubmersibles, in Civil War, 13
Sennet (SS 408); gun battery for wolfpack work, 218; history of, 302
SF designation, 179
Shad (SS 235), 295
Shark; history of, 286; periscope trials, 271
Shark (SS 174), 292, 310
Shark (SS 314), 298
Shears, fairwater and, 9
Shipyard participation in submarine design, 2
Signal ejector tubes, 131
Silencing submarines; diesel-electric engines, 260; in response to Japanese sonar, 247; SubLant emphasis on, 235
Silversides (SS 236); double-hull construction of, 5; history of, 295
Sims, Adm. William S. (as Comdr.); support for General Board, 2; ASW submarine, 157, 158; requesting Azores-based submarine division, 152; urging deployment of U.S. submarines against U-cruisers, 154
Single-hull submarines; A-1 submarine, 3; ballast tanks in, 6; Electric Boat's S-boat design, 119, 134, 135
Sirago (SS 485), 303
Size, submarine; see also displacement; attempts to cut cruiser, 180–186; dislike for V-4 boat's, 176; submarine performance vs., 77
SJ surface-search radar; Argonaut, 176; Bashaw, 238; credited with shift to night submarine attacks, 235–236; Gato, 206, 216; Mackerel, 225, 230; Marlin, 230; Nautilus, 180; S-28 boat, 146; S-35 boat, 131; S-44 boat, 145; S-boats rebuilt with, 147; Sturgeon, 212
Skate (F-4); history of, 286; sinking of, 264
Skate (SS 305), 298
Skegs; O-1 submarine, 95; removal from S-boats, 135, 143
Skipjack (E-1), 61; history of, 287; May 1915 exercise results, 69; range of installed radio, 76; re-engined with diesel, 257; SubDiv 4 Irish Sea deployment, 152
Skipjack (SS 184), 292
Small submarines; see also coastal defense submarines; 1942 revised design, 229–231; Adm. Hart's proposed, 221–223; Atlantic Fleet tests of, 228–229; Electric Boat's designs, 223; formal characteristics for, 224–227; lack of seaworthiness of, 77, 117; Lockwood's tentative characteristics for, 222–223; postwar successors, 231; WWII mobilization and, 227–228
Snapper; battery explosion, 264; new mufflers, 213

Snapper (C-5), history of, 286
Snapper (SS 185), 292
Snook (SS 279), 297
Snorkels; early proposals for, 75–76; proposed post-WWII submarine, 250; test of first experimental, 119; WWII German U-boat, 252, 253
Sonars; *see also* passive sonars; addition of deck units to submarines, 238–239; evolution of, 197–198; German, 252; jamming and confusing, 247–248; Japanese use of, 247; modified for torpedo and mine detection, 238; S-28 boat's keels, 146; S-35 boat's keel, 131; scanning, 240; universities involved in development of, 234
SORG (Submarine Operational Research Group), 234
Soviet Navy; Kilo class diesels, 260; wake-follower torpedoes, 246
Spadefish (SS 411); first 5-in/51 gun installed, 218; history of, 302
Spanish submarine purchases, 72
Spar torpedoes; defined, 11; *Hunley,* 15, 16
Spear, Lawrence Y.; 1909 presentation on design trade-offs, 76; collaboration with Holland on *Viper,* 29; designing *Octopus* class, 45; designs for small submarines, 223; fleet submarine designs, 100, 101
Spearfish (SS 190); history of, 293; new mufflers, 213
Speed; attacking convoys and high surface, 233; attempts to maintain high underwater, 75–76; British Royal Navy's fleet submarine, 104; Electric Boat's O-boats exceeding contract, 87; factors controlling maximum submerged, 119; Fleet Submarine 1919, 107; FY 18 submarines, 104; H class requirements, 78; heavy gun batteries and, 126; increase from FY 14 in FY 16/17, 87; maximum submerged for proposed cruiser submarine, 169–170; *Narwhal*'s slower than designed, 180; *Porpoise* class's high maximum, 198–200; primary Pacific submarine mission setting required, 189; proposed cruiser surface, 167–168; of proposed post-WWII submarine, 248; proposed post-WWII submarine submerged, 249; reduced by four-bladed propellers, 210; S-3 boat, 122–124; S-boat inability to keep up with cruisers, 137; sacrificed in Lockwood's proposed small submarines, 222–223; *Salmon* class, 202; *Sargo* maximum submerged, 204; Spear's guarantee of fleet boat surface, 101; Spear's trade-off of strategic vs. tactical mobility, 76–77, 119; study of tactical value of surface, 200; Submarine 1919, 104–105; *Tambor* class, 204
Spikefish (SS 404), 302
Spinax (SS 489), 303
Spot (SS 413), 302
Springer (SS 414), 302
Squalus (SS 192); history of, 293; overweight, 204
SS submarine designation, 179
SS surface-search radar; development of, 236; *Grouper,* 217
ST range-only radar; *Bashaw,* 238; *Crevalle,* 236; described, 236; *Gurnard,* 218

Stability; *see also* instability; blisters added for, 65; U-boat measures to improve, 161
Stadimeters, periscope; calibrating, 238; described, 269; as eyepiece attachments, 279
Standard Motor Construction Co., 255–256
Steam Engineering (SE), *see* BuEng (Bureau of Engineering); SE (Steam Engineering)
Steam submarines; 1920 revival of interest in, 113, 114; Alstilt's Confederate, 15; British Royal Navy's fleet submarine, 104; disadvantages of, 255; Nordenfeldt's, 21; proposed for FY 16 fleet submarine, 101–103; Submarine 1919, 104
Steelhead (SS 280), 297
Steering; *Adder* class, 30; *Holland VI*'s unsatisfactory, 25; *Tambor* class automatic, 204
Steering gear, ease of using U-boat, 160
Sterlet (SS 392), 301
Stern planes; introduction of electrically powered, 61; weak Electric Boat S-boat, 121
Sterns; Electric Boat's vertical-chisel, 100; L-8 boat's ship-type, 85; Lake submarines' distinctive, 87; M-1 vs. Electric Boat's single-hull boat stern, 88; O-1 submarine, 85; O-12 submarine, 93
Sterns Mechanical Laboratories, 261
Stickleback (SS 415), 302
Stingray (SS 186); described, 210; history of, 286, 293
Stocker, Capt. Robert, 170
Strategic mobility vs. tactical mobility, 76–77
Sturgeon (E-2); history of, 287; wartime modifications, 212
Sturgeon (SS 187), 293
SubDiv, 4, 8, 152, 154
SubDiv 5; conditions onboard submarines in, 152–153; Irish Sea patrol, 152–154; near loss of AL-4 boat, 153–154; operations against U-boats, 153; providing U.S. submariners with British Navy expertise, 155; transatlantic crossing, 152
SubLant; 1942 comparison of *Mackerel* and *Marlin* designs, 229; silencing submarines, 235
Submarine Officers' Conferences; 1941 support for small submarines, 228; estimate of number of small subs needed, 227; initiation of, 6; proposals leading to USS *Dolphin,* 139; proposed post-WWII submarine, 250–252; recommending characteristics for *Salmon* class, 200–201; V-boat characteristics recommendations, 180–181; voting down smaller submarines for FY 39, 221
Submarine Operational Research Group, *see* SORG
Submarine school (New London), founding of, 6
Submarine Signal Co.; C-tube development, 156; production of interwar U.S. sonars, 197
Submarine tankers, 137–139
Submarine warfare; *see also* attack tactics; during American Revolution, 11–12;

during Civil War, 12–17; WWI use of against trade, 151
Submarines; *see also* coastal defense submarines; cruiser submarines; harbor defense submarines; large submarines; midget submarines; small submarines; adoption of diesel engines, U.S., 62; agencies responsible for designing, 1; Allied, fueling each other, 137; assignment to European waters, 152; built by European navies for offensive operations, 55; changes in names and designations, 33; class designations and naming, 112; coastal defense, 75–97; commission dates, 285–304; conditions aboard WWI, 152–153; converted to "gunboats," 215; data, 305–311; decommission dates, 285–304; early U.S. Navy diesel, 257; fates of, 285–304; first designed by U.S. Navy constructors, 82–83; *Gato* as prototype of U.S. wartime, 206; *Holland VI* prototype of modern, 24, 25–27; introduction of permanent radios on U.S., 61; invention and deployment of first, 11–12; ironclads, 12–17; laid down dates, 285–304; last design of WWII, 248–252; major series tested in WWI, 105; modifications resulting from WWI experience, 124; number on station in 1930, 191; *Octopus* as first U.S. seagoing, 46; oldest retained for use in WWII, 96; proposal for army, 40–41; SS designation for general purpose, 179; strike dates, 285–304; submariners' 1910 requests for larger, compartmented, 79; as surface torpedo boats submerging at will, 66; treaty effects on numbers and types built, 163, 164, 170; underwater instability of 19th century, 6; U.S. government's consideration of abolishing, 158–159; U.S. interest in escape and salvage after foreign losses of, 73; ventilation systems installed in, 133–137; WWII reduction in silhouettes, 210
Sun Shipbuilding and Dry Dock, 261
Sunfish (SS 281); described, 167; history of, 297
Superstructures; *Adder*s vs. foreign near-duplicates, 30–31; addition of escape hatch to O-8's, 96; *Argonaut Junior*'s floodable, 31; B and C class floodable, 45; drawbacks of Lake's watertight, 151; G-1's floodable tankage on watertight, 51, 52; German U-boat measures compensating for floodable, 160; Laurenti's substantially watertight, 68; O-12 boat's flooding ports, 93; *Protector*'s floodable, 38; Simon Lakes' floodable, 7; thin Electric Boat's S-boat, 121
SV air-search radar; *Bashaw,* 238; described, 236; *Grouper,* 217; *Mero,* 209; *Sea Cat,* 215
Sweeney, Gen. T. W., 16
Swordfish (SS 193); full diesel-electric drive, 204; history of, 293

T-1 boat, 288
T-2 boat; 4-in/50 gun, 102, 103; Fessenden oscillator, 102; history of, 288
T-3 boat; chronic unavailability of, 104; history of, 288

T-boats; arising from proposal for fleet submarines, 80; hull form, 72; laid up, 104; obsolete when completed, 103–104; unreliable power plants, 103

Tactical mobility vs. strategic mobility, 76–77

Tactics; *see also* attack tactics; 1908 submarine, 75; evasive, 247–248; sonar changing, 197; TDC's potential transformation of, 197

Taft Board, 1904 review of coastal defenses, 55

Tambor (SS 198), 293; 5-in/51 gun, 214; depth charge tests, 205–206; TDC Mk 1 matured, 196–197

Tambor (SS 203), 311

Tang (SS 306), 298

Tankers, 137–139

Tarantula; flagstaffs and running lights, 42; history of, 286

Target bearing transmitter (TBT), 218

Targetting; British techniques taught to U.S., 155–156; periscope telemeter scales, 269; tactics formalized in 1908, 75; using fire-control systems, 218

Tarpon (C-3), 286

Tarpon (SS 175), 292

Tautog (SS 199), 293

Taylor, Chief Constructor David W., 110

Taylor, Rear Adm. David W., studies for airplane-carrying submarines, 170–172

TBT (target bearing transmitter), 218

TDC Mk 3/4, 240–241

TDCs (torpedo data computers); added to *Argonaut*, 176; described, 194–197; JT sonar and, 241; *Nautilus*, 180; prototype testing, 193

Tench (SS 417), 302

Tench (SS 417) class; data, 311; described, 209–214; vs. proposed fleet submarine, 251

Tenders, submarine; Congressional authorization for *Bushnell*, 81; General Board's FY 11 requirements for, 78; inclusion in FY 12 program, 79, 81; requirements under War College's 1909 proposal, 76

Test depths, 306–311; 1887 Circular of Requirements requirements for, 22; increase to 300 ft, 205; increase to 400 ft, 208–209; Navy's first specification of, 48; *Porpoise*'s survival of diving beyond, 30; proposal to increase in post-WWII submarines, 248; proposal for strengthening post-WWI submarines for 200 ft, 161; proposed cruiser submarine, 170; proposed post-WWII submarine, 249, 252

Thames class submarines (British), 200

Thornback (SS 418), 302

Thrasher (G-4); described, 64–68; history of, 287; May 1915 exercise results, 69

Threadfin (SS 410), 302

Thresher (SS 200); described, 201; history of, 293

Tiburon (SS 529), 304

Tigrone (SS 419), 302

Tilefish (SS 307), 298

Tinosa (SS 283), 297

Tirante (SS 419), 302

Tiru (SS 416), 302

TLR (triangulation listening ranging) set, 239

Tonopah, 152

Toro (SS 422), 302

Torpedo data computers; *see* TDCs

Torpedo directors, Mk, 14, 145

Torpedo impluse tanks, S-boat, 135

Torpedo salvos; automatically firing, 242; proposed 21-in bow tubes for firing second, 168; Spear's seeking smallest submarine providing largest, 77

Torpedo tubes; 1912 replacement of C and D class short with long, 50; abandonment of broadside, 107; aboard *Octopus*, 46; *Adder* modifications to improve loading, 34; dislike of H-boat stern, 78; EB 19B and 19E boats, 72; EB-19B's independently shuttered, 61; Electric Boat's B class, 90; end of fitting submarines with external, 210; evidence that Japanese and British were installing six bow, 187; first independent shutters on U.S., 51; fitted for angled fire, 119; FY 17/18 broadside, 104; FY 34 requests for six bow, 200; G-1 trainable deck, 51, 53, 54; gyro setting feature, 137, 195–196; *Kaimans*' trainable twin, 72; L class independent shutters, 84; *Narwhals*', 48, 50, 184–185; O-1 boat's bow caps, 93; proposed cruiser submarine, 166–167, 168, 169; proposed fleet submarine's trainable, 103; proposed post-WWII submarine, 248, 249, 250–252; proposed shift from four 21-in to six 18-in, 127; *Protector*'s single after, 40; purpose of four bow, 75; request for independent caps on, 80; S-boats redesigned with stern, 127–130, 133, 134, 136; *Salmon*'s four stern, 203; simultaneous flooding of both on *Viper*'s, 46; *Tambors*, 204; TDC and location of, 197; *Thrasher*'s, 67, 68; *Turbow*'s independently shuttered, 65; U-1 and U-2 submarines, 70; U-boat shutters for, 160; V-1 boat Fleet Submarine 1919 design, 111; V-8 and V-9 boat, 193; vulnerability of *Nautilus*' external, 180, 186

Torpedo War and Submarine Explosions, 12

Torpedo-firing (periscope) gear, 78

Torpedoes; *see also* spar torpedoes; TDCs; A- through D-class submarines, 50; British tactics using track angle, 155; chemical fuels, 245; contractors' refusals to test fire real, 50; defensive vs. offensive, 245–246; *Dolphin*'s, 188; E- and F-boat, 61; failures, 243; first self-propelled, 17; German work on wakeless (electric), 161; H class requirement to fire while surfaced in trim, 78; Holland's compensation for weight change when fired, 20; Mk VI magnetic pistol for triggering Mk XIV, 242–243; number of 21-in required to sink capital ships, 165; problems with T-boat, 104; proposed post-WWII submarine, 248, 249, 250; proposed SOB, 246; R- and S-boat 21-in, 118; redesigned cruiser's short, 185; running "hot" on *Nautilus*, 180, 186; *Salmon* class, 201–202; stowage cut in Hart's proposed small submarines, 222; submariners' desire for 21-in, 80, 81; submariners' desired improvements to, 246; *Tench*'s, 210; U.S. Navy vs. British,

155–156; wake-follower, 246; wakeless, 243–245; War College wanting more for Pacific submarines, 189

Torsional vibration; described, 256; diesel-electric drive solution, 259; heavier crankshaft solution, 258

Torsk (SS 423), 302

Track angle, torpedo; chance of counterattack vs., 155; vs. errors, 233–234; on TDC, 195

Trade-off studies, design; C&R and BuEng's, 119; Spear's 1909, 76–77

Transports; *Argonaut* conversion to, 176; *Nautilus* as, 180

Treaties; 1922 Washington Treaty, 163; depression-era attempts to limit naval spending by, 164

Trepang (SS 412), 302

Triangulation listening ranging (TLR) set, 239

Trigger (SS 237); additional holes cut into superstructure, 167; history of, 295

Trim; Holland's underwater "airplane" vs. rivals' submarines, 19; reloading torpedoes without changes in, 34; small vs. large partially filled tanks for maintaining, 25; weighted pendulums for maintaining, 21, 25

Trim pumps, 209

Triton (SS 201); 0.50-caliber machine gun, 205; history of, 293

Trout (SS 202), 293

Trumpetfish (SS 425), 302

Trutta (SS 421), 302

Tuck, Professor Josiah H. L., 21

Tullibee (SS 284), 297

Tuna (G-2); described, 61–62; history of, 287; May 1915 exercise results, 69; tandem pair gasoline engines, 255

Tuna (SS 203), 293

Tunny (SS 282), 297

Turbine torpedoes, multiple settings and, 156

Turbot (G-3); blisters added for stability, 65; described, 62–64; history of, 287

Turbot (SS 426), 302

Turtle, 11–12

Tusk (SS 426), 302

Twilight periscopes, 169

"Two-ocean navy," 165

U-1 boat, 70

U-2 boat, 70

U-3 *Eel* towed line array, 149

U-111 boat (German), 159–160

U-135 boat (German), 180–185

U-139 boat (German), 151

U-234 boat (German), 252

U-505 boat (German), 252

U-530 boat (German), 252

U-570 boat (German), 229

U-805 boat (German), 252

U-858 boat (German), 252

U-873 boat (German), 252

U-889 boat (German), 252

U-997 boat (German), 252

U-1105 boat (German), 252

U-1288 boat (German), 252

U-boats (German); alternative diesel power plant configuration, 107; British Q-ships sinking, 151; diesel power plant configurations, 107; effectiveness limited by British submarines, 152;

Electric Boat's B-boats, 90; heavy gun batteries, 126; inspiring desire for 800-tonners, 117, 151; "milch cows," 137; periscopes, 269; post-WWII exploitation of captured, 252–253; proposals to duplicate in V-boats, 180–181; purchase by Austria-Hungary, 69; results of U.S. inspection of captured, 159–161; SubDiv 5 operations against, 153; submariners impressed by small, 228, 229; WWI Allied submarine operations against, 151–152; WWI effectiveness in tying down Allied force, 151

U-cruisers (German); ASW operations off U.S. coast against, 154–155; forcing Allies to provide convoy escorts, 151, 154; inspiring fleet submarines as potential cruisers, 157

U-shaped ballast tanks, 60, 132

UB-88 boat (German), 160

UB-148 boat (German), 159

UC-97 boat (German), 160

Ulua (SS 428); diesel intakes, 262; history of, 302

Underwater airplane; buoyancy of, 6; vs. underwater "helicopters," 19

Unicorn (SS 429), 303

Unicorn (SS 436), 303

Union Iron Works; independent offer of EB designs, 86; R-boat completion time, 157

Union Navy; *Alligator*, 12–13; vs. Confederate submarines, 16; *Monitor*, 12

University of California Division of War Research, 234, 247

U.S. Navy; coordination of bureaus, 1; disputes with army over coast defense jurisdiction, 40–41, 55; first submarines designed by, 82–83; WWI reordering submarine priorities, 150

V-1 boats; described, 111–113; Fleet Submarine 1919 design, 111; ordered scrapped, 208; three periscopes, 279

V-2 boat, *see Bass* (V-2)

V-4 boat; *see also Argonaut* (V-4); design and construction of, 176; stern minelaying tubes, 174

V-5 boat; *see also Narwhal*; designs leading to, 182

V-6 boat, *see Nautilus*

V-7 boat; *see also Dolphin* (V-7); 1929 design alternatives, 187; 1930 design, 181; C&R 1928 design schemes, 186

V-8 boat, *see Cachalot* (V-8)

V-9 boat, *see Cuttlefish* (V-9)

V-boats; arising from proposal for fleet submarines, 80; characteristics

recommended by Submarine Officers Conference, 180–181; design evolution, 106–113; FY 17–19 authorization for, 104; torpedo gyro-setting, 196

Vendace (SS 430), 303

Vent holes, *see* limber holes

Ventilation systems; *see also* air conditioning; battery charging and, 264; German U-boat, 159, 160; installed for all submarines, 133–137

Ventilators; *see also* air conditioning; H-2 submarine, 59; S-1 submarine, 125

Venturis; *Grouper*, 217; *Marlin*, 230; S-17 boat, 129; S-20 boat, 138; S-45 boat, 146; *Sturgeon*, 212

Vickers, 35–36; 4-cycle diesel engines, 257; assembling H-boats in Montreal for Britain, 78; submarine completion time, 157

Vinson Act, 164

Vinson-Trammel Act, 164

Viper (EB 16); *see also* B-boats; change in designation to B class, 29; design of, 46; flagstaffs and running lights, 42; history of, 286; Holland-Spear collaboration on, 29

Virginia (ironclad), 14; *see also Merrimack* (CSS Virginia)

Volador (SS 490), 303

WAA (wide aperture array), 239

Wahoo (SS 238); after sinking Japanese ships, 232–233; history of, 295

Wahoo (SS 516), 303

Wake-follower torpedoes, 246

Wakeless torpedoes; German development of, 161; U.S. development of, 243–245

Walrus (K-4); history of, 287; hull form, 4

Walrus (SS 431), 303

Walrus (SS 437), 303

War Plans Division, OpNav; post-WWI plans for possible war with Japan, 163–164; support of tanker proposal, 139

Washington Navy Yard, 197

Washington Treaty (1922), 163

Watson, Baxter, 13

WBA sonar, 198

WCA sonar, 198; *Crevalle*, 236; described, 238; *Hoe*, 243

WDA sonar, 198, 238

Weights, submarine, 306–311

Welded construction; adoption of, 200; *Salmons*, 202

Westinghouse Corp.; chemical fuel torpedoes, 245; diesel engines, 259, 260

WFA sonar; described, 239–240; replacing JT and WCA sonars, 243

WFA-1 sonar, 240

Whale (SS 239), 16–17, 295

Wheels, bottom; *Argonaut Junior*, 31; G-1 (*Seal*), 51, 52; *Protector*, 39; U-1 and U-2 submarines, 70

Whitefish (SS 432), 303

Whitehead, Robert; building submarines with Marley F. Hay, 69; inventing first self-propelled torpedo, 17

Whiting (SS 433), 303

Wide aperture array (WAA), 239

Winton Engine Corp., 259, 261

Woods Hole Oceanographic Institution, 234

Woodward, J. W., 33–34

World War I; Allied innovations in listening gear, 156–157; ASW operations against U-cruisers off U.S. coast, 154; changes to submariners' conceptions of naval warfare, 149–150; Electric Boat's submarine sales during, 72; ending navy's suggestions for foreign boat purchases, 68; lessons learned from British Royal Navy, 155–156; major series of submarines tested, 105; new strategic roles and operating modes, 151–152; preventing building fleet submarines in FY 18, 104; replacement of signal bells with Fessenden oscillators, 85; SubDivs 4 and 5 deployments, 152–154; submarine modifications resulting from, 124

World War II; accelerating submarine production, 206–208; captured enemy submarines, 252–253; deployments of government S-boats, 147; guns, 214–219; increasing number of submarines built, 165; last submarine design, 248–252; modernization of Holland-type S-boats, 145, 146; O-boats retained for use in, 96, 97; pre-war preparations for Pacific war, 163–193; prewar technical developments, 234–235; radars, 235–238; retention of O-boats for use in, 96; S-boats in, 142; sonar and depth charge evasive tactics, 247–248; sonars, 238–240; torpedo attacks on shipping, 233–234; torpedo development during, 242–247

Y tube sonars, 149, 156–157

Y-5 tube sonars, 156–157

Yarnell, Rear Adm. H. E., 259, 260

Yeomans, Lt. E. E., 264

Zalinski, (U.S. Army) Lt. Edmund L., 21

Zweibel (onion) passive sonar array, 252